MOUNTAINEERING

The Freedom of the Hills

Fifth Edition

Mountaineering
The Freedom of the Hills

Fifth Edition

Editor: Don Graydon

Revision Committee Chairpersons:
Paul Gauthier
Myrna Plum

SWAN·HILL PRESS

© 1996 by The Mountaineers

First published in the UK in 1996
by Swan Hill Press, an imprint of Airlife Publishing Ltd

First published in the United States of America by
The Mountaineers Books

British Library Cataloguing in Publication Data
A catalogue record for this book
is available from the British Library

ISBN 1 85310 756 5

Swan Hill Press
an imprint of Airlife Publishing Ltd
101 Longden Road, Shrewsbury SY3 9EB

Edited by Maureen O'Neal
Illustrations by Bob Cram, Nick Gregoric, Ross
Prather, Ramona Hammerly
Cover design by Elizabeth Watson
Book layout by Barbara Bash

Cover photograph: Midnight on the summit of Mount
McKinley, Alaska. Photo by Patrick Morrow
Frontispiece: Climbers on Vowell Pinnacle, Howser
Spire in the distance, Bugaboos, Purcell Range,
British Columbia. Photo by Baiba Morrow

The following trademarks appear in this book: Ball Nuts, Band-Aids, Camalots, Chevron Blazo, Clog, Coleman, Diamox, Friends, Gibbs, Gore-Tex, Hexentrics, Jumar, Kevlar, Masonite, Mylar, Polypro, Quickies, RURP, Rock 'n Rollers, RPs, Spectra, Stoddard, Stokes, Stones, Stopper, Styrofoam, Teflon, Therm-a-Rest, TCUs, Tri Cams, Velcro, and Vibram.

Printed in the United States of America

A NOTE ABOUT SAFETY

Safety is an important concern in all outdoor activities. No book can alert you to every hazard or anticipate the limitations of every reader. Therefore, the descriptions of equipment and techniques in this book are not representations that a particular tool or technique will be safe for you or your party. When you participate in the activities described in this book, you assume responsibility for your own safety. Keeping informed on current conditions and exercising common sense are the keys to a safe, enjoyable outing.

CONTENTS

PREFACE

Mountaineering, the Freedom of the Hills is intended to present both introductory and advanced information on the sport of mountaineering. This fifth edition is an extensive revision of the fourth edition, the longtime, leading English-language text on mountaineering.

Each of the chapters from the fourth edition has been revised, rewritten, and, where necessary, expanded. These revisions reflect the rapid changes occurring in various areas of mountaineering and are due to increased popularity, the development of new techniques, and the introduction of new and improved equipment. Chapters considerably enhanced by these changes include: First Steps, Leading and Placing Protection, Rock Climbing Technique, Aid Climbing and Pitoncraft, and Belaying. This edition presents a completely new chapter on Winter and Expedition Climbing.

Many improvements make this edition more interesting to read, easier to use, and more accessible. A professional writer rewrote the material from all contributors, bringing the various parts and chapters together to form a comprehensive text. Additional headings clarify the topics and direct the reader to pertinent information. Completely new illustrations of techniques and equipment clearly and accurately illustrate the text. Line figure drawings were created from photographs of climbers demonstrating the precise technique.

SCOPE OF THE BOOK

As in previous editions, *Freedom* provides sound, clear, and current coverage of the concepts, techniques, and problems involved in the pursuit of mountain climbing. Individual topics, such as rock climbing technique or aid climbing, are detailed enough to be useful to readers with specific interests in those topics. The book provides a fundamental understanding of each topic. It is not intended, however, to be exhaustive or encyclopedic. In addition to presenting information for the novice, much of the material in this book can help experienced climbers review and improve their skills.

Mountaineering cannot be learned just by studying a book. *Freedom* was originally written as a textbook for students and instructors participating in organized climbing courses. The context of learning that is provided in a course of instruction, given either individually or in groups, and by competent instructors, is essential for beginning climbers.

Traditionally, climbing has been a thinking person's sport. The individual climber and climbing team bring their knowledge, skills, and experience to the problem at hand and apply their own solutions. In this fifth edition, *Freedom* presents widely used techniques and practices outlining both their advantages and limitations. It is presented not as dogma or the final word but as the basis for making sound judgments. This problem-solving approach is especially important in mountaineering because of the potential dangers that exist. Such dangers are inherently magnified by harsh conditions, insufficient skill, inexperience, and poor judgment.

Freedom characteristically describes not just simple climbing but wilderness mountaineering. Any person who becomes a wilderness mountaineer has a deep and abiding responsibility to help preserve the wilderness environment for present and future generations. Walking softly is a fair start. The mountain regions throughout the world constitute the domain of mountaineering. This dwindling and finite resource depends on the wilderness traveler for its future preservation.

ORIGINS OF THE BOOK

Freedom's direction and emphasis originated from the development of climbing in the Pacific Northwest. The wild and complex character of the mountains in this region, with their abundance of snow and glaciers throughout the year, furthered the mountaineering challenge. Access was inherently difficult. There were few roads, and the initial explorations were themselves expeditions, often with native guides.

When The Mountaineers was organized in 1906, one of its major purposes was to explore and study the mountains, forests, and watercourses of the Northwest. The journey to the mountain summit was a long and difficult one, and it required a variety of skills. With the knowledge of these skills, the competence that comes from their practice, and the experience gained through climbing mountains, more than a few had the exhilarating experience of the freedom of the hills.

As interest in mountaineering in the region grew, so did a tradition of tutelage. Increasingly, experienced climbers took novices under their wings to pass on their knowledge and skills. The Mountaineers formalized that exchange by developing a series of climbing courses. This book grew out of six decades' worth of teaching mountaineering and conducting numerous climbs in the Northwest and throughout the world.

LEGACY OF THE FIFTH EDITION

Issac Newton said, "If I see farther than others, it is because I stood on the shoulder of giants." The various editions of *Freedom* represent a tradition of bringing together and sorting through the knowledge, techniques, opinions, and advice of a large number of practicing climbers. Students, both in training and on actual climbs, have been an especially pivotal source of information.

Prior to the publication of the first edition of *Freedom* in 1960, The Mountaineers climbing courses had used European works, particularly Young's classic *Mountaincraft,* as required reading. These works did not cover various subjects unique and important to American and Pacific Northwest mountaineering. To fill in the gaps, course lecturers prepared outlines, which they distributed to students. Eventually these outlines were fleshed out and gathered together as the *Climber's Notebook,* subsequently published, in 1948, as the *Mountaineers Handbook.* By 1955, tools and techniques had changed so drastically, and the courses had become so much more complex, that the new and more comprehensive textbook was needed.

Members of the first edition editorial committee were: Harvey Manning, chairman; John R. Hazle; Carl Henrikson; Nancy Bickford Miller; Thomas Miller; Franz Mohling; Rowland Tabor; and Lesley Stark Tabor. A substantial portion of the then relatively small Puget Sound climbing community participated—some seventy-five as writers of preliminary, revised, advanced, semifinal, and final chapter drafts, and another one or two hundred as reviewers, planners, illustrators, typists, proofreaders, financiers, promoters, retailers, warehousemen, and shipping clerks. At the time, there were few Mountaineer climbers who did not have a hand in making or selling the book.

Efforts leading to the publication of the second edition (in 1967) began in 1964. Members of the second edition editorial committee were: John M. Davis, chairman; Tom Hallstaff; Max Hollenbeck;

Jim Mitchell; Roger Neubauer; and Howard Stansbury. Even though much of the first edition was retained, the task force was, again, of impressive proportions, numbering several dozen writers, uncounted reviewers, and helpers. Survivors of the previous committee, notably John R. Hazle, Tom Miller, and Harvey Manning, provided continuity to the effort. As he had with the first edition, Harvey Manning once more edited the entire text and supervised production.

The third edition editorial committee was formed in 1971 and headed by Sam Fry. Initially, a planning committee analyzed the previous edition and set guidelines for its revision. A steering committee, consisting of Jim Sanford, Fred Hart, Sean Rice, Howard Stansbury, and Sam Fry, directed the revision and had overall responsibility for the text. A large number of climbers contributed to individual chapters; the reviewing, revising, editing, and collation of chapters and sections was a true community effort. Peggy Ferber edited the entire book, which was published in 1974.

The fourth edition of Freedom involved a major revision and included the complete rewrites of many chapters, most notably the entire Ice and Snow section. A cast of hundreds was guided by a team of technical editors: Ed Peters, chairman; Roger Andersen; Dave Enfield; Lee Helser; John Young; Dave Anthony; and Robert Swanson. A large number of climbers submitted comments to the committee. Small teams of "writers" prepared a series of drafts for review by the technical editors. In addition to the substantial contribution of such writers, many others provided valuable help through critiques of subsequent and final drafts not only for technical accuracy and consistency, but also for readability and comprehension.

THE FIFTH EDITION

In late 1987, climbing committee chairman Ken Small responded to concerns of The Mountaineers Books staff and initiated an effort to assess the need for a new edition. A *Freedom* Ad Hoc Study Committee was formed to make specific recommendations to the club's board of trustees. The committee reported the need for a revision of many technique sections, overall improvement in the writing quality, and an upgraded visual format. It also recommended that this revision be carried out in the tradition of a volunteer committee. Chaired by Paul Gauthier, the committee's members were Ben Arp, Steve Costie, Nancy Jackson, Tom Merritt, and Susan Price. In order to assess the current strengths and the specific needs for improvements to the fifth edition, the committee solicited the opinions of Mountaineer members and well-known climbers and writers from outside the Club. The committee is grateful for the well-thought-out responses received from Greg Child, Randall Green, Michael Loughman, Eric Perlman, Doug Robinson, and Gary Speer. Many of their suggestions were incorporated into this latest edition of the book.

The board of trustees selected Paul Gauthier to spearhead a substantial revision of the fourth edition. The committee was organized into a coordinators' group, which took on the responsibility for overall guidance, and into subcommittees for subject areas. The individual subcommittees used various methods to produce detailed narrative "outlines." These were reviewed and modified by the coordinators' group to incorporate a wide range of critique by the whole committee. Professional writer Don Graydon wrote "drafts" from these narratives, which were reviewed and revised by the committee. Graydon showed extraordinary skill in working both with a diverse committee and the Books staff and in enhancing the overall style.

The coordinator group consisted of Paul Gauthier, chairman; Ben Arp, editorial coordinator; Marty Lentz, Safety and Rescue section coordinator; Margaret Miller, Rock section coordinator; Judy Ramberg, Approaching the Peaks section coordinator; and Craig Rowley, Snow and Ice section coordinator. In 1990, Paul Gauthier moved to England, and the committee was subsequently chaired by Myrna Plum.

The Approaching the Peaks Subcommittee jointly developed five chapters with major contributors as follows: "First Steps," Bill Deter and Judi Maxwell; "Clothing and Equipment," Judy Ramberg; "Camping and Food," Judy Ramberg and Judi Maxwell; ''Routefinding and Navigation,'' Bob Burns with consultation on maps section by Stewart M. Wright; and ''Wilderness Travel,'' Judi Maxwell, Bill Deters, and Judy Ramberg.

The Fundamentals and Rock Climbing Subcommittee jointly reviewed the revisions developed by the following lead individuals: ''Ropes, Knots, and Carabiners,'' Jack E. Bennett and Larry Longley; ''Belaying,'' Allen Frees; ''Rappelling,'' Ken Small; ''Rock Climbing Technique,'' Susan Price; ''Leading and Placing Protection,'' Dan Bean; ''Aid Climbing and Pitoncraft,'' Jeff Johnson; and Rating Systems appendix, Jan Green. Cal Magnusson of REI consulted on the ''Belaying'' chapter.

The Snow and Ice Climbing Subcommittee jointly revised each of their chapters with the major contributors as follows: ''Snow Travel and Climbing,'' Kurt Hanson, Jim Cade, and Don Heck; ''Ice Climbing,'' Don Heck; ''Glacier Travel and Crevasse Rescue,'' Craig Rowley and Nancy Jackson; and ''Winter and Expedition Climbing,'' Kurt Hanson, Nancy Jackson, and Jim Cade.

The Safety and Rescue Subcommittee, with contributions by Paul Gauthier and Ben Arp, condensed and revised materials into ''Safety and Leadership,'' revision led by Marty Lentz, and the ''Alpine Rescue'' chapter, led by Pete A. Bustanoby.

As the text was reaching a final form, Books staff organized efforts to revise figures and illustrations and provide artwork and photography. The committee end of this large effort was coordinated by Marilyn O'Callaghan. Concurrently, the professional design and layout was directed by Books production and design manager Marge Mueller.

THE MOUNTAINEERS, founded in 1906, is a non-profit outdoor activity and conservation club, whose mission is ''to explore, study, preserve and enjoy the natural beauty of the outdoors....'' Based in Seattle, Washington, the club is now the third largest such organization in the United States, with 12,000 members and four branches throughout Washington State.

The Mountaineers sponsors both classes and year-round outdoor activities in the Pacific Northwest, which include hiking, mountain climbing, ski-touring, snowshoeing, bicycling, camping, kayaking and canoeing, nature study, sailing, and adventure travel. The club's conservation division supports environmental causes through educational activities, sponsoring legislation, and presenting informational programs. All club activities are led by skilled, experienced volunteers, who are dedicated to promoting safe and responsible enjoyment and preservation of the outdoors.

The Mountaineers Books, an active, non-profit publishing program of the club, produces guidebooks, instructional texts, historical works, natural history guides, and works on environmental conservation. All books produced by The Mountaineers are aimed at fulfilling the club's mission.

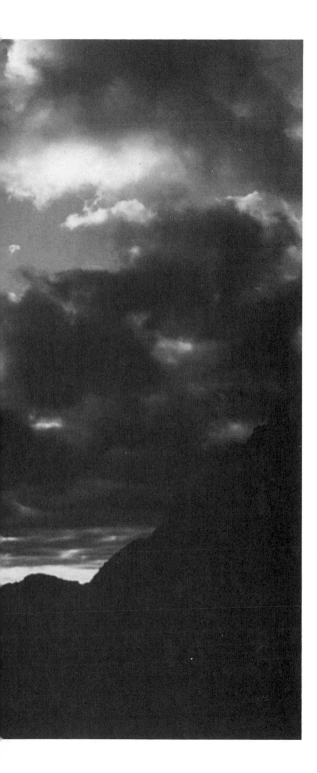

PART ONE

APPROACHING THE PEAKS

Stratocumulus front over the High Sierra, Mount Whitney region, California. Photo by Galen Rowell/Mountain Light

· 1 ·

FIRST STEPS

Mountaineering is more than climbing, panoramic views, and wilderness experience. It is also challenge, risk, and hardship. And it is not for everyone. Those drawn to the mountains can find them exhilarating and irresistible, as well as frustrating and sometimes even deadly. There are qualities to mountaineering that inspire us and bring us to revel in a pursuit that is more than a pastime, more than a sport; a passion, certainly, and sometimes a compulsion.

"What was the force that impelled me?" asks American mountaineer Fred Beckey. "Something complex and undefinable, the attraction of uncertainty." British climber George Leigh Mallory, many years earlier, offered another version of mountaineering's attraction: "What we get from this adventure," he said, "is just sheer joy."

Distant views of mountains may speak of adventure, but they seldom more than hint at the joys and hardships that await. If you want to climb mountains, be prepared for the totality of nature—storms as well as soft breezes, tangled brush as well as alpine flowers, biting insects as well as singing birds. Climbing mountains is a tough way to spend your spare time, and anyone who does it knows what Polish climber Voytek Kurtyka meant when he said that "alpinism is the art of suffering." Mountaineering takes place in an environment indifferent to human needs, and not everyone is willing to pay the price in hardship for its rich physical and spiritual rewards.

FREEDOM OF THE HILLS

"Freedom of the hills" is a concept that combines the simple joy of being in the mountains with the skill, gear, and strength to travel where we will without harm to ourselves, others, or the environment.

This book, with its roots in the mountains of the Pacific Northwest, champions this freedom by providing information for climbers of all levels, from novice to advanced. It represents the combined experiences of many climbers, who have traveled most of the major mountain ranges on earth. This does not make it gospel. Although learning from the experiences of others is valuable, time and again the student returns to instruct the teacher.

As you read, remember that new techniques and technical advances occur so frequently that any attempt to document the "state of the art" is quickly dated. With this caution in mind, this book can serve as your general passport to the freedom of the hills.

CARING FOR THE WILDERNESS

The beauty of wild places could be their undoing as they attract us to them—leaving them touched by human hands and eventually less than wild. We are consuming wilderness at an alarming rate, using it and changing it as we do so.

Though we sometimes act otherwise, the mountains don't exist for our amusement. They owe us

13

nothing and they require nothing from us. Hudson Stuck wrote that he and the other members of the first party to climb Mount McKinley felt they had been granted "a privileged communion with the high places of the earth." As mountaineers traveling in the wilderness, our minimum charge for this privilege is to leave the hills as we found them, with no sign of our passing. We must study the places we visit and become sensitive to their vulnerability, then camp and climb in ways that minimize our impact.

The privileges we enjoy in the mountains bring responsibilities. Therefore, the facts of mountaineering life today include permit systems that limit access to the backcountry, road and trail closures, environmental restoration projects, legislative alerts, and the clash of competing interest groups. While we tread softly in the mountains, it's also time to speak loudly back in town for support of wilderness preservation and sensitive use of our wild lands. As mountaineers, we need to be activists as well as climbers if we want our children to be able to enjoy what we take for granted.

KNOWLEDGE AND SKILLS

As part of our passport to travel the mountains, we need the skills for safe, enjoyable passage. For our sake and the sake of everyone we climb with, we learn the tools and techniques of camping, navigation, belaying, rappelling, glacier travel, safety, rescue, and climbing on rock, snow, and ice. This book is a guide to this learning.

PHYSICAL PREPARATION

Mountaineering is a demanding activity, both physically and mentally. Rock climbing, in particular, has become increasingly athletic, especially at the higher levels of difficulty. Climbers today accomplish what was considered impossible only a few years ago. Many serious rock climbers work out at specialized gymnasiums, and the sport features international climbing competitions. In the world of alpine climbing, the highest peaks are commonly climbed without supplementary oxygen, in record times, and by more and more diffi-

cult routes. Most of us, however, appreciate such world-class performance from the sidelines. It's not necessary to devote your life to mountaineering in order to enjoy the activity at a level that provides personal satisfaction.

Levels of performance are rising even among recreational climbers and mountaineers. Good physical conditioning is one of the keys and can make the difference between enjoying an outing and merely enduring it. More important, the safety of the whole party may hinge on the strength—or weakness—of one member.

Most mountaineers train regularly. Aerobic activities such as running, cycling, swimming, cross-country skiing, snowshoeing, hiking uphill with a heavy pack, and climbing stairs are popular exercises. Many climbers lift weights to build strength and perform stretching exercises for flexibility. Specific exercises, those closest to climbing itself, are probably the best preparation. Physical fitness is the foundation for all the strenuous activities of mountaineering.

MENTAL PREPARATION

Just as important as physical conditioning, our mental attitude often determines success or failure. Once physical fitness is adequate, the "mind games" we play with ourselves are what really get us past a difficult move or help us decide to back off.

We need to be positive, realistic, and honest with ourselves. There is a personal balance required here. A "can do" attitude may turn into dangerous overconfidence if it isn't tempered with a realistic appraisal of ourselves and the situation.

Many a veteran mountaineer says the greatest challenges are mental. Perhaps this is one of mountaineering's greatest appeals: while seeking the freedom of the hills, we come face to face with ourselves.

JUDGMENT AND EXPERIENCE

This book outlines the basics of equipment and techniques and suggests how to learn from practice. But judgment, the most important of all mental qualities in climbing, develops from how we integrate our knowledge and experience.

Much of what we need are coping skills—the ability to deal with adverse weather, long hikes, thick brush, high exposure, and the like. As we endure these situations, we become better decision-makers, and the experiences we gain are useful for comparison the next time the going gets tough.

New situations, however, will still arise for which we have no trustworthy precedent. We won't be able to make an automatic, confident response, so we will have to exercise careful judgment. In this uncertainty lies much of the charm and challenge of mountaineering—as well as the potential for tragedy.

Many years ago, The Mountaineers club of Washington State devised a set of guidelines to help people conduct themselves safely in the mountains. Based on careful observation of the habits of skilled climbers and a thoughtful analysis of accidents, it has served well for not only climbers but, with slight adaptation, for all wilderness travelers. It is not inflexible doctrine, but it has proven to be a sound guide to practices that minimize risk.

A CLIMBING CODE

• A climbing party of three is the minimum, unless adequate prearranged support is available. On glaciers, a minimum of two rope teams is recommended.
• Rope up on all exposed places and for all glacier travel. Anchor all belays.
• Keep the party together, and obey the leader or majority rule.
• Never climb beyond your ability and knowledge.
• Never let judgment be overruled by desire when choosing the route or deciding whether to turn back.

• Carry the necessary clothing, food, and equipment at all times.
• Leave the trip schedule with a responsible person.
• Follow the precepts of sound mountaineering as set forth in textbooks of recognized merit.
• Behave at all times in a manner that reflects favorably upon mountaineering.

This code is by no means a step-by-step formula for reaching summits, but rather a guideline to safe and sane mountaineering. Climbers sometimes question the need for such standards for a sport in which much of the appeal lies in the absence of formal rules. But many serious accidents could have been avoided or their effects minimized if these simple principles had been followed. This climbing code is built on the premise that mountaineers want strong chances of safety and success, even in risk-filled or doubtful situations, and that they want safeguards in case they have misjudged those chances.

Experienced mountaineers often modify the code in practice, taking an independent course that combines an understanding of risk with the skill to help control it. The code is recommended especially for beginners, who have not yet developed the judgment that comes from years of experience.

If we learn to climb safely and skillfully, body and spirit in tune with the wilderness, we will be able to accept the lifetime invitation that John Muir extended to us so many years ago.

"Climb the mountains," he told us, "and get their good tidings. Nature's peace will flow into you as sunshine flows into trees. The winds will blow their own freshness into you and the storms their energy, while cares will drop off like autumn leaves."

· 2 ·

CLOTHING AND EQUIPMENT

In packing for a wilderness trip, it's a simple matter of take it or leave it. The idea is to take what you need and to leave the rest at home. With thousands of choices widely available in outdoor clothing and equipment, it's no longer a question of how to find what you need, but rather of limiting your load to just the items that will keep you safe, dry, and comfortable.

To strike a balance between too much and too little, monitor what you take with you. After each trip determine what was used, what was really needed for a margin of safety, and what was not needed. As you buy equipment, go for lightweight alternatives if the weight reduction does not jeopardize the item's performance and durability. Whenever possible, look for versatile equipment you can use for several purposes.

If you're new to mountaineering, you don't have the experience yet to know what works best for you. So don't buy all your basic gear right away. Take it one trip at a time, one purchase at a time. Whether it's boots, packs, or sleeping bags, wait until you have enough experience to make intelligent decisions before spending your money. Rent, borrow, or improvise during your early outings until you learn what you need and what you don't need. Get advice by talking to seasoned hikers and climbers, by window-shopping at outdoors stores, and by reading mountaineering magazines.

This chapter is one useful source of information on basic wilderness gear, including guidelines on what constitutes good equipment. It won't tell you what brands to purchase, but it will help you find high-quality items among those thousands of choices.

FOOTGEAR

BOOTS

Not many years ago almost all boots were made of leather, but some modern materials have certain performance advantages. Plastic boots and lightweight hiking boots have now joined the classic leather boot as common footgear for wilderness travelers, although leather is still the first choice for general-purpose mountaineering.

Leather boots

A general mountaineering boot is a compromise between conflicting requirements. It should be tough enough to withstand the scraping of rocks, stiff and solid enough for kicking steps in hard snow, yet comfortable enough for the approach hike. In a single day of climbing, the boots may have to contend with streams, mud, logs, brush, scree, hard snow, and steep rock.

The classic leather mountaineering boot (fig. 2-1) has the following features: high uppers ($5^1/2$ to $7^1/2$ inches) to protect the ankles in rough terrain; Vibram-type soles for traction on slippery vegetation, mud, and snow; midsoles for insulation and shock absorption; and a semi-rigid shank.

The length and rigidity of a boot's shank (fig.

16

Fig. 2–1. A classic leather mountaineering boot

2-2) is a much-debated topic. The ideal length depends on how the boot will be used. For hiking, easy snow climbs, and rock routes, choose a boot with a half-length nylon or fiberglass shank, which keeps the sole reasonably flexible. Boots used primarily for technical ice climbing or difficult mountain routes benefit from being made of plastic or having a full-length shank. The rigid plastic or full-

length shank impairs walking but greatly reduces leg fatigue when front-pointing with crampons or standing on small rock nubbins.

The sole of the boot should be attached to the uppers by means of a durable method of stitching, with the Norwegian welt (fig. 2-3) considered the longest lasting. The welt should be narrw (fig.

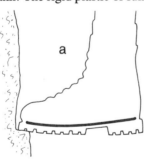

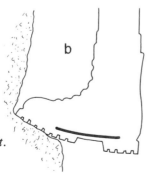

Fig. 2–2. The shank length determines the flexibility of the boot sole: a, full-length shank boot; b, half-length shank boot.

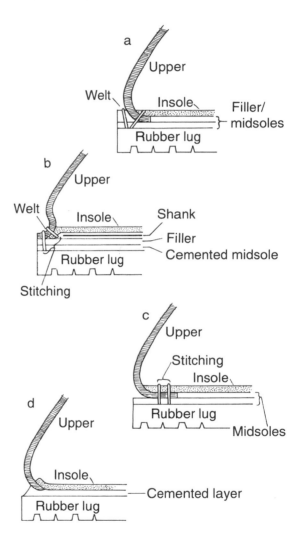

Fig. 2–3. Four common methods of boot construction: a, Goodyear welt; b, Norwegian welt; c, Littleway; d, cemented.

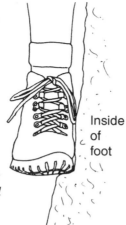

Fig. 2–4. A narrow-welt boot works well on small footholds.

2-4) to prevent it from bending on small holds.

Other desirable boot features include the following:

• Tops that open wide so that even when the boots are frozen or wet, they can be put on easily.
• A minimum number of seams, to decrease the places water can leak through.
• A gusseted tongue, or a bellows tongue, to keep water from easily entering the boot.
• Double- or triple-layered leather or fabric at areas of high wear (toes and heels).
• Hard toe counters (stiffeners) built in to protect the feet, reduce compression caused by crampon straps, and facilitate kicking of steps in hard snow.
• Hard heel counters (stiffeners) built in to increase foot stability and facilitate plunge-stepping down steep snow slopes.

Lightweight hiking boots

Improvements in boot technology have led to evolution of the medium- and lightweight hiking boot (fig. 2-5). Made of leather and nylon, these boots weigh one-third to one-half as much as traditional boots, yet are sturdy enough for three-season trekking on moderate terrain. The uppers of these boots typically are glued to the sole, eliminating the need for a welt. Check that the boots are high enough for ankle protection, that a stiff counter wraps the heel and toe, and that abrasion areas are reinforced.

Advantages of lightweight boots include reduced cost, increased breathability, improved comfort, shorter break-in time, and faster drying. However, they are not as durable and cannot be made as waterproof as leather boots, and they lack the weight and stiffness for kicking steps in firm snow. On difficult off-trail terrain and on snow, leather boots are still preferred.

Fig. 2–5. Lightweight trail boots: a, leather; b, synthetic.

Plastic boots

Plastic boots (fig. 2-6), originally designed for technical ice climbing, have found a much wider market among general mountaineers interested in snow routes or winter climbing. The plastic shell of the boot is waterproof, so the inner insulating boot remains dry and keeps your feet warm. This inner boot can be removed, which helps in drying out perspiration.

Plastic boots need to fit well from the start because their rigid shape will not mold around your feet over time. The boot's relative rigidity and its

Fig. 2–6. Plastic boot: a, waterproof shell; b, insulating inner boot.

high degree of warmth makes it a poor choice for general trail use. When fitting plastic boots, make sure that they do not constrict the feet. Feet swell at high altitude, and plastic boots are frequently used for high-altitude expeditions.

The proper fit

Whether you're looking at leather, plastic, or lightweight boots, the fit is critical. Try on several makes and styles, with socks similar to the ones you will wear on a climb. Be sure to bring along any orthotic devices, insoles, or other inserts you plan to use. Wear the boots in the store for several minutes to give your socks time to compress around your feet. Then note whether the boots have any uncomfortable seams or creases and whether they pinch against your foot or Achilles' tendon. In properly fitting boots, your heels will feel firmly anchored in place while your toes will have plenty of room to wiggle and will not jam against the toe box when you press forward. Boots that are too tight constrict circulation, causing cold feet and increased susceptibility to frostbite. Loose boots, on the other hand, cause blisters.

Most people's feet swell during the course of the day, so consider buying boots in the evening for the best fit. Given the choice between boots that are a hair too big and ones that are a bit too small, go with the larger boots. You can fill the space with a thicker sock, and most boots can shrink as much as a half size over time (because the toe of a boot has a tendency to curl).

Boot care

With proper care, good boots can last several years. Keep mildew at bay by washing the boots frequently. After washing, stuff them with a boot tree or newspaper, and dry them in a warm (not hot), ventilated area. Heat can damage the welt and the adhesive used on boot soles. Avoid drying or storing boots at high temperatures: the boots dried over a campfire are likely to be the ones that fall apart on a future trip. Boot soles usually wear out long before the uppers. High-quality boots can be resoled, although this may change the original fit because new soles tighten the size somewhat.

During an outing, water can get into boots over the top and through the leather and seams. Wearing gaiters keeps water from running into boots from the top. Waterproofing agents applied to the leather and seams stop water from going through the boots.

With new boots, treat the welt first with one of the waterproofing products designed for this purpose. It's a process that needs to be repeated periodically. Boots must be clean and dry, with any wax removed. Apply the material directly to the threads and stitching holes, and let it dry before applying waterproofing to the rest of the boot. Some boot makers use waterproof rubber rands to seal the welt, a desirable feature that simplifies boot maintenance and keeps your feet drier.

Apply waterproofing to the boots a day or two before a trip to give the agents time to penetrate the leather. The makeup of the waterproofing used on leather uppers depends on how the leather was tanned, so follow the manufacturer's recommendations. The nylon in many lightweight boots is difficult to seal completely, but you can make it more water resistant by applying silicone-based sprays. Whatever you use on your boots, apply it frequently if you expect your feet to stay dry.

After using plastic boots, remove the inner boots and clean them with mild soap and water. Remove any debris from inside the plastic shells to prevent abrasion and excessive wear between the outer and inner boots.

Specialized footwear

Depending on the trip, a climber may wear one kind of boot for the approach hike, another type of footwear in camp, and yet another on the climb. If you can afford additional footgear and are willing to carry the extra weight, consider these options:

• Lightweight, flexible trail shoes for long trails, easy approaches, stream crossings, and for wearing in camp. They are less likely to cause blisters and are less fatiguing to wear. (The rule of thumb is that 1 pound of weight strapped to the foot is comparable to 5 on the back.) However, these lightweight shoes may not provide the support you

need when carrying a heavy pack.
• Camp footwear (booties for comfort and warmer sleeping; running or tennis shoes, or sandals, for comfort and to give boots a chance to dry).
• Lightweight nylon-mesh socks for camp use and stream crossings. They are very light, have waffled soles for traction, and dry fast, but give no support.
• Special rock-climbing shoes for technical rock (see Chapter 9 for details).
• Full-shank boots that you can use with rigid crampons for ice climbing.

SOCKS

Socks cushion and insulate your feet, absorb perspiration, and reduce friction between the boot and the foot. Socks made of wool or synthetic materials can perform all these functions, while those made of cotton cannot. Cotton absorbs too much water, which destroys its insulating qualities and increases friction between the boot and the foot.

Most climbers wear two pairs of socks. Next to the skin, a smooth polyester or polypropylene sock transports perspiration from the foot to the outer sock. Over this goes a heavier, rougher sock made of wool or synthetics.

Of course there are many exceptions. A rock climber wants flexible rock shoes to fit like a glove, and so usually wears only one thin pair of socks. A hiker using trail shoes on a warm day keeps feet cooler by wearing just a single pair of socks, while a winter climber may wear three pairs of socks inside oversized boots. Always keep your toes free enough to wiggle. Three pairs of socks give less protection from the cold than two if the last pair constricts circulation.

Before donning socks, consider putting protective moleskin or tape on your feet at places prone to blisters, such as the back of the heel. Moleskin is especially valuable when breaking in new boots or early in the climbing season before your feet have toughened up. Another blister fighter is foot powder sprinkled on your socks and in your boots.

On expeditions or in cold weather, a vapor-barrier sock may be worn between the two main sock layers. Vapor-barrier liners keep moisture next to your foot and prevent perspiration from wetting your thick socks. They also keep your feet warmer by inhibiting the evaporation of sweat. In subfreezing temperatures, these socks reduce the danger of frostbite, but over time the moisture that is kept inside can result in trench foot—a serious problem. If you use vapor-barrier socks, dry your feet thoroughly at least once each day.

Insoles added to the inside of your boots provide extra insulation and cushioning. Synthetic insoles are non-absorbent, do not become matted when damp, and have a loose structure that helps ventilate your foot. Insoles made of felt, leather, and lambskin all absorb moisture and must be removed when drying boots. When trying on new boots, be sure to insert the insoles you intend to wear.

CLOTHING

Humans maintain body comfort by creating a microenvironment of warm air next to the skin. Combinations of cold temperatures, rain, and wind remove this warm air and can initiate a dangerous reduction in body temperature. If left unchecked, this condition, known as hypothermia, leads to uncontrolled shivering, loss of judgment, and eventually death.

Clothing protects you from the cold, wind, and wet and maintains a compatible environment next to your skin. Clothing also must help cool you when conditions become too hot. Over-exertion or excessive temperatures can cause the improperly clothed body to suffer heat exhaustion—an affliction that can be just as deadly as hypothermia.

LAYERING

Clothing maintains the body's microenvironment best when it is worn in multiple layers, letting you adapt easily to the fluctuating temperatures in the mountains. To keep pace with changing conditions, add or subtract layers of clothing one by one.

Three levels form the basis of this clothing system: a layer next to the skin, insulating layers, and an outer protective layer.

The layer next to the skin (long underwear) allows for ventilation so the body can cool itself. During the warmer parts of a day, many climbers wear just their long underwear and a pair of shorts. When it's cold, long underwear, covered by additional clothing, increases your insulation. This layer also transports perspiration away from your skin without absorbing the moisture. (Wet garments in contact with your skin draw away twenty-five times more heat than dry ones.)

The insulating layers (shirts, sweaters, pile coats) trap warm air next to the body. The thicker the layer of trapped or ''dead'' air, the warmer you'll be. However, several light, loosely fitting layers are usually warmer than one thick garment. They are also more versatile because the various pieces can be worn in different combinations depending on the temperature and your level of exertion.

The outer protective layer is essential for minimizing heat loss from wind and rain. Wind stirs up the warm air next to the body and blows it away, a process known as convection. The stronger the wind, the faster heat is blown away, producing a wind-chill effect that makes it feel much colder. When the air temperature is 10 degrees Fahrenheit, a 20-mile-per-hour wind produces a wind-chill effect (fig. 2-7) that is equivalent to −25 degrees. Rain dampens clothing and reduces its insulating

Fig. 2–7. Wind-chill chart

Wind Speed MPH	Temperature (°F)										
	50	40	30	20	10	0	−10	−20	−30	−40	−50
	Equivalent Chill Temperature										
Calm	50	40	30	20	10	0	−10	−20	−30	−40	−50
5	48	37	27	16	6	−5	−15	−26	−36	−47	−57
10	40	28	16	4	−9	−21	−33	−46	−58	−70	−83
15	36	22	9	−5	−18	−36	−45	−58	−72	−85	−99
20	32	18	4	−10	−25	−39	−53	−67	−82	−96	−110
25	30	16	0	−15	−29	−44	−59	−74	−88	−104	−118
30	28	13	−2	−18	−33	−48	−63	−79	−94	−109	−125
35	27	11	−4	−20	−35	−49	−67	−83	−98	−113	−129
40	26	10	−6	−21	−37	−53	−69	−85	−100	−116	−132
above 40	little additional effect										
Danger of Freezing Exposed Flesh if Dry and Properly Clothed:		Little Danger				Great			Extreme		

To use this table, which illustrates the intensely chilling effect of wind, find wind speed (in miles per hour) in left-hand column and temperature (in degrees F) in top row; the intersection of these is the equivalent temperature. For example, at a temperature of 0°F a breeze 15 mph has the cooling effect of a temperature of −36° on a calm day and precautions should be taken to protect exposed flesh from frostbite. The zones shown on the table indicate the danger of frostbite to any exposed flesh of an average person in good condition whose body is properly clothed for the conditions. When the effective temperature is −25°F or less, care should be taken to minimize exposure of bare skin to wind.

value, and wet clothing conducts heat from the body at an alarming rate. A waterproof shell over your insulating layers eliminates heat loss from conduction and convection. Wind cannot penetrate the shell, so warm air next to your body stays put. The shell also keeps the insulating layers drier so that body heat is not conducted away.

FABRICS

Clothing for the outdoors is made from a variety of fabrics, each with advantages and disadvantages.

Cotton is comfortable to wear when dry but absorbs many times its weight in water and loses its insulating qualities when wet. Because it absorbs so much water, it takes a long time to dry. In hot weather, however, cotton ventilates well and helps cool the body. Wet it down on a hot day, and the water evaporating from the cotton will cool you off.

Silk readily absorbs water, but not as much as cotton, so it dries faster. Silk is also useful in hot weather. Wetted down, it helps cool the body through evaporation.

Wool is far less absorbent than cotton, so it holds less water when wet. Consequently, it does not conduct away as much body heat and requires far less heat to dry. Wool is also warmer when wet because it does not collapse and therefore retains much of its dead-air space.

Synthetic pile does not absorb any water. Some moisture is held in suspension between the filaments of the fabric when it is wet, but most of the water can be wrung out. Garments made from synthetic pile are comparatively warm when wet, and they dry fast. Pile is also very light and fluffy so that, ounce for ounce, it traps more dead air than natural fibers like wool. All these features contribute to make pile a versatile and effective insulating material.

Polyester, acrylic, and polypropylene fabrics are used for a variety of long underwear and insulating garments. The synthetic filaments in these fabrics are also lightweight, non-absorbent, and quick drying. The filaments of some are also very good at transporting perspiration away from the body, making them well suited for use next to the skin. More and more fabrics are being designed to do this, and these fabrics have largely replaced wool, cotton, and silk for use in long underwear. When selecting items of clothing, consult the tags on individual garments or get help from a salesperson.

Down is still, ounce for ounce, the warmest insulation available. It is also the most compressible, so it packs away small yet quickly regains its loft—and therefore its warmth—when unpacked. These qualities make down an excellent insulator for cold-weather use. Unfortunately, down loses all its insulating value when wet and is almost impossible to dry in the mountains, making it a poor insulator in wet climates.

Spun synthetic filaments do not collapse when wet, as down does. Therefore they make excellent insulation for coats and sleeping bags used in moist climates. Although cheaper and more easily cleaned than down, they are not as warm, weigh more, and are less compressible. The useful life of synthetics is much shorter than down.

Nylon shells, which go over the insulating layers, give protection from the wind but are not waterproof unless the nylon is coated. Typically, polyurethane coatings are used to waterproof nylon. The thickness of the coating is measured by its weight per square yard, and a 1-ounce coating is the minimum weight you should consider. Polyurethane coatings are lightweight and effective when cared for but are not very resistant to abrasion or mildew, so some climbers prefer shells coated with synthetic rubber. These shells are more durable, but most rubber-coated raingear is too heavy for mountaineering.

Although most coatings keep rain out, they also seal sweat in. If you're working hard, the sweat generated can dampen your insulation from within. Microporous coatings were designed to attack this problem. These coatings have billions of microscopic holes per square inch. Moisture vapor from your skin has a much smaller molecular size than liquid water. The holes in the coating are large enough to let vapor escape but too small for liquid water to get in, so the coating breathes but is still waterproof. Gore-Tex, the first waterproof/breathable fabric on the market, works on the same theory but, rather than using a honeycombed coating, a Teflon film with microscopic holes is laminated to the inside of the nylon shell.

Many climbers see the waterproof/breathables as an improvement over the old-style coated nylons, but the new-generation materials are not perfect. If you work hard, you will exceed the garment's ability to blow off steam, and sweat will condense inside the shell. Once in liquid form, the sweat can no longer escape through the garment. Ventilating the garment helps keep you from overheating and building up perspiration. Most waterproof/breathables need maintenance. When water stops beading and rolling off the surface, the material should be washed, rinsed, dried, and treated with silicone or another waterproofing spray. Apply the spray generously three times over the course of three days.

HEADGEAR

When the rest of the body is covered in clothing, an unprotected head is like a radiator that accounts for more than half of the body's heat loss. The head is the first part of the body to uncover when you're overheated, and the first part to cover when you're cold. The old adage says ''If your feet are cold, put on a hat.'' There's some truth to this because as the head and trunk get cold, the body reduces blood flow to the arms and legs in an attempt to warm vital areas. To increase blood flow back to the arms and legs, you need to warm the vital head and torso areas.

Climbers usually carry several different types of hats. Cotton glacier hats and baseball caps are popular for sun protection. A bandanna can be draped from a hat to help shade your neck, ears, and face, or it can be dipped in water and tied around your head to cool you on a hot day. A lightweight rain hat is useful for warm-weather trips because it keeps your head dry while allowing ventilation at the neck of your rain parka.

Warm insulating caps of wool, polypropylene, or pile are standard for cold weather. Consider carrying two hats, because an extra hat affords almost as much warmth as an extra sweater but weighs much less. Warm hats should also be part of your summer wardrobe in case of a forced bivouac. Balaclavas are versatile insulating hats. Rolled down, they protect the face and neck from the cold; rolled up, they warm the head but allow ventilation of the upper body through the neck area.

THE UPPER BODY

Long underwear

Protection of the torso begins with appropriate underwear. Synthetics like polypropylene and polyester are currently the best fabrics for this purpose. They are soft, stretchy, ventilate well, and wick moisture away from the skin. The underwear comes in a variety of weights, and you can choose which suits your climate and metabolism.

It's smart to buy light-colored long underwear. Light colors absorb *and* radiate heat more slowly. If it is warm enough to strip down to your underwear, you will appreciate having a white rather than black or dark blue shirt exposed to the sun.

Insulating layers

In hot weather a thin cotton shirt will keep you comfortable and serve as a first line of defense against sunburn. Stick to light colors. In cold weather you'll carry several insulating layers for your torso. Shirts and sweaters should be made of wool or synthetics, such as pile, so they still provide warmth if they get wet. Cotton sweatshirts are useless once wet, so don't bring them.

Shirts and sweaters should be long in the torso so they tuck into or pull over the waist of the pants. Gaps between the pants and upper body let valuable heat escape. Similarly, turtleneck sweaters can keep much of the torso's heat from escaping. Tests show that the addition of a turtleneck alone can increase a garment's comfort level by 5 to 10 degrees Fahrenheit.

Jackets insulated with down or synthetic fills are not usually needed on summer trips but are valuable in cold climates and for winter travel. These jackets, weighing between 2 and 3 pounds, are seldom worn while climbing but are needed for emergencies, bivouacs, and the cold hours in camp.

Rain and wind protection

On top of everything comes a shell of nylon or other synthetic material as an outer layer to provide protection from rain and wind. The ideal shell is uninsulated, windproof, waterproof, and breathable. Another option is to carry both a lightweight, unlined nylon windshirt and a coated rain parka. The breathable wind shirt (which won't be completely windproof) will reduce heat lost to the wind yet let sweat pass out of your clothing. The raincoat goes on when the dampness caused by precipitation exceeds the dampness caused by perspiration.

Many of the qualities you should look for in a good rain parka (fig. 2-8)are the same whether or not the fabric breathes.

• A size large enough to allow for additional layers of clothing underneath without compressing your insulation or restricting your movement.
• A hood with a brim, neck flap, and good drawstring to keep water from dribbling down your face and neck. The hood should be large enough to accommodate a hat (or climbing helmet) and should not impair vision when you glance to the side.
• Seams sealed at the factory with tape. Check that the tape has bonded well to the coat. All seams need to be sealed to prevent moisture from entering along the stitching, and it's preferable to have factory-sealed seams rather than trying to seal them later yourself.
• Zippers with large, durable teeth and good flaps that keep the zipper dry.
• Pockets that are easily accessible with gloved hands and with a pack on. Pockets also need good rain flaps that keep water out.
• A coat length that extends below the hips, and a drawstring at the waist that allows you to seal off the bottom of the coat.
• Sleeves that cover the wrists. Snaps, elastic, or Velcro should keep the sleeve in place at the wrist.
• Ventilation: controllable openings at the front,

waist, underarms, sides, and cuffs that allow you to open up for ventilation or shut tight for trapping warm air next to your body.

Some climbers prefer anoraks, a pullover jacket with no front zipper, to standard rain parkas. The front zipper of a standard parka helps ventilation but can also leak, jam, or break. Cagoules (knee-length anoraks) are an option preferred by a few climbers. Ponchos, used by many hikers, are nearly useless in the wind and are not viable rain protection in the high mountains.

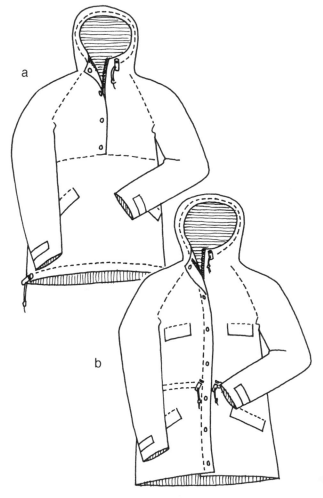

Fig. 2–8. Rain parkas: a, anorak (pullover parka); b, standard (zip-front parka).

THE LOWER BODY

Long underwear

Winter travel and cold alpine conditions call for long underwear, made of polypropylene, other synthetic material, or wool. Under these conditions, long underwear is not optional clothing, but an integral part of the layering system. The convenience and versatility of layering is compromised if a climber faced with a sudden storm has to strip to the skin to put on long underwear. Like your long underwear top, the bottoms should go on first and come off last. It is your heavier insulating pants that should be taken on or off as necessary. Down or synthetic pile underwear can also be carried and worn as outer wear during a bivouac. Synthetic briefs are an alternative to cotton.

Pants

Your insulating pants should be loose fitting for freedom of movement and made of a closely woven fabric with a hard finish so that it's resistant to wind and abrasion. Wool and wool/polyester blends work well. In cool, wet climates, synthetic pile is another good choice because it retains most of its insulating qualities when wet. Pile is not wind resistant, but a nylon shell, integral to the pants or separate, will remedy the problem.

To help layer your lower-body clothing, look for pants with full-length zippers that allow you to put the pants on while wearing boots. The life of your pants can be extended by reinforcing the seat and knees with patches of nylon or other durable fabrics.

Some climbers prefer knickers to long pants because knickers give better freedom of movement. By opening the leg straps and rolling down the socks, you can ventilate the knickers better than standard pants. Shorts are handy for hiking in the rain and for stream crossings, letting you keep your long pants dry inside the pack. Nylon shorts or gym pants worn over long underwear bottoms make a good summertime combination when shorts alone give inadequate protection against wind or cooler temperatures.

Wind and rain protection

Wind and rain pants should parallel your solution for protecting the upper half of your body. A pair of waterproof/breathable pants is one solution. Here again, full-length zippers are convenient. The zippers also help you ventilate the pants. An alternative to the waterproof/breathable fabrics is to carry both lightweight nylon wind pants and a pair of coated, non-breathable rain pants. Don the wind pants in blustery conditions, and the rain pants when it is raining hard.

Waterproof rain chaps are another outer covering for the legs, though they are now seen less and less frequently. Chaps protect the pant legs from rain, while the uncovered seat is protected by a long parka or cagoule. The system saves weight and improves ventilation but is more likely to fail in severe conditions, such as bushwhacking through wet brush or walking in blowing snow.

Some climbers use bibs made from waterproof/breathable fabrics and held up with suspenders. Bibs are best suited to winter snow and ice climbs, ski mountaineering, and cold-weather expeditions. They are considerably warmer than rain pants because they cover much of the torso and keep snow from melting around the waistline, but they are too warm for most summer uses.

Gaiters

The boundary between your trousers and boots is protected by gaiters (fig. 2-9). Climbers often carry gaiters both summer and winter to prevent wet brush, mud, or snow from saturating pant cuffs, socks, and boots. Gaiters are usually made from nylon packcloth and close with snaps, zippers, and/or Velcro. A cord running under the foot from one side of the gaiter to the other helps the gaiter hug your boot, while a drawstring at the top keeps the gaiter from sliding down. A tight fit around the boot is essential to prevent snow from entering underneath the gaiter. A tight fit also helps prevent catching your crampon points on the gaiters.

Short gaiters, those extending 5 or 6 inches over the top of the boot, are adequate for keeping corn

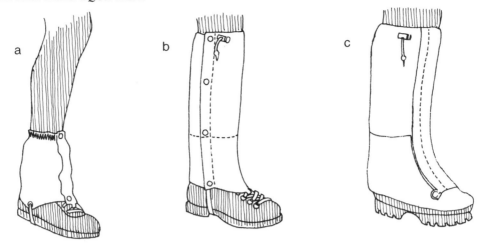

Fig. 2–9. Gaiters: a, short length; b, full length; c, supergaiter.

snow and gravel out of your boots in summer. The deep snows of winter, however, usually call for long gaiters that extend up over the calf.

The portion of the gaiter covering the boot should be made of coated nylon. The upper portion of long gaiters should be made of a waterproof/breathable fabric or an uncoated nylon so that the legs can breathe. Zippers are the usual failure point of a gaiter. Make sure yours are heavy-duty with large teeth. A flap that closes with snaps or Velcro protects the zipper from damage and can keep the gaiter closed and make it functional even if the zipper breaks.

The strap under the foot will wear out during the life of the gaiter. Neoprene straps work well in snow but wear quickly on rock, while heavy cord survives rock better but sometimes balls up with snow. Whatever you use, be sure the gaiter strap is designed for easy replacement.

Supergaiters completely cover the boot from the welt up but leave the lug soles exposed for good traction. Insulation built into these gaiters covers the boots and reduces the chance of frostbite during cold-weather climbs.

HANDS

Mittens are warmer than gloves because they allow your fingers to snuggle together and share warmth. A pair of synthetic pile or heavy wool mittens worn inside waterproof overmitts is fine for most non-technical climbs. Pile mitts can be wrung out when soaking wet and retain most of their insulating loft. Wool is not quite as effective once wet, so carry an extra pair of inner mitts (in a pinch, socks will work). Get inner mitts that cover the wrist.

Outer mitts can be made of a waterproof or waterproof/breathable nylon on the palm side. An increasing number of manufacturers use a non-slip coating on the palm to improve the climber's ability to grip ice tools. The backhand side of the overmitt should breathe, so choose a style that uses waterproof/breathable fabric. The overmitt should overlap the parka sleeve some 4 to 6 inches, and elastic or Velcro closures can cinch the overmitt around the forearm.

To prevent losing your mittens and overmitts, it's a good idea to sew on security cords (unless yours came so equipped). You'll find it's well worth the effort, especially when you need bare hands for snow or rock climbing, or if you take the mittens off in a high wind.

Many climbers wear polypropylene glove liners or a thin pair of fingerless gloves inside their mitts. Both give excellent dexterity for delicate chores. In very cold temperatures (around 0 degrees Fahrenheit, or −18 degrees Celsius), the polypropylene liners are better at keeping exposed flesh from freezing to metal. Fingerless gloves give slightly better dexterity and are preferred for cold-weather rock climbing when you don't want a layer of fabric between your fingers and the rock. You can buy fingerless gloves or make your own by cutting the fingers off a pair of army-surplus wool gloves.

Thin leather gloves are important for safety when rappelling or managing a hip belay because they prevent rope burns that could cause you to release the rope. These gloves are difficult to waterproof and they soak up water, so don't rely on them for warmth.

PACKS

Climbers usually own at least two packs: a rucksack to hold enough paraphernalia for a day climb and a large-capacity pack to carry the necessities for multiday trips. All packs should allow you to carry weight close to your body and center the load over your hips and legs.

INTERNAL AND EXTERNAL FRAMES

Soft packs with internal frames (fig. 2-10) that help maintain the pack's shape and transfer weight to the hips are by far the most popular packs among climbers and ski mountaineers. These packs allow the weight to be carried lower, and they do a better job of hugging the back. Internal frame packs are designed to move with you, while external frame packs tend to shift suddenly as you climb or ski. The sudden movement of 40 pounds or so can easily make you lose your balance.

The volume of most internal frame packs is easy to adjust. Most have compression straps so that the large-capacity pack used to approach a peak can be transformed into a compact, closely fitting summit pack. The clean, narrow profile of internal frame packs allows them to be hauled up rock pitches or taken through heavy brush with far fewer snags than external frame packs.

External frame packs (fig. 2-10) use a long rigid frame that is held away from the back by taut nylon

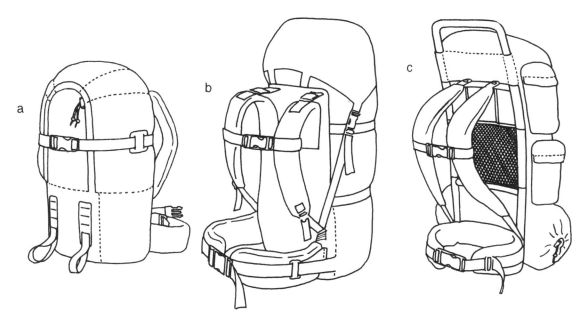

Fig. 2–10. Packs: a, small internal frame summit pack; b, large internal frame pack with padded hip band; c, external frame pack with padded hip band.

back bands. These packs provide excellent weight distribution by allowing the load to be carried high over the hips. This design lets the hips—not just the shoulders and back—share in the heavy work. Because the frame is held away from the back, these packs keep you cooler. External frame packs were designed for trail use and do a better job here than most internal frame packs. Some climbers use them for long, easy approaches and carry a small day pack for the summit day.

BUYING AN INTERNAL FRAME PACK

First and foremost, buy a pack that fits. The pack's adjustment range must be compatible with your back size, extending from the top of your sacrum to the top of your shoulders. Some packs adjust to a wide range of sizes, others don't.

Before buying a pack, loosen all the adjustments and load it up. Without a typical load, you can't tell how the pack rides or if the adjustments provide a good fit. Now put it on. The frame should follow the curve of your back. If it doesn't, can the stays or frame be bent so it does? The shoulder straps should attach to the pack about 2 or 3 inches below the crest of your shoulders and leave little or no gap behind your back. Check that the load-lifter straps work. These straps transfer weight between the shoulders and hips, allowing different muscle groups to share in the work.

Once the pack is adjusted to your liking, check the head clearance. Can you look up without hitting your head on the frame or top pocket? Can you look up if you're wearing a helmet? Next check for adequate padding wherever the pack touches your body. Pay particular attention to the thickness and quality of padding used in the shoulder straps and hip belt. Padding in the hip belt should extend beyond the hip bone. See that the hip belt goes around the top of the hip and not around the waist, because you want the bone structure of the hips to carry the weight of the pack.

Decide what capacity is right for your intended uses. A rucksack for day climbs and lightweight overnight trips usually has a capacity between 1,800 and 2,200 cubic inches. Longer trips and winter climbs require a pack with a capacity between 3,500 and 5,000 cubic inches.

Here are some additional questions to ask when shopping for a pack:

• Does it have a double bottom? This feature will greatly extend its life.
• Does the pack have haul loops and ice axe loops?
• Is there a means of increasing the pack's capacity for extended trips, such as an expandable snow skirt and an adjustable top pocket that will slide higher?
• Are there compression straps to reduce the pack's volume or to prevent the load from shifting while climbing or skiing?
• Does the pack offer a convenient way to carry crampons, skis, snowshoes, and other items?
• Are removable side pockets available? This feature can help convert a day pack into a weekender.
• Does the pack have a sternum strap, which will help keep the pack from shifting on difficult terrain?
• If you will be using the pack for technical climbs or in thick brush, does it have a smooth profile so it will not get hung up?
• Is the pack cloth durable enough for the activities you have in mind?
• How waterproof is the pack?
• Does the pack have load-restraining zippers? If the zippers fail, can you still use the pack?

TIPS ON PACKING

Packs constructed from waterproof materials are not necessarily waterproof. They can leak through seams, zippers, pockets, the top opening, and places where the coating has worn off. Individual plastic bags or good stuff sacks can protect the contents. You can use a large plastic bag as a liner, storing dry items inside the liner and wet clothing between the liner and the sides of the pack.

A climbing pack should allow you to carry the load closer to the pelvic area, the body's center of rotation. This prevents the pack's weight from shifting on the shoulders. On trails, however, the load should be carried high and close to the back.

ESSENTIAL EQUIPMENT

There is a selection of small but critical items that deserve a place in almost every pack. You won't use every one of these items on every trip, but they can be lifesavers in an emergency, insurance against the unexpected.

Exactly how much "insurance" you should carry is a matter of debate. Some respected minimalists argue that weighing down your pack with insurance items causes you to climb slower, making it more likely you'll get caught by a storm or nightfall and be forced to bivouac. "Don't carry bivy gear unless you plan to bivy," they argue.

The majority of climbers, however, take along carefully selected safety items to survive the unexpected. They sacrifice some speed but argue they will always be around tomorrow to attempt again what they failed to climb today.

The special items most climbers believe should always be with you have become known as the Ten Essentials. They are:

1. Map
2. Compass
3. Flashlight/headlamp, with spare bulbs and batteries
4. Extra food
5. Extra clothing
6. Sunglasses
7. First-aid supplies
8. Pocket knife
9. Matches, in waterproof container
10. Fire starter

Other critical items often join the list of essential equipment, depending on the trip. We will take a look at the Ten Essentials and at a number of these additional items in the sections that follow.

THE TEN ESSENTIALS

1. Map

Always carry a detailed map of the area you are visiting, in a protective case or plastic covering. (Chapter 4 gives details about maps, including how to interpret those all-important topographic maps.)

2. Compass

A compass is an essential tool of navigation and routefinding. (Chapter 4 explains the workings of a compass and describes how to use another navigation instrument, the altimeter.)

3. Flashlight/headlamp

Headlamps (fig. 2-11) and hand-held flashlights are important enough and temperamental enough to make it worthwhile to invest in only quality equipment. Waterproof flashlights are worth the added expense. They function reliably in all weather, and the contacts or batteries won't corrode even if stored in a moist garage for months.

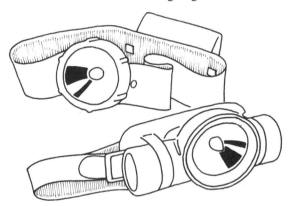

Fig. 2–11. Examples of headlamps

Few headlamps are waterproof, but some are more water-resistant than others. If you decide that a truly waterproof headlamp is important, start by buying a small waterproof flashlight. Sew a wide length of elastic into a headband, then sew several small retaining loops of thinner elastic onto the headband to hold the flashlight in place. The flashlight will be held on the side of your head, much like a pencil resting on top of your ear.

All lights need durable switches that cannot turn on accidentally in the pack, a common and potentially serious problem. Switches tucked away in a recessed cavity are excellent. So are rotating switches in which the body of the flashlight must be twisted a half turn. If it looks like your light switch could be tripped accidentally, guard against this danger by taping the switch closed or removing the bulb or reversing the batteries.

Adjustable focus is an excellent feature available on some lights. The reflector rotates so that the lamp gives flood lighting for chores close at hand or spot lighting for viewing objects far away. Adjustable focus permits maximum use of your light, often letting you see farther and accomplish more than a brighter light lacking this feature.

Flashlight bulbs don't last long, so carry spare bulbs in addition to spare batteries. You don't have to stick with the bulb that comes with your light. If it's a vacuum bulb, you can get a brighter beam with a replacement bulb filled with a gas, such as halogen, krypton, or xenon. These gases allow filaments to burn hotter and brighter than in vacuum bulbs, though they also draw more current (amperage) and shorten battery life.

Most bulbs have their amperage requirement marked on the base. You can get a rough idea of battery life by dividing the bulb's amperage figure into the amp/hours assigned to the batteries. For example, batteries rated at 4 amp/hours will burn about 8 hours with a .5-amp bulb.

It's a good idea to carry bulbs drawing different amperages. Conserve batteries by using low-amperage bulbs for tasks around camp. Switch over to high-amperage bulbs when you need a brighter beam.

Alkaline batteries are the best general-purpose batteries commonly available at mass merchandisers. They pack more energy than cheaper lead-zinc batteries. The major problems with alkalines are that voltage (hence brightness) drops significantly as they discharge, they can't be recharged, and their life is drastically shortened by cold temperatures (they operate at only 10 to 20 percent efficiency at 0 degrees Fahrenheit).

Nickel-cadmium batteries (nicads) can be recharged up to a thousand times, maintain their voltage and brightness throughout most of their discharge, and function well in the cold (about 70 percent efficient at 0 degrees Fahrenheit). However, they don't store as much energy as alkalines.

For climbing, look for high-capacity nicads, which pack two to three times the charge of standard nicads and are worth the added expense.

Lithium batteries have twice the voltage of regular batteries, so you'll need to rewire your light to run off half as many batteries. But one lithium cell packs more than twice the amp/hours of two alkalines. The voltage remains almost constant over the life of a lithium battery, and its efficiency at 0 degrees Fahrenheit is nearly the same as at room temperature. They are expensive.

4. Extra food

A one-day supply of extra food is a reasonable emergency stockpile in case you are delayed by foul weather, faulty navigation, injury, or other reasons. The food should require no cooking, be lightweight and easily digestible, and store well for long periods. A combination of jerky, nuts, candy, granola, and dried fruit works well. Some climbers also bring extra cocoa, dried soup, and tea if a heat source is available.

5. Extra clothing

How much extra insulation is necessary for an emergency? The garments used during the active portion of a climb and considered to be your basic climbing outfit are the inner and outer socks, boots, underwear, trousers, shirt, sweater or pile coat, hat, mitts or gloves, and raingear. These garments suffice over a wide range of temperatures and weather if the climber is active. Extra clothes for an unplanned bivouac are added to these basics according to the season. Ask yourself this question: what do I need to survive the worst conditions I could realistically encounter?

Extra underwear is a valuable addition that weighs little. During a strenuous climb, perspiration can soak the next-to-skin layer and conduct heat away from the core. It is important to get rid of wet garments in contact with the skin before donning thicker insulation, such as down or synthetic coats and an outer shell. Protection for the neck and head can be gained by using long underwear with a zippered turtleneck, and a balaclava. An additional thick hat will retain almost as much warmth as an additional sweater. For the feet, bring an extra pair of heavy socks; for the hands, an extra pair of polyester or pile mitts.

For winter and expedition climbing in severe conditions, you'll need more insulation for the torso as well as insulated overpants for the legs. In addition to your rain shell, carry some sort of extra shelter from the rain, such as a plastic tube tent, a Mylar ''space blanket'' taped into the shape of a bivy sack, or plastic trash-can liners. Carry an ensolite seat pad to reduce heat loss to the snow (some packs can double for this purpose).

Some climbers carry a bivouac sack, weighing about a pound, as part of their survival gear and go a little lighter on their insulating layers. It's a good strategy. (Chapter 3 has details on bivouacs and bivy sacks.) The sack protects your insulation from foul weather, minimizes the effects of convection by quieting the air surrounding you, and traps much of the heat escaping from your body so that the temperature of your cocoon rises.

6. Sunglasses

Eyes are particularly vulnerable to the brilliance of mountain skies, visible light reflecting off snow, and ultraviolet rays—which at 10,000 feet are 50 percent greater than at sea level. The retinas of unprotected eyes can be easily burned, causing the excruciatingly painful condition known as snow-blindness.

Because damage occurs to the eyes before discomfort is felt, it is essential to wear sunglasses to reduce the visible light and invisible ultraviolet rays. Don't let cloudy conditions fool you into leaving your eyes unprotected. Ultraviolet rays penetrate clouds, and the glare of reflected light can cause headaches. Sunglasses should filter 95 to 100 percent of the ultraviolet light. They should also be tinted so that only a fraction of the ambient light is transmitted through the lens to your eyes. For glacier glasses you want a lens with a 5 to 10 percent transmission rate. For more general outdoor use, the lenses should have about a 20 percent transmission rate. Look in a mirror when trying on sunglasses: if you can easily see your eyes, the lenses are too light. Lens tints should be gray or green if you want the truest color, and yellow if you want visibility in overcast or foggy conditions.

There is little proof that infrared rays (heat-carrying rays) harm the eyes unless you look directly at the sun, but any product that filters out a high percentage of infrared, as most sunglasses do, is added eye insurance.

The frames of sunglasses should have side shields that reduce the light reaching your eyes, yet allow adequate ventilation to prevent fogging. Problems with fogging can be reduced by using one of the many anti-fog lens cleaning products that are available.

Groups should carry at least one pair of spare sunglasses in case a pair is lost or forgotten. You can also improvise eye protection by cutting small slits in an eye cover made of cardboard or cloth.

A climber who depends on corrective lenses should carry a spare pair of glasses. Normal glasses with clip-on sunglasses can function as one pair, and good prescription sunglasses with extra-dark coatings can be the second pair. Alternatively, this climber can carry two normal pairs of prescription glasses plus a well-ventilated pair of ski goggles outfitted with a very dark lens.

Many climbers who need corrective lenses prefer using contact lenses instead of glasses. Contacts improve visual acuity, don't slide down your nose, don't get water spots, and allow the use of non-prescription sunglasses. Contacts do have some problems, however. Sun and blowing dust and dirt can dry out or irritate your eyes, though good side shields reduce the ill effects. Back-country conditions make it difficult to clean and maintain the lenses.

7. First-aid supplies

Don't let a first-aid kit give you a false sense of security. It cures very few ills. Doctors say that in the field there is often little they can do for a serious injury or affliction except initiate basic stabilizing procedures and evacuate the patient. The best course of action is to take the steps necessary to avoid injury or sickness in the first place. Still, you want to be prepared for the unexpected.

Your first-aid kit should be small, compact, and

sturdy, with the contents wrapped in waterproof packaging. Commercial first-aid kits are widely available, though many are inadequate. (Two of the best sources of information on items to include in a first-aid kit are *Medicine for Mountaineering*, by James A. Wilkerson, M.D., and *Mountaineering First Aid*, by Marty Lentz, Steven C. MacDonald, and Jan D. Carline, both published by The Mountaineers.)

The contents of your kit will be items you carry on all trips: Band-Aids or other small adhesive bandages, moleskin, adhesive tape, cleansers, soap, butterfly bandages, scissors, triangular bandages, a carlisle bandage, roller gauze, and gauze pads in various sizes. Carry enough bandages and gauzes to absorb a significant quantity of blood. Severe bleeding wounds are a common backcountry injury, and sterile absorbent material cannot be readily improvised.

In addition to the basics, consider the length and nature of your trip. If you are traveling on a glacier, for example, tree branches won't be available for improvised splints, so a wire ladder splint would be extremely valuable in the event of a fracture. For a climbing expedition, you may need to consider appropriate prescription medicines.

8. Pocket knife

Knives are so essential for food preparation, fire building, first aid, and even rock climbing that every climber needs to carry one. The knife should have two folding blades, a can opener, a combination screwdriver and bottle opener, scissors, and an awl. The tools and the inside of the casing should be made of stainless steel. Although you may carry a few additional tools on certain trips, the knife is your basic tool kit. A cord attached to the knife and secured to your belt lets you keep the knife in your pocket for ready access without danger of losing it.

9. Matches

An emergency supply of matches, stored in a watertight container, should be carried on every trip in addition to the matches or butane lighter used routinely. Storing waterproof or wooden matches and a strip of sandpaper in a film canister makes a good emergency system.

10. Fire starter

Fire starters are indispensable for igniting wet wood or starting a fire quickly in an emergency. They can even be used to warm a cup of water or soup, if you have a metal cup to heat it in. Common fire starters are candles or solid chemical fuel (such as heat tabs or canned heat).

OTHER IMPORTANT ITEMS

Water and water bottles

High peaks are often bone dry or frozen solid, so you usually carry the water that is needed to prevent dehydration and maintain energy. A single 1-quart bottle usually suffices, but if it's hot and you sweat a lot, you may need to carry two. Widemouthed polyethylene bottles are the most popular because they can be easily refilled with snow or water, and they impart no flavor to the water, unlike aluminum. If you do use an aluminum bottle, be careful not to mix up the water bottle with the bottle that carries fuel for the stove.

Giardiasis, a waterborne bacterial infection, is a major health concern for alpine travelers. The cyst of the bacteria has tainted many water sources in the wilds, and it takes only one swallow of contaminated water to get sick. The illness takes six to twenty days to manifest itself, with symptoms that include nausea, flatulence, diarrhea, cramps, belching, fever, and dehydration.

Several methods of water purification make water safe to drink by killing or filtering out *Giardia lamblia* and other contaminants. Chemical treatment with tablets of iodine or halazone is effective, and tetraglycine hydroperidide (TGHP) tablets are better yet. Follow directions closely. The required amount of chemical and soaking time increases dramatically with colder water. If you fill your bottle from a glacial stream, you may need to place the bottle in the sun or inside your shirt to raise the water's temperature.

Bringing water to a rolling boil will kill *Giardia*

cysts but may not kill other disease-causing bacteria and viruses unless the water boils for nearly 20 minutes. A combination of chemical treatment and a short boil makes water safe.

Water filters are another option. Filters with a pump can strain a quart of water in minutes and do not impart any unpleasant taste to the water. A good water-filtering device provides a method to clean and extend the life of the filter, which is replaceable. Buy only filters with pore sizes smaller than $4/10$ micron (.4 micron) to ensure you will filter out *Giardia* cysts, flukes, tapeworms, and protozoa.

Sunburn prevention

Sunlight at high altitudes has a burning capacity many times greater than at sea level, so much so that it is a threat to both comfort and health. Climbers cannot avoid long exposure to the sun so they must reduce the burning ultraviolet rays reaching their bodies by covering their skin with clothing or burn-preventing creams (sunscreens).

Individuals vary widely in natural pigmentation and the amount of protection their exposed skin needs. There is only one rule here: the penalty for underestimating the degree of protection needed is so severe, including the possibility of skin cancer, that you should always protect your skin.

Clothing is by far the best sun protection and is worth the discomfort it causes on a hot day. Skin not covered by clothing should be covered with sunscreen. Most sunscreens use *p*-amino benzoic acid (PABA), but if your skin is sensitive to PABA there are other chemicals that yield the same sun protection factor (SPF) as PABA creams.

For glacier travel or a snowy environment, get a sunscreen with an SPF of 15 or more. Cover all exposed skin, even if it's shaded, because reflected light can burn the underside of your chin and nose and the insides of your ears. Some sunscreens are advertised as waterproof and will protect you longer than regular products when you are sweating heavily. Regardless of the sunscreen used, reapply it occasionally if you are perspiring.

Actor's grease paint (clown white) or zinc-oxide pastes ensure complete protection, and the grease bases keep them from washing off. One application lasts the entire climb, except where fingers or equipment rub the skin bare. The disadvantages of these creams is that they are messy and so difficult to remove that you may need help from a cold-cream cleanser.

The area around the mouth is particularly susceptible to fever blisters caused by sun exposure. The lips should be covered with a total-blocking cream that resists washing, sweating, and licking. Zinc oxide and lip balms containing PABA are both good. Reapply lip protection frequently.

Insect repellent

The wilderness is an occasional home for people but the permanent habitat of insects. Some of them—mosquitoes, biting flies, ''no-see-um'' gnats, ticks, chiggers—want to feast on your body. You can protect your body and blood with heavy clothing, including gloves and head nets in really buggy areas.

In hot weather, covering your body with heavy clothing may be unbearable, and insect repellents become a good alternative. Repellents with *N,N*-diethyl-metatoluamide (DEET) claim to be effective against all these insects, but are really best for keeping mosquitoes at bay. One application of a repellent with a high concentration of DEET will keep mosquitoes from biting for several hours, though they will still hover about. Mosquito repellents are marketed under many names, have differing potencies, and come in liquid, cream, spray, and stick form. Be aware that DEET can discolor or dissolve plastics, paints, and synthetic fabrics.

Despite claims by manufacturers, DEET is not very effective at repelling biting flies. Products with ethyl-hexanediol and dimethyl phthalate are much more effective against black flies, deer flies, and gnats. Unfortunately fly repellents don't do much to ward off mosquitoes.

Ticks are a potential health hazard due to the diseases they can carry, such as Lyme disease and Rocky Mountain spotted fever. In tick country, check clothing and hair frequently during the day.

At night, give your clothes and body a thorough inspection to locate ticks before they embed themselves. If you find a tick on your body, cover it with heavy oil (mineral, salad, etc.) to close its breathing pores. The tick may disengage at once. If not, allow the oil to remain in place for half an hour, then carefully remove the tick with tweezers, taking care to remove all body parts. Once a tick is deeply embedded, you may need a physician to remove its buried head.

REPAIR KIT

It's helpful to carry an emergency repair kit for your equipment. It could include wire, tape, safety pins, thread, needles, yarn, string, patches, and small pliers. This kit will probably grow over time as you add items you wished were along on a previous trip.

ICE AXE

An ice axe is indispensable on snowfields and glaciers and on snow-covered alpine trails in spring and early summer. It also has great value when you are traveling in steep heather, scree, or brush, crossing streams, and digging sanitation holes. However, an axe is more dangerous than helpful in unpracticed hands. (Chapters 5 and 12 give the details on using an ice axe.)

EQUIPMENT CHECK LIST

Experienced climber or not, it's easy to forget an important item in the rush to get ready for the next trip. Seasoned climbers have learned that using a check list is the only sure way to avoid an oversight. The following list is a good foundation for formulating your own personal check list. Add to or subtract from this list as you see fit, then get in the habit of checking your own list before each trip.

Items in parentheses are optional, depending on your own preference and the nature of the trip.

Items marked with an asterisk can be shared by the group.

ALL TRIPS

The Ten Essentials

1. Map
2. Compass
3. Flashlight/headlamp, with spare bulbs and batteries
4. Extra food
5. Extra clothing
6. Sunglasses
7. First-aid supplies
8. Pocket knife
9. Matches, in waterproof container
10. Fire starter

Clothing

Boots
Socks: inner and outer
Long underwear
Pants: wool or pile
Sweater or shirt: wool or pile
Parka: wind and rain
Hats: wool, rain, sun
Mittens, gloves
Down or synthetic garments
Wind/rain pants
(Gaiters)
(Shorts)
(Hot-weather shirt)

Other

Rucksack
Ice axe
Emergency shelter or bivy sack
Water bottle/purification tablets
Lunch

Sunscreen and lip protection
Bandanna
Toilet paper
Whistle
(Cup)
(Insect repellent)
(Moleskin)
(Nylon cord)
(Altimeter)
(Watch)
(Camera and film)
(Binoculars)
(Insulated seat pad)

ADDITIONAL ITEMS FOR OVERNIGHT TRIPS

Internal- or external-frame pack
Sleeping bag and stuff sack
Sleeping pad
Spoon
*Shelter: tent or tarp
*Food
*Water container
*Repair kit
*Stove, fuel, and accessories
*Pots and cleaning pad
(Fork)
(Toiletries)
(Spare clothing)
(Camp footwear)
(Pack cover)

ADDITIONAL GEAR FOR GLACIER OR WINTER CLIMBS

Crampons
Carabiners

Slings: chest and prusik
Seat harness
Additional warm clothing: mittens, mitten shells, socks, balaclava, down or synthetic clothing, long underwear
Extra goggles
(Helmet)
(Supergaiters)
(Snowshoes or skis)
(Candles)
(Avalanche beacon)
*Climbing rope
*Rescue pulley
*Snow shovel
*Group first aid
*Alarm clock or alarm watch
*(Flukes, pickets, ice screws)
*(Wands)
*(Snow saw)

ADDITIONAL GEAR FOR ROCK CLIMBS

Helmet
Carabiners
Belay gloves
Runners
Seat harness
Prusik sling
*Climbing rope
*Rack: chocks, stoppers, etc.
*Chock pick
(Belay/rappel device)

---

* = equipment shared by the group
( ) = optional items

· 3 ·

CAMPING AND FOOD

Camping, like mountaineering in general, is part ecstacy, part drudgery. You can make life easier on yourself by learning the art of camping and alpine cookery. Setting up a temporary home in the wilds ought to be quick work and provide cozy shelter, a warm bag, and good food.

Camping has another critical component: respect for the wilderness. In fact, that's number one. Let's face it: our comfort is secondary to preserving the mountain environment. The peaks aren't there for us, they're just there, and it's really not hard to do the things that show our respect for the places that bring us such happiness. That's why this chapter includes a lot of tips on camping clean in addition to camping easy.

LOW-IMPACT CAMPING

THE CAMPSITE

Mountain climbers don't always set up camp in the most comfortable places. They may walk right past an idyllic spot in the forest in favor of a windy mountain ledge because that puts them closer to the summit. What other reasons might there be for picking a particular campsite? Because it's comfortable? Scenic? Environmentally sound? Sometimes you can have it all, but at other times you need to give a little to help preserve the wilderness.

Let's look at camps from the standpoint of the wilderness to see which sites are least damaging to the environment. From best to worst, they are:

Snow: The snow will melt and show no sign of your tenancy.

Rock slab: Solid rock resists most damaging effects of a campsite.

Sandy, dirt, or gravelly flat: This is the next-best choice.

Open, plant-sparse area in deep forest: This is less ideal than the first three choices.

Grass-covered meadow above timberline: Meadows above timberline have a brief growing season and are the most fragile of mountain ecosystems. A tent left on a grass-covered meadow for a week can wipe out an entire growing season for the covered patch. Moving a long-term camp every few days reduces the harm to any one spot.

Plant-covered meadow above timberline: Alpine plants grow very slowly. Heathers, for example, have only a couple of months to bloom, seed, and add a fraction of an inch of growth. They could take years to recover from the damage of a brief encampment.

Waterfront: Waterside plant life is especially delicate and water pollution is a growing problem as more people head into the backcountry. A large proportion of long-established campsites in American mountains are on the banks of lakes and streams, but many areas now ban camping within 200 feet of the water.

In general, you want to honestly visualize the impact of any campsite. Camp away from water, meadows, trails, and other campers. Look for a resilient, naturally bare site. Try to find a spot that has just the right natural slope so you won't have to level it or dig channels for drainage. If there happens to be an established campsite far enough back from a water source, use it rather than setting up a new one.

From the standpoint of comfort, wind is a big consideration in choosing a campsite. You will find that alpine breezes are capricious. An up-slope afternoon breeze may reverse at night to an icy down-slope draft from snowfields. Cold air, heavier than warm air, flows downward during settled weather, following valleys and collecting in depressions. Thus there is often a chill breeze down a creek or dry wash and a pool of cold air in a basin. Night air is often several degrees cooler near a river or lake than on the knolls above.

Consider wind direction in pitching your tent. It can be a good idea to face an opening into the wind so that wind blowing in will distend the tent, equalizing interior and exterior pressure and minimizing tent flapping. But alpine winds are reversible without warning. One consolation of foul weather is that storm winds are fairly consistent.

CAMPFIRES

The old romantic days of cooking over an open fire and lounging around a big campfire are just about over. The price is too high in old scarce trees, especially at higher elevations. And no matter where, campfire scars are a blemish. Mountaineers now cook almost exclusively on lightweight stoves they carry with them, a big step toward low-impact, no-trace camping.

Some simple rules apply in case you do build a campfire. Keep it small, within an existing fire ring, and only where it's safe and legal. Stay there until the fire is dead and the ashes cold. For firewood, use only dead or downed wood from outside the camp area; never cut a standing tree or snag. You might consider using a stove, even if campfires are permitted, because the stove fire doesn't mar the landscape and because it's more dependable than counting on finding firewood.

WASHING

You can keep dishes reasonably clean without soap. By taking moderate care in cleaning pots with hot water after each meal, parties commonly remain healthy on week-long trips without so much as a pinch of soap or biodegradable detergent. Fill pots with water as soon as they are empty and clean them right away or leave them to soak. Be sure to get rid of the cleaning water a long way from water sources, and if you do use soap, use a biodegradable product and keep it off the plant life. On weekend trips it can be easiest to carry dishes and pots home dirty.

Woven plastic or metal scouring pads are handy and weigh next to nothing. Teflon-coated pots are easy to clean, but of course they can be easily damaged with metal or abrasive cleaners. Using sand, gravel, or grass to clean pots can leave unsightly bits of food to attract flies and rodents. Carry leftovers out with you, and try to do better meal planning next time. Also as part of the cooking routine, it helps to have a large water container along to save yourself and the terrain from a lot of trips to the water source.

If you need to wash yourself or your clothing, stay at least 200 feet from water. Go without soap, or use only biodegradable soap in very small quantities.

SANITATION

Plastic bags can be indispensable. Mountaineers use them to package food, as emergency mini-tents, and sometimes to keep the water away from their feet. Keep a heavy-duty plastic bag on hand to carry the garbage. The old rule about food containers is that if you can carry it into the wilderness full, you can carry it out empty. Mountaineers clean up every bit of their garbage (yes, even aluminum-foil flecks from a campfire) and often pack out anything they find in camp or on the trail, no matter who left it. Never bury garbage or dump it in latrines. The golden rule of camping: Leave the campsite cleaner than you found it.

Heavily used campsites usually have a pit toilet,

set away from any source of water. Otherwise, go at least 200 feet from any open water (allowing for maximum level around lakes), dig a hole 8 to 10 inches in diameter and no deeper than 8 inches. Fill it after use with loose soil and tamp the sod back in place. Pack out used non-biodegradable items of personal hygiene, such as sanitary napkins, in airtight containers. In snow, find an unobtrusive toilet area, such as a clump of trees well away from camp, and wherever possible burn the used toilet paper. Pick up any trash before it gets covered with new-fallen snow, where it will lie hidden until the spring thaw.

ANIMALS AND FOOD

Bears and rodents will gnaw through plastic bags, packs, and even tents for food. A food sack or pack hung from a tree or suspended from a pole must be farther from the tree trunk and higher from the ground than a bear can reach. Watch out for mice that can walk a tight line and drop down to the food. Hanging food 4 feet from the tree trunk and 8 feet from the ground gives you a fighting chance against animals.

Some other tips: Keep the cooking area and food storage well away from where you sleep. Package food in containers with tight lids or in sealed plastic bags to conceal the smell. Don't encourage the wildlife by feeding them.

Hiding a food cache for your party in the wilderness is generally not acceptable. Animals can get into an improperly protected food cache and leave a big mess, which will only draw more animals.

SHELTER

When you settle in for a night in the mountains, your home away from home will be a tent, bivy sack, tarp, snow shelter, or hut. We will take a close look here at the kinds of shelters you can carry on your back or build from the snow. (Chapter 15 discusses tents, snow shelters, stoves, and sleeping bags as they are used in winter and expedition climbing.)

Tents are the most common shelter because of their many virtues. They are relatively quick and easy to put up, rainproof, private, usable almost anywhere, a refuge from wind or sun, and often roomy enough for you *and* your gear. They also are heavy and expensive. Tents are usually the best shelter above timberline and for glacier camps, winter camping, in strong winds, and in mosquito country. Alpine climbers in a hurry can get nighttime protection from a lightweight bivy sack, though the sack is not much help in heavy rain and has limited room inside for gear. A tarp in combination with a bivy sack increases protection from the elements. A snow shelter is a haven from wind and storm, but building it is hard work and time consuming.

Curiously enough, shelter is often more necessary on a clear night than on a cloudy one. When two opposing surfaces differ in temperature, the warmer radiates heat to the colder. Since the human body is usually warmer than the night sky, exposed portions of the body or sleeping bag radiate heat and grow cold. Any shelter at all serves as a baffle. Clouds often reflect heat back to earth, and thus have the effect of a huge tarp between sleeper and sky. The clear nights are the cold ones.

TENTS

The choice of a tent depends on what you like and what you plan to use it for. Will it be used only in the summer, or for three or four seasons of the year? Above or below timberline? For you alone, or for two people, or three, or four? Are you after luxurious space, or just the bare minimum? How much weight are you willing to carry? How much money are you able to spend? Manufacturers offer almost any combination of size, weight, and design. The choice is yours, after consulting catalogs, stores, your friends, and neighboring campers.

Water resistance

Tents are built with either single or double walls, of either waterproof or breathable materials. A completely enclosed unit must be well ventilated and preferably should "breathe." If the tent is waterproof, the moisture you exhale condenses on the cold walls and runs down to collect in puddles on the floor. In a single night, you and your tentmate can expel enough water vapor to drench the sleeping bags. Watch out for the cheap tents built of a single layer of unbreathable waterproof material. They are only good for the mildest of conditions below timberline where the door and windows can be left open for ventilation; even then, you can expect some condensation. Some single-walled nylon tents have a design that uses gravity to spread and remove condensation, but to be effective, the tents must be well ventilated.

The dilemma of a waterproof yet breathable tent is solved by using double walls. The inner wall is breathable: it is not waterproof, so it allows your breath and perspiration to pass through to the outside. The outer layer is a waterproof rain fly, usually separate, that keeps the rain off the tent and also collects and disposes of the body moisture from inside the tent. The rain fly must not touch the inner walls, because where it touches, water will condense inside. The fly should come fairly close to the ground to cover the tent and entrance, discouraging wind-driven rain. Even in a double-walled tent, sleeping bags can get wet from condensation that forms on the waterproof side panels that extend a foot or so up from the floor in some models.

An important step in keeping a tent dry is to close up the needle holes from stitching by painting all seams with waterproof seam sealer. Do this before the tent is ever used. Some tents come with factory-sealed seams; on others, it's up to you, but it's got to be done. In camp, put a plastic or nylon ground cloth under the tent to stop ground moisture from entering the floor of the tent and to keep the bottom clean and protected from abrasion.

Strength

Many tents are rated by a "relative strength factor," the speed of wind a tent can withstand before the frame deforms. If you expect to run into wind and snow, this is an important consideration. The tent should stand up to high winds and snow loads without structural failure.

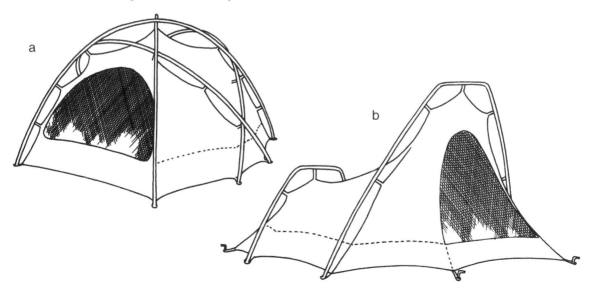

Fig. 3–1. Two types of mountain tents: a, dome; b, tunnel (hoop).

Weight

It's usually a tradeoff: light weight, or more comfort and durability. Lightweight tents are available, but the question is whether they are big enough or tough enough for your particular uses. Simply look for the lightest tent that meets your requirements for number of occupants, head room, floor space, gear storage, strength, climate, and weather conditions. A two-person tent for summer camping might be light, while a three-person, four-season expedition tent could weigh twice as much, and be two to three times as expensive.

Shape

The trend in tent shapes has been to tunnels and domes (fig. 3-1). These designs make maximum use of space and minimize the number of stakes and guy lines. The free-standing dome needs no guy lines at all and can be picked up and moved as a unit, but it still must be staked down so it won't blow away. The two- or three-hoop tunnel tent, usually not free standing, offers efficient use of space and has wind-shedding characteristics. The traditional A-frame doesn't give as much usable space, but it's a simple, proven design.

Size

The two-person tent is probably the most popular size and offers the greatest flexibility in weight and choice of campsite. For versatility in a group, it's generally better to bring, for example, two two-person tents rather than one four-person tent. Many two-person tents handle three in a pinch, yet are light enough to be used by one person occasionally. Some three- and four-person tents are light enough to be carried by two people who crave luxurious living. Larger tents, especially those high enough to stand in, are big morale boosters during an expedition or long storm. For carrying, you can distribute the weight among a group by dividing the tent into parts.

Color

Warm tent colors such as yellow, orange, and red are cheerier if you're stuck inside, and they make it easier to spot camp on the way back. On the other hand, more subdued hues blend into the landscape. One's an eyesore; the other may be camouflaged only too well if you're having a little trouble finding camp.

Other features

Entrance designs offer zip doors, tunnels, alcoves, vestibules, and hoods. Compare designs to find the one that looks like it will keep out the most rain and snow as you're coming and going. Vestibules can be nice as a way to shelter the entrance and provide more room for gear, cooking, and dressing. There are a lot of options in the arrangement and type of ventilation holes and windows. Mosquito netting can help keep out rodents as well as flies and mosquitoes.

Cooking inside a tent

Avoid cooking inside a tent, especially with stoves that use white gas. Fumes, spilled fuel, and stove flare-ups are fire hazards. Asphyxiation is a danger in a closed tent, particularly from the combination of a watertight coated-nylon tent and cooking fumes. Cooking also adds greatly to inside condensation.

If you must cook inside the tent, do it in an alcove or vestibule. Well-placed ventilation holes can lessen the danger. Always start the stove outside the tent and use an insulating pad under the stove once it's inside.

Care and cleaning

Your tent will give more years of good service if you are careful to air-dry it thoroughly before storing it away after each trip.

To clean a tent, hose it off with water, or wash with mild soap and water. Scrub stains with a sponge or brush. Don't put the tent in a washer or dryer. High temperatures or prolonged exposure to sun are damaging to tent material.

TARPS

A tarp is light in weight and low in cost, and may offer adequate shelter (fig. 3-2) from all but extreme weather in lowland forests and among subalpine trees. It gives less protection than a tent from heat loss and wind, none at all from insects or rodents, and demands ingenuity on your part and some cooperation from the landscape to set up.

Plastic tarps don't hold up very well, but are cheap enough that you can replace them often. Coated-nylon tarps come with reinforced grommets on the sides and corners for easy rigging. If your tarp doesn't have grommets, sew on permanent loops of fabric, such as nylon or twill tape, before leaving home. Alternatively, you can just tie off each corner (fig. 3-3) around a small cone or pebble from the campsite. Take along some lightweight cord to string the tarp and perhaps a few light stakes.

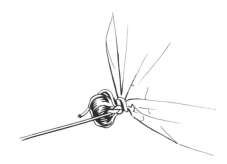

Fig. 3–3. Securing a tarp without grommets

The most versatile tarp size is about 9 by 12 feet—luxurious space for two people and their gear, and adequate for three, or even four. An 11-by 14-foot size will handle four campers comfortably. Since the outer margins of tarp-covered ground are usually only barely protected, usable space quickly approaches the vanishing point if your tarp is smaller than 9 by 12 feet. Put down a waterproof ground sheet, but if rain results in a surprise flood, be ready to move camp. A tarp is not meant to be used as a blanket, because perspiration will condense inside the waterproof material and leave you damp.

BIVOUAC SACK

For super-lightweight alpine traveling, the bivy sack takes the place of a tent in providing shelter

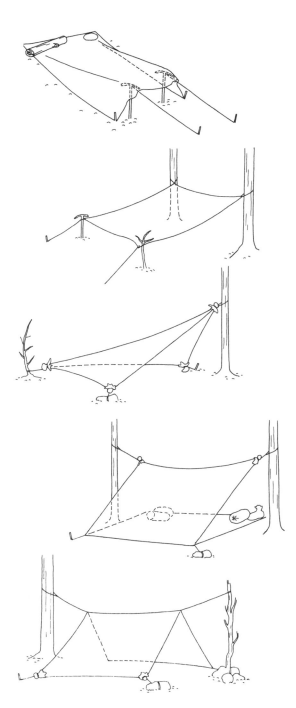

Fig. 3–2. Improvising a shelter with the basic tarp

from wind and rain. The sack is a large envelope of tightly woven fabric with a zipper entrance at one end. The bottom, usually of waterproof coated nylon, goes against an insulating ground pad. The upper side, of a breathable, waterproof material such as Gore-Tex, allows moisture to escape into the atmosphere. The bivy sack is designed for one person, two in an emergency. It needs no poles or stakes, but usually has strong loops for anchoring and can be used by itself or to add extra warmth to a sleeping bag.

SNOW SHELTERS

Newcomers to snow camping are sometimes surprised at what a warm, comfortable, and beautiful experience it can be. To make it work, a good shelter and insulation are essential. At the very least, every snow traveler needs the skills and equipment to survive overnight in the snow.

Tents in the snow

The most convenient snow shelter is a tent installed on a stamped-out platform slightly larger than the tent floor. It's easy to put up and gets you quickly out of the elements. When conditions are serious, a tent can shelter double to triple the usual number of occupants.

There are a few tricks to anchoring a tent in snow, where metal or plastic stakes can melt out during the day. Stakes can be replaced by "deadman" anchors (fig. 3-4), such as a rock, a bag filled with rocks, or a nylon stuff sack filled with snow. Attach a cord or sling to the deadman, bury the deadman in the snow, stamp down the snow above it, and then connect a tent guy line to the cord or sling. Stakes themselves can be used as deadman anchors by burying them horizontally in a snow trench, perpendicular to the guy line. Even better, prepare the deadman in advance by drilling holes in a stake or metal plate and attaching a bridle, to which the guy line can be tied. Snowshoes and ice axes also make solid anchors, but of course you can't use them for anything else while they're holding down the tent.

Snow campers have to watch out that heavy, wet snow does not pile up on the tent or fly, because too much force can break rigging or tent poles and bring the whole structure down. A heavy snow load can even bury a tent and its occupants, asphyxiating them. Shake the walls and shovel out around the tent as often as necessary to keep a big load of snow off. A snow wall built around the tent helps give protection from blowing snow and heavy wind.

Snow caves

A snow cave (fig. 3-5) provides more protection, comfort, and insulation from a storm than a flapping, gale-swept tent, and it's an emergency shelter when you have no tent. Knowing how to build snow caves is an essential mountaineering skill. Be prepared for the fact that it's a time-consuming job.

You can dig an emergency cave with a cooking pot, a hard hat, or whatever gear might be handy, but a lightweight snow shovel is the best tool. (A

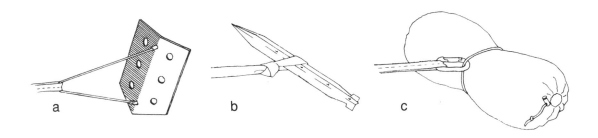

Fig. 3–4. Deadman anchors: a, metal plate; b, tent stake; c, nylon stuff sack.

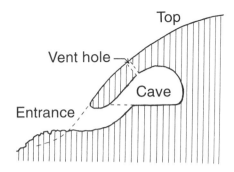

Fig. 3–5. Cross-section of snow cave

grain scoop—a lightweight shovel with a very broad blade—can move a lot of snow, but it's difficult to use in tight quarters.) Holes can be drilled in the shovel base to make it lighter, without sacrificing its scooping power. Even with two shovels in the party, it can take 2 or 3 hours to dig a shelter for four people.

Here's how to go about building a snow cave:

Find a location. Look for obvious hazards. Are you on a potential avalanche slope? Could wind blow snow over the opening and seal you in? Look for fairly firm snow at least 6 feet deep. A short steep slope, such as along a riverbank or on the side of a snowdrift, makes for a better cave than trying to dig one on the flat.

Get to work. Keep your clothing dry. Work slowly to avoid excessive sweating.

Dig an entryway into the slope, far enough to start a tunnel. Continue to dig inward about 3 feet to form the entrance to the cave, then angle upward to excavate a living area. There should be at least 1 foot of snow on the slope above the cave ceiling to provide enough strength to keep it from collapsing.

Put the cave floor above the top of the entry tunnel, in order to trap warm air inside. Make the ceiling smooth, with no bumps or protrusions, so melting snow will run down the walls rather than drip on the climbers. Put down a ground sheet to keep things dry and prevent loss of equipment in the snow. A small tarp over the entrance will help keep the weather out.

Punch a ventilation hole through the ceiling.

Enlarge the hole if it gets too warm inside.

There is even a way to build an emergency snow cave in shallow powder snow (fig. 3-6). You need at least 6 inches of snow, and it takes about 3 hours. Step by step, this is the way to do it. Drive a 6-foot stick vertically into the snow. Take another and draw a circle 12 feet in diameter around the stake. Lay the second stick on the snow, one end touching the vertical stick. (The second stick becomes a "guide" to point you toward the vertical stick after you've buried it within the cave.) Shovel snow into a big pile within the circle, packing it down until its center is about 1 foot above the top of the vertical stick. Let the pile sit for an hour or so, then tunnel into the pile following the guide stick. Excavate enough snow to make a small room, large enough for two or three people, with 2-foot-thick walls. Remove the vertical stake.

Fig. 3–6. Snow cave built in less than 6 inches of snow

Tree-pit shelter

With a little improvisation, natural shelters can be converted into snow hideaways in an emergency. Such shelters occur under logs, along riverbanks, or in the pits formed when snow melts and settles away from large trees. For a tree-pit shelter, enlarge the natural hole around the trunk and roof it with any available covering, such as ice blocks, tree limbs, or canvas. Boughs and bark can provide insulation (but don't cut live boughs unless it is a life-or-death emergency).

Snow trenches

When it is getting dark or the weather is especially bad, a snow-block shelter might be your answer. The trench igloo (fig. 3-7), built on either a slope or on the flat, is a quick emergency shelter for one or two people. Dig a narrow trench and then roof the trench, A-frame style, with snow blocks. (The blocks can be created as part of the process of removing snow for the trench, or they can be quarried nearby.) Then enlarge the interior and provide a vent hole. Smooth out any irregularities in the ceiling so that condensation will run down the blocks and not drip on the occupants. This shelter is not as easy to build as it looks, so practice first in good weather.

A more basic emergency snow shelter can be built by digging a trench some 4 to 6 feet deep and large enough for the party, then stretching a tarp over the top, perhaps gaining a slight angle by anchoring one side to a ridge of snow. This works well in wind or rain, but a heavy snowfall can collapse a roof that is so nearly flat. The smaller the trench, the easier it is to keep warm. Again, be sure to provide for ventilation.

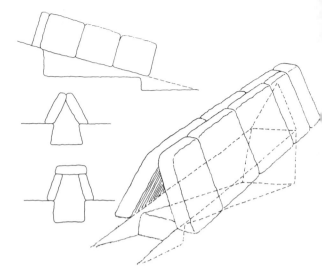

Fig. 3–7. Trench igloo

Igloos

Igloos are equal in protection to snow caves, but the traditional dome-shaped igloo (fig. 3-8) built of snow blocks that spiral upward to the top requires

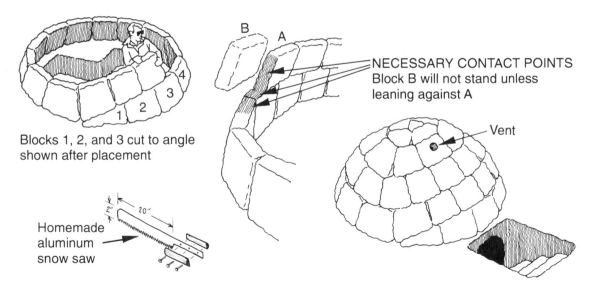

Blocks 1, 2, and 3 cut to angle shown after placement

Homemade aluminum snow saw

NECESSARY CONTACT POINTS
Block B will not stand unless leaning against A

Vent

Fig. 3–8. Construction of a traditional igloo

proper snow consistency or preparation, plus a builder with a good bit of expertise. Wet, packed snow provides blocks that stick together and stay in place, but makes them heavy and difficult to handle. Wind-packed snow is the easiest to work with. If the snow is soft, stomp it down and let it consolidate for a few minutes before starting to

saw blocks with a snow saw or shovel. Each snow block should measure about $2^1/_2$ feet by $1^1/_2$ feet by $1/_2$ foot. Bevel the bottom of each block so the wall will tilt inward at the proper angle. Hold each block in place as it is installed while the cracks are chinked with snow. The igloo entrance should be below floor level so that warm air is trapped inside.

SLEEPING BAGS

Your sleeping bag should be lightweight, warm, comfortable, easily compressible, have a hood or other way to keep your head covered, and generally suit the climate where you do your camping.

WARMTH

The warmth of a sleeping bag is provided by insulating material that traps dead air. How warm a particular bag is depends on the type and amount of this insulating fill, the thickness (loft) of the fill, and the bags's size, style, and method of construction.

Sleeping bags are generally categorized as recommended for summer, three-season, or winter expedition use. (See Chapter 15 for tips on sleeping bags for winter climbs.) Manufacturers give their bags comfort ratings, meant to indicate the lowest temperature at which the bag will be comfortably warm. Methods of rating the bags vary from manufacturer to manufacturer, so they can give only a general idea of how the bag will perform. Bags are usually rated to a minimum temperature of somewhere between 40 degrees and −20 degrees Fahrenheit (between about 5 degrees and −30 degrees Celsius).

How closely a rating matches you personally depends on whether or not you are in a tent, the clothing you are wearing, the ground insulation, and your body size, metabolic rate, and caloric intake. Look for a rating that matches your use. If you're mainly a summer backpacker, a bag rated to −20 degrees Fahrenheit will be too warm.

The warmest, lightest sleeping-bag design is the mummy bag—tapered toward the feet, hooded to

fit over the head, and with a small face opening secured with drawstrings. Whatever the design, your bag should have a form-fitting hood or a semicircular piece with drawstrings to keep your head warm and prevent heat loss. Some bags incorporate an insulated collar to provide extra warmth around the shoulders, and some include extra insulation at critical areas, such as chest or feet. You can buy a thin over-bag to put around the sleeping bag during colder weather to improve the bag's performance. Also available are vapor-barrier liners (for inside the sleeping bag) that can increase your bag's comfort range by 10 or 15 degrees Fahrenheit. However, figure that whatever clothing you have on in the bag is going to get damp from body vapor that has nowhere else to go. These liners are best used at below freezing temperatures.

There are some basic procedures for sleeping warmer, regardless of the bag you are in. Undress inside the bag. Wear a wool hat and dry socks to bed. Secure the bag closely around your face. Breathe through a sweater to reduce heat loss from exhalation. You can put your head inside the bag to help warm them both, though the water vapor from your breath will likely make it damper inside.

The comfort of the bag offers a chance to warm up not only you, but some of your things. Small items, like mittens and socks, can come into the bag to dry. Don't try to dry larger items of clothing by wearing them to bed, because they will just keep you cold and make the bag wet. In very cold weather, you may want to bring boots inside, wrapped in plastic. You may also need to make room for a water bottle, to keep it from freezing.

TYPES OF INSULATION

The warmth, weight, and cost of a sleeping bag depend chiefly on the kind and quantity of insulation, which is either goose down or a synthetic material.

Goose down is still the most efficient insulation per unit weight. Down bags are warm, very compressible, retain their loft well, and are long-lasting. Disadvantages? High cost and water absorbency. A wet down bag loses most of its loft and insulating value, making it almost worthless until it can be dried out. A down bag takes so long to dry—more than a day in good conditions—that it can't be dried during wet periods in the mountains. This characteristic makes down a questionable choice in a wet climate, unless you take extra care to keep it dry.

Synthetic insulation is resistant to moisture, retains most of its loft when wet, and dries relatively quickly. Bags with synthetic insulation are less expensive than down-filled designs. These bags are still slightly heavier than comparable down styles and do not compress quite as easily, thus making a weightier, bulkier load. Synthetic insulation does not last as long as down, and loses much of its loft with use.

CONSTRUCTION

Down bags are made with one of three basic construction methods (fig. 3-9) to keep the fill uniformly distributed: sewn-through, slant-tube, or overlapping tube. In sewn-through construction, the inner cover is stitched directly to the outer, a simple and inexpensive method but one with substantial heat loss at the seams. Most down bags are of slant-tube construction, which eliminates cold spots at the seams. The most efficient design, overlapping tubes, is used only in the most expensive bags. In addition, many designs incorporate channel blocks, baffles that prevent down from shifting.

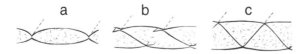

Fig. 3–9. Down sleeping bag construction: a, sewn through; b, slant tubes; c, overlapping tubes.

Synthetic bags are built using a variety of methods. There are two basic types of synthetic fills. The first is a long, stable polyester fiber, manufactured in batts that stand up well to use and laundering. A widely used construction method is the shingle style, in which sections of batting are sewn in the bag, overlapping like roof shingles to cover cold spots. The second type of fill is a short, stable polyester fiber that is quilted or sewn into fine scrims to keep it from wadding up or moving around. To avoid cold spots, these must be shingled, or quilted in double or triple layers with quilted lines offset (fig. 3-10).

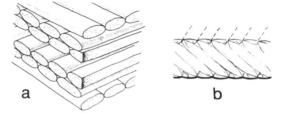

Fig. 3–10. Synthetic sleeping bag construction: a, triple-offset quilting; b, shingle.

Zippers are the almost universal means of closure even though they sometimes snag the fabric or go off the trolley. They are backed up with a tube of insulating material to reduce heat loss through the zipper. Long zippers make it easy to get in and out of the bag and are a big help in ventilating the lower portion. If you want to zip two bags together, be sure one zipper is right-sided and the other is left-sided.

EFFECTS OF WETNESS

Do yourself a big favor and keep your sleeping bag dry, especially if it is filled with down. Compared with down bags, polyester-filled bags retain much of their warmth when wet and are easier to dry, but a wet polyester bag is still a wet bag and colder than a dry one. You can buy a Gore-Tex sleeping-bag shell that lets body vapor escape while helping to protect the bag from condensation inside a tent or dripping water in a snow cave. Consider putting the sleeping bag inside a plastic sack before putting it on your pack, because most stuff sacks don't keep water out.

CARE AND CLEANING

Dirt decreases insulating efficiency. You should spot-clean soiled areas, especially around the head of the bag. A removable, washable liner or an outer cover of breathable material can provide protection from dirt and abrasion.

Both down and polyester bags can be hand-washed with any mild soap or with one of the excellent down soaps that are available. Rinse thoroughly to remove all soap. Squeeze water out gently by hand, or put the bag carefully through the spin cycle of a front-loading washing machine (with no agitator).

Down or polyester bags also can be washed in a front-loading washing machine on the gentle cycle because it doesn't have an agitator. The agitator will blow out the baffles in a down bag, which must be babied when wet to prevent damage to the inner structure.

Hang bags to air dry; do not dry either polyester or down bags in a dryer. Allow more drying time for a down bag (several days), and shake and turn the bag frequently to break up lumps of wet down. Both polyester and down bags can be put in a dryer after they have been line dried; use the fluff setting (air only—no heat), to fluff up the bag. A clean tennis shoe put in with the down bag may help break up any clumps of down.

A polyester or down bag can be dry-cleaned, but only by a professional who knows how to handle the material and only if it is thoroughly aired afterward to remove all traces of toxic fumes, which can cause illness or death. For best results, do what the manufacturer says.

GROUND INSULATION

The foundation for a comfortable night in the out-of-doors is a good piece of insulation under your sleeping bag. Summer or winter, in a tent or outside, that pad makes for a softer, warmer bed. On wet ground or snow, it's essential.

A thin pad of closed-cell foam, such as ensolite (more durable) or polyethylene (lighter weight), provides good insulation. Improved designs in closed-cell pads feature softer sleeping surfaces, lower weight, and an increased ability to trap air, resulting in greater thermal efficiency. Other pads use open-cell foam that offers $1^1/2$ inches of padding, but it makes for a bulky roll and must be protected from absorbing water.

An air mattress by itself is soft but provides no insulation. In fact, the air in the mattress carries heat away from the body. A pad, such as the Therm-a-Rest, that combines the insulation of open-cell foam with the softness of an air mattress is very popular and effective. Insulation pads come in a variety of lengths, but one that's only 4 feet long is usually adequate because you can use items of gear to support or insulate feet and legs. If you're stuck without a pad, use extra clothing, the pack, rope, or boots for padding and insulation.

BIVOUACS

A bivouac is a lightweight, no-frills overnight stay—sometimes planned, sometimes not. Climbers plan spartan bivouacs so they can travel fast and light and start high on the mountain. An unplanned bivouac comes as a not-so-pleasant surprise due to injury, bad weather, or getting off route.

Climbers at a planned bivouac camp make sure they have the essentials for a tolerable if not comfortable night, such as a bivy sack or cagoule, perhaps a tarp, some special food, and plenty of clothing.

Climbers at an emergency bivouac also carry everything necessary for survival—all the Ten Essentials and usually a good bit more. You can prepare for your own eventual unplanned bivouac by carrying an emergency shelter in your day pack, in the form of a very light bivy bag or plastic tube tent or even a couple of very large plastic trash bags. Another alternative for shelter from wind and rain is your pack. When it's time to settle down for a bivouac night, put your feet inside the empty pack, and pull the pack's load extension collar (the ''bivouac sleeve'') up over your legs and hips. Wear a waterproof parka or poncho to take care of the rest of your body.

A low-altitude bivouac might be a fairly comfortable affair, where you can get by comfortably by donning some extra clothing and sitting on a small insulating pad in front of a fire while you enjoy a hot drink. Most bivouacs aren't so pleasant. For a climbing bivouac, you may have to anchor yourselves and your gear to the mountain for safety during the night. Always conserve body heat by taking off wet boots, putting on dry socks and other dry clothes, keeping snow off your clothes, loosening belts and other items that can impede circulation, and putting on all the warm clothing you need or have. Huddle together with your bivouac-mates for as much warmth as possible.

How much clothing and gear should you carry to ensure that you survive a bivouac? The answer depends on a lot of other factors, including your experience, physical condition, and mental attitude. A mountaineer in top shape, who climbs 150,000 feet a year and has a positive outlook, might handle several planned bivouacs and perhaps a couple of emergency overnighters each year with no difficulty. Experience has shown this climber what we all can eventually figure out: how to distinguish that fine line between carrying too much and carrying too little.

FOOD

The art of camping includes the ability to set up a safe and comfortable camp and to provide food that's tasty and nutritious. Because mountaineering is such a strenuous and demanding activity, your body will need water and a variety of foods to provide sufficient carbohydrates, protein, and fats. With planning, it's not hard to choose foods that keep well, are lightweight, and meet your nutritional needs. But don't forget the other requirement of camping food: it must taste good, or you simply won't eat it. If fueling your body quickly and simply is the first aim of alpine cuisine, the enjoyment of doing so is a worthy secondary goal.

COMPOSITION OF FOODS

Each of the three major food components—carbohydrates, protein, and fats—provides energy, and each must be supplied in approximately the right amount to maintain a healthy mind and body. Food intake for mountaineers can go as high as 6,000 calories per day, possibly even more for larger folks. You will have to determine what is best for you depending on how demanding a trip you are planning and your own size, weight, metabolic rate, and level of conditioning.

Carbohydrates are easiest for the body to convert into energy, so they should constitute most of the total calories in your diet. Foods high in carbohydrates provide vitamins, minerals, protein, fiber, water, and essential fats. Good sources of carbohydrates include whole grains, rice, potatoes, cereals, pasta, bread, crackers, and granola bars. Eat small amounts but eat them often for sustained vigor and endurance.

Protein is important to include in your basic diet; the daily requirement is nearly constant regardless of activity. Your body cannot store protein, so once the requirement is met, the excess is either converted to energy or stored as fat. High-protein foods include cheese, peanut butter, nuts, beef jerky, canned meats and fish, powdered milk and eggs, and foil-packaged meals with meat or cheese.

Fats are also an important energy source, especially long-term. During moderate muscular exercise, energy is derived in approximately equal amounts from the body's stores of fats and carbohydrates. Fats occur naturally in small amounts in vegetables, grains, and beans, and when these are combined with fish, red meat, or poultry, your requirements for fat are easily met. High-fat foods include butter, margarine, peanut butter, nuts, canned bacon, salami, beef jerky, sardines, oils, meat, eggs, seeds, and cheese. Fats in the diet serve other functions in addition to providing energy. Stored body fats protect vital organs from shock and act as insulation to protect your body against the thermal stresses of a cold environment.

Eating for endurance

How efficient your body is in using its energy fuels is closely related to physical condition, rest, and nutrition. The better your condition, the greater the efficiency with which food and water will provide energy during heavy exercise. A well-rested, well-fed climber is less likely to experience difficulties from exertion, heat, cold, and illness.

WATER

Water is as vital to life as oxygen. You need it for energy metabolism, controlling your core and body temperature, and for eliminating metabolic wastes. During strenuous activity, particularly at high altitude, the amount of fluids lost through perspiration and evaporation of moisture from the lungs can be as much as 5 quarts or more per day.

If a substantial amount of fluid is lost and not replaced, the body's chemical equilibrium is upset and illness is more likely. The body can survive for a long time without food, but not without water. After hard exercise, replace fluids and carbohydrates as soon as possible. Then continue rehydration throughout the evening in preparation for the next day's activity.

Fluid intake for a 12-hour day of moderate activity in temperate climates should be at least 2 quarts (about 2 liters). For a longer climb or for more severe activity, you will need from 2 to 5 quarts.

The loss of salt through heavy sweating is normally not a problem, as most salts are replaced naturally in a well-balanced diet. If you're concerned about salt intake, you can use "sports drinks" that help replenish fluids and supply extra salt, sugar, calories, and minerals. Drinking additional water will also help.

Water sources

Water is sometimes at a premium in the wilderness. On a day trip, you can carry it from home. On longer trips, your sources will be lakes, streams, and snow.

You can often melt some snow for drinking by carrying it packed inside a water bottle. Start with a bit of water already in the bottle in order to hasten the melting time. When there is both sun and enough time, you can set out pots of snow to melt. Or, find a tongue of snow that is slowly melting into a trickle, dredge a depression below, let the water clear, and channel the resulting puddle into a container. You can also try catching the drips from melting overhanging eaves of snow. The most convenient and reliable way to get water on a snow-camping trip is to simply melt snow in a pot on the stove, though this obviously takes time and uses up cooking fuel.

Water purification

Clear, cold water looks pure, but may well be contaminated with harmful bacteria, *Giardia*, or other parasites that inhabit backcountry lakes and streams. For personal protection, it's best to purify all water. Common methods of purification are to put iodine in the water, to boil it (1 minute at sea level, or 5 minutes at 10,000 feet, will kill most bacterial or parasitic contaminants), or to use one of the filtration devices available at outdoors stores.

FOOD PLANNING

Put a reasonable amount of thought and effort into planning, and you should have no trouble ensuring the right combination of foods for optimum performance and enjoyment, whether your trip is for a day or for a week. As a rough general guideline, provide 2 pounds of food per person per day.

On very short trips, you can carry homemade sandwiches, fresh fruits and vegetables, and just about anything else you wish. For trips of two or three days—or longer if base camp is close to the road—any food from the grocery store is fair game. You can concoct a grocery-store stew from items selected almost at random, or by intuition. Canned or packaged items can be cooked together in one pot, then eaten with bread, a hot drink, and a dessert.

Cup-cooking works well for one-person meals. From one pot of hot water, eat each course in sequence from your cup, using instant foods such as soup, potatoes, rice, applesauce, or pudding.

For longer or more complicated trips, weight and packaging become more critical. Then freeze-dried foods are an easy, compact, lightweight option. Outdoors stores carry a large array of these prepackaged meals and snacks, and their variety and quality is constantly improving. They're expensive, but wonderfully convenient. Some require little or no cooking; you just add hot water, soak for a while, and eat from the package. Others are less easily hydrated, and require cooking in a pot. Freeze-dried meals include just about everything: main courses, potatoes, vegetables, soups, breakfasts, and desserts. Persons with access to a food dehydrator can make simple and nutritious foods from fruits, vegetables, and meat at a substantial savings.

Planning for a group

Because meals are social events, small groups often plan all food together. A common, carefully planned menu also reduces the overall weight carried by each person. Another typical arrangement is to leave breakfast and lunch to each individual, with only dinner, the most complicated meal of the day, as a group effort.

The number of people in a cooking group should rarely exceed four. Beyond that, group efficiency is outweighed by the complexities of large pots, small stoves, and longer cooking times. The ideal number is two to three people per stove. For longer trips, an extra stove is a good idea in case one breaks down.

Selecting the menu

A group can pack along just about whatever its members want on a short outing, but longer trips require precise food planning. It takes careful figuring to meet the conflicting goals of moderate-weight packs and plenty of good, nutritious food. You want to avoid unnecessary weight, but at the same time you need to ensure that right down to the last meal, there is enough food for all.

Meals can be planned by the group or by a chosen individual. In either case, the usual procedure is to write down a menu, discuss it with the group, compile an ingredients list, and then go shopping.

Packaging

The elaborate packages of commercial foods are too bulky and heavy for most trips, so repack the food in plastic bags. Place a label or cooking instructions inside each bag, or write on the outside with a felt pen. Smaller packages can be placed in larger ones that are labeled in broad categories, such as ''breakfast,'' ''dinner,'' or ''drinks.'' For precise planning and packaging, a small kitchen scale comes in handy. Items such as jam, peanut butter, and honey pack best in squeeze tubes or in small plastic containers with airtight lids.

MENU SUGGESTIONS

Breakfast

When you're in a hurry to get under way, breakfast is merely the first installment of lunch. For a fast start, prepackage a standard meal before the trip, measuring a prepared cold cereal (such as granola), raisins or other fruit, and powdered milk into a breakfast bag. Stir in water—cold for a cold meal, hot for a hot one—and breakfast is ready.

A hot drink is a pleasant addition to a cold breakfast and a standard element of a hot one. Common choices are instant cocoa, coffee, malted milk, coffee-cocoa (mocha), tea, eggnog, and instant breakfast drinks. Fruit-flavored drinks include hot cider and flavored gelatin.

Other possibilities for breakfast are cooked grains such as oatmeal or rice, toaster pastries, bakery items, dried fruits, nuts, meat or fruit bars, and applesauce. If there's time, you can prepare a full-scale breakfast, with such items as potato slices, hash browns, omelets, scrambled eggs, bacon (canned or bars), and pancakes with syrup (made with brown sugar or syrup crystals).

Lunch and snacks

As soon as breakfast is over, lunch begins and is eaten throughout the day. Eat small amounts and eat often. You should have plenty of food, as half of your daily allotment is for lunch and snacks.

A good munching staple is gorp, a mixture of nuts, candy, raisins, and other dehydrated fruits. One handful makes a snack, several make a meal. Also good for munching is granola, with its mixture of grains, honey or sugar, and perhaps some bits of fruit and nuts. Gorp and granola are available premixed at many food stores or you can make your own. Other snack items are fruit leather and fruit pemmican.

Your basic lunch can include any of the following:

Protein: Canned meats and fish, beef jerky, precooked sausage, meat spreads, cheese, nuts, and seeds (sunflower and others).

Starches: Whole grain breads, bagels, granola and other cereals, crackers, brown-rice cakes, chips or pretzels, and granola bars.

Sugars: Cookies, chocolate, candy bars, hard candy, muffins, pastries, and honey.

Fruit: Fresh fruit, fruit bars, jam, and dried fruit such as raisins, peaches, and apples.

Vegetables: Fresh carrot or celery sticks, cucumbers, etc.

Dinner

The evening meal should have it all. It should be both nourishing and delicious, yet easily and quickly prepared. To supplement your liquid intake, include some items that take a lot of water, such as soup. A cup of soup makes a quick and satisfying first course while the main course is being prepared.

One-pot meals with a carbohydrate base of noodles, macaroni, rice, beans, potatoes, or grains are easy and nutritious. To ensure adequate protein, fat, and flavor, you can add other ingredients such as canned or dried chicken, beef or fish, sausage, freeze-dried vegetables or fruits, butter or margarine, and a dehydrated soup or sauce mix.

Meals from the grocery store are relatively easy to fix and many are quick cooking, such as spaghetti, macaroni, rice mixes, ramen noodles, and instant salads. There are also meals prepackaged in Styrofoam cups: just add boiling water, cover, and let sit for a few minutes, and your dinner is ready.

Freeze-dried meals offer a lot of dinner choices: almond chicken, chili, shrimp newberg, turkey, beef stroganoff, and many more.

A hearty soup can serve as the main course for dinner. Good choices include minestrone, multibean, beef barley, or chicken. Add instant potatoes, rice, crackers, cheese, or bread and the meal is complete. Bouillon is an old favorite that has minimal food value but weighs little and is helpful in replacing water and salt.

Side dishes of freeze-dried vegetables or beans add variety and substance. They can also be added to soup, along with instant rice or potatoes. Precooked beans or processed soy products (in powdered or textured forms) are excellent low-cost protein additions. For those more interested in nutrition and health foods, there are packaged supplements and organic items at stores that specialize in natural foods.

Staples and seasonings

Sugar is a matter of preference. Brown is one-third heavier than white because of moisture, but it's preferred by many for flavor. Instant powdered milk is a good protein supplement that can be added to many dishes. Margarine, which keeps better than butter on long trips, improves the flavor of many foods and is available in liquid or canned form. Dried butter substitutes are available, but they don't have the fat content of the original. For seasonings, try salt, pepper, herbs, garlic, chili powder, bacon bits, dehydrated onions, Parmesan cheese, or a dash of soy sauce.

Drinks and desserts

Cold drinks after a hot day on the mountain are necessary and can be especially satisfying. Lemonade, orange juice, grape juice, and sugar-free drinks are all available in powdered mixes. Just add water. Hot drinks such as cocoa, tea, or mocha taste good after the evening meal.

Occasional full-scale desserts are possible if you've planned the menus carefully. They can include cookies, candy, no-bake cheesecake, applesauce, cooked dried fruit, and that old standard, instant pudding. Freeze-dried desserts include pies, ice cream, and berry cobblers.

HIGH ALTITUDE

High-camp cooking is often difficult because cooking times are longer and conditions can be challenging, at best. Cooking that requires boiling becomes a problem. As you gain altitude and the atmospheric pressure decreases, water boils at lower and lower temperatures. Therefore, it takes longer to cook things. For every drop of about 10 degrees Fahrenheit (or 5 degrees Celsius) in boiling temperature, cooking time is approximately doubled (fig. 3-11). The most suitable foods are those that require only warming, such as canned chicken and instant rice. The weight of the fuel you have to pack is another argument for simple menus.

The rigors of quick visits to higher altitudes require special attention to food. A typical quick gain to a relatively high elevation is the weekend ascent of Mount Rainier in Washington State, where climbers normally spend Friday night near sea level, Saturday night at 10,000 feet (about 3,000 meters), and perhaps only 20 hours after leaving tidewater, reach the 14,411-foot (4,392-meter) summit. Many climbers fall victim to symptoms of mountain sickness, ranging from a slight malaise to vomiting and severe headaches. The abrupt ascent doesn't allow time for acclimatization. Under these conditions it is more difficult to digest large meals because the stomach and lungs are competing for the same blood supply.

To repeat, eat light and eat often, stressing carbohydrates, which are easiest to digest. Bring foods that have proven themselves appealing at high altitude, because climbers often lose their appetite. Trial and error will teach you what foods your body can tolerate at altitude. You must continue to eat and drink, whatever the effort, for the loss of energy from a lack of food or water will only reinforce the debilitating effects of reduced oxygen.

Fig. 3–11. Boiling point of water

| Elevation | | Temperature | | Cooking Time |
ft	m	°C	°F	(sea level = 1)
sea level		100°	212°	1.0
5,000	1525	95°	203°	1.9
10,000	3050	90°	194°	3.8
15,000	4575	85°	185°	7.2
20,000	7000	80°	176°	13.0

UTENSILS FOR COOKING AND EATING

The simplest eating utensils are a spoon and a single large cup (or small pot). Some people like to add a bowl; bowls are available in plastic, stainless steel, metal, and lexan polycarbonate. Cook sets (fig. 3-12) should be durable and lightweight and nest for convenient carrying. You can get the cook sets in aluminum, stainless steel, and coated cookware for easy cleaning. The size of the set you pack along will vary depending on the needs of a particular trip, but generally you need at least two pots: one for food and one for water. You can even get it down to one if you use only freeze-dried dinners that are rehydrated in their own packaging. Be sure your pots have bails or handles for carrying and tight-fitting lids to conserve heat (and serve as makeshift fry pans).

Fig. 3–12. Cooking accessories: pots and lids; windscreen; utensils and cup.

STOVES

Stoves are now a necessity for backcountry travelers because many camping areas no longer have enough firewood, and others have banned natural-fuel fires. Stoves have a minimal impact on the wilderness and can be used in a variety of conditions.

In choosing a stove, consider a number of factors, including its weight, the altitude and temperature where it will be used, fuel availability, and its reputation for reliability. Whichever stove you select should be easy to start, operate, and maintain, even in cold, wet, or windy conditions.

Practice starting a new stove at home before a trip to be sure it's working and to be sure you know how to operate it. A stove kept in good working order will last for years. Check the stove frequently for dirt and carbon build-up. Stoves with pumps periodically need replacements for deteriorated pump leathers and gaskets. Mountaineering stoves typically weigh 1 to 1$^1/_2$ pounds and burn about an hour on approximately $^1/_2$ pint ($^1/_4$ liter or so) of fuel.

You'll be rewarded with a more productive stove if you make sure it has a wind shield to screen the flame and prevent heat from being blown away. If you don't have a shield for your stove, improvise a way to block the wind. Most mountaineering stoves will boil about 1 quart (approximately 1 liter) of water at sea level in 4 to 8 minutes. Wind can increase the time to as much as 25 minutes, or even prevent boiling.

Some preventive maintenance will help guard against dumping a pot of stew on the ground. Check the stability of the metal framework that supports the pot on the stove. Also see that the stove is solidly supported on the ground. In snow, a small square of Masonite or ensolite serves well as both a smooth base and insulation under the stove.

A direct flame under the pot is desirable for boiling water or melting snow. For heating food, you might consider some means to diffuse the direct heat of the flame, such as a large metal lid. Just place the lid on the burner, then sit the cooking pot on the lid. Some stoves have an adjustment valve that permits you to further control the stove's heat output and prevent scorched food and wasted fuel.

Mountaineers have a range of choices in stove designs (fig. 3-13) and in fuels (with white gas, kerosene, and butane being the most common). All stoves require a means of pressurization to force the fuel to flow to the burner. This is usually provided by a hand pump for white gas and kerosene stoves and by a pressurized cartridge for butane units. All stoves also need a way to vaporize the liquid fuel before it is burned. With white gas and kerosene stoves, a common method is to prime (preheat) the stove by burning a small amount of fuel in a priming cup to start the fuel vaporizing in the main supply line. With butane stoves, the fuel vaporizes inside the pressurized cartridge.

A pump on a stove lets you increase the pressure in the fuel tank; this causes the fuel to burn faster and hotter and brings water to a boil more quickly. Stoves that boil water fastest often do not simmer well, while those with a lower heat output

give you more control at lower cooking temperatures.

Stove fuels

White gas is probably the most popular fuel in the United States for mountaineering stoves. It tends to burn hotter than butane and is excellent for melting large amounts of snow, boiling water, or heating food quickly. Unlike kerosene, white gas

Fig. 3–13. Types of outdoor stoves

Kerosene stove: high heat output; requires white gas, alchohol, or lighter fluid for priming.

White gas stove with enclosure: compact carrier for safe, convenient packing.

Butane/propane cartridge stove: uses 80 percent butane/20 percent propane for better cold-weather performance.

White gas stove: white gas only; burns hotter and boils water more quickly than other fuels.

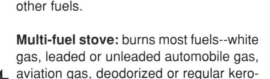

Multi-fuel stove: burns most fuels--white gas, leaded or unleaded automobile gas, aviation gas, deodorized or regular kerosene, Stoddard Solvent No. 1, diesel fuel or No. 1 stove oil; easy to clean; ideal when clean fuel not available.

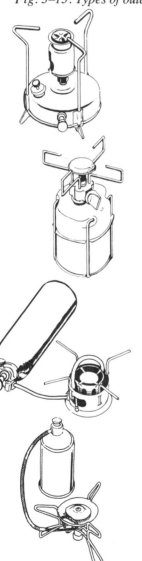

White gas/kerosene stove: burns either fuel; ideal stove for international use.

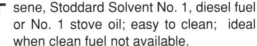

Isobutane stove: uses isobutane for best performance in cold weather.

can be used as its own priming agent. Use only refined or white gasoline prepared for pressurized stoves; don't use automotive gasoline, including unleaded gas. The correct fuel is less likely to clog jets, build up excess pressure, or emit toxic fumes. However, spilled white gas evaporates readily, with little odor, and is very flammable.

Kerosene is not as volatile as white gasoline and therefore is safer to transport and store. Kerosene stoves need to be pressurized in addition to being primed with either white gas, alcohol, or lighter fluid. (Liquid kerosene does not burn hot enough to preheat its own burner.) If the burner has not been heated sufficiently, the stove will burn with a sooty yellow flame, producing lots of smoke and carbon. But when it burns efficiently, a kerosene stove has a high heat output, equal to or greater than white gas.

Butane cartridge stoves are popular because of their convenience: easy to light, good flame control, immediate maximum heat output, and no chance of fuel spills. The pressure forces the fuel out as soon as the valve is opened, eliminating both pumping and priming. Most butane stoves are not recommended for temperatures below freezing unless the fuel is warmed. An exception is a stove that uses isobutane fuel, which has performed well at high altitude and in cold, wet conditions. With its windscreen/heat reflector, this stove has proven superior in the wind as well.

The disposable butane cartridges cannot be refilled. Therefore, you may end up leaving home with a cartridge that is only half full because it was already used on an earlier trip. The cartridges are bulky, and all too frequently the spent canisters are found discarded in the wilderness. Pack them out. Another drawback is that the maximum intensity of the flame declines as the fuel is used up (and the pressure in the cartridge drops correspondingly). This problem is partly compensated for at higher elevations, where lower atmospheric pressure means the interior cartridge pressure is relatively higher. Some cartridges cannot be changed until they are empty. Always change cartridges outside your tent because residual fuel in spent canisters can be a fire hazard.

Solid fuels such as candles and canned heat serve primarily as fire starters. They are lightweight and cheap, but provide only limited heat. Most are carried for emergency use only, along with a metal cup for heating small amounts of water.

Foreign travel

On foreign trips, fuel filters may be necessary because a high grade of fuel is often hard to find. Find out beforehand what fuels are available and take an appropriate stove. Kerosene is generally available worldwide, while white gas is not. Check airline restrictions about carrying fuel on planes. Most do not allow it.

Fuel storage

Carry extra fuel in a tightly closed metal container that has a screw top backed up by a rubber gasket. Plastic containers aren't good because fuel gradually diffuses out through the material. Plainly mark the fuel container and stow it in a place where it can't possibly contaminate any food. Some stoves have their fuel bottles directly attached to them, while others require a pouring spout or funnel to transfer the fuel from a storage container to a stove fuel tank.

How much fuel should you take along? It will depend on the conditions of the trip and the food you plan to cook. Will you have to melt snow for water? Will you cook your dinners on the stove or simply heat water for pouring into a food package? Practice and experience will eventually tell you how much fuel you need, but a good beginning would be to bring between $1^1/2$ and 2 quarts for two people for one week.

Fuel safety

Tents have been blown up, equipment burned, and people injured by careless stove use. Apply rules of safety and common sense. Don't use a stove inside a tent unless it is absolutely necessary. If you must cook in a tent, provide plenty of ventilation to minimize the danger of fuel escaping and igniting. Always change pressurized fuel cartridges, and fill and start liquid-fueled stoves, outside the tent and away from other open flames.

· 4 ·

ROUTEFINDING
AND NAVIGATION

Where am I? How can I find my way from here to there? Are we almost there? These are three of the most popular questions in mountaineering, and this chapter shows how to find the answers by using routefinding, orientation, and navigation.

By the time you finish this chapter, you will have a good handle on the tools of navigation and the proven, painfully acquired techniques of top-notch routefinders. You will have the basic knowledge to eventually head into the wilds, work out the way to the mountain, and find the way home.

These tools and techniques are simple and straightforward, but exacting. Study them carefully to help make your mountain adventures successful and keep you safe within the ranks of surviving routefinders. Before you immerse yourself in this chapter, remember two things: Navigation is easy. Navigation is fun. A positive attitude will get you through the learning phase in a hurry and out into the field to use these indispensable skills of mountaineering.

First, a few definitions:

Orientation is the science of determining your exact position on the earth. It requires mastery of map and compass. People who spend a reasonable amount of time and effort usually gain this mastery, even when they have little background or interest in math or science.

Navigation is the science of determining the location of your objective and of keeping yourself pointed in the right direction all the way from your starting point to the destination. Like orientation, this takes map and compass and is a required skill for all wilderness travelers.

Routefinding is the art of locating and following a route that is appropriate to the abilities and equipment of the climbing party. It takes a lot to be a good routefinder: an integrated sense of terrain, distance, and direction; a combination of good judgment, experience, and instinct; and a solid grounding in the technical aspects of orientation and navigation. As with other arts, routefinding skills can be sharpened through practice, regardless of your basic aptitude.

A related activity is *orienteering*, a sport in which participants compete with each other and the clock in finding the way with map and compass to destinations along a structured course. Orienteering is not a part of mountaineering, but mountaineers can learn from those who compete. It is no accident that many of the best routefinders are people who have engaged in orienteering.

TRIP PREPARATION

Routefinding begins at home. Before heading out the door, you need to know not only the name of your wilderness destination, but a great deal about how to get there. The information is accessible to anyone who takes the trouble to seek it out, from guidebooks and maps and from people who have already been there.

Prepare for each trip as if you were going to lead it, even if you aren't. Each person in a climbing group needs to know wilderness navigation and must keep track of where the party has been, where it is, and where it's going. In case of emergency, each climber must be able to get back alone.

Guidebooks provide critical information such as a description of the route, the estimated time necessary to complete it, elevation gain, mileage, and so forth. Climbers who have made the trip will tell you about landmarks, hazards, and routefinding hassles. Useful details are packed into maps of all sorts: Forest Service maps, road maps, aerial maps, sketch maps, and topographic maps. For a trip into an area that's especially unfamiliar, more preparation is needed. This might include scouting into the area, observations from vantage points, or study of aerial photos.

If the route comes from a guidebook or from a description provided by another climber, plot it out on the topographic map you'll be carrying along, noting junctions and other important points. It can help to highlight the route with a yellow felt-tip marking pen, which doesn't obliterate map features. Other maps or route descriptions should be taken along, marked with notes on any more up-to-date information. In selecting the route, consider a host of factors, including the season, weather conditions, the abilities of the party members, and the equipment available.

Before you've even shouldered your pack, you should have a mental image of the route. From experience, and from all the sources of information about the climb, you'll know how to make the terrain work in your favor. To avoid brush, try not to follow watercourses or drainages; select ridges over hillsides and gullies. Clearcuts are often full of slash or brushy second-growth trees, so stick to old-growth forest if possible.

A rock-slide area can be a feasible route—providing you watch carefully for new rockfall. One problem in planning the route, however, is that a rock-slide area may look the same on a map as an avalanche gully, which can have avalanche hazard in winter and spring and be choked with brush in summer and fall. If your sources aren't helpful, only a firsthand look will clear up this question.

The most straightforward return route is often the same as the route going in. If you plan to come back a different way, that route also needs careful advance preparation.

Don't let outdated information ruin your trip. Check beforehand with the appropriate agencies about roads and trails, especially closures, and about climbing routes and regulations, permits, and camping requirements.

THE MAP

A map is a symbolic picture of a place. In convenient shorthand, it conveys a phenomenal amount of information in a form that is easy to understand and easy to carry. No mountaineer should travel without a map or the skill to translate its shorthand into details on the route. Note the publication date of the map because roads, trails, and other features may have changed since that time. Try to use the latest information. A number of different types of maps are available.

Relief maps are the maps that attempt to show terrain in three dimensions by the use of shadings of green, gray, and brown tones, terrain sketching, or raised surfaces. They help in visualizing the ups and downs of the landscape and have some value in trip planning.

Land management and recreation maps are updated frequently and thus are very useful for current details on roads, trails, ranger stations, and other marks of the human hand. They usually show only the horizontal relationship of natural features, without the contour lines that indicate the shape of the land. These maps, published by the U.S. Forest Service and other government agencies and by timber companies, are suitable for trip planning.

Climbers' sketch maps are generally crudely

drawn but often make up in specialized route detail what they lack in draftsmanship. These rough and ready drawings can be effective supplements to other map and guidebook information.

Guidebook maps vary greatly in quality— some are merely sketches, while others are accurate modifications of topographic maps. They generally contain useful details on roads, trails, and climbing routes.

Topographic maps are the best of all for climbers. They depict topography, the shape of the earth's surface, by showing contour lines that represent constant elevations above sea level. These maps, essential to off-trail travel, are produced in many countries. As an example of this type of map, we will look in detail at the maps produced by the U.S. Geological Survey (USGS).

USGS TOPOGRAPHIC MAPS

It might be interesting to start this discussion of USGS maps with a refresher on how cartographers divide up the earth. The distance around our planet is divided into 360 units called degrees. A measurement east or west is called *longitude*; a measurement north or south is *latitude*. Longitude is measured 180 degrees, both east and west, starting at the Greenwich meridian in England. Latitude is measured 90 degrees, both north and south, from the equator.

By determining the intersection of longitude and latitude lines, any point on the earth's surface can be pinpointed. New York City, for instance, is situated at 74 degrees west longitude and 41 degrees north latitude. Each degree is divided into 60 units called minutes, and each minute is further subdivided into 60 seconds. On a map, a latitude of 47 degrees, 52 minutes, and 30 seconds north would probably be written like this: 47°52′30″N.

One type of USGS map used by mountaineers covers an area of 15 minutes (that is, $1/4$ degree) of longitude by 15 minutes of latitude. These maps are part of what is called the *15-minute series*. Another type covers an area of 7.5 minutes (that is, $1/8$ degree) of latitude by 7.5 minutes of longitude. These maps are part of the *7.5-minute series*.

The *scale* of a map is a ratio between measure-

ments on the map and measurements in the real world. A common way to state the scale is to compare a map measurement with a ground measurement (as in 1 inch equals 1 mile), or to give a specific mathematical ratio (as in 1:24,000, where any one unit of measure on the map equals 24,000 units of the same measure on the earth). The scale is usually shown graphically at the bottom of a map.

In the USGS 7.5-minute series, the scale is 1:24,000, or roughly $2^1/_2$ inches to the mile, and each map covers an area of approximately 6 by 9 miles. It is the standard topographic map for all of the United States except Alaska.

In the 15-minute series, the scale is 1:62,500, or about 1 inch to the mile, and each map covers an area of four times that of the 7.5-minute series (about 12 by 18 miles). The 15-minute maps are no longer in production and are being replaced by the 7.5-minute series for all states except Alaska. (Most 15-minute maps will be permanently out of print by the mid-1990s.) For Alaska only, the 15-minute maps are still the standard, and the scale is somewhat different: 1:63,360, or exactly 1 inch to the mile. The east–west extent of each Alaska map is actually greater than 15 minutes because the lines of longitude are converging toward the North Pole.

The 15-minute and 7.5-minute maps are the ones that mountaineers use for cross-country routefinding and navigation. The USGS also produces maps that cover larger areas (with such scales as 1:100,000 and 1:250,000), and these are suitable for some trip planning and trail navigation. In some areas, private companies produce maps based on USGS topographic maps, but they are updated with more recent trail and road details and sometimes combine sections of USGS maps. These maps are often useful supplements to standard topographic maps.

How to read a topographic map

Consider this a language lesson, but in a language quite easy to learn and one that pays immediate rewards to any wilderness traveler. Some of this language is in words, but most of it is in the form of symbols drawn on a map. The best way to follow the lesson is to study it along with an actual USGS topographic map. Any one will do.

Each map is referred to as a quadrangle (or quad) and covers an area bounded on the north and south by latitude lines that differ by an amount equal to the map series (7.5 minutes or 15 minutes) and on the east and west by longitude lines that differ by the same amount. Each quadrangle is given the name of a prominent topographic or human feature of the area.

What the colors mean

Colors on a USGS topographic map have very specific meanings. This is what the different colors stand for:

Red: Major roads and survey information.

Blue: Rivers, lakes, springs, waterfalls, and other water-related features. The contour lines of glaciers and permanent snowfields are in solid blue, with their edges indicated by dashed blue lines.

Black: Roads, trails, railroads, buildings, and other features not part of the natural environment.

Green: Areas of substantial vegetation. Solid green marks a forested area while mottled green indicates scrub vegetation. The lack of green doesn't mean there's no vegetation in the area, simply that it is too small or scattered to show on the maps. Don't be surprised if a small, narrow gully with no green color on the map turns out to be choked with slide alder or vine maple.

Brown: Contour lines and elevations.

Purple: Partial revision of an existing map.

Translating contour lines

The heart of a topographic map is its overlay of contour lines, each line indicating a constant elevation as it follows the shape of the landscape. A map's *contour interval* is the difference in elevation between two adjacent contour lines (usually 40 feet on 7.5-minute maps and 80 feet on 15-minute maps). Every fifth contour line is printed darker than other lines and is labeled periodically with elevation.

One of the most important bits of information a topographic map reveals is whether you will be hiking uphill or downhill. If the route crosses lines of increasingly higher elevation, you will be going uphill. If it crosses lines of decreasing elevation, the route is downhill. Flat side-hill travel is indicated by a route that crosses no lines, remaining within a single contour interval.

This is only the start of the picture that contour lines paint of your actual wilderness route. They also show cliffs, passes, summits and other features (fig. 4-1). You will get better and better at interpreting these lines by comparing actual terrain with its representation on the map (fig. 4-2). The goal is to someday glance at a topographic map and realize you have a rather sharp mental image of just what the place will look like. The following listing shows the main features sketched by contour lines.

Flat areas: No contour lines at all.

Gentle slopes: Widely spaced contour lines.

Steep slopes: Closely spaced contour lines.

Cliffs: Contour lines extremely close together or touching.

Valleys, ravines, gullies, couloirs: Contour lines in a pattern of "U's" pointing in the direction of higher elevation, if the valley or gully is gentle and rounded; a pattern of "V's," if the valley or gully is sharp and narrow.

Ridge or spur: Contour lines in a pattern of "U's" pointing in the direction of lower elevation, if the ridge is gentle and rounded; a pattern of "V's," if the ridge is sharp.

Saddle, pass, col: A low point on a ridge, with higher contour lines on each side and often with a characteristic hourglass shape.

Cirques, bowls: Patterns of contour lines forming a semicircle (or as much as three-quarters of a circle), rising from a low spot in the center of the partial circle to form a natural amphitheater at the head of a valley.

Peak: A concentric pattern of contour lines with the summit being the innermost and highest ring. Peaks often are also indicated by X's, elevations, benchmarks (BM), or a triangle symbol.

The margin of a USGS map holds important information, such as date of publication and revision, names of maps of adjacent areas, contour

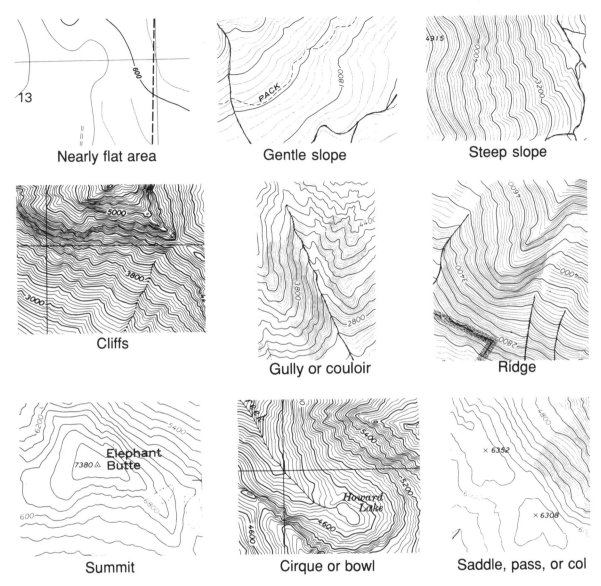

Fig. 4–1. Basic topographic features

interval, and map scale. The margin also provides a diagram showing the area's magnetic declination, which is the difference between true north and magnetic north.

Keep a couple of cautionary thoughts in mind as you study a topographic map, because they do have certain limitations. The map won't show all the terrain features you actually see on the climb because there's a limit to what can be jammed onto the map without reducing it to an unreadable clutter. If a feature is not at least as high as the contour interval, it may not be shown, so a 30-foot cliff may come as a surprise in an area mapped with a 40-foot contour interval. Check the date of the map

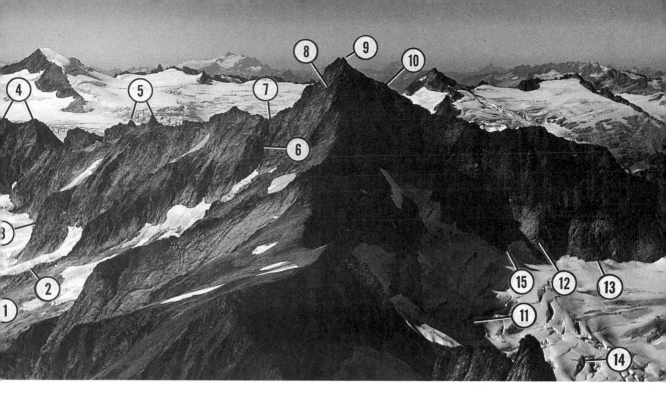

Fig. 4–2. *Photograph of a mountainous area; keyed features are represented on topographic map.*

KEY

1. Basin: moderate slope, camp spots
2. Snow or ice line: dashed line ends on cliffs, rock
3. Buttress: change in features of wall may provide approach to ridge
4. Twin summits: which is higher?
5. Gendarmes, aiguilles, or pinnacles
6. Gully or couloir
7. Saddle, pass, or col
8. Rock face
9. Summit: highest point on map
10. Ridge or arete
11. East slope: note shadows and ice accumulation
12. Cirque wall: glacier occupies this cirque
13. Moat
14. Crevasses: indicated by irregular contours, not smooth as near buttress, 3, above
15. Bergschrund: not seen on map but inferred possibility when rock and snow are steep

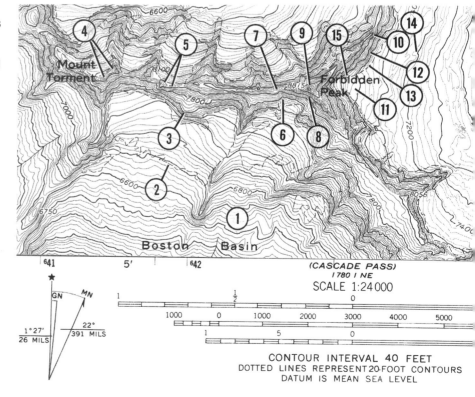

because topographic maps are not revised very often and information on forests and on roads and other manufactured features could be out of date. A forest may have been logged or a road either extended or closed since the last updating. Although topographic maps are essential to wilderness travel, they must be supplemented with information from visitors to the area, guidebooks, and other maps. As you learn about changes, note them on your map.

Sometimes a trip runs through portions of two or more maps. Adjoining maps can be folded at the edges and brought together, or you can create your own customized map by cutting out the pertinent areas and splicing them with tape. Include plenty of territory so that you have a good overview of the entire trip, including surrounding area. Photocopies, good for marking on, don't show colors and may distort, meaning they should be used only in addition to the real thing.

As the precious objects they are, maps deserve tender care in the wilds. A map can be kept in a plastic bag or map case. You can also laminate the map with plastic film or coat it with waterproofing, though these coatings are difficult to mark on. Some maps come already waterproofed. On the trip, carry the map in a jacket pocket or some other easily accessible place so you don't have to take off your pack to get at it.

ORIENTING A MAP

During a trip it sometimes helps to hold the map open so that north on the map is pointed in the actual direction of true north. This is known as orienting the map, a good way to gain a better feel of the relationship between the map and the countryside.

It's a simple process (fig. 4-3). Place your compass on the map, near its declination diagram. Turn the map and compass together until the north-seeking end of the compass needle is aligned with, or parallel to, the magnetic-north arrow on the diagram. The map is now oriented to the scene before you. (This orientation can give a general feel for the area but can't replace the precise methods of

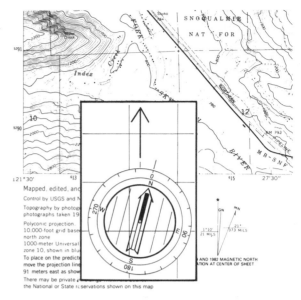

Fig. 4–3. Using the compass to orient a map

orientation and navigation that we will cover later in this chapter.)

ROUTEFINDING WITH THE MAP

Before the trip

Most wilderness orientation, navigation, and routefinding is done by simply looking at your surroundings and comparing them with the map.

One useful technique is to identify a navigational "handrail," a linear feature on the map that lies in the same direction you are traveling. The handrail should be within frequent sight of the route, so it can serve as an aid to navigation. Features that can be used from time to time as handrails during a trip include roads, trails, power lines, railroad tracks, fences, borders of fields and meadows, valleys, streams, ridges, lake shores, and the edges of marshes.

A handrail helps in staying on route. Another map technique can help in finding the way home if you've gone off track. This is the "base line," a long unmistakable line that always lies in the same direction from you, no matter where you are during the trip. Pick out the base line on the map during trip planning. It does not have to be something you can see during the trip. You just have to know that it is there, in a consistent direction from you. A base line (sometimes called a catch line) can be a road, the shore of a large lake, a river, trail, power line, or any other feature that's at least as long as your climbing area. If the shore of a distant lake always lies west of your climbing area, you can be sure that heading west at any time will get you to this identifiable landmark. It's not the fastest way to travel, but it saves you from being truly lost.

Also before the trip, anticipate specific route-finding problems. For example, if the route traverses a glacier, you may consider carrying route-marking wands, especially if the weather outlook is marginal. Make a note of any escape routes that can be used in case of sudden bad weather or other setbacks.

During the trip

Get off on the right foot by making sure that everyone understands the route. Gather the crew around a map and take time to discuss the route and make contingency plans in case the party gets separated. Point out on the map where you are and associate the surroundings with the piece of paper in front of you, orienting the map to true north if you wish. This is a good time for everyone to make a mental note of the main features the party will see during the trip, such as forest, streams, or trails.

Along the way, everyone needs to keep associating the terrain with the map. Ignorance of the territory is definitely not bliss for any daydreaming climber who gets separated from the party. Whenever a new landmark appears, connect it with the map. At every chance—at a pass, at a clearing, or through a break in the clouds—update your fix on the group's exact position. Keeping track of progress this way makes it easy to plan each succeeding leg of the trip. It also may turn you into an expert map interpreter because you'll know what a specific valley or ridge looks like compared with its representation on the map.

Look ahead to the return trip

The route always looks amazingly different on the way back. Avoid surprises and confusion by glancing back over your shoulder from time to time on the way in to see what the route should look like on the return. Fix in your mind this over-the-shoulder shape of the route. If you can't keep track of it all, jot down times, elevations, landmarks, and so on in a notebook. A cryptic few words—''7,600, hit ridge''—can save a lot of grief on the descent as a reminder that when the party has dropped to 7,600 feet, it's time to leave the ridge and start down the snow slope.

Think

Your brain is your most valuable navigational tool. As the party heads upward, keep asking yourself questions. How will we recognize this important spot on our return? What will we do if the climb leader is injured? Would we be able to find our way out in a white-out or if snow covered our tracks? Should we be using wands or other route-marking methods right now? Ask the questions as you go and act on the answers. It's a matter of think now or pay later.

Mark the route if necessary

There are times it may be best to mark the route going in so you can find it again going out. This situation can come up when the route is over snow-fields or glaciers during changeable weather, in heavy forest, or when fog or nightfall threaten to hide landmarks. On snow, climbers use thin bamboo wands with tiny flags on top to mark the path. (Chapter 12 explains the construction and use of wands.) In the forest, the recommended marker is brightly colored crepe paper in thin rolls. Plastic surveyors' tape is also used.

One commandment here: REMOVE YOUR MARKERS. Markers are litter, and mountaineers never, ever litter. If there's any chance you will not come back the same way and will not be able to remove the markers, be especially sure to use the crepe paper, which will disintegrate over the winter. The plastic tape, on the other hand, might outlive the careless climbers who put it there.

Rock cairns appear here and there as markers, sometimes dotting an entire route and at other times signaling the point where a route changes direction. These heaps of rock are another imposition on the landscape, and they can create confusion for any traveler but the one who put them together—so don't build them. If there comes a time you decide you must, then tear them down on the way out. The rule is different for existing cairns. Let them be, on the assumption someone may be depending on them.

Keep track

As the trip goes on, it may be helpful to mark your progress on the map. Some climbers even note on the map the time that streams, ridges, and other landmarks are reached. Keep yourself oriented so that at any time you can point out your actual position to within 1/2 mile on the map.

Part of navigation is having a sense of your speed. Given all the variables, will it take your party 1 hour to travel 2 miles or will it take 2 hours to travel 1 mile? The answer is rather important if it's noon and base camp is still 5 miles away. After enough trips into the wilds, you'll be good at estimating wilderness speeds. With a watch and a notebook (or good memory), you can monitor the rate of progress on any single outing. Here are some typical speeds for an average party, though there will be much variation:

• On a gentle trail, with a day pack: 2–3 miles per hour.
• Up a steep trail, with full overnight pack: 1–2 miles per hour.
• Traveling cross-country on gentle terrain, with a day pack: 1,000 feet of elevation gain per hour.
• Traveling cross-country up a moderate slope, with full overnight pack: 500 feet of elevation gain per hour.

In heavy brush, the rate of travel can drop to a third or even a quarter of what it would be on a good trail.

On technical portions of the climb

When the going gets tough, the tough forget about navigation and start worrying about the next handhold. But keep your map and other route information handy for the occasional rests. On rock climbs, don't let the mechanics of technical climbing overwhelm the need to stay on a particular route.

On the summit

Here is your golden opportunity to rest, relax, and enjoy—and to learn more about the area and about map reading by comparing the actual view with the way it looks on the map.

On the summit is the place to lay final plans for the descent, a journey often responsible for many more routefinding errors than the ascent. Repeat the trailhead get-together by discussing the route and emergency strategies with everyone. Stress the importance of keeping the party together on the descent, when some climbers will always want to race ahead while others lag behind.

During the descent

The descent is a time for extra caution as you fight to keep fatigue and inattention at bay. As on the ascent, everyone needs to maintain a good sense of the route and how it relates to the map. Stay together, don't rush, and be even more careful if you're taking a different descent route.

Now imagine your team is almost back to the car after a tough 12-hour climb. You follow a compass bearing right back to the logging road—but is the car to the left or the right? It's a bad ending to a good day if the car is a half-mile to the right and the climbers go left. It will be even worse if the car is parked at the end of the road and a routefinding error takes the party beyond that point and on and on through the woods (fig. 4-4a). The intentional offset (also called ''aiming off'') was invented for this situation (fig. 4-4b). Just travel in a direction that is intentionally offset some amount to the right or the left of where you really want to be. When you hit the road (or the river or the ridge), there will be no doubt about which way to turn.

After the climb

Back home, write a description of the route and of any problems, mistakes, or unusual features, and do it while the details are fresh in your mind. Imagine what you would like to know if you were

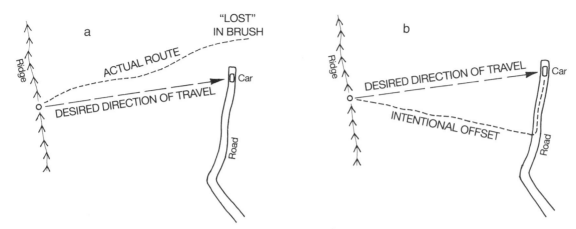

Fig. 4–4. Navigating to a specific point on a line: a, inevitable minor errors can sometimes have disastrous consequences; b, to avoid such problems, follow a course with an intentional offset.

about to make the climb for the first time, so you'll be ready with the right answers when another climber asks about it. If the guidebook was confusing or wrong, take time to write to the publisher.

THE COMPASS

The compass is a very simple device that can do a wondrous thing. It can reveal at any time and any place exactly what direction you are heading. On a simple climb in good weather, the compass may never leave your pocket. But as the route becomes more complex or the weather worsens, it comes into its own as a critical tool of mountaineering.

A compass is nothing more than a magnetized needle that responds to the earth's magnetic field. Compass-makers have added a few things to this basic unit in order to make it easy to read accurately. But stripped to the core, there's just that needle, aligned with the earth's magnetism, and from that we can figure out any direction.

These are the basic features (fig. 4-5a) of a mountaineering compass:

• A freely rotating magnetic needle. One end is a different color from the other so you can remember which end is pointing north.
• A circular rotating housing for the needle. This is filled with a fluid that dampens (reduces) the vibra-

tions of the needle, making readings more accurate.
• A dial around the circumference of the housing. The dial is graduated clockwise in degrees from 0 to 360.
• An orienting arrow and a set of parallel meridian lines. These are located beneath the needle.
• An index line. Read bearings here.
• A transparent, rectangular base plate for the entire unit. This includes a direction-of-travel line (sometimes with an arrow at one end) to point toward your objective. The longer the base plate, the easier it is to get an accurate reading.

The following are optional features (fig. 4-5b) available on some mountaineering compasses:

• Adjustable declination arrow. It's well worth the added cost because it's such an easy, dependable way to correct for magnetic declination.
• Sighting mirror. This provides another way to improve accuracy.
• Ruler. This is calibrated in inches or millimeters.

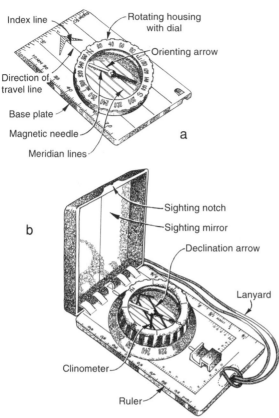

*Fig. 4–5. Features of mountaineering compasses:
a, essential features; b, useful optional features.*

Use it for measuring distances on a map.
• Clinometer. Use it to measure the angle of a slope. It can help resolve arguments over the steepness of slopes, and it can determine if you are on the higher of two summits. If there is an upward angle between you and the top of another mountain, then the other summit is higher.
• Magnifying glass. Use it to help read closely spaced contour lines.

The small, round, cheap compasses without base plates are not precise enough for mountaineering, nor can they be used for precise work with a map. For routefinding, the compass must be accurate to within 1 or 2 degrees. A larger margin of error, say 5 degrees, would land a moun-

taineering party 1/2 mile off target at the end of a 6-mile hike.

BEARINGS

A bearing is the direction from one place to another, measured in degrees of angle with respect to an accepted reference line. This reference is the line to true north.

The round dial of a compass is divided just as cartographers divide the earth, into 360 degrees. The direction in degrees to each of the cardinal directions, going clockwise around the dial starting from the top, is: north, 0 degrees (the same as 360 degrees); east, 90 degrees; south, 180 degrees; and west, 270 degrees.

The compass is used for two basic tasks regarding bearings:

1. The compass is used to *take* bearings. (You can also say that the compass is used to *measure* bearings.) To take a bearing means to measure the direction from one point to another, either on a map or on the ground.
2. The compass is used to *plot* bearings. (You can also say that the compass is used to *follow* a bearing.) To plot a bearing means to set a specified bearing on the compass and then to plot out, or to follow, where that bearing points, either on a map or on the ground.

Bearings on the map

The compass is used as a protractor to both measure and plot bearings on a map. Magnetic north and magnetic declination have nothing to do with these calculations. Therefore, ignore the magnetic needle. Never make any use of the magnetic needle when taking or plotting bearings on a map. (The only time the magnetic needle is used on the map is whenever you choose to orient the map to true north, which was explained earlier in this chapter. But there's no need to orient the map simply in order to measure or plot bearings.)

To take (measure) a bearing on the map: Place the compass on the map with one long edge of the base plate running directly between two points of interest. As you measure the bearing from

Point A to Point B, see that the direction-of-travel line is pointing in the same direction as from A to B. Then turn the rotating housing until its set of meridian lines is parallel to the north–south lines on the map. (Be sure the orienting arrow that turns with the meridian lines is pointing to the top of the map, to north. If you point it toward the bottom, your reading will be 180 degrees off.)

Now read the number that is at the index line. This is the bearing from Point A to Point B.

In the example shown in figure 4-6, the bearing from Point A, Panic Peak, to Point B, Deception Dome, is 40 degrees.

If your map doesn't happen to have north–south lines, just draw some in, parallel to the edge of the map and at intervals of an inch or two.

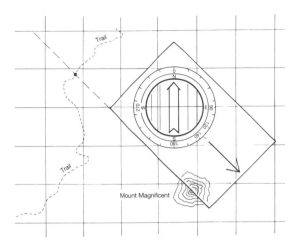

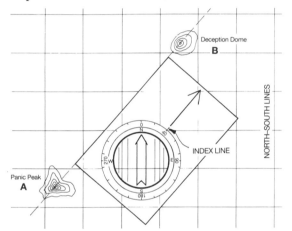

Fig. 4–6. Measuring a bearing on a map with the compass as a protractor

To plot (follow) a bearing on the map: In this case you are starting with a known bearing. And where does that bearing come from? From an actual landscape compass reading. Let's take a hypothetical example (fig. 4-7): A friend returns from a trip, disgusted at himself for leaving his camera somewhere along the trail. During a rest stop, he had taken some pictures of Mount Magnificent. At the same time, he had taken a bearing on Mount Magnificent and found it to be 135 degrees. That's all you need to know. You're heading into that same area next week, so get out the Magnificent

Fig. 4–7. Plotting a bearing on a map with the compass as a protractor

quadrangle, and here is what you do:

First set the bearing of 135 degrees at the compass index line. Place the compass on the map, one long edge of the base plate touching the summit of Mount Magnificent, with the direction-of-travel line pointing toward Mount Magnificent. Rotate the entire compass (not just the housing) until the meridian lines are parallel with the map's north–south lines, and make sure the edge of the base plate is still touching the summit. Again, be sure the orienting arrow points to the top of the map, toward north. Follow the line made by the edge of the base plate, heading in the opposite direction from the direction-of-travel line because the original bearing was measured toward the mountain. Where the line crosses the trail is exactly where your friend's camera is (or was).

Bearings in the field

Now the magnetic needle gets to do its job. All bearings in the field are based on where the needle points. For the sake of simplicity in these first two examples, we will ignore the effects of magnetic declination, a subject that will be taken up in the next section. Let's imagine we are taking the bearings in Ohio, which happens to be along the line of zero declination.

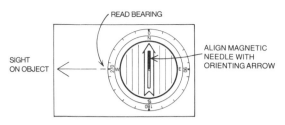

Fig. 4–8. Taking a compass bearing in the field in an area with zero declination

To take (measure) a bearing in the field: Hold the compass in front of you and point the direction-of-travel line at the object whose bearing you want to find. Rotate the compass housing until the pointed end of the orienting arrow is aligned with the north-seeking end of the needle. Read the bearing at the index line (fig. 4-8). And that's all there is to it.

If the compass has no sighting mirror, hold it at or near arm's length and at or near waist level. With a sighting mirror, hold the compass at eye level with the sight pointing at the object. Observe the magnetic needle and the orienting arrow in the mirror as you rotate the housing to align the needle and the arrow. In either case, hold the compass level. Keep it away from ferrous metal objects, which can easily deflect the magnetic needle.

To plot (follow) a bearing in the field: Simply reverse the process used to take a bearing. Start by rotating the compass housing until you have set a desired bearing at the index line, say 270 degrees (due west). Hold the compass level in front of you and then turn your entire body until the north-seeking end of the magnetic needle is aligned with the pointed end of the orienting arrow. The direction-of-travel line is now pointing due west. And that's all there is to that.

MAGNETIC DECLINATION

A compass needle is attracted to *magnetic north*, while most maps are oriented to a different point on the earth, the *geographic* north pole (''true north''). This difference between the direction to true north and the direction to magnetic north, measured in degrees, is called *magnetic*

declination. A simple compass adjustment or modification is necessary to correct for magnetic declination.

In areas west of the line of zero declination, the magnetic needle points somewhere to the east (to the right) of true north (fig. 4-9), so these areas are said to have *east declination*. It works just the opposite on the other side of the line of zero declination. Here, the magnetic needle points somewhere to the west (left) of true north, so these areas have *west declination*.

Consider a mountain traveler in Colorado, where the declination is 14 degrees east. The true bearing is a measurement of the angle between the line to true north and the direction-of-travel line. The magnetic needle, however, is pulled toward magnetic north, not true north. So instead it measures the angle between the line to magnetic north and the direction-of-travel line. This ''magnetic bearing'' is 14 degrees less than the true bearing. To get the true bearing, you must add 14 degrees to the magnetic bearing.

Like those in Colorado, climbers in all areas west of zero declination must add the declination to the magnetic bearing. In central California, for example, about 18 degrees must be added. In Washington State, it is about 20 degrees.

East of the zero-declination line, the declination is subtracted from the magnetic bearing. In Maine, for example, the magnetic bearing is 20 degrees greater than the true bearing. Subtracting the declination of 20 degrees gives a wilderness traveler in Maine the true bearing.

This is all very simple in theory but can be confusing in practice, and the wilderness is no place to practice mental arithmetic that can have life-and-death consequences. A more practical way to handle the minor complication of declination is to pay somewhat more for your compass and get one with an adjustable declination arrow instead of a fixed orienting arrow. The declination arrow can be easily set for any declination. Then the bearing you read at the index line will automatically be the true bearing, and concern about a declination error is one worry you can leave at home.

On compasses without adjustable declination ar-

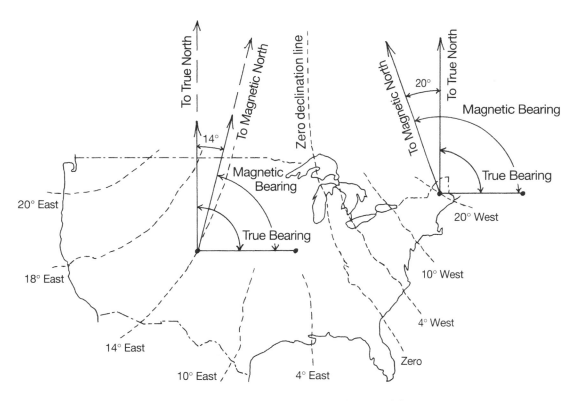

Fig. 4–9. Relationship between true and magnetic north in the United States

rows, you can get the same effect by sticking a thin strip of tape to the top or bottom of the rotating housing to serve as a customized declination arrow. Trim the tape to a point, with the point aimed directly at the specific declination for the area where you will be climbing.

In Colorado, your taped declination arrow must point at 14 degrees east (clockwise) from the 0 point (marked N for north) on the rotating compass dial (fig. 4-10a). In Maine, the declination arrow must point at 20 degrees west (counterclockwise) from the 0 point on the dial (fig. 4-10b). In Wash-

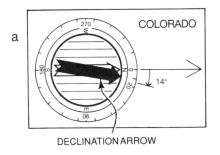

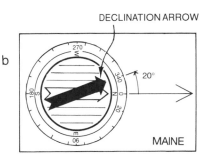

Fig. 4–10. Compass declination corrections: a, for the area west of the zero-declination line; b, for the area east of the zero-declination line.

ington State, the declination arrow must point at 20 degrees east (clockwise) from the 0 point.

To take or to follow a bearing in the field, follow exactly the same procedure used in the earlier examples from Ohio, where the declination is zero. The only difference is that from now on, you will align the magnetic needle with the declination arrow instead of with the orienting arrow.

From here on in this chapter, it is assumed you are using a compass with a declination arrow—either an adjustable arrow or a taped arrow that you have added. For all bearings in the field, you will align the needle with this declination arrow. Unless otherwise stated, all bearings referred to are true bearings, not magnetic.

PRACTICING WITH THE COMPASS

Before you count on your compass skills in the wilderness, test them in the city. The best place to practice is a place where you already know all the answers, like a street intersection where the roads run north–south and east–west.

Take a bearing in a direction you know to be east. When you have lined up the declination arrow with the magnetic needle, the number at the index line should be 90 degrees, or within a few degrees of 90. Repeat for the other cardinal directions, south, west, and north. Then do the reverse. Pretend you don't know which way is west. Set 270 degrees (west) at the index line and hold the compass in front of you as you turn your entire body until the needle is again aligned with the declination arrow. The direction-of-travel line should now point west. Does it? Repeat for the other cardinal directions. This set of exercises will help develop precision and self-confidence at compass reading and also is a way to check the accuracy of the compass. And if you make a mistake or two, well, no harm done.

Look for chances to practice in the mountains. A good place is any known location—such as a summit or a lake shore—from which you can see identifiable landmarks. Take bearings as time permits, plot them on the map, and see how close the result is to your actual location.

CAUTIONS ABOUT COMPASS USE

As you've gathered by now, there's a big difference between using a compass for working with a map and using a compass for field work. When measuring and plotting bearings on a map, the compass needle is ignored. Just align the meridian lines on the compass housing with the north–south lines on the map. In the field, you *must* use the magnetic needle.

You may have heard that metal can mess up a compass reading. It's true. Ferrous objects—iron, steel, and other materials with magnetic properties—will deflect the magnetic needle and produce false readings, as will a battery-powered watch that is within 6 inches of a compass. Keep the compass away from belt buckles, ice axes, and other metal objects. If a compass reading doesn't seem to make sense, see if it's being sabotaged by nearby metal.

Keep your wits about you when pointing the declination arrow and the direction-of-travel line. If either is pointed backward—an easy thing to do—the reading will be 180 degrees off. If the bearing is north, the compass will say it's south. Remember that the north-seeking end of the magnetic needle must be aligned with the pointed end of the declination arrow. And that the direction-of-travel line must point from you to the objective, not the reverse.

There's yet another way to introduce a 180-degree error in a compass reading. The way to do it is to align the compass meridian lines with the north–south lines on a map, but have the declination arrow pointing backward. The way to avoid this is to check that your declination arrow is pointing more or less to north (rather than more or less to south). This check has nothing to do with declination. It just happens that the arrow is placed in a convenient spot to serve as a reminder of which way to direct the meridian lines.

If in doubt, trust your compass. The compass, correctly used, is almost always right, while your contrary judgment may be clouded by fatigue, confusion, or hurry. If you get a nonsensical reading, check to see you aren't making one of those 180-

degree errors. If not, and if there is no metal in sight, verify the reading with other members of the party. If they get the same answer, trust the compass over hunches, blind guesses, and intuition.

THE MAP AND COMPASS: A CHECK LIST

Do you have the hang of it? Let's run through the whole procedure. Check off each step as you do it.

To take (measure) a bearing on a map:

1. Place compass on map, with edge of base plate joining two points of interest.
2. Rotate housing to align compass meridian lines with north–south lines on map.
3. Read bearing at index line.

To plot (follow) a bearing on a map:

1. Set desired bearing at index line.
2. Place compass on map, with edge of base plate on feature from which you wish to plot bearing.
3. Turn entire compass to align meridian lines with map's north–south lines. The edge of the base plate is the bearing line.

To take (measure) a bearing in the field:

1. Hold compass level, in front of you, and point direction-of-travel line at desired object.
2. Rotate housing to align declination arrow with magnetic needle.
3. Read bearing at index line.

To plot (follow) a bearing in the field:

1. Set desired bearing at index line.
2. Hold compass level, in front of you, and turn your entire body until magnetic needle is aligned with declination arrow.
3. Travel in direction shown by the direction-of-travel line.

And for the last time:

• Never use the magnetic needle or the declination arrow when measuring or plotting bearings on the map (except to check that the declination arrow is pointing more or less north on the map, not south, as a check that the compass meridian lines are not upside-down).

• When taking or following a bearing in the field, always align the pointed end of the declination arrow with the north-seeking end of the magnetic needle.

THE ALTIMETER

An altimeter (fig. 4-11), like a compass, provides one simple piece of information that forms the basis for a tremendous amount of vital detail. The compass merely points the direction to magnetic north. The altimeter merely gives the elevation. But by monitoring the elevation and checking it against the topographic map, mountaineers keep track of their progress, pinpoint their location, and find the way to critical junctions in the route. Every climbing party should have an altimeter.

An altimeter is basically a modified barometer.

A barometer measures air pressure (the weight of air) and displays it on a scale calibrated in inches or millimeters of mercury, or in millibars. Because air pressure decreases at a uniform rate with increasing altitude, a barometer can measure elevation if it is fitted with a scale calibrated in feet or meters instead of units of pressure.

To read a mountaineering altimeter, begin by holding it level in the palm of one hand. Look directly down on the needle, your eyes at least a foot above it, to reduce errors due to viewing

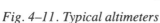
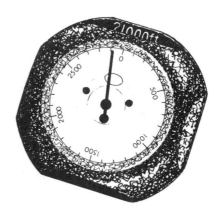

Fig. 4–11. Typical altimeters

angle. Tap it lightly several times to overcome slight friction in the mechanism, and then take an average of several readings. The elevations determined by an altimeter are only approximate because the instrument is strongly affected by variations in temperature and weather. Check the reading whenever you reach a point of known elevation so you can reset it if necessary.

HOW ALTIMETERS AID MOUNTAINEERS

The altimeter helps in deciding whether to continue a climb or to turn back, by letting you calculate your rate of ascent. Let's say you have been keeping an hourly check on time and elevation during a climb. It has taken the party 4 hours to climb 3,000 feet, an average of 750 feet per hour. But you know that the actual rate of ascent has been declining with each hour. In fact, the party gained only 500 feet in the past hour, compared with 1,000 feet the first hour. You know that the summit is at an elevation of 8,400 feet, and an altimeter reading shows you're now at 6,400. So you can predict that it will take roughly 4 more hours to reach the summit. Take that information, courtesy of the altimeter, combine it with a look at the weather, the time of day, and the condition of the climbers, and you have the data on which to base a sound decision.

An altimeter also can help determine exactly where you are. If you are climbing a ridge shown on the map, but don't know exactly where you are along the ridge, check the altimeter for the elevation. Where the ridge reaches that contour line on the map is your likely location.

Another way to ask the altimeter where you are is to start with a compass bearing to a summit or some other known feature. Find that peak on the map, and plot the bearing line from the mountain back toward the climbing party. You now know you must be somewhere along that line. But where? Take an altimeter reading and find out the elevation. Where the compass bearing line crosses a contour line at that elevation is your likely location. This could lead to an ambiguous answer, of course, because the line might cross that contour at several points. That's when you turn to further observations, common sense, and intuition.

Navigation gets easier with the aid of an altimeter. If you top a convenient couloir at 9,400 feet and gain the summit ridge, make a note of that elevation. On the way back, descend the ridge to that elevation and you will easily find the couloir again.

Guidebook descriptions sometimes specify a change in direction at a particular elevation. If it's on an open snowfield or a forested hillside, good luck in making the turn at the right place without an altimeter. The route you have worked out on a topographic map also may depend on course changes at certain elevations, and again the altimeter will keep the party on target. An altimeter obviously helps in mapping, providing elevations of key points along routes included on the map.

Last but not least, an altimeter will reveal if you're on the real summit when the visibility is too poor to be able to tell by looking around.

HOW TO GET THE MOST FROM YOUR ALTIMETER

Knowing all the facts about an altimeter—the pluses and minuses—will make it as valuable as possible in the wilderness. First of all, keep in mind that temperature and weather are always working their will on an altimeter's accuracy. A high-pressure weather area will tend to cause a lower elevation reading than a low-pressure area. Warmer, lighter air will tend to result in a higher elevation reading than colder, heavier air.

There's no need to be surprised if an elevation reading of 5,200 as you go to sleep turns into 5,300 when you wake up the next morning, even though the tent appears to be in the same spot. The elevation hasn't changed, but the weather has, and with it, the air pressure that is the basis for an altimeter's determination of elevation. That's just the way altimeters are, and as with any good friend, you've got to accept them despite their bad habits. The best way to keep them relatively honest is to check the reading at every known elevation point and reset the altimeter accordingly. Topographic maps give the correct elevations of many of the features you encounter on a trip, such as trailheads, lakes, and summits.

Try to keep the temperature of the altimeter relatively constant, perhaps by carrying it in your pocket. The altimeter expands and contracts due to variations in its temperature, causing changes in the indicated elevation. A bimetallic element in temperature-compensated altimeters adjusts for this effect of temperature when there is no actual change in elevation. The element counterbalances the effect on other parts of the instrument. When you are gaining or losing elevation, however, this adjustment sometimes is not enough, resulting in errors even in altimeters that are temperature-compensated.

The altimeter can help in predicting weather. The altimeter and barometer scales operate in opposition to each other. When one goes up, the other goes down. An altimeter reading showing an increase in elevation when no actual elevation change has taken place (such as at camp overnight) means a falling barometer, which generally indicates deteriorating weather. A decreasing altimeter reading, on the other hand, means increasing barometric pressure, generally associated with improving weather. This is an oversimplification, of course, as weather forecasting is complicated by the wind, local weather peculiarities, and the rate of barometric pressure change. Stay observant on climbing trips if you want to figure out the relationship between weather and altimeter readings in your area.

Because even the most accurate and costly altimeters bow to the weather, don't be misled into trusting them to accuracies greater than are possible. A typical high-quality altimeter may have a scale of resolution (smallest marked division) of 20 feet and a stated accuracy of plus-or-minus 30 feet. This doesn't mean the altimeter will always be that close to the truth. Get to know your own altimeter, use it often, check it at every opportunity, and note differences of opinion between it and the map. You'll soon know just what accuracy to expect, and it will then be a dependable aid to roving the wilds.

ORIENTATION BY INSTRUMENT

Figuring out exactly where you are is usually a relatively simple affair, just looking around and comparing what you see with what is on the map.

Sometimes this is not accurate enough, or there is just nothing much nearby to identify on the map. The usual solution then is to get out the compass and try for bearings to some faraway landscape features. This is orientation by instrument.

The goal of orientation is to determine that precise point on the earth where you now stand. Your position can then be represented by a mere dot on the map which is known as your *point position*. There are two lower levels of orientation. One is called *line position*: the travelers know they are along a certain line on a map—such as a river, a trail, or a bearing line—but they do not know where they are along the line. The lowest level is *area position*: they know the general area they are in, but that's about it. The primary objective of orientation is to find out your exact point position.

POINT POSITION

With point position known, there is no question about where you are, and you can use that knowledge in identifying on the map any major feature visible on the landscape. You can also identify on the landscape any visible feature shown on the map.

For example, climbers on the summit of Forbidden Peak know their point position. It's at the top of Forbidden Peak. (You can refer back to the Forbidden topographic map, fig. 4-2.) They see an unknown mountain and want to know what it is. They take a bearing and get 275 degrees. They plot 275 degrees from Forbidden Peak on their topographic map, and it passes through Mount Torment. They conclude that the unknown peak is Mount Torment.

However, if you start by wanting to find Mount Torment, do the map work first. The climbers measure the bearing on the map from where they are, Forbidden, to Mount Torment, and come up with 275 degrees. Keeping 275 at the index line on the compass, one climber holds the compass out and turns until the magnetic needle is aligned with the declination arrow. The direction-of-travel line then points to Mount Torment.

LINE POSITION

With line position known, the goal is to determine point position. Knowing they are on a trail, ridge, or some other identifiable line, the climbers

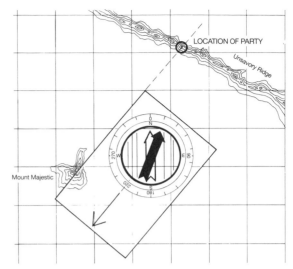

Fig. 4–12. Orientation with line position known

need only one more piece of information. For example, they are on Unsavory Ridge (fig. 4-12)—but exactly where? Off in the distance is Mount Majestic. A bearing on Majestic indicates 220 degrees. Plot 220 degrees from Mount Majestic on the map. Run this line back toward Unsavory Ridge, and where it intersects the ridge is exactly where the climbers are.

AREA POSITION

The climbers know their area position: they are in the general area of Fantastic Crags (fig. 4-13). They want to determine line position and then, from that, point position. To move from knowing area position to knowing point position, two trustworthy pieces of information are needed.

The climbers may be able to use bearings on two visible features. They take a bearing on Mount Majestic and get a reading of 40 degrees. They plot a line on the map, through Mount Majestic, at 40 degrees. They know they must be somewhere on that bearing line, so they now have line position. They can also see Unsavory Spire. A bearing on the spire shows 130 degrees. They plot a line on the map, through Unsavory Spire, at 130 degrees. The two bearing lines intersect, and that's where they are.

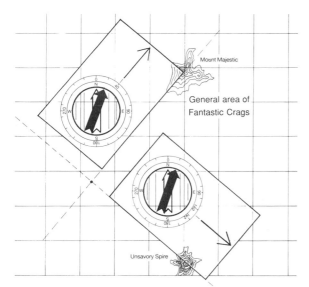

Fig. 4–13. Orientation with area position known

When you know the area position and there is just one visible feature to take a bearing on, the compass can't provide anything more than line

position. That can be a big help, though. Climbers in the general vicinity of Fantastic River then know they are near where the bearing line plotted from the one feature intersects the river. Perhaps from a study of the map they can then figure out just where they are. They can also read the altimeter and see on the map where the bearing line intersects the contour line for that elevation. The closer an angle of intersection is to 90 degrees, the more accurate the point position will be.

Use every scrap of information at your disposal, but be sure your conclusions agree with common sense. If the climbers who took bearings on Mount Majestic and Unsavory Spire find that the two lines on the map intersect in the river, but the climbers are on a high point of land, something is wrong. Try again. Try to take a bearing on another landmark, and plot it. If lines intersect at a map location with no similarity to the terrain, there might be some magnetic anomaly in the rocks, or you may have an inaccurate map. And who knows? Maybe those peaks weren't really Majestic and Unsavory in the first place.

NAVIGATION BY INSTRUMENT

Getting from here to there is usually just a matter of keeping an eye on the landscape and watching were you're going, helped by an occasional glance at the map. However, if the current objective is out of sight, you can take compass in hand, set a bearing, and follow the direction-of-travel line as it guides you to the goal. This is navigation by instrument. Sometimes this is the only practical method for finding the pass or base camp or whatever. It also serves as a supplement to other methods and a way of verifying that you're on the right track. Again, use common sense and challenge a compass bearing that defies reason. (Is your declination arrow pointing the wrong way, sending you 180 degrees off course?)

MAP AND COMPASS

The most common situation requiring instrument navigation comes when the route is unclear because the topography is featureless or because landmarks are obscured by forest or fog. You do know exactly where you are and where you want to go, and can identify both the current position and the destination on the map. Simply measure the bearing from your position to your objective on the map, then follow that bearing. Let's say you get a bearing of 285 degrees (fig. 4-14a). Read this bearing at the index line and leave it set there as is (fig. 4-14b). Hold the compass out in front of you as you rotate your body until the north-seeking end of the magnetic needle is aligned with the pointed end of the declination arrow. The direction-of-travel line now points to the objective (fig. 4-14c). Start walking.

COMPASS ALONE

Navigators of air and ocean often travel by instrument alone; so can climbers. For example, if

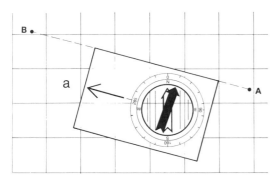

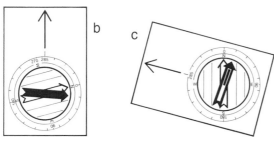

Fig. 4–14. Navigation using the map and compass: a, measuring the bearing from point A to point B on the map; b, bearing at index line; c, following the bearing.

you are scrambling toward a pass and clouds begin to obscure it, take a quick compass bearing. Then follow the bearing, compass in hand if you wish. You don't even have to note the numerical bearing; just align the magnetic needle with the declination arrow and keep it aligned. Likewise, if you are heading into a valley where fog or forest will hide the mountain that is your goal, take the bearing to the peak before you drop into the valley (fig. 4-15). Then navigate by compass through the valley. This method becomes more reliable if several people travel together with compass in hand, checking each other's work.

USING INTERMEDIATE OBJECTIVES

A handy technique is available for those frustrating times you try to stay exactly on a compass bearing, but keep getting diverted by obstructions such as cliffs, dense brush, or crevasses. Try the technique of intermediate objectives. Sight past the obstruction to a tree or rock or other object that is exactly on the bearing line to the principal objective (fig. 4-16a). Then you're free to scramble over to the tree or rock by whatever route is easiest. When you get there, you can be confident that you

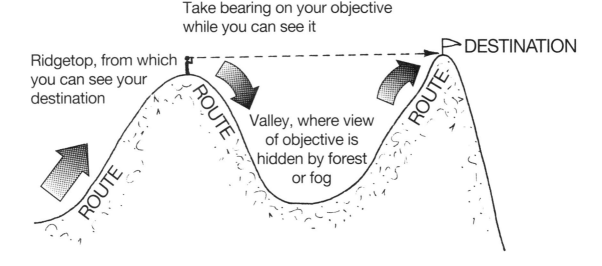

Fig. 4–15. Following a compass bearing when the view of the objective is obscured by forest or fog

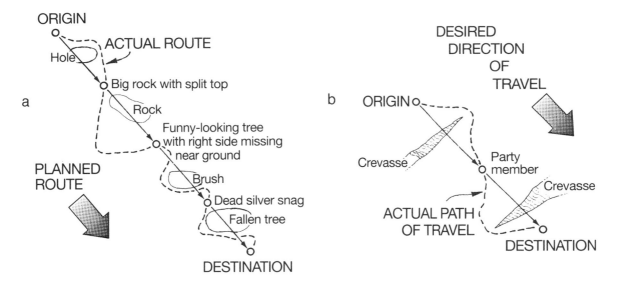

Fig. 4–16. Use of intermediate objectives: a, in a forest; b, on a glacier.

are still on the correct route. The technique is useful even when there is no obstruction. Moving from intermediate objective to intermediate objective means you can put the compass away for those short stretches rather having to check it every few steps.

Sometimes on snow or in fog, there *are* no natural intermediate objectives, just a white, undifferentiated landscape. Then another member of the party can serve as the target (fig. 4-16b). Send that person out to near the limit of visibility. Wave this new intermediate objective left or right, directly onto the bearing line. That person can then improve the accuracy of the route by taking a "back bearing" to you. (For a back bearing, keep the same bearing set at the index line, but for this purpose, align the *south-seeking* end of the magnetic needle with the pointed end of the declination arrow.) The combination of a bearing and a back bearing tends to counteract any compass error.

LOST

Why do people get lost? Lots of reasons. Some travel without a map because the route seems obvious. Others fail to check on recent changes in roads and trails. Some folks trust their own instincts over the compass. Others do not bother with the map homework that can start them off with a good mental picture of the area. Some don't pay enough attention to the route on the way in to be able to find it on the way out. Some rely on the skill of their climbing partner, who is just now in the process of getting them lost.

Why *do* people get lost? They don't take the time to think about where they are going, because they are in a hurry. They miss junctions or wander off on game trails. They charge mindlessly ahead despite deteriorating weather and visibility, fatigue, or flagging spirits.

Good navigators are never truly lost—but having learned humility through years of experience, they always carry enough food, clothing, and bivouac gear to get them through hours or even days of temporary confusion.

WHAT IF YOUR PARTY IS LOST?

The first rule is to STOP. Avoid the temptation to plunge hopefully on. Try to determine where you are. If that doesn't work, figure out the last time the group *did* know its exact location. If that spot is fairly close, within an hour or so, retrace your steps and get back on route. But if that spot is hours back and you can at least make an intelligent guess about the current position, continue forward, but cautiously and with a sharp eye out for landmarks. If the party tires or darkness falls before you find the route, bivouac for the night.

Groups of two or more rarely become dangerously lost, even if they have no wilderness experience. The real danger comes to an individual who is separated from the rest of the party. For this reason, always try to keep everyone together, and assign a rear guard to keep track of the stragglers.

WHAT IF YOU ARE LOST ALONE?

Again, the first rule is to STOP. Look around for other members of the party, shout, and listen for answering shouts. If the only answer is silence, sit down, try to regain your calm, and combat terror with reason.

Once you've calmed down, start doing the right things. Look at your map in an attempt to determine your location, and plan a route home in case you don't connect with the other climbers. Mark your location with a cairn or other objects, and then scout in all directions, each time returning to the marked position. Well before dark, prepare for the night by finding water, firewood, and shelter. Staying busy will raise your spirits. Keep a fire going to give searchers something to see, and try singing so you will have something to do and they will have something to hear.

The odds are that you will be reunited with your group by morning. If not, fight panic. After a night alone, you may decide to hike out to a base-line feature you picked out before the trip—a ridge or stream or highway. If the terrain is too difficult to travel alone, it might be better to concentrate on letting yourself be found. It's easier for rescuers to find a lost climber who stays in one place in the open, builds a fire, and shouts periodically, than one who thrashes on in hysterical hope, one step ahead of the rescue party.

FREEDOM OF THE HILLS

The wilderness awaits those who have learned the skills of routefinding and navigation. In large part, routefinding is the subject of this entire book because it is so essential to all off-trail adventure.

In medieval times the greatest honor a visitor could receive was the rights of a citizen and the freedom of the city, sometimes even today symbolized by presenting a guest with the ''keys to the city.'' For the modern alpine traveler, routefinding is the key to wandering at will through valleys and meadows, up cliffs and over glaciers, earning the rights of a citizen in a magical land, a mountaineer with the freedom of the hills.

· 5 ·

WILDERNESS TRAVEL

Climbing the mountain is one thing. Getting from the car to the mountain is another. Wilderness travel is the art of getting there—across streams, around brush, along trails, and over snow.

When climbers leave the trailhead deep in a valley of Washington State's Cascade range or head inland from the beach of a British Columbia fiord, tough wilderness travel may lie ahead. The techniques of muddling through brush are not as glamorous as fifth-class rock climbing, but many a peak has been lost in thickets of slide alder. The biggest barriers on the way to a mountaintop often appear below snow line. Learn the skills of wilderness travel and you open the gateway to the summit.

WILDERNESS ROUTEFINDING

Routefinding is the art of working out an efficient route that is within the abilities of the climbing party. Navigation, on the other hand, is the science of using map and compass, and often an altimeter, to determine the location of the objective and to keep moving in the right direction toward it. Navigation points the way from where you are to where you want to be, but it takes skill in routefinding to surmount the hazards and hurdles between here and there. Intuition and luck play a role in routefinding, but there also are principles that can be learned. And there is no substitute for firsthand experience. Climb with experienced mountaineers, watch their techniques, and ask questions. Routefinding is one of the most satisfying of mountain crafts to master.

Each mountain range has its own peculiarities of geology and climate that affect routefinding.

Mountaineers familiar with the Canadian Rockies, accustomed to broad valleys and open forests, will need to learn new rules to contend with the heavily vegetated, narrow canyons of British Columbia's Coast Range. The Pacific Northwest mountaineer used to deep snow at 4,000 feet in June will discover drastically different June conditions in the Sierra. Prolonged mountaineering in a single range teaches the lore of routefinding in that area, but a climber entering a new range has to be ready to learn again.

Some of the most detailed advice on routes will come out of conversations with local experts. Talk to geologists, rangers, and fellow mountaineers. Ask about climbers' trails that don't show on the map and about the best place to ford a stream. Stop at the ranger station on the way to the mountains and get word on current weather and route conditions. Spend a few minutes chatting with the other climbers who have stopped at the ranger station on the way to their own mountain adventure. Doing your homework makes for easier trips with fewer routefinding frustrations.

APPROACH OBSERVATIONS

Keep an eye on the mountain during the approach hike, studying it for climbing routes. The distant view reveals gross patterns of ridges, cliffs, snowfields, and glaciers, as well as the average angle of inclination.

As you get closer, details of fault lines, bands of cliffs, and crevasse fields show up. Gross patterns seen from far away usually are repeated in finer detail when viewed closer. Ledges revealed by snow or shrubs from a distance often turn out to be ''sidewalks'' with smaller ledges between. The major fault lines, or weaknesses, visible at a distance are usually accompanied by finer, less obvious repetitions.

If the approach skirts the base of the mountain, it can be viewed from various perspectives. A system of ledges indistinguishable against background cliffs may show clearly from another angle with the sky behind. The change of light as the sun traverses the sky often creates revealing shadows. A study of these lengthening or shortening shadows may disclose that apparently sheer cliffs are only moderately angled slopes.

The presence of snow often promises a modest angle and easy climbing, because it doesn't last long on slopes greater than 50 degrees. But beware of nature's illusions. Rime ice adhering to vertical or overhanging cliffs can at first appear to be snow. Deep high-angle couloirs (gullies) often retain snow or ice year-round, especially when shaded. And what look like brilliantly shining snowfields high on the mountain may actually be ice.

As you near the peak, look for climbing clues: ridges with lower average inclination than the faces they divide; cracks, ledges, and chimneys leading up or across the faces; snowfields or glaciers offering easier or predictable pitches.

Spot climbing hazards. Study snowfields and icefalls for avalanche danger, and cliffs for signs of possible rockfall. Snowfields reveal recent rockfall by the appearance of dirty snow or the presence of rock-filled ''shell-craters.'' If the route goes through avalanche and rockfall territory, travel in the cold hours of night, or very early morning before the sun melts the ice mortar bonding precariously perched boulders and ice towers.

Throughout the approach, follow the old mountaineering dictum to ''climb with your eyes.'' Keep evaluating hazards and looking for continuous routes. When the route information gets too complex to remember, begin making quick sketches during rest stops. These memory aids can prove invaluable during a climb when a critical exit gully, for example, becomes lost from view.

While you're at it, keep an eye out for emergency campsites, water supplies, firewood, and anything else that might make your return trip easier and safer.

WALKING

The basic skill for mountaineering is a simple act we all do every day: walking. But just as the ability to write doesn't mean you're a writer, the ability to walk doesn't mean you're a wilderness-ready walker. To walk efficiently in the mountains, you've got to take into account the varied terrain, the weight of your pack, and your physical condition.

PACE

Beginners often make one of two mistakes: they walk faster than they should, or they walk slower than they could.

The most common mistake is walking too fast, perhaps out of concern for the long miles ahead or from a desire to perform well in front of companions. But why wear yourself out on the first mile of a 10-mile hike if the whole day happens to be available for the walk? Take your time and enjoy it.

A simple test will reveal if your pace is too fast. If you cannot sustain it hour after hour, you're going too fast.

The other mistake is hiking too slowly. Your body complains long before it is hurt. Your muscles may ache but still have 10 miles left in them; your lungs may gasp but be able to go on gasping another 3 hours. A degree of suffering is inevitable on the way to becoming a good walker.

The most desirable hiking speed varies during a day. Get ready for a hike by stretching your legs, hips, back, and shoulders. Walk slowly at the start, letting the body become aware of the demands to come. Then start striding out, using will power to get through this period of increasing work until the body experiences its "second wind."

Physiologically, this means the heart has stepped up its beat, the blood is circulating more rapidly, the muscles have loosened. Psychologically, the hiker feels happy and strong.

Vary your pace depending on the trail. Plod slowly and methodically up steep hills; as the grade lessens, pick up the tempo. Your pace will slow late in the day as fatigue sets in. Adrenaline may fuel short bursts of exertion, but there is no "third wind."

THE REST STEP

The most valuable technique in wilderness hiking is setting the right pace. A very important way of controlling your pace is the rest step (fig. 5-1), used whenever legs or lungs need a little time to recuperate between steps on steep slopes. Once you learn it, you'll use it often.

The pace is slow, because for every step there is a pause. The rest takes place after one foot is swung forward for the next step. Support the entire weight of your body on the rear leg while relaxing the muscles of the forward leg. Important: keep your rear leg straight and locked at the knee so that bone, not muscle, supports the weight.

Synchronize breathing with the sequence. In a

Fig. 5–1. The rest step

typical sequence, you may take a new breath with each step—but the number of breaths per step will be less or more depending on how hard the work is. With one breath per step, inhale as you bring your back foot up to the front; exhale as your front leg rests and your rear leg supports the body's weight. Keep repeating this sequence. Where the air is thin, the lungs need an extra pause—sometimes three or four breaths per step. Make a conscious effort to breathe deeply.

Mental composure is important with the rest step. The monotony of the pace, especially on glaciers and snowfields, can undermine morale. You must trust the technique to slowly but steadily chew up the miles, even when the summit seems to be getting no closer.

RESTS

Even the strongest and most experienced hikers need occasional full rests.

During the first half-hour of a hike, stop for a shakedown rest. This lets hikers loosen or tighten boot laces, adjust pack straps, add or take off layers of clothing.

In groups that include both men and women, remember to declare regular party separations (toilet stops), especially out of courtesy to the hiker who may be too shy to express the need. With large groups, the day's first party separation should come before the hike begins, at a service station or outhouse near the trailhead.

During the early part of the day, while your body is fresh, take short, infrequent breathers. Rest in a standing or semi-reclining position, leaning against a tree or hillside to remove pack weight from the shoulders, take deep breaths, and have a bite to eat.

Later, with the body demanding more complete relaxation, the party can take a sackout rest every hour or two. When it's about time for a stop, look for a place with special advantages, such as water, view, flowers, and convenient slopes for unslinging packs. Don't prolong such lovely rests. It's agonizing to resume a march once muscles become cold and stiff. But do remember to eat small amounts of food and drink water during rest stops.

A climbing party sprawled along the trail is not getting any closer to its objective. Take rests when necessary. Otherwise keep moving, unless there's so much extra time in the day that you can afford a luxury rest.

DOWNHILL AND SIDE-HILL

Walking downhill is less tiring than walking uphill, but it's a mixed blessing. Going down a trail, body weight drops roughly and abruptly on legs and feet. Toes are jammed forward. Jolts travel up the spine to jar the entire body. The result can be blisters and knee cartilage damage, sore toes and blackened nails, headaches, and back pain.

Hikers use a few tricks to ease their way downhill. Tighten laces to reduce movement inside the boot (and keep your toenails trimmed). Maintain a measured pace that is slower than the one urged by gravity. Bend your knees to cushion the shock with each step, and place your feet lightly,

as if they were already sore. This restraint will tire your upper leg muscles, and you'll learn that rests going down a trail are just as essential as on the way up.

The ups and downs of hiking are far preferable to the torments of side-hilling (traversing). Walking across a side hill twists the ankles, contorts the hips, and destroys balance. If you can abandon a side hill in order to drop down into a brush-free valley or go up onto a rounded ridge, do it. It's worth going the extra distance. If you're stuck with side-hilling, switchback now and then to shift the strain. Work into your route any flat spots of relief provided by rocks, animal trails, and clumps of grass or heather.

ETIQUETTE

Walking with others requires certain courtesies that are nothing more than common-sense thoughtfulness.

• Avoid following too close. Instead of shadowing your companion, give the hiker ahead of you some space by staying perhaps seven or eight paces back.

• Avoid following too far back, so you don't lose contact with the other hikers or make them continually wait for you.

• Take a look back before you release the branches you've pushed aside along the route. If the hiker behind you has violated the first rule, that person is in danger of getting swatted.

• Step aside when you stop to tie a shoe lace, adjust your pack, or admire the view. (Step above those passing by, if possible.)

• Ask permission to pass, instead of elbowing your way forward.

• Step aside on the way downhill to let a party of uphill hikers continue forward without breaking their pace.

• Set a pace that everyone in the party can maintain. If someone can't keep up, slow the party's pace. Give the last person time to catch up with the party at rest stops—and time to rest after getting there.

TRAILS

The simplest way into the wilderness will always be a trail. They come in many shapes and sizes. One trail will be wide and well marked, while another will have a quality of magic about it: now you see it, now you don't. One big job of the wilderness traveler is to find trails and use them.

TRAIL FINDING

Very few trails were created for the use of climbers. Miners built trails to ore, fishermen to the high lakes, trappers along valleys, pioneers over passes, and animals to food and shelter. But the mine or the lake or the pass might make a good base camp, and any track is worth following as long as it heads the right way.

Even in popular areas with heavy foot traffic and lots of signs, keep alert to find the trail and stay on it. It's easy to stagnate mentally on a long, monotonous walk and miss a turnoff where a sign is missing or where logging has obliterated part of the trail.

Old blazes cut in tree trunks or ribbon tied to branches often mark the trail through a forest, and rock cairns may show the way above timberline. But these pointers don't last forever, and they aren't always reliable. A tiny cairn or a wisp of ribbon may reflect nothing more than the passage of a climber who was lost or was laying out a route to another destination.

As a trail-seeker, you become a detective who combines the clues (a bit of beaten path here, a tree blaze there) with the use of map, compass, and altimeter and with tips from guidebooks and the experts. You'll soon delight in rediscovering the trail just as your companions pronounce it lost forever. And you'll shock the lowland Sunday-afternoon hiker with your definition of the word "trail": any visible route, no matter how ragged, that efficiently gets you where you want to go without battling through brush.

The trick is to stay on the trail until the inevitable moment it disappears or until it becomes necessary to head off-trail in order to keep going in the right direction. Then create your own trail, choosing a course that a trail would follow if there were one. Trail builders look for the easiest way to go. Do as they do.

SOUND TRAIL PRACTICES

Finding the trail is only one half of trailcraft. Using it in a sensitive, caring way is the other. Here are some guidelines:

• Walk in single file to protect trail-side vegetation.
• Stay on the trail even if it's muddy, snow-covered, or rutted.
• Help save vegetation and prevent erosion by not cutting switchbacks.
• Select resilient areas instead of fragile vegetation for rest breaks.
• Look and photograph instead of picking or collecting.
• Guard against damage to stream banks.
• Do light trail maintenance and remove litter.
• Leave trailless areas free of cairns and flagging unless they're already there. Let others have the same adventure of routefinding that you experienced. If you need to mark your route, remove the markers on your way down.
• Choose talus instead of fragile meadows for cross-country travel.

BRUSH

Brush can be a backcountry horror, but there are ways to avoid it.

Wherever there is running water or sliding snow, brush thrives. The classic example is a low-altitude gully swept by avalanches in winter and a torrent in summer. Conditions are perfect for shrubs that flourish during the short summer season, bend undamaged under the snow, and quickly sprout again.

Along riverbanks, brush keeps a window on the sun and builds a narrow, dense thicket. A river that frequently changes course prevents large trees from growing but permits a wide belt of entangling brush. At subalpine elevations, avalanche snow that lasts late into summer prevents the growth of forests and leaves the valley floor crowded with brush.

Mountaineers prefer mature forests. The forests help by blocking sunlight, stifling growth of the deciduous brush that makes for rough going. Young forests, however, only add to the brush problem. The second-growth timber that springs up densely after a fire or windstorm or logging is at its worst when about 20 feet high. The branches fill the space between trees, and deciduous brush continues to thrive.

Blowdowns, avalanche fans, and logging trash are even tougher to get through. The chaotic jumble can slow progress to a crawl and justify a major change of route. Tough and twisted scrub cedar that clings to cliffs and bands of rock presents another hurdle.

When a skirmish with brush is inevitable, there are ways to minimize the hassle. Choose the shortest route across the brushy area. Use fallen trees with long straight trunks as elevated walkways. Push and pull the bushes apart—sometimes by stepping on lower limbs and lifting higher ones to make a passageway. On steep terrain, use hardy shrubs as handholds.

Brush can be dangerous: down-slanting vine maple or alder is slippery; brush obscures the peril of cliffs, boulders, and ravines; and brush snares ropes.

The best policy is to avoid brush. Here are some tips:

• Use trails as much as possible. Five miles of trail may be less work than 1 mile through brush.

• Consider traveling when snow covers brush. Some valleys are easy going in May when you can walk on snow but almost impossible in July when you must burrow through brush.

• Avoid avalanche tracks. The best route up a long valley may be on southern or western slopes, where avalanches hit less frequently than on northern and eastern slopes. When climbing a valley wall, stay in the trees between avalanche tracks.

• Aim for the heaviest timber. Brush is thinnest under the big trees.

• Travel on talus or scree and remnants of snow, rather than in adjacent thickets.

• Consider traveling on ridges and ridge spurs. They may be dry and brushless, while creek bottoms and valley floors are choked with vegetation.

• Consider climbing directly to timberline to take a high route above the brush. This may be worthwhile if the valley bottom seems impassable, and the valley sides are scarred by avalanche tracks.

• Consider going right into the stream channel. The stream bed could be a tunnel through the brush, though you may have to do some wading. Dry stream beds are sometimes ideal. In deep canyons, however, streams usually are choked with fallen trees or interrupted by waterfalls.

• Look for game trails. Animals generally follow the path of least resistance.

TALUS

Talus slopes can either help or hinder the climber. Most offer handy brush-free pathways to the mountains, but some are loose and dangerous.

The peaks constantly crumble, dropping fragments that pile up below as talus and scree. Most of the rubble pours from gullies and spreads out in fan-shaped cones that often merge into one another, forming a broad band of talus between valley greenery and the peaks. Talus fans also often alternate with forest.

Talus slopes build gradually over the ages. On the oldest slopes, soil fills the gap between rocks, making smooth pathways. But talus can be dangerous on volcanos and younger mountains, where rocks are only loosely consolidated because vegetation hasn't filled in the spaces. Move nimbly here, ready to leap away if a rock shifts underfoot. Disturbing one key stone on a glacial moraine or a talus slope can even set off a serious rock avalanche.

Climbers on talus slopes need to keep alert because almost everyone will knock loose a rock or two. Try to travel outside the fall line of climbers above and below. If you're in a narrow gully and this isn't possible, tread gently and be ready to shout ''Rock!'' if a stone is dislodged. Keep close together so a rock set off by one climber can't gain dangerous momentum by the time it reaches other team members. Or permit only one climber to move at a time, while the rest stay in a protected spot.

Slopes with the smallest fragments, called scree, are sometimes as loose as sand. This makes the uphill going a slow-motion torment, but on the way down it might permit some careful ''screeing.'' This involves shuffling your feet to start a minor slide of pebbles and riding it down, in a standing glissade. If there is any vegetation on the slope, skip the screeing out of regard for the plants.

SNOW

Snow can be a blessing in wilderness travel. Many peaks are best climbed early in the season because talus, brush, and logging slash are covered by consolidated snow, and snow bridges provide an easy way over streams.

There are hazards, however. Streams will melt the underside of a snow bridge until it can no longer support your weight. You may break through, the result being wet feet or, much worse, being carried under the snow by a swift stream. To guard against a dunking, watch for depressions in the snow and variations in color or texture, and listen for sounds of running water. Water emerging at the foot of a snowfield gives a clue to the existence and perhaps the size of a cavity beneath the snow. Probe thin spots with your ice axe.

The snow next to logs and boulders often covers holes and soft spots, caused when the snow melts partially away from the wood and the rock. Probe or avoid likely trouble spots, and step wide off logs and rocks. As spring merges into summer, the best route along a valley floor may be somewhat erratic, taking advantage of each remaining snow patch for the few steps of easy walking it provides.

The techniques of snow travel are the same whether the snow lies high in the mountains or deep in the woods. On steep slopes, you may need safeguards such as an ice axe, a rope, or crampons. With experience, you'll recognize both the dangers and the advantages of snow and learn to use the medium to make wilderness travel easier and more enjoyable.

STREAMS

In a wilderness without trails or bridges, streams can become a major impediment. In Alaska or the Canadian Coast Range, climbers may spend more time and energy crossing a perilous river than on their ultimate objective, the mountain.

FINDING THE CROSSING

When the peak lies on the far side of a sizable river, the crossing is a major factor in route selection. Try to get a distant overall view of the river, perhaps from a ridge before dropping into the valley. This view can be more useful than a hundred close looks from the riverbank. When a distant view isn't possible or isn't helpful, you're stuck with either thrashing through the river-bottom brush looking for a way across or sticking to the slopes high above the river in hopes of spotting a sure crossing.

In deep forest there's a good chance of finding

easy passage on a log jam over even the widest river. Higher in the mountains, foot logs are harder to come by, especially if the river changes course periodically and prevents growth of large trees near its channel.

A particular river may be impassable. If it's fed by snow, early morning is the time of minimum flow, and a party may camp overnight to wait for lower water. Sometimes it's necessary to hike for hours or days seeking a crossing. For the widest and deepest rivers, rafts are the only alternative short of hiking to the headwaters.

MAKING THE CROSSING

Unfasten the waist and chest straps of your pack before trying any stream crossing that would require swimming if you fell. You must be able to shed the pack in a hurry.

A foot log is a great way across, with an ice axe, stick, or tightly stretched handline to help with balance and support if the log is thin, slippery, or steeply inclined. Sit down and scoot across if that helps.

Boulders offer another way. Move from boulder to boulder—but only after mentally rehearsing the entire sequence of leaps. Safety lies in smooth and steady progress over stones that may be too slippery and unsteady for you to stop for more than an instant. Use an ice axe or pole for added balance.

If you must wade across, use the widest part of the river. The narrows may be appealing as the shortest way, but they're also the deepest, swiftest, and most dangerous.

If the water is placid and the stones rounded, put your boots in the pack and keep them dry as you wade across. In tougher conditions, wear your boots, but put socks and insoles in the pack. You can drain the boots on the far side, replace the insoles, and put the dry socks back on. You may decide to remove your pants or other clothing in deeper crossings. Loose clothing increases the drag from the water, but it also reduces chilling and may permit a longer crossing before your legs go numb.

The force of moving water is easy to underestimate. A swift stream flowing only shin-deep boils up against the knees. Knee-deep water may boil above the waist and give a disconcerting sensation of buoyancy. Whenever water boils above the knee, it is dangerous, and one false step could have you bouncing in white water from boulder to boulder. Frothy water, containing a great deal of air, is wet enough to drown in but may not be dense enough to float the human body. Streams fed by glaciers present an added difficulty because the bottom is hidden by milky water from glacier-milled rock flour.

If the stream is deep but not swift, you can cross by angling downstream at about the same speed as the current. But it's usually best to face upstream, lean into the current, and stab an ice axe or stout pole upstream for a third point of support. The leading foot probes for solid placement on the shifting bottom, the following foot advances, and the axe or pole is thrust into a new position.

Two travelers can cross together, taking turns securing the other as that person moves to a solid new stance. Team-crossing with a pole is another method. Team members enter the water, each grasping the pole, which is held parallel to the flow of the stream. The upstream member breaks the force of the current. Anyone who slips hangs on to the pole while the others keep the pole steady.

Using ropes for stream crossings is hazardous and not generally recommended. A taut handline can be helpful, but belaying someone across a river holds the danger that the person could be held by the belay and trapped under water.

THE ICE AXE

The tool is called an ice axe, but it's really an invaluable all-purpose item that often goes to work long before snow or ice is reached.

The axe has a lot of unsuspected uses. It pro-

vides a "third leg" during stream fording. It gives a brief touch-and-go balance point while you hop across talus. It also helps with balance on steep trails, serving as a heavy-duty cane going uphill and a brake going down. The axe held diagonally across the body, spike touching the slope, will help you hold a stable, vertical stance on steep hillsides. The ice-axe self-arrest is taught as a technique for snow, but many climbers have been happy to use their "dirt axe" to stop themselves in steep meadows, forest, and heather.

On open trails many climbers strap the axe on the pack. It comes off the pack and into the hands as the route gets rougher (and as the axe on the pack begins snagging on brush and tree limbs). The ice axe is truly the mountaineer's friend, but it's also probably the most dangerous implement of mountaineering. Its pick (the pointed end of the head), adze (broad end of the head), and spike are always ready to poke, gouge, and impale a climber or nearby companions. Leather or rubber guards are available to cover sharp points and edges when the axe is not needed. Be aware that these guards often get knocked off by brush. Remove the guards when on steep, slippery terrain, whether it's mud, needles, grass, or snow.

Carrying an axe without the skill to use it provides a false sense of security. All too often, climbers slip on hard snow and discover they don't know enough about self-arrest to stop their fall. This indispensable skill comes from practicing on slopes with safe run-outs. (See Chapter 12 for details on this technique and much more information on ice axes.)

The safe way to carry an axe while walking

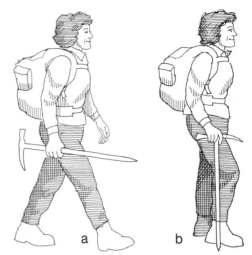

Fig. 5–2. Carrying an ice axe: a, in your hand on easy terrain; b, as a cane.

along a trail (fig. 5-2a) is to grasp the shaft at the balance point (shaft parallel to the ground), with the spike forward, and the head to the rear with the pick down. This way, the hiker behind is safeguarded against running into the spike and the pick is less likely to jab you in case you stumble. To use the axe as a cane while hiking (fig. 5-2b), grasp the head, with the spike toward the ground. It's usually easiest to have the pick pointing forward, permitting the palm of your hand to rest comfortably on top of the adze.

READY FOR THE WILDERNESS

Wilderness travel can be a complicated business because of all the variables of terrain, weather, snow, water, and vegetation. By putting the information in this chapter into practice, you can learn to travel safely and efficiently through some of the most awe-inspiring landscapes on earth. Combine this information with the advice in earlier chapters on navigation, camping, food, clothing, and equipment, and you should be ready for the wilderness.

PART TWO

CLIMBING
FUNDAMENTALS

Climbing at dawn on the Park Glacier, Mount Baker, Washington. Photo by Alan Kearney

• 6 •

ROPES, KNOTS, AND CARABINERS

The rope, more than any other piece of equipment, symbolizes climbing and the climber's dependence on another person. Most climbers remember that very first tie-in—and their sudden dependence on the rope and on their partner or partners who joined them on that length of lifesaving line.

The rope is a "safety net" to catch you when the difficulty of a pitch exceeds your abilities or when the unexpected happens—a foothold crumbles, a snow bridge collapses, or a falling rock knocks you off an exposed stance. It is also fundamental to climbing because, when anchored, it can be climbed or descended.

The rope does not work alone in protecting you, but is one link in your chain of safety. Other links in that chain include the knots that allow you to use the rope for specialized tasks, the seat harness the rope is tied to, the loops of webbing known as runners that help connect the rope to rock or snow, and the carabiners that join parts of the climbing system. These links are the topics of this chapter.

ROPES

During climbing's infancy, ropes made of natural fibers (manila and sisal) were used to protect climbers, but these ropes were not reliable for holding severe falls. The development of nylon ropes during World War II forever changed the sport. Suddenly, climbers were offered lightweight lines capable of bearing more than 2 tons. The nylon ropes also had the remarkable quality of elasticity. Rather than bringing a falling climber to an abrupt, jolting stop, the nylon ropes stretched to dissipate much of the force of a fall.

The first nylon ropes were of "laid" or "twisted" construction. Like braided hair, these ropes were composed of many thin nylon filaments bunched into three or four major strands which were then woven together to form the rope.

The early nylon ropes were light-years ahead of natural fiber ropes, but they were stiff to handle and created substantial friction when run through the points of protection used by climbers. Also, they were so elastic that direct-aid climbing with them was inconvenient; they stretched too much when climbers ascended the rope.

Gradually, twisted nylon ropes were replaced by kernmantle ropes, synthetic ropes designed specifically for climbing. Today's kernmantle ropes (fig. 6-1) are composed of a core of braided or parallel nylon filaments encased in a smooth, woven sheath of nylon. Kernmantle rope maintains the advantages of nylon but improves upon the problems associated with twisted ropes—stiffness, friction, and excessive elasticity. Kernmantle

Fig. 6–1. Construction of a kernmantle rope

ropes are now the only climbing ropes approved by the Union Internationale des Associations d'Alpinisme (UIAA), the internationally recognized authority in setting standards for climbing equipment.

PERFORMANCE TESTS

The UIAA tests equipment to determine which gear meets its standards. In a sport where equipment failure can be fatal, it's wise to purchase equipment that has earned UIAA approval.

A principal UIAA test checks the strength of single ropes, the basic ropes used in most climbing. These ropes generally measure between 9.8 and 12 millimeters in diameter. For the test, the UIAA attaches an 80-kilogram (176-pound) weight to one end of a 2.8-meter (9-foot) length of rope. The other end is attached to a fixed point after passing through a carabiner-type ring about 1 foot above the point of attachment. The weight is raised as high as it can go, which puts it 2.5 meters above the ring, and dropped for a free fall of 5 meters (fig. 6-2).

The test mimics a severe real-life climbing fall. To receive UIAA approval, a rope must survive at least five of these falls. The test also measures the impact force of the rope, which determines the stress of the fall on the climber's body and on the pieces of protection. UIAA standards require that the impact force not exceed 1,200 kilograms (about 2,700 pounds) on the first fall.

The UIAA also tests double ropes, those used in climbing techniques that utilize two ropes at a time. (Double-rope technique and twin-rope technique are explained in Chapter 10.) These ropes generally measure between 8 and 9 millimeters in

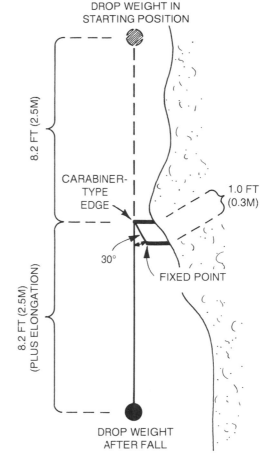

Fig. 6–2. UIAA drop test

diameter. The test for any individual rope used with two-rope technique is identical to the test for single ropes, except that a weight of only 55 kilograms (121 pounds) is used. Each rope must survive at least five falls, and the maximum permitted impact force on the first fall is 800 kilograms (about 1,800 pounds).

The UIAA also applies static tension tests to the ropes it approves, to keep rope stretch below a certain maximum. A load of 80 kilograms is applied to a 1-meter section of rope. A larger rope (between 9.8 and 12 millimeters in diameter) cannot elongate by more than 8 percent. A lighter rope used in two-rope climbing cannot elongate by more than 10 percent.

WATER-REPELLENT ROPES

Wet ropes are more than unpleasant to handle and heavy to carry. They can freeze and become difficult to manage. Equally important, studies show that ropes hold fewer falls and have about 30 percent less strength when they are wet.

Rope manufacturers treat some of their ropes to make them more water repellent and therefore stronger in wet conditions. The sheaths and cores of these ''dry'' ropes are treated with either a silicone-based or Teflon-based coating. The treatment improves the abrasion resistance of some ropes and also reduces friction of the rope as it runs through carabiners. The dry ropes cost about 15 percent more than untreated ropes.

ROPE CARE

When you consider what a climbing rope protects—your life—it's easy to understand why it deserves pampering. A new rope is extremely strong, but abusive treatment can soon destroy it.

Stepping on a rope is a common form of abuse that grinds sharp particles into and through the sheath. Over time, the particles act like tiny knives that slice the rope's nylon filaments. Stepping on the rope creates even more damage if it happens to be trapped between a sharp edge and your boot. Be doubly careful about keeping off the rope when you're wearing crampons. The havoc these metallic points can wreak is obvious, though not always visible. Crampons can damage the core of a rope without leaving any visible gash on the sheath.

Nonetheless, the sheath gives the best picture of the rope's overall condition. If a crampon wound, excessive abrasion, rockfall, or a sharp edge leaves the sheath looking tattered, the rope's integrity should be seriously questioned. Often the damaged portion of the sheath is near an end and cutting off a small segment of the rope solves the problem. But if the damaged section is closer to the center, retire the rope.

If no obvious blemishes scar the sheath, it's harder to decide when to retire the rope. Its actual condition depends on many factors including frequency of use, the care it has received, the number of falls it has endured, and how old it is. Following are some general guidelines to help you decide when to retire your rope:

- A rope used daily should be retired within a year.
- A rope used during most weekends should give about two years of service.
- An occasionally used rope should be retired after four years (nylon deteriorates over time).
- After one very severe fall, it may be wise to replace your rope. A *new* rope may be certified to take five falls, but if your rope is not new, consider all the other factors affecting its condition.

These guidelines assume proper cleaning and storage. A rope should be washed frequently with tepid water and a gentle detergent. Wash it by hand or in a side-loading machine (ropes can get caught under the agitator in top-loading machines). Rinse the rope several times in fresh water, and then hang it to dry in a shady area.

Before storing any rope, be sure it is completely dry. Remove all knots, coil the rope loosely, and store it in a cool, dry area away from sunlight, battery acid, and other strong chemicals.

Get in the habit of inspecting your rope frequently. Is the sheath clean? If not, wash the rope. Are the ends of the rope fraying or unraveling? If so, fuse them with a small flame. Are the ends and middle of the rope well-marked for easy detection? If not, mark them according to the manufacturer's guidelines.

COILING THE ROPE

For carrying or storing, the rope is normally coiled, most commonly in the mountaineeer's coil (fig. 6-3) or the butterfly coil (fig. 6-4). Most climbers prefer one or the other, but knowing both is useful. The mountaineer's coil is advantageous when the rope is carried over a pack. But the butterfly coil is faster, doesn't kink the rope, and ties snugly to your body if you are not wearing a pack.

Whatever your method, uncoil the rope carefully before use. Untie the cinch knot and then uncoil the rope, one loop at a time, into a pile. If you just drop the coils and start pulling on one end,

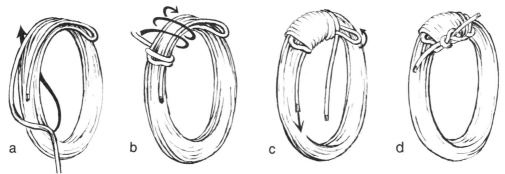

Fig. 6–3. Mountaineer's coil

you'll probably create a tangled mess.

Rope throw bags offer an alternative to coiling. These bags protect the rope, keep it cleaner and drier, and reduce chances of tangling. Throw bags have a loop of webbing sewn into the bottom of the inside. One end of the rope is tied into the loop before the rest of the rope is threaded and stuffed into the bag uncoiled. Do not connect the rope with a carabiner, because the carabiner could be damaged if the bag is thrown. Before tossing the bag—in preparation for a rappel, for example—don't forget to anchor the free end of the rope.

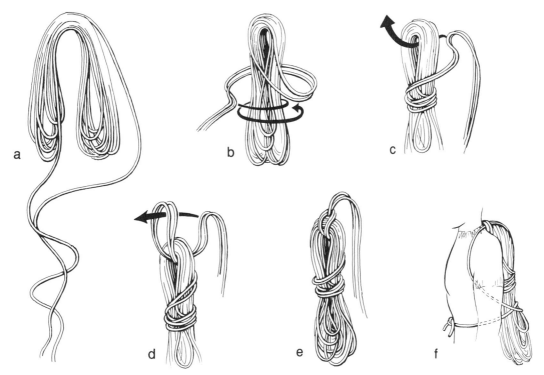

Fig. 6–4. Butterfly coil

KNOTS

Knots allow you to use the rope for many special purposes. They let you tie into the rope, anchor yourself to the mountain, tie two ropes together for long rappels, use slings to climb the rope itself, and much more.

Climbers rely most heavily on a dozen or so different knots (figs. 6-6 through 6-26). Practice these knots until tying them is second nature. If you really want a test, try tying them in a cold, dark shower to give you an idea of the conditions you may someday encounter on a climb.

In some cases, more than one knot can perform a particular task, and the knot chosen is a matter of personal preference. Some knots may be preferred because they have a higher breaking strength (fig. 6-5). Others may be chosen because they are easier to tie or are less likely to come apart in use.

Regardless of the knot, tie it neatly, keeping the separate strands of the knot parallel and free of twists. Cinch every knot tight, and tie off loose ends with the insurance of overhand knots.

	%		%
Without knot	100	Double fisherman's	65-70
Bowline	70-75	Water knot (ring bend)	60-70
Figure 8	75-80	Clove hitch	60-65
Fisherman's	60-65	Overhand	60-65

Fig. 6–5. Relative strengths of knots for single kernmantle rope (courtesy the American Alpine Journal*)*

Overhand knot

The overhand knot (fig. 6-6a) is most often used to secure loose rope ends after another knot has been tied. For instance, it can be used to secure rope ends after tying a square knot (fig. 6-6b) or a rewoven figure-8 (fig. 6-6c).

Overhand loop

The overhand loop (fig. 6-7) is often used for leg loops in prusik slings or to make a loop in a doubled rope or a length of webbing.

Fig. 6–7. Overhand loop

Water knot

The water knot (fig. 6-8), also known as the ring bend or tape knot, is used most often to tie a length of tubular webbing into a runner. This knot can work loose over time, so be sure the knot is

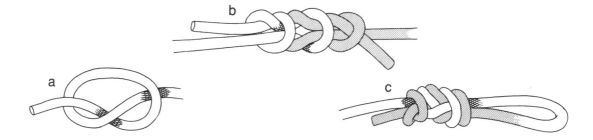

Fig. 6–6. Overhand knot: a and b, tying an overhand knot; c, overhand knot with a rewoven figure-8.

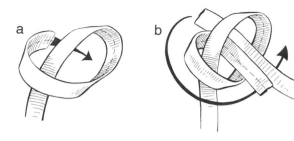

Fig. 6–8. Water knot

cinched very tight, and the tails of the knot are at least 2 inches long. Check the knot often in runners and retie any that have short tails.

Square knot

The general-purpose square knot (fig. 6-9) has many applications around camp. It is often used to finish off a coiled rope.

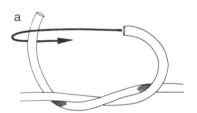

Fig. 6–9. Square knot

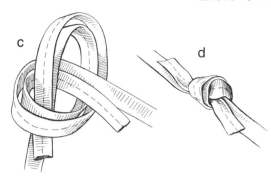

Fig. 6–10. Fisherman's knot

Fisherman's knot

The fisherman's knot (fig. 6-10) can be used to join two ropes together. It has been replaced to a large degree by the double fisherman's knot and is shown here primarily to provide a clearer understanding of the double fisherman's knot.

Fig. 6–11. Double fisherman's knot

Double fisherman's knot

The double fisherman's knot (fig. 6-11), also known as the grapevine knot, is the most secure and preferred knot for tying the ends of two ropes together for a rappel.

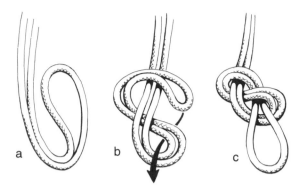

Fig. 6–12. Figure-8 loop

Figure-8 loop

The figure-8 loop (fig. 6-12) is a strong knot that can be readily untied after being under a load.

Rewoven figure-8

The rewoven figure-8 (fig. 6-13) is an excellent knot for tying into a seat harness at the end of the rope. Finish it off by tying one or two overhand knots in the loose end. This knot also can be used to connect a rope to an anchor.

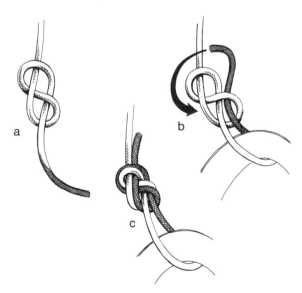

Fig. 6–13. Rewoven figure-8

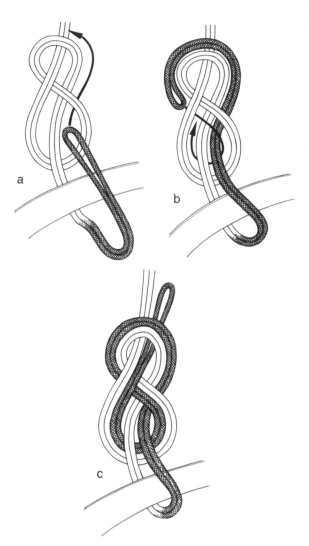

Fig. 6–14. Double rewoven figure-8

Double rewoven figure-8

The double rewoven figure-8 (fig. 6-14) is used by the middle person in a three-person rope team to tie the rope to the seat harness. Secure the resulting end loop with an overhand knot or a carabiner.

Single bowline

The single bowline (fig. 6-15) makes a loop at the end of the climbing rope that will not slip, and

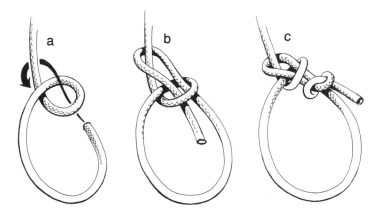

Fig. 6–15. Single bowline

it can secure the rope around a tree or other anchor. Tie off the loose end with an overhand knot. The free end of the rope should come out on the inside of the loop, because the knot is much weaker if this end finishes on the outside.

Rewoven bowline

The rewoven bowline (fig. 6-16) is another excellent knot for tying into a seat harness at the end of the rope. It can be used in place of the rewoven figure-8. If the rewoven portion of the bowline comes untied, you are still tied in with a single bowline.

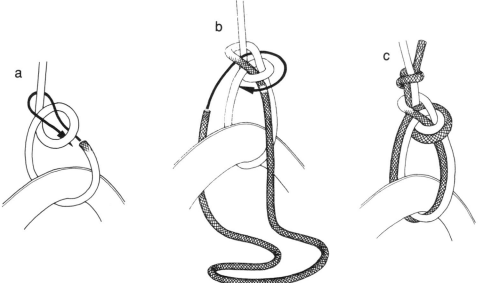

Fig. 6–16. Rewoven bowline

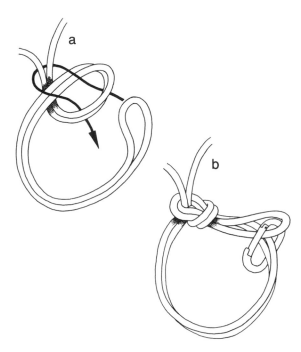

Fig. 6–17. Double bowline

Double bowline

The middle person on a three-person rope can tie the double bowline (fig. 6-17) to a seat harness. The resulting end loop should be secured with an overhand knot or a carabiner.

Fig. 6–18. Clove hitch

Clove hitch

The clove hitch (figs. 6-18 and 6-22) is a quick knot for clipping into a carabiner attached to an anchor. With the clove hitch, it is easy to adjust the length of the rope between the belayer and the anchor without unclipping.

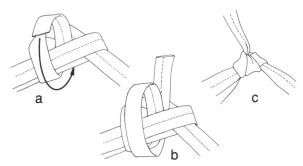

Fig. 6–19. Double sheet bend

Double sheet bend

The double sheet bend (fig. 6-19) is sometimes used instead of a water knot as the tie-off knot on homemade seat harnesses because it is easier to adjust. This knot has a tendency to work loose. Tie off the loose ends with backup overhand knots.

Girth hitch, overhand slip knot, and clove hitch

The girth hitch (fig. 6-20), the overhand slip knot (fig. 6-21), and the clove hitch (fig. 6-22) are simple knots that can be used to tie off partially driven pitons or ice screws.

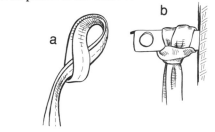

Fig. 6–20. Girth hitch

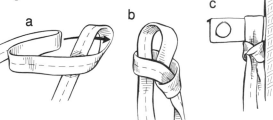

Fig. 6–21. Overhand slip knot

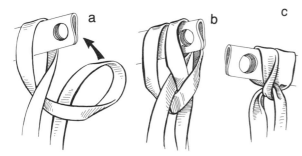

Fig. 6–22. Clove hitch

FRICTION KNOTS

Friction knots provide a quick and simple way to set up a system for ascending or descending a climbing rope. The knots grip the climbing rope when weight is on them, but are free to move when the weight is released. The best known friction knot is the prusik, but others such as the Bachmann and the Klemheist are also useful.

Prusik knot

The prusik (fig. 6-23) requires a few wraps of a light accessory cord around the climbing rope, and it's ready to go to work. The cord is usually a loop (sling) of 5-millimeter to 7-millimeter perlon, wrapped two or three times around the rope. Icy ropes or heavy loads require more wraps than dry ropes or light loads. The accessory cord must be smaller in diameter than the climbing rope, and the greater the difference in diameter, the better it grips. Webbing isn't used for prusik knots because it may not hold.

By attaching two slings to a climbing rope with prusik knots, you can "walk" up the rope. To do this, stand in one sling and take all your weight off the other; now you can slide that knot 1 foot or so up the rope. Then transfer your weight to the second sling, and slide the first sling another foot up the rope. Keep repeating the process and you'll slowly but steadily ascend the rope. (Chapter 13

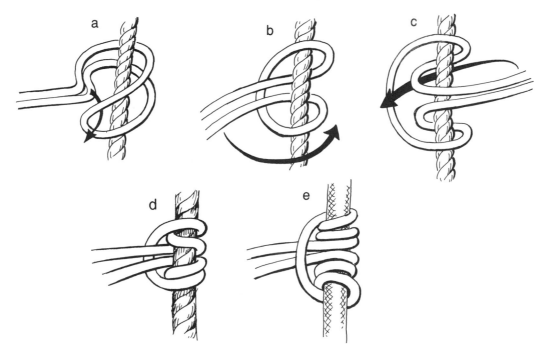

Fig. 6–23. Prusik knot: a–c, tying sequence for the prusik knot; d, a two-wrap prusik knot; e, a three-wrap prusik knot.

describes this process in detail as it is used in getting out of a crevasse.) The knot is also used to help in raising and lowering people and equipment during rescues.

Bachmann knot

The Bachmann knot is used for the same purposes as a prusik knot. The Bachmann (fig. 6-24) is tied around a carabiner, making it much easier to loosen and slide than a prusik. It has the virtue of sometimes being ''self-tending'' when it's being used to help hoist an injured climber.

Klemheist knot

The Klemheist (fig. 6-25) is another alternative to the prusik, with the advantage that it allows you to use a sling made from either accessory cord or webbing. This can be a big help to a climber caught with an ample supply of webbing but little cord.

The cord or webbing is wound around the main rope in a spiral and then threaded through the loop of the top wrap. The Klemheist tied off with a sheet bend is an improved version that is less likely to jam and easier to loosen and slide. The knot also can be tied around a carabiner, providing a good handhold.

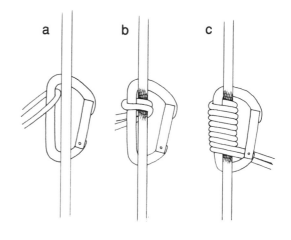

Fig. 6–24. Bachmann knot

The Münter hitch

The Münter is a simple hitch in the rope that is clipped into a carabiner to put friction on the line. It provides an excellent method of belaying a leader or lowering a climber because the hitch is

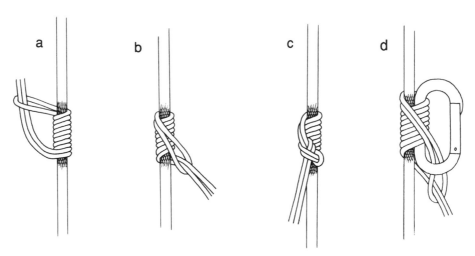

Fig. 6–25. Klemheist knot: a–b, winding and threading Klemheist knot; c, Klemheist tied off with a sheet bend; d, Klemheist tied around a carabiner.

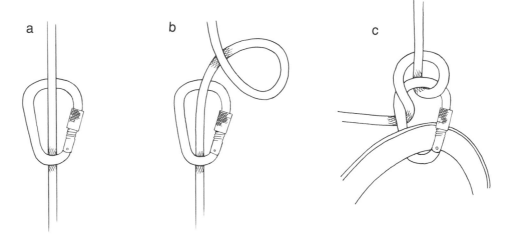

Fig. 6–26. The Münter hitch

reversible (you can feed rope out of the carabiner or pull rope back in) and because the hitch slides (yet is easy to stop if you hold the braking end of the rope). It can also provide the necessary rope friction for rappelling, though it puts more twist in the rope than other rappel methods.

The Münter hitch (fig. 6-26) is very easy to set up and use, and the only equipment needed is a large pear-shaped locking carabiner. Even if you prefer to use a specialized belay device, this hitch is worth knowing as a backup for the time you lose or forget the gear.

HARNESSES

In the old days, climbers looped the climbing rope around the waist several times and tied in with a bowline-on-a-coil (fig. 6-27). That practice is no longer encouraged because long falls onto waist loops can injure your back and ribs. Falls that leave you hanging, such as a fall into a crevasse or over the lip of an overhang, will constrict your diaphragm and suffocate you.

Nowadays, climbers who value their health tie the rope into a harness designed to distribute the force of a fall over a larger percentage of the body. (The bowline-on-a-coil is an option for emergency use if no harness or harness material is available.) The rope is tied into the harness with knots such as the rewoven figure-8 or rewoven bowline (for climbers at the ends of the rope) or with the double rewoven figure-8 or double bowline (for middle climbers).

COMMERCIAL SEAT HARNESSES

With properly fitted leg loops, a seat harness rides comfortably on the hips, yet transfers the force of a fall over the entire pelvis. It also provides a comfortable seat while rappelling.

Several features are particularly desirable in a mountaineering seat harness (fig. 6-28a). Adjustable leg loops allow you to maintain a snug fit no matter how few or how many layers of clothing you wear. The loops also can be unbuckled to permit toilet calls without having to remove the harness, or even untie from the rope. Having the waist buckle located toward one side helps avoid conflict with the locking carabiner clipped to the front of the harness, and lets you move the carabiner left or right of center. Hardware loops are desirable for carrying carabiners and other pieces of climbing

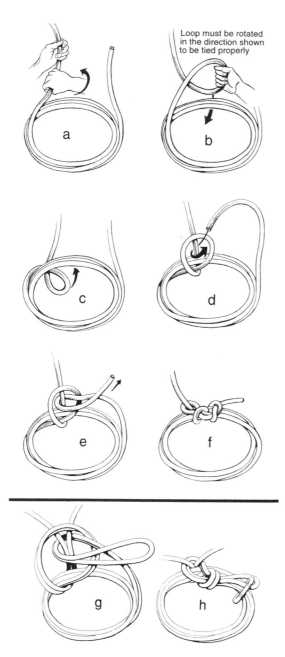

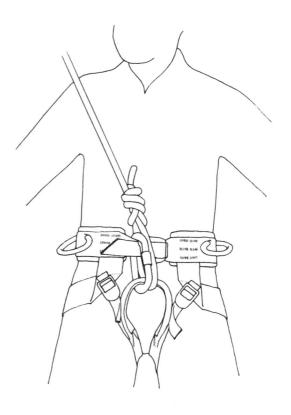

Fig. 6–28. Commercial seat harnesses showing principal features mentioned in text

gear, while padded waist and leg loops give added comfort.

Follow the manufacturer's instructions for buckling into these harnesses. For most harnesses, you will need to pass the waist strap back over and through the main buckle a second time for safety. Be sure that at least 2 inches of the strap extends beyond the buckle after reweaving it.

HOMEMADE SEAT HARNESSES

Homemade seat harnesses are an option for linking yourself to the rope, and you can make a simple one from 22 feet of 1-inch tubular webbing. Starting about 4 1/2 feet from one end of the webbing, tie two leg loops in the webbing using overhand loops. Make the loops just large enough to fit

Fig. 6–27. Bowline-on-a-coil: a–f, for climber at the end of a rope; g–h, for middleman. It is not recommended that this knot be used around the body except in emergencies.

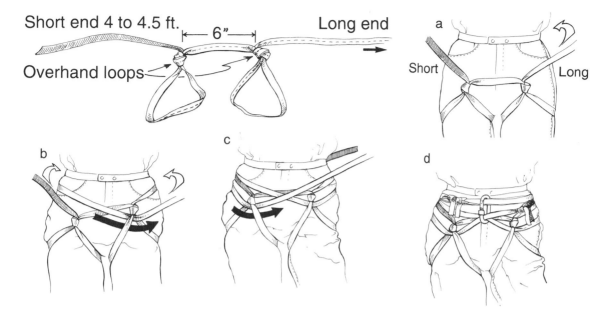

Fig. 6–29. Homemade seat harness

over your clothing, and leave about a 6-inch bridge between the loops. Once tied, leave the loops in place. That completes construction of the harness. To wear it, step into the leg loops and wrap the webbing as shown in the accompanying illustration (fig. 6-29). Use a square knot, water knot, or double sheet bend to tie off the harness, then secure the ends with overhand knots.

SWAMI BELTS

Swami belts (fig. 6-30), another method of tying into the rope, are usually commercially made and are secured to the waist with a buckle or a water knot. The climbing rope is tied through the belt with a rewoven figure-8 or a rewoven bowline.

The belts are wide enough to provide support around the middle of the waist and lower back and to help distribute the force of a fall. Still, if you are left hanging, the belt can creep up and restrict your breathing. Adding leg loops keeps a swami belt from creeping up and distributes the force of a fall to an even larger area, much like a seat harness. In fact, with leg loops attached, the swami belt becomes a seat harness.

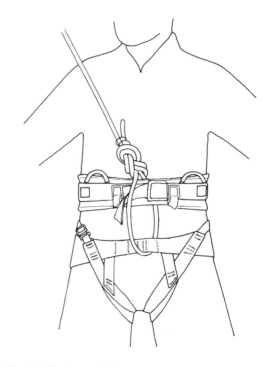

Fig. 6–30. Swami belt

BODY HARNESSES

The only commercial harnesses approved by the UIAA are full body harnesses (fig. 6-31). Body harnesses, which incorporate both a chest and a seat harness, have a higher tie-in point. This greatly reduces the chance of flipping over backward during a fall, especially if a pack makes you top heavy. Because a body harness distributes the force of a fall throughout the trunk of your body, there is less danger of lower-back injury.

Although they are unquestionably safer, body harnesses are resisted by many climbers. They are more expensive and restrictive, and make it hard to add or remove clothing. Instead, many climbers prefer a seat harness for most climbs, and improvise a chest harness when one is warranted, such as when climbing with a heavy pack, crossing glaciers, or aid-climbing under large overhangs.

CHEST HARNESSES

A chest harness can be readily improvised with a long loop of webbing (a long runner). One popular design depends on a carabiner to bring the ends of the harness together at your chest. Another uses a knot instead to attach the ends.

The carabiner chest harness: Start with a double-length runner. Give the runner a half twist to create two temporary loops, and push one arm all the way through each loop. Lift the runner over your head and let it drop against your back, then pull the two sides together and clip with a carabiner at your chest. Connect the chest and seat harnesses with a short piece of webbing or cord to keep the chest harness from riding up around your neck in a fall (fig. 6-32).

The final step is to link the chest harness to the climbing rope to prevent you from being flipped upside down during a fall. There are two ways to do this. You can simply run the climbing rope from your seat harness up through the chest carabiner. Or, you can tie a short prusik sling onto the rope in front of you and clip this into the chest harness. If you use the prusik, be sure it is carefully adjusted to help keep you upright, but still permit your weight to be borne by the seat harness (not by the prusik).

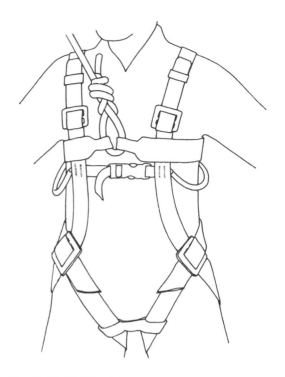

Fig. 6–31. Full body harness

The baudrier chest harness: The harness known as the baudrier also is made from a runner, though it will take a somewhat longer runner than the carabiner harness. Put your arm through the runner and hang it over one shoulder. Pull the other end around your back, under the opposite arm, and across your torso. Wind it around a short loop from the other side of the runner, push it through the loop, and cinch the knot tight. Clip the tail of this chest harness directly into the locking carabiner on your seat harness (fig. 6-33).

This harness is linked to the climbing rope in the same way as the carabiner chest harness: either by running the climbing rope up through a carabiner clipped to the chest harness or by attaching a short prusik sling from the rope to the chest harness.

Regardless of the system used, remember that harnesses also deteriorate with use, abuse, and disuse. Replace them about as often as your climbing rope.

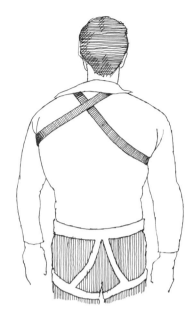

Fig. 6–32. The carabiner chest harness

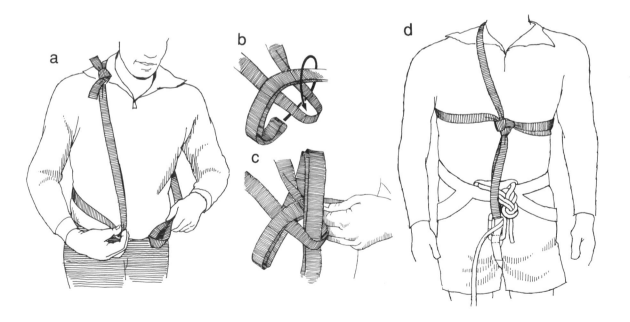

Fig. 6–33. The baudrier chest harness

RUNNERS

Loops of tubular webbing or cord, called runners, are among the simplest pieces of climbing equipment and among the most useful. You'll use them in endless ways as a critical link in climbing systems that involve you, your rope, safety anchors and carabiners.

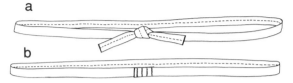

Fig. 6–34. Runners made of webbing: a, tied runner; b, sewn runner.

Runners are most commonly made by tying a loop with $9/16$-inch to 1-inch webbing or with 8-millimeter to 9-millimeter perlon accessory cord. With webbing, a water knot is typically used to make the loop; with cord, a double fisherman's knot does the job. Melt the ends of your runners with a match or candle to keep the nylon from unraveling.

Most standard runners are made from about $5^1/2$ feet of webbing. You will also need several double-length runners, which take $9^1/2$ feet of material. To help you quickly identify the different lengths, make standard runners from one color of webbing and double-length runners from another color. You should also write your initials and the "manufacturing" date on the tails of all your runners so that you know which are yours and when to retire them.

Tied runners (fig. 6-34a) have several advantages over commercially made sewn runners. They are inexpensive to make, can be untied and threaded around trees and natural chockstones, or can be untied and tied to another length of webbing to create extra-long runners. However, sewn runners (fig. 6-34b) also have some advantages. Sewn runners, always made of webbing, are stronger, lighter, and less bulky than knotted runners. They also eliminate the possibility of the knot untying, a continual concern with homemade runners.

Sewn runners come in four normal lengths: 2-inch and 4-inch "quick draws," 12-inch "half-lengths," and 24-inch "full-lengths." They also come in a variety of widths, with $9/16$-inch, $11/16$-inch, and 1-inch being most common. Runners made from Spectra—a high-performance fiber that is stronger, more durable, and less susceptible to ultraviolet deterioration—are usually made from $9/16$-inch webbing.

CARABINERS

Carabiners are another versatile and indispensable tool of climbing. These ingenious metal snap-links are used for belaying, rappelling, prusiking, clipping into safety anchors, securing the rope to points of protection, and a hundred and one other jobs.

Carabiners for climbing are made of aluminum alloy and require a UIAA minimum breaking strength of 2,000 kilograms (about 4,400 pounds) along the long axis and 400 kilograms (about 900 pounds) along the minor axis. The UIAA minimum breaking strength with the gate open is 600 kilograms (about 1,300 pounds) along the long axis.

Carabiners come in many sizes and shapes (fig. 6-35). Ovals (fig. 6-35a) are very popular because their symmetry makes them a good all-purpose shape. "D" carabiners (fig. 6-35b) also offer a good general-purpose shape and are stronger than ovals because more of the load is transferred to the long axis and away from the gate, the typical point of failure. Offset Ds (fig. 6-35c) have the strength advantage of standard Ds, but the gate on an offset D opens wider, making them easier to clip in awkward situations. Bent-gate carabiners (fig. 6-35d) are a specialty design most commonly used

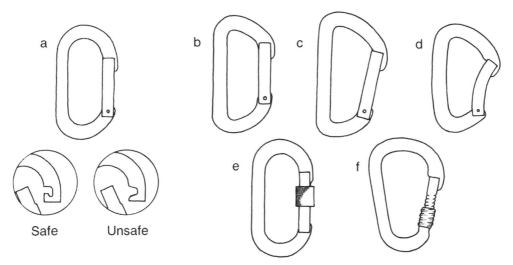

Fig. 6–35. Carabiners: a, oval carabiner, with inset showing safe (notched) and unsafe (unnotched) carabiner gates; b, standard D carabiner; c, offset D carabiner; d, bent-gate carabiner; e, standard locking carabiner; f, locking pear-shaped carabiner.

on difficult routes where it's important to quickly clip and unclip the carabiners from the feel of the gates alone. These carabiners should always be used with a runner so that they are free to rotate.

Locking carabiners (fig. 6-35e), with a sleeve that screws over one end of the gate to prevent accidental opening, give a wider margin of safety for rappelling, belaying, or clipping into anchors. Some locking carabiners even have a spring that automatically positions the sleeve whenever the gate is closed. You can't forget to lock these carabiners, but you must always unlock them as well, which can be a nuisance. Pear-shaped locking carabiners (fig. 6-35f) are much larger at the gate-opening end than at the hinge end and are ideal for belaying with the Münter hitch.

A few basics apply to the use and care of all carabiners. First, always make sure the force on a carabiner falls on the long axis, and be especially careful that the gate does not receive the load. Check the carabiner gates occasionally. A gate should open easily, even when the carabiner is loaded, and the gate should have good side-to-side rigidity when open. A dirty gate can be cleaned by applying a solvent or lubricant to the hinge (oil, kerosene, white gas), working the hinge until it operates smoothly again, and then dipping the carabiner in boiling water for about 20 seconds to remove the cleaning agent. Finally, remember that a carabiner that has fallen off a cliff onto a hard surface has probably suffered hairline fractures and should be retired. Resist using such a ''treasure'' found at the base of a cliff.

In fact, you should resist using any equipment discussed in this chapter if you don't know its history. Ropes, harnesses, runners, and carabiners are all vital links in your chain of protection. Second-hand equipment, whether found or passed along without an account of its use, increases the possibility of a weak link in the chain you depend upon for safe climbing.

· 7 ·

BELAYING

Belaying is a bedrock technique of climbing safety, a system of setting up the rope to hold a climber in the event of a fall. Belaying works like magic, but like any good magic trick, it takes a lot of practice to do well and requires a basic understanding of underlying principles.

In its simplest form, a belay consists of nothing more than a rope that runs from a climber to another person, the belayer, who is ready to put immediate friction on the rope to stop a fall. Three things make the magic work: a skilled belayer to apply friction to the rope, a stance or anchor to take the forward pull of the fall, and a method of amplifying the friction of the belayer's hand. There are many ways to amplify this friction, a variety of stances, and any number of methods for tying into the anchor. This chapter introduces the principal techniques and major options of belaying, so you can choose the methods that work best in your own climbing. The last section introduces the physics of belaying; you can skip this until you are thoroughly familiar with the procedures.

HOW BELAYS ARE USED IN CLIMBING

Before we move into the details of belay setups and procedures, it might be helpful to get a general feel of how belays are used on a climb (fig. 7-1). For the moment, picture just the essentials of a belay. There are two climbers, each tied into an end of a 150-foot rope. As one climbs, the other belays. The belay is connected to an anchor, a point of secure attachment to the rock or snow. The belayer pays out or takes in rope as the climber ascends, ready to use one of the methods of applying friction in case the climber falls.

Belay setups are usually established on the ground or on a ledge that is reasonably comfortable. One climber takes the lead, belayed from below, and moves up the route to the next desirable spot and sets up a new belay. The climber at the bottom then takes apart the belay and climbs up, belayed from above. The distance between belays is known as a pitch, or a lead. The climbers typically leapfrog their way up so that the one who goes first leads all of the odd-numbered pitches, and follows second on all of the even-numbered pitches. Each climber belays at the top of every pitch he leads, which allows a rest before following the next pitch.

The climber belayed from above—known as the follower, or the second—can climb aggressively, confident that any fall will be held easily by the belayer and will be very short, typically involving only a slight stretching of the rope.

It's a different matter for the leader of a pitch, who is belayed from below and will drop some distance before the rope begins to stop the fall. To reduce the distance of a potential fall, the leader attaches pieces of climbers' hardware—called protection—to the rock on the way up. The leader

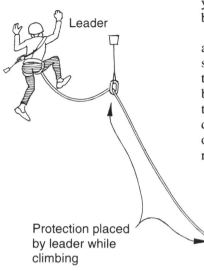

Leader

Protection placed
by leader while
climbing

Fig. 7–1. The belay system for two pitches of a climb

tage to pushing the first lead as far as possible, and you can just pick the most convenient intermediate belay spot.

The minimum belay location should have two attributes: good placement for anchors and reasonable comfort. Belayers also try to find a position where they can see the partner they are belaying. And they keep an eye out for rockfall if the climber is above. If there is significant rockfall danger, you might belay from the shelter of an overhang or bulge, or perhaps have your pack ready to hold above you, and wear a hard hat.

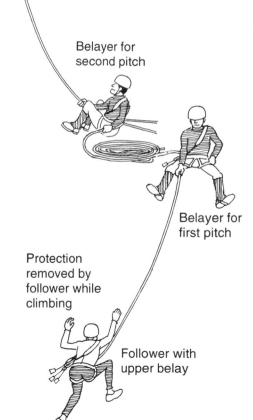

Belayer for
second pitch

Belayer for
first pitch

Protection
removed by
follower while
climbing

Follower with
upper belay

attaches a carabiner to each piece of protection and clips the rope inside the carabiner so the rope is free to be pulled through as the ascent continues. Now, a fall can be no more than double whatever the distance the leader is above the highest piece of protection (plus some rope stretch and sometimes belayer movement or a bit of rope slippage at the belay).

The length of each pitch is usually determined by the location of a comfortable, convenient spot to establish the next belay. Being the belayer can be tough work—long, awkward and boring, but requiring nearly constant vigilance—making it essential to find a secure belay spot that is as comfortable as possible. Longer leads are more efficient, so if there are several nice belay ledges within reach of the rope, go for the highest one. The conditions of the moment can change this general rule. You may decide to set up the next belay somewhat early because the drag of the rope through pieces of protection and over rock is becoming too annoying. Or if a huge, enticing ledge is only $1\frac{1}{2}$ rope lengths away, there is no advan-

BASIC TECHNIQUES

A climber who is just learning to belay should select and stick to one method, perfecting it to the point that setup is largely automatic. At that stage, some climbers become very opinionated about the choice they've made. But the most experienced climbers often learn other methods and use them whenever they offer an advantage.

As you learn belaying, you will discover your own favorite tools and techniques. However you belay, the methods all boil down to a means of stopping a fall by applying friction to the rope and by resisting the forward pull of the fall.

PREPARING FOR THE PULL OF A FALL

There are two general approaches to belaying, depending upon whether the forward pull of the fall goes first to your body, or directly to the anchor.

Belaying from the anchor: Belaying directly from the anchor (fig. 7-2a) requires, at a minimum, complete confidence that the anchor is bombproof; in short, it will not fail under any conceivable force. If you are using one of the many available belay devices for applying friction to the rope, you must be able to assume a specific brak-

Fig. 7–2. Belaying: a, directly from an anchor; b, from the harness, with support from the anchor.

ing position for a fall. You need to be near the anchor, and of course you should be comfortable for the entire time or your attention will be divided and a poor belay will result. (In belaying from the anchor, there are unique advantages to the Münter hitch as a way to apply friction. The Münter hitch will be covered later in this chapter.)

Belaying from your body: In the other approach, the pull of the fall goes directly to your body (fig. 7-2b). You assume a belay stance by bracing against solid features of the mountain, and back this up with a snug attachment from you to the anchor. Friction on the rope comes from a belay device or Münter hitch attached to the front of the seat harness, or from a wrap of the rope around your hips. Your body, supported by the stance, takes the initial pull of the fall and keeps the anchor—the ultimate line of defense—from being fully tested. The inevitable movement of the belayer a few inches under the force of the fall also helps reduce the forces. If the consequences of a fall have been correctly visualized ahead of time, the impact on the belayer is small. You may be surprised to discover how readily a small belayer can catch a big climber. Belaying from a stance, with the climbing rope running directly to your body, helps prevent "sleeping at the wheel" during the sometimes dreary duty of belaying.

Which method is most popular depends in part on both local tradition and geology. In some mountain ranges or on certain routes, you will find belay spots where every available anchor is suspect; here a stance is essential. In other situations there will be a bombproof anchor but poor stances. The belayer may still set up a stance to simplify rope handling, knowing full well that the pull of the fall goes directly to the anchor. The stance can be used almost anytime, even when the stance itself plays a minor role in controlling forces. Belaying directly from the anchor, however, is done *only* when the anchor is believed to be bombproof.

Parts of the setup, and the constant task of rope handling, are the same for every belay, whether it's from your body in a stance or directly from an anchor. All belays depend on applying friction to the rope, and all belays (with occasional exceptions) require an anchor, either to take the pull directly or as backup for a stance.

The belay anchor

As the ultimate security for any belay, the anchor should be able to hold the longest possible fall and the full weight of both climbers. Anchors are essential on rock, snow, and ice for belaying and rappelling. You'll get a few tips here on selecting good anchors for belays, but for full details on finding and using natural features, and on using artificial protection on rock, snow, and ice, study Chapters 10, 12, and 14. This chapter will concentrate on ways to tie in to one or more anchors for belaying.

A large natural feature, such as a tree or pillar of sound rock, is an ideal anchor. However, it's easy to overestimate the stability of large boulders, which may be more lethal than stable. More important than size is the shape of the boulder's bottom, the shape of the socket it is sitting in or the angle of the slope it is on, and the ratio of height to width. Imagine the hidden undersurface and the block's center of gravity: will it pull over under a big load? Test it, but don't send it over the edge.

The beginner should not necessarily accept the first anchors that look good enough, but search widely for simple and obviously solid placements. When placing hardware, bend down, feel deep in cracks, and include everything within arm's length above or to the sides of your ledge. To save time, don't immediately pull out earlier hardware placements that seem less than optimal, as you may find nothing better. If a single bombproof anchor can't be set up, try to establish two or three that in combination will be capable of holding a pull. If you find an old bolt or piton already in place at the belay site, back it up with a second anchor because of the danger that the old placement is weak.

When the belay depends upon a single carabiner, use one locking carabiner or two regular carabiners with the two gates forming an X when held open and the carabiners are aligned (fig. 7-3). In free climbing, avoid chaining carabiners in suc-

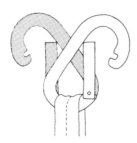

Fig. 7–3. How to use two ordinary carabiners instead of a locking carabiner

cession, as a twisting motion relative to each other weakens them and can open a gate.

Tying into the anchor

The belayer ties in to the anchor with the climbing rope itself, using the first few feet of rope as it comes from its tie-in at the belayer's harness. The rest of the rope is available for use by the climber. The belayer faces quite an array of choices when it comes to knots and methods for tying in to the anchor. Let's take a look at them to identify some of the more useful.

One method of dealing with a large natural anchor is the simple technique of looping rope around it and clipping the loop back on itself with a carabiner (in a quasi–girth hitch). Tie an overhand knot in the end of the loop and clip the carabiner through that (fig. 7-4).

When a knot is needed to tie to an anchor carabiner, the figure-8 knot or the clove hitch is usually preferred. The figure-8 is strong, stable, and easy to untie. The clove hitch has the advantage of being adjustable after it is tied, and is the easiest way to back up a stance with a taut line from you to the anchor.

An anchor is often backed up with one or two other anchors. Because of its adjustability, a clove hitch on the carabiner at each anchor is the most convenient way to minimize slack between the anchors (fig. 7-5a). (Make sure the clove hitch is tight, or normal rope play will make it expand and possibly open the carabiner's gate. Beware of any

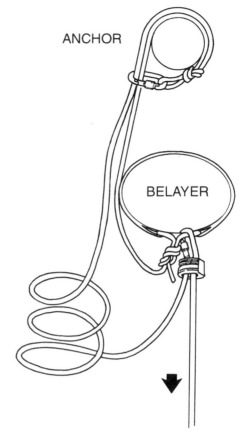

Fig. 7–4. Anchoring to a large object with a quasi–girth hitch

pull on a clove hitch that makes it slide away from the end of the carabiner, which could also make it expand and open the gate.)

There is quite a disadvantage, however, in tying separate knots in a series of anchor carabiners, as in the series of clove hitches. If the anchor takes the force of a fall, all the impact first goes to a single anchor. The other anchors come into play only if the first one fails.

There are a couple of ways to overcome this disadvantage and spread the load so that more than one anchor takes the initial impact.

One way is to tie a clove hitch to each anchor carabiner, as before—but to run the rope back to a

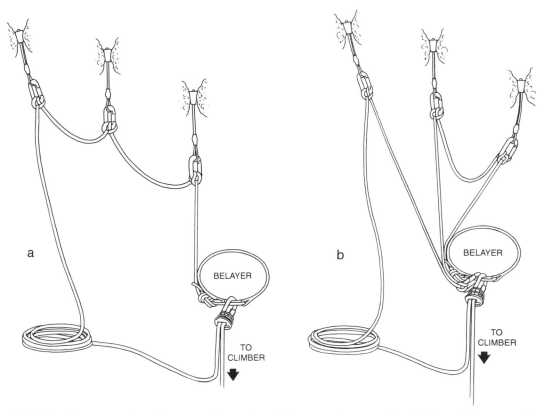

Fig. 7–5. Tying into several anchors: a, with a series of knots—only one anchor holds weight at any given time; b, so that they all hold weight simultaneously.

locking carabiner at the harness and tie in (with a clove hitch) after every other clove hitch at an anchor (fig. 7-5b). This results in a section of rope tied between your seat harness and each anchor carabiner. You can then adjust the clove hitches to snug up the strand to each carabiner. Then if the anchor takes the force of a fall, the impact will be shared by the multiple placements, and if one fails, no drop results before the others come into play.

Another way to spread the load is the technique of self-equalization, which automatically distributes any force among all the anchors.

Two-point equalizing, using two anchors, is the simplest method of self-equalization (fig. 7-6a). Put a half twist in a high-strength runner (such as one made of Spectra), which divides the runner into two parts, and clip each end into an anchor with a carabiner. Then clip a locking carabiner over the X formed in the middle, from one half of the runner to the other, and tie into that carabiner.

Multipoint equalizing, using any number of anchors, is another technique in setting up a secure belay (fig. 7-6b). Take one high-strength runner, and clip it into the carabiners on each of the three anchors. Grasp the runner between each anchor, twist it 180 degrees, and clip each resulting loop into the main carabiner. Such twists guarantee that the main carabiner is clipped into, and not around, the runner, so that it will stay attached to the runner even if two of the three anchors fail. The smaller the runner, the smaller the drop if one anchor fails. Therefore, if the anchors are widely

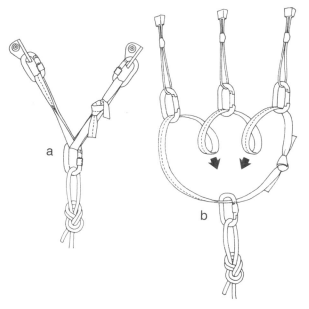

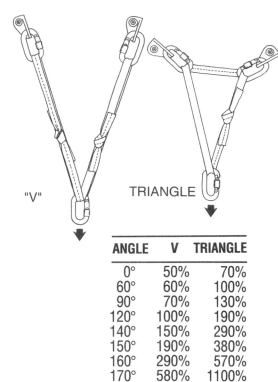

Fig. 7–6. Equalization: a, two-point; b, multi-point.

Fig. 7–7. The force on two anchors depends upon the method of sharing the force and the angle at the bottom of the sling.

ANGLE	V	TRIANGLE
0°	50%	70%
60°	60%	100%
90°	70%	130%
120°	100%	190%
140°	150%	290%
150°	190%	380%
160°	290%	570%
170°	580%	1100%

separated, bring them together with other slings before equalizing.

How well an equalization setup reduces the pull on each individual anchor depends on the angle at the bottom where the parts of the runner come together. The smaller the angle, the less force each anchor will have to absorb. As the angle increases, each anchor is subject to an increasing force. Be sure that the angle is always less than 120 degrees. Above that, each anchor will actually be subject to a greater force than if equalization wasn't even used. This is true whether it's two-point or multi-point equalization.

Climbers also use the "triangle" method, instead of equalization, to spread the weight between two separate anchors. In a triangle, the runner simply goes through each carabiner in turn, without returning to the main carabiner between each anchor. Just as in equalization, the angle at the bottom where the two sides of the runner come together is critical. But with triangles, a significantly greater force hits each anchor for any given angle, compared with equalization (fig. 7-7). With

triangles, the maximum angle can only be 60 degrees; beyond that, each anchor faces a greater force than if the method wasn't used at all. And for any given length of runner, the triangle puts more force on the anchors than equalization.

The triangle performs better when it comes to another aspect of hooking into two anchors. If one of the anchors fails in either the equalization or triangle methods, the belay will drop as far as needed to throw the weight onto the remaining anchor. This drop, though usually quite short, hits the remaining anchor with additional force. The drop will be less in a triangle setup, for any given length of runner used, than with equalization. This difference in the length of the drop increases with the length of the sling and with the distance between the two anchors.

Sometimes the length of the tie-in from you to the anchor is critical to the stability of your stance. Until now we have mainly discussed the situation in which the knots are located at the anchor. But if the anchor is out of reach, you can't adjust the knots while in your stance, so precise adjustment is tedious or impossible. The solution is to tie in with a knot only on your harness. Take the rope—after it has run from the harness and simply been clipped through the anchor carabiner—and tie it again at the seat harness. Make the new tie-in with a clove hitch, so you can easily adjust the tension on the rope between you and the anchor. In this option, the rope runs freely around a natural anchor or through a main anchor carabiner (fig. 7-8).

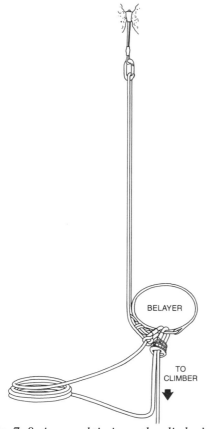

Fig. 7–8. A second tie-in on the climber's harness to allow convenient adjustment of tension on the anchor rope

The belay stance

If you belay from your harness or body rather than directly from the anchor, you usually will brace against the forward pull of a fall with a solid stance. The stance can help keep the anchor from being fully tested. You will usually support the stance with a short, tight rope to a strong anchor to greatly increase your stability. But for the moment we will consider the strength of the stance alone, based in part upon studies by the Sierra Club. Although the club's experiments used the hip wrap, the results apply to stances with modern belay devices (though perhaps a little on the conservative side). They give a good picture of the comparative value of different stances (fig. 7-9).

Located behind a solid object: In unusually fortunate situations, you can assume the strongest stance of all, directly behind an immovable object, such as a rock protrusion. Don't count on this luck often.

Sitting stances: The most common and versatile is the sitting stance, in which your feet and seat make three solid contacts with the mountain. It is most stable if the rope passes between your feet or legs, for it then resembles a tripod. The tripod's apex is the attachment of the belay to the front of your harness; one leg is your pelvic bones and seat, the other two your own legs. In that configuration, the average person can hold 350 pounds of tension on the rope for several seconds, or an impact about twice as great. Knees are strongest when the angle at the joint is nearly straight (180 to 140 degrees). The stance is only about half as strong if the knees are bent at an angle below 100 degrees, or if the rope runs over the foot support (directed slightly outside the tripod). The stance is suitable for rock, snow, or brush.

Standing stances: In the standing position there are only two points of contact with the rock. With one foot well forward, the average belayer can hold 200 pounds from below, but less than half as much with a pull to the side or with the feet together. Belaying a leader from a standing position (''slingshot'' belay) is extremely weak if the pull is forward. It should be done only with a short tight

Behind solid
object: very strong

Standing: weak

"Sling shot:"
very weak

Three-point,
sitting: strong

Three-point,
leaning: strong

Fig. 7–9. The strength of various types of stance, before adding support from the anchor

rope to the anchor, which will take most of the force, or when standing just below the first protection, so that you cannot be pulled over.

Even if your stance fails and you are pulled out of position, you *must* keep control of the rope. If you don't, it means loss of the belay and a disastrous plunge for the climber. Before tying in, visualize the consequences if you are pulled out of what you thought was a solid stance. Ask yourself if you will be able to keep charge of the rope and maintain the belay. The force on you will come from a new direction, pulling you into the straight line between the anchor and where the rope goes over the edge, or between the anchor and the first protection. The momentum of your body will carry you even farther; look to see whether you would strike something.

Imagine the results of being pulled in various directions, sideways or up or down, particularly if you are standing. There is less chance you will be jerked about, and you will be moved less, if you have a short tie-in from you to the anchor. This short tie-in is necessary if the direction of pull will change as the climber ascends. The longer the anchor tie-in, the more powerful and dangerous the pull. You must not be dragged, lifted into the air, or strike anything. It's OK to risk some movement in order to take advantage of a strong rock feature for a stance. But think it through. Visualize the possible consequences if you are pulled from the stance. If a loss of control of the rope is possible, find another solution.

Preparing to belay the follower

Because there are so many things to remember and balance, setting up the belay is one of the slower tasks for beginners. The more aggressively you search for anchors and stances, the more likely you will discover a simple solution. Don't rush the visualization stage. Here are factors to consider as you complete leading a pitch and have just reached a spot to set up a belay for the follower:

Establish an anchor for yourself and clip into it, and then call out "off belay" so the follower can stop belaying and start preparing to climb. Then attend to yourself. Take off your pack and the rack of climbing hardware. Put on extra clothes, if necessary, for the long period of staying stationary while you belay.

Search out available options for belay anchors and for a stance.

Visualize the consequences if your stance collapses.

Consider other factors. Assess the rockfall danger. Make the belay comfortable enough so you can belay without distraction. Try to be in position to watch the climber and route as you belay. An experienced climber can establish a belay that is also useful for belaying the next pitch, when the follower moves past and up into the lead.

Pick the best combination of anchor and stance, after weighing all the choices.

Check to be sure that knots are complete, that coils of rope won't snarl or catch on projections, and that your pack is conveniently nearby. For your very first belay, verify with your partner that you know the correct braking position—and that you are belaying the end of the rope that goes to the climber, not the end to the coils. (Partners should check each other's harness buckle and rope tie-in whenever roping up.)

Prepare to belay the next lead as soon as you have belayed the follower up to your position.

Preparing to belay the leader

Belaying the leader is a big change from belaying the follower because the pull is from a new direction, usually above. A new stance is often necessary.

The anchor for belaying the leader must hold a pull toward the first piece of protection, possibly straight up, so your existing anchor may have to be revised or augmented. Fortunately the follower has brought up all the hardware from the pitch below, so you should have plenty of gear to work with. Before setting up your belay, pull in all the slack rope, and pile it neatly to avoid snarls later.

The difference between a strong and weak stance is the direction of the expected pull in comparison with how your legs are placed. By putting in a piece of protection near you that the climber's rope will travel through, you can aim this pull to provide a stronger stance.

Aiming the pull is particularly useful with standing stances. If you are facing the anchor, a simple method is to add another carabiner to the anchor and clip the climbing rope through that. Later, after the climber has put in other protection higher up, this link becomes unnecessary, and you can remove it to reduce rope friction and increase your "feel" of the climber.

The belayer needs to be extra alert when the climbing is difficult right off a ledge because the leader may not be able to get in enough protection to prevent hitting the ledge in case of a fall. In fact, broken ankles are among the most common rock-climbing injuries. Of course, the climber should land with knees bent. Head injuries can be reduced by the belayer "spotting" the climber, preferably while tied in and otherwise ready to belay. Spotting does not mean cushioning the climber's weight with your body, but simply helping the falling climber land upright or preventing his head from hitting the ground.

The "zipper effect" is a concern for both belayer and climber. Whenever possible, the climber should position the lowest piece of protection to prevent this phenomenon, in which the bottom protection pulls out under the forces of a fall, and succeeding pieces up the route are yanked out one by one like the opening of a zippered jacket. To avoid it, the lowest protection should be multidirectional; that is, able to hold a pull from any direction, including outward or upward. If a zipper starts opening, you can only hope that a multidirectional piece of protection has been placed higher up that can put a stop to it. (Chapter 10 includes an illustration of the zipper effect.)

ROPE HANDLING AND COMMUNICATING

Ideally, when you are belaying the leader, the rope is never taut, which would impede the climber's next move. An alert belayer keeps just a hint of slack and responds immediately to the leader's advance by paying out more rope. When the climbing is easy, more slack is permissible.

As the leader climbs, it is inevitable that some friction will develop along the rope. This rope drag can greatly increase the difficulty of the climb or make the leader stop, creating time-consuming extra belays, often in uncomfortable spots. The problem can be caused by the terrain the climber passed, such as blocks of rock or rope-sized notches, or by poorly placed protection that forces the rope over convexities or into acute angles. Any friction applied by the belayer is multiplied by these, so if the leader tells you that rope drag is a problem, keep a few feet of slack in the rope and do everything possible to eliminate any pull. If the climber falls when there is a lot of friction in the system, the belayer may actually be unsure whether a fall took place. If it is impossible to communicate with the climber, you can find out by letting out a few inches of rope. If the same tension remains, then you are probably holding the climber's weight.

Ideally, when you are belaying a follower, there is no slack in the rope. At the same time, the rope should not be taut, which would hamper the climber's movement and balance.

When belaying a follower up to you, pile the rope where it won't be disturbed later. Don't let loops hang down if there are projections that could snag a loop. If the entire pile must be moved, picking it up is tempting but will produce snarls later. It is best to re-pile the entire rope twice, so the leader's end is on top. If the follower is climbing rapidly, you can take in more rope with each pull by leaning forward or bending over.

Your braking hand must never leave the rope. This is easier when belaying the leader because the leader is pulling up the slack. But when belaying a follower, you pull the slack in against gravity, and when you reset your braking hand, the natural tendency is to lift it off the rope. The correct procedure must be consciously learned (fig. 7-10).

To minimize falling distance, leaders preparing to make difficult moves often place protection well above their harness tie-in and clip in before moving up. This means the direction of rope movement will reverse twice. As you are belaying the leader and letting out rope, you will suddenly find yourself taking in slack as the climber moves up to the

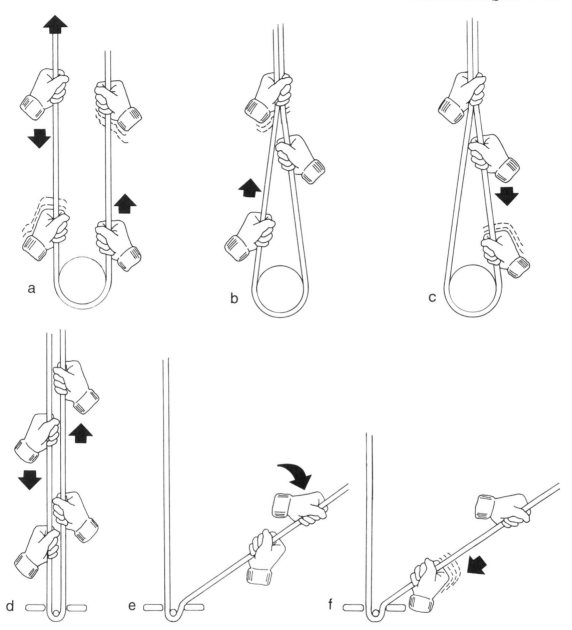

Fig. 7–10. How to take slack in from a follower so the braking hand is always on the rope: a, pull in the rope with both hands; b, extend whichever hand is near your body, and grab both ropes with it, so that; c, the braking hand can slide back toward your body while remaining closed and ready to brake. Although a through c is commonly used with belay devices, another method offers extra security, as when the climber is at a crux. Keep the ropes in steps b and c apart and grab only the braking rope, as shown in the lower row of illustrations (d, e, and f).

protection, then letting it out again as the climber moves past the protection and puts renewed pull on the rope. These switches call for extra attention, especially as this tends to happen at the most difficult spots.

As climber and belayer get farther apart and hearing begins to be difficult, stick exclusively to the set of short commands that have been developed to express essential climbing communications. Prefacing them with explanations or justifications makes them harder to recognize and defeats their purpose. Use the commands alone. They have been chosen so that the sounds and number of syllables produce a distinctive pattern. Toward the end of the rope, shout as loudly as possible and space out each syllable, using very big spaces if there are echoes. In a crowded area, preface commands with your partner's name. Don't expect an audible response; just do your best the first time.

Three problems are common at the end of each pitch, when hearing is most difficult. First, when calling out to your leader the length of rope remaining in the coils, the first syllable is often lost, and if normal word order is used, the leader hears only ''—ty feet.'' Instead, invert the word order and pronounce each digit separately: ''Feet: . . . three . . . zero,'' for 30 feet. The climber will pause upon the first word and have a better chance of understanding the remainder. Second, when the leader completes a pitch and calls ''Off belay,'' do not respond with ''Belay off'' to indicate you heard him, as is the natural reaction of a beginner. ''Belay off'' means you have taken apart your belay and the rope coils are ready to be pulled up, and you won't be ready to shout that command truthfully for a while yet. Third, avoid the impatient question ''On belay?'' unless a truly inordinate amount of time has passed. Usually the leader, at work on setting up anchors, is out of earshot anyway.

Commands are sometimes transmitted by rope pulls, but there is no universal system. Because of rope stretch at the end of long leads, it's necessary to greatly exaggerate the pulls. A simple tug will seldom be felt at the other end. Take in all slack and for each signal, yank 1 foot or more, holding it tight for awhile before releasing the tension. If there is much friction, pulls may not be distinguishable from normal rope movements. The most common commands correspond to the number of syllables in these verbal equivalents: one pull means ''Slack,'' two means ''Up rope,'' and three means ''Belay on.''

In reality the follower often decides when the belay is ready, based upon a partner's known rope-handling habits. Regular partners familiar with each other's habits can dispense with all normal commands, which is more aesthetic.

APPLYING FRICTION TO THE ROPE

In any belay method, the rope from the climber goes to a belay device or Münter hitch or around the belayer's hips, and then to the belayer's braking hand. This braking hand produces the belay, the controllable friction that is multiplied by a factor of as high as fourteen by the belay method and stops a falling climber.

Belay devices

Belay devices amplify the friction of the braking hand by passing the rope through an opening and wrapping it around a post. The opening guarantees a minimum of wrap, or bend, in the rope to produce enough friction on the post. The post is a locking carabiner or part of the device itself. The opening must be large enough to allow the device to touch the carabiner.

To stop a fall, the belayer pulls back on the free end of the rope to create a separation of at least 90 degrees between the rope entering the device and the rope leaving it. Nothing must be in the way of your braking hand or elbow carrying out this critical task, and it must not require an unnatural body twist or motion. The simplest way to learn to do this conveniently in all situations is to clip the device into a locking carabiner on your harness (currently the most popular belay method in the United States) rather than directly to the anchor. In this section on belay devices, we will stick to a description of their use when attached to the climber's harness.

Basic voice commands used by climbers:

Follower:	"That's me"	You have pulled up all the slack in the rope and are now tugging on my body; don't pull any more.
Belayer:	"Belay on"	I am belaying you.
Climber:	"Climbing"	I am, or will resume, moving up.
Belayer:	"Climb"	Response to "Climbing."
Climber:	"Slack"	Give me some slack in the rope and leave it out until I call "Climbing." (If you want to indicate how much slack you need, the command would be "Slack X feet," with X being the amount of slack.)
Climber:	"Up rope"	(Usually to upper belayer.) There is slack in the rope; pull it in.
Climber:	"Tension"	(Usually to upper belayer.) Take up all slack and hold my weight. (Should be used sparingly by beginners, to avoid overdependence on rope. Say "Watch me" instead.)
Climber:	"Falling!"	Assume your braking position and brace for a pull on the rope.
Belayer:	"Halfway"	About half of the rope remains.
Leader:	"How much rope?"	What length of rope remains?
Belayer:	"Feet ... four ... zero"	Forty feet of rope remains; find a belay soon (best used when 50 to 20 feet remain).
Leader:	"Off belay"	I am secure and no longer need your belay. Take it apart and prepare to follow the pitch.
Anyone:	"OK"	I heard you.
Follower:	"Belay off"	(After taking apart the belay.) You may pull in all the slack and remaining coils when you are ready.
Anyone:	"Rock!" "Ice!"	(Very loudly, immediately, and repeatedly until falling object stops; mandatory.) Falling objects. Look up or take cover.
Anyone:	"Rope"	A rappel rope is about to be thrown down by another party. Look up or take cover.

Climbers also use some discretionary voice commands, depending on local custom or prior agreement with a climbing partner. These are examples, and many idiosyncratic variations are also used.

Leader:	"Pro in"	I have just clipped into the first protection. Or I have clipped into protection located above my harness tie-in, so the direction of rope movement will reverse twice as I move up through a difficult spot.
Climber:	"Protection" or "Cleaning"	I am placing or cleaning protection and will not move up for awhile.
Climber:	"Good belay" or "Watch me"	I anticipate a fall or difficult move.
Climber:	"On top"	I have passed the difficulty.

Contrary to a popular misconception, there is no automatic clamping effect with a properly designed belay device. Your hand is the ultimate source of friction, and without your braking hand on the rope, there is no belay. The total friction is determined by the strength of your grip, the total number of degrees in the bends or turns the rope makes, and the rope's internal resistance to bending and deforming against the sides of the device and carabiner.

There are a number of popular belay devices (fig. 7-11). One general type may be referred to as an aperture device: It simply provides an aperture through which a bight (loop) of rope is pushed and then clipped to the locking carabiner on your harness or at the anchor. In one widely used version of this type, the aperture consists of a slot, or slots, in a metal plate. (The original and best known of these is the Sticht plate [fig. 7-11a].) In another version, the aperture is a cone-shaped tube (fig. 7-11b).

The figure-8 device (not to be confused with the figure-8 knot) was originally designed only for rap-pelling, not belaying. Some figure-8s now serve double-duty, for both rappelling and belaying. Figure-8s are seen in three different configurations as belay devices. One is the standard rappel configuration (fig. 7-11f). Another is set up like the Bachli (fig. 7-11e), described below. If the hole in the small end of the figure-8 is the size of a typical aperture device hole, it can also be used similarly to a slot or tube (fig. 7-11c). Make certain that your figure-8 was intended for belaying use by the manufacturer; most are not.

The Bachli device (fig. 7-11d) is, in appearance, a sort of streamlined figure-8. The bight of rope goes up through the large hole and is then clipped into a locking carabiner attached both to your harness and to the small hole in the device.

Your tie-in to the anchor should be on the braking-hand side when using a belay device. This way, your body rotation under the force of a fall will assist, rather than hinder, you in separating the ropes.

In belaying a lead climber, try to prepare for the possibility that before placing the first piece of pro-

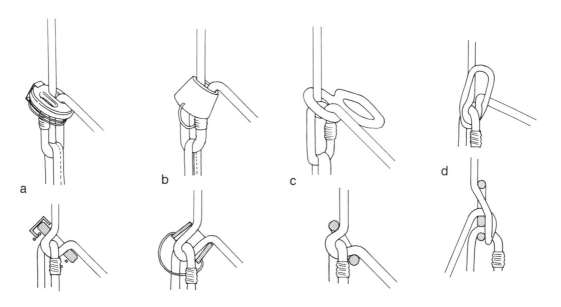

Fig. 7–11. Major categories of belay device: a, slot; b, tube; c, figure-8 in aperture configuration; d, Bachli; e, figure-8 in Bachli configuration; f, figure-8 in rappel configuration.

tection, the leader could fall, plunging below your position. The braking hand should be on the opposite side of this possible fall, or you won't be able to separate the ropes entering and leaving the device.

Belayers rarely wear gloves when using a belay device, in part because the device itself provides a greater proportion of the total friction. However, rope burns are a possibility, although they seem to be rare.

When taking in or letting out slack with an aperture device (slot or tube), keep the ropes strictly parallel. Otherwise, the rope will pull the device up against the carabiner, and braking begins. Eventually the practice becomes automatic.

Among devices, slots and tubes produce the least friction in routine rope handling, which allows you to take in rope faster when the climber is on easy ground, and a slightly improved feel for small movements of the climber and elimination of slack. The Bachli configuration, however, generates less friction than slots and tubes when it holds a fall. This characteristic lends the Bachli to use on

ice and snow, where stances and anchors are usually weaker and would benefit from a lower force, and where the consequences of a longer fall are often less important.

A belayer is called upon not just to stop falls, but to hold the climber stationary under tension, or lower him to a ledge. Devices vary significantly in how easily they perform these tasks. Slot devices require the least force to hold the climber's weight, but are the least smooth in lowering the climber.

Slots and tubes can be attached to a tether to keep them from sliding out of reach. Some of these devices include a hole for attaching the tether. A tether to your harness must be long enough so it doesn't interfere with belaying in any direction.

Like any piece of critical equipment made of metal, a belay device that is dropped a significant distance should be retired because internal stresses could cause it to break when holding a big fall.

Hard-anodized devices tend to glaze the outermost surface of the rope when stopping a fall, but this effect is purely cosmetic and not harmful. (The metallurgic process of hard-anodizing produces a thin layer of aluminum oxide whose surface is hard and microscopically pitted, and appears dull gray, black, or brown.)

Belay devices are also used for rappelling. Slot devices produce a jerky ride that puts unnecessarily high loads on the anchor. However, the slot design that has a spring may be OK, and tube devices may be acceptably smooth. The Bachli device and figure-8s are the smoothest for rappelling. However, figure-8s put one twist in the rope for every 10 feet of descent, producing snarls in the coils later.

The Münter hitch

The Münter hitch is a very effective method of using only the rope and a carabiner to provide the friction necessary to stop a fall. This method requires a large pear-shaped locking carabiner in order to allow the knot to pass through the interior. It amplifies the effect of your braking hand with the friction both of rope on rope and of rope on carabiner. When attached to the front of your harness it works much like a belay device. Although

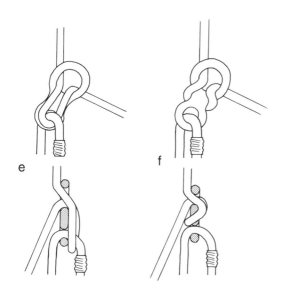

e

f

no belay method is foolproof, the Münter hitch requires the least skill and attention.

The Münter hitch is the only traditional belay method that provides sufficient friction regardless of the angle between the ropes entering and leaving it (fig. 7-12). This offers a number of advantages:

• No special braking position is required. Consider the situation of a belayer who cannot see the climber and is distracted at the moment of a fall. The belayer, caught by surprise, might merely squeeze the rope at the start, rather than immediately yanking it into the angle required by all other methods. This situation is unusual, but could occur at any time. The Münter hitch would hold. The other methods may not.

• If all of the slack rope is hanging down a wall, you may be unable to raise your braking hand high enough, as required by a standard belay device, to arrest a follower fall. The problem is caused by the weight of the rope, the extra force exerted by the falling climber, and the difficult arm position. But with a Münter hitch, it doesn't matter (fig. 7-13).

The friction of the Münter hitch is also unique in being less with the ropes 180 degrees apart than when 0 degrees apart. This usually means its friction is relatively less for leader falls than follower falls. But in absolute terms it often provides more friction than any other belay method, regardless of the angle between the ropes. This high friction means a quicker stop to a fall.

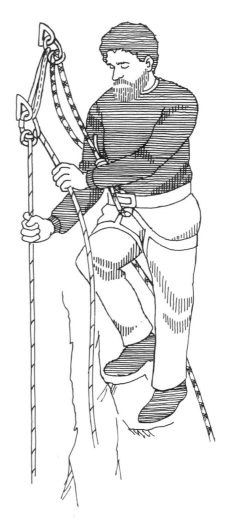

Fig. 7–13. The Münter hitch works when the ropes must be hanging down a wall.

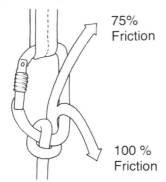

75% Friction

100 % Friction

Fig. 7–12. The friction provided by the Münter hitch does not depend greatly upon the angle between the ropes.

The Münter hitch has some drawbacks. Its friction, often higher than other methods, means more impact on a leader's protection and more danger that poor placements will pull out. It kinks the rope more than any other method, producing snarls in the last few feet of rope after several pitches, especially if the same person always leads. To unsnarl the rope, shake it out while it is hanging free. After a big fall, the outermost layer of the sheath is glazed (which, like the effect of hard-anodized devices, is probably only cosmetic). The Münter hitch isn't good for rappelling because it twists the rope once for every 5 feet of descent, and makes ropes very fuzzy if used regularly.

Every time the direction of pull on the hitch reverses, the entire knot first flip-flops through the carabiner oval. This can get a bit awkward when the leader clips into protection above, moves up toward it, and then passes it, because it requires the belayer to pay out, take in, and pay out rope in rapid succession, reversing the direction of pull on the Münter hitch each time. For a fall of a follower, or of a leader below a piece of protection, the Münter hitch produces an additional drop of 6 inches, as the knot pulls through the carabiner, before braking begins.

You may run across the Münter hitch under a variety of names, such as the friction hitch, Italian hitch, half ring bend, carabiner hitch, running R, half-mast belay, and UIAA method. It was introduced in Europe in 1973 as the *halbmastwurf sicherung* (half clove-hitch belay), now abbreviated as HMS. (Chapter 6 gives details on tying the Münter hitch.)

The hip wrap

The hip wrap (fig. 7-14) amplifies friction by passing the rope around your back—just below the top of your hips—and around your sides. Its main advantage is the speed with which you can belay a follower who is moving rapidly over easy ground. It can be set up quickly and requires no hardware.

The use of the hip wrap in climbing on upper fifth-class rock is rapidly declining. Because your back and sides provide most of the friction on the rope, you must wear a lot of clothes, preferably several thick layers—highly undesirable in hot climates. Even a short leader fall can cut through a polypropylene jacket. Although the belayer will feel the pain from the burn as it is produced, the fall will be completely arrested before he or she has time to react to the pain.

Because your hands provide a greater proportion of friction than in other methods, gloves are essential. Contrary to the usual expectation, burns

are reduced with a tighter grip and less rope slippage (because slower rope velocity and less rope slippage generates less heat), another reason for wearing gloves. However, gloves can make your hands damp and soft, the opposite of what is necessary for difficult rock climbing.

There are additional problems with the hip wrap: if the climbing rope runs over the anchor attachment, it may be burned. In a big fall, the outermost layer of the rope sheath may be glazed and covered with melted fabric from your clothes. Because more time is required to attain the braking position and because it has the least braking friction of any method, the hip wrap more often results in rope slippage, and the climber usually falls

Fig. 7–14. The hip wrap is often used for the impromptu belaying of a fast-moving follower.

farther. If your stance fails, you will probably also lose control of the rope, which is less likely with other methods.

To catch a fall with the hip wrap, your elbow must be straight before you begin to grip hard (fig. 7-15), so that bone and not muscle resists the pull of the rope. (Your natural reaction will be to grip the rope first, but this may pull your arm into a helpless position, requiring you to let go and grasp the rope again.) Then bring your braking arm across in front of your body, to increase the amount of wrap for maximum friction. An optimal braking position can only be learned with practice, for which schools and climbing clubs have constructed belay towers.

Several precautions must be observed to prevent the hip wrap from unwrapping in a fall. With frequent practice, they should become automatic.

1. Run your anchor attachment from the side opposite the braking hand (fig. 7-16). If you put the line to the anchor on the same side as the braking hand, the rotation of your body under the impact of a climber's fall can unwrap the hip wrap, decreasing friction and stability.

2. If you are facing toward the rock, belaying the leader, have the braking hand on the same side as any fall that could happen before the leader puts in the first piece of protection. If the fall is on the opposite side and the leader drops below you, the rope could be unwrapped from your hip.

3. Clip a control carabiner on your harness anytime the climbing rope goes straight up or down from your hips (fig. 7-17). The carabiner goes well forward of the hip bone, on the same side as the rope coming from the climber. Clipping the rope into this carabiner keeps the rope where you want it, at your hip, and also counteracts body rotation.

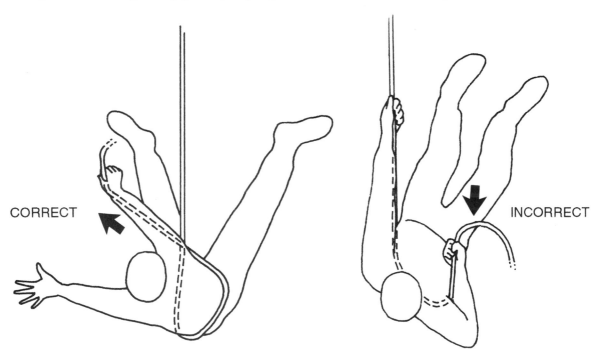

CORRECT   INCORRECT

Fig. 7–15. The correct braking arm position for the hip wrap must be achieved before braking begins, left; *or the arm will be pulled into a helpless position,* right.

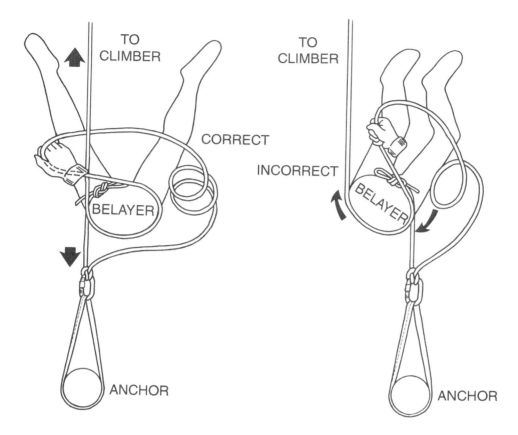

Fig. 7–16. The anchor attachment on the side opposite the braking hand, **left,** *keeps the hip belay from unwrapping.*

4. If you don't use a control carabiner, take advantage of your anchor attachment to keep the climbing rope from being pulled over your head or under your seat. If the pull will come from below, put the rope above the anchor attachment. If the pull will come from above, put the rope below the anchor line.

Of all braking methods, the hip wrap exerts the smallest force for a given grip of the braking hand. In a fall, this lower force might preserve questionable protection when any other method would pull it out. This would be extremely important if both your stance and anchor were weak. On the other hand, the climber will fall farther, increasing the danger of hitting something.

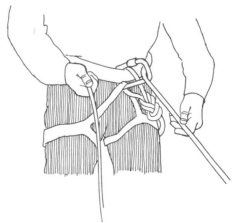

Fig. 7–17. *A control carabiner on the harness keeps the hip belay from unwrapping.*

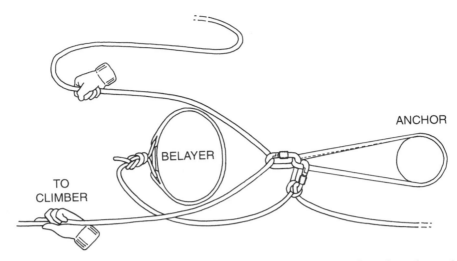

Fig. 7–18. A variant of the hip wrap, in which the forward pull of a fall goes directly to the anchor

As with belay devices, it is possible to arrange the hip wrap so that the forward pull of the fall goes directly to the anchor (fig. 7-18). This provides the same advantages as belaying directly from the anchor with a device. The friction of rope running against your back is replaced by the climbing rope's wrap of at least 90 degrees around the carabiner, a few inches to 1 foot or more behind your back. (If you are far from the anchor, a big fall could pull you toward it, especially on snow or wet rock.)

Fig. 7–19. Major belay options

METHOD	REQUIRES	FEATURES, ADVANTAGES	DISADVANTAGES
Resisting the pull of the fall			
Belay attached to harness	Ledge permitting a stance	Force is absorbed before reaching anchor	Relationship between stance and anchor must be carefully visualized
Belay attached directly to anchor	Bombproof anchor	Simple set-up (except hip wrap); easy to tie off	Anchor not always available, or conveniently placed for rope-handling
Applying friction to the rope			
Belay device	Device, locking carabiner	Some devices useful for rappelling	Figure-8s kink rope to some extent
Münter hitch	Large pear-shaped locking carabiner	Braking possible with ropes parallel	Slightly slower passing knot through carabiner; kinks rope; follower fall of at least 6 inches
Hip wrap	Protective clothes, gloves	Least braking friction; fast taking in rope	Burns possible unless much clothing worn; complex precautions required; greater chance of loss of control of rope if stance collapses

Fig. 7–20. Common beginner problems

PROBLEM	CORRECTION
Removes braking hand from braking rope (especially with hip belay)	Use the rope-handling procedure shown in fig.10, forcing yourself to be conscious of your braking hand at all times, until the technique becomes automatic.
Produces rope tension on leader	Watch leader or free-hanging sections of rope (if any) near your belay; keep hand on rope to feel movements; react quickly.
When belaying follower, unable to pull in rope fast enough	Bend over and extend your full reach for each cycle.
Great difficulty communicating when separated by a rope length	Stick to standard or agreed-upon commands; omit explanations; space out words more

OTHER TECHNIQUES

DECIDING WHEN TO ROPE UP

Climbers don't rope up and belay for every exposed place. There are occasions when it may be safer not to, even though you might wish you could. Rubble-strewn slopes are much more hazardous when dragging a rope. Some terrain has no suitable points for anchors. If you must pass through an area subject to rockfall or avalanche, roping is usually secondary to speed. Very experienced climbers may climb on solid rock well below their limit, "third-classing" what may nominally be a fifth-class route.

Anyone in the party may ask for a belay at any time, and must receive it immediately and without complaint from other members of the party. The primary exception is when roping up would significantly decrease the safety of the entire party. As difficulty and exposure increase on an alpine climb, natural differences in ability tend to spread the party out. It is just then, as the anticipated limit of the weakest member is approached, that the party must concentrate on keeping together, to enable roping up easily.

TYING OFF THE BELAY

There's at least one aspect of belaying you hope you'll never have to use: tying off the belay in order to help an injured partner. If your climbing partner is seriously injured and other climbers are nearby, it is usually best to let them help while you continue to belay. By staying there you could also help in raising or lowering the victim, if necessary. But if the two of you are alone, it is rare but conceivable that you may want to tie off the climbing rope to remove yourself from the belay system, so you can investigate, help your partner, or go for help.

If you are using a belay device or Münter hitch attached directly to the anchor, you need only to prevent rope from sliding through the belay. Simply form a knot such as the clove hitch in the braking rope and clip it to another carabiner on the anchor. You can now take your hand off the braking rope and it will be held by the knot.

If you are using a stance, with a belay device or Münter hitch attached to your harness, it is possible to tie off using one hand. However, it is easier and safer to put a clove hitch in the braking rope and clip it temporarily to your harness. Then while the clove hitch is doing the job of holding the belay rope, attach a normal sling to the climbing rope with a friction knot (prusik or Klemheist). Clip the sling into the anchor, chaining slings if necessary to make the connection long enough. If you can't reach the anchor, attach another sling with a friction knot to the rope that is holding you to the anchor, and join the slings with a carabiner. Transfer tension from the belay to the anchor by letting rope slip through the belay. But first tell the climber to expect being lowered a few inches, and not to worry.

With the hip wrap it may be impossible to tie off with one hand while in the braking position, so the first step may be to free yourself from holding the weight. Wrap the rope coming from your braking hand around the foot opposite the braking hand, keeping your knee locked (fig. 7-22). You can then proceed with both hands, attaching a sling to the climbing rope with a friction knot and clipping the sling to the anchor.

In any case, you should eventually back up the arrangement by tying the climbing rope itself directly to the anchor, with a figure-8 knot on a separate carabiner (fig. 7-21).

SELF-BELAYED SOLO CLIMBING

Self-belay devices, which allow roped solo climbing, have begun to appear. It is worn by the climber, and works like a ratchet, sliding up the rope during the climb, but not down it in a fall. To lead a pitch, the rope is first anchored at the bottom, and the climber protects as he ascends. Then

Fig. 7–22. Freeing the hands before tying off the climber when using the hip wrap

the rope is anchored at the top, and the climber rappels. Finally, the climber removes the bottom anchor and climbs the pitch a second time, retrieving the protection as he goes.

This is not just another belaying alternative to be chosen on occasion. It is a different form of climbing, requiring a commitment to relearn many fundamentals. Shortcomings compared to a belay by a live partner are almost inevitable. Read the manufacturer's literature critically, and practice in a safe situation. Is the belay static? Does it work if you fall in a horizontal or head-down position? When climbing, does the rope feed automatically, without producing extra slack or drag, especially at the top of a pitch, or on a traverse? Can you clip into protection above your waist without trouble? To fully evaluate the device, you should understand the basic physics of belaying, as described in the next section.

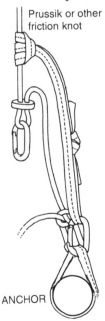

Prussik or other friction knot

ANCHOR

Fig. 7–21. Tying off a fallen climber

THE PHYSICS OF BELAYING: WHAT HAPPENS WHEN THE CLIMBER FALLS

Many years ago, the leader's main fear in a fall was the very real possibility that the rope would break. Ropes were made of the natural fiber hemp, and if a belayer held on too strongly, the rope would snap, even in a fall that by today's standard is not long. To prevent this, early editions of this book said that beginners had to study the theory of something called dynamic belay technique and practice it every year by holding simulated falls with heavy weights. Today, this is no longer necessary. Everyone takes for granted that a belay, correctly set up and executed, will eventually hold any fall. Modern ropes seldom, if ever, break (although they can be cut by a sharp edge of rock).

Today, the leader's main fear in a fall is the failure of his *protection*. Protection is explained fully in Chapter 10, but its general purpose is shown in figure 7-23. The topmost piece of protection stops a leader fall. If it is pulled out of the mountain, then the climber falls much farther, until the next protection gets a chance to hold the fall. Unfortunately, the protection is the weakest link in the belay system. This is partly because the force on the protection is greater than anywhere else, 50 percent greater than in the rope between the top protection and the climber. But the major factor is the uncertainty of the protection itself. Usually the limiting factor is not the breaking strength of the hardware, but the firmness of its fit in the rock and the quality of the rock (or ice) itself. Climbing lore is replete with true horror stories of supposedly "bombproof" protection that pulled out of the mountain in a fall, or even after a firm test tug. Therefore, the older belay techniques for reducing forces, described below, are still relevant. They are not necessary to save the rope and the climber's life, but many experienced climbers know them and occasionally use them to protect the protection. Be forewarned: there are few simple rules. Many decisions involve some trade-off between benefit and risk. The best choice is seldom clear. However, if you understand how a belay works,

Fig. 7–23. If the topmost protection fails, the climber will fall an additional distance, which is twice the distance to the next protection down.

you can, at least, decide what would be a bad choice in certain situations.

We will progress from simple concepts of belay physics to complex ones. A little history can illustrate the principles.

WHAT DETERMINES THE FORCES IN A FALL

Static belay

The simplest belay is the one the word originally meant. The sailor wraps rope around a cleat so that it cannot be pulled; the earliest climbers wrapped rope around or over a boulder or rock horn or the like, hoping for the same result. The only difference between this and tying the rope directly to an anchor was that the rope could be fed out or taken in without untying and retying a knot. Today, a firm grip on the rope, coupled with a sufficiently small protected fall, produces the same functional result—no rope is pulled through the belay. By definition, this is a *static* belay. In fact, most falls today are held by static belays.

In a static belay we encounter the strangest truth in all of belay theory. The forces are determined only by the distance of the fall, divided by the length of the rope between climber and belayer (see fig 7-24). This number is so important it has a name: the *fall factor*. It is a pure number, independent of the scale, such as feet, used to calculate it. Thus, for example, a 20-foot fall on 100 feet of rope has the same fall factor as a 2-foot fall on 10 feet of rope: 0.2. Both falls produce the same force in a static belay, if the climber's weight and the rope's characteristics are identical. If a climber falls before placing any protection, the fall factor is 2, the maximum possible. No matter whether the climber was just above the belayer, or if he was at the top of a 150-foot pitch on an ice face, the resultant forces are the same (neglecting friction on the rock and in the system, air resistance, etc.). The energy of the longer fall is absorbed by the proportionally longer rope.

The rope's characteristics are crucial, because in a static belay, the rope absorbs nearly all of the energy of the fall. The more the rope stretches, the

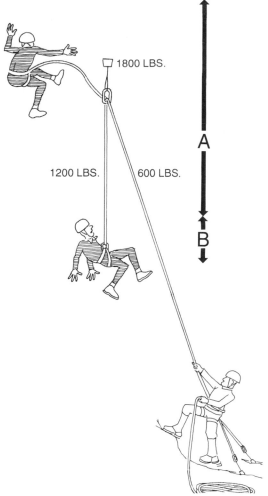

Fig. 7–24. Fall factor is defined as the fall length A, divided by the length of rope between the climber and belayer. (Slack rope contributes to A. B is due to rope stretch and/or slippage at the belay.)

lower the forces become. The effect is dramatic. An old hemp rope stretches little, producing forces so high that it will break if the fall factor is greater than about 0.25 and the belay is static! A modern climbing rope stretches so much that no fall should exceed its strength if the rope is new and undamaged. Therefore, manufacturers no longer specify rope strength by the force required to break it, but by the number of standard static falls it will hold before breaking. The standard is administered by the Union Internationale des Associations d'Alpinisme (UIAA). In order to pass this test, a rope must hold at least five such falls, spaced five minutes apart. The maximum force on the protection must not exceed 2,700 pounds (1,800 pounds for a half rope) on the first fall. However, this is still basically a rope-strength test. Because it uses a static belay and the extremely high fall factor of 1.7, it does not show the forces produced by real belays of typical falls. The only fall length tested is 16 feet long.

If all belays were static, fall factor alone would determine the forces of a fall, and forces could be controlled quite simply. The rule would be: it is more important to place protection at the beginning of a pitch, than at the end. This is because a given fall produces the highest force early in the pitch, the lowest force at the top. Although it is still good to keep that rule in mind, the forces in a real fall are reduced by two other factors. They constitute the difference between the static belay of the sailor and the actual belay given by the climber. These are: movement of the belayer, and friction on the rope at the belay. We will introduce them in their historical context.

The early climber's equivalent of a "cleat," a rock feature around which to belay a rope, was not always conveniently located near a place to stand or sit. The belayer, therefore, often substituted his own body for the cleat. It was quickly realized that if the belayer moved under the force of the fall, the force was significantly reduced. Sometimes called the *resilient belay*, this had one problem: the greater the movement, the greater the chance of collapse and total failure. Some authorities encouraged belayer movement, others warned against it. It is not surprising that up to the middle of the twentieth century, the situation was summed up in the golden rule of climbing, "the leader must not fall."

But world-famous climbers did in fact survive leader falls, which the theory of the day said should have broken their ropes. Some suspected that rope slip in the hands of their belayer played a role in saving their lives. But this was considered

to be a partial loss of control of the rope, embarrassingly close to total failure of the belay. Its implications were seldom even discussed.

Dynamic belay

The first real breakthrough in belaying was the full realization of the value of substituting a frictional grip on the rope for a static belay. When the rope was pulled through a belayer's gloved hand, the climber decelerated slowly. The energy of the fall, instead of being absorbed in a small fraction of a second, was spread out and thereby reduced. The Sierra Club, in the 1930s and 1940s, demonstrated the value of the new *dynamic belay* theoretically, experimentally, and by putting it into actual practice. It was so successful that it allowed modern rock climbing to begin in Yosemite. The new golden rule became, "the rope must run."

There is a fundamental trade-off in a dynamic belay. It decreases the forces on the top protection at the expense of a longer fall and a greater risk of hitting something before being stopped by the belay. However, the benefit can be surprisingly great, as you can see from figure 7-25, which shows the effect with modern ropes. For example, if the climber is 8 feet directly above the protection

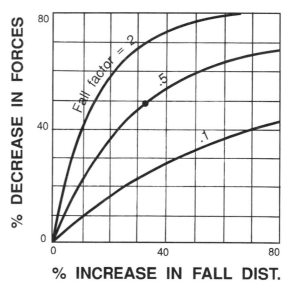

Fig. 7–25. The trade-off in a dynamic belay

and 32 feet from the belayer, the fall factor is 0.5. If rope slippage at the belay increases the fall 33 percent (5 feet), the force on the protection will be reduced by almost half. The benefit is greatest at high fall factors, which is also when rope slippage is most likely to occur. (This graph is based upon the current standard theory of belaying developed forty years ago by Wexler, which includes several simplifying assumptions, including simplifying the rope's characteristics and neglecting friction in the system and between the climber and the rock).

Modern kernmantle ropes stretch so well that they removed the necessity for the beginner to learn dynamic belay theory and technique. The golden rule "the rope must run" passed into history. Indeed, kernmantle ropes are frequently called "dynamic ropes." But that does not mean a dynamic belay—rope slippage—never occurs; it means only that it is now very uncommon. Rope slippage is still possible if the fall factor is high, or the belay friction is low. In either case, the pull on the rope exceeds the friction in the belay, so the rope slides.

We have just considered separately the three factors that determine the forces of a fall: fall factor, belayer movement, and belay friction. To see how they work together, we will use the graph in figure 7-26. A given fall held by a given belay

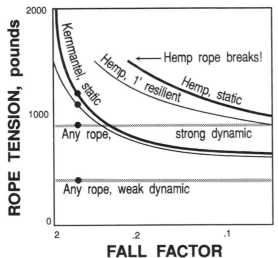

Fig. 7–26. Comparison of the major belay types

method produces a certain tension in the rope between the climber and the protection, which can be calculated using the current standard theory. The result is a point in this graph. A series of falls at different fall factors produces a line in the graph. In other words, each line shows the force produced by a given type of belay, at different fall factors. The solid lines represent static belays wherein all of the energy is absorbed only by rope stretch. There are two lines, showing the great difference between modern kernmantle and early hemp ropes. The dashed lines show the effect of 1 foot of belayer movement, holding an 8-foot fall, with each rope. The two horizontal lines show the effect of dynamic belays with two different levels of friction. These levels are the highest and lowest friction that have been suggested by various authorities in the past twenty years.

To illustrate, consider the previous example, whose fall factor was 0.5. If the belay is static, the peak tension is 1,200 pounds. If the belayer moves one foot during the fall, the tension is reduced by only 75 pounds. The "strong dynamic belay" in the graph reduces the force to 900 pounds, and the "weak" one reduces the force to 400 pounds. (The fall would be 2 and 12 feet longer, respectively). The same dynamic belays would, be definition, result in the same tensions in a hemp rope, regardless of fall factor. Of course, a static belay would break the hemp rope.

In summary, the friction applied to the rope at the belay places the real practical upper limit on the forces that a fall can produce. In other words, rope slippage at the belay dissipates excessive force, just like a safety valve on a boiler dissipates excessive pressure. How the belay is chosen and applied determines the force at which the rope slips, just as how the valve is designed determines the pressure at which it opens. Let's look more closely at how the belayer's "safety valve" works.

WHAT THE BELAYER CAN CONTROL

Three factors, which are at least theoretically under your control, determine the amount of friction that your belay will produce. The strength of your hand grip is one factor. Since the belay ampli-

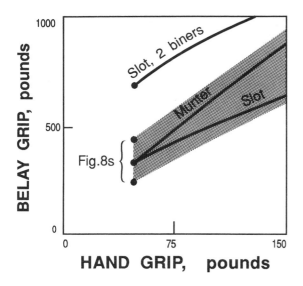

Fig. 7–27. Comparison of some dynamic belay methods

fies this grip, your choice of belay method is a second factor. Both of these factors are shown in figure 7-27. For example, virtually anyone can grip a rope hard enough to hold a 50-pound pull. A standard slot device or the Münter hitch will amplify this grip so that your belay can hold a 350-pound steady pull before the rope begins to slide. (But as you grip harder, the Münter hitch grips harder than slot devices do, as shown by the diverging lines.) Figure-8 devices come in a wide variety of sizes and surface finishes, so their belay varies from 250 to 430 pounds, with a 50-pound grip. A standard slot device with two carabiners holds 700 pounds. (Different ropes can produce somewhat different numbers. For example, using a half rope, forces are reduced by an average of 20 percent.)

The third factor determining belay friction is the angle between the ropes entering and leaving the belay device or the Münter hitch, or the total number of degrees in all the wraps of the rope in the hip belay. Varying this factor produces a continuous change in the total grip, with no angle at which a sudden change occurs, for any belay method.

The belay method is the most important of the three factors, because it operates for every fall. Hand strength and rope angle can usually be varied only when a fall is expected by the belayer. Taken by surprise, a belayer will react as he has trained himself to do, with full braking efforts.

Although you can predetermine the level of friction to some extent, it would be an overstatement to say that you can precisely control it. Probably the most you can do is to seek to avoid the extremes. High friction is justified whenever protection is known to be bombproof. Low friction might be called for when protection and anchors are poor, or rope drag (acting just like the belay itself) is very high, or for a very long fall on uncertain protection, provided the extra fall length is not itself a hazard.

Most belays are chosen and executed by a given belayer in that belayer's customary way, to allow concentration on other aspects of climbing, as it should be. But armed with a knowledge of how belays work, informed climbers can recognize extreme conditions and may decide to vary their belay accordingly.

· 8 ·

RAPPELLING

Rappelling can be so easy and exhilarating that you forget what a serious undertaking it really is. It's an indispensable activity in climbing, but it's also one of the more dangerous. If you learn it carefully from the start, you should have no trouble using this technique for sliding down a rope, controlling your speed with friction on the line. You will be able to descend almost any climbing pitch on rappel and, in fact, rappelling will be the only way to get down some faces of rock or ice.

You can get a sense of the danger by considering that as you rappel down a high cliff, full body weight on the rope, your life depends all the way on the anchor to hold the rope and on you to use the correct technique. If you fail or the anchor fails, you fall. Unlike belaying, where a large force comes on the system only if you fall, the force on the rappel system is always there. Despite the danger, it's easy to become cocky and careless after you learn how simple rappelling can be, and the exhilaration can encourage hazardous technique.

Coming down from a climb, there's often a choice between rappelling and downclimbing. Sometimes rappelling is the fastest and safest way to descend a particular pitch, but many times it is not. Think it through, considering the terrain, the weather, how much time is available, and the strength and experience of the party. If you decide to rappel, do it safely and efficiently. One of the hidden dangers of rappelling is that it can waste an awful lot of time in the hands of inexperienced rappellers.

RAPPEL SYSTEMS

A rappel system has four basic requirements: a rope, an anchor, someone to rappel, and a means of applying friction to the rope. The midpoint of the rope is looped through the anchor (a point of attachment to the rock or snow), with the two ends hanging down the descent route. The rappeller slides down this doubled rope and retrieves it from below by pulling on one end.

In mechanical rappel systems, the doubled rope passes through a friction device attached to your seat harness. In non-mechanical systems, friction is provided by wrapping the rope around your body. In either case, your braking hand grasps the rope to control the amount of friction. Gloves are usually worn to prevent rope burns.

Short rappels can be handled with just one rope, but longer rappels need the extra length of two ropes tied together, usually with a double fisherman's knot. The ropes are joined next to the anchor, with the two loose ends hanging down the cliff. With a two-rope rappel, you can even join ropes of different diameters, mating, for example, an 11-millimeter line with a 9-millimeter.

On rare occasions, climbers use a single-strand rappel, in which the rope is simply tied at one end to the anchor.

MECHANICAL SYSTEMS

Most climbers use a mechanical system (fig. 8-1) as their principal rappelling method, and all operate essentially the same. The two strands of rope are run through a rappel device attached to your harness. As you begin the rappel and gravity pulls you downward, the rope slides through the device. Your braking hand controls this natural pull by adjusting the amount of friction on the rope as it runs through the device. It does this through a combination of variations in grip and hand position. With some setups, you get additional friction by wrapping the rope partly around your back. You control the speed of descent, and you can come to a stop anytime you wish.

It takes less effort to produce friction at the top of a rappel than at the bottom, because the weight of the rope hanging below you puts added friction on the rappel device. This is especially so on very steep or overhanging rappels where most of the rope hangs free. But no matter how little grip strength may be required to control your descent, your braking hand must never leave the rope. Your other hand—the guiding, or uphill, hand—slides freely along the rope to help maintain balance.

To rappel with a mechanical system, you need to wear a seat harness, or an improvised diaper sling or figure-8 rappel seat. Never rappel with a simple loop of webbing tied around your waist, because it can constrict your diaphragm enough to make you lose consciousness.

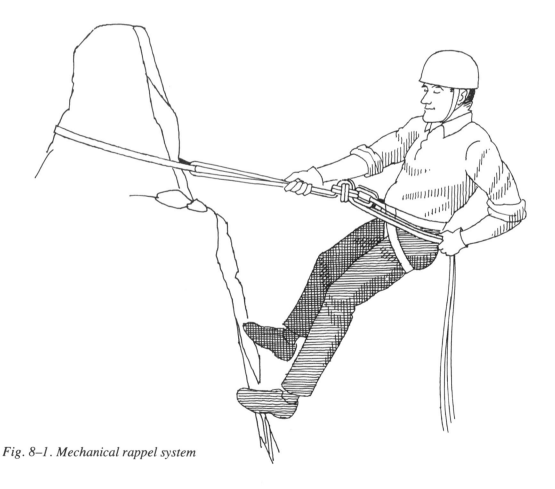

Fig. 8–1. Mechanical rappel system

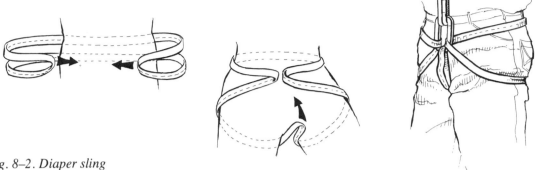

Fig. 8–2. Diaper sling

The diaper sling (fig. 8-2) takes about 10 feet of webbing tied into a large loop. With the loop behind your back, pull an end around to your stomach from each side. Bring a piece of the webbing from behind your back, between your legs, and up to your stomach to meet the other two parts. Clip them together in front with doubled carabiners or a locking carabiner. The diaper may also be clipped to a waist loop.

The figure-8 seat (fig. 8-3) is improvised from a standard-length runner. It must be clipped to a waist loop for stability.

Carabiner brake method

A very widely used mechanical system, the carabiner brake is somewhat complex to set up, but has the virtue of not requiring any special equip-ment—just carabiners. All climbers should know how to use the carabiner brake method, even if they normally use a specialized rappel device. It's a great backup if the device is lost or forgotten, and it's the safest method of rappelling without a special device.

To create the carabiner brake setup, start by attaching one locking or two regular carabiners to your seat harness. Any time a regular carabiner could be subjected to a twisting or side load, two carabiners or a locking carabiner are needed, and this is one of those cases. If you use two regular carabiners, position the gates to keep them from being forced open and accidentally unclipping (fig. 8-4). The correct position is with the gates on opposing sides, forming an X when they are opened at the same time.

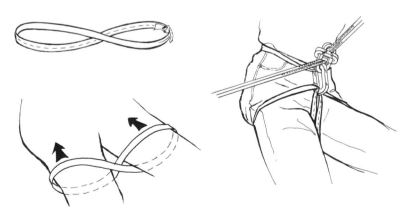

Fig. 8–3. Figure-8 sling

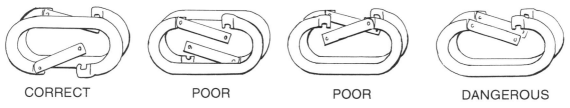

CORRECT   POOR   POOR   DANGEROUS

Fig. 8–4. Proper and improper positioning of gates on double carabiners

After attaching the harness carabiners (or locking carabiner), clip another pair of carabiners to that, in the same correct position. Then face the anchor, if you can. Lift a loop of the rappel ropes through the outer carabiner pair. Take yet another carabiner and clip it across the outer carabiner pair, beneath the rope loop. The rope then runs across an outer edge of this final carabiner, known as the braking carabiner.

One braking carabiner (fig. 8-5a) provides enough friction for most rappels on ropes that are 10 or 11 millimeters in diameter. You might need a second or even a third braking carabiner (fig. 8-5b) for thinner ropes, heavy climbers or heavy packs, or steep or overhanging rappels. The ropes must always run over the solid side of the braking carabiners, never across the gate.

There are a couple of things to watch for as you're setting up the carabiner brake system. First,

it's sometimes not possible to face the anchor as you pull the loop of rappel rope into the carabiner brake, and this can get confusing. A common beginner's mistake is to pull the rope into the system backward, as if preparing to rappel uphill toward the anchor.

Second, the weight of the rope hanging down the cliff may make it very difficult to pull the loop of rope up through the outer pair of carabiners and hold it while you clip in the braking carabiner. It helps to get that weight off the system. You can do that before pulling the loop of rope through by yanking up some slack rope and throwing a couple of wraps around a leg to take the weight. Or you can do it by pulling the loop through first, but making it extra large so you can lay it over your shoulder while you clip in the braking carabiner. Then drop the downhill strands back through the system so the brake remains close to the anchor.

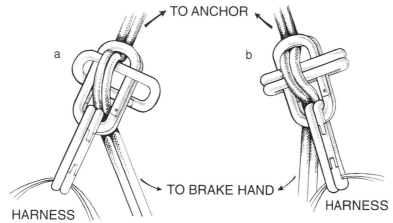

Fig. 8–5. Carabiner brake system: a, with one carabiner clipped across the outer carabiner pair; b, with two carabiners clipped across the outer carabiner pair in order to give greater friction.

If you are near the edge while setting up the carabiner brake or any other rappel method, you should be attached to an anchor for safety.

Figure-8 rappel device

The figure-8 is probably the most popular special device for rappelling (fig. 8-6). It is simpler to set up and requires less force to control than the carabiner brake method.

Keep in mind the disadvantages. It means carrying an extra piece of equipment, and most figure-8s are relatively heavy. If you lose or forget it, you must be prepared to use another rappel method. Most figure-8s require use of a locking carabiner and don't give you the option of using doubled carabiners. And the figure-8 puts some twists in the rope. The figure-8 was designed for rappelling, though some climbers use the device in one of several possible configurations for belaying.

Other rappel devices

Many other devices are used for rappelling. Most are primarily belay devices that can also be used for rappelling, such as belay plates (slots) and tubes. Some have disadvantages, such as being difficult to feed rope through or heating up easily. Before buying any new device, check climbing literature for evaluation and test data, and read the manufacturer's instructions closely.

Other mechanical systems

Several mechanical rappel systems require no special device, just a locking carabiner. It can be worthwhile insurance to learn at least one of them.

To set up the carabiner wrap system (fig. 8-7), clip a locking carabiner into the locking carabiner or doubled carabiners that are clipped to your seat harness. Run the rappel rope through the outer end of the outside carabiner, and wrap it around the carabiner's solid back, giving it more turns if you want more friction. Two turns are usually just about right. Position the outer carabiner so that the locked gate opening is at the far end. A hazard of the carabiner wrap system is that the carabiner could flip around, and the movement of the wrapped rope might then unlock it.

The Münter hitch used for belaying can also be used for rappelling (see Chapter 7 for details on

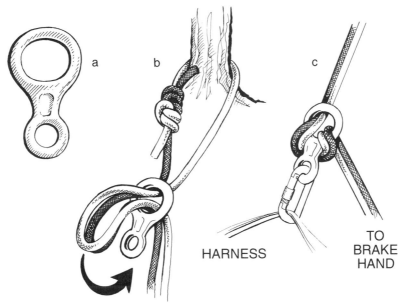

Fig. 8–6. Attaching a figure-8 device for use in rappelling: a, figure-8 rappel device; b, attaching rope to the figure-8 device; c, figure-8 rappel device in use.

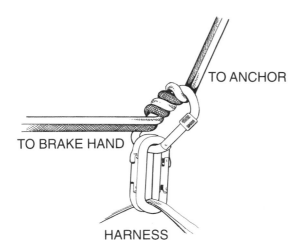

Fig. 8–7. The carabiner wrap system

using the Münter hitch while belaying). It's very easy to set up, but is the worst method for twisting the rope.

A method common in Europe merely runs the rappel rope through a locking carabiner at the harness, up over the climber's shoulder, and then down across the back to the opposite hand for braking. A danger is that, like non-mechanical systems, it is easy to fall out of.

NON-MECHANICAL SYSTEMS

Two traditional rappel methods use no hardware whatsoever to create friction on the rope. It's just the rope and your body.

The arm rappel (fig. 8-8) isn't used much, but it's occasionally helpful for quick descent of a low-angle slope. Lay the rappel rope behind your back, under your armpits, then wrap it once around each arm. Control your rate of descent by hand grip. For an arm rappel with a pack, be sure the rope goes behind the pack rather than on top or underneath.

Fig. 8–8. The arm rappel

The dulfersitz (fig. 8-9) is a simple all-purpose method that should be mastered by every climber for emergency use if you have no carabiners or seat harness. Face the anchor and step into the dulfersitz by straddling the rope. Bring it from behind around one hip, up across your chest, over the opposite shoulder, then down your back to be held by the braking hand on the same side as the wrapped hip. The other hand is your guiding hand to hold the rope above you to help stay upright.

The dulfersitz has a number of drawbacks compared with mechanical rappel systems. It can un-wrap from your leg, especially on high-angle rappels, though it helps to keep the wrapped leg slightly lower than the other. Stay under careful control and try to pad your body, because rope friction around your hip and across the shoulder will be painful, especially on steep rappels. Turn your collar up to protect your neck. If you're wearing a pack, the dulfersitz is even more awkward. The dulfersitz is used in modern climbing only when there is no reasonable alternative or for short, easy rappels to save the trouble of putting a seat harness back on.

RAPPEL ANCHORS

You will often be hanging your full weight on the rappel anchor, which is simply some point of attachment to the rock, snow, or ice. Set up the anchor as close as possible to the edge of the rappel route (providing you can get a solid anchor). This provides the longest possible rappel. It also makes it easier to pull the rope down from below after the rappel, and often reduces the danger of rockfall as

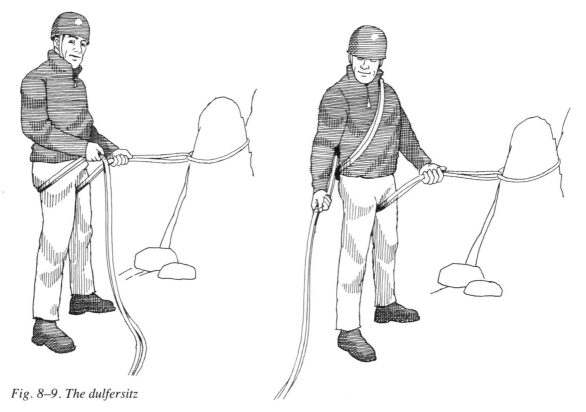

Fig. 8–9. The dulfersitz

you do so.

Think about possible effects on the rope as you are looking for an anchor. Locate the anchor so as to minimize chances of the rope being pulled into a constricting slot or otherwise hanging up when you try to pull it down from below. Check the position of the rope over the edge of the rappel route as the person before you finishes rappelling. If the rope moves near or into a slot in the surface that could restrict its movement, consider relocating the anchor.

You can use natural anchors or artificial (manufactured) anchors, just as you do for belaying or for placing points of protection during a climb.

NATURAL ANCHORS

The best natural anchor is a living good-sized, well-rooted tree. The rappel rope usually goes through a runner that is attached to the anchor. If you can attach this runner to a tree branch rather

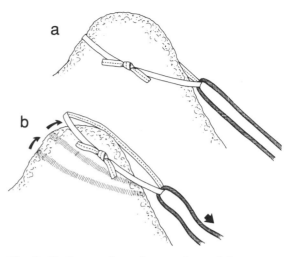

Fig. 8–10. Runner looped around a rock horn: a, a dangerous rappel anchor; b, runner rides up and off rock horn.

than low on the trunk, it helps limit the rope's contact with the ground, making it easier to retrieve the rope and reducing rope abrasion and the risk of rockfall. But note that connecting to a branch rather than the trunk puts more leverage on the tree, increasing the danger that it could be pulled out. Be cautious in using bushes as an anchor, and if you do use one you'll probably want an additional anchor or two for safety. Also be careful using trees and bushes in very cold weather, when they can become brittle. Rock features—horns, columns, chockstones, large boulders—are commonly used as anchors. On snow or ice, you can make bollards (see Chapter 12 for illustrations of snow bollards).

Test a natural anchor if there's any question about whether it can support the weight of the heaviest climber, plus a large safety margin in case a rappeller puts extra force on the anchor by stopping quickly. You can test rock horns and smaller trees by pushing against them with your foot. Test the anchor before rappel gear is attached, and never after the rope or the rappeller is hooked in.

If you run the rappel rope through a runner looped around a rock horn (fig. 8-10a), be rigorous in determining the angle of force on the horn. You must eliminate the deadly possibility the runner could ride up and off the horn during a rappel (fig. 8-10b). Most climbers use only a single anchor if it's a solid, dependable natural anchor—but add another anchor or two if there are any doubts.

ARTIFICIAL ANCHORS

As a rule of thumb, if you are using artificial (manufactured) anchors, use at least two and try to equalize the load between them.

In unknown alpine terrain, some climbers carry pitons and a hammer to set anchors. The most common artificial rappel anchors are bolts or pitons that have been left in place by previous climb-ers, and which must be evaluated for safety just as if you were using them for belaying or for protection while climbing.

The climbers' hardware known as chocks—nuts, hexes, and so forth—are usually used only if no good alternative is available, but better a couple of good chocks than a shaky rock horn. It's not a good idea to trust chocks that you find already in place, left behind by climbers who weren't able to work them loose from their crack in the rock. However, sometimes you can take advantage of an abandoned chock by using it like a natural chock-stone—looping a runner directly around it and making no use whatsoever of the sling attached to the old chock.

SETTING UP THE ROPE

To get the rope ready for rappelling, you attach it to an anchor. In the simplest case, you would untie a runner and retie it around a tree as a rappel sling. Then the midpoint of the rope is suspended from the sling (fig. 8-11a).

If you're using just one rope, put one end of the rope through the sling and pull it until you reach the midpoint. Or you can put the sling around the midpoint before you retie it around the tree. If you're joining two ropes together for the rappel, put one end of a rope through the sling and tie it to the other rope with a double fisherman's knot, backed up with overhand knots.

You could put the rope directly around the tree (fig. 8-11b), without use of a rappel sling—but this causes rope abrasion, makes it harder to retrieve the rope and, if done enough times, can kill the tree.

If your anchor is a rock feature or bolts or pitons, always attach a sling to the anchor, then run the rappel rope through the sling. Never put the rope directly around the rock or through the eye of the bolt hanger or piton, because the friction may make it impossible to pull the rope back down from below. Some climbers prefer to use two slings instead of one for added security. If you normally carry only sewn runners (which cannot be untied), you may want to bring along some 9/16-inch webbing to cut and tie as needed for rappel slings.

On popular climbs, you will find established rappel anchors encircled with the slings that must be left behind when a rappel rope is retrieved. Some of the older slings will feel dry and less supple. It's a good idea to cut out a couple of the oldest slings and add a new one before running your rappel rope around them. If you are using

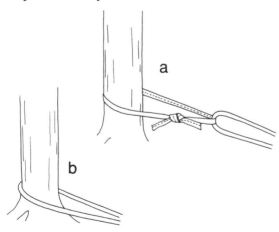

Fig. 8–11. Rappel rope attached to tree: a, rappel rope through a sling around a tree; b, poor—rappel rope directly around tree.

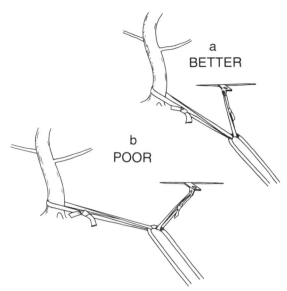

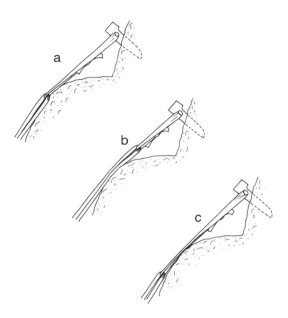

Fig. 8–12. The most common method of attaching the rappel rope to multiple anchors, with a separate sling attached to each of two anchors and meeting at the rappel rope: a, a narrow angle between slings is best; b, the angle between slings is too wide.

Fig. 8–13. The point of connection between the rappel sling and the rappel rope: a, poor—rope binds and abrades against rock; b, better; c, best.

more than one sling, try to use the same length to help distribute the load.

When using two anchors to support the rappel, the most common method is to run a separate sling from each anchor, with the slings meeting at the rappel rope. Generally try to adjust the slings so the force is the same on each anchor. For the strongest setup, keep a narrow angle between the two slings (fig. 8-12). (You can also use just a single sling run through the two anchors, employing either self-equalization or the triangle method. Both are described in Chapter 7.)

You can help to avoid binding and abrasion of the rappel rope by making sure the point of connection between the rappel sling and the rope is away from the rock (fig. 8-13).

You can use a tiny piece of rappel hardware known as a descending ring to help reduce rope wear and make retrieval easier. It's simply a metal ring, $1^1/_2$ inches or so in diameter. Thread the rappel sling through the ring before tying the sling.

Then thread the rappel rope through the ring until you reach the rope's midpoint (fig. 8-14). When you pull the rope down later, it slides more easily through the descending ring than it would directly over the sling, which also can be weakened by rope friction.

The descending ring, however, does add another possible point of failure. Newer rings are continuous non-welded designs, much better than the welded type, which cannot be trusted. Some

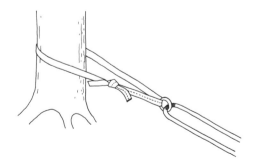

Fig. 8–14. Rappel rope through descending ring

climbers insist on two rings, even if both are non-welded. An alternative is a single ring, backed up by a non-weight-bearing sling from the anchor through the rope, ready to hold the rope in case the ring fails.

Throwing down the rope

After the rappel rope is looped at its midpoint through an anchor, it's time to get the rope ready to toss down the rappel route.

Beginning from the rappel sling, coil each half of the rope separately into two butterfly coils. You'll end up with four butterfly coils, two on each side of the anchor. Throw the coils out and down the route, one at a time. Start on one side of the anchor by tossing the coil nearest the anchor, then the rope-end coil. Repeat for the other half of the rope (fig. 8-15). This sequence reduces rope snags and tangling. Before tossing, have another climber hold onto the rope near the anchor to make sure your tosses won't cause the rope to pull through the anchor. (Commercial rope bags are available which make it easier to carry ropes and to keep them clean and tangle-free, and rope-tossing is usually easier if you are using a rope bag.)

You won't always end up with a perfect toss, with the rope hanging straight down the rappel route. If you end up with tangles, hangups, or bunching, it's usually best to pull it back up, re-coil, and toss again. But sometimes it's just as well to work with what you've got. For instance, in a high wind, you're not likely to get a perfect toss. So just rappel down to the first problem, recoil the strands below that point, toss again, and continue the rappel.

Shout ''Rope!'' before you throw the rope down a rappel route. Some climbers shout the word two times, to give anyone below a little time to respond or to watch out for the rope. Others shout just once, but wait for a moment for any response. Be sure you're attached to an anchor as you stand at the edge of the route to toss the rope.

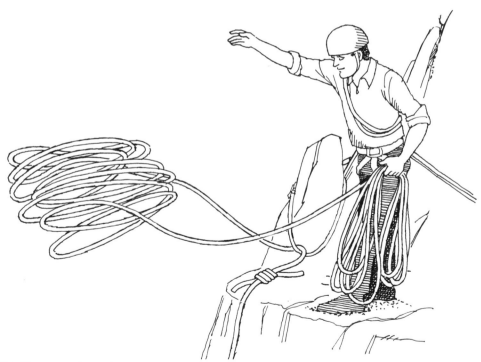

Fig. 8–15. Throwing down the rope

RAPPEL TECHNIQUE

In preparing to rappel, you will go through a sequence of establishing the anchor, attaching the rope to the anchor, throwing the rope down, and hooking yourself into the rappel system. At this point, you are facing the anchor, your back to the descent route, ready to head down the rope. Here's how to do it.

Start with a final check of the entire system: seat harness, rappel hardware, attachment to the rope, and anchor. Then, unless you're the last to rappel, wait while a partner checks your entire system. Pay special attention to the brake system: it's not set up backward, is it, as if you were rappelling uphill? Are the gates of carabiner pairs opposed correctly? Are locking carabiners securely closed? If another climber rappels before you, don't let the rappel begin until you've thoroughly checked out the setup.

GETTING STARTED

Now comes the most nerve-wracking part of most rappels. To gain stability, your legs must be nearly perpendicular to the slope. Therefore, at the very brink of a precipice, you're required to lean outward (fig. 8-16). In some cases you may be able to ease the transition by climbing down several feet before leaning out and putting your full weight on the rope to start the rappel (fig. 8-17).

With the carabiner brake or other mechanical systems, you may be able to sit on the edge of the

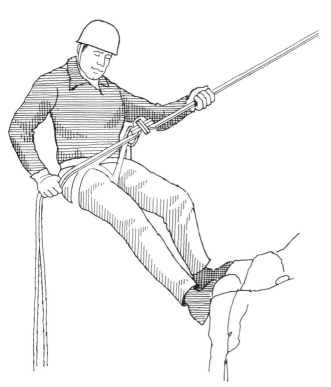

Fig. 8–16. Starting rappel from a high anchor

Fig. 8–17. Climbing below a low anchor before starting rappel

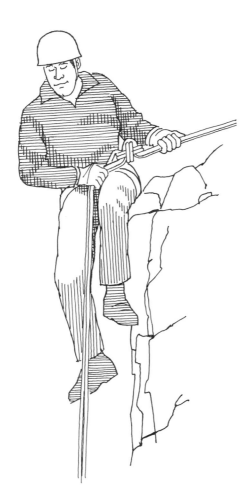

are keeping the feet together and failing to lean back far enough. (Some go to the other extreme and lean too far back, bringing the chance of tipping over.)

Move slowly and steadily, with no bounces or leaps. Higher speeds put more heat and stress on the rappel system, and it's especially important to

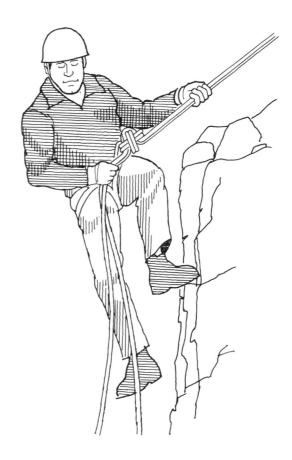

rappel ledge and wiggle gently off, simultaneously turning inward to face the slope. This technique is particularly useful when starting the rappel above an overhang (fig. 8-18).

POSITION, SPEED, AND MOVEMENT

As you move downward, your position should be something like this: feet apart, knees flexed, body at a comfortable angle to the slope, and facing a little toward the braking hand for a view of the route. The most common beginners' mistakes

Fig. 8–18. Sitting down on ledge and squirming off to get started

go slowly on any questionable anchor. If you have to stop quickly while moving fast down the rope, the anchor comes under a great deal of additional force. Use extreme caution rappelling a face with loose or rotten rock. The danger here is that rock can be knocked loose and hit you or chop the rope.

Overhangs on the route can be a problem. It's easy to end up swinging into the face below the overhang and banging your hands and feet. There also is the danger of getting the brake system jammed on the lip of the overhang. One way to help get past that difficult transition from moving down against the rock wall to hanging below the overhang is to bend your knees sharply while your

feet are at the edge of the overhang, then quickly drop three or four feet. This stresses the rappel system, of course, but it helps reduce both the chance of swinging into the face below and of jamming the brake on the lip.

Below an overhang, you will be dangling free on the rope. Assume a sitting position, hold yourself upright with the guiding hand on the rope above and continue steadily downward. Don't be surprised if you spin as twists in the rope unwind.

Sometimes, in order to reach the next rappel spot, you'll have to move at an angle to the fall line, walking yourself to one side instead of moving straight down. Be careful you don't lose your footing here. If you do, you will swing on the rappel rope back toward the fall line in what could be a nasty pendulum fall. And it could leave you in a position you can't recover from without climbing back up the rope with prusik slings or ascender devices.

POTENTIAL PROBLEMS

Shirttails, hair, chinstraps from a hard hat, and just about anything else have the potential to get pulled into the braking system. Keep a knife handy in case you have to cut foreign material out of the system.

If you run across a tangled or jammed rope on the way down, fix it while you're still above the problem. Stop at the last convenient ledge above the area, or stop with a leg wrap (explained in the next section). Pull the rope up, correct the problem, then throw it down again. Sometimes there's a simple solution. For instance, rappelling down blank slabs, you can often just shake out tangles as they are encountered.

STOPPING IN MID-RAPPEL

If it's ever necessary to stop partway down a rappel, wrap the rope two or three times around one leg (fig. 8-19a). The friction around your leg, increased by the weight of the hanging rope, is usually enough to hold you and to free your hands. Keep a braking hand on the rope until the wraps are completed and tested with your weight. Make the wraps tight, or you could end up a foot or two

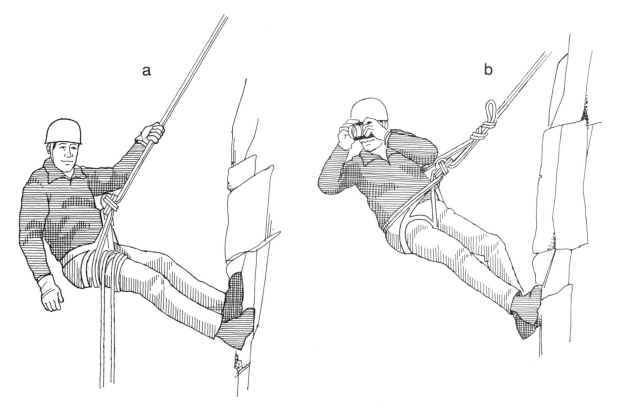

Fig. 8–19. Stopping in mid-rappel: a, with rope wrapped around leg; b, with a carabiner brake or other mechanical rappel system.

lower than you intended as you put weight on the wraps and they tighten.

With the carabiner brake or other mechanical rappel system, an alternative method is to pass the rope around your waist, and tie two or three half-hitches around the rappel rope above the brake system (fig. 8-19b). This can be released easily when you're ready to continue the rappel.

MULTIPLE RAPPELS

A descent route often involves a series of rappels. These multiple rappels, especially in alpine terrain, present special problems and require maximum efficiency to keep the party on the move.

The trickiest is a rappel into the unknown, down a route you're not familiar with. Avoid this kind of multiple rappel. If you cannot, take the time to check out the possible rappel lines as carefully as time and the terrain permit. Sometimes you can find a photo of the route before you leave on the climb and bring it with you. Keep in mind that the first couple of rappels down an unfamiliar route may commit you to it all the way, for better or for worse.

If you can't see to the bottom of an unfamiliar rappel pitch, the first person down has got to be prepared to climb back up in case the rappel leads nowhere. This rappeller should carry prusik slings or mechanical ascenders for going up the rope. As additional preparation, the rappeller can tie both strands of the rappel rope to the anchor with figure-8 knots before starting the rappel. This secures the strands so the rappeller can climb up either strand if necessary. The next rappeller unties the knots before heading down.

Rappelling down unfamiliar terrain brings an increased risk of getting the ropes hung up. You can minimize the problem by downclimbing as much of the route as possible, instead of rappelling. You might also consider doing rappels using just one rope, even if two ropes are available, be-cause one rope is easier to retrieve and less likely to hang up than two.

Even though it's nice to gain the maximum distance from each rappel, don't bypass a good rappel spot even 40 feet or so from the end of the rope if there are doubts about finding a good place farther down.

As a party moves through a series of rappels, the first person down each pitch usually carries gear to use in setting up the next rappel (after tying into an anchor at the bottom and trying to find shelter from rockfall). Climbers can take turns being first and last, though it's best for beginners to be somewhere in the middle.

SAFETY BACKUPS

Climbers have several options to increase the safety of a rappel. The options are occasionally useful in specific situations or for helping a beginner gain confidence in rappelling.

Knots in the end of the rope: It's possible to rappel off the end of the rope if you're not paying attention. Some climbers put a knot in the end of each rope, or tie the ends together, to eliminate this danger. If you add knots, don't rely blindly on them to tell when you've reached the end of the rope. The knots might come untied, of course, and in any case you want to keep an eye on the end of the rope so you can plan where to stop. The knots themselves can cause a problem by jamming in the rock if you ever find it necessary to pull the rope back up to work on it.

Pulling on the rappel ropes: A person standing below a rappeller can easily control the rappeller's movement, or stop it altogether, by pulling down on the rappel ropes, putting friction on the brake system. To safeguard the rappeller with this method, the person at the bottom simply holds the rope strands loosely, ready to pull them tight the instant the rappeller has difficulty (fig. 8-20).

Top belay: The rappeller can also be protected by a belay from above with a separate rope. If the belayer uses a separate anchor, the rappeller is safe

Fig. 8–20. Rappel halted by climber below, who is pulling down on the ends of the rope.

from even a total failure of the rappel anchor. A top belay is recommended for all beginners, for climbers with minor injuries, and for the first person down on a suspect anchor. The belays are too time-consuming for routine use because they drastically increase a party's descent time.

Prusik backup: Some climbers like the security of a prusik or Bachmann knot while rappelling, sliding the knot along the rappel ropes as they descend. The knot is in place above the brake system, and the prusik loop is clipped to a carabiner linked to your seat harness. If the brake system fails and you start to drop, the pull causes the prusik knot to automatically grip the ropes and stop the fall (fig. 8-21).

Backing up your rappel with a prusik knot has its dangers. Be careful it doesn't lock up unexpectedly—once it's under tension it can be tough to get loose—and keep the loop short so you can reach it if it locks. There's also the opposite danger: that the prusik knot will fail to lock when it should, particularly if you forget to release your

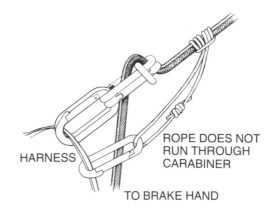

HARNESS

ROPE DOES NOT RUN THROUGH CARABINER

TO BRAKE HAND

Fig. 8–21. Prusik backup for a carabiner brake rappel system

hold on the knot. The prusik also has the unfortunate potential to burn through during a sudden stop from a high-speed rappel. Remember that controlling the prusik requires the full-time use of your guiding hand, which then isn't available for balance or protection.

RETRIEVING THE RAPPEL ROPE

Successful rope retrieval after a rappel depends on some important steps even before the last rappeller starts down the rope. It takes just one frightening experience with a stuck rappel rope to guarantee that you'll always take these precautions.

If you're using two ropes for the rappel, they will be tied together near the anchor. It's critical that you know which rope to pull on from below. Pull the wrong one, and you'll be attempting the impossible task of pulling the knot through the rappel sling. In some parties, the last two rappellers say out loud which rope is to be pulled, as an aid to remembering which is which.

The last rappeller should take a good final look at the rope and the rappel sling to see that everything is in order and that the rope isn't about to catch on the rock or the sling. Before the last person starts down, a climber at the bottom can test the rope by pulling to check that it can be moved and to see that the connecting knot in a two-rope

rappel can be pulled free of the edge.

With such a two-rope rappel, the last person who starts down may want to stop at the first convenient ledge and pull enough of the rope down so that the connecting knot is clear of the edge. This helps take some of the uncertainty out of the difficult business of recovering a long rappel rope. However, it also shortens one rope end, so be sure the rappeller still has enough rope to reach the bottom.

The last rappeller has the main responsibility for spotting any retrieval problems. This last person can get twists out of the rope by keeping one finger of the braking hand between the ropes throughout the descent. (The same purpose is served by splitting the two ropes through a carabiner on your harness, just uphill of the braking hand.)

With the last rappeller down, it's time to retrieve the rope. First take out any visible twists. Then give the rope a slow, steady pull. Other climbers should take shelter to stay out of the way of falling rope or rockfall. If you've taken all the right steps and luck is on your side, the rope will pull free.

A jammed rappel rope is among a climber's worst nightmares. If it hangs up, either before or after the end clears the anchor, try flipping the rope with whipping motions before trying to get it down with extreme pulling. If you can, move both left and right and try more flipping or pulling. If all else fails, it may be necessary to climb up and free the rope. Belay the climber if enough rope is available. As a final resort if the party can't proceed without the rope, a climber might decide to attempt the desperate and very dangerous tactic of ascending the stuck rope with prusik slings or mechanical ascenders.

After you've studied rappelling and tried it a few times, it will be easy to see why climbers approach the technique with a fair degree of caution. But it's one of the activities central to climbing, and if you know what you're doing, it works well.

PART THREE

ROCK CLIMBING

Sherpa climber rappelling on a crag with Ama Dablam in the background, Khumbu region, Nepal. Photo by Gordon Wiltsie

• 9 •

ROCK CLIMBING TECHNIQUE

Climbing is a joyous, instinctive activity. As children, we scurry up trees, garden walls, building facades, and anything else steep and enticing. Then we grow up. For some of us, however, the adult urge to climb finds a beautiful outlet in rock climbing.

It's an exciting activity you can go at in many different styles and many different settings. For many, the ultimate pleasure is scaling steep solid granite in an isolated alpine setting far from the city. For them, the crags close to home are only a practice ground to hone skills in preparation for an escape to the mountains. For others, the primary pleasure is the kinesthetic joy of moving on rock, executing the most difficult and gymnastic moves. Mastering the challenge of the rock may be more important than the setting, and a long alpine approach a nuisance rather than a pleasure. And there are those who treasure the whole range of rock-climbing experiences, from working out a single move in a difficult bouldering problem or training on an artificial climbing wall, to completing sustained challenging pitches on a towering rock wall or climbing short sections of rock during an alpine climb on a glaciated peak.

The joys of rock climbing are found in all these ways, and despite their differences, the skills and techniques are essentially the same.

PREPARATION

PHYSICAL CONDITIONING

Climbing is physically demanding, and if you don't have the needed strength, some climbs will be too difficult. However, many climbs are possible without an abundance of strength. To some extent, technique can compensate for a lack of strength, while extra strength can sometimes compensate for a deficiency of technique. Some climbs, especially at the higher end of the rating scale, demand a high degree of both strength and technique.

ATTITUDE

To climb rock well, you must have the desire. Rock climbing calls for a commitment of both mind and body, and making the necessary moves requires total concentration and complete confidence. This confidence can come by practicing with a top rope (belayed from above), which minimizes possible injury in case of a fall and allows you to safely attempt harder and harder moves, eventually finding the limits of your ability.

Confidence goes hand in hand with physical conditioning. If hand, arm, or leg strength is not sufficient, it doesn't matter that the mind is willing. Conversely, physical ability alone won't move you if your mind says no.

An equally important component of attitude is an awareness of safety. This includes knowing your limits, and knowing when and how to back off when you don't have the strength or technique for a given route on a given day.

GEAR

Footwear

Mountaineering boots are commonly used on alpine climbs of modest technical difficulty or where weather or conditions (such as presence of snow or ice) favor their use. Boots generally hold on larger edges quite well, but are less useful on tiny edges or for "smearing" on holds.

For more difficult rock climbs, there are shoes made specifically for rock climbing (fig. 9-1). For many routes, rock shoes are essential. They are generally superior for smearing, and often will edge quite well also.

Most rock shoes consist of a flexible upper, often made of soft leather or cordura and leather, and a smooth flexible rubber sole. In recent years, new rubber compounds have been developed to create "stickier" soles that provide greater friction between rock and sole, and have aided in success on increasingly difficult routes. Rock shoes should fit very snugly to allow maximum control and feel of the rock. Specialized rock shoes are now available that are especially well suited for certain types of climbing, such as edges, pockets, and friction.

Clothing

Clothing for rock climbing should be chosen for appropriateness to weather conditions and for freedom of movement. Some climbers prefer loosely fitting pants; others prefer body-hugging tights made of stretchy material such as Lycra. Some climbers find that knickers provide a desirable combination of freedom of movement and utility in an alpine environment. Remove jewelry and watches that can get caught in equipment or abraded on holds or in cracks.

Tape

Athletic tape can protect hands from abrasion against rock, especially when climbing difficult jam cracks. There are a number of different taping methods, but no matter what the method, the tape must stay securely in place and not begin to peel off part way up a pitch. The tape also must protect

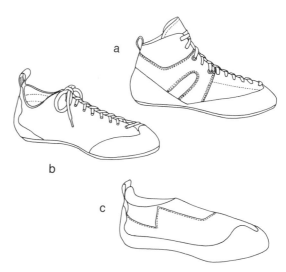

Fig. 9–1. Rock shoes: a, all-around shoe; b, more specialized edging shoe; c, slipper.

vulnerable areas, especially knuckles and the back of the hand, while allowing maximum freedom of hand movement (fig. 9-2). A common mistake is to wrap the tape too tightly.

Some taping methods leave most of the palm untaped to increase sensitivity to the rock. Tape can also be used to provide support and/or protection for finger joints that are easily overstressed by difficult rock climbing or vigorous training.

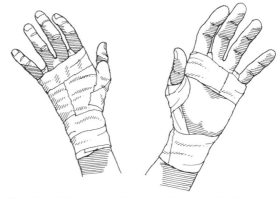

Fig. 9–2. Hand taped for climbing: back of hand and knuckles are protected; palm is mostly left open.

Chalk

Many climbers use gymnastic chalk to improve their grip, especially in hot sweaty weather. The chalk is usually carried in a chalk bag worn on the back of the harness or attached to a separate runner tied around the waist, so you can dip a hand in the chalk whenever you need it.

Some climbers feel that chalk detracts from the rock by leaving white smudges. They also argue that the chalk identifies the holds, robbing other climbers of the experience of finding the holds and figuring out the climbing sequence for themselves. A compromise solution used by some is colored chalk that blends in with the rock. Several colors are commercially available.

On frequently climbed pitches, sweat and chalk can leave holds slimy and difficult to use. Some climbers carry a small brush, such as a toothbrush, to clean the holds.

Other gear

Additional gear is covered in other chapters. This includes equipment that is less specific to rock climbing, such as ropes and harnesses, and the varieties of hardware specific to the skills of leading and placing protection.

BASIC CLIMBING TECHNIQUES

PRINCIPLES OF MOVEMENT

Climbing with the feet

Pay attention to footwork and balance and you'll reduce the need to rely on arm and hand strength.

Stand erect over your feet and fight the tendency to lean in and hug the rock. On very steep rock, however, pressing the hips close to the rock can help push body weight directly down onto small footholds.

When possible, keep arms outstretched to avoid hanging on bent arms, which is very tiring. As you raise your feet to the next foothold, try to keep your arms straight, avoiding the tendency to use them to haul yourself from one hold to the next. Legs are much stronger than arms. Let the legs lift the body.

Three-point suspension

In this elementary approach, you move one hand or foot at a time while the other three limbs remain stationary (fig. 9-3). Be sure you're in balance over your feet before releasing a handhold to reach for the next one. This is an especially useful approach when the rock may be unsound, because it allows you to balance securely on three

Fig. 9–3. Three-point suspension: hands and right foot provide secure stance; left foot is moved to a higher hold.

holds while testing the next one.

Know where your center of gravity is. The optimal position will vary, but it's often useful to keep a low center of gravity, with weight directly over the feet. Move your center of gravity over a new foothold before committing weight to it. Only when your body is in balance over the new hold should you transfer weight onto it.

As you try more difficult climbs, you'll learn moves that don't adhere to the principle of three-point suspension. There may be only one or two sound holds and body position will be used to maintain a delicate balance over those holds. For example, a hand or foot may be positioned over a non-existent hold, or hips may be thrust in one direction, to counterbalance other parts of the body.

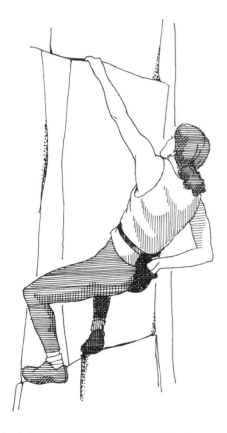

Fig. 9–4. "Resting" on an outstretched arm

CONSERVING ENERGY

Plan a move before trying to execute it. Move smoothly and deliberately, without wasted motion. Strive for fluidity, as if dancing a ballet with the rock, to conserve both time and energy.

Once you begin to step up on a foothold, transfer all your weight and complete the move. Avoid hanging with bent arms and bent knees in an awkward and tiring position while deciding what to do next.

Look for natural resting places such as ledges or secure footholds. If a no-hands rest isn't possible, try for a stance that uses as natural a body position as possible, and that requires the least amount of upper body strength.

If you must hang on handholds, the least tiring way is to hang on straight arms rather than bent arms (fig. 9-4). Do this either by lowering your center of gravity (bend knees, even squat) or by leaning out, away from the rock. Always maximize the proportion of weight being supported by the feet rather than the arms. It also helps to hang your arms down and shake them out, allowing a brief rest and return of circulation to stressed muscles.

USE OF HOLDS

Selection

In general, select holds based on solidness, convenience, and size. A visual inspection will often tell all you need to know. But if you doubt the soundness of a hold, test it with a kick, or with a blow from the heel of the hand. You can also push or pull on it. Keep alert to the consequences if the hold fails during testing: be sure it won't fall on people below, and be sure your stance is secure so you yourself won't fall. Remember that the hold must be useful in the context of the route. A large firm hold is useless if it leads away from the planned route and puts you into a position where you can't move to the next hold. A smaller but more conveniently placed hold may be a better choice.

Footholds should be comfortably spaced whenever possible. High steps are strenuous and make balance awkward, while steps close together waste energy without providing much upward progress.

Handholds at about head height provide a good stance and often are not as fatiguing as handholds above the head. They also let you lean away from the rock to view other potential hand- and footholds. Often, however, you won't have much choice in the matter, because the nature and difficulty of the rock may dictate where the holds are.

Footholds

Climbers use most footholds by employing one of two techniques, edging or smearing. On many holds, either technique will work, and the one to use depends on your own preference and type of footwear. We'll take up a third technique, called the foot jam, in a later section.

In edging, the edge of the boot or rock shoe is placed over the hold (fig. 9-5a). You can use either the inside or outside edge, but the inside is usually preferred for greater ease and security. The ideal point of contact may vary, but generally it's between the ball of the foot and the end of the big toe. Keeping the heel higher than the toes provides greater precision, but lowering the heel is a more restful position. Using the actual toe of the boot or rock shoe ("toeing in") may be very tiring. With practice, you will become proficient using progressively smaller footholds.

In smearing, the foot points more uphill, with the sole "smeared" over the hold (fig. 9-5b). The technique of smearing works best with rock shoes or flexible boots. On lower-angle rock, you may not need an actual hold, but will only have to achieve enough friction between sole and rock. On steeper terrain, smear the front of the foot over a hold, and see how even tiny irregularities in the rock can provide significant friction and security.

Fatigue, often aggravated by anxiety, can lead to troublesome vibrations in the muscles of the leg, known as "sewing-machine leg." The best way to stop it is to try to relax your mind and to change leg position, either by moving on, lowering the heel, or straightening the leg.

In using footholds, optimize the direction of

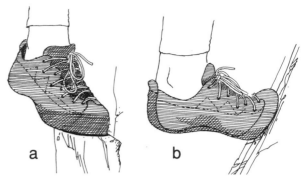

Fig. 9–5. Footholds: a, edging; b, smearing.

force on the hold. Flexing the ankle may increase the surface area of contact between sole and rock, giving maximum friction. Leaning away from the rock can create inward as well as downward force on the hold, increasing security.

Decide the best way to use a hold before you put your foot on it. Then maintain your position on the hold. Although it's sometimes necessary to reposition the foot into a better relationship to the hold, avoid thrashing and repeated repositioning to try to find something better. This wastes time and energy and may cause you to slip off altogether. On marginal footholds it may be mandatory to maintain the position exactly, as any movement or rotation could cause the foot to slip off. Keeping your foot in position can take a lot of concentration and skill as you move up on the hold and step above with the other foot.

With the large footholds called buckets, place only as much of your foot as necessary on the hold (fig. 9-6). Putting your foot too far into the bucket can sometimes force the lower leg outward, making for an out-of-balance stance.

Generally avoid using your knees, which are susceptible to injury and offer little stability. Nevertheless, even experienced climbers occasionally use a knee to avoid an especially high or awkward step. The main considerations are to avoid injury from pebbles and sharp crystals, and to avoid becoming trapped on your knees, unable to rise to your feet. This can be a big problem if you find yourself beneath an overhanging bulge with insufficient space to easily stand up.

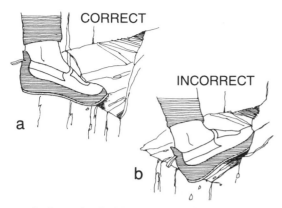

Fig. 9–6. Bucket hold: a, correct; b, incorrect.

Handholds

You can use handholds for balance, to help raise yourself by pulling up on the hold, or to provide various forms of counterpressure.

Handholds (fig. 9-7) offer maximum security when all fingers are used. Ways to use fingers aren't always obvious on small holds. For example, with fingers holding onto a tiny ledge, you may be able to use the thumb in opposition on a minor rugosity (fig. 9-7a). On a very narrow hold or a small pocket in the rock, you can stack fingers on top of each other to increase pressure on the hold (fig. 9-7b).

The most common handhold is the cling hold (fig. 9-7c). Large cling holds allow the entire hand to be cupped over the hold, while smaller variations (fig. 9-7e) may allow room for only the fingertips. Keeping fingers close together provides a stronger grip on the hold. If the hold is not large enough for all fingers to be placed on it, at least curl the other ones, which permits the fingers in use to get the most force from the muscle/tendon system (fig. 9-7f). When using cling holds, be aware that certain hand configurations put extreme stress on the fingers and may lead to injury (fig. 9-7e). (Other types of handholds will be discussed later in this chapter.)

DOWNPRESSURE

For this technique, place the finger tips, palm, side or heel of your hand on the hold and press down (fig. 9-8a). Pressing down with a thumb can

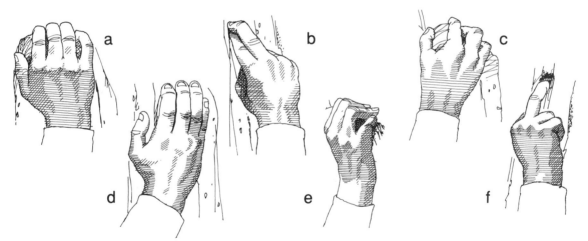

Fig. 9–7. Handholds: a, thumb used in opposition to other fingers; b, stacking fingers to apply greater pressure on a small hold; c, large cling hold; d, open grip. Keeping distal finger joints flexed puts less stress on joints and tendons. e, Cling grip on small hold. Extension of distal finger joints is more stressful and is more likely to cause injury than the open grip. f, Pocket grip: useful for small pockets only large enough to admit a single digit. Keeping other fingers curled helps get the most force out of the muscle-tendon system, but stresses the finger and may cause injury.

be useful on very small holds.

Holds are often used as cling holds from below, then as downpressure holds as you move above them. Downpressure holds may be used by themselves or in combination with other holds (fig. 9-8b), such as in counterforce with a lieback hold, or as part of a stemming move. With your arm extended and elbow locked, you can balance one-handed on a downpressure hold as you move the other hand to the next hold.

MANTEL

The mantel is a very specific use of the downpressure technique. It lets you use hand downpressure to permit your feet to get up onto the same hold as your hands when no useful handholds are available higher.

For the classic mantel (fig. 9-9), place both hands flat on a ledge at about chest height, palms down, with the fingers of each hand pointing toward the other hand. Then raise your body up onto stiffened arms. This will be easier if you can first walk your feet a ways up the rock, or if you can spring up from a foothold. Then lift one foot up onto the ledge and stand up.

This basic mantel, however, isn't always

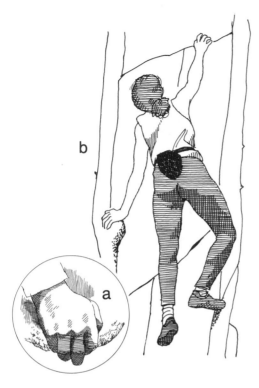

Fig. 9–8. Downpressure: a, using heel and palm of hand; b, used in combination with other holds.

Fig. 9–9. Mantel: the climber turns his hand with the fingers pointed down to make use of the natural shape of the ledge, then reaches up to use a face hold.

possible, because a ledge will often be higher or smaller or steeper than you might wish. If the ledge is narrow, you may be able to use the heel of your hand, with the fingers pointed down. If the ledge is over your head, you'll use it first as a cling hold, and then convert to a downpressure hold as you move upward. If the ledge isn't big enough for both hands, you'll mantel on just one arm while the other hand makes use of any available hold, or perhaps just balances against the rock (fig. 9-10). Don't forget to leave room for your foot.

Avoid using knees on a mantel because it may be difficult to get off your knees and back on your feet, especially if the rock above is steep or overhanging. Sometimes in mid-mantel you'll be able to reach up to a handhold to help as you begin standing up.

Fig. 9–10. Manteling with one hand while using a face hold with the other

COUNTERFORCE

Counterforce is the use of pressure in opposing directions to help keep you in place. For instance, with both hands in a vertical crack, you can create outward pressure by pulling in opposite directions on the sides of the crack—a pulling-apart action (fig. 9-11a). Or you can create inward pressure by pulling in on widely spaced holds—a pulling-together action—or by pressing in on both sides of a sharp ridge. You can also use the hands in counter-

Fig. 9–12. Undercling: converting from a pinch grip (a) to an undercling (b).

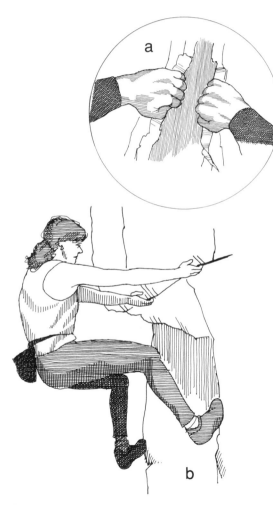

Fig. 9–11. Counterforce: a, outward pressure; b, hands in counterforce to feet.

force to the feet (fig. 9-11b). Counterforce plays a part in many of the climbing maneuvers described in this chapter.

UNDERCLING

In the undercling, the hands (palms up) push up beneath a lip of rock while the body leans out and the feet push against rock (fig. 9-12). The arms pull while the feet push, creating a counterforce. Try to keep your arms extended. Both hands can undercling at the same time, or one hand can undercling while the other uses a different type of hold.

An undercling hold may have multiple uses. For example, you can hold the bottom edge of a rock flake in a pinch grip from below, then convert to an undercling as you move up to the flake.

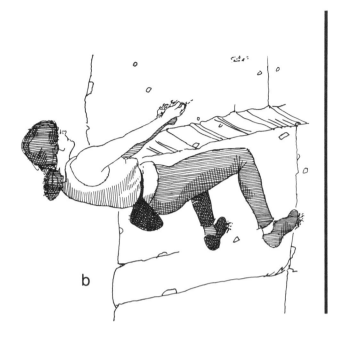

STEMMING

Stemming is a valuable counterforce technique that lets you support yourself between two spots on the rock that might be of little or no use alone. It often provides a method of climbing steep rock where no hold is apparent, simply by pressing in opposing directions with the feet or with a hand and a foot.

The classic use of stemming (also called bridging) is in climbing a rock chimney. It also comes into play in climbing dihedrals, where two walls meet in approximately a right-angled inside corner. One foot presses against one wall of the chimney or dihedral, while the other foot or an opposing hand pushes against the other wall (fig. 9-13a).

Stemming may also open an avenue of ascent on a steep face, where you can press one foot against a slight protrusion, while the other foot or a hand gives opposing pressure against another wrinkle in the rock (fig. 9-13b). When stemming between widely spaced holds on a steep face, be careful that your body doesn't rotate away from the

Fig. 9–13. Stemming: a, across a chimney; b, on a steep face.

a

b

INCORRECT

Fig. 9–14. The barn door effect: a, the climber is balanced over two footholds with the left hand on a hold up and to the side. When the right hand is removed from the hold, the climber can no longer hold herself into the rock, creating the "barn door" effect, b, with the climber swinging away from the rock.

CORRECT

Two methods of avoiding the barn door effect: c, the climber moves the right foot to the hold where the left was to keep her weight more centered under the secure left handhold; d, the climber flags the left foot behind the right. Both techniques allow the climber to release the right hand to reach up to a new hold.

c

d

rock the second you release a hand to reach for a new hold (fig. 9-14b). Several methods can be used to avoid the barn-door effect. Sometimes a strong stem against the foot below the hand being moved is effective. Other times centering your weight over the foot below the stationary hand is more helpful (fig. 9-14c). One method is to try rearranging the body position using a counter-balance technique such as flagging one leg behind the other (fig. 9-14d).

LIEBACK

The classic lieback technique, another form of counterforce, uses hands pulling and feet pushing in opposition as the climber moves upward in shuffling movements (fig. 9-15a). It's used to climb a crack in a corner, or a crack with one edge offset beyond the other, or along the edge of a flake.

Grasp one edge of the crack with both hands and lean back and to the side on straightened arms. Push your feet against the opposite wall of the crack. Then get a move on. It's a strenuous technique, and it's best to move as quickly and efficiently as possible.

Keep arms extended to minimize stress on tensed muscles. The right relationship of hands and feet will vary, but it becomes easier to determine with practice. In general, keep your feet high enough to maintain friction on the rock, unless a foothold is available. But the higher you bring your feet, the more strenuous the lieback becomes.

The lieback has variations. You can lieback on a single handhold in combination with other holds, or use one hand and foot in a lieback while utilizing face holds for the opposite hand and foot (fig. 9-15b).

Fig. 9–15. Lieback: a, a classic lieback; b, combining a lieback (right hand and foot) with face holds (left hand and foot).

JAMMING

The technique of jamming consists of wedging parts of the body, such as hands or feet, securely enough into a crack to bear weight. Jamming isn't as instinctive or natural-feeling as many other climbing techniques, but it works. It's the principal technique for working your way up the cracks that constitute a big part of rock climbing.

The basic procedure is to insert part of a hand or foot, usually just above a narrower part of the crack. Jams are usually locked by twisting (torquing) so the hand or foot is wedged against both sides of the crack.

Jamming can be used by itself, with both feet and hands utilizing jams, or in combination with other types of holds. As you move up on a jam handhold, you can maintain the jammed position but use it almost like a downpressure hold.

Cracks vary a great deal in size and configuration. The descriptions of jams that follow are just some basic techniques, with a lot of room remaining for creativity and ingenuity.

Finger jams

Finger jams make it possible to climb some of the narrowest cracks, where you may only be able to insert one or more fingers, or perhaps just the finger tips. Finger jams are commonly done with the thumbs down. Slip fingers into the crack and twist the hand to lock the fingers in place (fig. 9-16a). You get added strength by stacking fingers and also by pressing the thumb against the index finger in a ring jam (fig. 9-16b).

In slightly wider cracks, you can try a thumb lock. Place the up-pointing thumb in the crack, the

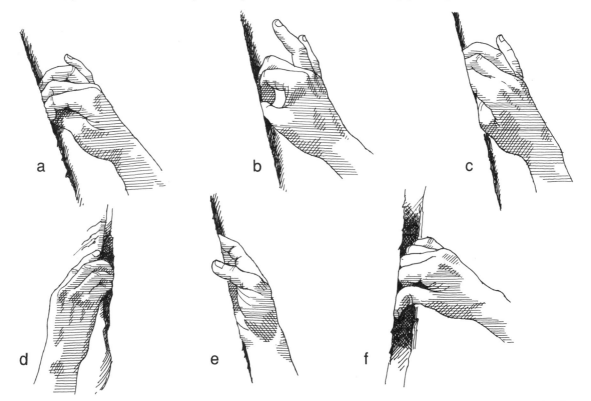

Fig. 9–16. Finger jams: a, thumb-down jam; b, ring jam; c, thumb lock; d, pinkie jam; e, jamming heel of hand as well as finger; f, using counterpressure with thumb.

pad against one side of the crack and the knuckle against the other. Slide the tip of the index finger tightly down over the first joint of the thumb to create the lock (fig. 9-16c).

Here are two other variations on the finger jam, done with the thumbs up (fig. 9-16d,e). You can put the little finger in a crack and stack the other fingers on top (finger tips down, nails up) for a "pinkie jam." In slightly larger cracks, you may be able to wedge the heel of the hand and the smaller fingers into a crack that isn't quite wide enough for a full hand jam. The weight here is borne by the heel of the hand.

For another variation, you can use counterpressure of thumb pushing against one side of the crack, fingers pushing against the other (fig. 9-16f).

Hand jams

With a wider crack, you'll gain the luxury of inserting your entire hand, cupping it as needed to provide adequate expansion against the walls of the crack (fig. 9-17a). To increase pressure against the walls, you'll sometimes tuck your thumb across the palm, especially in wider cracks (fig. 9-17b).

You can often improve the hold by bending your wrist so the hand points into the crack rather than straight up and down.

The hand jam is done either thumbs up or thumbs down. Thumbs up often is easiest and most comfortable for a vertical crack, and it works especially well when the hand is relatively low. The thumbs-up configuration is most secure when the body leans to the same side as the hand that is jammed.

The thumbs-down technique may allow a more secure reach to a jam high above your head, because the hand can be twisted for better adhesion, and you can lean in any direction off this jam (fig. 9-17c). Climbers use a combination of thumbs up and thumbs down, especially in diagonal cracks where it's often useful to jam the upper hand thumb down and the lower hand thumb up (fig. 9-17d).

With both finger and hand jams, keep alert to the effect of your elbow and body position on the security of the hold. As you move up, you may have to rotate your shoulder or trunk to keep sufficient torque and downward pressure to maintain the jam. Direction of force should be pulling

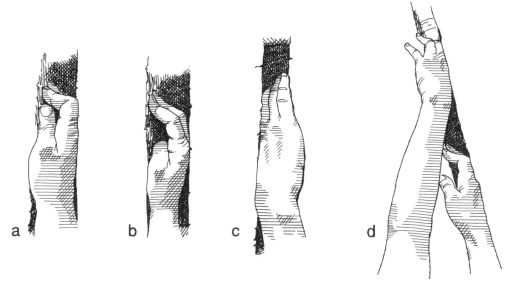

Fig. 9–17. Hand jams: a, thumb-up jam; b, with thumb tucked across palm; c, thumb-down jam; d, combining thumb-down and thumb-up jams in a diagonal crack.

down, and not out of the crack.

In dealing with hand jams, you'll run across variants at both ends of the size scale: thinner cracks that won't admit the entire hand but are larger than finger cracks, and wider cracks that aren't quite large enough for a fist jam but require extra hand-twisting to create enough expansion for a secure jam. The size of your hand is a major factor in determining the appropriate technique and the degree of difficulty for any particular crack.

Fist jams

In a crack that's too wide for a hand jam, you can insert your fist (fig. 9-18). The thumb may be inside or outside the fist, depending on which provides the best fit. Your palm may face the back of the crack, the front, or either side. Flexing the muscles in the fist can expand the fist slightly to help fit the crack. Fist jams are often painful, but

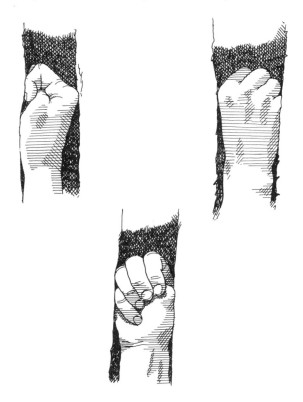

Fig. 9–18. Fist jam: three different positions

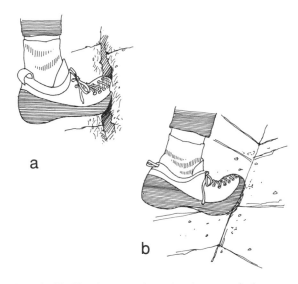

Fig. 9–19. Toe jams: a, jamming in a crack; b, smearing in a corner.

can be very useful. For the most secure hold, try to find a constriction in the crack that you can jam your fist above.

Toe jams

You can wedge your toe into a crack by turning your foot sideways—usually with the inside ankle up—and inserting the toe in the crack, then twisting the foot to jam it (fig. 9-19a). You can also wedge the toe into a steep inside corner with a smearing technique, keeping the heel lower than the toe and putting pressure down and in to keep the toe in place (fig. 9-19b).

Foot jams

If the crack is wide enough, jam more of the toe or even the entire foot into the crack. As with the toe jam, insert the foot sideways with the sole facing the side of the crack, then twist to jam (fig. 9-20a). Avoid twisting the foot so securely that it gets stuck, leaving you open to serious injury in case of a fall.

In even wider cracks, you can jam the foot diagonally or heel-to-toe (fig. 9-20b).

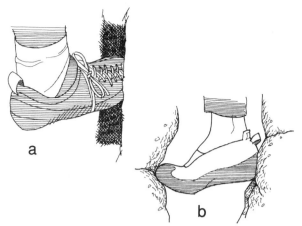

Fig. 9–20. Foot jams: a, foot jam in a crack; b, heel and toe jam.

Body jams

Climbers have figured out ways to jam arms, shoulders, hips, knees, and just about anything else into cracks that are too large for fist jams but too small to accommodate the entire body. These are the awkward off-width cracks, so called because they aren't the right width for any of the more standard jamming techniques. Details of off-width climbing are outlined later in this chapter.

COUNTERBALANCE

Counterbalance is not a specific type of move, but rather a principle that can be used in all kinds of climbing. It's the principle of distributing your body weight in a way that maintains your balance.

This means selecting holds that do the best job of keeping your body in balance. But it also sometimes means putting a hand or foot in a particular location, even if no hold is available, in order to provide counterbalance to the rest of the body. The hips and shoulders also come into play as you move them to provide counterbalance (fig. 9-21).

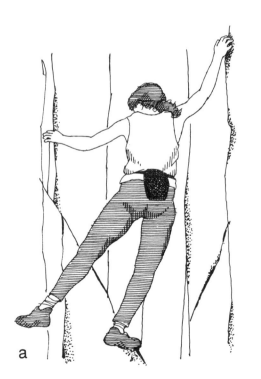

Fig. 9–21. Two examples of counterbalance: a, the left foot is extended to the side to provide counterbalance; b, the left foot is flagged behind the right for counterbalance.

LONG REACHES

What do you do when the next available handhold is a long reach away—or even out of reach?

The climber has several techniques available.

First, make the most of available holds, by using one or more of these tips: stand up on your toes; pull your body into the rock to achieve maximum extension of the body; use a foot for counterbalance to help in standing up completely on the other foot; move your foot higher on a sloped hold; move your foot more to the side that the next handhold is on. Additional tips: move your foot to the edge of a foothold for a traversing move; lean your body and hips out or to the side to allow a longer sideways reach; use a handhold for downpressure to allow maximum upward reach with the opposite hand. Sometimes a longer reach is possible by standing on the outside edge of your boot, which tends to turn your body somewhat sideways to the rock. And remember that the longest reach is possible with the hand that is opposite of the foot you're standing on.

Another option is to consider quick intermediate moves, using holds that are marginal but will be used just long enough to scamper up to the next good hold.

The last resort may be a dynamic move that could involve a lunge or simply a quick move before you lose your balance or grip. The time to grab the next higher handhold while making a dynamic move is at the "dead point"—at the apex of your arc of movement when the body is weightless for a fraction of a second before it begins to fall. Movement is most efficient at that point.

There's a built-in danger if a dynamic move fails: you're no longer in complete control and a fall is likely. Make a dynamic move only after calculating and accepting the consequences of failure. You should know beforehand that the protection is secure and that a fall onto the protection won't result in hitting a ledge or the ground or otherwise risking injury. Keep in mind that dynamic moves are for accomplished climbers, not for desperate novices.

EXCHANGING PLACEMENTS ON A SMALL HOLD

Sometimes you need to move one foot onto a small hold already occupied by the other foot, or one hand onto a hold being used by the other hand. Either move can be made several different ways.

To exchange a foot placement, you can make an intermediate move, using a poorer, even marginal hold to get the one foot off the good hold long enough for the other one to take it over. And there's the hop, in which you hop off the hold as you replace one foot with the other.

You can also try sharing the hold by matching feet, moving one foot to the very edge of the hold to make enough room for the other. Another technique is the crossover, in which you cross one foot in back of the other to occupy the far side of the hold (fig. 9-22).

Fig. 9–22. Foot crossing to change feet on a small hold

To trade hands, you can make an intermediate move, much as you might in exchanging feet. You have the option to match hands, placing both hands on the same hold. If space is limited, you can also try picking up the fingers of one hand, one finger at a time, and replacing them with the fingers of the other hand. The crossover technique also is occasionally useful.

PUTTING IT ALL TOGETHER

Once you've learned the basic climbing techniques, you are ready to begin combining them in ways that make different types of climbs possible.

You'll soon discover the value of planning before you start up a new pitch. Always plan several moves ahead to help you conserve energy and stay on route. Identify and examine difficult sections before you get to them, make a plan, then move through them quickly. Look ahead for good rest spots.

Many climbs require a variety of techniques, rather than pure jamming, or pure stemming, or pure anything. You'll often use one technique with one hand, or one side of the body, and another technique with the other. You can be jamming with one side of the body as you use face holds with the other. A single pitch may require different techniques in sequence: a jam followed by a lieback, then face climbing followed by a mantel onto what had been a cling hold.

Basic techniques are combined in various ways for climbing faces, slabs, cracks, dihedrals, chimneys, and overhangs.

FACE CLIMBING

In some ways, face climbing is the most natural type of climbing (fig. 9-23). You move up a series of handholds and footholds, somewhat like climbing a ladder.

Remember that a single hold may be used in a variety of ways, by feet and hands. What initially appears to be a good cling hold may allow a lieback, a mantel, or a stemming move. Be creative.

SLAB CLIMBING

Also referred to as friction climbing, slab climbing (fig. 9-24) requires liberal use of smearing moves. Balance and footwork are the keys to success, and smearing with the feet is the primary technique.

Remember to flex the ankle (lowering the heel) and keep weight directly over the ball of the foot for maximum friction between rock and sole. Avoid leaning into the slope with your body, which pushes your feet away from the rock. Instead, keep weight over the feet, bending at the waist to allow your hands to touch the rock, and pushing hips and buttocks away.

Fig. 9–23. Face climbing

Fig. 9–24. Slab climbing

Take short steps to maintain balance with weight over the feet. Look for the small edges, rough spots, or changes in angle that provide the best foot placements. On the toughest slabs, footholds may be so subtle you'll have to feel with your hand or foot to find the roughest surface.

Don't forget that other techniques can be useful on slabs. Face holds may be intermittently available, as well as cracks. You can use downpressure on small edges or irregularities, with the finger tips, thumb, or heel of your hand. A lieback with one hand might be possible using tiny edges. Look for an opportunity for stemming, which could mean a chance to rest.

CLIMBING CRACKS AND DIHEDRALS

Cracks may be climbed with a pure jamming technique or by a combination of techniques. A very potent combination is to jam with one side of the body and use face holds with the other (fig. 9-25).

Cracks also may be climbed with a pure lieback technique or by liebacking with one arm in combination with face holds for the other hand (fig. 9-26). This may result in a kind of stemming action.

Dihedrals (inside corners) may be climbed by pure stemming. You can also use various combinations, such as hands jammed in a crack splitting the dihedral combined with feet stemming on opposite sides of the dihedral (fig. 9-27). You may even use

Fig. 9–25. Combining jamming with face climbing

classic chimney technique, described later in this chapter.

Useful edges or other holds may be found hidden within cracks—on the sides or even at the back of wide cracks. Remember that horizontal cracks can also be used as cling holds.

Off-width cracks

Cracks that are too wide for standard jamming, but too narrow to admit the entire body for chimneying, call for specialized off-width technique. You stand sideways to the crack, and one full side of your body goes into the off-width.

When confronted by an off-width, first decide which side of your body to put inside the crack.

Fig. 9–27. Climbing a dihedral using stemming and jamming

This depends on several things, such as holds in the crack or on the face, and the lean, flare, and offset of the crack.

After you've settled on which side to use, the inside leg goes inside the crack and forms a leg bar, usually with counterpressure between foot and knee or foot and hip. This foot is often placed in a heel-toe jam.

The outside foot also is inside the crack in a heel-toe jam. Try to keep the heel above the toe (for better friction) and turned into the crack (to allow the knee to turn out).

Fig. 9–26. Liebacking combined with face holds

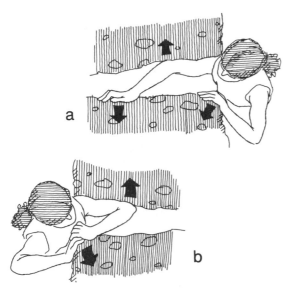

Fig. 9–28. Off-width technique: a, arm bar; b, arm lock.

As for the arms, a primary body-jam technique is the arm bar (fig. 9-28a). With the body sideways to the crack, insert the arm fully into the crack, with the elbow and the back of the upper arm on one side of the crack giving counterpressure to the heel of the hand on the other side. Get the shoulder in as far as possible, and have the arm lock extend diagonally down from the shoulder.

In a variation, the arm lock, fold the arm back at the elbow and press the palm against the opposite side in counterforce to the shoulder (fig. 9-28b).

The outside arm is used to give downpressure to help hold you in the crack, or is brought across the front of the chest and pushed against the opposite side of the crack, elbow out.

You're now wedged securely in the crack. To climb, move the outside leg upward to establish a higher heel-toe jam. When this jam is set, stand up on it. Then re-establish the inside leg bar and arm bar (or arm lock), and reposition the outside arm. This again wedges the body in the crack. You're now ready to move the outside leg upward again to establish a yet higher heel-toe jam. Continue repeating this procedure (fig. 9-29).

You may use your outside foot occasionally on face holds, but watch out for the tendency for these outside footholds to pull you out of the crack.

CHIMNEY TECHNIQUE

A chimney is any crack big enough to climb inside, ranging in size from those that will barely admit the body (squeeze chimneys) to those the climber's body can barely span.

The basic principle is to span the chimney somehow with the body, using counterforce to keep from falling. Depending on the width of the crack, you will either face one side of the chimney, or face directly into or out of the chimney. The best body position and technique to use depends on the situation and on the size of the climber. Which direction you face may depend on what holds are available outide the chimney and on how you plan to climb out of it.

Fig. 9–29. Climbing an off-width crack

In squeeze chimneys, wedge your body in whatever way works best and squirm upward. Look for handholds on the outside edge or inside the chimney. Arm bars and arm locks may be useful. It's helpful, sometimes, to press the left foot and knee, for example, against opposite sides of the chimney. You might try stacking your feet in a T configuration, with one foot placed parallel to one side of the rock, while the other is placed perpendicular to it, jammed between the first foot and the opposite wall. Squeeze chimneys can be very strenuous, and the best approach here may be to look for an alternative way to climb that section.

In a crack that's somewhat wider than a squeeze chimney, you begin to have some room to maneuver (fig. 9-30a). You can then press your back and feet against one side of the chimney as your knees and hands push against the other side. You can move upward by squirming your way. Or try a sequence of wedging the upper body while raising the feet and knees, then wedging them and raising the upper body.

A wide chimney calls for stemming technique, with the climber facing directly into or out of the chimney (fig. 9-30b). Counterforce is between the right hand and foot on one side and the left hand and foot on the other. Press down as well as against the sides, especially if there are holds on the sides of the chimney. Ascend by alternately moving arms and legs, or by moving each leg, then each arm.

In a standard moderate-width chimney, perhaps 3 feet wide, you'll again face one wall of the chimney, your back to the other. For the upper body, your hands may push against one wall in counterforce to your back pressed against the other. Or the

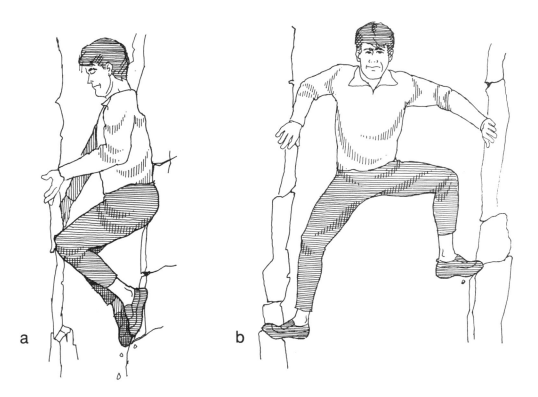

Fig. 9–30. Chimney techniques: a, in a narrow chimney; b, in a wide chimney.

counterforce may be between hands on opposing walls. For the lower body, your feet may push against one wall in counterforce to your buttocks against the other. Or the counterforce may be between your two feet.

To climb this moderate-width chimney, use the following sequence (fig. 9-31): Start with your back toward one wall. Press one foot against each wall and one hand against each wall. Move upward by straightening your legs and then re-establishing hand positions. Immediately bring your back leg across to the same side as the forward leg. Then swing the forward leg across to the back position. You're now again in position to move upward by straightening your legs.

Beware of getting too far inside a chimney. Although psychologically it may feel more secure, you can get lodged deep inside and find it difficult to move back out. You have a better chance of finding useful hand- and footholds if you stay near the outside of the chimney.

Climbing deep inside the chimney also can make it harder to exit at the top. The transition from the top of the chimney to other types of climbing is often challenging and may require extra thought and creativity.

Chimney technique may be useful in places that don't look like classic chimneys. It can be used to climb dihedrals (fig. 9-32), or short wide sections of otherwise narrower cracks.

NEGOTIATING OVERHANGS AND ROOFS

Depending on the situation, overhangs and roofs require a variety of techniques such as manteling, face climbing, or crack climbing.

There are two important points to remember: maintain balance and conserve strength.

Fig. 9–31. Chimney techniques in a moderate-width chimney

To maintain balance, look for good footholds and make the most of them. This often means keeping feet high and hips low to help press weight against footholds (fig. 9-33). In some situations, it means pressing your hips into the rock, with back arched, to keep weight over the feet while poised under an overhang. While balanced over your feet beneath the overhang, locate the handholds you will use to move up and over the bulge. A cling hold, a jam, a lieback, or a combination of these may be the key.

Fig. 9–32. Chimney techniques in a dihedral

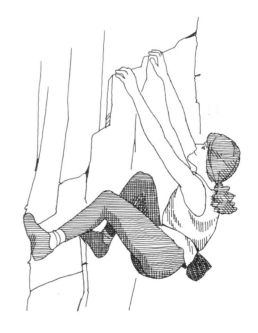

To conserve strength, weight your feet as much as possible. Keep arms straight while raising the feet. When the feet are as high as possible, lift the body with your legs rather than pulling up on your arms. Avoid hanging on bent arms, as this will quickly exhaust arm strength. Move quickly through crux sections of the pitch to minimize the time spent in strenuous positions (fig. 9-34).

Occasionally you may need to raise up on your feet while making a dynamic reach (a lunge) to a handhold. Another trick is to throw one foot up

Fig. 9–33. Climbing an overhanging route

Fig. 9–34. Climbing over a roof: a, the climber is poised under the roof with hips close to the rock; b, she leans out on an outstretched arm to locate a hold above the roof; c, she has both hands above the roof and feet are high, pushing against the rock; d, finally, she brings one foot up and begins to pull over the roof.

onto a ledge, perhaps hooking the heel on it while pushing with your other foot and pulling with your arms to swing up onto the top foot.

TRAVERSING

Traversing—going sideways across a section of rock instead of up or down—again calls for a catalog of climbing techniques (fig. 9-35). The main ones are side clings, liebacks, and stemming. And counterbalance is important when making a long sideways reach.

The climber usually faces into the rock, toes pointed away from each other. Hands and feet are commonly shuffled sideways, although exchanging one hand for the other, or one foot for the other, on a single hold can be very useful. You may occasionally cross one foot behind the other to reach the next hold, or cross one hand over the other.

On a steep pitch it's very tiring to hold yourself into the rock on bent arms. When possible, lean out from the rock on straight arms. This conserves arm strength, and it gives a better view of where you're going.

A specialized type of traverse is the hand traverse, used when footholds are marginal or nonexistent (fig. 9-36). The hands grip a series of holds or shuffle along an edge, while the feet provide a counterforce by pushing against the rock, as in a lieback or undercling. Keep the feet high and the center of gravity low so the feet are pushed into the rock. And once again, keep the arms straight to

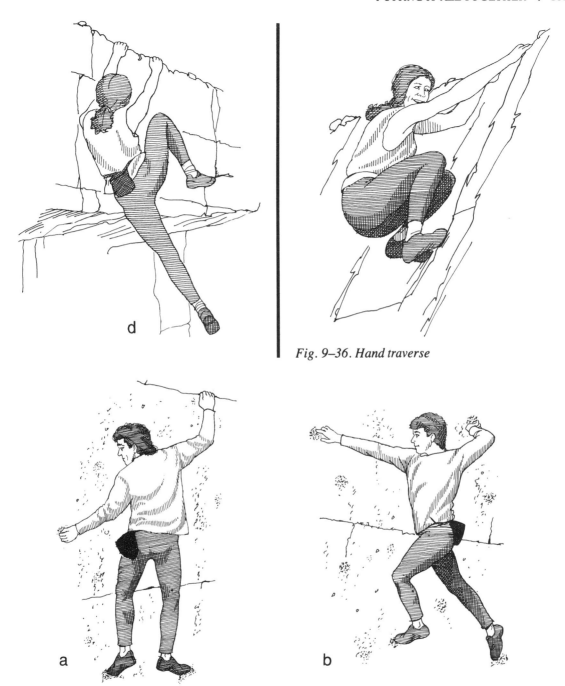

d

Fig. 9–36. Hand traverse

a

b

Fig. 9–35. Traversing a steep face: a, lieback with one hand, leaning out to reach another hold with the other hand; b, climber twists body to take long sideways reach—an advanced technique.

conserve arm strength and to let the legs do as much of the work as possible.

EXITING ONTO LEDGES

As you approach a ledge, avoid the temptation to reach forward and pull yourself onto it. This may throw you off balance and also make it impossible to keep an eye on your footholds (fig. 9-37a).

Instead, continue to walk your feet up the rock, and then use downpressure with the hands near the edge of the ledge. You might do a classic mantel. Be careful not to exit onto the ledge on your knees and then find yourself beneath an overhang, unable to stand (fig. 9-37b).

DOWNCLIMBING

While you're learning lots of ways to climb upward, also allow some time to learn the valuable technique of downclimbing (fig. 9-38). Downclimbing at times is faster, safer, or easier than rappelling, such as when rappel anchors aren't

readily available. Downclimbing provides a way to retreat when you find yourself off route or on a pitch where the rock above is more difficult than you care to attempt.

Downclimbing has its special difficulties, however, which helps explain why some climbers resist learning the skill. Holds are harder to see than when you're climbing upward—and holds on the steepest, most difficult sections are the most difficult to see, especially if the rock is undercut below a bulge or small roof. It's hard to test holds without committing to them, an unpleasant fact if you doubt the soundness of the rock. And unless you climbed up the same way, the terrain below is unknown, and you may not be able to anticipate the consequences of a fall.

For downclimbing on low-angle rock, face outward for the best visibility. Keep hands low and use downpressure holds whenever possible. Going down friction slabs, keep weight over your feet to maximize friction. It may help to keep your center

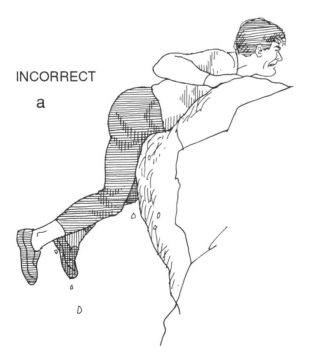

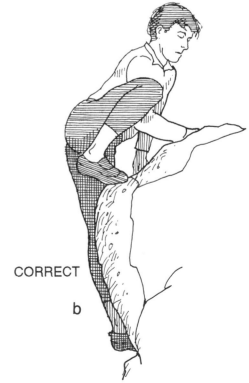

Fig. 9–37. Exiting onto a ledge: a, incorrect; b, correct.

Fig. 9–38. Downclimbing: a, facing out; b, facing sideways; c, facing in.

of gravity low, with knees well bent.

As the rock steepens, turn sideways, leaning away from the rock for better visibility. If the cliff gets even steeper, face into the rock. Keep hands low, and lean away from the rock to look for holds below.

SPECIAL DEMANDS OF ALPINE ROCK CLIMBING

GENERAL CONSIDERATIONS

When you take the rock-climbing skills you've learned during pleasant days on small nearby crags out into the mountains proper, some of the conditions of the game change. There are new things to keep in mind when it comes to alpine climbing which involves a mix of hiking, scrambling, routefinding, snow and ice climbing, and rock climbing.

First of all, you'll probably be climbing with a pack, a significant impediment to speed and performance. With a pack, it can be a challenge to climb rock several levels easier than what you lead comfortably on the crags. For a real test, try climbing a chimney or an off-width crack. Sometimes it's necessary to haul the pack up separately with a rope, and this again slows the climb.

Decisions about how much gear to take become extremely important as each extra pound cuts into speed and performance and, ironically, adds to the possibility that the extra gear may be needed to survive an unplanned bivouac or accident.

On the crags, you use light, flexible shoes specially designed for rock climbing. But on alpine climbs, heavy mountaineering boots are the usual footwear for approaches, for snow travel, and often for much or all of the climbing. As with carrying a pack, climbing in mountaineering boots adds to the challenge of otherwise moderate rock. If you decide to change to rock shoes for the more technical portions of a climb, you're stuck with packing the mountaineering boots. If you're wearing boots and crampons for hard snow or ice and encounter a short section of rock, you may have to ascend the rock in crampons, adding yet another dimension to the climb.

Use special care in testing holds on alpine climbs, where loose rocks may not have been discovered and discarded by previous climbers the way they are at popular crags. Unsound rock is common on alpine climbs because of the many different types and the constant weathering it receives. You may want to place protection even on rock that appears easy to climb. However, occasionally on low-angle loose rock, using the rope may be more hazardous than climbing unroped, because the rope can dislodge rocks onto climbers below.

Unpredictable weather, arduous approaches, high altitude, and routefinding problems all add to the commitment and challenge of alpine rock climbing.

SPEED AND SAFETY

A speedy ascent is sometimes an important part of safety on an alpine climb. On long routes, speed minimizes the risk of being caught by darkness. It provides extra time to deal with equipment breakdown, routefinding problems, injury, or illness. It lessens the length of exposure to rockfall, storms, or lightning.

Speed doesn't mean careless rushing. It means developing efficiency in such activities as testing holds, belaying, exchanging gear, and rope management. It means looking ahead at the route, formulating a plan, and moving smoothly ahead without thrashing over routefinding dilemmas.

As a team, climbing efficiently requires planning and practice, as well as development of a systematic approach to all basic activities. Moving efficiently over the rock saves a lot of time, promotes safety, and conserves energy for each member of a climbing team.

A light pack helps in completing a route quickly. Safety lies in having enough gear to do the climb and survive unexpected situations—not in carrying every piece of gear and shelter that might possibly come in handy.

The size of the climbing party and of the rope teams has an important bearing on speed. The more rope teams there are, the slower the party generally will move. However, rope teams of two are considerably more efficient than teams of three on an alpine route. Other things being equal, two rope teams of two can move much more quickly than a single team of three.

TRAINING FOR ROCK CLIMBING

Rock climbers need a fitness program tailored to their needs. Overall fitness is helpful, but general conditioning programs don't usually promote the forearm and finger strength needed by climbers.

TRAINING GOALS AND REGIMENS

A training program should be designed to develop and maintain strength, endurance, balance, and flexibility. Added benefits will be greater confidence and fluidity on the rock.

The energy required for muscular contraction is derived from three energy-producing systems (each of which produces adenosine triphosphate [ATP], the final common source of chemical energy for muscle).

The primary source of energy for sustained or repeated muscular contraction requires oxygen and is referred to as the aerobic system.

The other two systems do not utilize oxygen and are referred to as anaerobic. They are important when the demand for energy temporarily exceeds the capacity of the aerobic system, or during sudden muscular contractions demanding energy before the aerobic system can supply it.

Training should include use of all three of these energy-producing systems.

Be careful you don't hurt yourself while you

train. Common causes of injury are overtraining, trying to increase strength too quickly, and failing to pay attention to early signs of overuse or acute injury, especially to tendons of the elbows and of the fingers.

Strength

Strength refers to the maximum force that can be exerted against a resistance. A practical example might be the heaviest weight you could lift a single time.

Developing strength is useful for individual moves or short sequences when maximum strength is required for a brief time. Maximum muscular effort requires use of the anaerobic energy systems. These can be trained using routines that alternate periods of intense muscular work, from seconds to less than 2 minutes, with periods of rest.

The best approach is progressive muscular overload exercises. This includes weight training with heavy loads and few repetitions, or other short-duration, near-maximal efforts, such as hanging from small holds for brief periods. A description of training regimens is beyond the scope of this chapter, but climbers can consult books and magazine articles devoted to strength training.

Endurance

Endurance is the ability to sustain muscular effort over time. Although crux sections of a pitch may require considerable absolute strength, climbing a full pitch, or more particularly a multipitch route, requires muscular endurance.

The primary energy system involved is aerobic, and the best training approach is lower-resistance, higher-repetition exercises than the ones used for strength training. You can adapt this approach to weight training, finger-board routines, or sustained bouldering.

Aerobic activities—such as jogging, bicycling, swimming, or rowing—help develop cardiovascular fitness, which aids in any sustained rock climbing effort. This is particularly true for alpine climbs, where the approach may be strenuous and where rapid progress up a long route can be essential.

Balance

Perhaps the best way to improve your balance is simply to climb. Try climbing exercises, such as moving up a slab without the use of hands, or working on difficult boulder problems that require balance. You can also devise other exercises, such as walking across a tightly stretched rope suspended above the ground. Many dancers take readily to climbing; dance lessons might improve both balance and flexibility.

Flexibility

Flexibility is essential for all rock climbing beyond an elementary level. Many books are available that describe stretching exercises to improve flexibility. They should be done regularly, like any training exercise. Take care to avoid injury.

Weight loss

You can increase your relative strength and endurance by losing excess weight, thereby decreasing the number of extra pounds you have to lift with your arms and legs. A lower body weight may enhance balance and flexibility as well.

USING AVAILABLE RESOURCES

Climbers can take advantage of natural resources to train specifically for the strength, endurance, and technique required in climbing.

Look for opportunities to climb on boulders at local crags or at developed climbing areas. Bouldering lets you practice close to the ground without needing a belay. Work on low-level traverses and on short but difficult problems.

Buildering is the same idea as bouldering, but using the sides of buildings instead of the sides of rocks. Beware of conflicts with authority.

Top-roped climbing is another training tool. In top roping, you are belayed so that any fall will result in only a short drop—just the distance the rope stretches when it takes your weight. Because you're safe, you can practice techniques and push the limits of your ability, increasing strength and confidence. You can try moves you wouldn't be willing to go for if you were leading a climb, belayed only from below and risking a leader fall.

SPECIALIZED EQUIPMENT

Climbers now have access to a growing catalog of manufactured climbing aids. They let you train whenever you want and tailor a fitness program to your own needs.

Artificial climbing walls are appearing both indoors and out, where you can boulder in the absence of readily available natural areas. The walls help develop both strength and technique, and they allow creation of specific problems to work on. These problems can even simulate a difficult sequence on an established natural route. Of course, indoor walls are especially welcome during bad weather.

Manufactured finger boards (fig. 9-39) have a selection of hand and finger holds to hang from or pull up on. Using a finger board improves upper

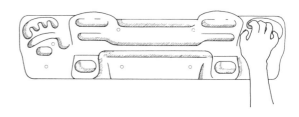

Fig. 9–39. Finger board

body strength and also lets you concentrate on developing the finger strength needed to take advantage of small holds.

Other training tools have been developed and more are on the way. There are rope ladders and peg boards for improving upper body strength. There also are artificial cracks designed to improve strength and endurance with hands in specific configurations.

STYLE AND ETHICS

Climbing generates endless debate over which styles are fair and which are less than sporting, over which practices are harmful, and which are "none of your damn business." The terms "style" and "ethics" are sometimes used interchangably by climbers, but style usually refers to a person's mode of climbing, which is principally a personal decision. Ethics usually refers to issues where preservation of the rock itself, and thus the experience of other climbers, is at stake.

Climbers soon discover that getting to the end of the pitch or the top of the peak isn't the only goal—that it's also getting there in a way that feels right, that respects the rock, and that tests a person's skill and resolve as a climber. These are questions of style and ethics.

DIVERSITY OF STYLES

Styles change and attitudes evolve, but the core of the debate on climbing styles is about how to maintain the challenge of climber against rock and

how to play the game in a way that fairly tests the climber.

Climbers adhering to traditional style prefer to climb each route strictly from the ground up, with no help from such aids as top ropes or preplaced protection. New routes are explored and protected only on the lead. After a fall, the climber returns to the start of the climb or at least to a no-hands resting place.

Climbers following the European-influenced sport-climbing style are more likely to find other techniques acceptable as well. This can include inspecting the route on rappel before trying to lead it from below. It can also mean cleaning the route and perhaps placing protection on rappel. Routes may be climbed with multiple falls, by resting on the rope while checking out the next move ("hang-dogging"), or by rehearsing moves with the help of a top rope.

These sport-climbing techniques have made it possible to climb harder and harder routes. A particular climbing area may lend itself more to one style than another because of the type of rock, the difficulty of the routes, or the conventional style of the local climbers. In the world of climbing, there's room for a diversity of styles, and most climbers will experience a variety of them.

No matter what the style, a climber will work to eventually climb the route by putting no weight on the rope or on any piece of protection. The goal is to "redpoint" the route; that is, to eventually lead a complete no-falls ascent. Better yet is to "flash" the route, leading it all the way with no falls on the very first try. Best of all is to flash it "on sight"; that is, without prior inspection or knowledge.

ETHICS AND THE ROCK

The subject of ethics has to do with respecting the rock and every person's chance to use it. Unlike climbing style, ethics involves personal decisions that do affect the experience and the enjoyment of others. This includes the sticky question of the manner in which bolts are placed on a route. Are bolts placed on rappel different—less "ethical"—than bolts placed on the lead? Traditional climbers may argue that bolts placed while on rappel rob others of the chance to try the route from the ground up. But other climbers may say that placing the bolts gives a chance at a route that otherwise would be unclimbable.

Each area has its own tradition of what styles and ethics are acceptable, and visiting climbers should observe the local standards. It's not hard to find out what they are. The guidebook will say, the locals can tell you, and you can always just look around at what the other climbers are doing.

This book won't try to resolve issues of style and ethics. But there is general agreement on a couple of principles.

First of all, preservation of the rock is paramount. Chipping the rock to create new holds is almost universally condemned. And while bolt-protected routes are common in many areas, bolting should not be indiscriminate. In the mountains or other wilderness areas, away from concentrated centers of rock climbing, it's particularly important to preserve the environment for those who follow.

If possible, stick to clean climbing, using only removable chocks for protection.

Secondly, it's almost never justified to add a bolt to an existing route. If you feel you can't safely climb the route as it is, don't try it. Exceptions may occur when a consensus of local climbers, usually including the person who first climbed the route, agree that another bolt should be placed to promote safety and enjoyment. There's rarely any objection if you replace an old bolt with a newer, stronger one or add a bolt at an established belay or rappel point.

COURTESY

Keep other climbers in mind when you're out climbing. If your party is moving up a multipitch route much slower than the people behind you, let them pass at a safe spot, such as a belay ledge.

Beware of tackling climbs that are beyond your abilities. You may prevent more capable climbers from enjoying the route. And if your inexperience gets you in trouble, you may end up dragging the other climbers into your rescue.

CLIMBING ACCESS

Access to many climbing areas is threatened and two issues are usually at stake. The people who own or manage the land are worried about liability for accidents and are concerned that climbers are defiling the environment.

As climbers, we can help by taking responsibility for our own actions. It's up to us to put in dependable anchors and otherwise promote safety—and to provide rescue services when they're needed, rather than expecting others to do it for us.

It's also up to us to leave areas in as natural a state as possible. Chalk, rappel runners, fixed protection, and litter can be eyesores. We can help by establishing rappel anchors that don't require leaving slings, using colored chalk that blends in with the rock, keeping bolt placements to a minimum, and removing all litter. These efforts can promote public acceptance of the sport and help maintain access to climbing areas.

· 10 ·

LEADING AND PLACING PROTECTION

Climbers who have learned the basic techniques of rock climbing and who know how to belay and rappel are ready to take up the study of leading and of placing protection.

Leading is the skill of climbing first up a pitch, utilizing a belayer, rope, and intermediate protection for added safety. To many climbers, leading is one of the most satisfying activities in all of climbing. As leader, you're not just following; you've taken on the challenge and responsibility of determining the direction of the climb.

Placing protection is the skill of establishing points of protection along the route by using natural features such as trees and rock horns or by lodging safety devices in the rock. It's the technique that makes safe leading possible. The leader clips the rope through each piece of protection, while the belayer at the bottom of the pitch waits in position to hold the leader with the rope after any fall.

The skills of belaying, leading, and placing protection are combined in a two-person team for safe rock climbing. One climber, belayed by the second, leads up a pitch, placing protection along the way, and establishes a belay station at the top. The leader belays the second climber up. The leader then starts the next pitch, or alternates the lead (swings leads) with the second. The process is repeated until the end of the climb.

It's easy to picture how placing protection can save your life by limiting the severity of a fall.

Unless there's an obstruction to stop the fall, you as the lead climber will fall just a bit more than twice the distance between you and your belayer. If you are climbing 20 feet above your belayer and have placed no protection, you could fall 40 feet: 20 feet back down to the level of the belayer, and another 20 feet to straighten the rope out again—plus a bit more due to rope stretch (fig. 10-1b). But add an intermediate point of protection, and the length of the fall is dramatically reduced. The fall now will be shortened to just twice the length of the rope between you and the last point of protection (fig. 10-1a).

The leader accepts more risk than the second, who has the luxury of a belay from above. The second doesn't have to place protection, and doesn't have to worry about dropping more than a short distance before the belayer stops a fall. The leader, on the other hand, has to place protection at intervals along the route and has to face the possibility of a longer fall.

Unless the leader falls, a piece of protection usually gets no use whatsoever. This is free climbing, in which the leader climbs free of the protection, never holding onto a piece of protection and never putting weight on the rope. In another type of climbing—aid climbing—the climber purposely hangs from the protection. (Aid climbing is covered in Chapter 11.)

Climbers distinguish between two main types of protection: natural protection and artificial protec-

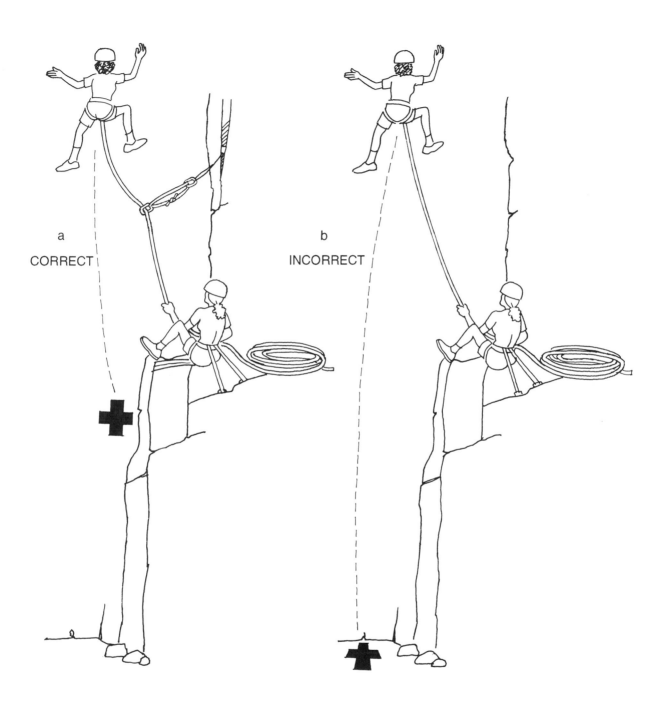

Fig. 10–1. Leader fall: a, with protection in place; b, no protection in place.

tion. With natural protection, you're relying on nature to provide something to connect the rope to. When natural protection is not available, you rely on metal wedges and cams (known as artificial chockstones, or chocks), and bolts and pitons, to establish artificial protection.

NATURAL PROTECTION

Some of the very best protection is already in place, just waiting for you. It's natural protection: trees and bushes, horns and flakes, chockstones, boulders, and other natural features. The leader can save the fancy hardware for later in the climb. Only the simplest tools—runners and carabiners— are needed to take advantage of these gifts from Mother Nature.

The basic technique for using all natural protection is identical: position a runner around the natural feature, clip a carabiner to the runner, clip the rope into the carabiner. And that's it.

Some things to pay attention to in using natural protection:

• **Test** every potential piece of natural protection before you trust your life to it. Take a close look at every tree and every rock. Does the tree look healthy? Does the rock appear unfractured, without cracks or other weaknesses? Carefully push them and pull them, tap and prod, kick and shake. Is everything solid?

• **Remember** the climbers down below as you're kicking and prodding. Be careful not to dislodge anything.

• **Try** to identify the type and composition of a rock feature as clues to its strength.

• **Check** to see if the protection will hold a pull in only one direction, or if it can take a tug from multiple directions. That is, is the protection one-directional or multidirectional? Multidirectional protection, such as a tree, is best because it can withstand an outward and upward pull.

• **Choose** an appropriate method of attaching the runner (fig. 10-2). You'll usually start by looping the runner around or over the natural feature. A runner that is looped around is secured by using a

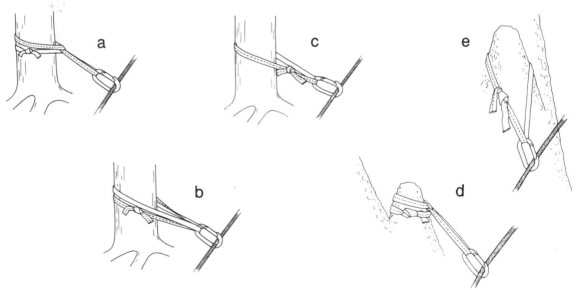

Fig. 10–2. Methods of attaching a runner to natural protection: a, secured around a tree using a girth hitch; b, looped around a tree with the ends clipped together with a carabiner; c, retied around a tree trunk; d, attached to a rock horn using a clove hitch; e, looped over a flake.

girth hitch (fig. 10-2a) or by connecting the two ends with a carabiner (fig. 10-2b). If you clip the ends together with a carabiner, be sure the runner is long enough to permit the carabiner to extend out from the natural feature; this reduces the chance that the weight of a fall will be taken directly on the carabiner gate. Another method of attachment is to untie a runner and then retie it around the protection (fig. 10-2c). With rock horns, you also have the option of attaching the runner with a clove hitch (fig. 10-2d).

• **Position** carabiners with the gates down and facing out to lessen the chance that the rock will force the gate open during a fall. If there's danger of a carabiner being forced open, use a locking carabiner or two carabiners with opposing gates.

• **Pad** all sharp edges that the runner may touch.

TREES AND BUSHES

Trees and large bushes offer the most common and obvious natural protection. To judge their trustworthiness, look for vigorous growth and a well-developed root system. Avoid trees or bushes rooted in shallow soil, gravel, talus, or cracks. If you can identify the tree or bush, you may then know if it's one that tends to be shallow-rooted or especially brittle. Shake it. If the dirt or roots move, avoid it.

Select the largest tree or clump of bushes possible. Be wary of bushes, in general, and back them up with another point of protection if there's any doubt.

To reduce the leverage on a tree or clump of bushes—leverage that could bend or break them—it's best to position the runner as low as possible. However, sometimes it's desirable on a large tree to place the attachment point higher on the trunk, or even on a large branch, to avoid putting a sharp bend in the rope. If the runner is placed on a branch, keep it close to the trunk to reduce the leverage.

HORNS AND FLAKES

Horns are the most common type of natural rock protection. They also are called spikes, knobs, bosses, chicken heads, and rock bollards. They're small protrusions in the rock, and they come in handy.

Flakes are narrow pieces of rock partially detached from the main rock, and they also provide natural protection (fig. 10-2e).

Be aware that a horn or flake that was solid when you climbed the same pitch a year ago might have been weakened by frost action over the winter. Test the rock by pushing or pulling, gently at first, then with more force. Finally, hit it with your hand or foot and listen for a hollow sound. If it moves or creates a hollow sound, avoid it. If you use a girth hitch to secure the runner to a horn or flake, be sure it's placed so it can cinch up tight (fig. 10-3).

Horns and flakes frequently offer protection in only one direction. The runner may stay in place if there is a downward tug, but come loose if the pull is upward or sideways.

There are several ways to help overcome this problem. Attach some extra climbing gear to the runner in order to weight it and help keep it in place. Use a longer runner (or extend a short run-

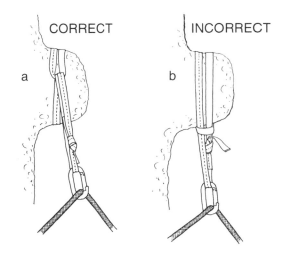

Fig. 10–3. Runner attached to a horn: a, correct, attached by a correctly placed girth hitch. Girth hitch will cinch properly; b, incorrect, attached by an incorrectly placed girth hitch. Girth hitch will not cinch.

ner), a trick that will minimize the chance that rope movement will pull the runner off the rock. Place opposing protection that can take an upward pull. (We'll get into the theory and practice of opposing protection later in this chapter.)

CHOCKSTONES

A chockstone is a rock wedged in a crack. It can make a great protection point—if it passes a few tests. Does it have substantial contact with the sides of the crack? Is the chockstone, and the walls of the crack, of a non-friable type of rock (that won't tend to crumble and let the chockstone fall)? Does the crack narrow below the chockstone, causing it to be well-wedged? Will it jam even tighter if it must withstand the force of a fall?

Arrange a runner around the chockstone so the runner can't be pinched or jammed in case the chockstone comes under such a load. Be sure it can't be pulled sideways through a point of contact between the chockstone and rock. If you choose to simply clip the ends of the runner together with a carabiner, twist one end before clipping in. This ensures that if the runner does pull through one side of the chockstone, the carabiner won't drop off (fig. 10-4a). You also can attach the runner by a girth hitch around the point of contact between chockstone and rock, which can help hold the chockstone in place (fig. 10-4b).

You may be able to use an artificial chock to help thread the runner behind the chockstone.

Sometimes you can move a chockstone to a spot in the crack where it's more secure. Be careful you don't knock it loose and send it hurtling down the climbing route.

BOULDERS

A boulder, or a block detached from the main body of rock, can be used as a protection point if it's well-embedded or too heavy to move. Steer clear of boulders that look chancy—ones that lean, are perched precariously, or rest (temporarily) on a slope.

A runner is usually looped around the boulder to create the protection placement. Keep the runner low to reduce leverage and to keep it from being

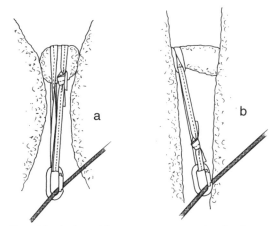

Fig. 10–4. Attaching a runner to a chockstone: a, looped around a chockstone; b, using a girth hitch on one side of a chockstone.

pulled off the top of the boulder. Use extreme care in using a boulder as a protection point because of the danger it poses to others if it comes loose.

THREADED PLACEMENTS

Threaded protection can be created from natural tunnels (fig. 10-5), arches, or the contact point between two blocks of rocks. If the rock feature is strong, the protection is usually a good choice because it is multidirectional; it can take a pull in any direction.

If you decide to use the contact point between two rocks, be sure the rocks can't move under the force of a fall. However, it's often difficult to test threaded protection, and you will usually have to rely on visual inspection and good judgment.

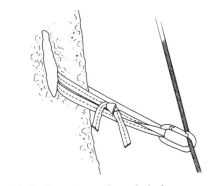

Fig. 10–5. Creating a threaded placement using a rock tunnel

ARTIFICIAL PROTECTION

In the absence of natural protection, climbers use artificial protection devices. These devices include chocks (artificial chockstones), bolts, and pitons. In most cases, the leader will use a chock or bolt, although pitons still have their uses. On a climb, the leader secures the piece of protection in the rock, providing a point of attachment for a runner, which is then connected to the climbing rope using carabiners.

CHOCKS

Chockcraft—the art of placing and removing chocks—is the preferred technique for protecting climbs. This supports the ethic of clean climbing, which is climbing that does not permanently alter the environment. Chocks are relatively easy to place and to remove and, unlike bolts and pitons, leave no scars on the rock.

Chocks are either wedges or cams (fig. 10-6). Wedges hold a fall by wedging against a constriction in a crack or against another wedge. Cams hold a fall by rotating slightly within a crack, creating a camming action that jams the chock against the rock.

Wedges and cams are either passive or spring-loaded. Passive wedges and cams are single pieces of metal, without moving parts, that are simply placed firmly in an appropriate location in the rock. Spring-loaded wedges and cams are chocks with moving parts that are retracted in order to fit them into a spot, then allowed to open fully again to hold them in that place.

To become proficient at chockcraft, a climber learns the strengths and weaknesses of different types of chocks and learns to place them correctly.

The lead climber should know the breaking strength of each chock, information published by manufacturers or independent testers. Larger chocks are usually heavier and stronger than smaller chocks, and therefore have a higher breaking strength. Some smaller chocks aren't even meant to hold a fall, but are strong enough to support a climber's weight in aid climbing.

All chocks are designed to use in a rock feature—usually a crack, sometimes a pocket. Before placing a chock, the climber inspects the rock, both to judge its soundness and to decide what chock to use.

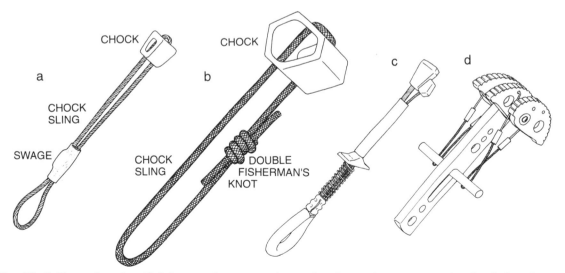

Fig. 10–6. Examples of artificial protection: a, passive wedge; b, passive cam; c, spring-loaded wedge; d, spring-loaded cam.

The type of rock and its condition help indicate whether the chock will hold a fall. Specifically, chocks tend to hold well in solid rock. Crumbling or deteriorating rock is unreliable, and should be avoided.

If you're thinking of putting a piece of protection behind a rock flake, remember the hollow-sound test. Hit it with the palm of one hand, and if you hear a hollow sound, don't use the flake. Under load, it takes only a slight movement of the rock for the chock to lose its grip and fail.

The size, shape, and orientation of the crack or pocket determines what chock to use. Does the crack or pocket flare outward, flare inward, or have parallel sides? Is it shallow or deep? Is it vertical or horizontal? Some types of chocks work well in one situation, not so well in another.

Some other general considerations in placing chocks:

• **Learn** to estimate the right chock size for a particular placement. The better the estimate, the faster the placement—and the less chance the climber will tire and fall.
• **Choose** the best chock, not necessarily the largest one possible. A larger chock usually will hold a harder fall, but first decide if it actually provides the soundest protection or if a smaller piece would be more secure.
• **Decide** whether a particular chock is likely to be adequate, based on the characteristics of the rock and the magnitude of a possible fall. If not, reinforce it with another chock or find a better placement.
• **Check** out every chock after it's in place. Look to see that it's placed correctly. Tug on it to help determine the strength and security of the placement, especially in the likely direction of pull.
• **Guard** against the chock being dislodged by rope movement. A runner is usually attached, with carabiners, between the chock and the rope. This helps reduce the effect of rope movement. Wired chocks are more affected by rope movement and have a greater tendency to rotate out of place.
• **Guard** against the chock being dislodged by an outward or upward pull. Many chock placements are one-directional; they will take a load in only one direction. If a one-directional placement could come under a load from multiple directions, make it multidirectional by placing opposing chocks. (This procedure gets a full explanation later in this chapter.)
• **Remember** the climber who will be following behind you and removing the protection. Make your placements secure, but also try to make them reasonably easy to remove.

Chock slings

A climber's high-priced pieces of protection won't do any good until they're connected to the rope. So every chock must include some type of sling as a part of the attachment system from the chock to the rope. The sling is usually made from accessory cord, tubular webbing, or wire cable.

Smaller chocks usually come with a wire cable sling, which is much stronger than cord or webbing of the same size. The ends of the cable are swaged together. Larger chocks come pre-drilled with holes for accessory cord, which is usually added by the climber. Some chocks come pre-slung with tubular webbing.

There is a bonus advantage to using wire cable with passive wedges, such as Black Diamond (formerly Chouinard) Stopper nuts or Wild Country Stones. The wire's relative stiffness makes the wedges easier to handle and to place.

However, with passive camming chocks, such as Black Diamond Hexentric nuts, it's better to have accessory cord, providing it's strong enough. The cord permits the chock to rotate and cam freely as it's meant to do. Most modern hexes are drilled to accept 5.5-millimeter accessory cord.

For many years, climbers used 6- to 9-millimeter nylon cord and 1-inch nylon webbing to make chock slings. Nylon is durable and inexpensive but requires relatively larger diameters for strength, creating bulky and heavy chock slings.

An alternative fiber called Kevlar came into use for accessory cord. Kevlar cord at 5.5 millimeters in diameter is smaller, lighter, and stronger than nylon. However, Kevlar cord is weakened by repeated bending. Consequently, the manufacturer recommends it only for tying chock slings, because these slings are knotted just once and are not subjected to repeated bending.

A new fiber, Spectra, is even lighter, stronger, and more abrasion resistant than Kevlar. For use as chock slings, the Spectra fiber is used in 5.5-millimeter cord or $9/16$-inch webbing.

Here are some things to keep in mind when attaching accessory cord as a sling to a chock:

• **Inspect** the holes that are drilled in the chock for the cord. They should have rounded edges to reduce the chance the sling could be cut under stress.
• **Tie** the ends of the cord together with a double fisherman's knot. Check it frequently in use to be sure it stays tight.
• **Determine** the right length for the sling. A sling is usually between 8 and 14 inches long, and some manufacturers provide information on how much sling material is needed for chocks of different sizes. One caution: If you make a chock sling too long, it could hang down far enough to interfere with footwork during climbing.

Passive wedging chocks

Out on a climb, no one will mention anything called a "passive wedging chock." Out there, passive wedging chocks go by a lot of catchier names: brands such as Stoppers, Stones, and RPs, and terms such as nuts, steel nuts, micronuts, tapers, and just plain chocks.

Wedging chocks are tapered down from top to bottom so they will fit into a constriction in a crack. They have a wide side and a narrow side, and are strongest when the wide surface area is touching the rock (fig. 10-7). The object is to get the greatest possible contact between chock and rock. Many wedging chocks, especially the smaller sizes, are not designed to be placed with the narrow side in contact with the rock.

A passive wedging chock has no moving parts to hold it in place. It sits passively in a constricting crack until it takes a load—such as a leader fall.

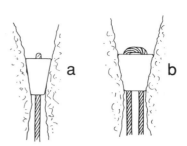

Fig. 10–7. Wide-side and narrow-side placement of passive wedging chocks: a, wide sides are in contact with the rock, a stronger placement; b, narrow sides are in contact with the rock, a weaker placement.

Then the chock wedges into the crack, generating expansion forces and increased friction. It holds tight.

Though they all taper, there are variations in the shapes of wedging chocks (fig. 10-8). Manufacturers try subtle changes in design to improve performance, and new designs continue to appear.

Some wedging chocks are straight-sided, some

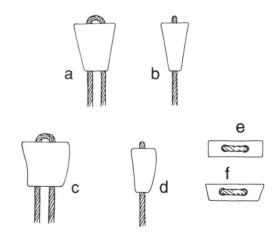

Fig. 10–8. Design variations in passive wedging chocks: a, wide side, straight sides; b, narrow side, straight sides; c, wide side, curved sides; d, narrow side, curved sides; e, top view, rectangular; f, top view, trapezoidal.

have slightly curved sides. They can also have a combination of straight and curved sides. Smaller wedging chocks are usually straight-sided, while larger chocks may have pronounced curvature. Viewed from the top, wedging chocks can be rectangular or trapezoidal.

The goal in using any wedging chock, regardless of shape, is to create a stable and secure point of protection—something you can stake your life on. A straight-sided chock may not place well in a crack with an uneven surface, whereas a curved chock may fit nicely. In another spot, the straight-sided chock could be just the thing.

A curved-sided chock creates three points of contact, which adds to stability (fig. 10-9). However, it may seat so securely that it can be tough to remove. If the edges on a wedging chock are slightly rounded, it tends to be easier to remove.

Fig. 10–9. Curved-sided chock, with three points of contact with the rock

The Hexentric passive camming chock can also be used as a passive wedge. Even though it doesn't look like a wedge, the ends of the Hexentric are tapered, allowing it to wedge in a constricting crack (fig. 10-10).

In an emergency, the knot of a runner can be jammed into a constricting crack and serve as a wedging chock.

Vertical cracks

Here's where wedging chocks work the best. Put the chock above a constriction in a vertical crack. A downward pull wedges the chock more tightly into the crack.

If the sides of the crack are generally smooth, a

Fig. 10–10. Hexentric used sideways in a crack as a passive wedging chock

straight-sided chock works well. If the sides are rougher or slightly curved, a curved-sided chock works better.

For the most secure placement, slot the wedge completely into the crack (fig. 10-11).

Passive wedging chocks usually are able to hold a load only in one direction. However, if the chock is slotted deeply into a crack and seated correctly, it can handle pulls from multiple directions.

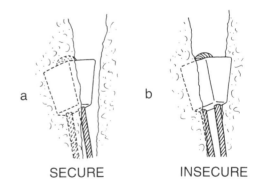

a   b

SECURE   INSECURE

Fig. 10–11. Passive wedge slotted in a vertical crack: a, secure, slotted completely into a vertical crack; b, insecure, slotted partially into a vertical crack.

Passive wedging chocks do not work in parallel-sided vertical cracks (fig. 10-12). If the sides of the crack are straight and parallel, the chock has very little contact with the rock, and a severe downward pull can cause the contact points on the chock to shear.

Fig. 10–12. Incorrect, a passive wedge placed in a parallel-sided vertical crack with little contact to the rock

There's a way around this problem: use two wedges in a method called stacking. Stacked chocks can be created from two independent chocks or from a specially made chock stack.

The theory is the same in either case. The chocks are placed in opposition in a parallel crack. A downward pull on the larger chock causes it to wedge between one side of the crack and one side of the opposing chock. All stacked chocks should be seated with a firm tug before use.

If two independent chocks are used (fig. 10-13a), they should be connected with a carabiner so that if the placement fails, a chock will not be lost.

A chock stack (fig. 10-13b) is constructed by putting two passive wedging chocks on the same sling. The chocks are different sizes, with the smaller chock at the end so that either can be used in a non-stacking chock placement.

Stacked wedges aren't used so much any more because climbers now have the option of spring-loaded wedges or spring-loaded cams, which work better and are easier to place.

Horizontal cracks

Although wedging chocks work best in vertical or near-vertical cracks, horizontal cracks sometimes can be used. The horizontal crack should constrict at the lip of the crack. The chock can be slotted in a wider section and then slid behind the constriction (fig. 10-14). A well-placed wedging chock in a horizontal crack can be very secure because it tends to be multidirectional.

The chock should be well recessed, and the sling should not be able to contact a sharp upper or lower lip on the crack. A chock set at the lip of a

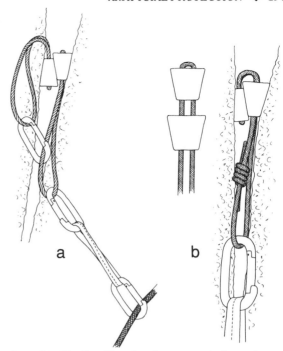

Fig. 10–13. Stacking chocks: a, two independent chocks stacked together; b, chock stack.

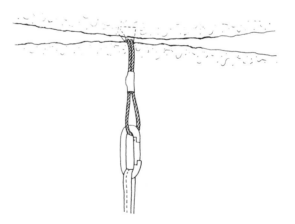

Fig. 10–14. Passive wedge slotted behind a constriction in a horizontal crack

crack is more likely to fail. The edge of the chock can cause the sling to shear, and the chock itself will create a camming action at the lip of the crack that could cause it to crumble (fig. 10-15).

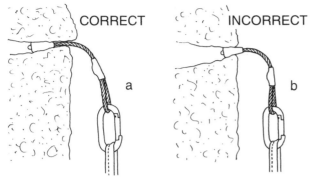

CORRECT a   INCORRECT b

Fig. 10–15. Passive wedge placed in a horizontal crack, side view: a, correct, slotted deep within the crack; b, incorrect, slotted at the lip of the crack.

Flaring cracks

A wedge that's trapezoidal in shape from a top view may work well in a crack that flares outward. Used with the narrow sides of the chock against the rock, this shape can provide a stronger and more stable placement in this particular situation because it increases surface contact with the rock (fig. 10-16a).

A crack that flares inward can cause a seemingly strong placement to be insecure (fig. 10-16b). If you keep alert you should be able to see this situation before making a bad placement.

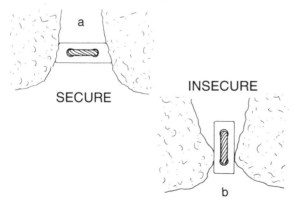

SECURE a

INSECURE b

Fig. 10–16. Using passive wedges in flaring cracks: a, a secure placement in an outwardly flaring crack; b, an insecure placement in an inwardly flaring crack.

Pockets and threaded placements

Passive wedging chocks don't work well in pockets.

For a threaded placement, where a crack constricts to form a tunnel, a wedging chock can sometimes be threaded through to form a protection point (fig. 10-17). The chock can be threaded upward or downward. A wired chock will thread more easily than a chock that has accessory cord for a sling.

Be sure the crack does not widen too much behind the constriction, possibly permitting the chock to pull through. Good threaded placements, however, can be very secure because they are often multidirectional.

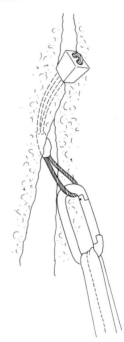

Fig. 10–17. A passive wedge threaded through a tunnel in a crack

Passive camming chocks

Climbers also have a batch of popular names and brand names to use in referring to passive camming chocks: hexes, hex nuts, Hexentrics, Tri Cams.

A passive camming chock is placed in a crack in such a way that when it takes a load—from, for example, a 160-pound climber at the end of a 30-foot leader fall—it tries to rotate. The rotation causes the chock to cam and lock in place.

The shapes of camming chocks vary. One manufacturer will use a design completely different from that of another, and designs continue to evolve.

Traditional camming chocks had a balanced hexagonal shape. Both pairs of opposing sides used for camming were the same distance apart. These hex nuts could cam and lock in place, but had limited versatility because each nut could fit only a small range of crack sizes.

Chouinard Equipment (now Black Diamond Equipment) modified the basic hex nut in creating its Hexentric nut, in which each pair of opposing sides is a different distance apart. The Hexentric can be used in a greater range of crack sizes because it can be placed for narrow camming or wide camming and provides different camming angles (fig. 10-18). It can also be used endwise as a passive wedge.

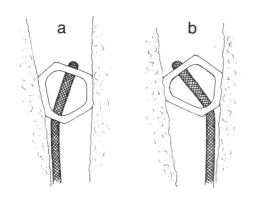

Fig. 10–18. Camming modes of a Hexentric chock: a, narrow camming; b, wide camming.

The Lowe Tri Cam is another design, using a completely different shape to generate the camming action. Because of its shape, the Tri Cam can be used in a range of crack sizes (fig. 10-19).

Any single camming chock works only within a

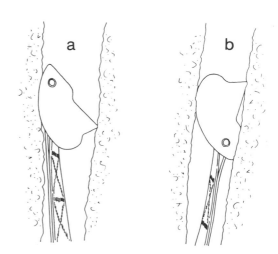

Fig. 10–19. Camming modes of a Lowe Tri Cam chock: a, major cam mode; b, minor cam and wedging mode.

specific range of crack sizes. If a crack is too wide, the chock can fall out. An excessively tight fit, on the other hand, can prevent the camming action from occurring. Then the camming chock would simply act like a passive wedging chock.

After you've placed a passive camming chock, give a sharp tug on the sling. This will initiate some camming action and seat the chock in place.

Vertical cracks

Passive camming chocks work well in vertical cracks that are parallel or that do not expand too much. Place a chock that is tight enough to have maximum contact with the rock, but that has enough room for proper camming action to take place under load.

If the chock is too small, only its edges may be in contact with the rock and, under load, these edges can shear off. A loose chock also can be dislodged by rope movement. The fit should be snug, which will help hold the chock in place when it's not under load (fig. 10-20).

One trick that can create a stable placement is to build a combination stack using a passive wedging chock with a passive camming chock—a Stopper with a Hexentric (fig. 10-21).

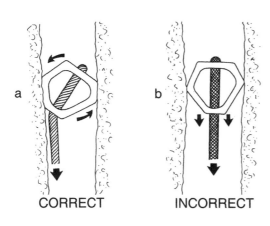

CORRECT   INCORRECT

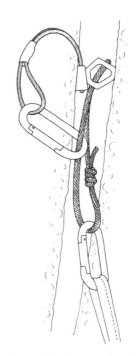

Fig. 10–20. Placement of a Hexentric in a vertical crack: a, correct, Hexentric in proper camming mode with sides fully contacting the rock; b, incorrect, Hexentric is too small for the vertical crack. No camming will occur.

Fig. 10–21. A combination stack using a passive wedge and a passive camming chock

Horizontal cracks

Passive camming chocks also like parallel cracks that are horizontal. Place the chock so the sling leaves the crack closer to the roof than to the floor of the crack (fig. 10-22a). Otherwise, it won't cam (fig. 10-22b). Be careful that the chock isn't rotated out of position by sideways forces.

The crack shouldn't widen inward too much or proper camming action won't take place (fig. 10-22c).

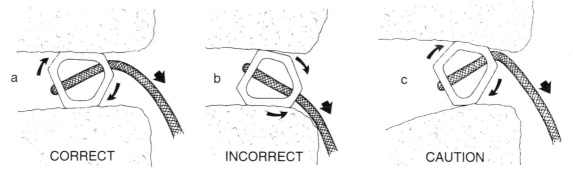

CORRECT   INCORRECT   CAUTION

Fig. 10–22. Placement of a Hexentric in a horizontal crack: a, correct, chock sling exits near roof of crack, proper camming will occur; b, incorrect, chock sling exits near bottom of crack, little or no camming will occur; c, caution, if the Hexentric moves back in the inwardly flaring crack, proper camming will not occur.

Flaring cracks

Passive camming chocks don't work well in flaring cracks, where they tend to be unstable and don't make maximum surface contact. Tri Cams work in some flaring cracks. However, all points must still be able to contact the rock and that may not be possible.

Pockets and threaded placements

If the pocket is deep enough, a Tri Cam will work, but it must be recessed completely into a pocket for maximum surface contact and stability (fig. 10-23). Rope movement can easily dislodge this placement.

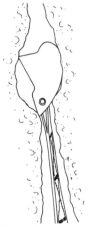

Fig. 10–23. Tri Cam placed in a pocket

Like passive wedging chocks, some passive camming chocks can be threaded through a small rock tunnel to create a protection point. In this case, the chock is relying on wedging and not camming action to hold a load.

Spring-loaded wedging devices

This is another of those technical terms you won't usually hear while moving up a rock face: spring-loaded wedging devices (fig. 10-24). That's what they're called here, because it's a good technical description. In action, you'll hear them referred to under such names as Quickies, Rock 'n Rollers, and Ball Nuts.

These gadgets use variations on the chock stacking theme to create protection in tiny finger

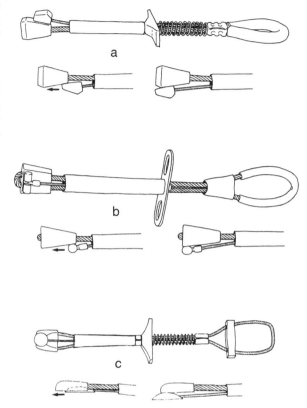

Fig. 10–24. Examples of spring-loaded wedging devices: a, D. Best Quickie, contracted and expanded; b, Go-Pro Rock 'n Roller, contracted and expanded; c, Lowe Ball Nut, contracted and expanded.

cracks. A spring-loaded wedging device features two sliding pieces in opposition. A trigger mechanism held by a spring controls the position of the smaller sliding piece.

Pull the trigger, and the smaller piece slides lower against the larger piece—narrowing the profile of the device so it can fit into the thin crack. Release the trigger, and the smaller piece springs back higher against the larger piece—expanding the profile and wedging the pieces against each other and against the walls of the crack. The force of a fall wedges the pieces even tighter.

You can place a spring-loaded wedge in a vertical crack using only one hand, a big improvement in efficiency over passive chock stacks. After placing a spring-loaded wedge, give it a tug to seat it securely.

Spring-loaded wedges also can be used in horizontal cracks. Try to place them so the stem of the device won't be bent sharply around a rock edge in case of a fall. The stems are flexible, but may not be designed to hold a fall if they are bent too much.

Some spring-loaded wedges are designed to be separated and used as individual wedges if you wish. This makes the device more versatile, but be sure that's what the manufacturer had in mind before you try it.

The orientation of the smaller piece on some spring-loaded wedges, such as the Quickie, is fixed in relation to the larger piece, limiting these devices to parallel-sided cracks. But the smaller piece on designs such as the Rock 'n Roller and the Ball Nut rotates relative to the larger piece. This allows the smaller piece to conform better to un-even or flaring cracks and reduces the possibility it will be dislodged by rope movement.

Spring-loaded wedges don't work in pockets and threaded placements.

Spring-loaded camming devices

First came Friends. The original spring-loaded camming device was developed in the mid-1970s and dramatically expanded the limits of free climbing by providing protection that could be placed with one hand and that could adapt to a variety of cracks. Climbers now could take on tough routes that would be very difficult to protect with conventional chocks.

Since the development of Friends, variations on the basic design have been created. Newer designs tend to use cable stems, more flexible than the solid stems of the original Friends. Some include three cams instead of the four used in each Friend. Among today's most popular spring-loaded camming devices (fig. 10-25) are Friends and Flexible Friends (manufactured by Wild Country), Camalots (made by Black Diamond Equipment), and TCUs (Three-Cam Units, by Metolius).

The three or four cams in a spring-loaded camming device are connected to a trigger mechanism.

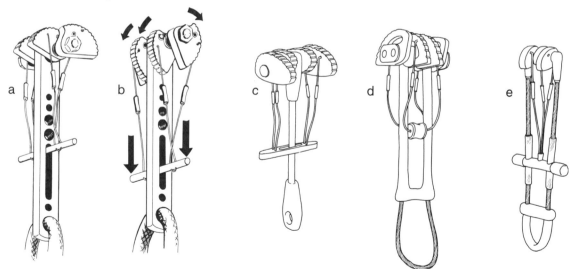

Fig. 10–25. Examples of spring-loaded camming devices: a, Wild Country Friend, expanded and b, contracted; c, Wild Country Flexible Friend; d, Black Diamond Camalot; e, Metolius TCU (tri-cam unit).

Pull the trigger and the cams retract—narrowing the profile of the device so it can fit into a particular crack. Release the trigger and the cams again rotate outward—expanding the profile until the cams grip the sides of the crack (fig. 10-25a). In a fall, the cams try to rotate and expand again, gripping the crack even more securely.

The three or four cams rotate independently of each other, permitting each to expand to the maximum, wherever it may sit in a particular crack.

All is well if you've placed a spring-loaded camming device and all the cams, expanded to their midpoint, are in contact with the rock and the stem of the device is pointing in the likely direction of pull (fig. 10-26a).

But beware of these potential problems:

1. All the cams don't touch the rock. The placement will be unstable. Find a better spot.
2. The cams are over-retracted in the crack (fig. 10-26b). The device may be jammed in so tightly that it can't cam, and it may be very hard to get the thing out. Use a smaller spring-loaded cam.

3. The cams are over-expanded, with only the tips of the cams touching the rock (fig. 10-26c). No camming action can take place, and the device will serve only as a passive wedging chock. Under load, most devices will structurally fail. Use a larger spring-loaded camming device. (An exception is the Camalot, which is strong enough in the "umbrella" position to be used as a passive chock.)
4. The stem does not point in the likely direction of pull (fig. 10-26d). A fall can force the device to rotate, perhaps causing the cams to lose their grip.

In an uneven crack, the independent cams can expand to different widths. This is good. It means the device will adjust to variations in the crack. But if the cams are too unbalanced, proper camming action won't occur and the placement could fail. This is bad. So always try to make sure that each pair of cams is symmetrically oriented and that all cams contact the rock.

The spring-loaded camming devices that use

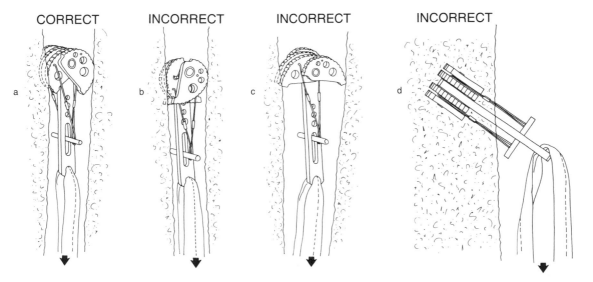

CORRECT INCORRECT INCORRECT INCORRECT

Fig. 10–26. Correct and incorrect placement of spring-loaded camming devices: a, correct, cams expanded to midpoint, stem in likely direction of pull; b, incorrect, cams are over-retracted, proper camming may not occur; c, incorrect, cams are over-expanded, no camming will occur; d, incorrect, stem is not pointed in likely direction of pull.

only three cams, instead of four, are smaller and narrower. They're designed for shallower placements, though they can also be used more conventionally. The four-cam devices have a bad habit of "walking" into cracks as a result of rope movement, making them sometimes difficult to retrieve. The three-cam units will rotate more and are less likely to walk.

Vertical cracks

Spring-loaded camming devices really come into their own in parallel-sided vertical cracks. They're easier, faster, and safer than stacked wedges or passive cams. When correctly placed, the stem of the device will point in the anticipated direction of pull, allowing the load to be transmitted along the axis of the stem and maximizing strength of the placement.

Horizontal cracks

You can also use spring-loaded cams in horizontal and diagonal cracks, but watch out for stem breakage.

The original Friends design uses a solid stem. This is fine as long as the direction of pull is along the axis of the stem, which is usually the case in a vertical crack. The picture changes with horizontal cracks.

Newer designs from the makers of Friends and from other manufacturers use flexible cable stems, which can bend and adjust if the direction of pull is not along the axis (fig. 10-27a). However, the original Friends are still being made and are in wide use, so it's important to know how to minimize the danger of having a solid stem break in a horizontal placement.

If the solid stem doesn't extend beyond the edge of the horizontal crack, the stem won't come under any dangerous forces. However, if the crack is shallow and the stem extends beyond the edge of the crack, the stem would be forced against an edge during a fall and could shear at the lip of the crack.

You can reduce the danger of breakage by adding a tie-off loop, of accessory cord or webbing, to the largest hole in the stem. Make it slightly shorter than the regular chock sling. Clip into the tie-off loop so the force of any load will be taken closer to the cams (and farther from the end of the stem). As a backup, also clip in the regular sling in case the tie-off loop fails (fig. 10-27b).

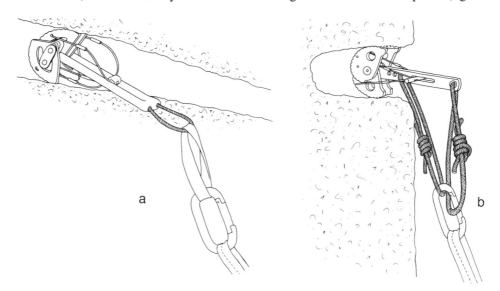

a   b

Fig. 10–27. Spring-loaded camming device placement in a horizontal crack: a, flexible cable stem can bend and adjust to the direction of pull; b, a tie-off loop can reduce the danger of solid-stem breakage.

Flaring cracks

Because each cam works independently, they can individually expand to fit a flaring crack. Problems occur if the crack flares too much. Some of the cams could over-expand, making for an unstable placement. The device may then be more susceptible to rotation or rope movement and less able to cam properly under load.

Pockets and threaded placements

Spring-loaded camming devices don't work for threaded placements.

They are usable in some pockets, but only if the pocket is deep enough to allow all cams to touch the rock.

Spring-loaded tube chocks

It's difficult to place protection in wide cracks because most chocks aren't big enough.

Sometimes the answer is a large spring-loaded camming device, but these can get awfully heavy. An alternative spring-loaded device for protecting wide cracks is the telescoping tube chock.

The tube chock has a spring-loaded inner sleeve. Release the spring and the sleeve pops out

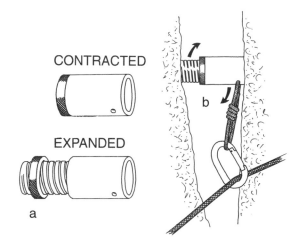

CONTRACTED

EXPANDED

a

Fig. 10–28. Spring-loaded tube chock: a, Mountain Hardwear Big Bro, contracted and expanded; b, Big Bro correctly placed in a vertical crack.

far enough for the tube to bridge the crack (fig. 10-28a). A locking collar keeps the tube extended. After setting the chock, the climber clips in to a sling attached to one end. With a load on that end resulting in an upward force on the other end, the device acts like a passive camming chock (fig. 10-28b).

The wedging factor

Under load, a chock creates expansion forces. The relative amount of expansion force created by a chock—whether it's a wedge or a cam—is known as the wedging factor.

Splitting firewood with a wedge is an illustration of wedging action. A chock is a wedge in the rock. Put a load on the chock, and it tries to expand the rock—just as hitting a wedge with a hammer causes it to split firewood.

The relative amount of expansion force depends on the angle of a chock face (fig. 10-29a). If the taper angle is smaller, the wedging factor will be higher and it will put more force on the rock (fig. 10-29b). Conversely, if the taper angle is larger, the wedging factor will be lower (fig. 10-29c).

Friction between the rock and the chock affects the wedging factor. Rougher rock increases friction, which decreases the wedging factor. Dirt or vegetation can lubricate the chock, reducing friction and increasing the wedging factor.

The applied load and the wedging factor combine to determine the actual amount of expansion force generated. A high applied load, such as a falling climber, taken on a chock with a high wedging factor results in a very large expansion force.

A couple of examples can give an idea of how the wedging factor affects expansion forces. A chock with a taper angle of 14.4 degrees will cause it to push against the walls of a crack with a force equal to four times the load. Therefore, a 170-pound climber who puts full weight on this chock would generate 680 pounds of expansion force (and a little hop could easily double the force). Now take a smaller chock, with a taper angle of 4.5 degrees. The wedging factor goes much higher, now equal to 12 times the load. The 170-

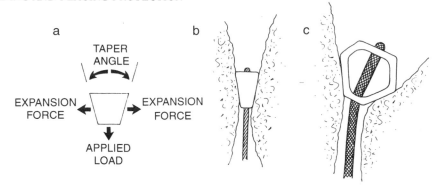

Fig. 10–29. The wedging factor: a, illustration of taper angle and expansion forces; b, narrow chocks have small taper angles and generate greater expansion force under load; c, wide chocks have large taper angles and generate less expansion force under load.

pound climber who puts full weight on the chock now generates 2,040 pounds of expansion force.

The wedging factor becomes particularly important when placing a chock behind a flake. Expansion force could push the flake outward, loosening the protection. It could even knock the flake off, destroying the protection point. Chocks with higher wedging factors are more likely to generate this magnitude of expansion force.

A flake best resists expansion force near its point of attachment. Consequently, it may be better to use a smaller chock (with greater wedging factor) near the attachment point, than a larger chock (with lower wedging factor) higher up. The tradeoff in using a smaller chock is that it is a weaker piece of protection.

The camming action of a spring-loaded camming device generates very concentrated expansion force. Be cautious in using them behind flakes.

BOLTS AND PITONS

Bolts and pitons are protection devices that are drilled into the rock or pounded into cracks. They sometimes provide protection where there's no place to lodge a chock.

A bolt is a permanent piece of protection driven into a hole drilled in the rock (fig. 10-30a). A bolt hanger provides attachment for a carabiner, and a threaded nut is sometimes needed to attach the hanger to the bolt.

A piton is a metal spike that is pounded into a crack to provide a point of protection (fig. 10-30b). The blade of the piton is the part driven into the rock; the eye is the point of attachment for the carabiner.

Placing pitons is called pitoncraft, a skill that will be studied in Chapter 11. Pitons and bolts are being introduced here because it's necessary to know how to deal with ones you will encounter on climbs, put in place by previous climbers. You need to know how to check these placements to determine if they can be trusted as protection for your climb.

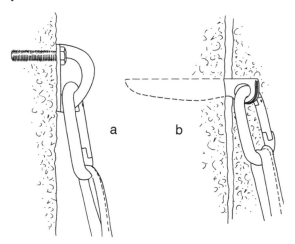

Fig. 10–30. Bolts and pitons: a, bolt with a bolt hanger; b, piton driven into a vertical crack.

Pitons are seldom used in modern free climbing. They still get some use on climbs in remote areas or on routes requiring mixed free and aid climbing.

Bolts are now widely used to protect some of today's severe free rock climbs. The bolts create artificial protection where there are no rock features to accept either chocks or pitons. However, climbing ethics encourage the use of clean-climbing techniques when possible, to prevent the permanent scarring caused by pitons and bolts.

Bolts

Look at fixed bolts with a skeptical eye.

How safe a particular bolt may be is going to depend on the quality of the hardware, the type of rock, the skill of the climber who placed the bolt, and so forth. It's to your advantage, to say the least, to carefully check out every bolt you encounter before clipping into it.

Check to see that the bolt is placed in rock that is solid, not crumbling or deteriorating. Be sure the hanger is flush to the rock. Look for corrosion or cracks on the bolt or hanger. Beware of aluminum hangers because they can become brittle with use. Steel hangers tend to be stronger.

Do not tap on a bolt to test its strength or security as repeated hammering only loosens the bolt. The bolt can be partially tested by hand or by clipping a runner onto it and tugging. If it moves, or if for any reason the placement doesn't seem solid, forget it except possibly for backup protection.

If you like the bolt, use a carabiner to clip a runner to the bolt hanger. In some climbing areas, bolt hangers are customarily removed by climbers after use, so it may be necessary to carry along a few hangers and nuts in $1/4$-inch and $3/8$-inch sizes.

If a hanger is not available, a hangerless bolt can be used by sliding a wired chock down its cable sling so the resulting wire loop can be placed over the bolt. Slide the chock back up the sling to create a snug noose, then clip into the sling (fig. 10-31). Rope movement easily dislodges this type of placement, so don't use it for protection unless it's an emergency. Nevertheless, it can be used in

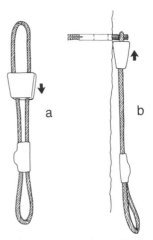

Fig. 10–31. Placing a wired chock on a hangerless bolt: a, create a loop by sliding the chock down the chock sling; b, slide the chock up the sling to form a noose around the hangerless bolt.

aid climbing or in constructing opposing chock placements.

Pitons

Can you trust an old piton? Well, it depends …

A fixed piton that you run across during a climb may be a quick and easy way to get some good protection. It may also be old and in bad condition. Over the years, pitons rust, weaken, and become loose.

Take a close look at the piton. Is the eye broken or badly rusted? Is the piton rusting in the crack or perhaps even loose enough to pull out by hand? Is the piton bent?

Ideally, the fixed piton is perpendicular to the likely direction of pull, and it's driven in all the way, with the eye up close to the rock. Examine the condition of the rock, looking for deterioration. Test the piton first by hand. Then tap on it with a piton hammer or a large chock. If it moves, it's unreliable. Beware of older pitons that use iron rings as an attachment point because the rings tend to be very weak. If there is any doubt about a piton's strength or security, try to find other protection.

If the piton seems to be strong, secure, and in good condition, use it. Attach a runner with a carabiner clipped to the piton eye. Be sure the carabiner will not bind against the rock under load, which could cause carabiner failure.

If a piton is only partially driven, tie it off next to the rock with a runner, using a girth hitch or clove hitch (fig. 10-32). The tie-off reduces the leverage on the piton under the impact of a fall. It's also possible to get a marginal attachment by using a cabled chock in the same manner as in connecting to a hangerless bolt. (Slide a wired chock down its cable sling, place the resulting wire loop over the piton, and slide the chock back up the sling to make a snug noose.)

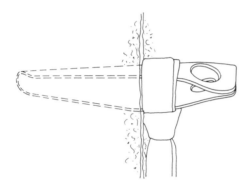

Fig. 10–32. Partially driven piton, with a tie-off next to the rock to reduce leverage

If a piton eye is bent so much that the carabiner won't fit through, it may be possible to thread a cabled chock through the eye. Don't count on it to hold a hard fall, however, and avoid this placement if you have an alternative.

The best judge of fixed pitons is the climber who knows how to place them correctly in the first place. (See Chapter 11 for information on placing pitons.)

DOUBLE PLACEMENTS

Two pieces of protection are sometimes linked in order to do a better job than a one-piece placement. This technique is commonly used in two different ways: to set up opposing chocks so the placement gives multidirectional protection, or to equalize the load over two pieces of protection.

Multidirectional protection

Most chock placements will hold only a downward pull. They are one-directional, providing protection for a load from only a single direction.

No problem, you might say. If I fall, I'll only fall downward. True. But there are times a chock must be able to hold an upward or sideways pull. When the route changes direction at or above a placement, the resulting bend in the rope may simply pull a passive chock up and out of the crack. In some cases a fall taken on a higher chock will put upward and outward forces on lower chocks.

What's needed in these situations is multidirectional protection—placements that will hold fast whether the pull is down, up, or out. The most obvious multidirectional protection is provided by trees, natural tunnels, pitons, and bolts. Otherwise, the standard method of providing multidirectional protection is to place a pair of opposed chocks—chocks that are linked so that they pull toward each other. This method also is used to hold passive wedging chocks in horizontal cracks that won't take a simple placement.

Vertical opposition

An "iffy" chock in a vertical crack needs help from an opposed "keeper" chock.

The basic procedure is simple. Place one chock in the crack so it can take a downward pull. Below that, place a chock that can take an upward pull. Clip a carabiner to each chock sling. Using a clove hitch or half hitches, tie the two carabiners together with a runner so there is tension between the two chocks, which helps hold them in place (especially the bottom chock—the keeper—which otherwise might drop out). Then clip the rope into this arrangement. Three methods are shown here in figure 10-33.

Another setup, recommended in some climbing

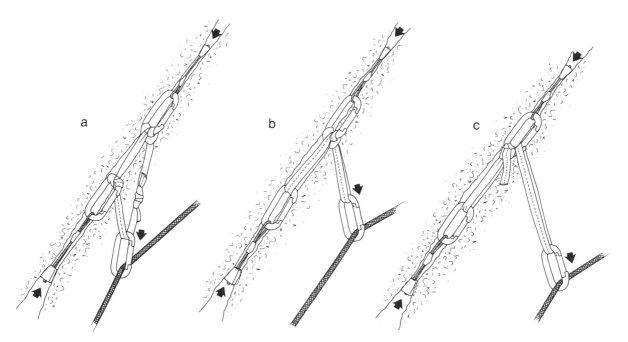

Fig. 10–33. Three methods for creating vertical opposition: a, using one runner, chocks are held by tension on one side of the runner using clove hitches; b, using one long runner, a clove hitch or two half hitches holds the tension between the chocks; c, using two short runners, one runner creates the tension between the chocks using a clove hitch or two half hitches, the other runner clips to the rope.

texts, should be avoided (fig. 10-34). This setup has two principal disadvantages compared with the preferred methods.

First of all, it places a dangerous multiplication of forces on the upper chock. Because the runner is not tied off to the upper chock, the runner moves freely through the carabiner, which acts like a pulley. This will double the usual force on the upper chock, perhaps causing it to fail.

Secondly, the bottom chock has nothing to hold it in place. This chock may stay put if it's set securely or if there is some tension on the rope. Otherwise, it could simply drop out.

The preferred methods (illustrated in figure 10-33) avoid the dangers of load multiplication. Each preferred method creates tension between the chocks to hold them in place and includes a tie-off at the upper chock to prevent the carabiner from acting like a pulley and multiplying the load.

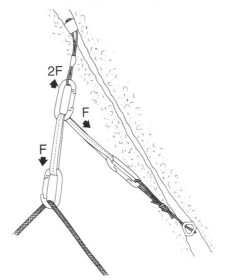

Fig. 10–34. Incorrect method of creating vertical opposition

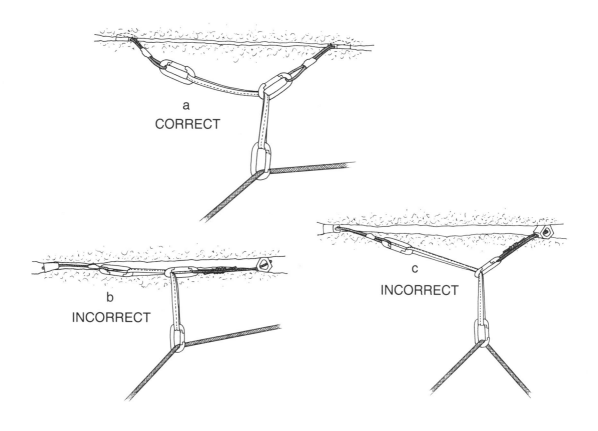

Fig. 10–35. Creating horizontal opposition in a crack: a, correct, chocks are slotted back into the crack and angled to resist rotation and outward pull under load; b, incorrect, chocks are slotted at the lip of the crack and face directly at each other; c, incorrectly placed chocks in vertical opposition can be rotated out of the crack under load.

Horizontal opposition

If a horizontal crack doesn't have a nice constriction to slot a passive wedging chock behind, you can try to set up opposing chocks. Under load, the opposition pulls the chocks toward each other, creating tension that keeps them in the crack.

Here's the basic procedure: slot two chocks back in the crack. They should face in the general direction of each other, yet be set at enough of an angle to withstand some outward and downward loading. If at least one chock cannot withstand some downward loading, the horizontal opposition is likely to fail.

There are a couple of ways to link the chocks to each other and to the rope. In one method, a runner clipped to the carabiner at one chock sling simply runs through the carabiner at the other sling and then is clipped to the rope (fig. 10-35a). Be *sure* the chocks are slotted back into the crack and are partially angled outward. If not, the chocks could rotate out of the crack and fail under load (fig. 10-35b and c). Also, be aware that the usual force felt by the right-hand chock in figure 10-35a will be increased because its carabiner will act like a pulley. Choose a strong chock for this placement.

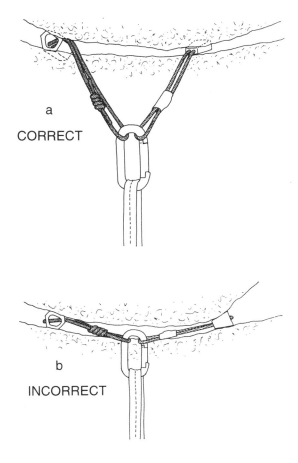

a

CORRECT

b

INCORRECT

Fig. 10–36. Clipping two chocks together to create horizontal opposition: a, correct, chocks are slotted back into the crack and angled to resist rotation and outward pull under load; b, incorrect, chocks are slotted at the lip of the crack and face directly at each other. The chocks are susceptible to rotation and outward pull under load.

Another method is to clip the two chocks together with a carabiner (fig. 10-36). The carabiner can either be clipped into both chock slings or into runners that extend from the slings.

In either case, there are two important things to remember:

First, slot the chocks back in the crack, facing in the general direction of each other but angled partially outward. At least one must be able to withstand outward and downward loading.

Second, keep the angle between the chock slings as small as possible. When two chocks are connected and subjected to a load, the angle between the slings determines how much force they will experience. The larger the angle, the greater the force on the chocks (fig. 10-37). Too large an

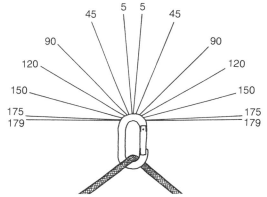

If the load on the carabiner is 100 lbs., then each anchor will be subjected to X pounds of force depending on the angle:

ANGLE BETWEEN PROTECTION (DEGREES)	LOAD ON PROTECTION (LBS.)
179	5727
175	1147
150	200
120	100
90	71
45	54
5	51

Fig. 10–37. How the angle between protection affects the force exerted on the protection under load

angle and the protection could fail. The angle should be kept below 90 degrees, and ideally around 45. Using runners to extend out from the slings will reduce the angle, helping minimize the force felt by the chocks during a fall.

Equalizing protection

Faced with a hard move and questionable protection, a leader may decide to place two pieces of protection close together. If the upper chock fails, the lower chock is there as a backup (fig. 10-38).

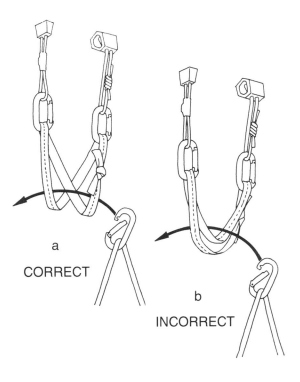

Fig. 10–39. Constructing the two-point equalizing protection: a, correct, the carabiner is clipped from one loop of the twisted runner to the other; b, incorrect, the carabiner is clipped across the twisted runner.

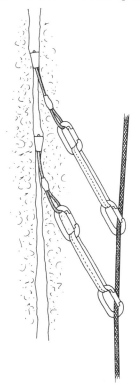

Fig. 10–38. Placing a backup chock to help protect a questionable placement

Another option is to equalize the load over two protection points, subjecting each to only a portion of the total force. (A more complicated version of equalizing protection, with three or more protection points, can be used at belay points to establish an anchor. See Chapter 7.)

Two-point equalizing protection can be placed

with one hand and requires the use of only one runner. Twist the runner into two halves, then clip each end into a protection point. Clip a carabiner between the two halves, providing an attachment point for the rope (fig. 10-39a). A load on the rope causes this carabiner to slide between the questionable protection points, adjusting the runner to equalize the force exerted on each point.

Important: clip the carabiner from one loop of the twisted runner to the other loop, not crosswise (fig. 10-39b). You'll find out why if you fall and one of the protection points fails. If you've done it right, the carabiner will stay connected to the runner, which stays connected to the remaining protection. Do it wrong, and the carabiner, with you attached, will plummet.

TECHNIQUES OF PROTECTION: LEADING A PITCH

A SAFE LEADING STRATEGY

After you get to know the tools for protection and how to place them, it's time for the next move—literally.

It's one thing to recognize a Stopper and a hex and a Friend and to be able to use them in individual placements. You can learn all this at home or while standing safely at the base of a cliff.

It's another thing to get up on the cliff and take the lead. You now need to learn the protection techniques that let you use these tools safely in mapping strategy for an entire pitch.

You'll learn to think of the entire pitch as you make each placement. How will this placement affect the total climbing system—and vice versa? Learn these techniques and you shouldn't have any nasty surprises in a fall. That beautifully placed chock won't pop out, because you used the right tricks to make it do its job in the context of protection for the entire pitch.

Leading is a complex business. Beginners usually need an apprenticeship, moving behind seasoned climbers, before they can safely take the sharp end of the rope. Don't ever take a lead if you don't feel ready, and don't pressure others into leading. Keep the art of leading what it ought to be: exciting, challenging, satisfying, and safe.

DECIDING FREQUENCY OF PROTECTION

The universal fear of falling leads many climbers to place protection before almost every move. They deplete their hardware and waste valuable time. They also miss one of the great attractions of rock climbing, the exhilaration of moving smoothly and continuously up the rock.

Other climbers under-protect, sometimes to show off their strength and daring. They get a psychological lift that doesn't do a thing to counteract the law of gravity.

But the sensible climbers—you and I—base our decisions about protection on a careful assessment of our personal abilities, the character of the rock, and the time and equipment available.

The closest thing to a general rule is to place protection where you feel uncomfortable without it. Of course, comfort level isn't always determined by a rational assessment of danger. A climber who feels comfortable making a difficult move a mere 6 feet above the last piece of protection may risk a nasty fall onto a sharp rock horn, while a climber on a low-angle friction slab with no projections to hit if he falls may be terrified at running out 20 feet beyond the protection.

In coming to your own decision on when to place another piece of protection, keep in mind the quality of the placements on a pitch. If they're tending to be poor or questionable, you'll probably put in more to increase the likelihood that at least one will hold. Knowing the fall factor, discussed next, also helps in deciding the next placement.

DETERMINING THE FALL FACTOR

The relative forces generated by a leader fall are measured by the fall factor, determined by dividing the length of a fall by the length of rope run out from the belay. The higher the fall factor, the greater the force.

The fall factor is lower when the length of rope run out from the belay is relatively great, because a long length of rope stretches more and absorbs more energy than a short length. The practical effect of this fact is that when the length of rope between belayer and climber is great, a fall will usually result in a smaller force than the same fall on a short length. Therefore, it's possible to place protection less frequently toward the end of a pitch without increasing the fall factor.

The fall factor is an important concept for the lead climber to understand because it provides an estimate of the relative forces that will be generated in a fall. The lead climber—not the belayer—determines the fall factor by deciding when to place protection. Therefore, the leader should keep the fall factor in mind and take steps to minimize it. Place protection as soon as possible after leaving the belay stance, in order to eliminate chances of a fall with the maximum fall factor of two. Then place intermediate protection as the opportunity arises while you climb. You can roughly estimate the potential fall factor at different points during the lead, to help in deciding when to place more protection. Just remember that a fall near the start of a pitch puts relatively more force on you and the protection, so it generally promotes safety to place more protection near the beginning.

Your belayer has the capability to adjust the belay technique to help accommodate the fall factor and minimize the effects of the fall on you and the climbing system. However, if you allow too much friction to develop in the climbing system or lead out the full length of the rope, the belayer will not be able to dynamically feed out rope to reduce the fall forces. This can create a static belay and cause the actual fall forces experienced by the leader to be higher.

SELECTING A PLACEMENT

As you lead a pitch, moving up from the belay station or from the last piece of protection, you'll reach a point where you would like to put in another piece—either because you want the extra protection at that point, or because a good opportunity for a placement presents itself. Find a stance for yourself that is secure and comfortable as possible. It can take some time to put in a good placement, so you need a stance where you won't slip off or become dangerously tired.

If there's no good stance, you're stuck with some unpleasant options: downclimb and ask the belayer to lead the pitch; hang on desperately and hope to get in a placement before arms or legs give out; or charge on to the next available placement point. This unhappy situation usually can be avoided by planning ahead and placing protection before it's urgently needed. When such a situation does develop, however, don't panic. Make a decision and stick with it. Surprisingly often, the correct decision is to continue without protection to the next possible placement.

When you find a good stance, however, go ahead with the protection placement. Sometimes you'll be faced with a choice between two or more

usable cracks for placing chocks. It's tempting to always place the largest possible chock, but which one you use should depend on considering several factors. Which placement would be the strongest? What size chocks should be conserved for use higher on the pitch? Which placement will be easiest for the second climber to remove? Choose your placement after thinking through all the consequences of your choice.

ATTACHING THE ROPE TO THE PROTECTION

The normal method of attaching the rope to any piece of artificial protection is very simple and very important. A runner clipped by a carabiner to the artificial protection is also clipped by another carabiner to the rope. The finished chain of protection is this: a piece of protection, a carabiner, a runner, another carabiner, the rope (fig. 10-40a).

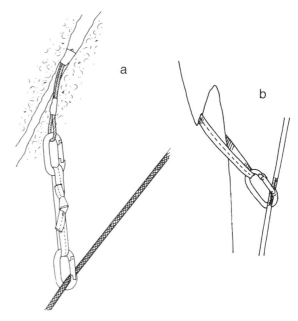

Fig. 10–40. Attaching the rope to the protection: a, attaching the rope to a piece of artificial protection (artificial protection, carabiner, runner, carabiner, rope); b, attaching the rope to natural protection (natural protection, runner, carabiner, rope).

With natural protection, the usual method of attaching the rope is to clip it to a carabiner that is clipped to a runner around the point of natural protection—whether it's a tree, flake, rock horn, or whatever. The finished chain of protection is: the point of natural protection, a runner, a carabiner, the rope (fig. 10-40b).

These standard methods of extending the protection point with a runner have two critical virtues: they reduce the effect of rope movement on the protection, and they reduce the drag on the rope as it moves through the climbing system.

Carabiners

The carabiner is a basic tool for connecting parts of the climbing system. A carabiner's reliability in the event of a climber's fall is largely determined by how it is placed and used.

Clip each carabiner so the solid side is against the rock and the gate is down and facing out. This helps ensure that contact with the rock won't force the gate open—resulting in a much weaker carabiner—and makes it easier to clip a runner or rope into the carabiner.

The carabiner should allow the rope to run smoothly without twists or kinks. Avoid chaining carabiners, which can become unclipped if severely twisted. Use locking carabiners, or two carabiners with gates opposed, if there's danger of a carabiner being forced open as the result of a fall.

It's always best to use a carabiner to attach the runner to a chock sling, rather than tying the runner directly to the sling (fig. 10-41a). This is particularly important with wired chocks because the wire cable under load could cut the runner. In an emergency, you can loop a runner through a wire sling (fig. 10-41c). But never attach the runner to a wire sling with a girth hitch (fig. 10-41b).

When a carabiner is clipped directly into protection (usually a bolt or piton), see that the carabiner

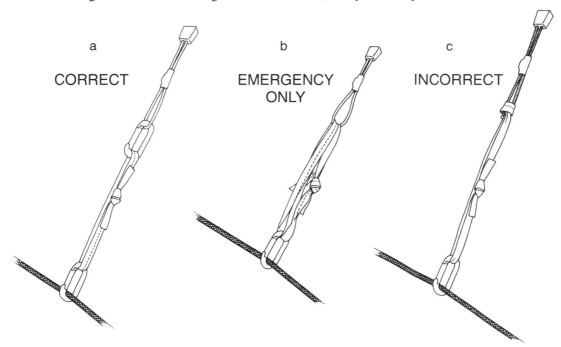

Fig. 10–41. Attaching a chock to a runner: a, correct, a carabiner is used to connect the chock to the runner; b, emergency only, the runner is looped through the chock sling; c, incorrect, the runner is girth-hitched to the chock. A cable chock sling could cut the runner under load.

will not bind against the rock. A fall could subject the carabiner to loads from several directions and cause carabiner failure.

Runners

Single runners and the shorter runners known as quick draws are usually used with artificial protection. Double runners are often used to loop around natural protection such as trees and boulders.

You can create a large runner by connecting one runner to another with a girth hitch. Two single runners connected together like this will be about the length of a double runner.

For single runners or quick draws, there's a choice of using sewn or tied runners. Each has certain advantages and disadvantages. Sewn runners are stronger, lighter, less bulky, and have no knot that needs rechecking or retying. However, they cannot be untied and retied around a protection placement. Tied runners are cheaper and have a knot for use as a passive wedging chock in emergencies. They also can be untied and then retied around a tree or other point of protection. But tied runners are bulkier, and the knot (the weakest part of a tied runner) must be checked regularly for looseness.

Energy-absorbing runners can be used to reduce the load on marginal protection. This type of runner has a series of bar tacks designed to rip out as they absorb some of the load in a fall (fig. 10-42).

A safety consideration in using energy-absorbing runners: as each bar tack breaks, it can cause vibration that opens the gate of the attached carabiner. If all the bar tacks break, the final load could be on an open carabiner. (A locking carabiner would be insurance against this problem.) With these special runners, it's important to study the manufacturer's instructions.

KEEPING THE ROPE IN A STRAIGHT LINE

Keeping the rope in roughly a straight line from the belayer to the climber is the best way to reduce rope drag and to guard against unanticipated fall forces. Rope drag is at best an annoyance and at

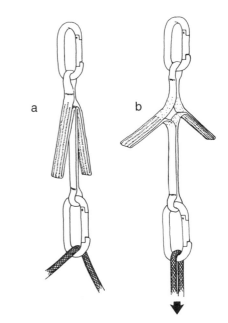

Fig. 10–42. Energy-absorbing runner: a, Yates Screamer energy-absorbing runner in use; b, during a fall, the bar tacks will break to absorb energy and help reduce the load on marginal protection.

worst can cause a leader fall. Fall forces, if they're not anticipated and planned for, can yank your protection right out of the rock.

Reducing rope drag

Rope drag causes all sorts of problems. It can hold a climber back. It can throw a climber off balance. It makes it hard for the leader to pull up enough rope to clip into the next protection. It adds friction to the climbing system, which can increase the force on the top piece of protection in a fall. Also, rope drag can affect how well a belayer responds to a fall, by reducing the ability to provide a dynamic belay.

If the protection placements do not follow a straight line up the pitch and if the rope is clipped directly in to these placements, it will zig-zag up the cliff, causing severe rope drag (fig. 10-43b). That's one main reason to extend runners from protection to rope, allowing the rope to hang straighter and run more freely through the protection system (fig. 10-43a).

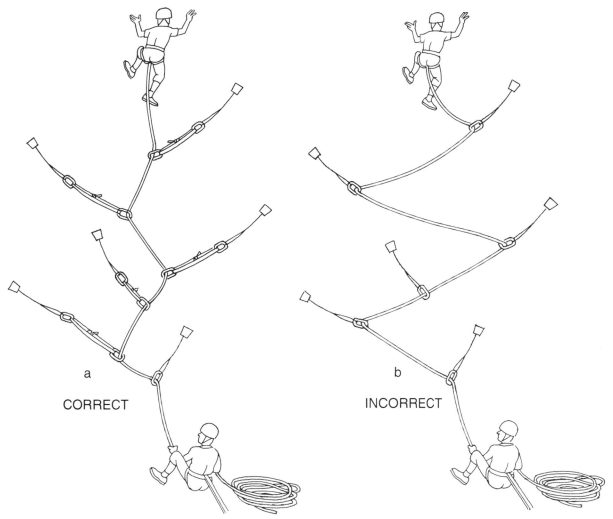

a
CORRECT

b
INCORRECT

Fig. 10–43. Reducing rope drag: a, correct, the protection placements are extended using runners to straighten the rope and reduce rope drag; b, incorrect, the rope was allowed to excessively zig-zag, causing severe rope drag.

There's another problem that can occur here: the increased fall distance when using an extra-long runner. The extension may help keep the rope in a straight line. But it may also add dangerous extra feet to the length of a fall. In such a case, it's sometimes better to accept some rope drag in order to get better security in case of a fall.

If the protection placements happen to be in a straight line, the rope will, of course, be straight and experience less rope drag, even if it's clipped directly to the protection. And by clipping the rope directly to the protection, the distance of any fall is minimized. However, be aware that rope movement might jiggle a chock out of position in this situation. When a rope is clipped directly to bolts or pitons, a short runner (known as a quick draw) or two linked carabiners are normally used to separate the rope from the protection.

Judging the direction of fall forces

The mechanics of placing protection is only one skill a leader must acquire. The leader must also anticipate the direction of forces that will be created by a fall and how they affect the protection placements.

Climbers can be so wrapped up in placing the next piece of protection that they fail to analyze the effect it will have on the entire climbing system. This can create a false sense of security. A protection point may seem solid and secure—but it may not withstand a fall that generates forces in directions not anticipated. It's the responsibility of the lead climber to anticipate and protect against these fall forces.

The dangers of a zig-zagging rope again command our attention. The zig-zag not only puts a dangerous amount of drag on the rope, but also can bring unanticipated forces to bear on the protection. The pieces of protection may have been placed only with the thought of holding a downward pull. Now they are in danger of taking sharp pulls from a number of directions during a fall.

Consider this: when a climber falls, the rope becomes taut in an attempt to form a straight line from the belayer up to the highest protection and then back down to the falling climber. The zig-zag rope tries to go straight—tugging sideways or up or outward on every piece of protection as it does so (fig. 10-44). If the placements are designed to take a pull in only one direction, they may come loose. If the highest piece of protection fails, the whole system could collapse.

During a fall, the top piece of protection is

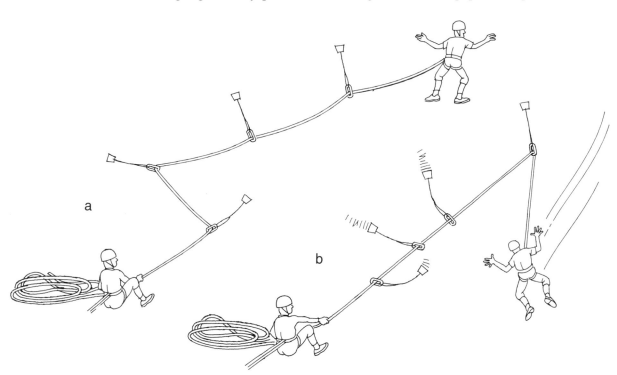

Fig. 10–44. Judging the direction of fall forces: a, a zig-zagging rope can bring unanticipated fall forces to bear on the protection; b, as the rope tries to straighten, it can pull up or outward on the protection, causing it to fail, especially if it was placed only for a downward pull.

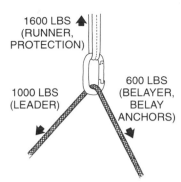

Fig. 10–45. The combined force on the top protection placement during a fall

loaded with the sum of two forces: the impact of the falling climber and the force exerted by the belay in arresting the fall (fig. 10-45). If a fall is taken by a weak piece of protection, it could fail. In this situation, it would be nice to know the protection below could be counted on to stay in place. But with the rope zig-zagging all over the hill, this might not be the case.

As in the problem of rope drag, keeping the rope in a straight line will prevent most of the problems caused by fall forces. Try to make all the protection placements form a straight line back to the belayer, or extend the protection with runners to permit the rope to run straight.

Work for placements that will take some upward or outward pull. Try to ensure that all awkward placements are multidirectional by using natural protection, such as a tree or a tunnel, or by setting up opposing chocks.

Consider ending the pitch early, before the normal belay point, to avoid awkward placements. Two smaller pitches may be better than one long meandering pitch.

GUARDING AGAINST THE ZIPPER EFFECT

The full-scale zipper effect is a dramatic demonstration of the importance of anticipating force directions. It happens most readily where the belay is established away from the base of the climb. The rope runs at a low angle from the belayer to the

Fig. 10–46. The zipper effect in action: force on the bottom chock is up and out.

first piece of protection on the cliff. There, the rope changes direction and goes abruptly upward. In a leader fall, the rope goes taut and tries to run in a straight line from the belayer to the top piece of protection—putting great outward pressure on that bottom chock. If it pulls out, the line of chocks could be yanked out one by one from the bottom up—the zipper effect in action (fig. 10-46).

The zipper effect can also occur at placements higher on the pitch. Danger points are found on overhanging and traversing routes.

The zipper effect can be prevented by making the suspect placement multidirectional, using natural protection or opposing vertical chocks. At the bottom of the pitch, another method of prevention is to move the belay to the base of the climb. (This may not be possible, however, because of the danger of falling rock.)

PROTECTING SPECIAL SITUATIONS

Overhangs

That overhang looks intimidating, doesn't it? But for purposes of placing protection, simply pay close attention to the consequences of every placement, just as you've been doing on the rest of the pitch. Keep the rope running as free of the overhang as possible. Extend the rope with runners in order to reduce rope drag, prevent dangerous fall forces (the zipper effect), and keep the rope from being cut by the edge of the overhang (fig. 10-47). On small overhangs, it may be possible to lean out and place protection above it.

Traverses

A lead climber often places protection both before and after a hard move, which guards not only the leader but the climber who follows (fig. 10-48). This is particularly important on traverses, where the second climber could otherwise face a long pendulum fall. In addition to the danger of injury, that kind of fall could leave the second in a tough spot, off route and with no easy way back.

As you lead a diagonal or traversing section, keep in mind the effect each placement could have on a second. Put yourself in the second's shoes and ask, Would I like some extra protection here? If so, place it.

It's possible to belay the second with an extra rope, which may help protect against a pendulum

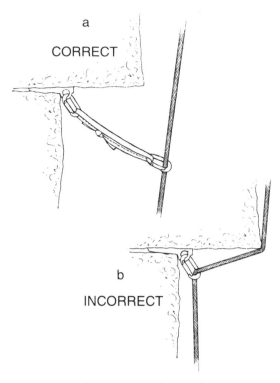

Fig. 10–47. Placements under overhangs: a, correct, rope runs free of the overhang; b, incorrect, bends cause rope drag and rope could be cut by rock edge during a fall.

fall and provide better protection than the leader's rope. If you happen to be using the double-rope technique (described later in this chapter), do not clip in both ropes during the traverse so that the follower can receive a belay from above on the free rope.

PLANNING A FULL CLIMB

WHAT GEAR TO BRING

You're planning a climb. And the question before you is: what should we carry along for protection?

If you're in an established climbing area, no problem. A guidebook will often tell what you

need to know before deciding what to carry: type of rock, width of cracks, amount of fixed or natural protection, length and direction of each pitch, difficulty rating—even the precise sizes of chocks needed.

It's a different matter on first ascents or in remote climbing areas. The leader then has much

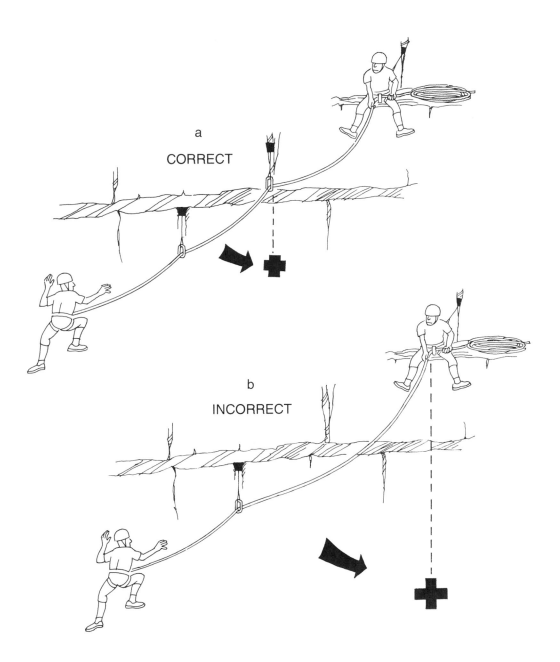

Fig. 10–48. Protecting a traverse: a, correct, placing protection after a hard move on a traverse can reduce the potential pendulum fall for the second climber; b, incorrect, if the second climber falls on a traverse with inadequate protection, he faces a long pendulum fall.

less information to use in estimating what to take along. Take too much, and the extra weight and equipment make the climbing awkward and harder than necessary. Take too little, and you may be forced to ''run it out''—to climb higher above the protection than is safe.

For protection, a leader always packs a selection of chocks, carabiners, and runners. But how many and what kind? These questions can't be answered without knowing some specifics of the climb at hand. However, there are some general considerations in choosing what to bring.

First of all, there's an endless variety of protection available—in the climbing shops. Because of the cost, most climbers own only a moderate number of protection devices. So the two climbers in a typical rock climbing team can really choose only from the protection they own (or borrow). The climbers usually combine their equipment to increase the choices of protection.

Chocks: It's very difficult to know just what size you'll need. Pick sizes and types that fit a wide range and offer more options.

Carabiners: In most cases, each protection placement requires at least two carabiners. Non-locking carabiners are the norm, though locking carabiners can be used in cases where the gate might be forced open during a fall. Many climbers carry extra carabiners (free carabiners) for contingencies.

Runners: These will be in three lengths: short (quick draws), medium (single runners), and long (double runners). Each point of protection commonly requires one runner. The proper runner at any point is the one that helps the rope stay in as straight a line as possible. Additional runners are needed for belay anchors and unanticipated protection placements.

Chock picks: Sometimes chocks are harder to get out than to put in. That's why each climbing team needs a chock pick—a thin metal tool that helps the second climber remove pieces of protection from a pitch (fig. 10-49). The second climber uses the tool to pry and poke and tap and tug at chocks that are too tightly lodged to come out by hand. Even with the pick, it often takes persistence

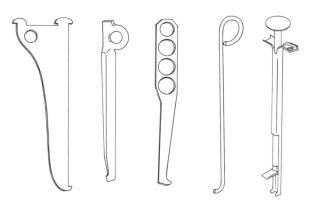

Fig. 10–49. Chock picks, left to right: shelf bracket, piton type, Leeper, skewer type or tent stake, Friend of a Friend.

to remove a chock. Give up if it refuses to budge. Wasting time trying to remove a badly stuck chock only tires you out and delays the climb.

In addition to chocks, carabiners, runners, and a chock pick, a rock climber often carries a belay device, a chalk bag, and tie-off loops (for such uses as emergency prusiking and for tying off a climber after a fall).

HOW TO CARRY THE GEAR

Once you've decided what gear to take, it must be organized for carrying. The technique of organizing the gear is called racking. The collection of gear is the rack.

Typically, pieces of protection are carried on a gear sling which is slung over the head and under one arm. (Climbing shops sell gear slings, or you can make your own by sewing 2-inch flat webbing into a loop and then rolling and sewing about half of it into a rope-like shape.) Single runners are grouped together and slung over the head—on top of the gear sling and under the opposite arm (fig. 10-50a).

Double runners are too long to handle without a little extra work. A double runner can just be doubled before it goes over your head. An alternative method, which makes it easier to get it when you need it, is to drape the double runner over one shoulder and then clip the two ends together under the opposite arm with a carabiner. Make one twist in the runner before attaching the carabiner, which will eliminate the possibility of the carabiner falling off when the runner is removed. When you need the runner, simply unclip the carabiner from one end and yank; the double runner will pull free.

Typical ways to rack gear

The ideal racking method would permit the leader to place protection efficiently and to climb without awkwardness despite carrying the gear. No such ideal method exists, but a variety of compromises are in use.

One carabiner per chock

In one common method, each chock and each runner gets its own carabiner (fig. 10-50b). In this setup, the gate of each carabiner that carries a chock should be up and toward your body, making

it easier to unclip the carabiner from the gear sling.

This method can be very efficient for placing protection. The leader simply places the chock in the rock, clips the chock's carabiner to a runner, and clips the runner's carabiner to the rope. Easy.

Disadvantages of this method are bulkiness and poor weight distribution. The rack tends to be wider and more cumbersome, and there are fewer free carabiners. With a carabiner on each runner, the runners are more weighted and tend to shift, making climbing awkward.

Several chocks on one carabiner

In a second method, pieces of protection are grouped together, each group held by a single carabiner (fig. 10-50c). In this setup, the gate of each carabiner that carries a set of chocks is down and facing away from your body. In this method, single runners don't have carabiners, and extra

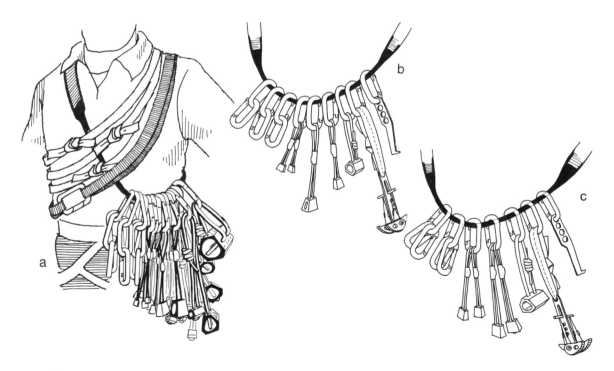

Fig. 10–50. Example racking methods: a, a climber carrying runners and a typical rack; b, a racking method where most pieces of protection get their own carabiner; c, a racking method where most pieces of protection are grouped together, each group held by a single carabiner.

carabiners are clipped to the gear sling in chains of two or three.

This second method can make climbing easier because it results in a less bulky rack with better weight distribution. But it also can make it more difficult to place protection. First of all, you have to decide whether to remove a single piece from the group of chocks on a carabiner, or to unclip the carabiner and hold the whole batch of chocks up to the placement.

If you've got a good eye and know what you'll want, you can remove a single chock and place it. But a wrong guess means you've got to put the chock back and try again.

On the other hand, if you unclip the carabiner with its batch of chocks, you can easily try out each chock and place the one that fits. You can then clip the carabiner to the rope for safekeeping while you finish constructing the placement. Finally, unclip the carabiner from the chock and return the carabiner and the unused chocks to the gear sling.

This method of racking gear with several chocks per carabiner usually means slower placements and more equipment handling. Even after placing a chock, the leader must handle two free carabiners and a runner to create the extension to the rope. All this increases the danger that the leader will drop gear or become exhausted. But some climbers feel the increased ease of climbing is worth the extra work.

Other methods

There are other ways to rack gear. Some climbers clip a separate carabiner to each larger chock, but group the smaller chocks so that several will be attached to one carabiner.

Some climbers carry part of the equipment on the gear loops of their harnesses. This helps distribute the weight of the rack, but be sure the gear doesn't hang down far enough to interfere with footwork.

Whatever the method, rack the protection in a systematic order that never varies, so you can find a particular piece in a hurry. The usual order is to start at the front with the smallest wired wedges and to work back with larger-size chocks.

A final point on runners

It's a good idea to carry a couple of runners readily accessible on the harness gear loops in case you can't get to the ones slung under one arm. (If that arm is being used in a jam crack, you won't be able to remove the runners.) You can carry quick draws on the gear loops. To shorten a longer runner so it won't trip you up, you can double it or "chain" (fig. 10-51) the runner and attach it to the

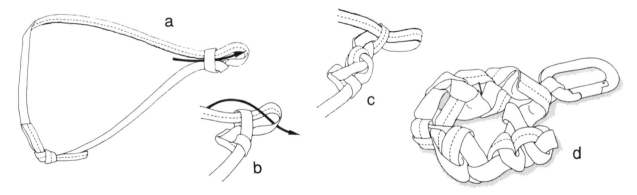

Fig. 10–51. "Chaining" a long runner: a, form a slip knot; b, pull runner through the loop formed by the slip knot; c, repeat this process until the runner is "chained"; d, the final loop can be attached to a carabiner for carrying and to ensure it does not unravel.

harness. When needed, just shake out the chained runner to remove the knots.

PLANNING THE ROUTE

The question of finding your way to the top depends on where you're climbing. If you're sport climbing in a popular spot, just follow the line of fixed pins and bolts, or look up the climb in the guidebook.

There's more involved in finding the route in alpine rock climbing. Even with a guidebook, the description may be sketchy: ''Ascend NE Buttress for several hundred feet of moderate climbing.'' Figure on some planning and routefinding.

Start working out the route as soon as you can see the buttress, face, ridge, or whatever you plan to climb. Look for major features that the line of ascent might follow: crack systems, dihedrals, chimneys, areas of broken rock. Note areas of small trees or bushes that could indicate belay ledges.

Keep an eye out for deceptively tempting lines that lead to broad roofs or blank walls. These may not be visible from near the start of the ascent and if the climbers don't pay attention on the approach, they could climb four or five pitches only to hit a dead end.

Develop a flexible plan for the line of ascent, keeping in mind likely alternatives. Continue planning and routefinding as the actual climb begins, looking for more local features. The general principles are the same: look for natural lines to follow, such as cracks, chimneys and ledges; form a tentative plan for the pitch, perhaps including a place for the first piece of protection and a spot for the next belay station; and note alternative moves in case the planned line leads to a blank wall. Be prepared to look around the corner for easier alternatives not visible from below.

Faced with a choice between pitches of differing difficulty, look at the next pitch before deciding. It's better to climb two moderate pitches than to go for an easy pitch and then be faced with one that exceeds the party's ability.

On the way up, keep track of retreat possibilities in case the climb is aborted, as well as good descent routes from the summit if you don't know of any established route.

PLANNING THE BELAY

It's simple enough: if it's a one-pitch climb, the second belay setup only needs to be directed against a downward pull from the second climber. If it's a multipitch climb, the belay station will also be used to belay the next lead. The climber who sets up this dual-purpose station should try to arrange anchors that will handle the downward pull from the second climber and then, with minimal change, the upward pull of the leader. An efficient belay setup is faster, safer, and leaves more time for climbing.

CLEANING A PITCH

The climber who follows and cleans a pitch should be neat and efficient. A second who is slow and sloppy can drop chocks, allow dangling protection to dangerously interfere with the next move, and hold up the climb while the hardware is untangled at the belay station.

Here are some suggestions for the second:

Start preparing to climb as soon as the leader is off belay. Get out of the belay setup and break down the anchor system (staying clipped into one anchor until you are on belay).

Put on the pack before anything else, except perhaps a hardware sling. Rack all chocks and carabiners on a hardware sling or runner worn over one shoulder and under the opposite arm; then put your runners over the other shoulder and under the other arm. Give the area a last look to make sure nothing is left. Then, once you are on a belay, start climbing.

Remove a chock in reverse order of the way it was placed. If it was slotted down and behind a constriction, remove it by pushing back and up.

Be persistent. Although vigorous pulling or tugging may only set the chock more solidly, it may be necessary to tap or wiggle the chock to free it. Sometimes it takes a lot of work.

Carry a chock pick. You'll need it to tug and

push on stubborn placements. Some chock picks also can be used to pull the retraction trigger on a spring-loaded camming device that has ''walked'' back into a crack. Wired chocks can also sometimes be used for that purpose.

Consider leaving the chock behind if it won't budge. Sure, they're expensive. But you can waste too much time and energy on a chock that won't come out.

The second can minimize the risk of dropping gear by using a careful cleaning procedure, which may depend on how you prefer to rack the hardware. In general, cleaning from the rock to the rope is best.

Consider a typical placement consisting of chock-carabiner-runner-carabiner-rope. If your rack features one carabiner on each chock and on each runner, the following cleaning procedure is very efficient. First, remove the chock from the crack. Hold the carabiner that is clipped to the chock, unclip it from the runner, and clip the carabiner-chock combination directly to your gear sling. Then loop the runner over your head, unclip the carabiner from the rope, slip the carabiner-runner combination under one arm and continue climbing.

If your rack features several chocks per carabiner, the following cleaning procedure works well with that method. First, remove the chock from the crack, unclip it, and rack it. Then remove the carabiner from the runner and rack it, then the runner, and finally the carabiner on the rope.

TRANSFERRING EQUIPMENT AT THE TOP OF A PITCH

If the second was neat and efficient in cleaning the pitch, organizing gear as it was removed, the transfer at the belay station will probably go quickly and the fun can resume.

First reconstruct the original leader's rack. The second clips the removed pieces to the leader's rack or hands them to the leader, who can rack them. Caution: don't drop any gear. The second then passes over the removed runners. If the original leader plans to lead the next pitch, the climbers

then carefully switch places in the belay setup. This is one way to do it, but if the second is also a competent leader, it's a lot more efficient to swing leads, with the second now taking the lead.

To swing leads, the second usually takes over the leader's rack and runners. The original leader hands the runners to the second (an arm makes a good ''post'' to place the runners on). The rack is next, passed to the second, who places it over the head and under one arm. The runners then go over the head and under the other arm. The new leader checks and adjusts the rack to ensure that everything is ready for the new lead. During this whole procedure, the new leader stays clipped into a separate anchor and, as a backup, can remain on belay.

RUNNING BELAYS

The running belay is an old technique that is still occasionally used for the time it saves. Both climbers tie in and move simultaneously. There is no belayer. The leader places occasional protection and clips the rope through it. The leader also can weave between blocks and spires to take advantage of natural protection. The climbers can reduce rope friction and also stay closer together for communication by carrying some of the rope coiled. In any case, the follower usually carries a few coils in hand to avoid unpleasant jerks when the leader moves fast.

In a fall, the rope—running through the protection—will be held at some point by the weight of the other climber, because the rope is tied to both climbers' harnesses and neither is anchored. The friction of rope running over rock or snow also helps slow the fall. This technique probably only makes the difference between serious injury and total disaster. If either climber falls, both may fall—and a big fall is arrested only by dragging one's partner.

A running belay is not to be confused with moving in coils, which is simply carrying the rope over truly easy ground without using intermediate protection and when any type of belay is unnecessary.

HAULING PACKS

You may decide to shed your pack sometime because you can't fit inside a chimney with it or because the weight would make a pitch too difficult. Then you'll have to haul the pack up after you.

One way to handle this chore is to trail a rope behind you as you climb, tied to the pack down below. This can be either the unneeded end of the climbing rope, if the pitch is short enough, or a separate rope. At the end of the pitch, put in an anchor, haul the pack up hand-over-hand, untie it, and throw the end of the rope down to haul up your partner's pack. If you lack extra rope, have your partner untie from the climbing rope so you can pull it up through the protection and toss the end down for pack hauling.

Ice axes are often hauled separately so there is less danger the pack will snag as it is being pulled up. Tie the ice axe, and any other gear, securely to the rope.

Be sure you have a compelling reason for shedding your pack. If you're doing it only because climbing without it is more fun, think twice. Hauling packs takes valuable time, especially when they get stuck, and they do. It's also hard work that can rob you of precious arm strength. And remember, packs launch rocks.

CLIMBING WITH A PARTY OF THREE

Most rock climbing is done in teams of two, but occasionally a party will end up with three climbers. This works, though it's usually more awkward than climbing with just two.

A three-person team climbing on one rope is limited to pitches of only 70 to 80 feet, just half the rope length. Because many climbs have pitches much longer than this, a three-person team may need to carry two ropes.

With three climbers, the leader climbs while the second belays and the third remains anchored at the belay station. At the top of the pitch, the leader sets up a belay and brings up the second (who can also be belayed from below by the third).

If the pitch follows a straight line up, the second can clean the pitch. But if the line includes some traversing, the protection should stay in for the third climber, to help prevent a pendulum fall. In this situation, the second climber unclips each piece of protection from the first rope and clips it to the second rope. At the top of the pitch, the belay is reset to bring up the third climber. The climbers then may decide to swing leads, with the third climber leading the next pitch. The second generally doesn't do any leading in a party of three.

With all the anchors, ropes, and climbers involved, it can get messy and confusing at the belay station. A lot of time can be taken up setting and resetting belays. Throughout the commotion, it's critical that each of the three climbers be securely anchored. (The belay stations on some tough climbs are so small they couldn't accommodate a three-person team in the first place.)

There are occasional advantages to a three-person team, such as the added help in hauling packs and the availability of an extra rope if a full-length rappel is required. But the disadvantages usually outweigh the advantages.

SPECIAL ROPE TECHNIQUES

Much of this book describes climbing situations in which only a single rope, with a diameter between 10 and 11 millimeters, is used. However, climbers can opt for a system that uses two separate ropes (double-rope technique) instead of a single rope, or another in which two smaller-diameter ropes are used as one to replace the single rope (twin-rope technique).

Double-rope technique

Double-rope technique uses two ropes that serve as independent belay lines. The leader clips each rope into its own protection points on the way up, and a single belayer manages the ropes separately.

Yes, it's complicated, but the system offers some important rewards, such as reduced rope drag and safer traverses. The technique is widely used by British climbers and by an increasing number of climbers everywhere to protect highly technical routes. Double-rope technique usually employs color-coded 9-millimeter ropes.

The leader clips one rope into one series of protection placements and the other rope into another series, the goal being to keep each rope in as straight a line as possible so rope drag is at a minimum (fig. 10-52). The drag is usually less than what it would be on a single rope on the same pitch because the single rope would have to follow a more meandering route. The double ropes typically run in roughly parallel routes, and do not cross. However, if both ropes must be attached to one protection placement, each rope should be attached using a separate carabiner.

The system also helps reduce the worries of the leader who is straining to clip in to the next piece of protection. In single-rope climbing, the rope is slack as the climber pulls up a big hunk of it to clip the next placement. But on a double rope, only the one rope is slack if the belayer is holding the other snug. If the climber falls at this point, the fall will be taken on the nearest placement used by the snug rope, usually making for a shorter fall.

The system has the advantage that both ropes are unlikely to be cut by sharp rock edges or

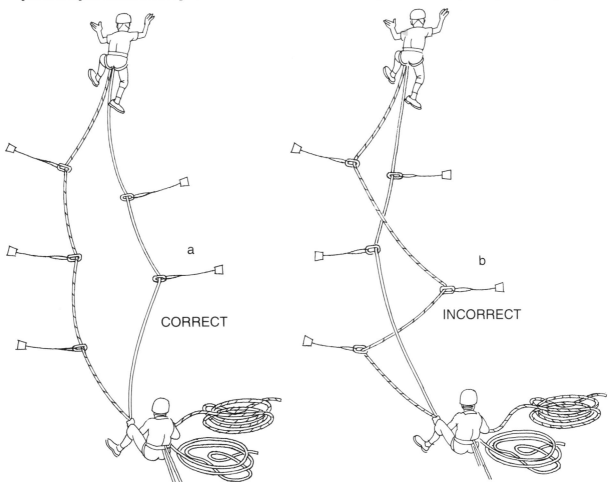

Fig. 10–52. Double-rope technique: a, correct, the two ropes do not cross but run straight to reduce rope drag; b, incorrect, the two ropes cross and run in a zig-zag, increasing rope drag.

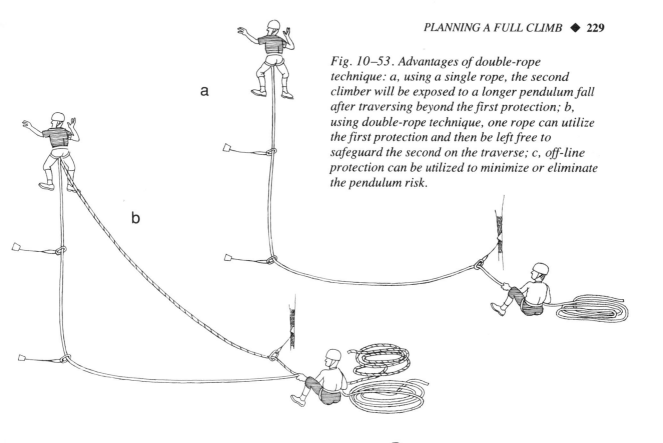

Fig. 10–53. Advantages of double-rope technique: a, using a single rope, the second climber will be exposed to a longer pendulum fall after traversing beyond the first protection; b, using double-rope technique, one rope can utilize the first protection and then be left free to safeguard the second on the traverse; c, off-line protection can be utilized to minimize or eliminate the pendulum risk.

rockfall, or to otherwise fail, at the same time. And it provides two ropes for rappels.

The double ropes can also be used to protect a traverse, particularly one at the start or the middle of a pitch which then goes straight up. In the event of a fall, without a second rope the second climber risks a long pendulum (see Fig. 10-53a). With double ropes, the pendulum can be minimized or avoided. The leader can use one of the ropes for protection on the traverse and leave the other free to protect the second from above (see Fig. 10-53b, 10-53c).

Disadvantages of the double-rope technique? The two ropes weigh more and cost more than the single rope (though often each climber will contribute one rope). The principal problem is that the belayer's job is more complex as he must handle the movements of two ropes, often letting out slack on one rope while taking it in on the other. For this type of climbing a double slot Sticht belay plate is particularly useful, though other belay techniques can be used. Moreover, the rope has to be constantly monitored to avoid tangling or kinking. With practice these difficulties are soon mastered, and on long and complex rock pitches the advantages vastly outweigh the disadvantages.

Twin-rope technique

Twin-rope technique—with two ropes used as one—features ropes that are 8 to 8.8 millimeters in diameter. Both ropes are clipped into each piece of protection, just as in single rope technique (fig. 10-54).

The twin ropes absorb more energy and thus can withstand more falls than a single rope. Two ropes also are safer running over an edge, as it's unlikely that both ropes would be cut through at the same time. The smaller-diameter ropes are individually easier for the lead climber to handle than a standard single rope.

However, the technique means the belayer has to handle and belay with two ropes, so rope management is tricky. As with the double-rope method, both belayer and leader need a good bit of practice before taking this technique out on the cliffs. And again, twin ropes cost more than a standard single rope.

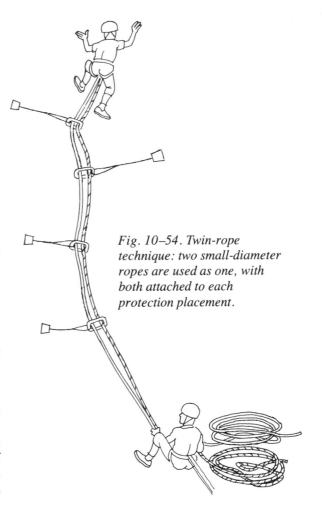

Fig. 10–54. Twin-rope technique: two small-diameter ropes are used as one, with both attached to each protection placement.

PERSONAL RESPONSIBILITY

ETHICS AND STYLE OF PLACING PROTECTION

Local climbers at each area have usually settled on some basic rules to play by, including standards for placing protection. Some climbing areas are more traditional, encouraging leading and placing protection "from the ground up." Other areas have embraced newer techniques, such as inspecting a route on rappel before climbing it, or placing bolts on rappel. You'll have your own opinions regarding protection, of course, but be sensitive to the climbing ethics and styles developed and demonstrated by local climbers.

ENVIRONMENTAL IMPACT

Everything about mountaineering, including rock climbing, is linked to affection and respect for the environment and consideration for the travelers who come after you. The general rule is the same whether you're hiking, backpacking, alpine mountaineering, or rock climbing: leave the world the way you found it. Specifically on a rock pitch, this means avoiding permanent scarring of trees, rock, and vegetation. If possible, stick to clean climbing, using only chocks for protection.

SAFETY

You know by now that climbing is a balancing act in more ways than one. There's not always one ''correct'' technique for doing something, and you often need to balance different factors in deciding on a course of action.

Likewise there's no simple set of commandments to memorize and mechanically follow to ensure safety. You may be called on to make life-and-death decisions despite incomplete knowledge, with no clear rule to follow, and without the luxury of being able to consult your favorite expert, even if that expert is on the other end of the rope.

Controlling the risks of climbing is a matter of understanding the reasons that underlie the techniques you've learned, being aware of everything that affects a safe choice, and being able to gauge all the consequences of your actions. And then making a decision as thoughtfully as time allows.

The important thing is that you'll be acting on knowledge, not ignorance; on deep understanding, not superficial rules. A climber who uses techniques without understanding them or who mechanically follows a set of safety rules is not thinking and is a danger to himself and fellow climbers. But learn the principles, make them yours, and you'll be free to do what we all want to do: climb hard, climb high, climb safe.

· 11 ·

AID CLIMBING AND PITONCRAFT

Aid climbing is the technique of using gear to support your weight as you climb. It can be as simple as using a bolt as a single handhold, or as complex as climbing an entire route with your full weight on pieces of specialized gear you have placed.

Aid climbing is clearly a sharp departure from free climbing, where weighting the rope or the protective hardware is poor style. Free ascents are one of the goals of the sport of climbing, while aid climbing is a valuable skill for ascending currently "unfreeable" routes and for use in emergencies.

As standards of difficulty continue to rise, top climbers are freeing many of the routes originally climbed with aid. But despite the rise in free-climbing standards, there will always be tempting routes that are more difficult still—and so devoid of natural features that a climber will need some artificial assistance.

Skills in aid climbing and pitoncraft can also help overcome unexpected difficulties during normal free climbing. They can provide a way to move safely up or down when weather or accident puts your party in jeopardy. Knowing how to use pitons for aid also helps you in evaluating the soundness of fixed pitons you encounter while free climbing. In winter mountaineering, pitons may be the only protection that will hold in ice-filled cracks.

Any advice to use pitons always comes with a stern caveat: pitons permanently damage the rock. Don't use them unless you must. And don't use them at all on established free routes.

Aid climbing and pitoncraft require skill, judgment, and a lot of practice. To learn both the basics and the many "tricks" of the techniques, try to work with an experienced partner, and climb often.

CLEAN AID CLIMBING

Aid climbing takes a lot of gear, but it needn't be damaging to the rock. With all the chocks and camming devices on the market, you now have a better chance to climb routes clean, without putting in a single piton or bolt. The chocks and other devices can be removed without defacing the rock, and the next climber won't even be able to tell you were there.

Aid climbing may still require bolts and pitons, but keep them to a minimum. Pitons (also called

pins) chip the rock, especially when you remove them. On popular routes, tiny cracks sometimes evolve into finger or hand cracks after generations of climbers force them to accept pitons.

When climbers make the first ascent of a major wall, they often carry bolts and pins to make it go. Once placed, the best approach is to leave them so future parties can use them without marring the rock further. In general, make clean climbing your goal.

TYPES OF AID CLIMBING

We can roughly categorize aid climbing based on the extent of its use on a particular climb.

Mountaineering alpine aid climbing uses a minimal amount of aid techniques and equipment to overcome short, blank (or extremely difficult) sections of a route that otherwise goes free. This type of climbing requires little or no specialized aid equipment. Usually you'll just use the free-climbing gear you have along.

General aid climbing often uses aid for extended distances, although artificial and free-climbing techniques may be interspersed. Long one-day climbs may involve "fixing" the initial pitches—putting up ropes and leaving them in place so they can be climbed quickly with mechanical ascenders the following morning to reach the previous high point.

Big-wall aid climbing involves ascents that take longer than one day to complete, even if the initial pitches are fixed. These climbs include either a hanging bivouac or ledge bivouac and require sack-hauling techniques.

Take a look at Appendix 2, Rating Systems, for a discussion of the various grades of difficulty in aid climbing.

AID CLIMBING EQUIPMENT

Probably more so than in any other type of climbing, you're now in for the true "nuts and bolts" of the sport. This section details the range of equipment used in aid climbing, and builds on all the gear and techniques described in Chapter 10. If you're not interested in aid climbing, this section may hold all the drama of a hardware catalog. But if you've become intrigued with the subject, you'll find this material both thorough and fascinating.

BASIC EQUIPMENT FOR CLEAN AID CLIMBING

Clean aid relies heavily on standard free-climbing equipment. You'll simply need more of it.

Chocks and camming devices: Because you'll be setting placements every several feet, a long pitch can require more than 50 assorted chocks and camming devices. The sling attached to each piece should be as short as possible to help you get the maximum elevation gain out of each placement.

Carabiners: While a minimum of 40 free carabiners are needed on an aid rack, it's not unusual to use 80 on a long pitch and more than 100 on a particularly difficult pitch. Many aid climbers prefer oval carabiners rather than D carabiners because ovals minimize the unnerving shifting that occurs when a D takes your weight. Regardless of the shape, you should be able to open the carabiner gate whenever you wish, even while it is holding your weight.

Small nuts: Aid racks include specialty small nuts, beyond those on free-climbing racks. These tapered nuts are often used instead of thin pitons, but they are not as strong. They are designed to support body weight, and may fail if fallen upon.

Two general styles of nuts are available. The first is a smaller version of a normal tapered Stopper. The second style has both horizontal and vertical taper and is more secure in flaring cracks and old pin scars (piton scars).

The heads of small nuts are made from aluminum, brass, or stainless steel. Aluminum and brass bite into the rock and hold better in marginal placements, but steel nuts are less likely to deform and fail if you take a fall on one of them.

Ropes: The tough duty of aid climbing usually requires 11-millimeter or 12-millimeter kernmantle ropes, 165 feet long. The haul line is typically an 11-millimeter or 9-millimeter line which doubles as a backup rope and a second rope for long rappels. If your route entails pendulums or other unusual problems, you may need a third rope.

Hero loops: Very short slings are useful for aid climbing. These tie-off (hero) loops—4 to 6 inches long—are threaded through fixed protection in place of a carabiner. Climbers usually tie their own out of 1/2-inch webbing. You'll use many of them if the route has a lot of fixed bolts or pitons. They are also used to prevent the loss of stacked pieces (described later), and to tie off partially driven pins. Also carry at least six regular-length slings for establishing anchors, extending placements to reduce rope drag, and other normal rock-climbing uses.

Chock picks: Picks used for aid climbing should be sturdy, because you'll often hammer on the pick to tap out lodged nuts.

Gloves: Over and above their value for belaying and rappelling, gloves protect your hands while "jugging" (ascending the climbing rope with mechanical ascenders) and removing protection placements.

Rock shoes: If the route involves only a small amount of aid, normal free-climbing rock shoes perform best. If sustained aid is anticipated, boots with greater sole rigidity provide a better working platform and more comfort. Some new boots on the market provide a rigid arch support and good torsional rigidity for aid climbing, yet have a flexible toe and a sole of soft friction rubber for good free-climbing capabilities.

Energy-absorbing slings: These slings increase security when climbing above placements of questionable strength. In a fall, the slings limit the shock delivered to the protection. Their use, however, limits the amount of elevation gained from the placements to which they are attached.

UNIVERSAL AID-CLIMBING EQUIPMENT

In addition to equipment normally used in free climbing, you will need a selection of gear that is used for both clean aid climbing and for aid that involves placing pins.

Etriers: These ladder-like slings (fig. 11-1) allow climbers to step up from one placement to the next when they are clipped to a chock, piton, or other aid piece. Consider the intended use when

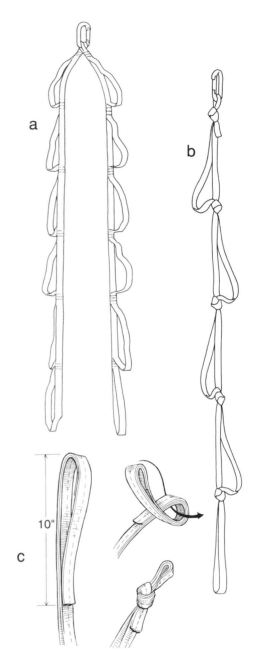

Fig. 11–1. Types of etriers: a, sewn; b, tied; c, the frost knot. Tied etriers require twice their finished length plus 10 inches for each step (overhand knot) and the frost knot. A 60-inch etrier with five steps (four overhand knots) takes 170 inches of runner.

Fig. 11–2. Tied daisy chain

making or buying etriers. For alpine climbs, minimize weight by using a single pair of etriers made of $^9/_{16}$-inch or $^{11}/_{16}$-inch webbing. For most aid climbing, four- or five-step etriers made of 1-inch webbing are standard. Etriers should be long enough to let you step smoothly from the top step of one to the bottom step of another that has been clipped into a piece at arm's reach above.

Tying your own etriers lets you tailor their size to your own. However, commercially made or home-sewn etriers are preferred for routes with extensive aid because they remain open for foot placement when weighted. Metal-rung etriers have the same advantage and are less prone to blow in the wind, but they can cause more pain if they do hit you or your partner.

Some climbers use two pairs of etriers while aid climbing; others use a single pair—it depends on the nature of the route and on personal preference. Likewise, some climbers prefer to attach a short grab sling to the carabiner loop of their etriers.

Daisy chains are tied or sewn slings with a loop—formed by a knot or stitching—every 3 to 6 inches (fig. 11-2). The proper length for you is a daisy chain that, when attached to your harness, reaches as far as your raised hand. Attach a carabiner to every loop (or every other loop) in the chain so you can quickly clip into an aid placement and rest on your harness.

Carry a second daisy chain, without carabiners in each loop, for other purposes, such as attaching yourself to your ascenders while jugging or for preventing loss of etriers if a hook placement fails.

Fifi hooks function somewhat like daisy chains but are attached to your harness with a sling only 2 to 6 inches long (fig. 11-3). You can quickly clip the hook into an aid piece, allowing you to rest on your harness. Be careful. If you release the tension or change the angle, it could come unhooked. Aid

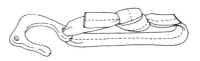

Fig. 11–3. Fifi hook with sling

climbers usually carry one fifi hook for use on bolt ladders and fixed pitches.

A double rack, with equipment slings on both sides of the body, distributes the weight of the hardware (fig. 11-4). It improves your balance and

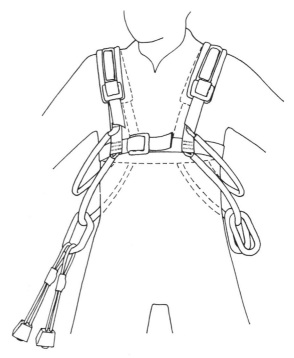

Fig. 11–4. Double rack

comfort and reduces the neck strain caused by a single rack. If it's built right, a double rack can also serve as a chest harness as you jug up a rope with mechanical ascenders. Some climbers carry a single rack in addition, for their free carabiners or as a supplemental free-climbing rack.

A belay seat with two- or three-point attachment is a great creature-comfort during hanging belays (fig. 11-5). One urgent warning: never let the belay seat be your sole means of attaching to an anchor. Clip in from your harness to the anchor with the climbing rope as usual—and then set up the belay seat for comfort.

Mechanical ascenders (fig. 11-6) serve the same function as prusik knots but are stronger, safer, faster, and less tiring. The devices are a requirement for sack hauling on big walls.

All ascenders employ a cam, allowing the ascender to slide freely in one direction on a rope but to grip tight when pulled in the opposite direction. They also have a trigger or locking mechanism to keep them from accidentally coming off the rope. Some triggers are difficult to release, decreasing the chance of accidental removal but making it harder to get them off when you want to. If your ascenders are made of cast aluminum, back up their frames with webbing to reduce the danger created should they break.

If you plan to use ascenders for cold-weather climbing, look for a pair with openings large enough to accommodate heavily gloved hands. Carabiner holes at the top and the bottom of the ascender come in handy for a number of purposes, such as sack hauling. If the ascender doesn't have

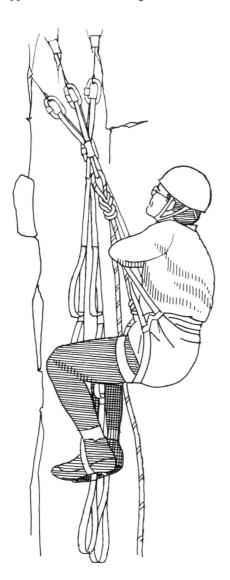

Fig. 11–5. Two-point belay seat; note the anchored climbing rope.

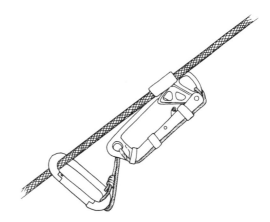

Fig. 11–6. Mechanical ascender with backup sling; ascender is attached in preparation for diagonal ascent.

these holes, you'll have to attach slings for clip-in points.

Piton hammers have a flat striking surface for cleaning and driving pitons, and a blunt pick for prying out protection, cleaning dirty cracks, and placing malleable pieces (fig. 11-7). Hammer shafts should be long enough to forcefully drive pins, and short enough to fit comfortably in a belt holster. The shafts should also be sturdy and taped for protection. A carabiner hole in the head is useful for cleaning pins and malleable pieces.

Attach a sling to your hammer that allows full arm extension when the hammer is in use (fig. 11-8). If you happen to drop the hammer, it will just hang below your feet on the sling. Be sure to check the sling regularly for wear.

Hooks come in many shapes and forms, and are most commonly used to grip ledges or small holes

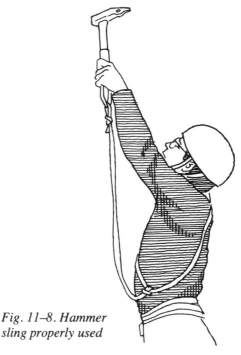

Fig. 11–8. Hammer sling properly used

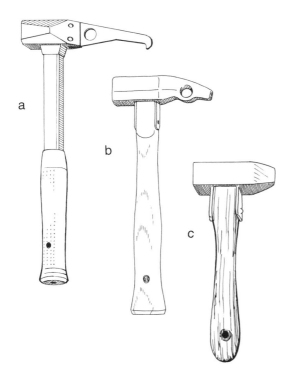

Fig. 11–7. Piton hammer styles: a, Mjollnir; b, Chouinard; c, less adequate.

(fig. 11-9). With etriers attached to the hook, you have a rather delicate placement for moving upward. Hooks should be made of chrome-moly steel (for strength), and the non-hook end should be wider and curved (for stability). Attach slings to the bottom of your hooks with a girth hitch, positioned so that when the sling is weighted, the "legs" (lower end) of the hook are pulled into the

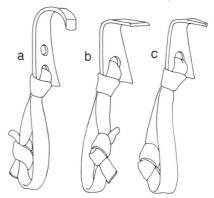

Fig. 11–9. Hook types: a, sky hook; b, Logan hook; c, bat hook.

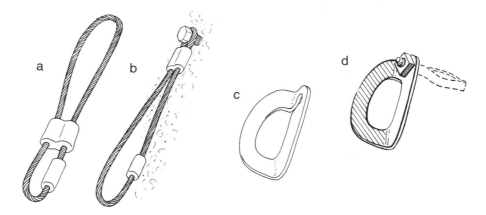

Fig. 11–10. Hangers: a, wire; b, wire hanger on a bolt; c, keyhole; d, regular hanger on a bolt.

rock. To accomplish this, the sling should hang from the rock side of the hook.

Sky hooks look almost like giant fish hooks and are useful for small flakes and ledges. Greater stability is achieved on some routes if the tip of the hook is filed to a point, which can be set into small holes drilled at the back of tiny ledges. Fish hooks, or ring claws, are like large sky hooks and are used to grip larger flakes and ledges. Logan hooks are L-shaped: the wide style is stable on tiny ledges and flakes, and the narrow style can be used in shallow pockets. Bat hooks are basically a narrow-style Logan hook with a pointed blade, allowing their use in shallow 1/4-inch holes drilled for their use.

Wire hangers (fig. 11-10a and b) are loops of wire 1/8 inch or 3/32 inch in diameter, with a slider to cinch the wire tight over bolt studs and rivets (basically, bolts with a wide head). Small tapered chocks (Stoppers) with wire slings can also be used for this purpose, with the chock itself acting as the slider to tighten the wire against the bolt stud. However, because the chocks have a longer wire loop than the wire hangers, you won't get as much elevation gain from them.

Regular hangers and keyhole hangers serve a similar function to the wire hangers, but are shaped pieces of metal rather than wire loops (fig. 11-10c and d). They are useful, especially at belay anchors and for fixed bolts that have no hangers. Keyhole hangers have the metal between the bolt hole and carabiner hole filed out to allow placement over rivets and buttonhead bolts.

IRONMONGERY FOR FULL AID CLIMBING

To master the full range of aid-climbing techniques, climbers must have a knowledge of pitons and bolts.

Pitons

Modern pitons—or pins—are made of chromemoly (hard) steel. Rather than molding to cracks like the malleable pitons of old, they mold the crack to their form. Because of the damage that pitons cause and because of improvements in clean-climbing hardware, piton use has declined greatly. They are still important, however, on overhanging rock and very thin cracks. For winter mountaineering, when cracks are filled with ice, they may offer the only viable means of protection. To fit the diverse cracks encountered on rock walls, pitons vary tremendously in size and shape (fig. 11-11).

The Realized Ultimate Reality Piton (RURP) is the smallest piton, a postage-stamp-sized, hatchet-shaped pin used in incipient cracks. It will usually support only body weight and derives what little strength it has by minimizing the leverage between the piton and carabiner supporting your etriers. Some styles come with offset sides for use in corners.

Birdbeaks are similar to RURPs but have a longer arm for attaching a carabiner or sling. Generally they are easier to place and remove.

Knifeblades are long thin pitons that have two eyes—one at the end of the blade and a second in the offset portion of the pin. They come in different lengths and in thicknesses between $1/8$ inch and $3/16$ inch, and they are commonly used to fit many cracks that are too thin for tiny nuts.

Lost arrows are similar to knifeblades but have a single eye which is centered and set perpendicular to the end of the blade. These too are commonly used pitons that come in several lengths and thicknesses ($5/32$ to $3/8$ inch). They are very good in horizontal cracks.

Angles are pitons formed into a "V." The V varies in height from $1/4$ inch to $1^1/2$ inches (smaller ones are most popular). Their strength is derived from the metal's resistance to bending and spreading. Angles and other large pitons have largely been replaced by modern free-climbing hardware.

Leeper Z pitons obtain their thickness through their Z profile as opposed to the V profile of an angle. These pitons are very solid and work well for stacking because of their short length, useful in bottoming cracks.

Bongs are large angle pitons that vary from 2 to 6 inches in width. In addition to their use as pitons, they can double as large chocks. Camming devices like Friends have largely replaced bongs.

Sawed-off pins are handy on routes that have been heavily climbed using pitons, leaving shallow pin scars. Several $3/4$-inch and 1-inch angles with a few inches cut off the end are useful for shallow placements.

Malleable hardware (bashies)

Malleable hardware (fig. 11-12) is designed to hold weight by melding the soft head of the placement to the irregularities of the rock. The security

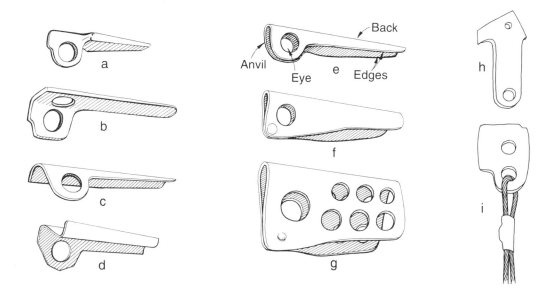

Fig. 11–11. Piton (pin) types: a, lost arrow; b, knifeblade; c, shallow angle; d, Leeper Z; e, angle; f, large angle; g, bong; h, birdbeak; i, RURP.

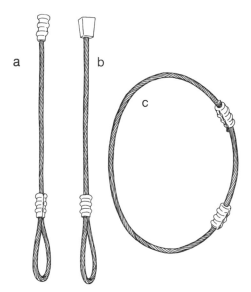

Fig. 11–12. Malleable head types: a, copperhead; b, aluma-head; c, circlehead.

of these bashies varies greatly, and it is difficult to gauge their strength, making them last-resort equipment.

Copperheads (fig. 11-12a) have a swage of copper attached to one end of a short cable that has a loop at the other end. They are placed by pounding the copper head into an irregularity in the rock. They tend to form well and are more durable than similar pieces with aluminum heads (aluma-heads).

Aluma-heads (fig. 11-12b) are not as tough as copperheads but are more malleable, so they tend to be used for the larger sizes, while the smaller heads are usually copper.

Circleheads (fig. 11-12c) consist of a wire loop with an extra copper swage on the loop, which is pounded into the rock like a copperhead. They are used in horizontal cracks.

Bolts

Chapter 10 includes a section on the use of existing bolts found on climbing routes. Bolts permanently scar the rock and alter the style of a climb, and very serious consideration should be given before placing one. Proper bolt placement is a special skill, beyond the scope of this book. Bolt placement is best left to the skill and judgment of very experienced climbers.

BIG-WALL EQUIPMENT

Climbers undertaking a big wall have other specialized equipment to consider.

Pulleys will be required to ease the chore of sack hauling. They receive much abuse, so they must be durable. Pulleys with bearings and larger wheels operate more smoothly.

Haul bags carry your clothing, water, food, sleeping bag, and other non-climbing paraphernalia. A good haul bag should have adequate cargo capacity, a solid haul suspension, durable fabric, an absence of snag points, and a removable backpacking harness system. Duffels can be converted into haul sacks by reinforcing the wear areas. A top cap to the haul bag is a good idea to protect the knot connecting the sack to the haul line and help reduce snagging problems while hauling.

Cheater sticks allow you to clip a carabiner into a piece of hardware beyond your reach. Although rarely needed, they are often used to avoid "top stepping" in etriers. Cheater sticks should have a means of holding a carabiner solidly while you clip in with your arm fully extended.

Knee pads protect your knees, which are regularly in contact with the rock during aid climbing. Pads should be comfortable and allow good circulation.

Portaledges or hammocks: Portaledges, which are lightweight cots, offer greater comfort from a single point of suspension than hammocks. Unfortunately, they are much heavier and bulkier. As with belay seats, climbers must *always* be anchored to the rock when using this equipment.

If you take on a big wall, safeguard important equipment with tie-in loops to attach anything you might drop. Bring gear that will get you through the worst possible weather, because there's not likely to be any easy way to retreat. Be sure your equipment is durable and beef up any item that could fail, such as water containers. Select only the sturdiest, and reinforce them with duct tape.

AID PLACEMENTS

The main rule for aid climbing is to place each aid piece as high as possible. If you make placements at 5-foot rather than 4-foot intervals, over the course of a 160-foot pitch you'll save eight placements, many more carabiners, and much time.

Most of the techniques for placing free-climbing protection apply to aid climbing. For aid climbing, if possible, you'll shorten the slings to your pieces and often use hero loops on fixed protection rather than clipping in directly with a carabiner.

Placing small nuts during an aid climb is similar to placing larger ones on a free climb. But because aid nuts take the weight of the lead climber and because they may be smaller than the chock pick, they can be difficult to remove. If you place small nuts near the outside of the crack, they will be easier to remove and there will be less danger of damaging them in the process. Test small nuts gently before committing your weight to them.

Fixed pins, bolts, or rivets must be evaluated before use (see Chapter 10). If you decide to use a fixed piece, thread a hero loop through its eye and clip a single carabiner into the two ends of the loop. This saves a carabiner. Note: use a direct carabiner clip-in every three or four pieces as a backup. The hero-looped pieces are not as safe for stopping a fall because of the danger the loop could be cut by the edge of the metal eye. It's also wise to carry a few bolt hangers and nuts (in both $1/4$-inch and $3/8$-inch sizes) for bolts with missing or damaged hangers.

PITON PLACEMENT

Here are some basic guidelines for the sound placement of pitons (pins) (fig. 11-13):

• Horizontal placement of pins is generally more secure than vertical placement because rotation is reduced or eliminated.

• Ideally, the eye should point downward.

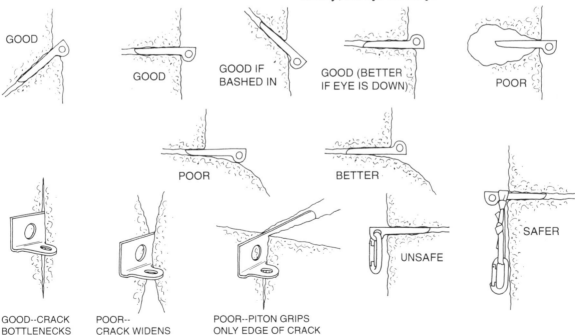

Fig. 11–13. Piton placements and problems

• As with chocks, place pins in locally wider portions of a crack. If the crack is thinner below and above the pin, the pin will be supported when it has to take a climber's weight.

• A properly sized pin can be placed one-half to two-thirds of the way by hand. The remainder of the pin is hammered in place. Select the correct pin to fit the crack. Don't try to make the crack fit the pin; this practice causes needless destruction of the rock.

• A sound piton rings with a higher-pitched "ping" with each strike of the hammer. After the pin is driven, tap it to test for rotation. Rotation indicates the pin is not biting the rock. Replace such pins with a larger size.

• Knowing just how much to hammer a piton is a matter of touch and experience. Excessive hammering wastes energy, makes it harder for the second to remove the piton, and needlessly damages the rock. Under-driving a piton, however, increases the risk of it pulling out. If several pins are under-driven, the failure of one could result in a long fall as the series of pins zippers out.

• When possible, avoid placing a pin in a three-way corner. Such placements are often impossible to clean because the pin cannot be tapped back and forth for removal. Just leave it as a fixed pin.

• If the position of the piton causes the connecting carabiner to extend over an edge, add a hero loop to the piece (fig. 11-14). This prevents loading the carabiner across its sides.

• On overhangs, place pins with some horizontal orientation when possible (fig. 11-15). This reduces the odds of total failure should the pin shift when weighted.

• Place knifeblades in vertical cracks with the offset eye down.

• When placing angles, keep the three points of the V in contact with the rock (fig. 11-16). The back (point of the V) *always* must contact one wall, while the edges (two tips of the V) contact the opposing wall. In a horizontal crack, put the back of the angle up and the edges down.

• Bongs (fig. 11-17), being made of aluminum, are quite fragile, so pound them as little as possible. Bongs are often placed as chockstones,

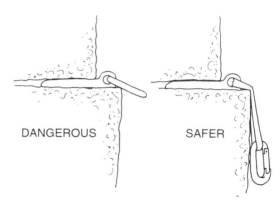

Fig. 11–14. Safely extending a piton; right figure eliminates side loading the carabiner.

and you can add a sling to a bong before using it that way.

• Expanding cracks present problems for pins because as subsequent pins are placed, lower ones loosen. When possible, use chocks in such situations, because they minimize flake expansion. If pins must be used, try to work with long minimum-taper pins placed lightly in natural slots, to minimize expansion of the rock flake.

• In shallow cracks and flutings, a piton may be driven over a chock. The chock creates a second "wall" against which the pin wedges. Because the chock would fall and be lost if the pin failed, attach a "keeper" sling to the chock and clip it into the

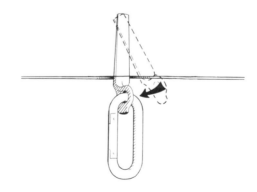

Fig. 11–15. Overhang piton placement

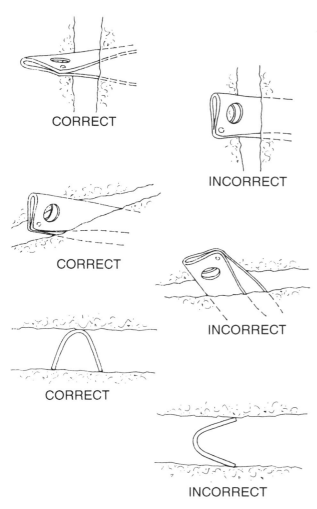

CORRECT

INCORRECT

CORRECT

INCORRECT

CORRECT

INCORRECT

Fig. 11–16. Proper placements for angle pitons

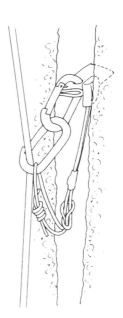

Fig. 11–18. Sawed-off piton driven over a Stopper; note the non–load-bearing keeper sling on the Stopper.

sling or carabiner of the load-bearing pin. The keeper sling must not bear any weight (fig. 11-18).
• When a pin ''bottoms out'' in a crack (that is, cannot be driven in all the way), stop hammering, to avoid loosening it. The piton must be tied off around the shaft at the point where it emerges from the rock. A hero loop tied to the piton with a girth hitch or clove hitch supports your weight and re-

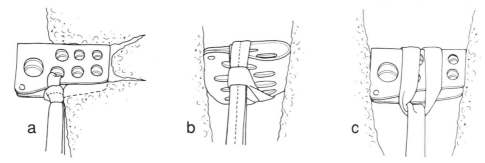

a   b   c

Fig. 11–17. Bong placements: a, driven and tied off through lightening holes; b and c, girth-hitched for use as a large chock.

duces the levering action on the pin (fig. 11-19). Bongs can be tied off through their lightening holes. Loop a longer keeper sling (or a second carabiner) through the eye of the pin and clip it into the hero loop or hero-loop carabiner. The keeper sling doesn't bear weight, but will catch your pin if it pops.

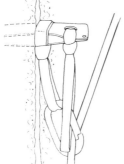

Fig. 11–19. Tied-off piton; note the use of a keeper sling through the piton eye.

STACKING AND NESTING

When no single pin or chock fits the crack at hand, aid climbing gets very creative. Whether you've run out of the proper-sized pieces or are facing a shallow flaring crack, it's time to improvise by stacking or nesting your hardware in whatever combination works (fig. 11-20).

Blades are nested back to back and are usually driven together. If a third blade is necessary, the first two are inserted by hand, and then the third is driven in between.

Some disagreement exists about the best way to stack angles. Most climbers stack them by keeping the backs of both angles against the rock, but any combination will work. Try to avoid stacking angles by simply placing one over the other, as these may be very hard to separate once removed. Leeper Z pitons are especially useful in stacking.

It may be possible to use a camming combination of a pin and a chock—or a pin and a wire hanger—in very difficult situations (fig. 11-21). The concept relies on the camming force exerted by the chock or wire on the back of the pin. The chock or wire loop is partially inserted into the

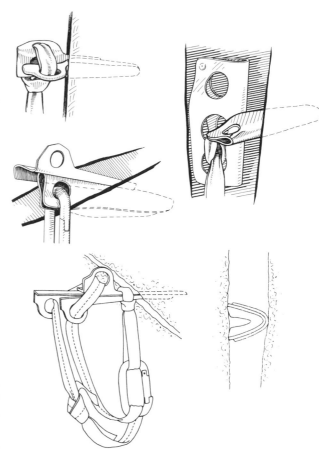

Fig. 11–20. Examples of pitons stacked and nested (some keeper slings omitted for clarity); inset, angles stacked over each other.

crack. Then, the pin is inserted to anchor the chock or wire and to create an artificial wall against which the chock or wire can cam. You can often achieve a solid aid placement this way with minimal use of the hammer. Note, however, that wires used this way wear quickly.

These special combinations present another situation that requires non-load-bearing keeper slings to catch any pitons should the placement fail.

HOOK PLACEMENT AND USE

Before placing a hook, clip an etrier to it. Also make sure to connect a sling (or daisy chain) between the etrier's carabiner and your harness. The

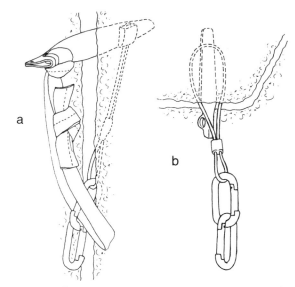

Fig. 11–21. Camming combinations: a, piton and chock; b, piton and wire hanger (keeper sling omitted for clarity).

sling will prevent the loss of your gear if the hook pops off its purchase.

Now set the hook on the ledge, flake, or hole where it will be used. Test it gently before applying full body weight (or gently "ooze" onto the hook). Avoid standing with your face directly in front of the hook because it could pop out with a good deal of force.

If the hook is used in a shallow bolt hole, a very slight tap to set the point is sometimes useful. However, this practice increases the possibility the hook will pop out. It also erodes the existing hole, and eventually a bolt will need to be placed.

MALLEABLE PLACEMENTS

Because you often can't tell how secure they are, do not use malleable heads unless you're dealing with a pocket or flare where other protection just won't work.

Copperheads, aluma-heads, and circleheads take more practice to place than other types of aid and require some specialized tools. The hammer pick works for setting large heads, but small heads require a striking tool like a blunt chisel or, in a pinch, a lost arrow.

Figure 11-22 illustrates the following procedure for placing a head:

1. Place it. Insert a head as you would a chock—in a narrowing portion of a flare or seam.
2. "X" it. Pound it in using angled strokes that form an X pattern on the head.
3. Paste it. Now pound the right and left sides to "pin" the head.
4. Rotate it. Hit the bottom and top to see if the head rotates. If so, X it and paste it again.
5. Sniff it. If the head emits a metallic odor, it is under-driven or over-driven; do not use it. The smell arises from the cutting or cracking of the head rather than its molding to the rock.
6. Use it. Heads are used like any other aid piece—but remember their inescapable weakness. Inspection cannot guarantee the molding of the head to the rock. Some heads may hold a short fall, others will just support body weight, and others might fail. All malleable-head placements are suspect, and an acceptance of this fact is inherent in their use.

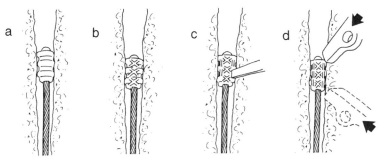

Fig. 11–22. Placing a malleable piece: a, place it; b, "X" it; c, paste it; d, rotate test it.

BASIC AID TECHNIQUES

Before starting up any aid pitch, study the terrain and make a plan. Determine the best rest spots, figure how to minimize rope drag, plan what gear you'll need and what you can leave for the second to carry, spot any obstructions that might plague sack hauling, and decide whether to save certain sizes of aid pieces for the end of the pitch.

Then gear up for the pitch. Place pitons (between three and six to a carabiner) on one side with the larger pieces to the rear. Place chocks and other gear for clean aid climbing on the other side, again with the larger pieces to the rear. Balance the

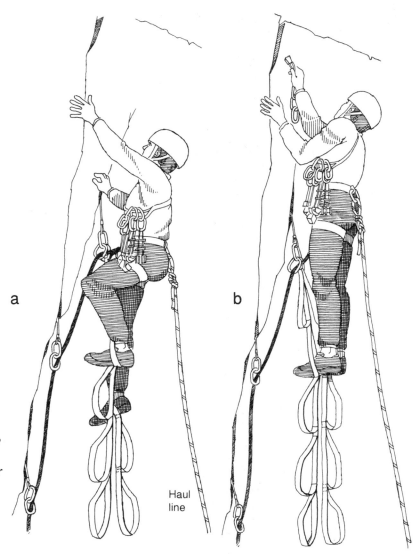

a

b

Haul line

Fig. 11–23. The basic sequence (some equipment omitted for clarity): a, climb high; b, place piece; c, clip etrier to carabiner on higher piece; d, test, move onto new placement, remove lower etriers; e, clip rope into lower carabiner on new piece and clip in daisy chain if desired.

weight with free carabiners racked in groups of four (two pairs). Short slings are best racked (several to a carabiner) and clipped to an easily accessible part of your harness. Finally, check that the hammer is accessible, with its sling untangled.

THE BASIC SEQUENCE

The basic aid sequence (fig. 11-23) is the same whether you are starting from the ground, a comfortable free stance, or the top step of your etriers:

1. Look and feel the terrain above and select an aid piece to place at the highest spot within reach (fig. 11-23a).
2. Place the piece (fig. 11-23b).
3. Clip in a free carabiner. Some climbers prefer to clip in a two-carabiner chain (fig. 11-23c);

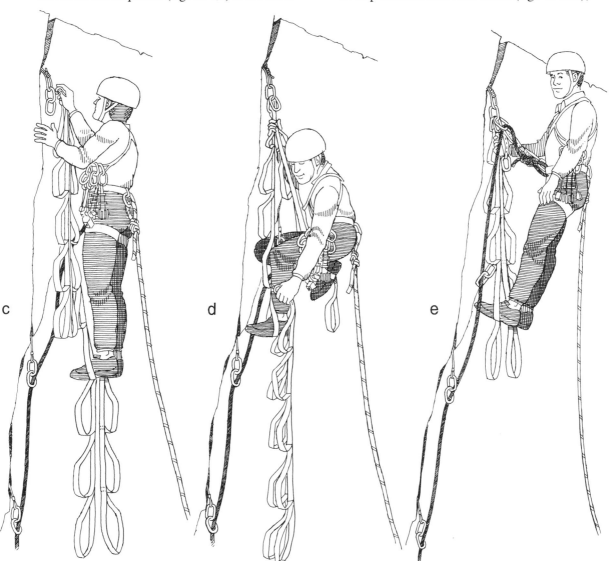

the second carabiner will later take the climbing rope. Other climbers feel two carabiners get in the way at this point. If you are moving onto a pin, first attach a hero loop to the pin, and then clip a carabiner to the loop.

4. If the aid piece you are currently weighting is questionable, you may want to clip the rope to the second carabiner of the higher piece if you are positive the higher placement is solid. Otherwise, the rope is not clipped into the higher piece yet.

5. Clip your free etrier(s) to the carabiner on the higher piece (the higher of the two carabiners if you used two) (fig. 11-23c). If moving onto a pin, clip the etrier(s) directly into the hero loop.

6. Test the new piece with a gentle, one-footed hop (the other foot is kept in an etrier on the lower piece). If the new piece is questionable, you may decide to avoid the test and simply "ooze" onto the new placement, applying your weight as gradually and smoothly as possible. Warn your belayer when you are about to test or move onto a dubious placement.

7. Move onto the higher etrier(s) (fig.11-23d). Clip the daisy chain into the new piece while in the lower step, if you wish.

8. Remove the lower etrier(s) (fig. 11-23d). For extended aid climbing, you will normally carry two pairs of etriers, so now you will remove the lower pair and clip it to your harness. (If you are climbing with just a single pair of etriers, remove the lower etrier and clip it to the highest aid piece.) Climb up the etriers until the daisy chain (or fifi hook) can be clipped in close to the new piece, if you wish.

9. Add a second carabiner (in chain fashion) to the new piece and clip in the rope. If you initially clipped two carabiners to the piece, clip the rope into the lower carabiner (fig. 11-23d).

10. Study the area immediately above to determine likely spots for the next placement. Then climb as high as possible, reclip the daisy if desired, and begin the process anew. Note: how high you climb in your etriers depends on

the terrain, but ideally you want to place the new piece from the top step.

Top stepping

Moving onto the top step of your etriers can be unnerving, but the ability to do so greatly improves the efficiency of aid climbing. The process is simple on low-angle rock where the top steps are used like any other foothold, and the hands provide balance.

Vertical and overhanging rock makes top stepping difficult because your center of gravity moves away from the rock *and* above the point where the etriers are clipped to the aid placement. If the rock offers any features, your hands may provide the balance. If the rock is blank, keep your weight on your feet while leaning back and applying tension to the daisy chain between your harness and your aid placement. That tension provides the means of balancing yourself (fig. 11-24).

Special considerations

Problems encountered while aid climbing may cause you to add variations to the basic sequence. As in free climbing, rope drag can become a problem. Use long slings to keep the rope running straight. Add the slings after you have moved to the next higher piece so that you obtain the maximum gain out of each placement.

You may also realize you're short of certain-sized pieces and that you will need to reuse these sizes. As you move onto a higher placement, you may opt to pull the piece you were just using and save it for future use. As a general rule, however, leave at least every other piece as your protection against a fall.

RESTING

Don't wear yourself out. Climb in a relaxed fashion and take rests as often as necessary to conserve your strength or plot the next series of moves.

Here's a quick and easy rest: with each foot in separate etriers and one foot one step below the other, bend the knee of the higher leg and bring that foot under you. Most of your weight rests over the bent leg. The outstretched leg takes minimal weight but maintains balance (fig. 11-25).

You can also clip your daisy chain or fifi hook into the piece supporting you and rest in your harness.

Once the climbing rope is clipped into the supporting piece, you can also ask the belayer for tension and rest on the climbing rope. This is not an efficient method, however, due to stretch in the

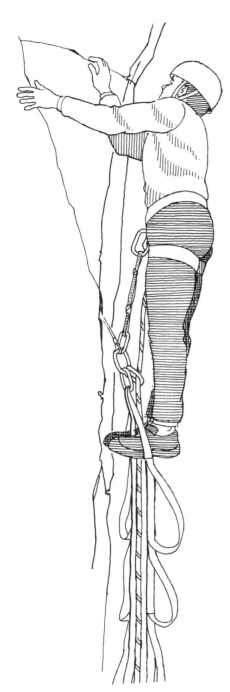

Fig. 11–24. Top stepping; note the use of daisy-chain tension.

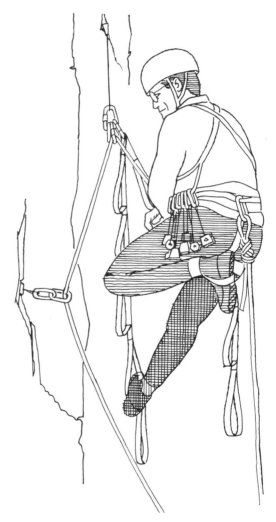

Fig. 11–25. Resting on a foot

rope. It also places unnecessary strain on the belay system.

Finally, you can often find relaxing stances in your etriers. Generally, the greatest stability is obtained with the heels together and the toes spread apart against the rock.

SWITCHING BETWEEN AID AND FREE CLIMBING

Timing is the key problem in switching between the techniques of aid and free climbing.

From free to aid: Free climbers must remember that the switch to aid requires some preparation. Begin the aid sequence before stretching yourself to the limit of your ability. This is easy if you know you will be changing to aid, but problems arise if you are not expecting to use aid but suddenly need it. Finding yourself in this bind, you can improvise etriers by interconnecting several slings and aid your way over the blank area. Such creativity is particularly important when climbing in a remote alpine environment. The climb's style may be damaged, but your body will be spared.

From aid to free: To free-climb a few moves during an aid pitch, simply clip the etriers to the back of your harness, and then make the moves. It is best to continue climbing on aid until you can comfortably switch to free techniques. If the change is made too early, you may have trouble retrieving your etriers from the last aid placement.

When beginning a longer section of free climbing, clip etriers, daisies, and so forth to your harness and be sure they will not hinder your movement. This may entail removing most of your aid implements and hanging them behind you.

TENSION TRAVERSES AND PENDULUMS

These techniques allow you to move horizontally across blank sections of a wall that would normally require placement of bolts.

Tension traverses are the simpler technique, useful for short traverses. The leader takes tension from the belayer, then leans to the side and uses friction on small holds to work sideways.

Pendulums let you cross wider blank sections without bolts but often require more ropes and pose special problems for the second climber. Start by placing a bombproof anchor at the top of the planned pendulum. The equipment used for this anchor cannot be retrieved unless it is possible to come back to it from above.

Next, you'll be lowered by the belayer (or rappel while on belay) until you have enough rope to run back and forth across the rock and swing into a new crack system. If a rappel is used for the pendulum, an extra rope will be required. When being lowered by the belayer, it is best to be lowered too little than too much, because if you're too low it may be very difficult to correct the error.

Once in the new crack system, climb as high as safety allows before clipping your belayed climbing rope into aid pieces for protection. The higher you get, the easier and safer it will be for your belayer, who will second the pendulum.

See the section later in this chapter on seconding pendulums for more details and an illustration of pendulum technique.

OVERHANGS

Before leading an overhang, check that you have enough equipment for the job. It may be impossible to obtain more gear later from the second climber. Keep your ascenders handy, because if a piece pulls and you end up hanging, you'll need ascenders to climb back up to your last secure piece. Also, check that your belayer is securely anchored, or you could both end up hanging free in the event of a fall.

Balance will be difficult as you scale an overhang because you can't effectively place your feet against the rock. Use of a daisy chain or fifi hook, however, allows you to hang from the harness and achieve a stable position. As an overhang approaches the horizontal, you can achieve greater balance still by clipping a sling from a chest harness to the supporting aid piece (fig. 11-26).

Despite the difference in balance, the basic sequence for aiding over a roof is the same as described earlier, but you may find it more comfortable to sit with your legs through the middle

Fig. 11–26. Aiding under a roof; note the use of a chest harness for support, and the availability of ascenders.

step of the etriers rather than standing in the bottom steps. Expect to experience some swinging. Finally, because your belayer will probably aid over the overhang rather than use ascenders, consider the length of your partner's reach when making your placements.

Rope drag is a common side effect of overhangs, but liberal use of longer slings will help. You may also want to pull along a second belay rope and start climbing on it after clearing the lip of the overhang.

Finally, try to relax when working out over a big roof. Have confidence in your pieces. Clutching at them won't keep them in place but will drain your strength.

HANGING BELAYS

Upon reaching the end of the pitch, the leader establishes an anchor as a new belay station (fig. 11-27). Place this anchor, when possible, to the side of the route (especially if you are sack hauling) so that your second can easily climb through. Also try to place at least one aid piece at the start of the next pitch to give the second a stance while changing leads.

When establishing your anchor, make sure *all* anchor points (including the haul anchor) are connected to *all* other anchor points. If an existing anchor system is in place do not simply place a sling over the system. This is an easy mistake to make and experienced climbers have paid for this error with their lives. Clip in, instead, in such a way that should any portion of the anchor fail, your attachment won't slide off the failed end.

Similarly, complete anchor systems have failed when a separate haul anchor, which was not interconnected with the main anchor, failed. In these cases the force generated by the falling haul sack overloaded the main anchor.

Once you are clipped in, anchor the climbing

Fig. 11–27. Hanging-belay sequence: a, leader establishes anchor; b, with climbing rope anchored and the haul system set, the second frees the haul sack (note that the first piece of the next pitch is set); c, while the second "jugs," the leader hauls the sack; d, the haul sack is anchored, and the second moves onto the first piece of the next pitch; e, after re-racking, the new leader begins to lead.

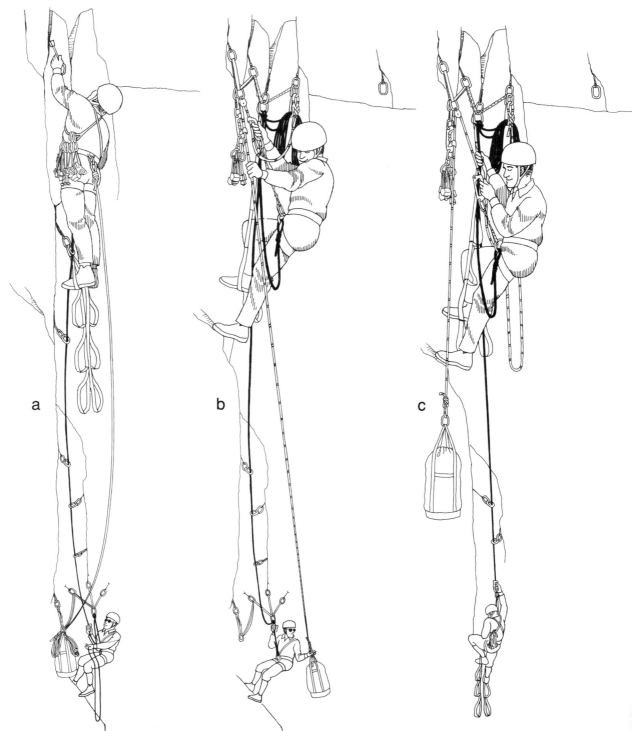

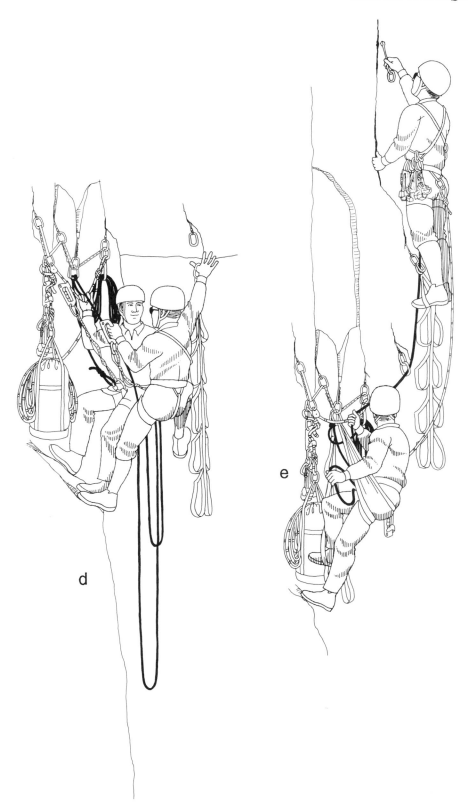

d

e

rope so that the second can ascend it as a fixed line. Now prepare the hauling system, if you are hauling. Remove the aid rack and use it as the counterweight for the hauling system. Inform the second to free the haul sack so that you can hoist it while the second ascends the fixed climbing rope.

After the hauling is completed (or after the climbing rope was fixed if you are not hauling), establish your belay seat, get comfortable, and prepare for the exchange of leads. Sort the rack, organize the ropes, prepare your belay system, and so forth.

TYROLEAN TRAVERSES

Tyrolean traverses are most often used to return to a main wall after ascending a detached pillar. Ropes are strung between the main wall and the top of the pillar, allowing you to traverse through the air, attached to the rope.

You can establish a Tyrolean traverse like this:

1. After setting up a bombproof anchor on the main wall—one that can take both a horizontal and vertical pull—rappel on two ropes to the saddle between the main wall and the pinnacle. (You can use just one rope for the rappel if the traverse will be short enough.) Do not pull down the rappel ropes. If it takes more than one rappel to reach the saddle, you'll have to tie a light line to the two ends of the main rappel rope to give you a way to retrieve the ends once you're on top of the pinnacle.

2. Climb the pinnacle using an additional climbing rope. The second climber brings up the free ends of the rappel ropes.

3. Once atop the pinnacle, the free ends of the rappel ropes (now the traverse ropes) are stretched tight and anchored to the pinnacle.

After the traverse, you will not be able to recover the equipment used for the pinnacle anchor.

4. While belayed, one climbers now "jugs" across the open area on *one* of the ropes, using the Texas prusik (which is explained in Chapter 13, in the section on crevasse rescue). The forward ascender is attached to the harness with a daisy chain. To the rear ascender is attached an etrier, and a second daisy chain attached to the climber's harness. Finally, the climber connects an additional safety sling between the traverse rope and the harness. This sling rides on a carabiner between the two ascenders. What would normally be the lower ends of the ascenders must be clipped to the rope with a safety carabiner (as shown in figure 11-6, earlier in this chapter).

5. After the first climber has jugged across, the second climber unties the ropes at the pinnacle anchor, threads the end of one rope through the anchor, and ties the ropes together as if preparing a rappel. This climber notes which rope will be pulled when it comes time to retrieve the ropes. (If it's a short traverse and you are using just a single rope, the climbers on each side of the traverse need to pull the rope around so that its center moves to the pinnacle anchor and the two ends are back on the main wall. Otherwise you will have problems retrieving the rope later.)

6. The first climber then tightens and anchors the rope ends on the main wall and belays the second, who will traverse in the same manner as the first.

7. Once both climbers are reunited, the ropes are untied at the main wall and retrieved by pulling on the appropriate rope.

SECONDING

As the second climber on short sections of aid, you will usually follow the same sequence as the leader, while belayed from above. You will, however, unclip the rope from a placement before clipping on the etriers, and clean the placement below

you after stepping up higher. If you cannot reach a lower piece after moving up, lengthen your etriers with another sling, and then step down to clean the piece.

When climbing long sections of aid, a different

strategy is called for. You will use mechanical ascenders to jug the fixed climbing rope and clean
the route as you go. Before heading up, free the
haul bag so the leader can start hauling it up the
route. If it hangs up along the way, you will be the
one to free it.

USING ASCENDERS

Although you could ascend fixed climbing
ropes on slings attached with prusik knots, mechanical ascenders are both safer and more efficient (fig. 11-28). Attach an etrier and a daisy
chain to each ascender. The etriers give you a platform to stand on, and the daisy chains positively
connect the ascenders to your harness. Use a carabiner—not a fifi hook—to clip each daisy chain to
an ascender. To expedite the process of preparing
your ascenders, mark the loops in both the daisies
and etriers where the gear is properly adjusted for
length while jugging.

You do *not* untie from the end of the climbing
rope while ascending. Remaining tied in serves as
a backup in case both ascenders fail. To further
decrease the likelihood of a long fall, you should
periodically "tie in short."

Tying in short is an easy precaution that has
saved lives. As the second ascends, an ever-length-
ening loop of climbing rope forms below him,
making for a long fall if the ascenders fail. To
avoid this danger, stop periodically and, using the
climbing rope just below the ascenders, tie a fig-
ure-8 loop and clip the loop into your harness with
a locking carabiner. This guarantees a much
shorter fall. Repeat this procedure about every 20
feet. Each time, unclip and untie the last figure-8
loop *after* the new figure-8 loop is clipped into
your harness. Even when tying in short, *do not
untie from the end of the rope.*

Often while jugging, it is necessary to remove
the upper ascender from the rope and place it above
a piece from which the rope cannot be unclipped
while weighted from below. This same situation
arises when the rope runs over an edge. Before
removing the ascender, tie in short; this is a convenient time to do so.

After reattaching the upper ascender above the

*Fig. 11–28. Use of
ascenders; note daisy
chains from each
ascender to harness,
and climber tied in
short.*

piece, check that the cam trigger is fully locked or the ascender could pop off the rope. This is especially true if you are jugging on a diagonal rope because the ascender has a tendency to twist to a vertical position once weighted. This twisting can be minimized by clipping a carabiner between the ascender and the rope as well (fig.11-6). Once the upper ascender is reattached and your weight is on it, you will be able to unclip the rope from the problem piece of aid.

Other precautions should also be taken while ascending. First, carry a spare prusik sling just in case an ascender fails. And, as in all climbing, beware of sharp edges. Jugging places the rope under tension and sharp edges can damage it. Ascend as smoothly as possible to minimize the sawing motion of the rope running over an edge.

CLEANING

Efficiency in aid climbing is very much related to organization. While ascending and cleaning a pitch, rack the equipment as it will be placed on the lead rack. This greatly facilitates the lead changes.

Clean protection and aid placements that are lightly set often pop out if you jug right through them. Lift up on the placement as you slide your ascender up the rope. If clean aid has been used, you can often ascend from one tying-off-short spot to the next without stopping. After tying in short again, rack the pieces that have accumulated on the rope above your ascender.

This general system works even if a placement does not pop out as you move the ascenders upward. Keep the piece clipped into the climbing rope and use a chock pick and hammer to dislodge it. Once it pops free, continue ascending without reracking until you tie in short again. If, however, you must remove the upper ascender frequently, you should rack the pieces as they are removed.

Fixed pins found on the route should be left in place unless they are obviously unsafe or interfere with a chock placement. Take care not to break the eyes off these old pins, leaving a useless pin.

When cleaning one of your own pins, pound it back and forth along the axis of the crack, as far as it will go in each direction. Once the pin is loose enough to move easily back and forth, you can remove it by any of several means (fig. 11-29):

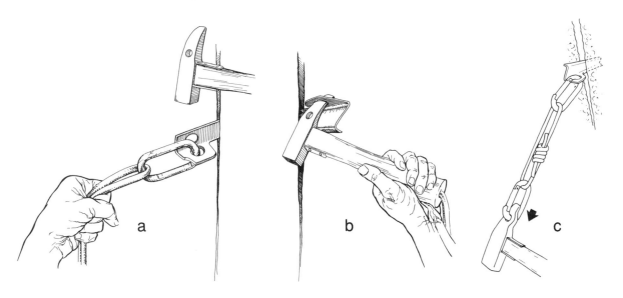

Fig. 11–29. Piton removal: a, use of "cleaner biner"; b, hammer used to pry; c, hammer swing.

1. Attach a "cleaner biner"—a carabiner no longer used for climbing—and a sling to the pin. Pull out on the sling while tapping the pin back and forth until it pops out (fig. 11-29a).
2. Pry out on the loose pin with the pick of the hammer, taking care not to break the hammer (fig. 11-29b).
3. Attach a "cleaner biner" and sling to the loose pin, then attach the sling to the hammer with another carabiner. Starting with slack in the sling, swing the hammer in the direction the pin should come out (fig. 11-29c).

Because the heads of malleable placements can only be reused a limited number of times, it is often best to leave them fixed. This is especially true if you think the wire will pull off the head as you remove the piece. If you decide to remove a malleable piece, attach a cleaner biner and sling between the head and your hammer. Then, as with pins, give the hammer a quick swing outward. It may take several swings before the head pops out. Inspect the head closely before reusing it because they deteriorate quickly. But if your attempt to remove the head merely strips the wire away, take the time to clean the head out of the rock. It is easier for you to do so on a fixed rope than for another climber on lead.

SECONDING TRAVERSES AND OVERHANGS

When traversing a long distance, it is generally more efficient if you aid across the traverse as if leading. Aiding in this fashion, you can receive a belay from above or self-belay by attaching ascenders to your harness with slings and sliding the ascenders along the climbing rope as you aid. When using the latter method, tie in short from time to time.

Short traverses, and those that are more diagonal than horizontal, can be crossed using normal jugging (mechanical ascender) techniques. The nearer the traverse is to horizontal, the less efficient this technique becomes, for at each piece you are faced with a small pendulum.

When jugging, remove the upper ascender at each placement and move it as far as possible above the currently weighted piece. This practice minimizes the pendulum that will result when you transfer your weight onto the upper ascender. Before doing this, however, allow some distance between the lower ascender and the placement so that the lower ascender does not jam into the piece as you transfer your weight to the upper ascender. Also, be sure to still tie in short at regular intervals.

The same basic methods just described for traverses also apply to seconding overhangs.

SECONDING PENDULUMS

The best method to second a pendulum depends on the length of the pendulum and the ropes available. The placements, slinging, and carabiner for the pendulum anchor usually will all need to be left behind, unless they can be reached from above after completing the pendulum.

Seconding long pendulums

All long pendulums require at least one rope in addition to the climbing and haul ropes. There are a number of ways to second a long pendulum, but the method shown in figure 11-30 will handle all such cases.

Figure 11-30a: All pendulums begin with a leader, of course, who rappels off a bombproof pendulum point using either one rope or two ropes tied together, depending on the width of the pendulum. The rappel rope should be clipped into the anchor so there's no danger of losing it. While on the pendulum, the leader is belayed on the climbing rope, which is not clipped into the pendulum anchor. At the bottom of the rappel, the leader runs back and forth across the rock to gain enough momentum to swing into the new crack system. On a very long pendulum, the leader may haul along an extra belay rope. The belayer keeps one end of this rope as the leader drags the other end.

Figure 11-30b: The leader ascends the new crack system and sets up an anchor. The leader attaches the climbing rope and the extra belay rope to the new anchor, the latter to serve as a belay

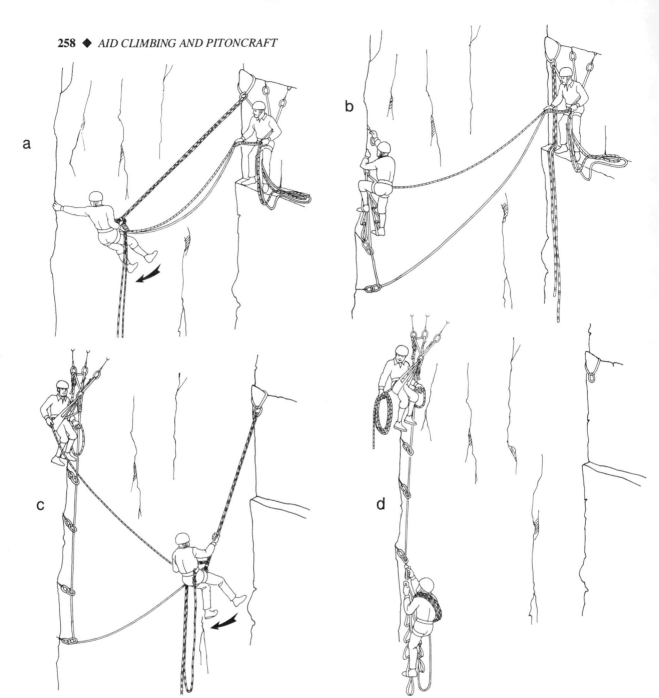

Fig. 11–30. Long pendulum sequence: a, leader rappels on two ropes while belayed on two; b, leader begins climbing, clipping in one of the belay ropes; c, with anchor set, leader belays with rope not clipped to aid pieces (the second rappels across the pendulum—note that the end of one rappel rope is attached to the second climber to prevent its loss); d, the second pulls the rappel ropes, ties in short, and "jugs" anchored climbing rope.

rope for the second climber. With the first climber now set to belay, the second climber frees or lowers the haul bag. The follower also unclips the rappel rope tie-in from the pendulum anchor so the rope can be retrieved later. (The follower can clip one end of the rappel rope to an out-of-the-way place on the seat harness to again ensure the rope can't be dropped.)

Figure 11-30c: The follower rappels the pendulum, with the first climber belaying and helping to pull the follower toward the new crack system at the end of the pendulum. (There's an alternative if the leader didn't drag an extra pendulum rope across. The second can pull across the pendulum on the lead climbing rope by hand, or with the help of mechanical ascenders.)

Figure 11-30d: Safely across, the second attaches ascenders to the climbing rope, ties off short, retrieves the rappel rope, and is ready to climb up the new crack system.

Seconding short pendulums

Climbers also have a variety of ways to handle the challenge of seconding a short pendulum. One clever and useful method is shown in figure 11-31. For this method to work, the slack rope from the pendulum anchor to the follower's harness must be at least double the arc of the pendulum. The follower stays tied in to the climbing rope during the sequence.

As shown in figure 11-31, here's how you as the follower could second a short pendulum:

Figure 11-31a: Connect the upper ascender with its attached etrier to the climbing rope beyond the pendulum anchor, facing across the pendulum. Clip a daisy chain from your harness to the ascender. Connect the lower ascender and etrier to the section of rope between the pendulum anchor and yourself. Clip it in with another daisy chain. Place your weight on the upper ascender. Next, attach a rappel device to the rope, below the lower ascender, and grasp the rope where it exits the device. Then, while keeping the safety trigger locked, release the cam of the lower ascender by pulling on the rope below it (this will take some effort). You're now ready to move.

Figure 11-31b: With one hand grasping the climbing rope as it leaves the rappel device and the other hand sliding the lower ascender, lower yourself across the pendulum. To put the brakes on at any time, simply let go of the lower ascender and the cam will again lock. (In fact, if a rappel device is not used, this ascender will often lock onto the rope by itself, requiring you to repeat the previous tactic of pulling hard on the rope below it.)

Figure 11-31c: Once across the pendulum, tie in short and move the lower ascender above that point. Now untie yourself from the end of the rope so you can pull it through the pendulum anchor. Once you've re-tied into the end of the climbing rope, you're set to ascend the climbing rope again.

The rappel device makes it easier to hold the rope while lowering yourself across the pendulum. However, you can also second a short pendulum this way without the device.

CHANGING LEADS

Unorganized belay stations can become a rat's nest of tangled ropes, twisted slings, and assorted hardware. Basic organization keeps the belay station manageable and the team functioning efficiently. Following are several methods to improve organization:

• All ropes should be different colors.
• After hauling the sack, the leader stacks the haul line and organizes the other ropes and hardware at the anchor.
• Once the second arrives at the anchor and begins consolidating the lead rack, the old leader (now the belayer) makes butterfly coils in the climbing rope and stacks these coils at the anchor with a sling. This prevents the climbing rope from getting snagged below and from tangling, and helps it pay out smoothly.
• If the second was carrying a rucksack, it can be packed with gear that won't be utilized on the next pitch and clipped into the anchor.
• Finally, the second (now the new leader) clips the free end of the haul rope to his or her harness, is placed on belay, and starts climbing.

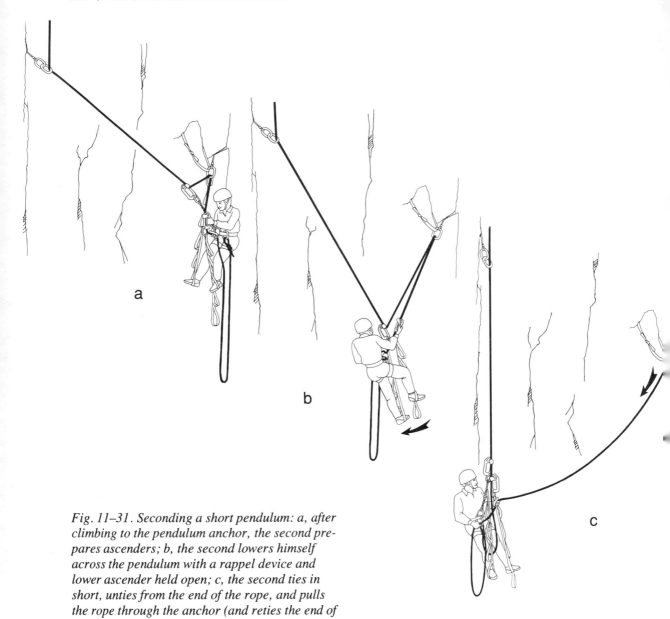

Fig. 11–31. Seconding a short pendulum: a, after climbing to the pendulum anchor, the second prepares ascenders; b, the second lowers himself across the pendulum with a rappel device and lower ascender held open; c, the second ties in short, unties from the end of the rope, and pulls the rope through the anchor (and reties the end of the rope).

BIG-WALL MULTIDAY TECHNIQUES

"Big walls," the saying goes, "are 90 percent work and 10 percent fun." Not everyone agrees with those percentages, but few climbers will say big walls are easy. There's no question that proper conditioning is essential for the hauling of heavy loads and the scaling of multiple aid pitches.

Big walls also call for a high degree of mental composure. Inexperienced wall climbers easily find themselves the victim of heightened fears brought on by prolonged and severe exposure. If you're new to the game, perhaps you can soothe your fears by realizing that techniques for dealing with major walls are much the same as those needed for smaller climbs. Concentrate on the problem at hand and work away at the objective one move at a time.

In preparing for a big wall, guidebooks and other climbers are often helpful sources of information. Beware, however, of overdependence on climbers' topographic maps and equipment lists. Routes do change over time, especially if pins are used regularly.

Solid, efficient aid technique is a prerequisite if a major wall is to be completed within the time constraints dictated by reasonable food and water supplies. For success on the big walls, you must develop competency in hoisting heavy sacks up the route, and you should be able to live comfortably in a vertical world for days at a time.

HAULING

After anchoring yourself and fixing the climbing rope for the second, it's your job as the leader to begin hauling (fig. 11-32):

1. Attach a pulley, through which the haul line passes, to the anchor.
2. Attach an upside-down ascender to the haul line on the haul-sack side of the pulley. The end of the ascender closest to the pulley (normally the bottom) is clipped into the anchor, while the end pointing toward the haul sack is counterweighted with the remains of the rack (or another weight).
3. Attach a second ascender, in the normal direction, to the haul line on the opposite side of the pulley (between yourself and the pulley). Use a daisy chain to connect this ascender to your harness.
4. Push back from the wall using your legs and palms; your body weight will raise the haul sack. When you stop pushing, the upside-

Top end
of haul line

Fixed
climbing
rope

Fig. 11–32. Sack-hauling system; hauler is preparing to move ascender up haul line and ascend etriers for next power haul.

down ascender acts as a brake to prevent backward slippage of the haul bag. You'll need a little slack in the climbing rope between yourself and the anchor to allow your hauling movement.

You can also haul by allowing slack of 6 to 8 feet between you and the anchor. Then, with the daisy chain connected between your harness and the haul line ascender, walk down the wall 6 to 8 feet until the anchor rope tightens. Climb back to your original position by stepping upward in etriers attached to the anchor, pulling the ascender with you. Repeat the process.

This method is also used if two people are needed to lift a very heavy bag. Both of you clip to the ascender on the haul rope, give yourself 6 to 8 feet of slack, and walk down the wall together. Regardless of the method used, *always* connect yourself to the anchor with the climbing rope.

FIXING PITCHES

On multiday climbs, you will often fix two or three pitches beyond the bivouac site and leave gear not needed for the bivouac at the high point. The lower end of each fixed rope is attached to the anchor of the previous pitch.

The next morning the pitches are jugged—one climber on a rope at a time. This gives a head start on the day and lets you warm up before new climbing begins.

RETREATING

Before a major climb, plan retreat lines in case of bad weather, accident, or other emergency. Locate other routes that are easy to reach to speed the ascent or that have fixed retreat lines.

If no retreat route exists, consider carrying a bolt kit for emergencies, allowing you to place rappel anchors. Also, as you climb each pitch, consider how you would descend it. On major walls rescues may be slow and difficult, if possible at all. It may be up to you to get back down in an emergency.

LIVING IN THE VERTICAL WORLD

Living for days on a vertical wall of rock brings some intriguing problems.

Dropped gear, for instance. Once dropped, it's gone. All vital items must have clip-in loops. Learn your gear so you can work it confidently. Get acquainted with unfamiliar items, such as Portaledges or hammocks, beforehand.

It's usually necessary to carry all your water with you. Each climber generally needs 2 quarts per day. For hot weather, especially if the route gets a lot of sun, you will need to carry even more.

Waste disposal poses another challenge. Tossing garbage down the wall is not acceptable, so you'll have to haul it up and off the climb. On popular routes, use paper bags for your excrement and toss these off the wall—warning climbers below when you are about to launch a bag. On seldom-climbed routes (or when no portion of a popular route is in your fall line), you can let your excrement fall out into space because this waste will decay far more quickly when not bagged. Keep all bivouac sites clean and sanitary, with no sign of your passing.

After completing a major wall, you need to get your gear back down. In the past, common practice was to toss the haul bag loaded with gear off the wall. Today, sack tossing is illegal at popular climbing areas like Yosemite; it endangers climbers below. Furthermore, many climbers have had their gear stolen by the time they got down to it. Carry down what you hauled up.

THE FUTURE OF AID CLIMBING

Free-climbers may feel that aid climbing isolates the climber from the rock. But anyone who has struggled to place a piece of aid while standing above a series of marginal placements understands that aid is not only climbing but a test of technical abilities and nerves.

To ensure that these routes will continue to be a test of skill and nerves, aid climbers are asked to respect certain ethics. If you are climbing an established route, adhere to the ethics of the first-ascent climbers. If they did not need a piton or bolt, *don't place one*. Use creativity and boldness to overcome the difficulty. A party following you on a route should find it in the condition you found it.

If you're putting up a new route, you are establishing the style for those who follow. Remember that routes once considered difficult using pitons are now free-climbed and that old bolt ladders are often viewed with disdain. Make it your goal to climb cleanly and in a style that climbers can respect. As time goes on, more of today's aid routes will be free-climbed, while aid climbers will push their limits on ever thinner and more remote climbs.

PART FOUR

SNOW AND
ICE
CLIMBING

Ice climbing on Habegger Falls, Bishop Creek in California's Sierra Nevada. Photo by Gordon Wiltsie

· 12 ·

SNOW TRAVEL AND CLIMBING

Climbing in snow is a fundamental part of mountaineering. Snow adds beauty and challenge—but even if you wanted to avoid snow, it wouldn't be easy. Climbers work in a world in which their medium, the mountains, is sculpted by the action of snow, ice, and water. To avoid snow would mean climbing in only a select few mountain ranges or for only a few months each year.

Climbers like snow for at least a couple of reasons. First of all, it makes many climbs a lot easier by providing a pathway over brush and other obstacles on the approach hike and reducing the danger of loose rock on the ascent. It also brings new beauty to the mountains at the same time that it conceals the impact of people.

Snow is a complex medium that shows up in many forms that continually change, making snow travel trickier than trail hiking or rock climbing. Snow falls in a form that varies from tiny crystals to coarse pellets, depending on temperature and wind. Once fallen, snow begins to change as it is acted upon by sun, wind, temperature variations, and precipitation.

A rock face stays basically the same, while snow goes through many changes. It may start as a dusting of snow over a brush slope, progress to an unconsolidated powder bowl waiting to avalanche, then to a solid surface offering rapid ascent to a ridge top, and finally back to a brush slope with only scattered snow patches. Even in the course of a day, the snow can change from rock hard in the morning to thigh-sucking slush in the afternoon.

The changeable nature of snow means mountaineers have to be flexible in their mode of travel, ready to use snowshoes, skis, or crampons instead of boots alone. Snow conditions also affect decisions on route and climbing technique. Should you hike up the comfortable, snow-covered valley bottom or on the ridge top away from avalanche hazard? Should you go for the easy step-kicking of the sunny slope or the firmer, more stable snow of the shaded hill? Do the conditions mean it is safer to travel roped or unroped?

In this chapter we'll take a look at the equipment you need to travel in snow and techniques for traveling quickly and safely—with special emphasis on avalanche recognition and rescue.

EQUIPMENT

At the top of the list of basic snow-climbing equipment are ice axes and crampons. Snowshoes, skis, and ski poles are other important snow-travel aids. Climbers also use equipment for snow anchors, which will be taken up later in this chapter in the section on roped climbing.

ICE AXE

The ice axe (fig. 12-1) is one of the most versatile and important pieces of mountaineering equipment a climber owns. Without it, safe alpine travel is restricted to easy scrambles. With an axe,

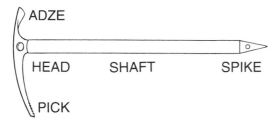

Fig. 12–1. Parts of the ice axe

and the skill to use it, you can can venture onto all forms of snow and ice, enjoying a greater variety of mountain landscapes during more seasons of the year.

The modern ice axe is an inherently simple tool with many uses. Below the snow line, it's used for balance, as a walking cane, and to help brake going downhill. But its main role is in snow and ice travel, where it provides balance or a point of security to prevent a fall and serves to stop any fall that takes place.

The design of an ice axe often is a trade-off between features that make the tool better for particular uses. A longer axe may be OK for cross-country travel and scrambling, where it's used as a cane and to provide security in low-angle climbing. You'll probably want a shorter axe for the steeper slopes in alpine climbing. For ice climbing, the axes get shorter still and other design aspects become more specialized, such as the droop of the pick, placement of the teeth, and shape of the adze. These specialized axes are covered in Chapter 14.

Parts of the ice axe

The head of an ice axe—which includes the pick and the adze—is usually made of steel, a material strong enough for snow and ice climbing. Although the hole in the head of the axe is commonly called a carabiner hole, most climbers attach their wrist leash through it.

The pick on most ice axes (fig. 12-2) is curved or drooped, a design that provides better hooking action in snow or ice, causing the axe to dig in faster when you're trying to stop yourself (self-arrest) after a fall. A moderate hooking angle of 65 to 70 degrees from the shaft is right for general moun-

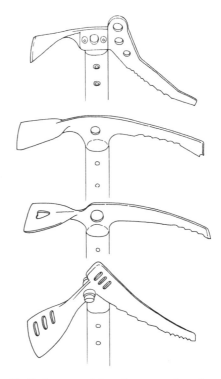

Fig. 12–2. Ice-axe picks: shapes and teeth patterns

taineering uses. A sharper angle of 55 to 60 degrees is better for technical ice climbing as it coincides with the arc followed by the axe head when it is planted in steep ice. Teeth on the pick provide grip for ice and hard snow.

The pick's hold for self-arrest is affected to some degree by its clearance (fig. 12-3). If the end edge of the pick is parallel to the shaft, the pick has neutral clearance. If the angle of the pick end tends toward the shaft, it has negative clearance. If the angle tends away from the shaft, it has positive clearance. Picks with neutral or negative clearance can skate or drag on an icy surface and not penetrate reliably during self-arrest. Picks with positive clearance tend to pull into the surface when pressure is applied—so much so that they can bite into hard snow with such suddenness that the axe may be yanked out of the climber's hands. To beat this

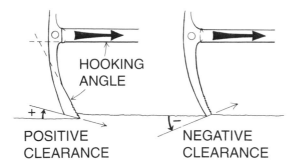

Fig. 12–3. Ice-axe clearance

problem, some climbers prefer a negative clearance to help with a more gradual stop in hard snow. But in most cases, the clearance probably makes little difference because self-arrest on ice is almost impossible regardless of the clearance, and in softer snow the pick will dig in whether the clearance is positive or negative.

The adze of the axe is used mainly for step-chopping on hard snow or ice. The flat top of the adze is also a firm, comfortable platform for the palm of your hand while holding the axe in the self-belay grasp during snow climbing. Adzes for general mountaineering may be flat or curved, straight-edged or scalloped, straight-out or drooped. A flat, straight-edged, non-drooped adze with sharp corners is probably the best all-around tool for step-chopping.

The shaft of your axe will most likely be made of metal (aluminum or titanium) or a composite (fiberglass, Kevlar, or carbon filament), or a combination of both. The wooden shafts of yesterday—often dense, straight-grained hickory—have been replaced by these stronger materials. Even the historical advantages of wood in dampening vibrations and offering a warmer grip have been minimized by the new composites.

Some shafts are covered at least partly by a rubber-type material for a better grip. The material helps give surer command of the axe during self-arrest and also dampens vibrations and increases control in placing the pick in ice. You can improve your hold on a shaft that doesn't have a rubber grip by adding athletic grip tape or using gloves with rubberized palms. However, the gripping material

on the shaft can keep the axe from slipping as easily into the snow when you're using it for a boot-axe belay, probing, or self-belay. For this reason, it is recommended that ice axes for basic mountaineering not have this grip.

The spike, the metal tip of the axe, must be kept sharp so that it pokes readily into snow and ice. The axe does come in handy on rocky trails and talus slopes by helping with balance, but beware of dulling the spike.

Ice-axe length

Ice axes range in length from 40 centimeters (about 16 inches) to 90 centimeters (about 3 feet)—still much shorter than the 5-foot alpenstocks of the alpine pioneers. The shortest axes are for technical ice climbing; the longest ones are for tall mountaineers using the axe as a cane on easy terrain.

The optimal length for an ice axe may depend more on what you plan to do with it than on how tall you are. Axes less than 60 centimeters long are ice-climbing tools, excellent for placements on steep slopes but not so good for self-arrest. An axe of 70 centimeters is the longest that is generally useful for ice climbing. A length of 60 to 70 centimeters works well in most alpine situations, where you are climbing moderately steep snow slopes and using the axe for self-belay and self-arrest. Longer axes are better for cross-country travel and scrambling, and also are good as snow anchors and for probing for cornices and crevasses.

Ice-axe leash

The leash provides a way to attach the ice axe to your wrist or your harness when you want to ensure it won't be dropped. The leash also has other uses that we'll get to. Although the length of a leash can vary, it usually consists of a piece of accessory cord or webbing attached through the hole in the head of the ice axe (fig. 12-4).

The leash is valuable insurance on crevassed glaciers or long steep slopes where losing an axe would leave you without a principal tool for safety and put climbers below in danger from the runaway axe. The leash also lets the ice axe hang freely

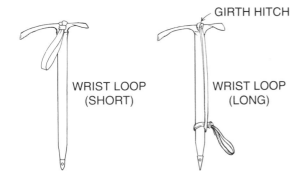

GIRTH HITCH

WRIST LOOP
(SHORT)

WRIST LOOP
(LONG)

Fig. 12–4. Ice-axe leashes (wrist loops), attached through carabiner hole in head of axe

while you make a move or two on occasional rock during a snow climb.

Short wrist leashes are favored by those who find them adequate for basic snow and glacier travel—easy to use and an aid to quicker control of the ice axe during a fall. During an uncontrolled fall in which you lose your grip on the axe, the short leash prevents the axe from flailing around as dangerously as it would on a longer leash. Ice axes sometimes come with a short wrist loop attached by the manufacturer.

A longer leash is now preferred, however, for all but the most basic of snow travel. With a long leash, you no longer have to switch the leash from wrist to wrist as you move the axe to the other hand for a change in direction up a snow slope. The long leash also makes the axe more versatile for climbing steep snow or ice.

A long wrist leash is usually about as long as the axe itself, and if it's just the right length, it can help reduce arm fatigue during step-chopping and ice climbing. It should be long enough to let you grasp the shaft near the spike through the wrist loop as you hold the leash taut from the head of the axe. This way, the wrist can share the work of the arm, and the head of the axe will be more stable. You can shorten the leash when you don't need it by wrapping it around the shaft.

With the long leash attached to your seat harness, the axe can serve as a personal anchor.

If you buy an ice axe without a leash, one can easily be made from a length of 5- or 6-millimeter accessory cord or 1/2-inch to 1-inch flat webbing, tied into a sling, and then girth-hitched through the hole in the axe head. Tie a slip knot at the end of the sling to form the wrist loop. Ready-made leashes are also available at climbing stores.

Ice-axe maintenance

Modern metal-shaft ice axes require very little special care. Inspect the shaft before each use for deep dents that might weaken it to the point of failure under load (but don't worry about minor nicks and scratches). Clean mud and dirt off the axe after each climb and remove any rust.

Check the pick, adze, and spike regularly. To sharpen, use a small hand file instead of a grinding wheel, which could change the temper and strength of the metal.

CRAMPONS

Mountaineering is unthinkable without crampons, but when the first 10-point crampons came on the scene in Europe in the early 1900s, many alpinists thought the gadgets took unsporting advantage of the peaks. However, crampons proved to be the one aid that could relieve climbers of the tremendous burden of step-cutting and open up a vast array of new snow and ice faces. They have since evolved into the 12-point crampons of today, with 10 bottom points and 2 front points.

As with ice axes, the different crampon designs involve a trade-off between what's good for general alpine use and what's good for technical ice climbing. Most crampons are made from chrome-molybdenum steel, an extremely strong, lightweight alloy.

Climbers face a number of questions in shopping for crampons. What type of crampons should I buy? How will I know when the crampons fit my boots? Which attachment system should I use? This section provides information to help answer these questions and offers tips on crampon maintenance.

Crampon points

The early 10-point crampon has long-since been eclipsed by the addition of two forward-slanting points in the 1930s to create the 12-point crampon. The 12-point models eliminated even more step-chopping and permitted "front-pointing" up steep snow and ice. Because 10-point crampons usually don't have front points, they're no good for very steep ice and are no longer available except as used equipment.

The angles of the first two rows of points determine the best use for a set of crampons. When the first row (front points) is drooped and the second row is angled toward the toe of the boot (fig. 12-5), the crampons are better suited for front-pointing than for general mountaineering. This configuration allows the boot heel to be lower without additional calf strain. Straight points are better for flat-footing and general use.

Tiny instep crampons with four or six points are sold for use by backpackers who need to cross an occasional short snowfield. Because there are no points at the heel or toe, they're unsuitable for

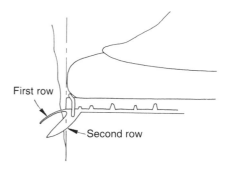

Fig. 12–5. Angle of first two rows of points, best suited for front-pointing

mountaineering and can be dangerous on steep snow or ice.

Hinged vs. rigid crampons

Mountaineers have a choice of either hinged or rigid crampons (fig. 12-6). Rigid crampons are for technical ice climbing. For most mountaineering, hinged crampons are preferable.

A hinged crampon flexes at the instep and is

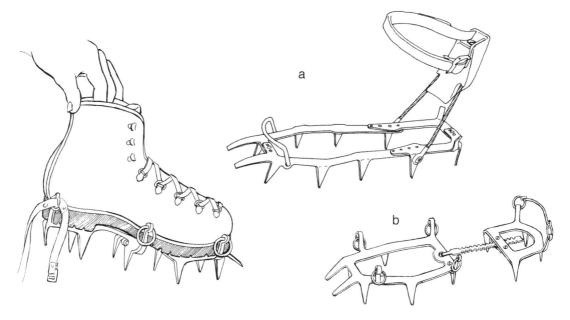

Fig. 12–6. Types of crampons: a, rigid; b, hinged.

meant to bend with the natural rocking action of walking. It can be attached to any mountaineering boot, full shank or not, and to plastic boots. Attached to a full-shank or plastic boot, hinged crampons perform nearly as well for ice climbing as rigid crampons, because the boot provides the stable climbing platform that's required. If you buy only one set of crampons, buy hinged. If your goal is steep technical ice, then you can consider a rigid crampon. Some hinged crampons can be made rigid simply by adding a screw to each side of the crampon.

A rigid crampon is inflexible and not meant to bend at the instep. In most cases, it must be used with full-shank or plastic boots because it could break from the natural flex of another boot. Rigid crampons don't perform well in mixed terrain, where some flexibility is desired, and they can be heavier than hinged crampons. Rigid crampons come into their own when you're front-pointing up technical ice. They vibrate less than hinged crampons when you swing them into the ice, and their stiffness makes for less tiring front-pointing by allowing you to keep your heel lower.

Crampon attachment

Anyone who has had a crampon come loose in the middle of a steep slope of hard snow on a dark,

cold morning knows the urgency of keeping crampons attached until you really want them off. To keep the crampons on the boots, climbers can choose from a variety of traditional strapping methods or the newer step-in/clamp-on bindings. The various systems are available on either hinged or rigid crampons.

Straps

Buckled straps do a good job of attaching crampons to boots. Neoprene-coated nylon is the best strap material because it is strong, doesn't absorb water, won't stretch, and can be easily transferred from one pair of crampons to another. Leather straps are less expensive but stretch when wet and will eventually rot or break. Nylon or fabric webbing is least desirable, since it readily accumulates snow and may freeze to the buckle.

Three strap-on designs are in general use:

Four independent straps per crampon are used in one design: two short straps, with buckles, attached to one side of the crampon and two longer straps attached to the other side. One long strap then connects the front four attachment posts over the instep of the boot, while the other wraps around the ankle and connects the two rear posts (fig. 12-7a).

Two independent straps per crampon are used

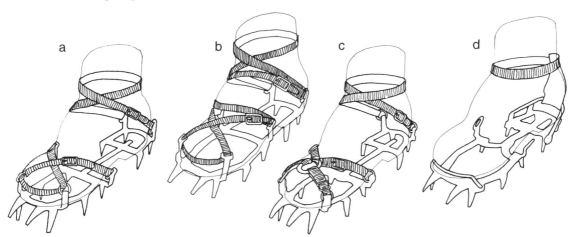

Fig. 12–7. Systems for attaching crampons to boots: a, four-strap; b, two-strap; c, Scottish; d, step-in/clamp on.

in an alternative strapping system: one connecting the front four attachment posts over the instep and the other wrapping around the ankle from the two rear posts (fig. 12-7b).

The Scottish system is a third strap-on method that is quicker than the other two and is gaining widespread use. A strap with a ring in the middle is permanently connected to the two front posts. A strap then runs from one side post through this ring to the other side post. The rear strap is the same as in the two-strap system (fig. 12-7c).

When strapping on crampons, position the buckles on the outward side of the boots to minimize the chance of catching a buckle with your foot as you walk. To reduce the danger of the front straps loosening on the two-strap and four-strap systems, thread the strap through the hole at each front attachment post *from the outside in*, and then give the strap an extra twist.

A word to beginning mountaineers: whatever you do, don't head out on a climb until you practice strapping on your crampons in the comfort of home. You'll have plenty of chances later to put the crampons on in the dark by feel, or by flashlight, with cold, numbed fingers. Lay the crampons on the floor with all straps started through the hole at an attachment post, put on your boots, place each boot in turn on its crampon, and attach the straps. Do the crampons fit? Do the straps have holes punched in them at the right places for attaching to the buckles? Do the straps need to be longer to accommodate insulated gaiters or overboots? Are they tight enough to keep the crampons on through thick and thin, but not so tight that they restrict blood flow? As best you can, work out all the wrinkles before you get out on that steep slope of hard snow in the cold, dark morning.

Step-in/clamp-on bindings

The old agony of fumbling with crampon straps and buckles is largely eliminated by the newer step-in/clamp-on bindings (fig. 12-7d). The crampons attach to the boot with a wire toe bale and a snap-up bale on the rear. They're fast and easy to put on, and each crampon has a safety strap so you won't lose it if it ever comes off. However, there are a couple of considerations in addition to higher cost to keep in mind before you decide to use step-in/clamp-on bindings.

The fit to the boot is more critical than with crampons that are strapped on. The boot must have a pronounced welt at both the heel and toe and, therefore, the step-in/clamp-ons fit especially well on plastic boots. Crampons with straps often work better on leather boots, particularly those without a decided heel welt. And some climbers, nervous about the possibility of the clamp-ons releasing, continue to use straps for technical ice.

Crampon fit

To ensure that crampons stay attached and perform well, it's essential they fit just right. Here are some tips to help in fitting crampons, either the kind that attach with straps or the step-in/clamp-on type.

• When buying crampons, try them on with the boots you'll be wearing. If you plan to use them on more than one pair of boots, check the fit on all pairs.
• If you'll be wearing gaiters with a rubber band that fits around the welt and instep of the boot, be sure to wear the gaiters when you fit the crampons.
• The front crampon points should protrude about 3/4 inch to 1 inch beyond the toe of the boot.
• Many crampons are adjustable to one degree or another. This can include adjustments for length and for the width of instep, heel, and toe. Being able to adjust the heel and toe widths can be especially important if you're using telemark boots (for a climbing/skiing trip) or overboots.
• The attachment posts at the sides and rear of strap-on crampons should hug the boot snugly without significant bending to fit. Test the fit by lifting the boot upside down by the crampon. The posts should hold to the boot without the use of straps.
• The heel wire found on some strap-on crampons helps keep the boot heel in place by preventing it from slipping through the rear post, especially when using plastic boots.
• The welt on a boot is especially important with

step-in/clamp-on bindings, which grip the welt at toe and heel. Most desirable are Norwegian-style double-stitched welts on heavy leather boots and the indented toe and heel on plastic boots.

• Some climbers place a flat piece of foam, shaped like the bottom of the boot, between the boot and crampon to help insulate the foot from the snow. If you want to do this, take it into account when you fit your crampons.

Crampon maintenance and safety

Regular simple maintenance is required for safe, dependable crampons. Keep the points sharp, clean the crampons after every climb, and inspect them before the next outing.

Snow and ice routes often include short sections of rock that you'll climb with crampons on. The crampons should be able to take the punishment, but too much of this will dull the points. As with ice axes, sharpen crampon points with a hand file, not a grinding wheel (fig. 12-8).

After you return home from each climb, wipe dirt and water from crampons to prevent rust. Check the points before each climb. They should be clean and reasonably sharp, though very sharp points are needed only for technical ice climbing. Also check alignment of the points, because splayed points make the crampons less efficient at gripping the snow and more effective as a weapon that can slash pants and legs. It's probably best to retire a pair of crampons with badly misaligned points. Check the tightness of nuts and bolts on adjustable crampons. And while you're looking over the crampons, don't forget to inspect the straps if you have the strap-on type. Look for rotting, abrasion, cracks, or cuts.

In the mountains, following a few easy rules can protect you, your gear, and your companions from sharp crampon points. Walk carefully to avoid snagging your pants, gashing your leg, or stepping on the rope. When you're carrying the crampons, use a set of rubber protectors to cover the points, or keep the crampons in a special pouch. Both the 12-point protectors and the crampon pouch are available commercially.

One little trick makes crampons safer and more effective in soft, sticky snow. Just wrap the bottom of the crampon with duct tape to minimize the amount of snow that balls up under the crampon. This balling of snow can be dangerous, particularly where slushy snow overlays an icy base. Or you might be able to just take the crampons off.

WANDS

To find their way back over snow and glacier routes, mountaineers often mark the path with tiny flags atop thin bamboo wands. Climbers usually make their own, using the green-stained bamboo sticks sold at garden supply stores for plant supports. Convert them to wands by attaching a piece of bright, durable, water-repellent material to one end; plastic route-marking tape or coated nylon is best (fig. 12-9). A common method is to slit the first couple of inches at one end of a wand, slip the flag in the slit, tie it, then tape the slit closed. Be sure the flag is secure enough to withstand the high winds of open snow slopes and glaciers.

Wands usually vary in length from 30 inches to 4 feet. Less than 30 inches and the flag may not be high enough to be easily seen; longer than 4 feet and the wands are awkward to carry. Use your longest wands in winter when they have to be

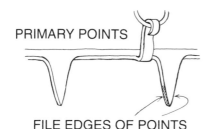

PRIMARY POINTS

FILE EDGES OF POINTS

Fig. 12–8. How to sharpen crampons

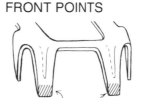

FRONT POINTS

FILE TOP OF POINTS

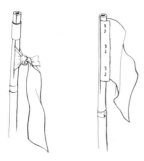

Fig. 12–9. Wand construction

pushed in farther because of soft snow and when new snowfall can bury them even deeper.

SKI POLES

Ski poles aren't only for use with skis. They beat an ice axe for balance when you're trudging with a heavy pack over level or low-angle snow, slippery ground or scree, or when you're trying to cross a stream or boulder field. They also can take some of the weight off your lower body. And the basket at the bottom keeps the poles from slipping deep into soft snow, a favorite trick of ice axes unless they're fitted with a special snow collar.

A variety of ski poles have features helpful to the trekker or mountaineer. Some poles telescope for adjustability on slopes and ease of strapping on a pack. With removable baskets, they can serve as a probe for crevasses or avalanche victims. Some poles fasten together to form an extra-long probe (fig. 12-10). Some poles both telescope out and fasten together. You can also buy a special self-arrest grip that has a pick protruding forward from the top, but this definitely is not a substitute for an ice axe on technical terrain. Most of these poles can be used whether you're traveling by foot, snowshoes, or skis.

SKIS

Mountaineering has become a popular four-season pursuit with the widespread use of Nordic and mountaineering skis fitted with climbing skins.

The Nordic ski, light and skinny, is worn with a special boot held in a toe binding that leaves the heel free (fig. 12-11a). Depending on the design

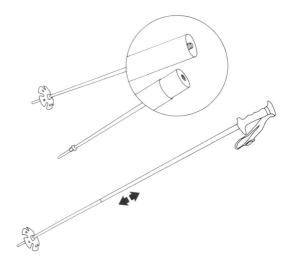

Fig. 12–10. Adjustable-length ski poles that can be fastened together to create an avalanche probe

and purpose of the ski, it may be referred to as a cross-country, touring, or telemark ski. Because the heel is not attached, Nordic skiers need the special skill of telemark turning for going downhill.

Ski mountaineering employs a wider, heavier ski (sometimes called a randonée ski) that is closer to a traditional alpine (downhill) ski (fig. 12-11b). It has a binding that leaves the heel free for uphill travel but can secure the heel for standard downhill technique. Special boots are sold for use with mountaineering skis, though plastic mountaineering boots are often adequate.

Both kinds of skis will get you into the backcountry in winter for touring or mountain approaches. To provide uphill traction, both are used with removable climbing skins, in a textured material known as nylon plush, that adhere to the bottom of the skis (fig. 12-11c).

If you're accustomed to using only boots or snowshoes for backcountry snow travel, you may find certain disadvantages to skis. During the times you have to pack them, there's extra weight. It's difficult to self-arrest on steep slopes, though self-arrest grips on your ski poles can help. The skis are awkward on rocky or forested snow slopes; skiing can be difficult if you have a heavy pack; and

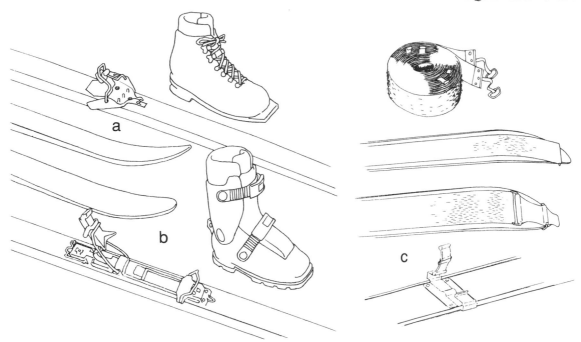

Fig. 12–11. Ski equipment for mountaineering: a, Nordic skis; b, mountaineering skis, boots, and bindings; c, climbing skins for skis.

you'll need a well-matched party in terms of skiing ability in order to keep a steady pace, especially for roped glacier travel.

But after all is said and done, skis are undeniably easier and faster for basic snow travel. They are giving more and more mountaineers a way to get to areas they couldn't readily reach before and to travel at more times of the year. Skis also can offer a safety bonus for crevasse crossings because with your weight distributed over a wider area, there is less danger of breaking through. They can also come in handy for rescue work, converting into a makeshift stretcher or sled.

Backcountry ski travel is a complex activity, with special techniques and equipment. For detailed information, take a look at articles or books devoted to the subject.

SNOWSHOES

Snowshoes (fig. 12-12) are a traditional aid to snow travel that have been updated into the small lightweight designs of today. Bindings hold your boots on the snowshoes, and metal claws or crampon-like devices improve traction on hard snow and ice.

Snowshoes are better than boots alone for traveling across fields of soft snow, where snowshoers float over the surface while hikers laboriously post-hole. But snowshoes are cumbersome for step-kicking uphill, even though modern snowshoes have an opening that lets you get the toe of your boot into the snow. Of course, when you're not wearing the snowshoes, they add extra weight to your pack.

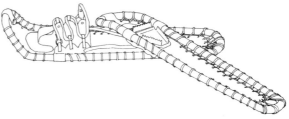

Fig. 12–12. Snowshoes

Although snowshoes are a lot slower than skis, they can be used on mixed terrain where skis would be awkward, and they're often more practical than skis if you have a heavy pack. If your climbing party includes some people who aren't very good on skis, it's probably more efficient for everyone to travel on snowshoes, which are easy to learn. You wear normal mountaineering boots with snowshoes, unlike Nordic skis and some mountaineering skis that call for special footwear.

SHOVEL

A broad-bladed shovel is a utility and safety tool for snow travel (fig. 12-13). It's the only practical tool for uncovering an avalanche victim. Shovels are also used for digging snow shelters and leveling off tent platforms and have even been used as a climbing tool to shovel a pathway up a particularly snowy route.

A good snow shovel has a blade large enough to move snow efficiently and a handle long enough for good leverage but short enough for use in a confined area. It should strap easily to the pack for quick access in an emergency. Some shovels come with a detachable handle or with a blade that locks perpendicular to the handle so it can be used as a

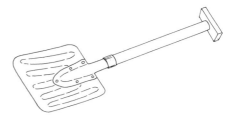

Fig. 12–13. Snow shovel

trenching tool. For projects such as building snow caves, mountaineers sometimes carry a grain scoop, a broad-bladed shovel that can move a lot of snow.

SNOW-CLIMBING TECHNIQUES

USING THE ICE AXE

How to carry an ice axe

The first rule is to carry your ice axe carefully. Keep in mind what its sharp points and edges could do to you or your partners. Whenever the axe is not in your hands, be sure it's secure against slipping down a snow slope or cliff.

When you're on the move and don't need the axe, the best bet is to slip it through the ice-axe loop on your pack and strap it down (fig. 12-14a). It's a good idea to keep rubber or leather guards on the pick, adze, and spike, particularly on an axe that's sharp as an axe should be. If you're simply carrying the axe in one hand, grasp the shaft at the balance point (shaft parallel to the ground), the spike forward and the pick down (fig. 12-14b).

During travel on snow that alternates with rocks or steep brush where you need both hands free, you can get the axe out of the way by sliding it diagonally between your back and the pack (fig. 12-14c). The spike is down and the pick, between the two shoulder straps, is well seated, clear of your neck, and pointing in the same general direction as the angle of the shaft. The axe can be stowed and retrieved quickly, and this works fine for short stretches. To avoid chances of a runaway axe, retrieve it before taking off the pack.

How to grasp an ice axe

How you hold the head of the axe when climbing in snow depends on your preference and on the climbing situation.

There are two principal ways to grasp the axe:

Self-arrest grasp: The thumb goes under the adze and the palm and fingers go over the pick, near the shaft (fig. 12-15a). As you climb, the adze points forward.

Self-belay grasp: The palm sits on top of the adze and the thumb and index finger drop under the pick (fig. 12-15b). As you climb, the pick points forward.

The self-arrest grasp puts you in perfect position to use the axe instantly to brake a fall down a steep

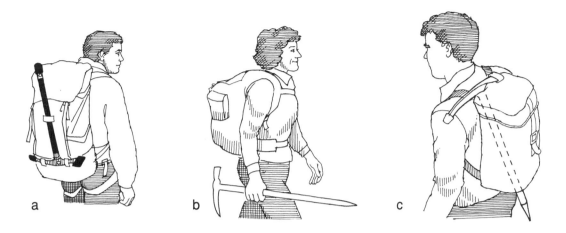

Fig. 12–14. Carrying an ice axe: a, attached to a pack by an ice-axe loop, with guards on the pick, adze, and spike; b, in the hand while walking; c, temporarily between back and pack.

slope. However, you're not going to fall very often, and in the meantime all the pressure of planting the axe as you climb is concentrated where the narrow top edge of the pick meets your palm. That hurts after awhile, and therefore you may not plant the axe as securely as you might otherwise. This compromises the safety of your critical self-belays (which are explained in the next section).

The self-belay grasp is much more comfortable because the pressure of placing the axe is spread over the wide, flat top of the adze, where your palm now rests. If you fall, you'll have to immediately flip to a self-arrest grip to put the brakes on. (This is something to practice during self-arrest drills.)

How to self-belay

The technique of planting the ice-axe shaft to help guard yourself against falls while snow climbing is called self-belay. We'll learn later in this chapter about what to do in the event you or a ropemate start sliding down a steep snow slope. Then self-arrest and other techniques come into

their own. But knowing how to avoid the slide in the first place with a self-belay is as important as knowing what to do if it occurs.

Self-belay (fig. 12-16) is a way to lessen the likelihood that a simple slip or misstep on a snow slope will turn into a long fall. It is used repeatedly to help safeguard the way up or down a steep snow

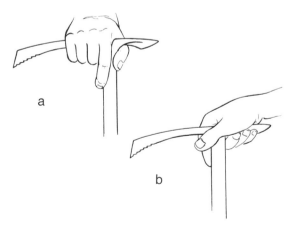

Fig. 12–15. Grasping an ice axe: a, self-arrest grip; b, self-belay grip.

Fig. 12–16. The self-belay: a, climbing; b, falling; c, recovering.

slope when the potential for a fall is the highest: when you are moving or when you are in an out-of-balance position. You can create the belay with either a self-belay grasp or a self-arrest grasp on the axe, though you'll probably find more power and ease in the self-belay grasp.

Here's how to do the self-belay: be sure both feet are secure (in the position of balance described in the next section). Then jam the spike and shaft of the axe into the snow and continue to grip the head of the axe with one hand as you move a step forward with each foot. When both feet are again secure, pull the axe out and replant it farther along (fig. 12-16a). Continue this procedure until you feel it's safe to proceed without it.

Used like this, the ice axe is ready as a safety post as you are moving your feet. To be reliable, the shaft must be placed deep enough, in snow that's firm enough, to hold your full weight. If you slip, keep one hand on the head of the axe as you grab hold of the shaft at the surface of the snow and trust your weight to it (fig. 12-16b). The key to a successful self-belay recovery is the grabbing of the shaft right where it emerges from the snow, so that your pull is against the buried shaft while the hand on the head of the axe minimizes the risk of it levering out.

Practice this technique on a slope of hard snow with a safe runout to develop the confidence to know when a self-belay will hold while you replant your feet after a slip. If you're on a climb and begin to doubt your self-belays, it's time to make a critical decision: whether to back off, to rope up, or to climb on, recognizing the risk you're taking.

ASCENDING SNOW

Climbing up—and down—snow slopes takes a set of special skills. Different techniques come into play depending on how hard or steep the slope is. (The related skills of cramponing and step-cutting are covered in Chapter 14.)

Climbing in balance

As with rock climbing, staying in balance while moving on snow is less tiring, more efficient, and safer than struggling to keep from falling only by clinging to something—in this case, the ice axe or the snow. Snow climbers move from one balanced position to another, avoiding any prolonged stance in an unbalanced position.

On a diagonal uphill route, the most balanced position is with the inside (uphill) foot in front of and above the trailing outside (downhill) leg,

which is fully extended to make use of the skeleton and minimize muscular effort. In that position, let the trailing leg bear most of your weight. Always grip the ice axe with your uphill hand.

The diagonal ascent is a two-step sequence: from a position of balance through an out-of-balance position and back to a position of balance (fig. 12-17). From the in-balance position, place the axe above and ahead into the snow. Move up two steps before repositioning the ice axe. The first step brings the outside (downhill) foot in front of the inside (uphill foot), putting the climber out of balance. The second step brings the inside foot up from behind and places it beyond the outside foot, putting the climber back in the balance position. Keep your weight over your feet and avoid leaning into the slope.

If you're heading straight up the fall line instead of moving diagonally, there's no longer an uphill or downhill leg, or an uphill or downhill hand. So carry the axe in the hand that feels most comfortable and climb in a steady, controlled manner. Regardless of the direction of travel, placing the axe firmly before each move will provide self-belay protection.

Fig. 12–17. Ascending a snow slope, diagonally, in balance

The rest step

Climbing a long featureless snow slope can give you the frustrating sensation that you're getting nowhere. Few landmarks help measure your progress, so distances are deceiving. Novice climbers try a dash-and-gasp pace in an attempt to rush the objective. But the only way to the top of the slope is to find a pace you can maintain, and then maintain it.

The solution is the rest step, a technique that conserves energy as it moves you methodically forward. (The rest step is illustrated in Chapter 5.) Use the rest step whenever legs or lungs need a bit of recuperation between steps. At lower elevations it's usually the leg muscles that require a break. At higher elevations, the lungs need the pause.

Here's a review of the rest step: the rest takes place after one foot is swung forward for the next step. Support all body weight on the rear leg while the unweighted forward leg muscles relax. During each mini-rest, the weighted rear leg must be kept straight and locked at the knee so that bone, not muscle, carries the load. The climbing pace is slow, because for every step there is a pause. Synchronize breathing with the sequence. At higher elevations you'll need to make a conscious effort to breath deeply and often.

Step-kicking

The technique of step-kicking is basic to snow climbing. It's a way to create a path of upward steps that provide the best possible footing with the least expenditure of energy. It is all that's needed for footing when the snow is yielding enough to permit security without the help of crampons or chopped steps.

The most efficient kick to create snow steps is a swing of the leg that lets its own weight and momentum provide the needed impact, with little muscular effort. This works fine in soft snow. On harder snow, you'll end up putting in more effort, and the steps will usually be smaller and less secure.

The definition of a secure step varies with the climber's skill and strength and with the effects of such factors as wind, altitude, and the weight of the pack. An average climber probably needs steps deep enough to take the ball of the foot when going straight up and at least half of the boot on a diagonal ascent. Steps that are kicked level or tilted slightly into the slope are more secure. The less space there is on a step, the more important it is that the step slope inward.

When you're kicking steps, keep the other climbers in mind. They can follow up your staircase in good balance if your steps are spaced evenly and somewhat close together. Make allowance for climbers whose legs aren't as long as yours.

Followers use the same leg swing as the leader, improving the steps as they climb. The follower must kick into the step, because simply walking onto the existing platform will not set the boot securely in position. In compact snow the kick should be somewhat low, the toe driving in and deepening the step. However, in very soft snow it is usually easier to bring the boot down from above, shearing off an edge of snow, which helps build a stronger step.

A basic principle of snow travel is that parties move in single file when ascending. If you're in the lead, you will be doing by far the hardest work. You also have to think harder in order to avoid potential hazards to the group and to choose the best route. Take turns leading so that no climber is worked to exhaustion.

Direction of ascent

You can either go directly up a snow slope or ascend it diagonally. If you're in a hurry, a direct ascent is usually the way to go. Speed is a primary consideration on a long snow climb, and a fast, direct ascent is the order of the day if you face bad weather, avalanche or rockfall danger, poor bivouac conditions, or a difficult descent.

When time permits, most climbers prefer a diagonal ascent, switchbacking up moderately angled slopes. They reason that the lower angle of ascent requires less energy for each step while it ends up gaining the same elevation as the fewer—but steeper—steps of a direct ascent. The strength of this argument probably depends on snow conditions. In good step-kicking snow, the energy you save at each step on a diagonal ascent can be used to kick the additional steps required by that angle. But in marginal step-kicking conditions, many climbers figure that a diagonal route is more difficult because of the work of kicking edged, traversing steps in hard snow.

Ice-axe technique: direct ascent

In a straight shot up a snowfield, step-kicking is the basic technique for your feet. Ice-axe technique, however, will vary depending on snow conditions and steepness.

Cane position: On a slope that is at a low or moderate angle (roughly up to 30 or 35 degrees), climb with the axe in the cane position, holding it in one hand by the head and using it for balance (fig. 12-18). You can continue in the cane position as the snow gets even steeper, as long as you feel

Fig. 12–19. Direct ascent, ice axe in stake position

secure with it. Setting the axe firmly before each move will provide a self-belay.

Stake position: At some point as the snow steepens, a climber may choose to switch to the two-handed stake position, a more secure stance often used for angles over 45 degrees (fig. 12-19). Before moving upward, plant the axe, with both hands, as far as it will go into the snow. Then continue to grasp it with both hands on the head, or with one hand on the head and one on the shaft. This position is particularly useful on steeper soft snow.

Horizontal position: This is a technique effective on steeper, harder snow that is covered with a soft layer. Hold the axe with both hands, one in the self-arrest grasp on the head and the other near the end of the shaft. Jab the axe horizontally into the

Fig. 12–18. Direct ascent, ice axe in cane position

Fig. 12–20. Direct ascent, ice axe in horizontal position

Fig. 12–21. Diagonal ascent, ice axe in cross-body position

snow above you, the pick down and the shaft at right angles to your body (fig. 12-20). This jabs the pick into the harder base while the shaft gets some purchase in the softer surface snow. (Don't forget to take advantage of the rest step as you head up the hill, regardless of the ice-axe technique being used.)

Ice-axe technique: diagonal ascent

On a diagonal route, remember to climb in balance as you kick steps up the slope. (Figure 12-17 shows the sequence of moves in a diagonal ascent.) For slopes angled less than about 40 or 45 degrees, the axe usually works fine in the cane position. As the slope steepens, the cane position becomes awkward and it's time to switch to the cross-body position.

Cross-body position: For this position, hold the axe perpendicular to the angle of the slope, one hand grasping the head and the other holding the shaft, which is jabbed into the snow (fig. 12-21). The axe will cross diagonally in front of you. (Be sure the pick does not point toward your body.) Most of the weight placed on the axe should bear on the shaft, while the hand on the head merely stabilizes the axe. Move your feet upward in the same manner as with the cane position.

Diagonal ascents often mean switchbacks, which mean changes in direction. There's a specific sequence of steps for a safe change in direction on a diagonal route, whether you have the axe in the cane position or the cross-body position (fig. 12-22).

Start from a position of balance, the inside (uphill) foot in front of and above the outside (downhill) foot. Jab the axe shaft straight down into the snow at a spot as directly above your location as possible. Grasp the head of the axe with both hands as you move your outside foot forward, bringing you into the out-of-balance position. Continue holding onto the head with both hands as you move into a stance facing uphill, moving your inside foot toward the new direction of travel, and ending with splayed feet. Finally, a turn in the new direction of travel returns you to a position of balance, with the new uphill foot now in front and above. With the cane position, the new uphill hand now grasps the axe head. With the cross-body position, the hands holding the head and the shaft are now reversed. If splayed feet feel unstable as you change direction at a steep angle, kick the steps more directly into the slope.

Traversing

Long horizontal traverses, which neither gain nor lose elevation, are rarely any fun. This "sidehill gouging" works OK on soft snow at low and moderate angles, though it's still not as comfortable or efficient as a diagonal route. On horizontal traverses over harder or steeper snow, you can face into the slope and kick straight forward for more secure steps. But try to avoid horizontal traverses in the first place.

DESCENDING SNOW

One mark of a skillful snow climber is the ability to go downhill efficiently and confidently. Many otherwise competent and aggressive climbers blanch at the prospect of going forward down a steep snow gully. Why? Because there's a superb view—perhaps too superb—of the exposure. And because on steep snow the axe must be placed very low to move down, leaving the climber without the comforting stance and handhold that was there on the way up. You can minimize those downhill jitters by mastering a few descent techniques.

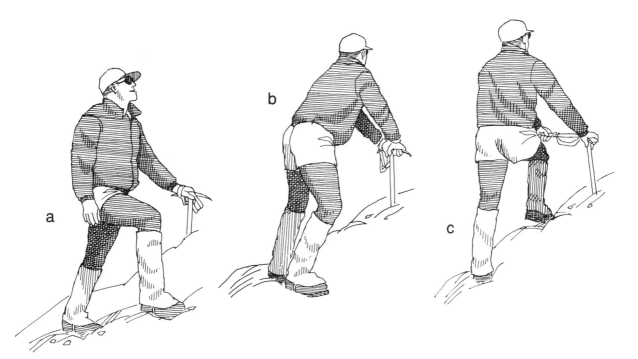

Fig. 12–22. Changing direction on a diagonal ascent: a, jab axe shaft straight down; b, face uphill with feet splayed; c, turn in new direction of travel.

Plunge-stepping

In going down, just like going up, technique is determined mainly by the hardness and angle of the snow. In soft snow on a moderate slope, simply face outward and walk down. With harder snow or a steeper angle, use the plunge step (fig. 12-23).

The plunge step is a confident, aggressive move. Face outward, step assertively away from the slope and land solidly on your heel with your leg vertical, transferring weight solidly to the new position. No timid steps allowed. Avoid leaning back into the slope, which could result in a glancing blow, less secure steps, and perhaps an unplanned glissade. Plunge-stepping can be secure with steps that hold only the heel of the boot, but most climbers do not trust steps more shallow than that.

When plunge-stepping, keep the knees bent a bit, not locked, to maintain control of balance. The degree of bending depends on the angle of the slope (the steeper the slope, the greater the bend) and the firmness of the surface (the harder the snow, the greater the bend). With bent knees, a forward lean is also needed to help with balance. An aggressive stride creates a deep step, so be careful in very soft snow that a plunging leg isn't injured by being buried so deep it can't be yanked back out as you take the next step.

The plunge-stepping climber holds the ice axe in one hand in either the self-arrest or self-belay grasp, with the spike close to the surface, well forward and ready to plant in the snow. You can spread and move the other arm for balance. Some climbers hold the axe in both hands in the full self-arrest position—one hand on the head, the other near the end of the shaft—but this allows less movement of the arms to maintain balance.

At some point, on harder or steeper snow, this style of plunge-stepping will not feel secure. Then it's necessary to plant the axe as low as possible in a self-belay before each move and advance the feet in a sort of crouched, modified plunge step (fig. 12-24).

Glissading

Glissading is one of the joyous bonuses of mountain climbing, offering the fastest, easiest, and most exhilarating way down many snow slopes for a climber on foot. It's an alternative to walking or plunge-stepping, for use on slopes where you can keep your speed under control. There are three principal methods of glissading. Which one you use will depend on how hard and steep the slope is, how safe the runout is at the bottom of the hill, and how good you are at glissading.

The sitting glissade (fig. 12-25a) is the easiest to learn and works on soft snow where you would bog down if you tried a standing glissade. You'll get the slickest and driest ride by wearing coated-nylon rain pants. For the sitting glissade, simply sit in the snow and let 'er rip, holding the axe in self-arrest position as you slide downhill. The standard posture is to sit fairly erect, knees bent and boot soles planing along the surface. However, to get started and maintain momentum in snow that

Fig. 12–23. Plunge-stepping, moderate slope

Fig. 12–24. Plunge-stepping with self-belay

is quite soft, it helps to stretch out your legs, spreading body weight over a greater area.

Run the spike of the axe, like a rudder, along the snow on one side of you. Putting pressure on the spike helps reduce speed and thwarts any tendency of your body to pivot head-downward. The standard posture, with knees bent and feet flat, also reduces speed. This posture is the most helpful in uncomfortable conditions: when the snow is crusted or firmly consolidated, pitted with icy ruts or small suncups, or dotted with rocks or shrubs. It provides more stability and control than with your legs straight out in front, and it helps minimize wear and tear on your bottom.

To stop, use the spike to slow down, then dig in your heels—but not at high speed or a somersault may be the result. For an emergency stop, simply self-arrest by rolling into position toward the side opposite the spike. (The indispensable technique of self-arrest will be explained in the next section of this chapter).

Turns are almost impossible in a sitting glissade. The spike, dragged as a rudder and assisted by body contortions, can exert a change in direction of a few degrees at most. The best way to get around an obstruction is to stop, walk sideways to a point that is not directly above the obstacle, and take off again.

The standing glissade (fig. 12-25b) is the best one, if you know how to do it and conditions are right. This position offers the earliest look at hazards of the route, is the most maneuverable, and saves your clothes from wetness and abrasion. The standing glissade is most effective on a firm base with a softer layer on top. The softer the snow, the steeper the slope needed to maintain speed. You can do a standing glissade down slopes of harder snow, but these will usually be at lower angles and with a safe runout. Slopes at very low angles can be skated, if the snow is firm.

Correct standing glissade technique is very similar to downhill skiing. The position is a semi-crouch over the feet with bent knees and outspread arms. The feet can be together or spread, as needed for stability, with one foot advanced slightly to further improve stability and prevent nose dives. Increase speed by bringing the feet closer together and leaning farther forward over the feet. Slow down and stop any number of ways: stand up and dig in the heels; turn the feet sideways and edge; crouch and drag the ice-axe spike as in the crouching glissade (described next); or perform a turn similar to skiing in which you rotate the shoulders, upper body, and knees in the direction of the turn and roll the knees and ankles in the same direction to rock the feet onto boot edges.

Transition areas, where the snow texture changes, are tricky. If you hit softer, slower snow, your head and torso will suddenly be outpacing your legs, so move one boot forward for stability. If you hit harder, faster snow or ice below the surface, lean well forward to prevent a slip. Keep speed under control by regular braking and traversing.

The crouching glissade (fig. 12-25c) is done

Fig. 12–25. Glissades: a, sitting; b, standing; c, crouching.

much like the standing glissade, except the climber holds the axe in the self-arrest position to one side of the body, sits back, and drags the spike in the snow. It's slower than a standing glissade and easier to learn. With three points of contact, it is also more stable. However, turning is more difficult, as is controlling speed with edging.

As in much of mountaineering, efficiency in glissading takes a smooth blend of several techniques. In particular, climbers who lack finesse in the standing glissade often use a combination: breaking into a plunge step to control speed, stepping off in a new direction rather than making a

ski-style turn, and skating to maintain momentum as the slope angle lessens.

Glissading can be hazardous. Glissade only when there is a safe runout, close enough that if you slide out of control, you won't be injured before reaching it. Unless there is a view of the entire run, the first person down must use extreme caution and stop frequently to look ahead. The biggest risk is losing control at such high speed that self-arrest is not possible. This is most likely to happen on the best glissading slope, one with firm snow. Maintain control of speed.

Adjust equipment before beginning the descent,

and stow crampons and other hardware in the pack. Don't try a sitting glissade while wearing crampons, because it's too easy to catch a point in the snow. Wear mittens, even on a warm day; snow is so cold and abrasive it can chill and flay the hands until they lose control of the axe.

Sometimes in soft snow, a glissader accidentally sets off a mass of surface snow, which slides down the slope with the glissader aboard. These are really small avalanches, known as avalanche cushions. The trick is to decide if it's a cushion safe to ride or if it is about to become a serious avalanche. If the moving snow is more than a few inches deep, self-arrest won't work because the ice-axe pick can't penetrate to the layer below. Sometimes the spike can be driven deep enough to slow, though probably not stop, the glissader. Unless you're sure the cushion is safe and your speed is under control, get off. Just roll sideways a few feet out of the path of the moving snow, then self-arrest.

Downclimbing

On steep snow where you may not feel secure glissading or plunge-stepping, you can face into the slope and downclimb backward by kicking steps straight into the slope. Use the axe in the stake position as a self-belay.

SELF-ARREST

Self-arrest is the lifesaving technique of using the ice axe to stop your own uncontrolled slide down a snow slope. It's used when you slip on the snow without a self-belay or when your self-belay fails. If you are unroped, it offers your only chance to stop the slide. It's the single most important snow-climbing skill, one you should continue to practice as long as you climb so that it remains an automatic response to a fall.

The technique also serves to brace you solidly in the snow if you have to hold the fall of a ropemate. Therefore a climber's own life and those of fellow climbers could hinge on self-arrest skills. Every climber must be proficient and reliable at self-arrest, learned through practice on increasingly steep and hard snow with a safe runout.

Strength obviously helps in self-arrest, but knowing the correct methods is more important than simple muscle power.

The first rule of self-arrest is: act fast. Good self-arrest form may be aesthetically satisfying, but fast is better than pretty when instantaneous action is critical. From the self-arrest position, get the ice-axe pick in as hard and as quickly as possible, before you've accelerated to an unstoppable speed.

Here's what you should look like as you complete a successful self-arrest, lying face down in the snow, head uphill, with the ice axe beneath you (fig. 12-26, last panel):

The hands hold the axe in a solid grip, one hand in the self-arrest grasp with thumb under the adze and fingers over the pick, the other hand on the shaft just above the spike.

The pick is pressed into the snow just above your shoulder so that the adze is near the angle formed by neck and shoulder.

The shaft crosses your chest diagonally and is held close to the opposite hip. Gripping the shaft near the end prevents that hand from acting as a pivot around which the spike can swing to jab the thigh. (A short axe is held the same way, although the spike will not reach the opposite hip.)

The chest and shoulder are pressed strongly down on the ice-axe shaft.

The spine is arched slightly away from the snow. This arch is critical; it places the bulk of your weight on the axe head and on your toes or knees, the points that dig into the snow to force a stop. Pull up on the end of the shaft, which starts the arch and rolls weight toward the shoulder by the axe head. (Note: the arch can be carried to excess by those unwilling to get their chest and face down into the snow.)

The knees are against the surface, helping slow the fall in soft snow. On harder surfaces, where they have little stopping power, they help stabilize your body position.

The legs are stiff and spread apart, toes digging in. But if you have crampons on, keep them above the snow until you've nearly come to a halt. A crampon point could catch on hard snow or ice and flip you over backward.

CORRECT

Fig. 12–26. Correct self-arrest technique, head uphill, on your back

Self-arrest from different positions

The position you find yourself thrown into when you fall determines how you self-arrest. You'll likely be sliding in one of four positions: head uphill or head downhill and, in either case, face down or on your back. The immediate goal is to get your body into the only usable self-arrest position: with your head uphill and your face down. And the first move toward that goal is to grasp the axe in both hands, one hand on the axe head in the self-arrest grasp and the other at the base of the shaft. From that point, here is how to handle each of the four situations:

Head uphill, face down: You're already in the desired self-arrest position. All you have to do is get your body over the axe shaft, as described above.

Head uphill, on your back: This isn't much more difficult than the first version. Roll toward the head of the axe and jab the pick into the snow at your side as you roll over onto your stomach (fig. 12-26). If the axe head is on the right, roll to the right. If it's on the left, roll to the left. Beware of rolling the other way, toward the spike, which could jam the spike in the snow before the pick and wrench the axe from your hands (fig. 12-27).

Head downhill, face down: self-arrest from

INCORRECT

Fig. 12–27. Incorrect self-arrest technique; do not roll toward spike

head-first falls is more difficult because the feet have to first be swung downhill. In this face-down predicament, reach downhill and off to the axe-head side and get the pick into the snow to serve as a pivot to swing the body around. Work to help swing the legs around so they are pointing downhill (fig. 12-28). Never jab the spike into the snow and pivot on that end of the axe. That would bring the pick and adze of the axe across your slide path and on a collision course with your chest and face.

Head downhill, on your back: Hold the axe across your torso and slide the pick into the snow, then twist and roll toward it (fig. 12-29). Once again, the pick placed to the side serves as a pivot point. But merely planting the pick won't bring you around to the final self-arrest position. You must work at rolling your chest toward the axe head at the same time as you help your legs to swing around and point downhill. A sitting-up motion helps the roll.

Variations: In the loose snow of winter and early spring, the pick may not be able to reach compact snow, making the usual self-arrest useless. The best brakes in this case are feet and knees and elbows, widely spaced and deeply pressed into the snow. In this case the greatest drag potential of

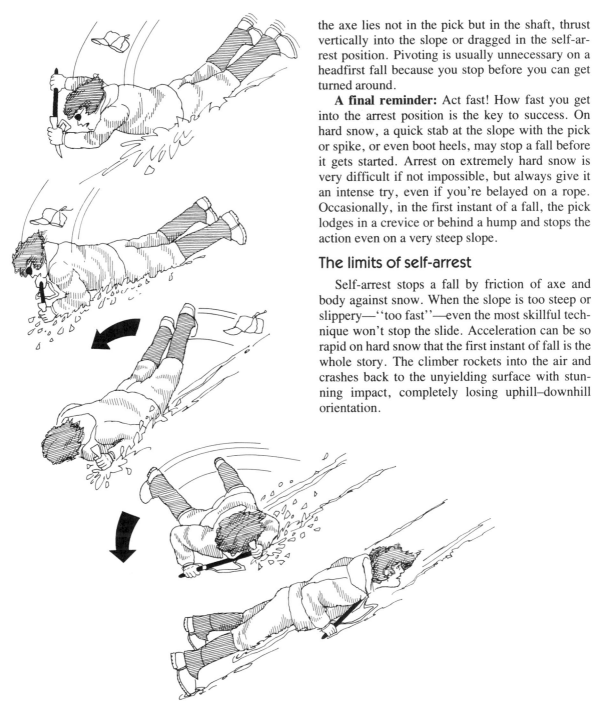

the axe lies not in the pick but in the shaft, thrust vertically into the slope or dragged in the self-arrest position. Pivoting is usually unnecessary on a headfirst fall because you stop before you can get turned around.

A final reminder: Act fast! How fast you get into the arrest position is the key to success. On hard snow, a quick stab at the slope with the pick or spike, or even boot heels, may stop a fall before it gets started. Arrest on extremely hard snow is very difficult if not impossible, but always give it an intense try, even if you're belayed on a rope. Occasionally, in the first instant of a fall, the pick lodges in a crevice or behind a hump and stops the action even on a very steep slope.

The limits of self-arrest

Self-arrest stops a fall by friction of axe and body against snow. When the slope is too steep or slippery—"too fast"—even the most skillful technique won't stop the slide. Acceleration can be so rapid on hard snow that the first instant of fall is the whole story. The climber rockets into the air and crashes back to the unyielding surface with stunning impact, completely losing uphill–downhill orientation.

Fig. 12–28. Self-arrest technique, head downhill, face down

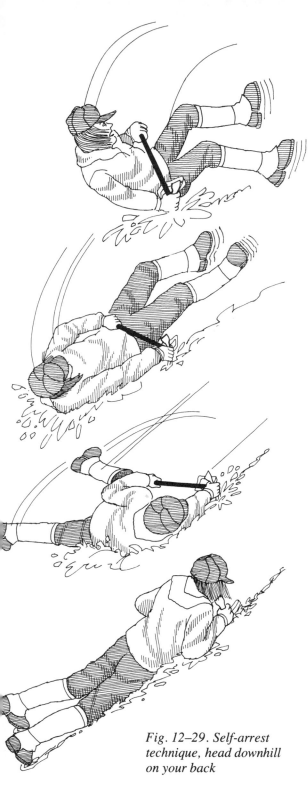

Fig. 12–29. Self-arrest technique, head downhill on your back

Even successful arrests require at least a little time, during which the climber slides some distance. Therefore the effectiveness of the self-arrest is limited by the climber's speed of reaction and the steepness and length of the slope.

If all initial efforts at self-arrest are unsuccessful, don't give up. Keep fighting. Self-arrest might work in softer snow or at a lower angle farther down the slope. Even if you don't stop, the attempt may slow you down and help prevent rolling, tumbling, and bouncing. It may also help keep you sliding feet first, the best position if you end up hitting rocks or trees. And if you are roped to other climbers, anything you can do to slow your fall increases the chance that their self-arrests or belays will hold.

Keep alert at all times to the limits of self-arrest. If a slope seems too fast or too short, or members of a climbing party doubt their strength or skill, use one of the techniques of roped protection outlined later in this chapter.

The uses of self-belay and self-arrest

Self-belay is preventive; self-arrest is a recovery measure. Some climbers who learned self-arrest as the primary security technique on snow fear too much emphasis on self-belay. But the purposes of the two techniques are different and you need them both. Where the axe can be planted securely, self-belay is usually all that is needed, so any fall is prevented in the first place. If self-belay fails, you can then self-arrest.

While self-belaying on a climb, keep alert to changes in snow conditions that make the belays insecure. If the snow on a steep slope is so hard that axe placement might not hold a slip, it may be best to change to the self-arrest grasp, ready to instantly self-arrest. Of course, under these conditions, a self-arrest will also be very difficult. Even with the self-arrest grasp, you can continue to make self-belay placements, though they will be a little more difficult because your palm will no longer be on the flat, comfortable top of the adze.

One important skill comes into play if you are using the self-belay grasp and slip into a fall. You must be able to instantly flip the ice axe from the self-belay grasp to a self-arrest grasp. Grab the shaft of the axe just above the spike, then change the hand to the self-arrest grasp—and arrest. This takes practice. If you don't have the skill or confidence to do it, then it will be safer to do your self-belays holding the axe head in the self-arrest grasp.

ROPED CLIMBING TECHNIQUES

When is it time to rope up on a snow climb? In general, when the overall risks to the climbing party of continuing unroped are higher than those of roping up. It's often an issue of trade-offs, weighing the pros and cons of both choices.

On a glacier, the risks to unroped climbers of falling into a crevasse clearly exceed the risks to the team of roping up. So teams rope up.

As slopes steepen and snow hardens, the easy decisions disappear. It becomes a matter of deciding whether the risks to unroped climbers of being unable to stop their own individual falls exceed the risks to the team of roping up. These team risks are not trivial. They include the possibility of one person's fall pulling the entire rope team off the mountain and the danger that roped climbing will slow the climb, adding to avalanche and rockfall exposure and the likelihood of an unplanned bivouac. It becomes a delicate decision involving an evaluation of each climber's skills and the variety of alternatives for roped team protection.

OPTIONS FOR ROPED TEAM PROTECTION

If your party decides it would be safer overall to rope up, there are several different ways to match the type of rope protection to the conditions of the climb and the strengths of the climbers.

Team arrest (roped but unbelayed)

Team arrest depends on each climber to stop a personal fall and on the rest of the rope team to provide backup in case the attempt fails. Everyone involved uses self-belay or self-arrest.

Relying on team arrest as the ultimate team security makes sense only in selected situations, such as on a low- or moderate-angle glacier or on a moderate snow slope where a less skilled climber could be saved from a dangerous slide by the more proficient members of the rope team. On steeper, harder slopes you face that appraisal of risks, trying to decide which is safer: continuing to rely on team arrest, unroping and letting each climber go it alone, or switching to a more secure mode of roped travel.

You may be able to increase the odds that team arrest will work on a snow slope by trying the following procedures:

• Carry a few feet of rope coiled in your hand if there are any climbers below you. If a climber falls, drop the loose rope and it will give you an extra instant to get the axe into self-belay position and to brace yourself. (Note: do not carry coils on a glacier, because the extra rope simply increases the distance the victim will fall into the crevasse.)

• Put the weakest climber on the downhill end of the rope. As a rule, the least skilled climber should be last on the rope while ascending and the first on the rope while descending. This puts the climber most likely to fall in position where a fall will be of the least serious kind: below the other climbers and coming quickly onto the rope. Unfortunately, it also means the weakest climber will be the team's last hope if the climbers above fall.

• Climb on a shortened rope. This is most applicable to a two-person rope team. If a climbing pair uses only a portion of the rope—say 60 to 75 feet instead of the full length—they will reduce the sliding distance and the tug from the fall if one partner falls while above the other.

• Climb in separate parallel tracks. This is also most applicable to a two-person rope team. The climbers will be abreast of each other, separated by the rope. A falling climber will pendulum down, putting force on the rope to the side of and below the partner. The tug on the rope will be less than if the climber fell from high above. Also, the friction of the rope as it pendulums across the snow will absorb some of the force. Traveling in separate tracks may be impractical on ascents where kicking two sets of steps would be a waste of time and energy. However, it might be used on ascents of harder snow and should be considered for any descent.

Running belays

The use of running belays (fig. 12-30) offers a middle level of protection, somewhere between team arrest and fixed belays. It can help in situations where a successful team arrest is improbable but where fixed belays aren't practical because they would take too much time. For example, running protection may do the job on long snow faces and couloirs.

To place running belays, the leader puts in pieces of snow protection as needed and uses a carabiner to clip the rope into each one. (Types of snow protection are discussed in the next section of this chapter, on snow anchors.) The climbers continue to make good progress because all members of the rope team climb at the same time, just as in unbelayed travel. Except that now there's protection in the snow that, if it is securely placed, will put an end to any fall. Traveling this way, the last

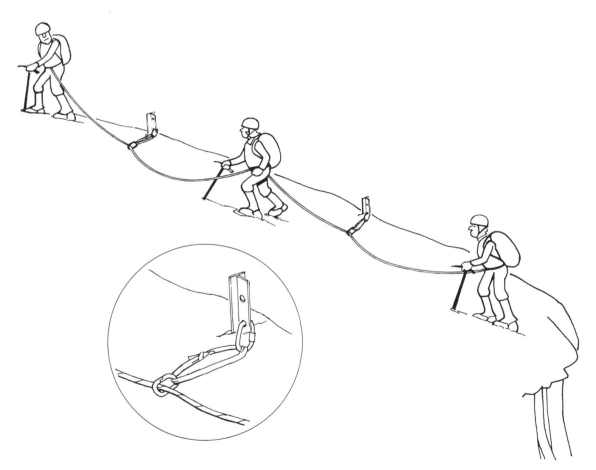

Fig. 12–30. A running belay setup

climber on the rope removes each piece. Of course the use of running protection means the team must pack the extra weight of the gear and must take the time to place it.

Fixed belays

The ultimate in safety comes from having climbers belay each other up snow pitches, in the same manner as in rock climbing. The catch is that this procedure may be so time-consuming it becomes impractical on the snow faces of major alpine routes. However, there is a wide variety of snow belays, varying in security and in the amount of time they take to set up. They are described later in this chapter.

Combination protection techniques

The reality of most serious snow climbs is that success calls for a combination of protection techniques. It's not likely a party will take on an entire climb unroped. It's just as unlikely that the party will use fixed belays all the way.

In deciding when to rope up, a climbing team is actually asking itself a series of questions. The team always ropes up on glaciers. But on snow or mixed terrain, the team asks:

1. Is each member of the party able to use self-belay or self-arrest to save himself or herself in case of a fall? If the answer is yes, the party can continue unroped. If the answer is no, the team asks:
2. Can we stop all falls by roping up and depending on team arrest? If so, rope up and continue climbing, unbelayed. If not, then ask:
3. Is it feasible to use some form of belay (a running belay or a fixed belay) and will this belay provide adequate protection? If so, begin belaying. If it's not feasible, because of poor terrain or lack of time, then the party must ask itself:
4. Shall we turn around, or shall we proceed unroped and assume the risks?

In practice, long snow routes are climbed roped and mostly unbelayed, with belays of some kind on steeper, harder snow or when climbers are tired or

hurt. Most of the reliance is on team arrest or running protection, though some sections may lend themselves to unroped travel.

The option of turning around is always worth considering. If things aren't going well, select a new route, another destination, or just head home.

SNOW ANCHORS

Anchors are needed in snow for the same reasons they are needed on rock. The equipment is different but the purposes are the same: to anchor belays and rappels. But rock anchors are usually easy to inspect and predictable in performance. Snow anchors are not. They vary widely in strength depending on snow conditions and placement, and their strength changes during the day with changes in the snow. This uncertainty makes it even more imperative than on rock to check and recheck any belay or rappel anchor. Snow anchors can also require a lot of time to put in place. They include deadman anchors (such as snow flukes), pickets, and bollards.

A deadman anchor is any object you bury in the snow as a point of attachment for the rope. The most common is the snow fluke, a specially shaped aluminum plate with a metal cable attached (fig. 12-31a). Snow flukes are available in various sizes, their holding ability generally increasing with size. For maximum strength and reliability, a buried fluke should be angled back about 45 degrees from the direction of pull (fig. 12-31b). Dig a slot in the snow to permit the cable to be pulled in as direct a line as possible.

In theory, the fluke serves as a dynamic anchor, burrowing deeper into the snow when it takes a load, such as the weight of a climber on rappel. In practice, it may behave in more complicated ways, even coming out if it is tipped too far forward or back, or if the load is to the side rather than straight out. If the plate or the cable travels down into the snow and hits a harder layer, the fluke could be deflected and pull out. Flukes are available with bent faces, flanged sides, or fixed cables—features intended to make them maintain the correct orientation and to make them self-correct if deflected.

Flukes are most reliable—but also more diffi-

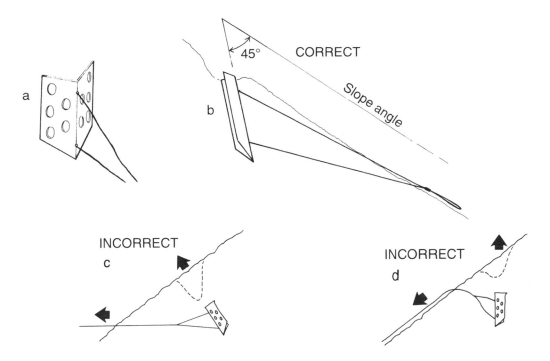

Fig. 12–31. Placing snow flukes: a, typical snow fluke; b, correct angle for fluke placement; c, incorrect, not angled back sufficiently; d, incorrect, no slot for cable.

cult to place—in the hard homogeneous snow of summer. They are generally used in a softer but dense pack, snow that is moist and heavy. They are least reliable under typical winter conditions, with snow layers of varying density where they may deflect off harder layers. Neither do they do well in dry, unconsolidated snow.

Ice axes, ice tools, and snow pickets can serve as deadman anchors (fig. 12-32). Bury the implement horizontally in the snow, with a runner attached at the midpoint. Cut a slot in the snow to let the runner lie in the direction of pull, and then clip into the runner.

A picket is a stake driven into the snow as an anchor (fig. 12-33). Aluminum pickets are available in lengths from 18 to 36 inches and are found in different styles, including round or oval tubes and angled or T-section stakes.

Pickets work well in snow too firm for flukes but too soft for ice screws. As with flukes, angle

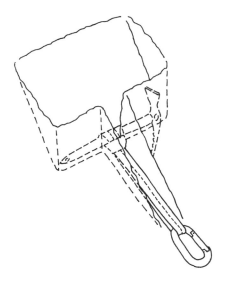

Fig. 12–32. Ice axe buried as deadman anchor

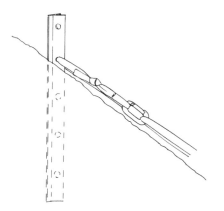

Fig. 12–33. Picket placement

them back about 45 degrees from the direction of pull. Attach a carabiner or runner to the picket at the snowline—not higher on the picket, or a pull may lever it out. You can drive a picket into the snow with a rock or the side of an ice axe, but a North Wall hammer or other ice hammer works best and reduces the chance of equipment damage. An ice axe or ice tool can serve as a makeshift picket.

A bollard is a mound of snow that serves as an anchor when rope or webbing is positioned around it (fig. 12-34). Snow bollards provide highly reliable anchors for belaying or rappelling in soft snow and are possibly the most reliable in all snow conditions. There's a significant trade-off here, however. It takes a long time to build one.

Create the mound by making a trench around an oval area of snow. In hard snow, chop out the trench; in soft snow, just stamp it out. The bollard should end up as an oval-shaped island of snow. The softer the snow, the broader and deeper the bollard must be: up to 10 feet wide and $1^1/_2$ feet deep.

Try to use webbing around the bollard instead of rope because it's less likely to saw into the mound. For the same reason, avoid pulling on the rope or webbing after placing it. For more security, pad the rope or webbing with packs and clothing and whatever, especially in soft snow. For safety, inspect the bollard after each use to see it hasn't been damaged. You can also back up the bollard with a picket or fluke (which the last person on a rappel removes before rappelling).

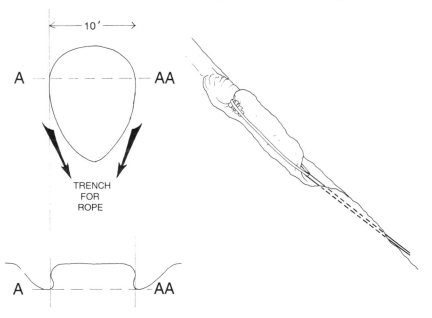

Fig. 12–34. Snow bollard

Multiple anchors are the best insurance because of the inherent weakness and unpredictability of snow anchors. As with questionable anchors in rock, multiple anchors are safest. Two anchors can be chained sequentially so that the first takes the hit, but has a backup to absorb any remaining force. Or they can be connected in a way that will permit them to share any load (fig. 12-35). (More details and illustrations on joining multiple anchors are in Chapters 7, 8, and 10.) In general, place multiple snow anchors one behind the other to reduce the angle of pull and the potential load on the surviving anchor if the other one fails. Keep the anchors several feet apart so they don't end up sharing any localized weakness in the snow.

BELAYING ON SNOW

Snow climbers choose from a catalog of techniques that provide belay protection to their ropemates. They sometimes give belays using established snow anchors, and sometimes they give quicker and less formal belays using the ice axe. The changeable nature of snow and the difficulty of inspecting snow protection usually result in anchors that can't be considered bombproof like a good anchor in rock. But they are still effective because most mishaps on snow do not generate the high loads of rock-climbing falls. Snow falls are usually slides on relatively moderate (30- to 60-degree) slopes, with help from the friction of rope against snow and with no direct vertical pull.

No matter what the belaying technique, every snow belay should be as dynamic as possible to help limit the force on the anchor. The dynamic, shock-absorbing quality of climbing rope helps minimize chances of an abrupt, static stop to a fall. As a belayer, plan your stance so the force is taken on your body and dissipated as much as possible by the belay and the dynamic quality of the rope. The standard hip belay provides a more gradual, dynamic belay than mechanical belay devices. Think of the consequences if a heavy hit on a question-

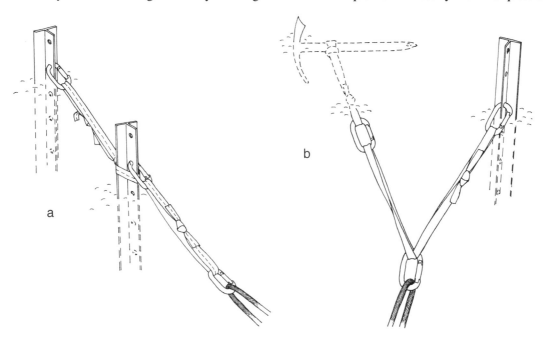

Fig. 12–35. Two methods of connecting snow anchors: a, two pickets linked serially, top anchor supports lower anchor; b, two independent anchors with equalized connecting runner.

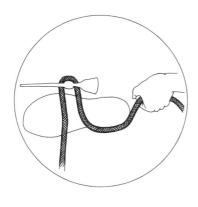
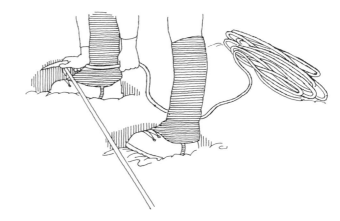

Fig. 12–36. Boot-axe belay

able snow belay yanks you and any anchor off your perch.

Set up a belay close to the climbing difficulties. If you're belaying the lead climber, get out of the line of fire by setting up the belay stance to one side of the fall line—not within it. If the leader is heading up on a diagonal, get outside any point where the climber's route could cross directly above you. On a ridge crest, it is not always possible to predict a fall line and plan a belay in advance. If a ropemate slips off one side of the ridge, the best reaction may actually be to jump off the opposite side, with the rope running over the ridge saving you both.

Quick belays

Snow climbers have a couple of quick belays for times the consequences of a fall would not be great, as in a sliding pendulum across a snow face. They are useful for belaying a climber who is probing a cornice or crevasse edge, or for providing a top belay to a weaker climber.

The boot-axe belay is a fast and easy way to provide protection as a rope team moves up together (fig. 12-36). Despite some naysayers, it has proven to be useful, provided its principal limitation is understood: it can't be expected to hold a high fall force. With thorough practice, you should be able to set up this belay in a couple of seconds with a jab of the ice axe and a quick sweep of the rope.

Step by step, here is how to do it (and after trying it a few times, you'll realize it is not as complicated as it sounds):

1. Stamp a firm platform in the snow, big enough for the axe and uphill boot.
2. Jam the ice-axe shaft as deeply as possible into the snow at the rear of the platform, the shaft tilted slightly uphill against a possible fall. Have the pick perpendicular to the fall line, thus applying the broadest side of the shaft against the force of a fall.
3. Stand below the axe, at approximately a right angle to the fall line and facing the side on which the climber's route lies.
4. Plant your uphill boot into the snow against the downhill side of the shaft, bracing it against a downward pull.
5. Plant the downhill boot in a firmly compacted step far enough below the other boot so that the downhill leg is straight, providing a stiff brace.
6. Flip the rope around the axe. The final configuration will have the rope running from the direction of potential load, across the toe of the uphill boot, around the uphill side of the axe, then back across the boot above the instep.
7. Hold the rope with the downhill (braking) hand, applying extra friction by bringing the rope uphill behind the heel, forming an S-

bend. The braking hand must never leave the rope.

8. Use the uphill hand for two jobs: to grasp the head of the axe to further brace the shaft and then, as the belayed climber moves upward, to take in rope.

Climbers must be equally adept at setting up the boot-axe belay with either foot uphill, because it is essential that the belayer face the climber's fall line. If a lead climber falls behind the belay, the rope unwraps from the axe and there is no belay.

The carabiner/ice-axe belay provides the same level of security as a boot-axe belay, with easier rope handling (fig. 12-37). To set it up, plant the axe as deeply as possible, the pick perpendicular to the fall line. Attach a very short sling with a girth hitch to the axe shaft at snowline and clip on a carabiner. Stand at right angles to the fall line, facing the same side as the climber's route. Brace the axe with your uphill boot, standing atop the sling but leaving the carabiner exposed. (Keep crampons off the sling.) The rope runs from the

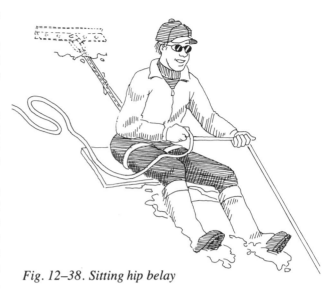

Fig. 12–38. Sitting hip belay

potential direction of pull up through the carabiner, then around the back of your waist and into your uphill (braking) hand. One nice thing about the carabiner/ice-axe belay: the force of a fall pulls the belayer more firmly into the stance.

Anchored belays

Other snow belays usually are used with formal anchors, such as flukes, pickets, or bollards.

The sitting hip belay, with an anchor, is inherently dynamic and very secure on hard snow or deep, heavy, wet snow (fig. 12-38). The sitting belayer may face the prospect of a cold, wet assignment, and the belay can be difficult to work if the rope is frozen.

To set up the belay, stamp or chop a seat in the snow plus a platform to brace each boot against. Put down a pack, ensolite pad, or other material as insulation from the snow, then settle into a standard hip belay, with outstretched, stiffened legs.

The standing hip belay is easier to set up than a sitting hip belay, as it needs only deep, secure slots for each boot. However, it is far less secure because the belayer tends to be toppled under the force of a fall. Standing hip belays must be backed up with an anchor.

These belays can be arranged so the climber

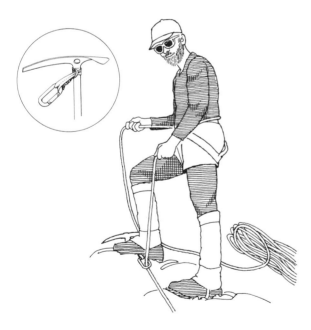

Fig. 12–37. Carabiner/ice-axe belay

faces into the slope, out from the slope, or side-ways. Facing into the slope is the poorest choice because the belayer will be completely wrapped by the rope if the climber falls below the belay stance. And it is difficult to pay out rope for a smooth belay. Facing out is an improvement because it gives a less complete wrap around the belayer and also permits a view of a fall below, important in timing a dynamic belay. But it shares a major weakness with the face-in stance: no way to brace the legs against toppling downhill. In both stances, the belayer should lean into the slope, against a downhill pull.

For the most reliable standing hip belay, stand sideways, facing the same side as the climber's route (fig. 12-39). The downhill leg is straight, locked at the knee, and braced in a snow slot. The uphill leg is on a line with the downhill leg and the direction of a potential fall. The downhill hand should be the braking hand to allow best control for a gradual dynamic belay.

Mechanical belay devices can be used in snow belaying. They are easy to set up and operate even with wet or icy ropes. With a device, you can belay

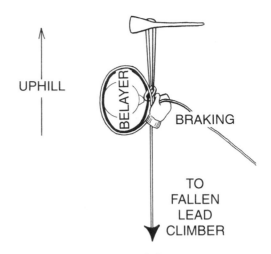

Fig. 12–39. Standing hip belay

directly from the anchor rather than from your seat harness, permitting you to get into a drier, more comfortable position. Be aware that belay devices provide a less dynamic belay than a hip belay, increasing the peak force of a fall on questionable snow anchors.

ROUTEFINDING ON SNOW

Snow gives us passage over some frustrating obstacles, such as tundra, talus, brush, streams, and logging debris. At its best, it provides a smooth, uniform surface and a straight shot up the mountain. But because its very nature means it constantly changes, we always have to study typi-cal seasonal weather patterns as well as current reports for an idea of what conditions to expect on any climb.

Snow can be too soft to support our weight, or it can be hard and slick. It covers obstacles in our path, but it also obscures trails, cairns, and other guideposts to the route, especially above tree line. Dangers often lie beneath the surface: crevasses, moats, or creeks hidden by a thin snow cover. Unstable slopes avalanche.

You can minimize the frustrations and dangers

of snow by studying the medium. (The appendix in this book on ''The Cycle of Snow'' provides infor-mation on snow formation, types of snow, and the creation of glaciers.) Mountaineers let the snow work for them. They read the snow surface and terrain features to determine a safe, efficient route.

SURFACE CONSIDERATIONS

Evaluating the snow surface begins before you even leave home, by considering the effects of both the current weather and of conditions over the last several months.

If you are climbing during a cold, snowy spring following a prolonged late-winter thaw, the thaw's thick crust could hold a heavy load of spring snow ready to avalanche. If spring is cold but sunny, and follows a winter with little snow, a gully that usually offers good step-kicking in May could be filled with rock-hard consolidated snow. However, much of the change in the snow surface takes place rather quickly, so the weather just before and during a climb is the most important.

The best snow, from a mountaineer's point of view, is snow that is safe from avalanche and that will comfortably support a climber's weight for easy step-kicking. Such snow exists, but you have to seek it out. Location of the best snow varies from day to day, even from hour to hour. If the snow is slushy in one spot, or too hard or too crusty or too something, look around: there may be better snow a few feet away.

Here are some tips for making best use of the snow surface:

• Find patches of firmer snow on a slushy slope by walking in shade or using suncups as stairs.
• Try to find patches of softer snow on a slope that is too firm for good step-kicking.
• When the going is difficult, detour toward any surface with a different appearance and possibly more comfortable support.
• Use a different descent route if necessary to find the best snow.
• If you want a firmer surface, look for dirty snow, which absorbs more heat and therefore consolidates more quickly than clean snow.
• Remember that south and west slopes in the Northern Hemisphere, bearing the heat of afternoon sun, consolidate earlier in the season and quicker after storms. They offer hard surfaces when east and north slopes are still soft and unstable.
• Get an early start after a clear, cold night that follows a hot day, in order to take advantage of strong crusts on open slopes before they melt.
• Beware of the hidden holes next to logs, trees, and rocks, where the snow has melted away from these warmer surfaces.
• If you don't like the snow conditions on one side of a ridge, gully, clump of trees, or large boulder, try the other side. The difference may be just what you need.

TERRAIN CONSIDERATIONS

Major terrain features present both obstacles and opportunities (fig. 12-40). Some you use, some you avoid, but they all have to be reckoned with.

Couloirs

A main avenue for all mountain climbing is provided by angled gullies (couloirs). They can hold the key to upward progress because their overall angle is often less than that of the cliffs they breach, offering less technical climbing.

Deeply shaded couloirs are more often lined with ice than snow, especially in late season. Even in spring, however, when open slopes are deep in slush, the couloirs are likely to hold hard snow or ice caused by freezing or avalanche scouring.

Safe passage through a couloir usually depends on the time of day. They can be safe in early morning when the snow is solid and rocks and ice are frozen in place. It's often a different story later in the day, when they can turn deadly. Gullies are the garbage chutes of mountains and with the arrival of the sun they begin to carry down such rubbish as avalanching snow, rocks loosened by frost-wedging, and ice blocks weakened by melting. Most of the debris comes down the center. But even if you keep to the sides, listen for suspicious sounds from above and keep an eye out for quiet slides and silent falling rock.

Avalanches erode deep ruts in many steep couloirs. Climbers usually avoid these ruts or cross them rapidly. However, early in the year the floors of the ruts offer the soundest snow available, and in cold weather they may be quite safe, particularly for a fast descent. Try to be out of a couloir before the sun hits. This means an early start for a round trip, or else a bivouac or an alternative descent route.

Couloirs can become increasingly nasty the higher they are ascended, presenting extreme steepness, verglas, moats, rubble strewn loosely over smooth rock slabs, and cornices. Many lead to difficulties, as when the gentle angle at the bot-

Fig. 12–40. Alpine terrain features

1. Horn or aiguille
2. Ridge
3. Rock arete
4. Cornice
5. Glacier basin
6. Seracs
7. Fallen seracs
8. Erratic blocks
9. Icefall
10. Glacier
11. Crevasses
12. Lateral moraine
13. Snout
14. Moraine lake
15. Terminal moraine
16. Glacial runoff
17. Rock band
18. Shoulder
19. Col
20. Coulior or gully
21. Bergschrund
22. Hanging glacier
23. Buttress
24. Cirque or bowl
25. Headwall
26. Flutings
27. Ice wall
28. Summit
29. Ice arete
30. Towers or gendarmes
31. Avalanche chute
32. Avalanche debris
33. Snowfield

tom is more than balanced by a frosty vertical chimney at the top. However, when the couloir ends at a col (small, high pass), it can offer a lower average angle than the face.

If the bed of the couloir is too steep, try the moat along the sides, formed when the snow melts and settles away from the rock. Moats can be rather deep and will vary in width. Portions of a moat can require bridging between the snow and the rock wall, while other parts present either a tight squeeze or a gap too wide to bridge. You might crampon or step-cut up the couloir, and then drop into the moat on the way down to avoid a nerve-wracking descent on steep ice and exposure to rockfall.

Despite the problems, many snow and ice routes follow couloirs. The techniques are usually simple cramponing and step-kicking, but the frequent presence of moats, crevasses, suncups, and blocks of fallen rock and ice make rock-climbing techniques useful. Some of these irregularities are welcome as a good place to set up a belay.

Ridges

Routes along a ridge crest are free of rockfall and avalanche hazard, so they can be the best choice for a long ascent in a region of moderate to heavy snowfall. Routefinding on a ridge top is generally easier than other places on the mountain, and you can usually find a safe way to retreat. Ridge routes take the full brunt of wind and bad weather, but the most significant hazard of ridge routes is presented by cornices.

Cornices

The shape of a ridge crest helps determine the extent of cornice-building (fig. 12–41). A ridge that slopes on one side and breaks into an abrupt cliff on the other is a good candidate for a gigantic cornice. A knife-edge ridge or one gentle on both sides will have only a tiny cornice, if any at all.

When the physical features are right for building cornices, wind direction decides their exact location. Because storm winds have definite patterns in each mountain range, most cornices in the same area face the same way. In the Pacific Northwest

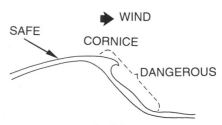

Fig. 12–41. Cornice building

region of the United States, for example, most storms blow from the southwest so the wind-drifted snow of the cornices mostly overhangs on the north and east. These same northern and eastern exposures were steepened by past glaciation, making the ridges ideally shaped for cornice formation.

Temporary or local wind deflection can contradict the general pattern. In rare instances cornices are even built one atop the other, facing in opposite directions, the lower one partially destroyed and hidden by later formations.

Approaching from windward: A cornice gives little sign of its presence as you approach from windward. It simply appears to be a smooth snow slope that runs out to meet the sky. Look at nearby ridges for an idea of the frequency, size, and location of cornices in the area.

Not every snowy ridge conceals a cornice—but be sure to find out whether the ridge you are on does. Try to view the lee side of the ridge from a safe vantage point, such as a rock or tree jutting through the crest. If you can't, have a belayed climber approach the ridge at right angles while probing with an ice axe or reversed ski pole to see if the snow is solid. Look for a crack or indentation in the snow, which could indicate a cornice that has partially collapsed.

It's hard to judge the extent of a cornice overhang and the danger it presents. Don't be misled by appearances. For a mature cornice, the probable line of fracture could be 30 feet or more back from the lip—no doubt farther back than an examination would lead you to expect. And although rocks and trees projecting from the snow suggest safety, they could be on the tops of buttresses with a connecting ridge that curves far back into bays supporting wide cornices. Lots of climbers have had the enlightening experience of looking back along a ridge and discovering their tracks on snow poised above a chasm. The safe course along a corniced crest is well behind the probable fracture line.

Approaching from leeward: You can't miss a cornice from the leeward side. Resembling a wave frozen in the act of breaking, a large cornice close above you is an awesome sight. If you doubt the stability of the cornice, stay among trees or on spur crests as you travel below it. At times, it's quite safe to climb under a cornice. The colder the weather, the more secure the cornice. A late-season cornice, almost completely broken down, is not a problem.

Climbers sometimes even push directly through a cornice to force their way to a ridge crest or pass. It's easiest to penetrate an overhang at a rock spur or where the cornice already has partially collapsed. The leader cuts straight uphill at the point of least overhang, undermining as little of the mass as possible. Generally though, the safest bet with cornices is to avoid traveling on them, under them, or through them.

Bergschrunds

A bergschrund is the giant crevasse found at the upper limit of glacier movement, formed where the moving glacier breaks away from the ice cap. The downhill lip of the bergschrund can be considerably lower than the uphill edge, which may be overhanging. Sometimes the bergschrund is the final problem of the ascent.

Moats

The gap that separates a snowfield from its rock borders is a moat, formed when the snow melts and settles away from the warmer rock. Crossing a moat at the top of a snowfield can be as tough as getting past a bergschrund, with the main difference being that the far wall of a moat is rock instead of snow.

Rockfall hazard

Snowfields and glaciers are prime targets for rockfall from bordering walls and ridges—especially on volcanic peaks, where the rock is often rotten and unstable. Climbers can reduce rockfall danger by wearing hard hats in hazardous areas and by timing climbs for less dangerous periods.

Early-season outings usually face less rockfall than summer climbs because snow still helps cement loose rock in place. Whatever the season, the general rule for glacier climbs is "early on and early off." Nighttime cold often freezes rock in place and prevents most rockfall, but direct sun melts the bonds. The greatest hazard comes in the morning when sun melts the ice, and in evening when meltwater expands as it refreezes, breaking rocks loose.

In the Northern Hemisphere, southern and eastern slopes get the sun first, and therefore should be climbed very early. The shadier northern exposures usually offer less rockfall danger.

ROUTEFINDING AIDS

Crossing a snowfield or glacier, especially at night or in a white-out, can feel like being at sea, without landmarks. However, mountaineers have a couple of navigational opportunities denied to mariners. Mountaineers have a solid surface for planting their own landmarks (wands), and they experience changes in elevation that can be measured by an altimeter as a way to show progress.

The thin bamboo wands topped with tiny flags are left to mark the return route. Try to place wands so that on the return, the next one is visible when the last member of the party is at the previous wand. Coordinate communication so the last person doesn't leave that wand until the next one is sighted. The wands can also be used to mark points of danger (such as moats and crevasses), changes in direction, the boundaries of safe areas for unroped walking in camp, and the location of buried supplies (caches).

An altimeter helps determine your progress and location when you use it along with a topographic map and compass, especially above timberline on a large snowfield with few natural features. You may know that an established camp is located at 11,000 feet, 5 miles due east of the trailhead. By determining the elevation periodically with an altimeter and then finding that elevation on the map along the route, you can find just where you are and how far you have to go. Also relate the altimeter's findings to natural features whenever possible. If you know you are supposed to cross a ridge at an elevation of 9,500 feet in order to keep on the right track to the camp, check the altimeter when you hit the crest. You'll get a good indication of whether you have topped the ridge at the right spot.

A good routefinder uses a variety of tools to stay on route or reach a destination, including compass, map, altimeter, wands, cairns, sun, and visual landmarks. The creative use of several methods becomes especially important when visibility is poor.

AVALANCHES

Avalanches are the number-one hazard facing snow travelers. Avalanche hazard and the conditions that create it are fairly easy to recognize, though there's no way to predict an individual avalanche. Whenever the strength and cohesion of snow on a slope are no longer enough to support the accumulated weight of the snow, an avalanche is due.

Evaluating the stability of a specific snow pack is highly technical work, beyond the scope of this book. A little knowledge about digging snow pits or studying snow crystals sometimes does nothing but give climbers a false sense of security as they rely on an evaluation that may be little more than guesswork. However, climbers do need to learn to recognize generally hazardous terrain and weather.

Four out of five avalanches strike during and just after a storm. Danger increases rapidly with snowfall of an inch or more per hour, or accumulations of a foot or more. Storms starting with low temperature and dry snow, followed by rising temperatures, are even more likely to set up avalanche conditions. The dry snow forms a poor bond, without strength to support the heavier snow that falls later in the storm. Rainstorms, or spring weather with warm winds and cloudy nights, can result in water percolating into the snow and causing wet-snow avalanches. Rapid changes in temperature and wind increase avalanche danger.

Be prepared for two types of avalanches.

A slab avalanche has an obvious fracture line at the top (fig. 12-42). The avalanche is a large area of snow that begins to move suddenly at the same time, sliding on a weak layer within the snowpack or on the ground. The snow in a slab

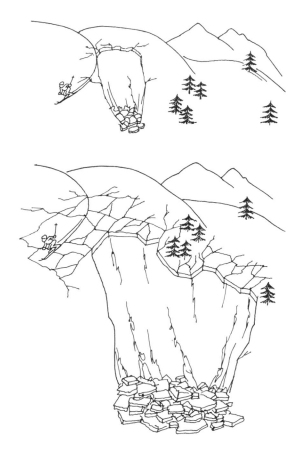

Fig. 12–42. Slab avalanche

avalanche can be from soft to hard, from wet to dry.

A loose-snow avalanche, on the other hand, starts at one point and grows in size as it slips

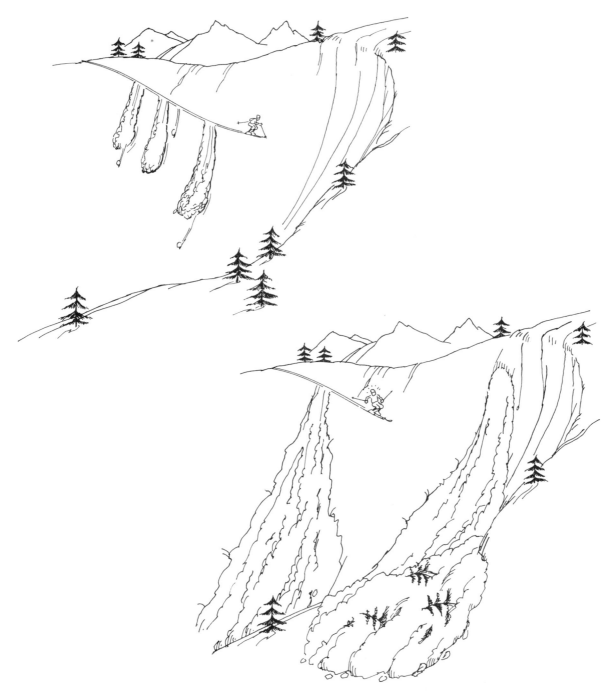

Fig. 12–43. Loose-snow avalanche

Hazard Evaluation Summary

Note: **Bold type** indicates the most critical factors in the evalution.

1. COULD THE SLOPE PRODUCE AVALANCHES?

   Is the slope steep enough to slide?

   ☐ **Slopes greater than 25°**

   ☐ Variations in incline — cliff bands

   What's the orientation of the slope to wind?

   ☐ **Lee slopes**

   What's the orientation of the slope to sun?

   ☐ **S and SW slopes exposed to strong radiation.**

   ☐ First major thaw of spring

   What's the nature of the slope?

   ☐ **Open slopes**

   ☐ Thin forest

   ☐ Confined slide path — gully or bowl

   ☐ Weak areas that might initiate failure

2. IS THE SNOW STABLE? COULD IT FAIL?

   How deep is the snowpack?

   Are there any signs of avalanche activity?

   What layers are there in the snowpack?

   ☐ **Very hard or soft layers**

   ☐ Weak bond between layers

   ☐ 30 cm or more of snow above a weak layer

   ☐ Loose, cold snow

   ☐ Wet snow

   How much snow has fallen?

   ☐ **Snowfall greater than 2 cm (3/4 in.) per hour**

   ☐ New snow depth greater than 30 cm (12 in.)

   ☐ Slow settlement of new snow

   ☐ Very light or very heavy snow

   ☐ Heavily rimed crystals, graupel

   ☐ Heavy stiff layer above a light weak layer

   ☐ Heavy rain

   ☐ Very easy or easy shovel test on new snow layer

   Wind

   ☐ **Moderate or strong wind**

   ☐ Cracking and settling of snow

   Air temperature

   ☐ **Rapid rise in temperature**

   ☐ Above freezing temperatures

   ☐ Sun on slope under consideration

   ☐ Sun with hazy sky

   ☐ Temperature inversions

   Humidity

   ☐ **High relative humidity during snowfall or during periods of moderate and strong wind.**

3. WHAT WILL HAPPEN TO ME IF THE SLOPE AVALANCHES?

   Depth of avalanche

   ☐ **Deep weak layers in snowpack**

   ☐ Foot penetration greater than 60 cm

   Type of avalanche

   ☐ **Stiff slab above weak layers**

   ☐ Slope has not yet avalanched recently

   Terrain

   ☐ **Long open slope above**

   ☐ Restricted deposition zone

   ☐ Drop-off below

   ☐ Trees to wrap around

4. WILL CONDITIONS GET WORSE?

   ☐ **Continuing snowfall**

   ☐ Increasing temperature

   ☐ Strong wind

Fig. 12–44. Hazard evaluation summary (reproduced by permission of the author from Avalanche Safety for Skiers & Climbers *by Tony Daffern, Rocky Mountain Books, 1983)*

downhill (fig. 12-43). The snow has little internal cohesion. There is no obvious fracture line and no clear layer where the sliding snow separates from snow beneath. A loose-snow avalanche can be wet and loose or soft and dry.

RECOGNIZING HAZARDOUS TERRAIN

It's easy to spot large slopes and wide swaths of avalanche activity. You'll get a lot of additional information on hazardous terrain by taking into account the time of year, previous weather, prevailing winds, snow characteristics, and the lay of the land (fig. 12-44). The classic law of avalanches says mountaineers face the least danger on ridges, more on the valley floor, and most on the slopes. Let's look first at the biggest danger zone.

The slopes

On slopes, danger comes in many shapes, angles, and sizes.

Slope angles between 30 and 45 degrees are the main originators of avalanches, although slides can start on inclines from 25 to 55 degrees (fig. 12-45). Angles above 55 degrees are generally too steep to collect a lot of snow, which tends to sluff off immediately after falling. Angles lower than 25 degrees are usually safe except for danger from

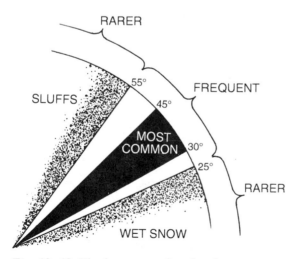

Fig. 12–45. The frequency of avalanches on slopes of various angles

very wet, and usually slow, avalanches. Climbers commonly overestimate the angle of a slope. Get a clinometer, built into a compass or as a separate instrument, if you want to end the guesswork.

Slope shapes also affect the hazard (fig. 12-46). Snow on a slope that is straight, open, and moderately steep presents the most obvious danger. Snow on a convex slope, under tension as it stretches tightly over the curve of the hill, is more prone to avalanche than snow on a concave slope. Coming down a convex slope, you may not know how steep it will get until you're past the curve obstructing your view and are down on the face. Regardless of the shape of the slope, look at them all, large and small, for avalanche hazard. They all can slide.

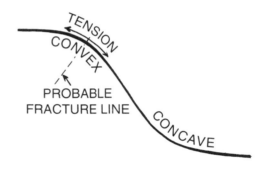

Fig. 12–46. Convex and concave slopes

Bowls and cirques have a shape that invites wind-deposited snow. Once an avalanche starts, it often spreads to an entire face and dumps a great depth of snow into the constricted area below.

Couloirs are enticing, because they offer a direct route up a mountainside, and intimidating, because they are natural avalanche chutes. Always weigh the merits of these gullies against the dangers, and trust them only at certain times under certain conditions. Take into acccount the snow conditions and the amount of snow both in the couloir and adjoining slopes. A slide on a slope within the drainage system of a couloir can sweep the main channel. This slide, by undercutting every tributary on its descent, may pick up bigger loads or leave the tributaries poised and ready to dump their loads at the slightest provocation. Beware of lower-angled couloirs and canyons that are obvious collection areas for avalanche debris.

Forested slopes offer some protection but don't put too much trust in trees. Slides aren't likely to originate in a dense forest, but they can smash through from above. Look around as you climb. Do you spot shattered trees in avalanche fans, and wide swaths cut through old timber? This is evidence of large avalanches penetrating even thick forest. Does a slope grow only brush and small trees, all downslanting? This is probably a slope that avalanches so often that timber has no chance to grow. Are tree limbs missing from the uphill side in open timber? It might be the result of avalanches. There's little or no avalanche protection in open timber, such as you can easily ski through. Another type of vegetation—grass—can increase avalanche danger by providing a slick surface for a slide.

Valleys and flat terrain

In a valley, the question to ask is whether an avalanche on the slopes above could reach you. The danger is obvious in a narrow-floored canyon, but large avalanches have swept for more than a mile across a valley, even climbing the opposite wall. As you trek through a valley, keep an eye out for damaged trees and other signs of avalanching. Remember to pitch tents outside the potential reach of an avalanche.

A route beneath a cliff is a gamble unless you're convinced that conditions are in your favor. Cliffs above flat terrain may harbor cornices, icicles, or ledges piled high with snow—temporarily. All this stuff is ready to drop, and if it doesn't get your party, it could start an avalanche that will.

Ridges

Safe at last! Well, perhaps not quite. A ridge, especially a forested ridge, is usually the safest route when the avalanche hazard is high. However, a ridge presents its own problems of cornices and of crests that can be too jagged to serve as a practical route.

The elements

Climbers pay attention to how sun and wind hit a slope for invaluable clues to avalanche danger.

The sun

The direction a slope faces determines how much sun it gets—and this tells a great deal about its avalanche potential. Here's how it works in the Northern Hemisphere, and of course it's just the opposite on mountains south of the equator.

South-facing slopes receive more sun, and therefore snow settles and stabilizes faster than on northern slopes. In general (with plenty of local exceptions), this makes south-facing slopes safer in winter. They also release avalanches sooner after a storm, so if they are avalanching it's an indication that slopes facing in other directions may soon follow their lead. As warmer spring and summer days arrive, south slopes become prone to wet-snow avalanches and north-facing slopes may be safer.

North-facing slopes receive little or no sun in the winter, so consolidation of the snowpack takes longer. Colder temperatures cause depth hoar within the snowpack, creating weak layers. Therefore, in general (again with local exceptions), north slopes are more likely to slide in midwinter. In spring and summer, as south slopes become dangerously soft, look to the north side for firmer, safer snow.

The wind

Windward slopes—those that face into the wind—tend to be safer. They retain less snow because the wind blows some of it away, and what snow remains is compacted by the blast of the wind.

Lee slopes—those that face the same way the wind is blowing—collect snow rapidly during storms and on windy days as snow blows over from the windward slopes. The result is cornices on the lee side of ridges, snow that is deeper and less consolidated, and formation of wind slabs ready to avalanche.

The snow is full of clues to the prevailing wind

direction. Cornices face the same way the wind is blowing. Deposits of rime, on the other hand, face into the wind: the larger the deposits, the stronger the wind. The steep faces of sastrugi and the rounded ends of snow drifts around trees and rocks also head into the wind (fig. 12-47).

Snow characteristics

Take a close at the nearby snow for more information on avalanche hazard. Are there new avalanches in the area? Do you see cracks close by, indicating you are on an unstable slab? Does an area of snow settle as you walk across it, again warning of a slab that could slide? Does the snow settle with a loud thump, indicating a hard slab ready to release?

The stability of the snow can be tested by probing with an ice axe or ski pole to feel for layers of varying solidity or by digging a pit to examine the layers for weakness. Specialized publications give details of these tests, which are mainly used during winter travel.

MINIMIZING THE RISK

Climbers have many ways to minimize the risk of avalanches and increase their chances of survival if one hits. These efforts begin before they leave home and continue throughout the climb. It's obvious advice, but check the weather report before starting the trip. Heed the detailed avalanche hazard reports prepared by agencies in many mountain areas. Talk to people with local knowledge.

Plan the route before getting under way, but be ready to adjust it depending on conditions. Lots of factors influence avalanche safety, and a problem with any one of them should be grounds to rethink your well-laid plans. During periods of general danger, are you willing to travel only in the morning and evening, when avalanche danger is lowest? Do you have a retreat route in mind? Are you prepared for an emergency bivouac? And don't let summit lust outweigh safety. The safest course might be to go home, or not to leave in the first place.

How to cross a questionable slope

Nobody likes it, but sometimes there's no way to avoid questionable avalanche terrain. The problem then is to make the passage with the least danger of disturbing the slope, and to minimize the consequences if the climbers set off an avalanche or one sweeps down from above.

Before heading out onto a questionable slope, check that your electronic avalanche rescue beacon is switched to the transmit position. Everyone in

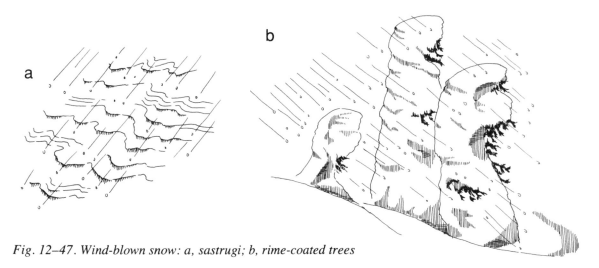

Fig. 12–47. Wind-blown snow: a, sastrugi; b, rime-coated trees

the party should carry one of the small battery-powered devices. If one climber is carried away by an avalanche, the others switch their devices to receive and then use the signal from the buried beacon to find the victim.

After you've checked your avalanche beacon, put on mittens and warm clothing. Get set to jettison your gear so it can't drag you down in the event of an avalanche. Loosen the shoulder straps and undo the waist and chest bands on your pack.

When the route lies up a slope, head straight up the fall line instead of switchbacking, which undercuts the snow. Only one person moves at a time, and everyone else watches from safe places, ready to shout if a slide starts. If the climber is on belay, don't tie the rope directly to the belayer, who would risk being pulled in if it proved impossible to stop a climber hit by a wet, heavy avalanche.

On a traverse, it's usually best to take it as high up the slope as possible, above most of the dangerous snow. Again, only one person moves at a time. Cross gingerly, with long, smooth strides, being careful not to cut a trench across the slope. Each climber follows in turn, stepping in the leader's footprints. Everyone listens and watches for an avalanche.

How to survive an avalanche

If you're caught, don't give up. Yell to your partners. Throw off equipment, pack, skis, anything and everything you can get rid of. At the start, grab a rock or tree, or stab your axe or ski pole into the underlying snow, and hold on. Try to stop before you're swept away. If that doesn't work, swim. Stay on the surface by using swimming motions, flailing arms and legs, or by rolling.

Close your mouth if your head goes below the surface. As the snow slows, try to stand up if your feet are below you. If you are buried, try to make a breathing space by putting your elbow or hand in front of your face. Inhale deeply before the snow stops, in order to expand your ribs. As the snow closes around you, it will become impossible to move. Don't shout or struggle. Conserve oxygen and energy. Your partners know what to do, and they have begun rescue efforts.

RESCUE

The rescue effort starts even before the avalanche has stopped. The first step in a successful rescue is a tough one in the shock of the moment: someone must pay attention to where a victim is first caught, where the person disappears beneath the snow, and where the point of disappearance on the moving surface of the avalanche finally stops—and be able to relate these three points to fixed objects, such as trees or rocks. With this information, the search area is immediately reduced in size.

Then mark these three points and search. Do NOT go for help. This is a critical principle of avalanche rescue. Do not go for help. The chance of a person surviving depends almost certainly on everyone staying put, searching efficiently, and digging the victim from the snow. You can go for help after the victim is unburied or all search efforts turn out to be futile.

Select a search leader so the operation will be thorough and methodical. Approach the scene carefully, posting an avalanche lookout in case of another slide. Start with a quick scuff search of the snow surface, looking for someone partially buried, any castoff equipment, or any logical spot the victim might have come to a stop against a tree or rock. The missing climber could turn up in this quick and immediate search. If not, the next step is a thorough search with avalanche beacons, if the climbers are carrying them, or with snow probes if they are not.

Probing

A probe is anything you can use to poke into the snow in hopes of feeling the victim's body, such as wands, ski poles, ice axes, or commercial snow probe poles. Probing is a slow and uncertain mechanical process, but it's all there is in lieu of avalanche beacons. Probe first at likely areas—near pieces of the victim's equipment, at the marked points of disappearance, and around trees and rocks. Then set up a probe line.

The probe line must be highly organized and methodical. Searchers stand elbow to elbow in a line and insert their probes once between their feet. They take one step forward, uphill along the most likely search route, and probe again. Another step, another probe, each movement in unison at the spoken command of the leader. If a searcher hits something, they dig in that spot. After one run up the slope, the probe line moves to one side of the original course and probes some more, again starting at the bottom and probing uphill.

Searching with avalanche rescue beacons

The small electronic device known as an avalanche rescue beacon is the principal tool for finding buried victims.

A rescue beacon can be switched to either transmit or receive signals at a set radio frequency. Rescue depends on each member of a climbing party carrying a beacon, which during the climb is left switched on to the transmit mode. Searchers switch their beacons to the receive mode to zero in on the automatic transmission from a victim. A rescuer who has taken the time to practice with the battery-powered beacon, also called an avalanche transceiver, should locate a victim in short order.

Climbers will encounter beacons that use a frequency of 2275 hertz (most common in North America) or 457 kilohertz. The United States is switching to the world-standard 457 kilohertz frequency, with the change to be completed at the end of 1995. In the meantime, to avoid incompatibility, the American Association of Avalanche Professionals recommends the use of only 2275 hertz or dual frequency beacons through the end of 1995, and 457 kilohertz or dual frequency beacons only after 1995. Some models transmit both frequencies at the same time.

The main thing is that all the beacons in a climbing party transmit and receive a frequency in common. The workings are packaged in a crush-proof case inside a pouch that a climber typically straps around the neck and carries under the shirt. The device comes out for rescue work, and the searcher listens for transmissions through a tiny earphone carried with the beacon.

Initial beacon search

If the original quick scuff search for an avalanche victim turns up nothing, start an organized beacon search. The leader checks every beacon to be sure they are switched from transmit to receive. A line of searchers spaced no more than 60 feet apart across the slope starts where the victim was last seen and works its way downhill.

Put the volume control all the way up on every beacon. Move in unison, stay in a straight line, and keep talk to a minimum. Searchers stop every 10 paces and slowly rotate their beacons left and right, then front and back, listening closely for a signal. When a signal is picked up, one or two persons start to track down the sound with a final beacon search. (If there is more than one victim, the rest of the line continues its work. As each victim is found, turn off his or her beacon so searchers won't continue to pick up those signals.)

Final beacon search

Using a single rescue beacon, the final searchers follow a very critical series of steps to zero in on the signal from the buried victim (fig. 12-48). This is what they do:

First of all, orient the beacon for maximum signal strength, moving the unit back and forth, front and back, to find the best position. Then reduce volume as low as possible while still hearing the signal. Keep the beacon in the same orientation as you walk in any straight line. As soon as the signal reaches a peak and begins to drop, again reorient the beacon for maximum signal, and then reduce the volume as low as possible. Holding this orientation, continue on the same path. When the signal fades out, mark the spot.

Without changing orientation of the beacon, turn yourself around and retrace the same pathway. When the signal fades out again, mark that spot. You now have a straight line bracketed at the end by points where the signal disappears. Run to the center of this bracketed line and make a 90-degree turn. Repeat the process. Reorient the beacon for maximum signal, reduce volume to the minimum, and walk in a straight line until the signal fades out. Mark the spot, turn around without disturbing

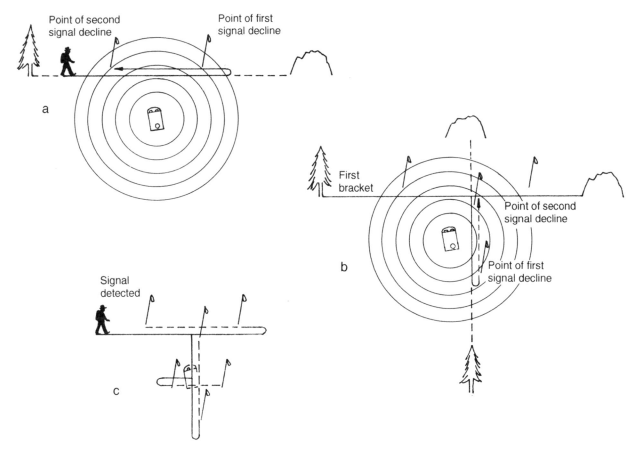

Fig. 12–48. Beacon search bracketing: a, first bracket; b, second bracket; c, summary of beacon search bracketing. (Illustrations by Ray Smutek, reprinted by permission, from "Avalanche Beacons." Summit [March–April] 1984.)

orientation of the beacon, and retrace your steps until the signal again disappears. You now have another straight line bracketed by two fade-out points. Run to the center of this new line and again make a 90-degree turn.

Work fast and efficiently, without worrying too much about precision. Continue this process of making bracketed lines until the distance between fade-out points on a line is less than 6 feet. You are now very close to the victim.

Finally, on hands and knees pinpoint your missing partner by moving the beacon from side to side and front to back in a small criss-cross. A loud signal when the volume control is down means you are close. Then dig. Use the beacon to recheck the victim's location with each 2 feet that you dig down. You have successfully found your stricken partner as quickly as possible.

· 13 ·

GLACIER TRAVEL AND CREVASSE RESCUE

Traveling on a glacier is just like crossing any other field of snow, except for the crevasses. They say there's nothing worse than fear of the unknown, and perhaps that's what makes crevasses special. Many of them are hidden, they are deep and cold and scary, and they will kill you if you don't know what you're doing. The purpose of this chapter is to show you how to spot crevasses and stay clear of them, and how to get out if you fall in.

HOW CREVASSES FORM

Think of a glacier as a frozen river flowing slowly down the mountain (figs. 13-1 and 13-2). When the slope steepens, the glacier flows faster.

Just as rivers form rapids, glaciers form crescentic crevasses when ice on steeper pitches flows faster and breaks away from slower moving ice above.

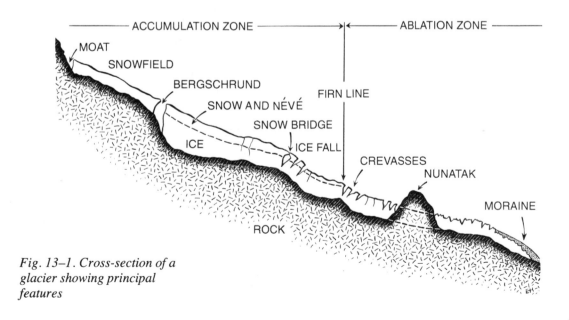

ACCUMULATION ZONE   ABLATION ZONE

MOAT
SNOWFIELD
BERGSCHRUND
FIRN LINE
SNOW AND NÉVÉ
SNOW BRIDGE
ICE
ICE FALL
CREVASSES
NUNATAK
MORAINE
ROCK

Fig. 13–1. Cross-section of a glacier showing principal features

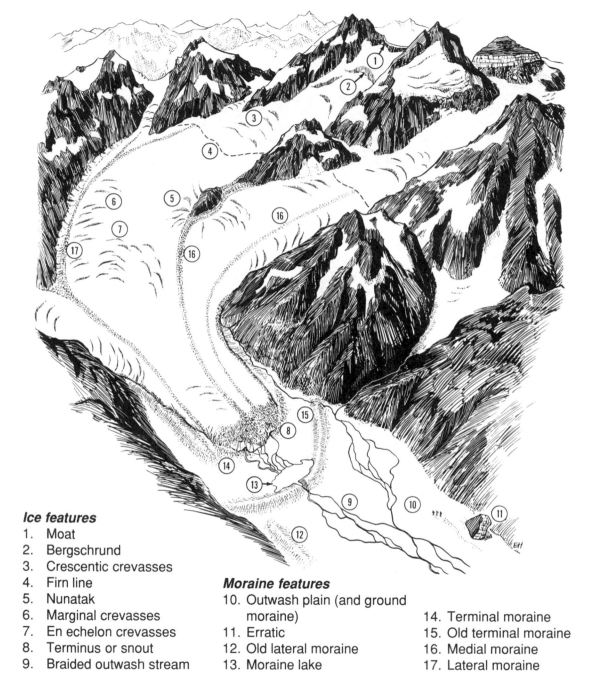

Ice features

1. Moat
2. Bergschrund
3. Crescentic crevasses
4. Firn line
5. Nunatak
6. Marginal crevasses
7. En echelon crevasses
8. Terminus or snout
9. Braided outwash stream

Moraine features

10. Outwash plain (and ground moraine)
11. Erratic
12. Old lateral moraine
13. Moraine lake
14. Terminal moraine
15. Old terminal moraine
16. Medial moraine
17. Lateral moraine

Fig. 13–2. Aerial view of a glacier showing principal features

EQUIPMENT FOR GLACIER TRAVEL ◆ 317

The crevasses form at a right angle to the direction of flow.

In a river, a steep drop brings a waterfall; the glacial counterpart is an icefall. Crevasses shoot out in all directions from the base of an icefall, and large ice towers (seracs) hang above. Gradually, gravity combined with the forward movement of the glacier will bring these seracs crashing down.

Below steep sections, the glacier slows again, and there may be no crevasses at this point. But if the decrease in slope is too sudden, the glacier may buckle, creating broken, uplifted waves (pressure ridges) as fast-moving ice rams slower ice.

The glacier moves faster in the center than along the sides, where friction along the walls of its route slows it down. This difference in speed often creates lateral (marginal) crevasses, which trend up-valley, near the sides of the glacier. Both lateral and crescentic crevasses tend to angle upstream toward the glacier center, a good clue in guessing the hidden extension of a crevasse from a single hole on the surface. (Any series of crevasses that are parallel to each other are known as *en echelon* crevasses.)

Unfortunately, minor irregularities underneath a glacier can produce random fractures with no pattern. For example, protuberances of rock under the ice, called nunataks, usually form a halo of crevasses. If the rock doesn't actually reach the surface so you can see it, you may be at a loss to explain the odd crevassing. Because of bottom irregularities like this, the only absolute rule about crevasses is that they can form just about anywhere, anytime.

Crevasses are most dangerous in the accumulation zone, that portion of a glacier high enough to receive more snow every year than it loses to melting. Here, crevasses are frequently covered with snow, either filling the hole or forming bridges over the void. Some of the bridges are too weak to support a climber. Others are strong enough for the moment, but will weaken as the bridge melts or the crevasse widens.

Below the accumulation zone is the area of the glacier called the ablation zone, where annual melting matches or exceeds the yearly snowfall. Between the two zones is the firn line (also known as the névé line), named for the words that designate old snow.

Often a giant crevasse known as a bergschrund forms at the glacier's upper limit, where it pulls away from a stationary ice cap. Sometimes a bergschrund presents the final problem in a climb, with the summit a short stroll beyond. Other times, a snowfield above a bergschrund is separated from a higher rock face by a moat, formed by melting and the downhill creep of the snow. A moat can be every bit as hard to cross as a bergschrund.

EQUIPMENT FOR GLACIER TRAVEL

Take a look at your gear with glaciers and crevasses in mind. Here are some considerations in getting ready for glacier travel.

THE ROPE

The rope you need depends on the glacier. If steep technical climbing is expected, with the possibility of severe leader falls, use a standard 10- to 11-millimeter climbing rope or two 9-millimeter ropes. But for "easy" glaciers, a single 9-millimeter rope will handle crevasse falls. For the snow, use one of the "dry" ropes treated by the manufacturer to reduce moisture absorption. This keeps the rope lighter, drier, stronger, and easier to handle.

Some parties carry an additional 100-foot rope, 8 or 9 millimeters in diameter, as an emergency rescue line.

HARNESS

For glacier travel, tie your climbing rope into a seat harness combined with a separate chest harness, or into a full body harness. You don't want to simply tie into a rope around your waist because it would dangerously constrict breathing if you fell into a crevasse and dangled from the rope. The chest harness keeps you from being flipped backward by the weight of your pack during a fall. (Chapter 6 gives details on this equipment.)

ICE AXE AND CRAMPONS

An ice axe and crampons are as important for safe glacier travel as a rope and harness. Crampons help you keep your footing if the snow is icy or the glacier slope gets steep. The ice axe does its usual job of aiding with balance and providing a tool for self-belay and self-arrest. It's also what you use to stop a ropemate's tumble into a crevasse, by falling into self-arrest position with the axe.

In order to keep the axe with you in case *you're* the one who falls in, attach a leash of accessory cord or webbing through the hole in the head of the axe. You can attach the other end of the leash around your wrist with a snug loop or to your waist harness with a locking carabiner. A short wrist leash can be somewhat inconvenient because you need to shift it from one wrist to the other when you change hands on the axe, while a long leash attached to one wrist or to your harness lets you switch hands freely. With the leash clipped to your harness, the axe can provide a quick personal anchor. (Chapter 12 includes a more complete discussion of ice-axe leashes.)

PRUSIK SLINGS AND ASCENDERS

Among the most important gear to help a climber out of a crevasse are slings, tied with prusik knots or other friction knots, and mechanical ascenders.

A prusik sling can be as simple as a mere loop of 5- to 7-millimeter accessory cord. One of these slings tied to a climbing rope with a prusik knot will slide up or down the rope when loosened but grip the rope firmly when tightened. The Bachmann knot does the same thing, but is tied around both a carabiner and the climbing rope. The Klemheist knot works best if the sling is made of webbing instead of cord. (Check back to Chapter 6 for refreshers on any of these knots.)

The simplest prusik slings are used as the link between a snow anchor and the rope that holds a fallen climber. More complicated prusik slings, with foot and safety loops, will be described later in this chapter in the section on crevasse self-rescue.

Mechanical ascenders (such as Jumars and Clogs) attached to slings can be used to replace friction knots such as the prusik for self-rescue and for anchoring an accident rope. Ascenders attach to the rope more easily than the knots. They work better on icy ropes and they can be operated more readily with gloved hands.

On the debit side, ascenders are heavy and expensive. As mechanical devices, they are more prone to failure than knots are and have popped off the rope under unusual circumstances.

On an expedition that fixes some of its ropes in place, most climbers will carry one or two ascenders for self-belay on the fixed lines. These climbers usually use the ascenders for glacier travel as well.

Other rescue gear: At a *minimum,* every glacier climber should carry a single-length runner and a double-length runner of 1-inch tubular webbing to attach to buried anchors; enough carabiners for rappelling (or two carabiners plus a belay device); and one rescue pulley (a carabiner will work in a pinch, but it adds considerable friction). Each rope team should carry at least one snow picket or ice screw (depending on snow conditions) for setting up a solid anchor. Anchors that use two placements are preferred for security, so a rope team may want to pack more anchoring hardware along, or they may have to borrow some from another team in an emergency.

CLOTHING

Dress for the crevasse, not for the glacier. It's frigid in the crevasses even when it's sunny and windless topside, and you want to be ready in case of a fall.

Even on a hot day, wear long trousers and a long-sleeve shirt (they can be wool or synthetic). Try to wear garments that can be ventilated, such as pants with side zippers or a parka with underarm zippers. You can zip these closed if you end up in a crevasse.

As further insurance against hypothermia, keep a jacket on the outside of your pack, where you can reach it easily. Stash a cap and gloves in your pockets. And wear light-colored garments that reflect the heat of the sun while you are on the glacier but will still provide insulation inside a crevasse.

SKIS AND SNOWSHOES

Skis or snowshoes are usually essential for winter or arctic mountaineering because they keep you from sinking too deeply into the snow by distributing your weight over a larger area. This same feature makes them helpful on some glacier climbs by reducing your danger of breaking through the snow bridging a hidden crevasse.

WANDS

Bamboo wands are valuable aids in marking the location of crevasses, identifying turns, and showing the climbing route for the return. Even on climbs where you intend to descend a different route, consider marking the ascent with these flag-topped sticks in case you're forced to retreat.

(Chapter 12 explains how to make your own wands.)

If the visibility is poor, the safest spacing for the wands is a distance equal to the total length of your party (when roped and moving in single file). On the way down, the party can "feel" its way if necessary. The last person in the line stops at each wand and doesn't continue until it is confirmed that the next wand has been found. If visibility is fairly good, space the wands farther apart.

A few other tips on wands: if you tilt each wand as you place it so that it points toward the one below, the search will be narrowed on the way down. Remember that you'll be looking from above for the wands on the return trip, so avoid placing them in hollows or on the down side of ridges where they'll be hard to see. Mark critical spots with some kind of code, such as two wands pointing in the new direction for a turn, or two wands crossing each other for a snow bridge or hidden crevasse.

FUNDAMENTALS OF GLACIER TRAVEL

On a cold, clear morning in late spring, 2 hours before dawn, the glacier is a place of peace and beauty. Above this great silent sweep of ice and snow, the mountain stands silhouetted against a star-filled sky. Climbers fiddling with their headlamps or adjusting their gaiters or squirming into their seat harnesses are too busy and too sleepy to think much about the adventure that lies ahead. But from training and experience, they know just what to do to get ready for a long day on a big glacier. It's one of those days when all the training and preparation for staying out of trouble around crevasses will pay off.

USING THE ROPE

The first rule of glacier travel is very simple: rope up. This holds whether or not you're familiar with the glacier and whether or not you can see any crevasses.

It's tempting to walk unroped onto a glacier that looks like a benign snowfield, especially if you've gone up similar routes time after time without mishap. Avoid the temptation. The extra time and trouble of dealing with the rope, like wearing a seat belt in a car, greatly increases your chances of surviving the most likely accident on a glacier, falling into a crevasse.

Rope teams

Rope teams of three climbers each are a good size for moderate glaciers because they provide two people, not just one, to arrest a ropemate's fall into a crevasse. Glacier rope teams usually keep 40 or 50 feet between climbers, putting three people on a 120-foot rope and three or four on a 150-foot or 165-foot rope. Putting the climbers much closer together increases the danger that more than one will be dragged into a crevasse before a fall can be arrested.

On severely crevassed or very steep glaciers where frequent belaying is required, rope teams of only two climbers (as in rock climbing) are the most practical.

A minimum of two rope teams is recommended for glacier travel so that a rope team involved in an accident will have backup help. While the team with the fallen climber concentrates on holding the rope fast, the second team can set up a snow anchor and then help with the rescue, including providing a second rope.

Tying in

Every climber ties into a seat harness. For glacier travel, each person also needs to wear a chest harness. (Review the details in Chapter 6 about making and tying in to chest harnesses). Here are some general glacier tie-in procedures, depending on the size of the rope team:

Three-person rope: This is the standard size for a rope team on a moderate glacier. The middle climber ties into the very center of the rope, most commonly with a double bowline through the tie-in loops of the seat harness. The small loop that remains at the end of the double bowline should be clipped with a locking carabiner to the harness to ensure the knot can't come loose. The two other climbers tie in at the very ends of the rope, usually with a rewoven figure-8.

Four-person rope: Divide the rope into thirds. Two climbers tie in at the ends, the other two tie in at the one-third points.

Two-person rope: Although a three-person rope is preferred for moderate glacier travel, ropes will sometimes have only two climbers. The most convenient procedure is to use only a part of the rope so you don't have to drag the whole thing through the snow. Each climber ties in anywhere from 25 to 50 feet from an end of the rope; then each carries a loose end on top of the pack or around the shoulders. This keeps the loose rope out of your way while you climb, but ready for use in a crevasse rescue.

Rope management

Keep the rope extended, without slack. This is the most important rule of rope management on a glacier. A rope that is fully extended between climbers is your insurance against taking a long plunge into a crevasse. A slack rope means you drop farther, increasing chances of hitting the sides or bottom or becoming wedged where the crevasse narrows. For the climbers on top, it can mean a much greater hit on the rope from the fallen climber and the danger of being pulled into the hole.

To help keep slack out of the rope, a rope leader needs to set a pace the others can follow for a long time. For their part, the second and third climbers must try to closely match the pace of the leader so the rope stays extended—but not taut. A taut rope is annoying because it pulls back on the climber ahead. You'll need to pay extra attention at turns, where the rope will start to go slack as the climber in front of you heads in a new direction, then tightens as you near the turn yourself. Throughout the turn, adjust speed as necessary, and avoid following the leader's footsteps; select an independent route that will keep the rope taut.

Don't forget safety when you reach a rest stop or campsite. The rope must stay extended and slack-free until the area has been thoroughly probed for crevasses. At a campsite, mark boundaries of the safe area with wands. Always belay climbers into and out of all rest and camp areas.

Another rope-management technique is to keep the rope running at right angles to crevasses. This makes it less likely that two climbers on the same rope will be walking dangerously near the edge of a particular crevasse at the same time. A rope team traveling in single file parallel to a crevasse runs the risk of one climber taking a long fall or of more than one climber tumbling in. Therefore, the second and third climbers on a rope should again avoid the footsteps of a leader who is walking parallel to a crevasse (perhaps looking for a snow bridge or for the end of the cavity). Instead, the followers should stay downhill of the leader and walk on their own separate courses, trying to keep the rope at a right angle to the crevasse.

The same technique is a good safety idea for traveling sideways across a glacier even if no crevasse is in sight. A sideways (traversing) route puts climbers parallel with the most likely direction of any hidden crevasse. Once again, the second and third climbers can blaze their own trail, staying downhill of the leader so the rope is at right angles to the most likely danger.

DETECTING CREVASSES

The first step in staying out of crevasses is to know where they are. Sometimes you can even get a head start before the trip by studying photos of the glacier, because crevasse patterns remain fairly constant from year to year.

On the approach hike, try for a good up-valley or cross-valley look at the glacier before reaching it. You may see an obvious route that would be impossible to discover once you're there. Consider making notes or sketches to help in remembering major crevasses, landmarks, and routes.

These distant views are useful, but prepare to be surprised. What appeared to be small cracks may be gaping chasms, and major crevasses may have been hidden from the angle of your view. Plan alternative routes if you can.

Once you're on the glacier, it's a continuous game of Find the Crevasse. Just because you can't see them doesn't mean they aren't there. Here are some important tips for detecting crevasses:

• Keep an eye out for sagging trenches in the snow that mark where gravity has pulled down on snow that covers a crevasse. The sags will be visible by their slight difference in sheen, texture, or color.
• Take advantage of the low-angle light of early morning and late afternoon to spot the characteristic shadows of sagging snow trenches. They may be impossible to detect in the flat light of a fog and difficult to see in the midafternoon sun.
• Be wary after storms in fall or late spring, when new snow can mask the thin sagging roof of a crevasse.
• Be especially alert in areas where you know crevasses form, such as around nunataks, at the sides of the glacier, and where slopes steepen.
• Check regularly to the sides of your route to determine whether open cracks to your left or right could possibly extend, beneath the snow, under your path.
• Remember that where there is one crevasse there are often many.

Snow probing is the technique to use if you have found a suspicious-looking area and want to search it for crevasses. If your probe locates a crevasse, continue probing to find its true lip.

Probe with your ice axe, thrusting the shaft into the snow a couple of feet ahead of the snow you are standing on. Keep the axe perpendicular to the slope and thrust it in with a smooth motion. You need an axe with a uniform taper from the spike to the shaft, because a blunt spike or jutting ferrule makes it hard to feel the snow.

If resistance to the thrust is uniform, you have established that the snow is consistent to at least the depth of your axe. If resistance lessens abruptly, you've probably found a hole. If your route must continue in the direction of this hole, use further axe thrusts to establish its extent. The leader should open up the hole and mark it with wands.

The value of probing depends on your skill and experience at interpreting the changes felt in the snow layers. An inexperienced prober may think the shaft broke through into a hole when all it really did was hit a softer layer of snow.

The length of the ice axe becomes a limiting factor in probing. The lead climber can also carry an avalanche probe ski pole, which is lighter, longer, and thinner than the axe for easier, deeper probes.

CROSSING CREVASSES

Climbers have a number of ways to get past a crevasse that lies across their route.

The end run

When a crevasse pinches to a close at one end, the safest and most dependable technique is the end run (fig. 13-3). A quarter-mile walk may gain you only 20 or 30 feet of forward progress, but it often beats a direct confrontation with the crevasse.

In late summer when the winter snow has melted down to the ice, you may be able to see the true end of the crevasse. But if fresh snow still blankets the glacier, the visible end of the crack is usually not its true end. Make a wide swing around the corner and probe carefully.

Snow bridges

If an end run is impractical, look for a bridge (fig. 13-4). Remnant snowcover sagging over the void forms one type of bridge. Other, sturdier bridges are really thin isthmuses between two crevasses, with foundations that extend deep into the body of the glacier.

Study a bridge carefully—try for a side view— before putting any faith in it. If you're in doubt, belay the leader in for probing and a close-up look. After the leader gets across, you can follow exactly in the original tracks, belayed from both sides of

Fig. 13–3. End run around a crevasse, keeping the rope taut by not following in the leader's footsteps

Fig. 13–4. Crossing a bridged crevasse under belay

the crevasse if you're the middle person on a three-person rope. Then belay the third climber across.

The strength of a snow bridge varies tremendously with temperature. An arch that might support a truck in the cold of winter or early morning may collapse under its own weight during an afternoon thaw. Cross every bridge with caution every time. Don't assume that because it held in the morning during the ascent that it's safe as you head down in the afternoon.

Jumping

Jumping is the final common tactic for crossing a crevasse (fig. 13-5). Most jumps across crevasses are short, simple leaps. If you're planning a desperate lunge, be sure you've ruled out all the alternatives and see that you are well belayed.

Before any significant jump, remove your pack. While belayed, probe to find the true edge of the crevasse. If you need a running start, tramp down the snow for better footing. As final preparation, put on parka, mittens, and hat, check prusiks and harness, and spool out the amount of rope slack needed from the belayer. Then jump—with your ice axe in the self-arrest position, ready to help you claw over the edge if you're shy of a clean landing.

With the rope now linked to the landing side, the other climbers have a less dangerous job ahead. The belay rope can help pull up on any jumper who falls just short of the target.

Use caution and common sense if the leap is from the high lip of a crevasse over to a lower side.

Fig. 13–5. Jumping a crevasse (belay not shown)

(Bergschrunds, for example, often have a high overhanging wall on the uphill side.) You can be injured in a long, hard leap. If you go for it, keep your feet slightly apart for balance, knees bent to absorb shock, and ice axe held ready for a quick self-arrest.

CREVASSE RESCUE

The depths of a great crevasse exhibit an awful beauty, both enticing and repellent. On a fine day, the walls are a sheen of soft blue ice in the filtered light from high above, and the cavern is cool and still as a church, or a tomb. It's a place every climber should visit once in a lifetime—for crevasse rescue practice. But if there's a second time, we hope it will be in the company of climbers who know the rescue techniques spelled out in the rest of this chapter.

RESCUE RESPONSE

You're the middle person on a three-person rope team traveling up a moderately angled glacier. The climber walking 50 feet in front of you suddenly disappears beneath the snow. What do you do?

Do not stop and think. Your immediate reflex must be to drop into self-arrest in the snow (facing away from the direction of pull) and hold the fall.

The climber at the end of the rope will be doing the same thing. (Chapter 12 details all the steps in self-arrest with the ice axe.)

After that, you and your ropemate topside, along with any other climbers in the neighborhood, get started on the rescue operation, working together with your fallen friend. The principal steps you will take (fig. 13-6), starting right from the instant of the fall, are:

1. Arrest the fall.
2. Set up an anchor.
3. Attach the rope to the anchor.
4. Check the fallen climber.
5. Devise a rescue plan.

Set up an anchor

Once the fall is stopped (fig. 13-6a), the middle climber on the three-person rope stays in self-arrest to support the weight of the fallen climber. The end climber slowly gets out of self-arrest, making sure the middle climber can hold the weight alone, then sets to work establishing an anchor (fig. 13-6b). However, if another rope team is on hand, both climbers can stay in self-arrest while the other team sets up the anchor.

The anchor goes between the middle climber and the lip of the crevasse. (If it's placed instead on the other side of the climber, eventual tension on the rope could make it impossible for that person to untie.) It takes a bombproof anchor because at least one life will be riding on it. Whoever establishes the anchor must work quickly, but without taking shortcuts.

Solid anchors can be made from the following types of protection: pickets pounded into firm snow; ice screws placed in ice; or snow flukes, ice axes, or skis buried as deadmen in soft snow. Ideally, put in two independent anchor placements (or more), with slings to equalize the load. A solitary ice axe driven vertically into the snow is not a good candidate as an anchor to carry the loads of a rescue.

Attach the rope to the anchor

The climber who set up the anchor now attaches a short sling to the climbing rope with a prusik knot, Bachmann knot, or mechanical ascender, and clips the sling to the anchor (fig. 13-6b). The knot or ascender is then slid down the rope, toward the crevasse, until the sling is tight. Now anyone who is still in self-arrest can ease the load off the ice axe and onto the anchor. Do it slowly to confirm that the anchor is solid and that the ascender or friction knot is gripping the climbing rope tightly. (Keep in mind that if you choose to use a prusik knot, one rescuer will have to tend the knot later to keep it open any time the fallen climber is being pulled up. The Bachmann knot and ascenders, on the other hand, usually require less tending.)

Check the fallen climber

Belay one rescuer to the edge of the crevasse to check out the climber's situation closely (fig. 13-6c). The rescuer can be belayed from the anchor by a teammate. Or the rescuer can operate with a self-belay—attaching a prusik loop to the rope that runs from the anchor to the fallen climber, then sliding this prusik along the rope as the rescuer moves toward the crevasse edge. On the way, the rescuer can probe the area and check for any other hazards that might endanger the rescue.

The rescuer will try to talk with the fallen climber. If there is no response, one person can rappel or be lowered on belay into the crevasse to help the fallen climber. But if there is a response, the rescuer can ask if the climber needs clothing, is injured, is able to get into prusik slings, and so forth. The person who fell in should be able to say whether self-rescue is a good possibility—by ice-climbing out or prusiking out—or whether a hoist from above will be needed.

Devise a rescue plan

With all the groundwork out of the way, it's time to get the climber out of the crevasse. There are a lot of methods to choose from, as you will see later in this chapter. Just use the one that looks the best for this particular case, depending on the condition of the climber, the number of rescuers, the equipment available, and any other variables.

Fig. 13–6. Rescue response: a, arresting the fall;
b, setting up the anchor and attaching the rope to
the anchor; c, checking on the fallen climber
(anchor of the climber giving a boot-axe belay not
shown for clarity).

Look for the best method that combines simplicity, speed, and safety.

First of all, a climber who falls into a crevasse doesn't necessarily have to come back up at the same spot. Sometimes there's another way out. Check the possibility of lowering or swinging the fallen climber to a ledge. It might be a good spot to rest and perhaps a gateway to a different part of the crevasse where rescue will be easier. Consider whether the bottom of the crevasse looks solid. This could offer another resting spot and a possible path to a climbing route or a snow ramp to the surface.

Whatever the rescue method, be sure the rope is padded to keep it from digging into the lip of the crevasse. A buried rope will sabotage either the rescuers' efforts to hoist the climber up over the lip or the climber's own attempts to prusik out. For padding, slide an ice-axe shaft, a ski, an ensolite pad, or even a pack under the rescue rope at the edge of the crevasse. (Anchor the padding so it can't fall into the crevasse.)

Throughout the rescue, everyone on top must be tied to the anchor or clipped into a prusik sling tied to an anchored rope or on belay at all times. If your party is large enough, assign one climber to brace and guard the anchor. Establish additional anchors if necessary.

Always remember who you're trying to help. Avoid knocking snow or ice down on the person in the crevasse. Keep talking to the fallen climber. Give reassurance and information about what's going on and enlist ideas for making the rescue go more smoothly.

INSIDE THE CREVASSE

While rescuers are busy topside, the person down below has work to do. Here's how you can prepare for rescue if you are the fallen climber:

Set up your prusik slings on the climbing rope so you can alternate between standing and sitting as you dangle. You will be a lot more comfortable, and will be ready to climb up the rope using the slings if that seems the best way out. (The next section in this chapter outlines self-rescue using prusik slings.)

Clip the climbing rope through a carabiner at your chest harness, if you didn't do so earlier. It will help you maintain an upright position.

Get your pack and ice axe out of the way. You may be able to send them up on a rope from the rescuers. You can also clip the axe to your seat harness, letting it hang so it doesn't interfere with your movement. For the pack, you have the option of attaching a sling to its haul loop and clipping the sling onto the climbing rope with a carabiner, just above your seat harness (but below the prusik attachments). Then the pack will just hang below you. Later, if you climb up the rope using a friction knot or ascenders, the hanging pack will slide freely along the bottom of the loop of climbing rope and weight the rope, making it easier to climb.

Keep warm. Close your parka, put on the hat and gloves you had stuffed in your pockets, and try to put on additional layers of clothing.

SELF-RESCUE

Self-rescue is often the easiest and fastest form of crevasse rescue. This is especially true for small parties that lack the muscle power to hoist you out or that may be pinned down holding the rope. It may be the only practical rescue method for a two-person party. Self-rescue has the added advantage of keeping the fallen climber active and warm.

In some cases, you may be able to climb the crevasse wall to safety, while on belay. Or you can climb back up the rope that held your fall. Two good self-rescue methods of ascending the rope are the stair-step prusik and the Texas prusik. They both use slings of accessory cord attached to the climbing rope with a prusik knot. However, they also work well if they are attached with the Bachmann knot, which incorporates a carabiner that makes a good handhold for loosening and sliding the slings. Mechanical ascenders also can be used instead of the friction knots.

If you ever use slings made of tubular webbing rather than accessory cord, the Klemheist knot is a better friction knot to use than the prusik or Bachmann.

Don't start up the rope until you get an OK from topside. Your movement could interfere with the work of rescuers who may be struggling to hold the fall and set up an anchor.

The stair-step prusik

This system of climbing the rope uses a separate sling for each leg. You can make a set of slings for yourself, and 25 feet (about 8 meters) of 6-millimeter accessory cord is plenty of material for both of them. Getting the size right requires some experimentation. When all the work is done, you should end up with two slings—one as long as the distance from your foot to your ears, the shorter one as long as from foot to elbow.

Each sling consists basically of a single strand of cord, tied with equal-sized loops (1 foot long or so) at each end. One will be the prusik loop, used in attaching the sling to the climbing rope with a prusik or Bachmann knot. The other is a foot loop, large enough to fit over any footwear, including crampons and overboots. Add a slip knot to this loop to prevent tightening down on the boot and cutting off circulation (fig. 13-7a-c).

You need to incorporate one little difference in the longer sling. Leave a 5-foot tail after you tie the loop that will be used for creating the prusik. Tie a small overhand loop at the end of this tail. When you use the slings, clip this small loop to your seat harness as a safety strap to catch you in case both feet slip out of the slings.

Before you head out onto a glacier, attach the prusik loops to the climbing rope so the slings are ready for immediate use in an emergency (fig. 13-7d,e). Attach them at a point beyond where the climbing rope leaves the carabiner at your chest harness, the longer sling attached beyond the shorter. (Pass the long sling through the chest carabiner as well.) Shove the other end of the long sling under the belt of your seat harness. Put the

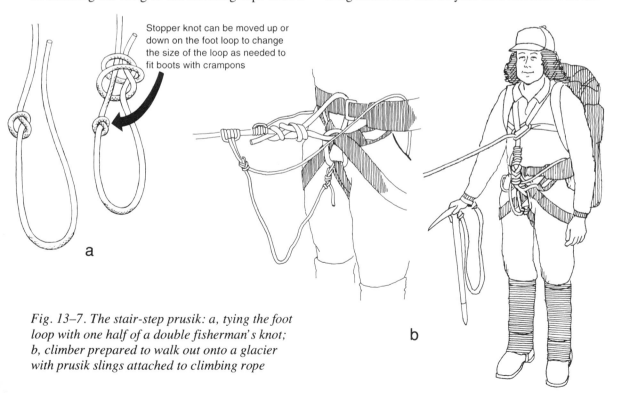

Stopper knot can be moved up or down on the foot loop to change the size of the loop as needed to fit boots with crampons

a

b

Fig. 13–7. The stair-step prusik: a, tying the foot loop with one half of a double fisherman's knot; b, climber prepared to walk out onto a glacier with prusik slings attached to climbing rope

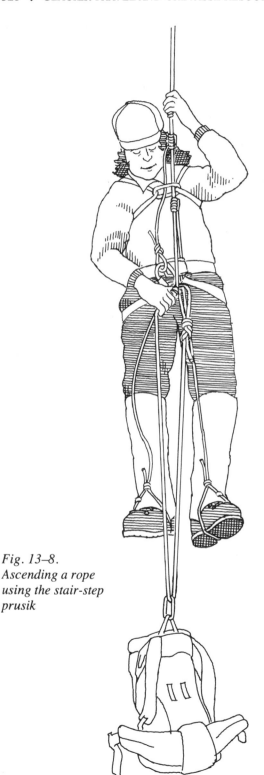

Fig. 13–8. Ascending a rope using the stair-step prusik

ends of both slings into your pockets, ready to be pulled out and slipped onto your feet when needed.

(If you are using mechanical ascenders instead of prusik loops to hold the sling to the rope, carry the ascenders on your seat harness and the slings in your pockets. After a crevasse fall, attach the ascenders to the rope.)

This is the sequence to follow if you need to climb the rope (fig. 13-8):

1. Take the foot loops from your pockets and slip them over your boots, cinching up on the slip knots.
2. Stand up in the short prusik sling, putting all your weight onto it.
3. Lift the leg attached to the long prusik sling, then loosen the knot attached to that sling and slide it up the rope some 18 inches.
4. Stand up in the long sling, shifting all your weight to it.
5. Lift the leg attached to the short sling, then loosen the knot attached to that sling and slide it about 18 inches up the rope.
6. Stand up again in the short sling.
7. Keep repeating the process and you'll walk up the rope, somewhat as if it were a flight of stairs.

The Texas prusik

This alternative method of ascending the rope also uses two slings, but this time only one goes to the feet while the other attaches directly to the seat harness (fig. 13-9). The foot sling has a separate loop for each foot (though an option is to provide just a single loop used by only one foot.)

As with the stair-step method, attach the slings to the climbing rope before you start walking on the glacier. The seat sling should extend to head level when you slide the prusik knot upward. The prusik for the foot loops should be tied below the seat prusik, with the knot at waist level when you are standing on the sling. (Attach a safety loop from the top of the leg sling to the locking carabiner at your seat harness.) Experiment to find the sling lengths that are best for you.

Fig. 13–9. Texas prusik dimensions

This is how to use the Texas prusik after a fall into a crevasse (fig. 13-10):

1. Remove the foot loops from your pocket and slip one over each boot, cinching up on the slip knots. (If you have a sling with just a single foot loop, slip it over one boot.)
2. Stand up in the foot slings.
3. Loosen the prusik knot attached to the seat sling and slide it up the rope until it is taut.
4. Sit down in the waist harness, putting all your weight on the seat sling.
5. Loosen the prusik knot attached to the foot slings and slide it up the rope (18 to 24 inches, if the sling is adjusted properly).
6. Once again, stand up in the foot slings.
7. Keep repeating the process.

Fig. 13–10. Ascending a rope using the Texas prusik: a, leg-raise position; b, stand-up position; c, rest position.

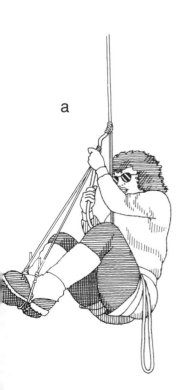

The Texas prusik is a simple system that permits more progress per cycle and more comfortable rests than with the stair-step prusik. A climber with an injured leg can still ascend the rope because only one leg is required if you choose to make use of only one foot loop. This method is harder to perform than the stair-step in very narrow crevasses.

With either the stair-step or the Texas prusik, some climbers attach etriers rather than conventional slings. The steps in these ladder-like slings can help you climb up and over a crevasse lip if the rope is entrenched in the snow.

TEAM RESCUES

All rescues are team rescues to some degree, because the fallen climber needs some help even for a self-rescue. However, a full team rescue usually involves hauling the climber to safety. Following are the principal team-rescue methods.

Brute force

Here's a technique we can all understand. Just grab the rope and pull. This is an excellent method for large groups because it's fast, uncomplicated, uses minimal equipment, and requires little or no help from the fallen climber. It works best when perhaps half a dozen strong rescuers can haul on the rope and when the working platform for the pullers is flat or downhill.

After the rescuers have established an anchor, checked the fallen climber, and padded the rope at the lip of the crevasse, they line up along the accident rope and grasp it. They haul by pulling on the rope hand over hand or by moving step by step away from the crevasse.

One rescuer tends the anchor and its tie-in point to the accident rope (where it is attached with a prusik knot, Bachmann knot, or a mechanical ascender). As the rope is pulled up, this rescuer sees that it moves smoothly through the tie-in point. The knot or ascender is then in position to grip and hold the rope if the rope is dropped or the pullers need a rest.

Rescuers should pull the rope at a slow, steady pace, especially when the fallen climber reaches the crevasse lip. If the rope has cut into the lip, the climber could be hurt by being pulled into the wall. At this point, rescuers may ask the climber to scramble over the lip while they hoist.

The single pulley (C-pulley)

Smaller groups without enough muscle to pull the climber out by brute force need a more sophisticated system. The single pulley gives rescuers a 2-to-1 mechanical advantage, doubling the amount of weight that each puller can raise (although friction somewhat lowers this ratio).

Several considerations enter into a decision to use the single-pulley (also known as the C-pulley). The fallen climber must be conscious in order to help by clipping into the rescue pulley. A separate length of rope is needed, either an unused end of the accident rope or another rope entirely. This method is, in fact, a good alternative to consider if the accident rope itself is embedded in the edge of the crevasse and won't move.

To carry out a single-pulley rescue (fig. 13-11), follow these steps:

1. Find a rescue rope. It must be at least twice as long as the distance from the anchor to the fallen climber.
2. Attach one end of the rescue rope to the existing anchor or to a new rescue anchor. (If the unused end of the accident rope is long enough to be used, tie a figure-8 loop in it a few feet beyond the rope's attachment to the anchor. Clip this loop into the anchor.)
3. Double the rescue rope into a big loop and attach a pulley with a locking carabiner.
4. Lower the loop with the pulley and carabiner down to the fallen climber. Tell the climber to clip the carabiner into the seat harness. Confirm that this has been done. Then tell the climber to take the strand of rescue rope that you will be pulling on and to run it through the carabiner at the chest harness, to help stay upright. Tell the climber *precisely* what to do.
5. Be sure the rescue rope runs over an ice axe or

Fig. 13–11. Setting up and raising a climber with the single pulley (rescuer's personal anchors omitted for clarity)

other padding at the crevasse edge to keep it from digging in.

6. Haul on the unanchored end of the lowered loop. As you haul, the climber can grab the anchored half of the loop and pull up. This relieves weight on the rope and makes hauling much easier.

7. A rescuer must attend to the original accident rope at the anchor and pull slack through the friction knot or ascender as the climber is raised. This keeps the accident rope ready at any time to accept the climber's weight again, in case of emergency or if the pullers need a rest.

The Z-pulley

The Z-pulley (fig. 13-12) magnifies the muscle power of small climbing parties by offering a 3-to-1 theoretical mechanical advantage through the use of two pulleys. It can be set up and operated with no help from the fallen climber, making it valuable in rescuing an unconscious person.

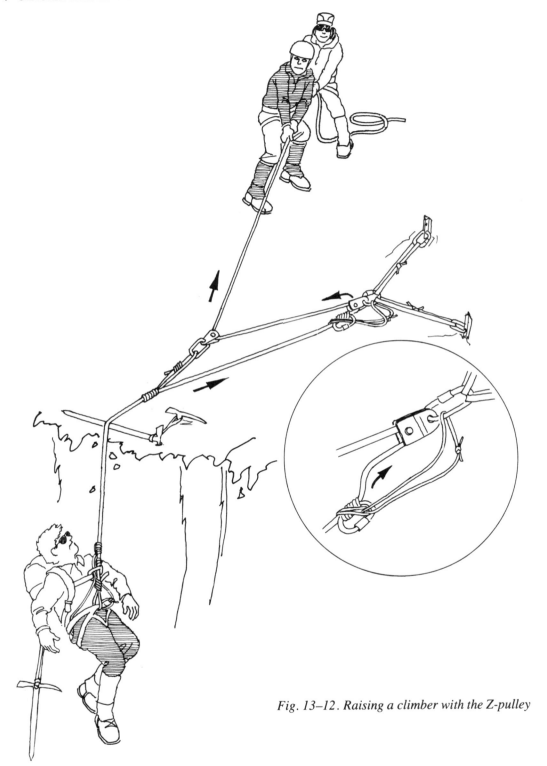

Fig. 13–12. Raising a climber with the Z-pulley

The Z-pulley system, which uses the accident rope, requires more equipment and is somewhat more complicated than the C-pulley.

You can get to work on the Z-pulley as soon as you have set up the anchor that is established after any crevasse fall. As usual, the accident rope will be secured to this anchor via a sling tied to the rope with a friction knot (prusik or Bachmann) or an ascender.

Take the loose end of the accident rope and lay out a long loop on the snow, in front of the anchor, so that the loop and the taut line leading to the fallen climber form a giant flat Z.

At the first bend in the Z (by the anchor), place a rescue pulley. Clip a locking carabiner through the pulley and attach the carabiner to the anchor with a short sling. (Some climbers prefer to establish a second anchor to secure this pulley.) The pulley will be located on the climbing rope, between the friction knot and the anchor.

At the second bend in the Z (closer to the crevasse lip), place a second pulley on the rope. Clip this ''floating'' pulley into a short sling that also is attached with a friction knot to the taut rope going to the fallen climber. You may have to see it to believe it, but you now have a Z-pulley setup, ready for use.

To work the system:

1. Pull hand over hand on the free end of the rope, hauling the climber upward.
2. Be sure the rope slides freely through the friction knot or ascender that is linked to the climbing rope near the anchor. This will be the friction brake that holds the accident rope whenever you reset the pulley. If it's a prusik knot, one rescuer needs to help keep it in the open, sliding position. If it's a Bachmann knot or mechanical ascender, it should be able to tend itself.
3. As the floating pulley is hauled in close to the other pulley, slowly relax your pull on the rope in order to let the friction brake take the weight of the climber. Don't let the two pulleys touch because that will undo the Z con-

figuration and convert your system to a direct pull—the old brute-force method.
4. Reset the Z-pulley by loosening the friction knot that is attached to the floating pulley and sliding it way out toward the crevasse lip once again.
5. Haul again on the free end of the rope.
6. Keep repeating the process.

Remember that in any rescue system calling for pulleys, you can substitute carabiners if necessary. However, they create far more friction and the rope will be much harder to pull.

Piggyback systems

To get even more mechanical advantage out of a rescue hauling setup, you can piggyback two systems. For example, establish a separate single-pulley setup to haul on the rope coming from a Z-pulley system. This now gives you a 6-to-1 theoretical mechanical advantage. Or set up a single pulley to haul on another single-pulley system for a 4-to-1 advantage.

To piggyback two systems, set up your initial hoist to the fallen climber, either a single pulley or a Z-pulley. Now establish a second anchor some distance behind the main one, to anchor the second system. Attach the second hoist, again either a single pulley or a Z-pulley, to the accident rope at the point where the rescuers would normally pull.

As you might guess, piggyback systems require an ample supply of slings, pulleys, carabiners, anchor material, and rope.

The Bilgeri rescue

The Bilgeri (fig. 13-13) is a sort of ''team self-rescue.'' It involves the rope-climbing techniques used in the stair-step prusik and the Texas prusik—except that the friction knots or ascenders are operated by a rescuer topside, not by the fallen climber.

Here's how to do it:

1. Secure the accident rope to an anchor with a friction knot or ascender—the standard procedure after any crevasse fall.

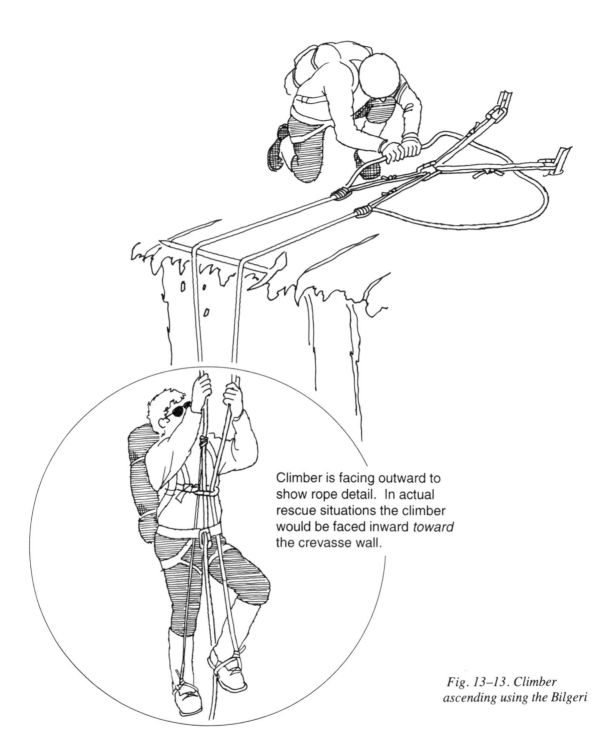

Climber is facing outward to show rope detail. In actual rescue situations the climber would be faced inward *toward* the crevasse wall.

Fig. 13–13. Climber ascending using the Bilgeri

2. Tie a foot loop in the end of a length of rope (either a spare rope or the loose end of the accident rope).

3. Lower this loop to the climber.

4. Attach the upper end of this rope to the anchor with a friction knot or ascender.

5. Tell the climber to put one foot in the foot loop you lowered and the other foot in a prusik sling attached to the accident rope. The climber should now be standing in two foot loops—each on a separate strand of rope that is secured topside by separate friction-knot slings clipped to the anchor.

   (To complete the picture, the fallen climber should take all the precautions associated with self-rescue: thread the foot loops through the seat harness and then down to the feet; run the ascent ropes through the chest carabiner to help maintain an upright position; clip a safety loop from the prusik sling to the seat harness.)

   Everything is now ready for the ascent:

6. Shout "Right," and the climber lifts (unweights) the right foot. You pull in 12 to 18 inches of slack through the friction knot anchoring that rope.

7. Next, shout "Left." The climber lifts (unweights) the left foot while transferring all weight to the opposite rope. You pull in 12 to 18 inches of slack through the friction knot anchoring that rope.

8. Repeat the sequence until the climber is up and out.

This version of the Bilgeri is similar to the stair-step prusik. There's also a "Texas prusik" variation, useful for a person with an injured leg. The climber puts a boot into the foot loop that is lowered from above. The other foot is left free. To ascend, the climber alternates standing in the foot loop on one rope with sitting in the seat harness attached to the accident rope.

The Bilgeri can be a good idea if the fallen climber is in pretty good shape and can communicate readily with rescuers, but isn't particularly adept at working prusik slings. The Bilgeri rescue has an advantage over prusiking methods when the crevasse lip is reached. Because the knots are being handled up top, the fallen climber does not have to force prusik knots up a rope burrowed in the snow. If either of the Bilgeri ropes digs into the crevasse lip, you can free it from up top while the climber's weight is on the opposite line.

SPECIAL SITUATIONS

The realities of a rescue are bound to bring a few snags and surprises on the way to a successful conclusion. You may need to improvise on the basic techniques of rescue. The following are some special situations you could encounter and ideas on how to deal with them.

The middle person

It's an awkward situation when the middle person on a three-person rope team falls in a crevasse, and there are no other teams around to help. The fallen climber is temporarily left hanging while the only two people who can help are separated by the crevasse, each in self-arrest.

To get out of this fix, the climbers start by deciding which side of the crevasse is the rescue side; that is, which side should the fallen climber come out on? Usually, one of the two rescuers in self-arrest is holding more weight than the other. The one holding the least weight usually has the best chance to get up and establish an anchor while the rescuer on the other side stays in self-arrest to hold the fall.

With the anchor set up, the rescuer in self-arrest is ready to get free. This rescuer can ease back until the fallen climber's weight is on the anchor (keeping alert to the danger of also being pulled into the crevasse). Or this rescuer can try to set up a temporary anchor that will take the weight being held by the self-arrest.

Next step: the climber at the anchor tries to belay the climber on the wrong side over to the rescue side, if that person is needed to help in the operation. The loose end of the rope on the rescue side can be used for belaying, if it happens to be long enough. Or if they thought to bring along a lightweight 100-foot accessory line (a good precaution for a rope team traveling alone), this can provide the belay.

However, the climber on the wrong side could be stuck there if no belay or safe route is available. This climber should then set up an anchor and stay put.

On the rescue side, the ideal option now is for the fallen climber to ascend the rope on prusik slings. The rescuer can also use the Bilgeri technique, providing there's enough rope. If a hoist is necessary, the single rescuer can try a Z-pulley or a piggyback system. (For the friction brake at the anchor, be sure to use a Bachmann knot or an ascender, which require less tending than a prusik knot.)

In case one of the two middle members of a four-person rope team falls into a crevasse, conduct the rescue from the side that has two climbers topside.

Two-person rope team

Glacier climbers on a two-person rope team traveling alone really need to know their stuff when it comes to crevasse rescue. Each climber must carry enough equipment for an anchor and a hauling system. The topside climber not only stops the fall but must set up the anchor while staying in self-arrest.

As the sole rescuer, first secure your arrest position by digging in your feet and pressing the ice axe firmly into the snow.

Try to free one hand by rotating the upper half of your body—but keep leaning on the axe. Use your free hand to place a fluke, picket, or ice screw. At this point, you'll see the value of keeping the anchors easily accessible.

Then attach the rope to the anchor with a prusik sling. Ease the weight onto the anchor, keeping ready to resume self-arrest if the anchor doesn't hold. Once you're safely out of self-arrest, back up the anchor.

Now the fallen climber can ascend on prusik slings. Another option for the fallen climber is to work with the rescuer on a Bilgeri ascent—pro-

vided the rescuer is carrying enough spare rope (either extra line, or the coiled and unused rope end carried by climbers in a two-person team). If neither of these methods works in this particular situation, the rescuer will set up a hoist, either a Z-pulley or a piggyback system, using the extra rope resulting from tying in 25 to 50 feet from the rope end. The climbing rope must have a self-tending attachment to the anchor (either a Bachmann knot or an ascender). The rescuer can lighten the hoisting job by first pulling up the fallen climber's pack.

If the rescuer isn't able to set up an anchor in the first place, the fallen climber has no choice but to ascend on prusik slings while the rescuer remains in self-arrest.

Special rescues

New considerations come into the picture when you have to deal with an unconscious victim or with more than one fallen climber at a time.

To help an unconscious climber, first send someone down by rappelling or being lowered on belay. The helper can administer first aid and also get a fallen climber right-side up if necessary. The unconscious climber can be pulled up by brute force or with the Z-pulley. To help get the unconscious climber over the lip of the crevasse, a rescuer may have to work right at the edge or from inside the crevasse.

To rescue more than one fallen climber, assess each person's condition and the best method for getting each one out, and then decide the order of rescue. Be sure each fallen climber is given warm clothing, if needed, and keep them informed of rescue plans as they develop.

Working space

Rescue procedures can be modified to help give you the working space needed to carry out a successful operation.

Temporary anchor

This is a solution to a situation where there is very little working space between the edge of the crevasse and the person who is in self-arrest position to hold the fall. Normally, the anchor and then the Z-pulley would be set up in this space. But now there's not enough room.

The answer is simply to set up the main anchor *behind* the climber in self-arrest (instead of between the climber and the crevasse). Attach the climbing rope to the main anchor with a friction knot or ascender—but at this point, leave a couple of feet of slack between the main anchor and the climber in self-arrest, so that this climber isn't trapped in the system by tension on the rope.

This is where a temporary anchor comes in. Between the climber and the crevasse, set up a temporary anchor and use a prusik sling to secure the rope to it. This permits the climber to ease off from the self-arrest position, let the temporary anchor take over the weight, and untie from the climbing rope.

Now the rescuers can set up a normal Z-pulley in front of the main anchor. They now have plenty of working space. Once hauling begins, the prusik attached to the temporary anchor can be untied.

Difficult areas

Rescuers trying to work in a very narrow area between two crevasses can consider moving the operation. The rescue might proceed better if it is run from the opposite side of either crevasse.

Another option in a tight spot is to change the direction of pull on a Z-pulley system. Hook another pulley to the anchor and run the hauling end of the rope through it. Now the rescuers can pull in a direction more parallel to the crevasses.

Rescues from the uphill side of a crevasse are harder than those from the downhill side. If possible, move the operation to the lower side, where it will be easier for rescuers to haul and for the fallen climber to get over the lip of the crevasse.

Entrenched ropes

The upward progress of a person climbing out or being pulled out of a crevasse can be stopped cold by a rope that has dug itself into the lip.

The situation calls for some improvisation. For instance, a rescuer can attach prusik slings or etriers above the entrenched portion of the rope and drop them down for the climber to step into.

Another option is to switch to a new rescue rope. A rescuer can lower a new rope to the climber. Or the fallen climber can, in effect, provide a new rope by tossing the loose end of the climbing rope up to the rescuers. This is done by prusiking up to the lip, untying from the end of the climbing rope (after first tying in higher up), and throwing the loose end up to the rescuers.

A new rescue rope, carefully padded at the lip of the crevasse so it doesn't also get entrenched, opens up several rescue possibilities. The climber can switch prusik slings from the original climbing rope to the new free rope. Or the rescuers can haul the climber up and out on the new rope. Or the climber can merely transfer all weight to the new rope to give rescuers a much better chance of freeing the entrenched line.

Roofed crevasses

Wide roofed crevasses present special problems. The fallen climber may be hanging free, without a stabilizing wall for support, and the accident rope typically entrenches itself deeply into the snow of the crevasse roof. The climber may be bombarded by snow and ice dislodged by the rescuers above, who will be working in an area of proven instability.

Sometimes it's necessary for a well-belayed rescuer to take a shovel or axe and enlarge the hole the climber fell through. Do your best to keep snow and ice from hitting the climber.

Knowledge and preparation will minimize the hazards of roofed crevasses and the other problems of traveling near crevasses. Glacier travelers who learn about crevasses and regard them with a healthy respect may never fall in. If they do, they will know the techniques that give them the best chance to get back out.

· 14 ·

ICE CLIMBING

The world of the ice climber embraces all the forms in which ice exists. In the high mountains, snow and other frozen precipitation endures pressure and heat over time to become the *alpine ice* of glaciers, icefields, and couloirs. This alpine ice is sometimes seen as *blue ice*, a hue born of its exposure to very low temperatures during formation. Blue ice is good for climbing and placing protection. *Black ice* is another alpine variation—old, hard ice, mixed with dirt, pebbles or other debris, often found in gullies and couloirs, and very difficult to climb.

When water freezes, the result is *water ice*. It can be as dramatic as a frozen waterfall or as common as *verglas*, the thin, clear coating that forms when rainfall or melting snow from upper cliffs freezes on rock. Verglas is difficult to climb because crampons have little to penetrate. Water ice is usually harder, steeper, and more brittle than alpine ice, but at high altitudes and low temperatures, the two may be indistinguishable.

Rock also comes in various forms, but is very stable when compared with ice. Yesterday's crack and slab problem will likely be there next year, but this morning's ice route may be only wet rock by afternoon. The ice climber learns to anticipate the ever-changing character of the climbing medium.

Ice-climbing techniques vary depending on steepness of the slope. You can walk without crampons on flat ice fairly easily, especially if rocks are embedded in the surface. On short slopes, you can use an ice axe to chop steps, but longer sections call for crampons. French technique—"flat-footing"—works well on steepening ice, up to a limit. But the steepest routes require the German technique of front-pointing.

This chapter will use some descriptive terms in referring to the approximate steepness of ice slopes. Here's roughly what they mean, in degrees of angle:

- Gentle: Up to 30 degrees
- Moderate: 30 to 45 degrees
- Steep: 45 to 60 degrees
- Extremely steep: 60 degrees and over
- Vertical: 80 to 90 degrees
- Overhanging: Over 90 degrees

EQUIPMENT

Ice climbers refine and expand their techniques and use them on greater climbing challenges with the help of modern equipment. Manufacturers offer a steady stream of specialized clothing, boots, crampons, ice tools, and ice anchors. Review Chapter 12 for a good general rundown on gear such as crampons and ice axes. Building on Chapter 12, this chapter will outline equipment features that are especially important for ice climbing.

CLOTHING

Clothes for ice climbing should offer a combination of comfort and function. In choosing a jacket or anorak, check to see that you can reach high and not have the anorak or jacket bottom rise above your waist. You don't want your waist exposed to the elements as you're reaching up to make a high ice placement. Reinforce the knees and ankles of rain pants or bibs.

Some climbers wear bibs or a body suit as an alternative to the conventional outfit of jacket (or anorak) and pants. A one-piece body suit of synthetic material retains warmth and rebuffs debris. For ventilation, it needs zippers that open from elbow to ankle, and another that opens the suit from stomach to back via the crotch. The body suit should not be confused with the expedition suit, essentially an insulated body suit.

For the hands, mittens with rubberized palms can help in gripping the bare-metal shaft of an ice tool—a tough job with a snow-coated nylon mitten. One option for covering your hands is high-density wool mittens (such as Dachsteins), which are not only warm but offer an unusual secondary feature. If you hit a difficult section of climbing and have only one ice tool, you can temporarily freeze a mittened hand to the ice for help through a move. For safekeeping, always attach wrist loops to your mittens and gloves.

BOOTS

Ice climbers use plastic (synthetic) boots more commonly than leather footwear. The plastic boots are warmer than leather and provide a rigid platform for crampons, which is especially important for front-pointing. Many plastic boots have indented toes and heels that help keep step-in/clamp-on crampon bindings securely attached.

Three-quarter-shank leather boots usually are adequate for general alpine ice climbing. However, leather boots used for extensive front-pointing should have a full shank.

Because ankle rotation is so important in French technique (flat-footing), you need a boot that permits good rotation. Leather boots often are better in this regard. And like any boots, you want ice-climbing footwear to fit well: snug in the heel and instep, and with room for toes to wiggle.

Make sure your gaiters fit your boots. You'll need full-length gaiters that extend from your foot to just beneath the knee. Insulated gaiters are available for added warmth.

CRAMPONS

Properly fitted hinged crampons are adequate for most alpine ice climbing. They work well with most types of climbing boots and are less expensive than rigid-frame designs. They should have medium-length points and require front points for ice climbing.

Climbers who do a lot of front-pointing (especially waterfall climbing) prefer rigid-frame crampons, which vibrate less than hinged crampons when kicked into water ice. Most rigid crampons should be worn with full-shank or plastic (synthetic) boots to prevent over-stressing the frame, although some newer models are strong enough to be worn with boots having less than full shanks. (For a fuller discussion of crampons, see Chapter 12.)

Crampon points must be sharp, and the harder the ice, the sharper the points need to be. Check the points before each climb and sharpen them if they need it.

The angle of the front points and of the first row of downward points is critical in determining the best penetration. For regular ice, the front points are shaped straight but bent slightly downward, and the first row is angled slightly forward (fig. 14-1a).

For waterfall ice, the front points are curved downward, and the ends of the first row are angled more forward than those used for regular ice (fig. 14-1b).

Some waterfall climbers prefer crampons with

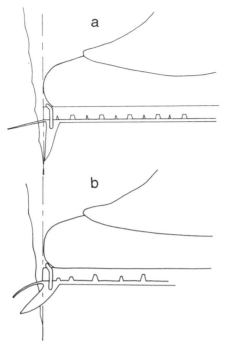

Fig. 14–1. Angle of front points: a, for regular ice; b, for waterfall ice.

just a single front point, which makes for easy placement (fig. 14-2). However, the single front point has more tendency to rotate than the normal double front points.

ICE TOOLS

Part of the fun of ice climbing is experimenting with the large variety of ice-climbing hand tools and learning how to use them. You can borrow, rent, or buy ice tools in order to discover which ones work best in your own climbing.

Most ice tools have shorter shafts than the standard axes used in snow climbing. The short shaft, commonly 50 to 60 centimeters, helps in accurate placement of the pick and reduces the shaft vibration that can fatigue arm muscles. Ice tools that feature a hammer in place of the adze (fig. 14-3) often have a shaft length even shorter than other tools (as short as 35 centimeters).

Many alpine ice climbers use a full-length ice axe partnered with a shorter hand tool. On more technical ice routes, many climbers choose to use two shorter hand tools. A versatile combination is to use one tool that has an adze and one that has a

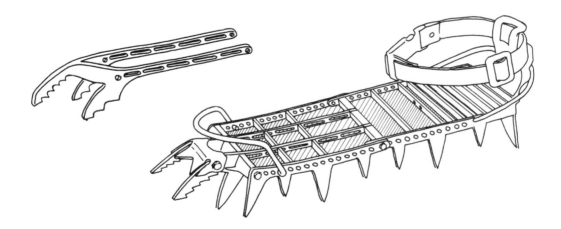

Fig. 14–2. Rigid crampon with interchangeable single front point

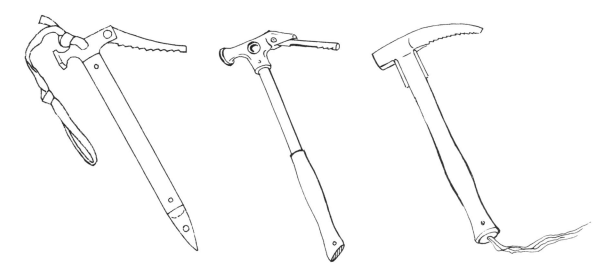

Fig. 14–3. Typical ice hammers

hammer. The adze chops and scrapes ice for steps, belay positions, or ice bollards; the hammer pounds in pieces of protection. Some climbers prefer to hold the ice hammer in their dominant hand, which makes it easier to use in starting ice screws or placing ice and rock pitons.

For a long and demanding ascent, some climbers bring along a third tool. It can be used as an anchor at belay points, as a protection placement, or to replace a lost or broken tool. If your hand tools feature replaceable picks, you can carry a lightweight spare as insurance against a broken pick.

To help in gripping the ice tools, you can wear gloves with rubberized palms or use tools with a covering on the shaft that improves the grip. Inspect your tools before each outing to see that adzes, picks, and spikes are as sharp as possible. Keep these sharp edges covered with guards when they're not in use.

There is great variety in the styles of ice tools. Following are the principal design variations, categorized by the parts of the tool: pick, adze, shaft, and spike.

Picks

The job of the pick is to penetrate the ice, hold against a pull along the shaft, and release easily when its grip is no longer needed. The holding and releasing characteristics of a pick are determined by its weight and shape and by its teeth.

A tool with a relatively heavy head cuts and penetrates most readily, but may be difficult to extract because of its greater penetration. Removable weights can be added to the head to help balance your swing and give better ice penetration.

The steeper the droop of a pick and the sharper, deeper, and more frequent the teeth, the better the pick will hold; but the smoother the pick, the easier it is to remove. The teeth should be shaped to bite into the ice as you pull on the end of the shaft. Although thin, sharp edges penetrate and hold best, they are especially vulnerable to damage when they hit rock. A thin pick may place well, but is more prone to break from the twisting that often occurs when a climber tries to extract the tool. A thick-bladed pick, on the other hand, requires more force to place and is more likely to chip out plates

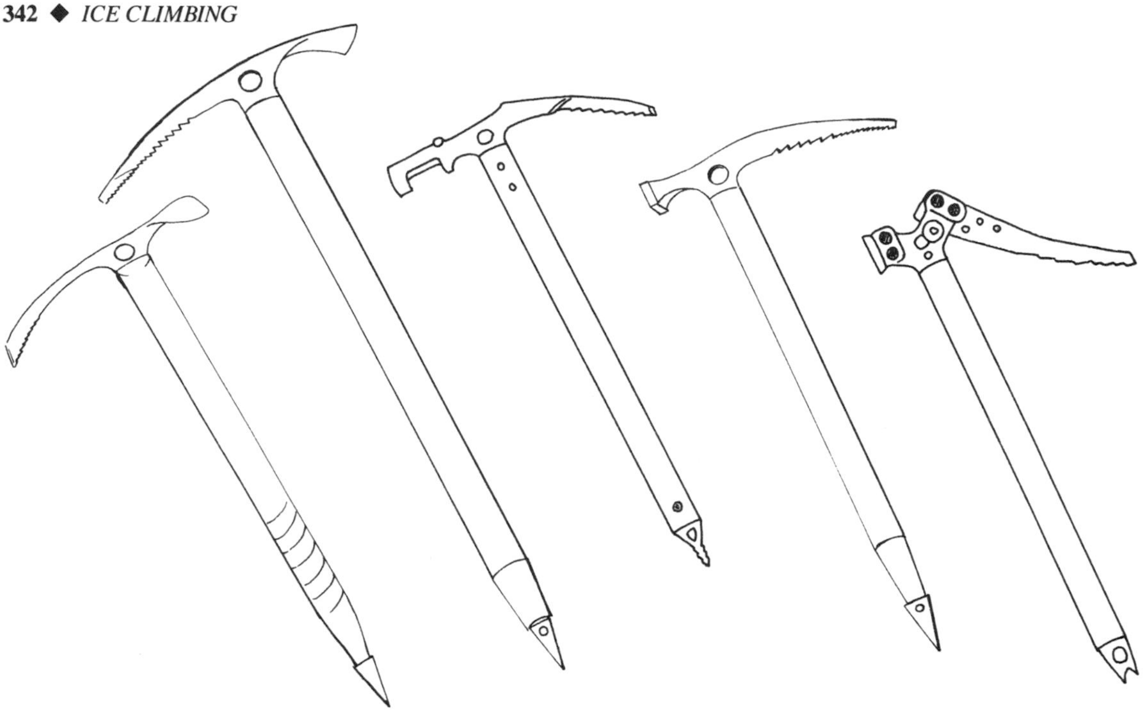

Fig. 14–4. Ice tools with various pick designs

of ice, but is less prone to break as you work to remove it.

With the conflicting demands on an ice tool, it's no wonder there is wide variation in pick design (fig. 14-4). Many tools are available with interchangeable picks, so you can choose the right one for a particular climb and replace a broken pick instead of discarding the tool. Talk to experienced ice climbers for help in choosing pick designs suitable for you. Here are the principal pick designs you will encounter.

Technically curved: The pick on a standard ice axe used in snow climbing curves slightly downward. But many of the shorter axes used in ice climbing feature a pick that curves down more sharply and holds better in ice. This technically curved pick is most often used on alpine and glacial ice. A good choice is an ice tool with a pick whose curvature matches your natural swing. The angle at the very end of the pick (which determines whether it has negative or positive clearance) is not a major consideration. The main thing is to keep the pick sharp.

Reverse curved: The ease of removal of a drooped pick that has some reverse curve (an upward curve) makes it a frequent choice for waterfall and other steep ice routes.

Straight drooped: An ice tool with a straight but sharply down-angled pick penetrates well in soft to hard ice.

Tubular: Tubular-nosed picks—thin and sharp—are popular for hard water ice because the tube shatters the ice less than a conventional pick.

Adzes

With the adze of an ice tool, you can chop steps, clear ice to make a good surface for screw placement, and cut footholds at belays. As with picks, adzes come in an array of shapes and sizes (fig. 14-5). Many ice tools accept interchangable adzes, letting you replace a broken adze or change adzes depending on ice conditions. You can even

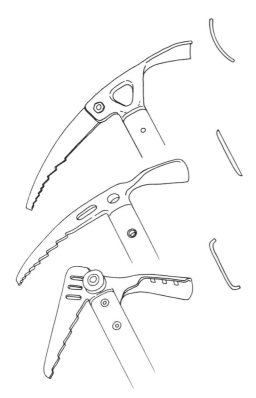

Fig. 14–5. Side and end views of three adze designs

replace an adze with a hammer head.

The most common adze is straight, extending perpendicular to the shaft or drooping somewhat downward. The straight adze is excellent for cutting steps with sharp corners. Some adzes curve downward like the technically curved pick. The very end—the working edge—of some adzes curves slightly inward, although this impedes step-cutting because the full force of a swing is diffused. Tubular adzes are available, mainly for use on waterfall ice.

Shafts

The shafts of most ice tools are straight, but a few designs feature curved shafts (fig. 14-6). Be sure the curve of the shaft complements your natural swing. Curved shafts are designed to keep your knuckles from banging against the ice, aiding in a better placement.

Spikes

To penetrate ice, the spike on an ice tool must be sharp, and the joint between spike and shaft must be smooth. Spikes are solid or tubular. Solid spikes consist of a flat plate or a cone-shaped tip, and cone-shaped spikes point either straight down

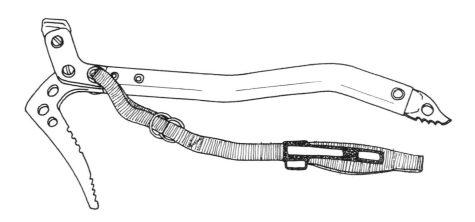

Fig. 14–6. Curved-shaft ice tool

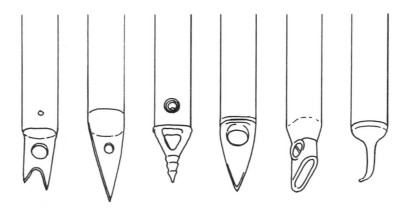

Fig. 14–7. Various ice-tool spike designs

or somewhat forward. Most spikes have carabiner holes, which you can clip to as a temporary anchor when setting up a belay anchor (fig. 14-7).

Attachment

A wrist leash from you to each ice tool serves several purposes. The leash secures a dropped tool, helps in the work of swinging the tool, and lets you rest your grip by hanging your weight from it.

A wrist leash is an energy-saving necessity on extremely steep or vertical ice. The leash attached through the carabiner hole at the head of the tool should be just long enough to let you grasp the shaft near the spike. The leash needs an end loop to slip your hand through. You may tie or tape the loop to the shaft at the desired hand position, to help hold your hand in the right spot at all times and direct the downward pull straight along the shaft (fig. 14-8). Used like this, the leash shares in the work of holding and swinging the axe.

The wrist leash also makes it possible to hang from an ice tool without maintaining a forearm-killing grip. To do this, let your arm hang straight, with hand and arm relaxed and body weight on your skeleton.

You can also rest by hanging from a tether that runs from the carabiner hole in the spike to your harness or gear sling. Make the tether long enough that it won't hinder your swing but short enough

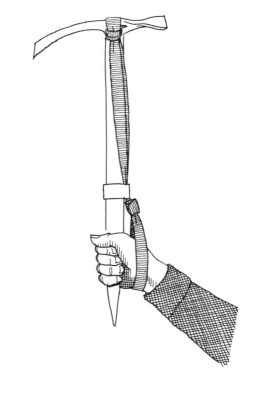

Fig. 14–8. Wrist leash for ice tools

that it doesn't get in the way (perhaps catching on a crampon). Put an ice tool in a holster or tool loop when it's not needed.

ICE SCREWS

Ice screws evolved from ice pitons, which were extra-long, blade-type rock pitons with holes, notches, or bulges to increase their grip in ice. After World War II, climbers experimented with new designs that featured a greater shaft area to decrease the load per square inch on the ice and more holes to help the shaft freeze into the slope.

When ice screws first appeared in the early 1960s, enthusiasts claimed they would revolutionize ice climbing, bringing security to the slopes. Critics scoffed that the screws weren't much better than the older ice pitons. This proved particularly true of the lightweight, relatively weak "coat-hanger" ice screw, rarely used today. But ice screws continued to improve and now are considered reliable leader protection (fig. 14-9).

The modern tubular ice screw is the strongest and most reliable design. Commonly 7 to 9 inches long (18 to 23 centimeters), this screw works well in temperatures of both winter and summer. It is relatively easy to screw in and to screw out, with some models including a built-in ratchet for faster placement and removal. The hollow design minimizes fracturing of the ice by allowing the displaced ice to work itself out through the core of the screw.

After the screw is removed, ice inside the core must be cleaned out immediately or it may freeze to the interior, making the screw temporarily useless. The interior of some ice screws is slightly conical, permitting easier ice removal. If ice freezes to the inside, push it out with a length of stiff wire.

The shape and size of an ice screw have a great bearing on its strength. A large-diameter screw supports more weight than a smaller-diameter screw of the same length. A tubular screw holds a greater load than a solid one.

Another type of ice screw is hammered into place, but screwed back out. This type—developed in an attempt to make an easy-to-place and easy-to-remove screw—is available in both solid and tubular versions.

The solid versions can offer good protection in water ice at temperatures below freezing, but are less effective in other forms of ice and at higher temperatures. Melt-out is sometimes rapid because of limited thread displacement and, under load, they tend to shear through the ice. They can break

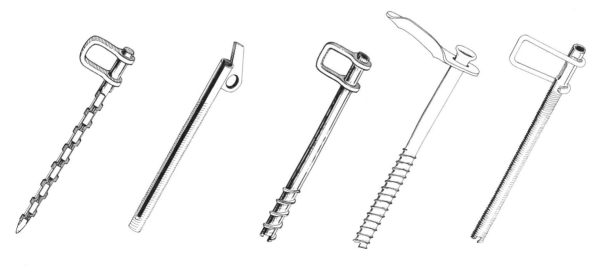

Fig. 14–9. Types of ice screws

if they aren't hammered in all the way, and they are sometimes tough to remove.

Hollow-core versions of pound-in, screw-out designs have the advantage of allowing the displaced ice to come out through the core instead of being forced aside by a solid screw. This design, with its small threads, can be placed with a series of light blows and removed relatively easily by unscrewing or by levering out with an axe pick. It works best in hard ice, but can be unreliable in temperatures above freezing.

OTHER GEAR

Holsters

You can add two holsters or a double-size holster to your seat harness for carrying ice tools. Try out the tools in the holster before you use it. The tools may be hard to remove if the holster was designed for small rock-climbing implements.

Ropes

Standard 10- to 11-millimeter climbing ropes are the most commonly used for ice climbing, though this depends on the type of climb and the preference of the climbers. Some ice climbers use a rope longer than the standard 50 meters (165 feet) to permit longer pitches. Some use double-rope or twin-rope techniques (outlined in Chapter 10).

Water-repellent ropes may be worth the extra cost because they won't freeze like regular ropes (though they can still become ice-coated). However, experience indicates the water repellency may not last the lifetime of the rope.

Head and eye protection

Your head and eyes need protection from the chunks of ice that start flying when climbers begin swinging their tools into ice. Helmets and goggles are both strongly recommended. The helmet, which also protects from rockfall, must adjust enough to make room for a stocking cap or balaclava. The goggles must fit when your helmet is on, provide protection from ultraviolet rays, and have adequate ventilation to minimize fogging. Sunglasses with side shields are an acceptable substitute.

TECHNIQUES OF ICE CLIMBING

A rock climber taking up ice climbing may find some striking similarities in the two pursuits. In both, climbers progress by moving their weight from one point of balance to another, support themselves as much as possible on their legs, and plan several moves in advance, climbing ''with their eyes.'' On ice, as on rock, climbers use surface features, seeking out buckets and protrusions for handholds, footholds, and ice-tool placements. Of course, the differences are at least as striking. Ice climbers must rely on hand tools and on crampons. They learn to make do with anchors that can be uncertain, and they work in a medium that changes throughout the day and throughout the season.

TECHNIQUE OVERVIEW

Ice climbers usually employ features of two basic techniques, depending on steepness of the slope, conditions of the ice, and their ability and confidence level. They are known as the French and German techniques. The techniques are not mutually exclusive, and most climbers use aspects of both in working out the best way to handle a climb.

French technique (flat-footing)

French technique is the easiest and most efficient method of climbing gentle to steep ice and hard snow—once you learn how to do it. Good French technique demands balance, rhythm, and the confident use of crampons and axe.

French climbers developed the flat-footing technique, thus their terminology is commonly used. Terms using the French word *pied* refer to the feet; terms using *piolet* refer to the ice axe. *Pied à plat*, for example, is French for flat-footing. The name describes the technique: you must keep your feet as flat against the ice as possible at all times to keep all crampon points on the ice. It can be a difficult style to master because it requires severe rotation of the ankle on steep slopes.

The various French placements will be detailed later in this chapter. For now, here is an abbreviated directory of French ice-climbing terms, along with the approximate steepness of slope for each type:

For the feet:

- *Pied marche* (marching)   Gentle, 0 to 15 degrees
- *Pied en canard* (duck walk)   Gentle, 15 to 30 degrees
- *Pied à plat* (flat-footing)   Moderate to steep, 30 to 65 degrees and higher

For the ice axe:

- *Piolet canne* (cane)   Gentle to moderate, 0 to 40 degrees
- *Piolet ramasse* (cross-body)   Moderate, 35 to 50 degrees
- *Piolet ancre* (anchor)   Steep, 45 to 65 degrees and higher

German technique (front-pointing)

Developed by the Germans and Austrians for climbing the harder snow and ice of the eastern Alps, front-pointing can take an experienced ice climber up the steepest and most difficult ice slopes. With this technique, even average climbers can quickly overcome sections that would be difficult or impossible with French technique.

Front-pointing, in contrast to the choreography of flat-footing, is straightforward and uncomplicated. The technique is much like step-kicking straight up a snow slope, but instead of kicking your boot into the snow, you kick your front crampon points into the ice and step directly up on them.

Just as in French technique, however, good front-pointing is rhythmic and balanced, with the weight of your body over the crampons. Efficiency of movement is essential, whether it's planting your front points, placing your hand tools, or moving on the ice.

Although the Germans and Austrians developed it, German technique is frequently described with the general vocabulary of the French technique. Here is a brief directory of German technique, with approximate slope angles for each type. As you can see, aspects of French and German technique overlap in the steepness of slopes for which they are recommended. The proper technique to use depends on ice conditions and the preference of the climber.

For the feet:

- Front-pointing   For all angles from 45 degrees through vertical and overhanging

For the ice tools:

- *Piolet panne* (low dagger)   Steep, 45 to 55 degrees
- *Piolet poignard* (high dagger) Steep, 50 to 60 degrees
- *Piolet ancre* (anchor)   Steep, 45 to 60 degrees
- *Piolet traction* (traction)   Extremely steep, 60 degrees through vertical and overhanging

CLIMBING WITHOUT CRAMPONS

Climbing gentle ice slopes without crampons is balance climbing, moving up from one position of balance to the next. At each point of balance, your inside (uphill) foot is in front of and above the trailing outside (downhill) leg, which is fully extended so you can put most of your weight on the bone of that leg, minimizing muscular effort. The axe, in your uphill hand, moves only after your body and feet are in balance, and your feet move only after the axe has been moved forward. As you climb, look for irregularities in the surface of the ice to use as footholds.

Step-cutting

The earliest method of ascending steep ice was simply to cut steps. The invention of crampons reduced the need for step-cutting, but never eliminated it. Climbers still encounter sections of ice when they are not carrying crampons or face short ice problems that may not merit taking the time to put on crampons. A broken crampon, or an injured or inexperienced climber, may be reason enough to cut steps. Even if you're wearing crampons, you might welcome a slight step chipped out by the axe for added security or to serve as a small platform to rest on.

A stairway chopped up an ice slope will consist of steps cut diagonally up the hill or of "pigeonhole" steps cut straight up the slope. In either case, the steps are cut from a position of balance. The usual sequence is to cut two steps from a position of balance, place the axe for security, move up to a new position of balance, cut two more steps, and so on.

A single line of diagonal steps is usually cut up gentle slopes, while a double parallel line of diagonal steps is put in on moderate slopes where balance is more of a problem. Pigeonhole steps are used on steeper slopes.

To make diagonal steps in relatively soft ice, such as summer serac ice, stand in a position of balance with the axe in your outside (downhill) hand (fig. 14-10). Swing the axe from your shoulder, cutting with the adze and letting the weight of the axe do most of the work. On harder ice, this takes extra muscle, and two hands may be necessary. With successive swings, slice ice out of the step. The swings cut away from your body, starting at the heel-end of the new step and working toward the toe. Scoop out chunks of ice with the adze and use the adze and pick to finish the step. (On steeper sections, you can cut small fingerholds to use while you are cutting steps.)

On hard ice that fractures easily, swing the pick horizontally into the ice to define the bottom of the step so that vertical chopping doesn't destroy the

Fig. 14–10. Cutting diagonal steps

foothold. If you jerk outward on the axe just as the pick penetrates the ice, the pick should chip out the ice successfully rather than sticking in it. Make the step slope slightly inward to help keep your boot from slipping out. On gentle slopes, it may be OK if it holds only a small part of the boot, but steps on steeper slopes should be roomy enough for the entire boot. Space the steps so they are convenient for all members of your party.

When you're ready to change the direction of a series of diagonal steps, chop a hold large enough for both feet as a secure position for turning and for switching hands on the axe. For all step-cutting, you must attach the ice axe to your wrist with a leash to help support your hard-working hand and to prevent loss of the axe if you drop it.

Pigeonhole steps for the direct ascent of steep ice are placed about shoulder-width apart and within easy stepping distance of each other (fig. 14-11). Each step functions as both a handhold and foothold, so each should be large enough to hold the front half of a boot and should have a small lip to serve as a handhold. Cut the step, then create the lip with small chops of the adze.

If you decide to chop steps down an ice slope, the easiest method is to cut ladder steps that descend straight down the hill (fig. 14-12). To cut two steps in sequence, start in a position of balance, facing down the slope. Chop two steps directly below the ones you are standing in. When they are ready, step down with the outside (downhill) foot, and then the inside (uphill) foot. To cut just one step at a time, again start in a position of balance. Cut the step for the outside (downhill) foot and move that foot down into the step. Then cut the step for the inside (uphill) foot and move that foot down into it.

The step-cutter works at a tiring, difficult job on a slippery surface, often in an exposed location,

Fig. 14–12. Cutting steps on descent

and therefore usually needs to be belayed. The only way to be ready for that emergency when the skill of step-cutting can be a life-saver is to take the time once in a while to practice using your axe to chop steps.

CLIMBING WITH CRAMPONS

Modern crampon technique, evolving from the French and German styles, moves an ice climber efficiently upward with minimum fatigue. Flat-footing is generally used on lower-angle slopes and where point penetration is easy; front-pointing is most common on slopes steeper than 45 degrees and on very hard ice. In practice, most climbers blend them into a combination technique. In any technique, the most important element is confident use of the crampons. Practice on gentle and moderate slopes helps develop skill, confidence, and

Fig. 14–11. Cutting pigeonhole steps

the aggressive approach needed at steeper angles.

A skilled ice climber, whether flat-footing or front-pointing, displays the same deliberate movement as a skilled rock climber on a difficult slab. The crampon points must be carefully and deliberately placed on the ice, the weight transferred from one foot to the other smoothly and decisively.

Boldness is essential to skillful cramponing. Exposure must be disregarded and concentration focused solely on the climbing. But boldness is not blind bravado. It is confidence and skill born of time and enthusiasm, nurtured in many practice sessions on glacial seracs and on ice bulges in frozen gullies, and matured by ascents of increasing length and difficulty. (See Appendix 2 for an explanation of rating systems that are used in assessing the difficulty of ice climbs.)

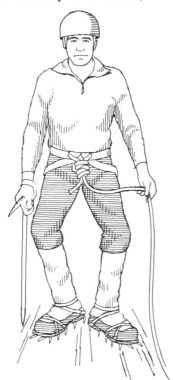

Fig. 14–13. French technique: duck walk combined with ice axe in cane position (pied en canard/piolet canne).

Gentle to moderate slopes

French technique (flat-footing)

Many climbers find flat-footing awkward and needlessly complicated when they first try it. Once mastered, however, it provides great security because it keeps you in balance over your feet, with maximum penetration of all vertical crampon points.

Ankle strain can be eased by pointing your boots downhill more and more as the slope steepens, so the flex needed to keep your feet flat comes from the more normal forward flex of the ankle and from the knees, which are bent away from the slope and spread well apart. Boots that are flexible at the ankle help. In addition, unlacing the upper part of the boot may permit more ankle flex.

Walking on gentle slopes with crampons requires little more technique than walking anywhere else. Keep your feet slightly farther apart than normal to avoid snagging a crampon point on clothing or on a crampon strap on your other foot. Press all bottom points of each crampon firmly into the ice and walk straight forward (in the manner known as *pied marche*, or marching). Use the ice axe in the cane position (*piolet canne*), holding the axe in the self-belay grasp, with the pick forward and your palm on top of the adze.

As the slope steepens slightly, it will begin to get awkward to keep your toes pointing directly uphill. So splay them outward, duck fashion (*pied en canard*). Continue to use the axe as a cane, in *piolet canne* (fig. 14-13).

As the slope gets steeper still, heading straight upward in pied en canard causes severe ankle strain. Then it's time to turn sideways to the slope and ascend diagonally for a more relaxed, comfortable step. Keep the feet flat (*pied à plat*), with all bottom crampon points stamped into the ice (fig. 14-14). Don't try to edge with crampons. Start with your feet pointed in the direction of travel. As the slope steepens, you'll have to rotate your feet more and more downward in order to keep them flat on the ice. On the steepest slopes they may be pointing downhill.

As the slope angle changes from gentle to mod-

Fig. 14–14. French technique, on a diagonal ascent: flat-footing combined with ice axe in cane position (pied à plat/piolet canne).

erate, using the axe in the cane position becomes awkward. You can now get greater security by holding the axe in the cross-body position (*piolet ramasse*), as shown in figure 14-15. Grip the shaft just above the spike with the inside hand and hold the head of the axe in the self-belay grasp, pick pointing forward, with the outside hand. Drive the spike into the ice, the shaft perpendicular to the slope and roughly horizontal across your waist.

In the cross-body position, most of the force on the axe should be at the hand on the shaft. The hand on the head stabilizes the axe and is a reminder not to lean into the slope. You need a full-length ice axe, rather than a shorter ice tool, to keep your body from leaning into the ice. Even experienced ice climbers have difficulty maintaining proper French technique with a short axe.

Move diagonally upward in a two-step sequence, much the same as ascending a snow slope without crampons. Remember to keep your feet flat at all times (fig. 14-15). Start from a position of balance, your inside (uphill) foot in front of

Fig. 14–15. French technique, on a diagonal ascent: flat-footing combined with ice axe in cross-body position (pied à plat/piolet ramasse).

and above the trailing outside (downhill) leg. From this in-balance position, bring the outside foot in front of and above the inside foot, into the out-of-balance position. The outside leg crosses over the knee of the inside leg, because if the cross is made at the ankle, stability is compromised and the next step will be difficult to make. To return to a position of balance, bring the inside foot up from behind and place it again in front of the outside foot. Keep the weight of your body over the crampons. Avoid leaning into the slope and creating the danger of crampon points twisting out of the ice. Step on lower-angled spots and natural irregularities in the ice to ease ankle strain and conserve energy.

During this diagonal ascent, plant the axe about an arm's length ahead of you each time before moving another two steps. Whether you're using the axe in the cane or the cross-body position, plant it far enough forward so that it will be near your hip after you move up to the next in-balance position.

To change direction (switchback) on a diagonal ascent of an ice slope, use the same technique as on a snow slope where you aren't wearing crampons, but keep your feet flat (fig. 14-16). From a position of balance, place the axe directly above your location. Move your outside (downhill) foot forward, into the out-of-balance position, to about the same elevation as the other foot and pointing slightly uphill. Grasping the axe with both hands, turn into the slope, moving your inside (uphill) foot to point in the new direction and slightly uphill. You are now facing into the slope, standing with feet splayed outward. (If the splayed-foot position feels unstable, you can front-point.) Return to the in-balance position by turning your attention to the foot that is still pointing in the old direction. Move this foot above and in front of the other foot. Reposition your grasp on the ice axe, depending on whether you are using the cane or cross-body method. You're now back in balance and facing the new direction of travel.

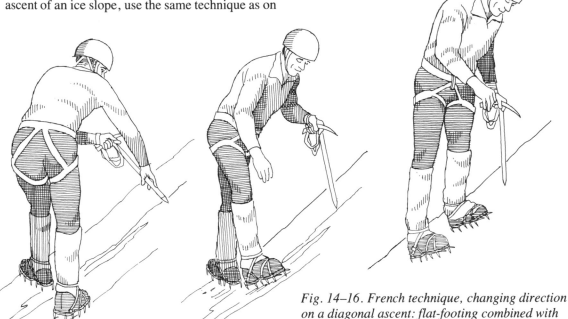

Fig. 14–16. French technique, changing direction on a diagonal ascent: flat-footing combined with ice axe in cross-body position (pied à plat/piolet ramasse).

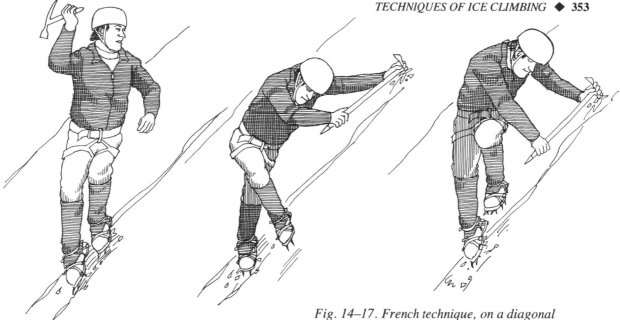

Fig. 14–17. French technique, on a diagonal ascent: flat-footing combined with ice axe in anchor position (pied à plat/piolet ancre).

Moderate to steep slopes

With steeper ice, other variations of the French technique are called for. At some point, the German technique of front-pointing comes into play.

French technique (flat-footing)

On moderate to steep slopes, you can switch the axe from the cross-body position (*piolet ramasse*) to what is known as the anchor position (*piolet ancre*) for more security. Your feet remain flat, with all bottom crampon points stamped into the ice at each step.

To place the axe in *piolet ancre*, begin in a position of balance. Grip the ice-axe shaft just above the spike with your outside (downhill) hand. Swing the axe so that the pick sticks into the ice in front of and above your head, with the shaft parallel to the slope (fig. 14-17a). With your other hand, take hold of the axe head in a self-arrest grasp. Now pull on the axe as you move two steps forward to a new position of balance (fig. 14-17c). A gentle and constant outward pull sets the teeth and keeps the axe locked into the ice. When you're ready to release it, push the shaft toward the ice as you lift the pick up and out.

In order to keep your feet flat at these angles, your body must lean farther away from the slope, knees and ankles flexed, and the toes of your boots will increasingly point downhill. Try to continue advancing upward in the standard sequence, moving two steps at a time. At the steepest angles, however, your feet will be pointing downhill, and you will have to begin shuffling your feet instead, moving backward up the slope. But continue to plant and remove the pick from a position of balance. The foot that is on the same side as your direction of travel should be at least slightly higher than the other foot, allowing the upper body to rotate for a smooth, strong swing of the axe.

You can change diagonal direction when the axe is in the anchor position by using the same sequence as with the cane or cross-body positions. However, on the steepest slopes, where you are shuffling backward, you can change direction simply by switching hands on the axe and planting it on your other side. There won't be much diagonal movement at this point, because you'll mainly be moving backward straight up the slope.

The French also devised a position—called *pied assis*—that gives leg muscles a rest and provides more security for replanting the axe (fig. 14-18). From a position of balance, bring your outside (downhill) foot up and beneath your buttocks, with the boot (flat as always) pointing straight downhill. Then sit down on that foot. You'll discover a balanced position, a relatively comfortable one.

The invaluable technique of flat-footing, used with the ice axe in the cane or cross-body positions, will serve an experienced climber for many alpine routes. For short stretches of steeper ice, flat-footing combined with the ice axe in anchor position will often work, but this marks the upper limit of French technique.

German technique (front-pointing)

On moderate to steep ice slopes, use of the French and German techniques begins to overlap. They both have a place on these slopes.

The French technique (flat-footing) takes a lot of practice to perfect, but most people pick up front-pointing quickly because it feels natural and secure. Unfortunately, this encourages climbers to use it excessively on moderate slopes where flat-footing would be more efficient and just as secure. In flat-footing, most of the stress is on the thigh muscles, where people usually have more strength than in the calf muscles strained by front-pointing. Even climbers who strongly prefer front-pointing would benefit from alternating the techniques to give calf muscles a rest.

Front-pointing uses not only the two forward points of each crampon, but also the two vertical points immediately behind them. These four points, properly placed, provide a platform to stand on.

Synthetic (plastic) boots provide a firm base for crampons and make front-pointing easiest. Full-shank stiff-soled leather boots also are good. Three-quarter-shank boots can be used in some cases, but require more muscular effort, while soft-soled boots are not suitable at all (fig. 14-19).

The best placement of the boot is straight into the ice, avoiding the splayed feet that tend to rotate the outside front points out of the ice. Boot heels need to be level in order to push the first set of vertical points into the ice and complete the four-point platform for standing (fig. 14-20).

Fig. 14–18. French technique: pied assis. The ice climber is using this position for rest and balance.

Fig. 14–19. Problems of trying to front-point with soft-soled boots

Resist the temptation to raise your heels higher. This pulls the stabilizing vertical points from the ice, endangering placement of the front points and fatiguing calf muscles. Your heels will normally feel lower than they really are, so if you think your heels are too low, the odds are that they are in the correct horizontal position. This is especially important coming over the top of steep ice onto a gentler slope, where the natural tendency is to raise your heels, relax your level of concentration, and hurry. This is a formula for trouble because it could cause the crampon points to shear from the ice.

Except in extremely hard ice, a firm, deliberate kick is usually enough to make sharp points bite. Kicking too hard or too often wastes energy and may shatter the ice. After placing the points, avoid foot movement because it can make them rotate out of the ice.

Front-pointing encompasses a selection of ice-axe positions.

Low-dagger *(piolet panne)*: This position is helpful in tackling a short, relatively steep section that requires only a few quick front-pointing moves. For *piolet panne*, hold the axe by the adze in the self-belay grasp and push the pick into the ice near your waist, to aid balance (fig. 14-21). This position tends to hold you away from the

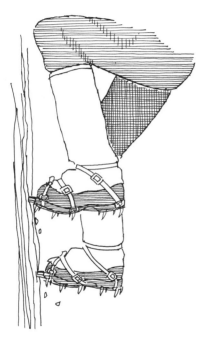

Fig. 14–20. Correct boot position in front-pointing

Fig. 14–21. Front-pointing, with axe in low-dagger position (piolet panne)

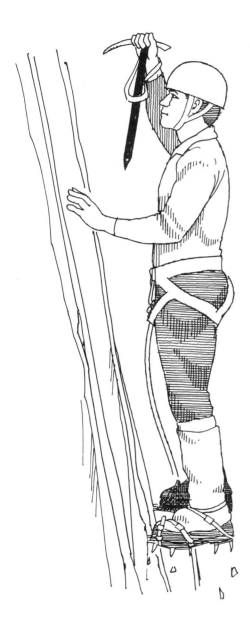

Fig. 14–22. Front-pointing, with axe in high-dagger position (piolet poignard)

slope and out over your feet, the correct stance for front-pointing.

High-dagger *(piolet poignard):* If the slope is a bit too steep to insert the pick effectively into the ice at waist level, in low-dagger, move it into the high-dagger position (fig. 14-22). For this method, hold your hand on the axe head the same as if you were in self-arrest and jab the pick into the ice above your shoulder. Use the high-dagger in hard snow or relatively soft ice that the pick can penetrate easily.

Anchor position *(piolet ancre):* For harder ice or a steeper slope, you can abandon the high-dagger position for the anchor position that is also used in flat-footing. As you stand on front points, hold the axe shaft near the end and swing the pick in as high as possible (fig. 14-23). Front-point upward, holding on higher and higher on the shaft as you progress, adding a self-arrest grasp on the adze with the other hand when you get high enough. Finally, switch hands on the adze, converting to the low-dagger position. When the adze is at waist level, it's time to remove it from the ice and replant it higher.

Piolet traction: The steepest and hardest ice calls for piolet traction (fig. 14-24). The axe is held near the spike and planted high; the ice is then climbed by pulling down on the axe as you front-point up.

It becomes necessary to use a second ice tool on very hard or extremely steep ice when it gets too difficult to balance on your front points while replanting the axe. It's possible to use two tools at the same time because, except for the anchor position, all ice-axe techniques associated with front-pointing require only one hand.

Using two tools provides three points of support—two crampons and one ice tool—as you replant the other tool. The placements must be secure enough that if one point of support fails, the other two will hold you until the third point is replaced. The legs carry most of the weight, but the arms help with both weight and balance.

In double-tool technique, you can use the same ice-axe method for both hands or a different method for each. For instance, you can climb with

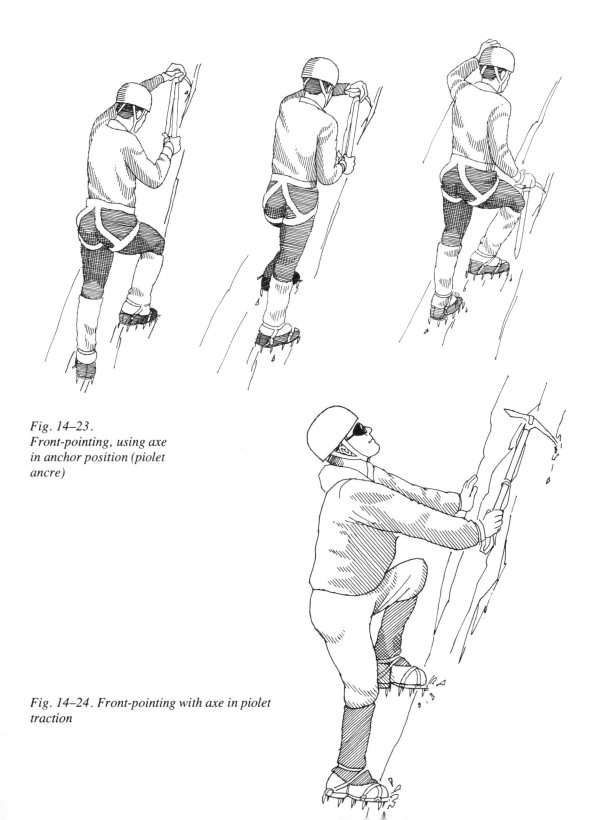

Fig. 14–23.
Front-pointing, using axe
in anchor position (piolet
ancre)

Fig. 14–24. Front-pointing with axe in piolet
traction

both tools in low-dagger (*piolet panne*), as shown in figure 14-25. Or you can place one tool in high-dagger (*piolet poignard*) and the other in *piolet traction*, as shown in figure 14-26. The upcoming section on vertical ice spells out details of double-tool technique using traction with both tools.

Combination techniques

One fast and powerful technique combines flat-footing and front-pointing. It's called the three-o'clock position because as one foot is front-pointing, the other is flat and points to the side (to three o'clock if it's your right foot, or nine o'clock if it's your left). The French term for the position is *pied troisiéme* (fig. 14-27), literally "third foot."

Pied troisiéme is a potent resource for a direct line of ascent, much less tiring than front-pointing alone. The position lets you distribute the work over more muscle groups by alternating techniques with each leg. As you climb, seek out irregular flatter spots and any nooks or crannies for flat-foot-

Fig. 14–26. Front-pointing, using piolet traction with the tool in the left hand and high-dagger (piolet poignard) with the tool in the right hand

ing, allowing you to rest calf muscles. With the ice axe, use whatever position is appropriate to the situation.

Climbers alternate crampon techniques depending on ice conditions. Flat-footing is usually more secure on frozen snow, ice crust over snow, and soft or rotten ice, because more crampon points dig into the surface. For soft snow over ice or hard snow, front-pointing or the three-o'clock position lets you blast through the surface to get points into the firmer layer beneath. Front-pointing is often the most secure technique for the average climber to use with very hard ice on all but gentle slopes. If you are having serious problems on a climb with flat-footing—perhaps due to fatigue, winds, high altitude, or fear—switch to front-pointing or the three-o'clock position.

Fig. 14–25. Front-pointing, using low-dagger position (piolet panne) with two tools

Fig. 14–27. Three-o'clock position (pied troisiéme)

Vertical ice

The basic method of climbing vertical ice is front-pointing combined with use of two ice tools in piolet traction, in which you pull down on both tools as you ascend (fig. 14-28).

The standard position for the feet is about shoulder width apart and level with each other, a stable and relatively comfortable stance. Reach up and plant the pick of one ice tool as high as possible—but off to the side a bit so you're not hit by dislodged ice or by a tool that comes loose. Then plant the other tool, in the same manner.

From the back, your body at this point resembles an "X" against the ice wall. Your feet are level with each other, heels slightly down, and your arms are straight. As you pull down on the tools, also pull slightly outward to keep their teeth set in the ice and apply inward pressure on the

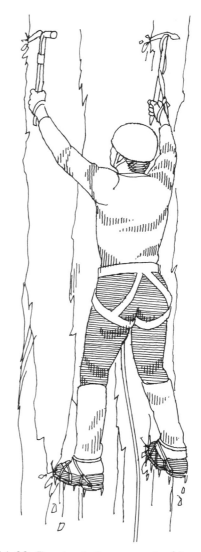

Fig. 14–28. Front-pointing on vertical ice, piolet traction with two tools

crampon points. You can liken this to a mild lie-back on rock. To conserve energy, you can now hang your weight from the wrist loops rather than gripping the tools tightly.

To ascend, grasp the tools and pull yourself higher as you step upward on the front points to a new level position. You're now ready to replant the ice tools higher, one at a time, returning you to the X body position. Repeat this sequence. Concentrate on efficient, methodical placement of crampon points and hand tools. Rhythm is as important as balance.

To overcome ice bulges and small overhangs, you can try the monkey hang (fig. 14-29). Starting from the X body position, walk your front points up the ice without raising your body. Loosen—but do not remove—one of the hand tools. Rise to a standing or nearly standing position by pushing with your feet and pulling on the tools, and in one smooth, continuous motion, remove and replant the loosened tool. Quickly rest that arm by relaxing the hand and letting the arm hang from the tool's wrist loop. Loosen and replant the other

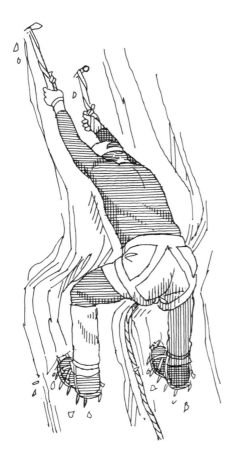

Fig. 14–29. The monkey hang

tool. You're now back in the X body position, ready to repeat the sequence.

Traversing steep to vertical ice

The principles for traversing are much the same as for front-pointing up steep ice. However, because you're moving to the side instead of straight up, it's more difficult to keep one foot perpendicular to the ice as you replace the front points of the other foot. If the heel rotates, the front points will also rotate and come out of the ice. Hand tools also tend to rotate out in sideways travel.

Start from a secure position—feet on the same level, with front points and hand tools in place (fig. 14-30). Replant the leading tool in the ice at about a 45-degree angle from your body. This puts it lower than if you were ascending, but not so far to the side that it causes your body to rotate out from the wall as soon as you remove the trailing tool. With the leading tool in place, you can shuffle sideways on front points. You also have the option of making a two-step move, crossing the trailing foot over the leading foot, and then bringing the other foot back into the lead. Most climbers prefer the shuffle, which is less awkward and feels more secure. After moving your feet, replant the trailing tool closer to your body. In good ice, the trailing tool can often be securely planted in a hole left by the leading tool—especially if the first tool leaves a small hole that can serve as a starter for a larger-nosed second tool.

Descending

Flat-footing

To descend gently sloping ice, simply face directly downhill, bend the knees slightly, and walk firmly downward (*pied marche*). Plant all bottom crampon points into the ice with each step. Hold the axe in the cane position (*piolet canne*).

As the descent angle steepens, bend your knees more and spread them apart, with body weight over your feet so all crampon points bite securely (fig. 14-31). Thigh muscles do the bulk of the work. For greater security, plant the axe perpendicular to the slope in the cross-body position (*piolet ramasse*), as shown in figure 14-32.

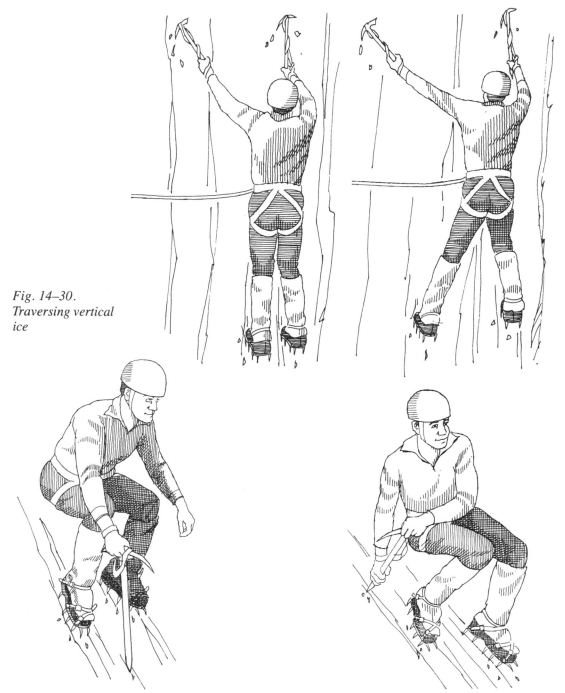

*Fig. 14–30.
Traversing vertical
ice*

*Fig. 14–31. Flat-footing on descent, with ice axe
in cane position (piolet canne)*

*Fig. 14–32. Flat-footing on descent, with ice axe
in the cross-body position (piolet ramasse)*

For the next level of security, use the axe in the support position (*piolet appui*), as shown in figure 14-33. Here's how to do it: grasp the axe near the middle of the shaft and hold it beside you as you descend. The axe head points uphill, with the pick down and the spike downhill.

As the slope steepens, switch the axe to the bannister position (*piolet rampe*), as shown in figure 14-34. To do this, grasp the axe near the end of the shaft. Swing the axe to plant the pick as far below as possible. Walk downward, sliding your hand along the shaft toward the head of the axe. It's important to maintain a slight outward pull on the shaft to keep the pick locked in the ice. Keep moving down until you are below the axe head.

Then push the shaft against the ice to help release the pick, and replant the axe farther down.

On a slope too steep to safely descend facing outward, turn sideways and descend diagonally. Your footwork changes to the same flat-foot technique used to ascend diagonally. Use the axe in the anchor position (*piolet ancre*), as shown in figure

Fig. 14–34. Flat-footing on descent, with ice axe in the bannister position (piolet rampe)

Fig. 14–33. Flat-footing on descent, with ice axe in the support position (piolet appui)

14-35. With your outside arm, swing the axe out in front and plant the pick in the ice, take hold of the head with the other hand in the self-arrest grasp, and then flat-foot diagonally down below the axe. The shaft rotates as you pass below it.

Front-pointing

It's often tiring and ineffective to try front-pointing down a gentle to moderate slope. A climber tends to be bent over, facing the moderate slope, and to vacillate between flat-foot and front-point technique.

On steep slopes, front-point and hand-tool techniques are generally the same for going down as for going up. But just as on rock, downclimbing is more difficult. There is a tendency to step too low, which keeps the heel too high, so front points may

Fig. 14–35. Flat-footing on descent, with ice axe in the anchor position (piolet ancre)

shear out or fail to penetrate in the first place. It's awkward to plant the ice tools because they must be placed closer to your body, so you lose the power of a good full swing. You don't get a good view of the route on a descent (although descending on a slight diagonal will help).

Climbers don't often front-point a descent, but it's still a valuable skill for occasions such as retreating from a route. Downclimbing ability also builds confidence in ascending.

Rappelling

Ice climbers often descend on rappel, sliding down a doubled rope attached through an anchor, just as in rock climbing. They use natural anchors whenever possible, of course, because snow flukes or other manufactured anchors used for rappelling usually must be left behind, a costly way to go.

PLACING ICE TOOLS

With any ice tool, the goal is accuracy and a solid placement—the first time. One or two swings saved at the bottom of a pitch mean that much more energy at the top. It takes a lot of practice to learn pinpoint placement. But with a combination of proper technique and equipment, you should be able to place a tool easily and precisely, keep it secure for as long as it's needed, and extract it with less effort than you took to place it (fig. 14-36).

Study the ice for a good placement. A slight depression above and slightly to the side is likely to be good. Ice is more compact and holds the pick better in depressions than in bulges, which shatter or break off under the impact of an ice tool. Try to make placements in opaque ice, less brittle than clear ice because it has more air trapped inside. Minimize the number of placements by planting the axe as high as possible and by moving upward as far as you can with each placement.

Different climbers will have different experiences, though they may be using identical tools on the same climb, because of differences in ability and climbing background. The more experienced climber, for instance, may climb confidently with only a small bite of the pick into the ice, while another climber might not feel comfortable without

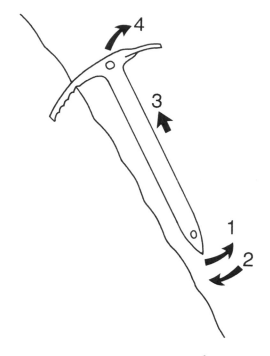

Fig. 14–36. How to remove an ice tool

slamming the tool deep. On most tools, only the first few teeth provide any useful bite in the ice, and the upward angle of the pick in the ice provides most of the holding power. (On an ice tool, small teeth often perform better than large teeth.) Keep your tools sharp.

Placement and removal techniques will vary somewhat, depending on the type of pick that is on the ice tool:

Technically curved: These picks result in an ice tool that is most like a standard ice axe. However, the picks are curved more than on a regular axe to hold better in ice, and the shaft is shorter to permit an easier swing on steep surfaces. A tool with a technically curved pick requires a natural swing, from the shoulder. The first swing should result in a satisfying, solid "thunk"—the sound and feel of a well-placed ice tool. This tool is used in conditions ranging from soft serac ice to hard water ice, though you may need to weight a lighter tool (perhaps with lead sheet taped to the head) for good penetration on hard ice. The pick is usually removed from the ice by lifting straight up on the shaft.

Reverse curved: While technically curved picks take a natural swing, the sharp angles of the reverse-curved and straight-drooped picks require a shorter, choppy swing. A reverse-curved pick, featuring a drooped pick with a slight upward curve, penetrates waterfall ice with a straight, downward hooking motion. It is usually easy to remove.

Straight drooped: This sharply angled pick re-quires a decisive downward flick at the end of a short swing, making it penetrate well in ice from soft to hard. It is fairly easy to remove by using an up-and-down levering motion. Avoid sideways twisting.

Tubular: A tubular-nosed tool works best with a short-arc swing and often grips securely on the first try. A tubular pick is moderately easy to re-move by twisting sideways while holding the head (up-and-down levering can fracture the nose). The nose dents easily and is particularly vulnerable if the climb involves ice with sand or rocks close to the surface.

ROPED CLIMBING TECHNIQUES

Climbers usually rope up on ice. The principal exception comes when they decide that overall team safety is served best by climbing unroped. Late on a stormy day, for example, or while as-cending a couloir threatened by rockfall, the greater speed of unroped travel might offer rela-tively more safety than continuing on the rope. It is also sensible to unrope through a section so diffi-cult to protect that a fall by one roped climber would sweep them both away.

Ice climbers can get a measure of protection that is somewhere between climbing on belay and climbing unroped by setting up a running belay. It's another way for a team to move faster when storms or avalanches threaten and, more than ever, speed is safety. It can also be useful on gentle to moderate terrain where danger of falling is minimal and actual belays would be too time-consuming.

A running belay on ice is created very much the same as a running belay on rock (described in Chapter 10) or snow (described and illustrated in Chapter 12). Team members move simul-taneously. The leader places protection as they climb and clips the rope through it; the follower removes the protection. The idea is to keep at least two points of protection between them at all times to hold the rope in case of a fall. Because this technique sacrifices much of the safety of true belaying, the decision to use it takes fine judg-ment, based on extensive experience.

Full belaying on ice requires a belayer, belay anchor, and intermediate points of protection, just as it does on snow or rock. A belay anchor is set up and the leader climbs the pitch on belay, sets up another anchor, and then belays the follower up the route. The climbers can either swing leads or have a single climber continue as the leader.

PROTECTION ON ICE

Modern ice screws offer dependable security on ice climbs. However, there is some sacrifice of safety in the time and energy it takes to put them in place. Leaders, therefore, commonly place fewer points of protection in a rope length on ice than they would in a rock pitch of the same length. Ice climbers also make some use of natural protection.

Natural protection

Ready-made natural protection is hard to come by on an alpine ice route, although climbers make use of the medium to fashion ice bollards. Good natural protection may be available not on the ice itself, but in rock bordering the route or protruding through the ice.

Natural protection is often found on frozen wa-terfalls, where runners can be placed around ice columns. Climbers also devise some slightly un-conventional protection points. On frozen water-falls or high alpine routes, where large ice columns may form only an inch or two apart, an ice screw tied off with webbing can be inserted behind the columns and turned sideways as a deadman. You may find a sheet of ice separated from the underlying rock by an inch or two, leaving a slit that can be enlarged enough to insert a screw tied off with webbing; again, turn the screw sideways to function as a deadman. You can also punch two holes in the sheet of ice, thread a runner through them, and clip the rope into it. On mixed rock and ice climbs, rock-climbing chocks may be wedged into ice holes.

Ice bollards

A bollard can be among an ice climber's most useful anchors. It can be used for rappelling or belaying. By linking together two bollards, one cut for an upward pull and the other for a downward pull, you have a multidirectional anchor. The strength of a bollard is proportional to its size and the hardness of the ice. Made of hard, solid ice, it can be stronger than the rope.

A completed ice bollard is teardrop-shaped when viewed from above, and horn-shaped when viewed from the side (fig. 14-37). All you need for a bollard is an ice axe and good ice, uniform and without cracks or holes. Cut the outline of the bollard with the axe pick. In hard ice, give it a diameter of 12 to 18 inches (30 to 45 centimeters) across the wide end of the teardrop. Cut a trench around the bollard at least 6 inches (15 centimeters) deep, working outward from the outline with both the pick and the adze.

Undercut the sides and top half of the bollard to form a horn that prevents the rope from popping off over the top. This is the most sensitive part of the construction because you can easily fracture or break the bollard if you're careless with the axe.

Ice screws

A favorable location for an ice-screw placement is the same as for an ice tool. A good choice is a natural depression, where fracture lines caused by the screw are not as likely to reach the surface (fig. 14-38a).

A screw placed into a bulge in the ice, on the other hand, can cause serious fracturing that weakens the placement or makes it useless. If this happens, move the screw a foot or two and try again. Generally keep screw placements at least 2 feet apart—more in rotten ice—to reduce chances that fracture lines from one placement could reach the other, weakening both.

The procedures for placing a screw vary somewhat with ice conditions, but the basic routine is

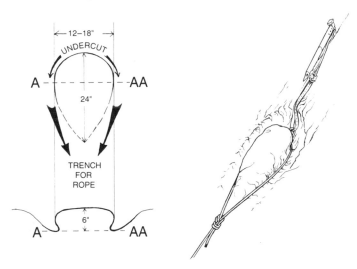

Fig. 14–37. Ice bollard: a, diagram; b, with backup ice-tool anchor.

much the same in any case: punch out a small starting hole with the pick or spike of a hand tool, to give a good grip for the starting threads or teeth of the screw. Make the hole gently, with light taps, to avoid fracturing the ice. Start the screw in the hole, angled uphill 45 to 60 degrees against the anticipated direction of pull. (On hard ice, it may take a few light taps to make the threads catch.)

On ice topped with a layer of soft snow or rotten ice, scrape down with the adze to get to a hard, trustworthy surface before making the starting hole (fig. 14-38b). In extremely rotten ice, make a large horizontal step with a hand tool and place the screw vertically at the back of the step, in a starting hole (fig. 14-38c). Press the screw firmly and twist it into the ice at the same time.

When glacier ice fractures and shatters at the surface, you may still be able to get a secure placement by continuing to install the screw and gently

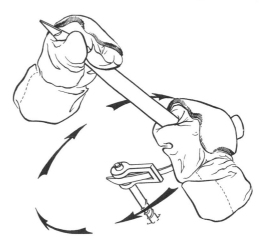

Fig. 14–39. Screwing in an ice screw with an ice tool

chopping out the shattered ice with sideways strokes of the pick.

A screw with sharp cutting teeth can sometimes be screwed in all the way by hand. If not, do it with the help of a lever through the screw eye; another ice screw or the pick of a hand tool works well (fig. 14-39). Some screws provide a kind of built-in ratcheting capability, simplifying the work of screwing them in.

Twist the screw all the way until the eye is against the ice, tight and solid. Clip a carabiner into the eye, with the carabiner gate down and out. To slow melt-out in soft summer ice or direct sun, pack ice around the screw head. If the screw doesn't go in all the way, reduce leverage on it by tying it off at the surface of the snow with a runner, and then clipping into the runner.

Climbing extremely steep ice is fatiguing, physically and mentally. To conserve energy and keep moving upward efficiently, climbers work to minimize the number of screw placements. If the ice is hard and solid, or the slope not extremely steep, only one or two protection points may be placed on an entire pitch. Unless the ice is rotten, only one screw is placed at each protection point.

It usually takes two hands to place an ice screw, ticklish business on extremely steep, exposed ice. For extra support, you can slip one arm through the

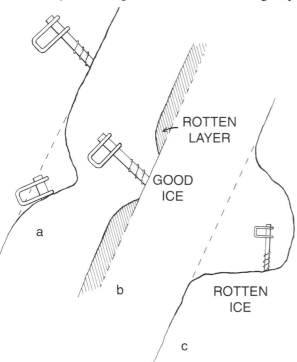

ROTTEN LAYER

GOOD ICE

ROTTEN ICE

a

b

c

Fig. 14–38. Ice-screw placements: a, in solid surface; b, with soft or rotten surface layer; c, in extremely rotten ice.

Fig. 14–40. Support from hand tools while placing an ice screw: a, through wrist leashes; b, from runners between tools and seat harness.

wrist loop of a solidly planted hand tool (fig. 14-40a). Or clip a runner from your seat harness to one or two securely placed hand tools (fig. 14-40b).

On a moderate to steep slope, it may help to chop a step for standing in as you place the screw. On extremely steep ice, however, it's too difficult a job, so save your energy. When it's time to place an ice screw, do it from your front points, and then continue climbing.

BELAYING ON ICE

Near the end of a pitch that you are leading, keep an eye out for a good belay spot, perhaps at a slight depression or where the ice is not so steep. Place a hand tool off to one side and clip in for temporary protection while you chop a step large enough to permit you to stand facing the ice with both feet flat and splayed.

Belay anchors

A standard anchor set-up for an ice belay takes two ice screws. Place the first screw in the ice in front of you, a bit to one side, at about waist to chest level. Clip in a carabiner and tie into it with the climbing rope as it comes from your seat harness. Use a clove hitch or figure-8 knot.

Unclip from the hand tool that was placed as a temporary anchor and replant that tool above and to the outside of the ice screw. Clip the tool to the screw (via the wrist leash or a runner) as a backup to the anchor. Then tell your belayer down below that you are off belay.

Now you can place the second ice screw. Put it

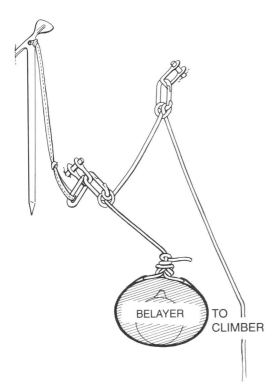

Fig. 14–41. Anchor set-up for an ice belay

above you and about 2 or 3 feet higher than the first one. Extend the climbing rope from the first screw to the second screw and tie in with a clove hitch. There should be little or no slack between the two screws. This completes the anchor set-up (fig. 14-41).

The next step in establishing your belay is to clip another carabiner into the second ice screw and clip the belay rope through the carabiner. This directs the pull from the climber through this screw. And after the follower ascends to the belay station and starts upward to take the lead, that screw becomes the first piece of protection on the new pitch.

Belay methods

You have the choice of using a mechanical belay device, a Münter hitch, or a hip belay. The anchor set-up is the same in any case. Your choice will probably depend on what you're accustomed to and on your degree of confidence in the anchor. The hip belay tends to be somewhat dynamic, with a bit of movement at the belay—resulting in a slower stop to a fall but less force on the anchor and intermediate protection points. Belay devices and the Münter hitch, on the other tend, tend to be less dynamic, stopping a fall faster but putting more force on the anchor and intermediate protection points. (See Chapter 7 for details on the various belay methods.)

Mechanical devices

A Münter hitch, or a belay device such as a slot, tube, or Bachli, is easy to set up and efficient in use. Many ice climbers use such a method as standard procedure. The mechanism is usually situated at your seat harness (fig. 14-42), though you also have the option of belaying directly from the anchor.

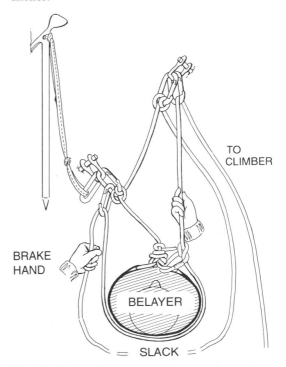

Fig. 14–42. Ice belay set-up for a mechanical belay device or Münter hitch at the climber's seat harness

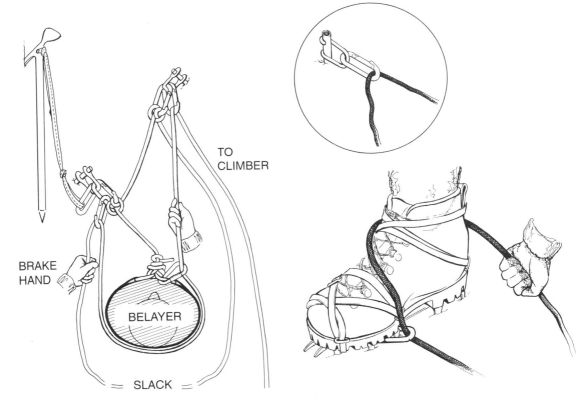

Fig. 14–43. Ice belay set-up for a hip belay

Fig. 14–44. Boot/ice-screw belay

Hip belay

You can establish a hip belay as you stand facing the ice by running the belay rope through a control carabiner at your waist, around your back, through an extra carabiner on the first screw, and then into your braking hand (fig. 14-43). This arrangement is especially favored when the rope is stiff and frozen and could jam in belay devices.

Boot/ice-screw belay

For flat or gentle ice slopes, the boot/ice-screw belay is very useful (fig. 14-44). Here's how to do it: start by twisting an ice screw into place, then clip in a carabiner and run the belay rope through the carabiner. Plant your uphill boot over the screw, perpendicular to the direction of pull. Place the boot so that the inside point of your mid-boot row of crampons goes through the carabiner. Don't

jab the rope. Bring the belay end of the rope over your instep, around the back of your boot ankle, and into your uphill hand.

You control friction on the rope by the amount of wrap on the ankle, much as in a boot-axe belay. You can also adjust the space between the edge of the boot and the outside edge of the carabiner. If the climber falls, slowly tighten the rope low against the ankle with your uphill hand.

Helpful variations of the boot/ice-screw belay include two that utilize the Münter hitch. Use a large pear-shaped carabiner, which has the correct diameter for the Münter, instead of a standard carabiner. In one method, simply use a Münter hitch at the carabiner instead of running the belay rope around your ankle (fig. 14-45). Another method permits you to operate the belay while standing (fig. 14-46).

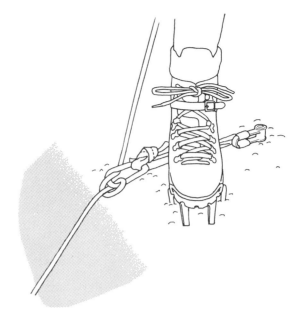

Fig. 14–45. Boot/ice-screw belay using Münter hitch

Fig. 14–46. Boot/ice-screw belay using Münter hitch while standing

THE ICE CLIMBER

To climb steep ice, you'll use a lot of what you learned in rock and snow climbing and add in the special tools and techniques for ice. As an ice climber, you will especially share the joys of snow climbing, along with its perils: avalanches, hazardous couloirs, and unstable cornices, ice blocks, and icefalls. (Chapter 12 provides a full catalog of snow-climbing dangers and how to avoid them.) You can find climbing opportunities year-around, from the winter challenge of waterfall ice on short dark days in cold weather to the summer experience of alpine ice on days that are long and warm.

Skill and confidence in ice climbing comes from long practice. If you can link up with a steady partner, so much the better. Practice together often. Work on pinpoint ice-tool and crampon placement, which conserves energy so you can meet the rigors of serious routes. Also work to increase the speed and efficiency of your climbing, gearing it to the conditions of the ice and the current strength of your body. Learn to determine when you and your partner should rope up for protection—and when it's safer not to. An experienced ice climber learns these skills and applies them with confidence and good judgment.

· 15 ·

WINTER AND EXPEDITION CLIMBING

Climbers enter a new world of effort and commitment when they take on winter or expedition climbing. There are big differences between the weekend alpine climbing practiced by most climbers and the winter and expeditionary mountaineering of the serious amateur climber or the professional alpine mountaineer. Winter climbing brings severe conditions that require specialized equipment, a high level of skill, and a tremendous will to succeed. Expedition climbing demands the skills of winter climbing in addition to the logistics of an extended trip, often in a foreign country.

The weather takes on a new importance during winter and on expeditions. On a typical weekend summer climb, weather is seldom a big issue. If the weather is poor, you can cancel the climb and try again when it gets better. If the weather turns poor on the climb, a bit of unpleasantry usually gets climbers down from the route and a wet walk brings them back to the trailhead. In the winter, however, good weather is harder to come by and frustrated climbers may give it a try despite a marginal forecast. If the weather does turn poor, descending the route and returning to the cars may become a mini-epic, with routefinding difficulties and increased danger from cornices and avalanches. On expeditions, the climbing team rarely has the luxury to pick and choose the weather. Once the team leaves town, the trip schedule grinds on inexorably and weather be-

comes a condition that must be dealt with like any other obstacle on the trip.

Extremes of hot and cold are common. You expect low temperatures during the winter, but it can get hot, too. On windless, cloudless days the temperature soars as sunlight reflects from the snow. Then, as quickly as a cloud can sail across the sky, the temperature plummets. At night, radiative cooling into a cloudless sky can create temperatures that test the mettle of the finest sleeping bag.

The shorter length of day is another obvious challenge of winter climbing. At the winter solstice, in the higher latitudes, the hours of daylight may be only half the hours available in summer. This means fewer hours for climbing and more hours of sack time in camp waiting for daylight. The winter camp must be made more comfortable for the long hours of waiting, and goals must be scaled back from summer expectations. You may decide to put off the most challenging climbs until late winter, when the day is longer. On expeditions, especially at higher latitudes during the summer, the shortness of day isn't usually a problem. However, climbers often adjust their own internal clocks, traveling in the cooler hours of early morning, late day, or even at night to reduce the problems of soft snow, rockfall, or avalanche.

If your goal is one of the high mountains of the world, acclimatization to the altitude is essential.

Schedules must match not only your ability to climb the route but the ability of your body to meet the rigors of living at high altitudes. More than one climber on the ''dog'' route of a high peak has turned back not because of weather or technical difficulties but because of too rapid an ascent.

To pull off a successful winter climb or expedition, it often takes a lot of extra gear. For a one-day summer rock climb, you may need little more than a rope, rack, lunch, water bottle, and windbreaker. But the pack for even the simplest winter climb is heavier, with more equipment and clothing. The pack for an overnight trip must accommodate a warm sleeping bag for the low temperatures, a comfortable four-season tent for the long nights and more severe weather, and an ample stove and cook kit. An expedition multiplies the amount of food and fuel by the length of the trip. The expedition also may require extra climbing equipment for ''fixing'' parts of the route, leaving ropes in place for the safety of climbers and porters.

Looking at all the special demands of winter and expedition climbing, it's no surprise you need exceptional endurance. This is different than the intense short-term effort made by weekend climbers, who are accustomed to the early Saturday morning drive to the trailhead and the bleary-eyed drive back home Sunday night or early Monday morning. It's the marathon run compared with the 100-yard dash. On an expedition, bursts of intense effort cannot be sustained, as the body does not heal or recover quickly at high altitudes. Team members need to find levels of physical and mental effort they can sustain for the entire trip. Save the climbing ''burnout'' of the weekend climb for the final summit push, and don't waste it on hauling a load between base camp and Camp 1.

Winter travelers often find the season's solitude a virtue of their adventures. Likewise, the expedition climber may cite the distance from civilization as a benefit. With this remoteness comes the need for self-sufficiency. The climbing team must rely on its own resources to get out of a jam because self-rescue is the only option when the nearest help is days or weeks away.

Winter mountaineering and expedition climbing have much in common. Most expeditions are to places where the climbing is decidedly wintery, such as Mount McKinley or the Himalaya. The best way to learn winter climbing is through multiday trips in your own part of the world. These climbs are obviously cheaper and easier to schedule than trips to Alaska or Nepal, but they get you fit and skilled for expedition climbing.

WINTER MOUNTAINEERING

Climbing in winter is a natural extension of climbing at other times of the year, with a lot of similar techniques and equipment and many of the same goals and rewards. It's just more complicated. This chapter goes into a number of topics that were taken up in earlier chapters, such as clothing, tents, and routefinding—but covers them in the specific detail needed to help you stay safe and comfortable in winter.

CLOTHING

Climb often enough in the mountains, and even in the summer you will encounter winterlike conditions. Likewise, many of the best winter climbs are done when the weather resembles spring. Your clothing and equipment must be prepared to accommodate both extremes.

For winter, summer clothing serves as the starting point. Begin with a wicking layer of underwear, followed by whatever layers of insulating clothing the weather dictates, topped off by a windbreaking layer. How much extra clothing you bring, and what kind, depends on the type of winter you can expect at your destination. Additional layers of synthetics work best in the cold damp of maritime climates. Where winter is drier and colder, you can take advantage of the lightness and compactness of down, which must be kept dry.

The dangerous chilling effect of wind means you must always pack a complete layer of windproof clothing during the winter. The wind layer needs to fit over all the insulating layers you are likely to wear at one time, and should overlay or tuck together for a solid shield against the wind. If you've left any chinks in the armor, the wind will find them. Fabrics vary in their windproofness so get recommendations from other climbers and from the people at outdoors stores. Laminated materials such as Gore-Tex are among the most windproof. (Chapter 2 has more information on clothes for mountaineering.)

Keeping dry

On a hot summer day, a sweaty shirt dries quickly in the sun and heat after you've stopped working. But in winter, there is little warmth from the sun to dry out wet clothing. The only other source of heat to dry a shirt is your own body, and tremendous amounts of energy are necessary to evaporate water. Wearing damp clothing is the quickest way to chill yourself.

Avoid dampness by regulating your pace and not allowing yourself to overheat. If clothes get damp, either from perspiration or precipitation, change as soon as camp is reached. If several layers of clothing are damp, at least change the layer closest to your skin.

CARE OF THE FEET

Because of their distance from the body core, extremities have the poorest circulation. To make matters worse for your feet in winter, they are always close to snow or ice. The same factors that keep your body warm—adequate insulation and staying dry—will also warm your feet.

The advent of plastic double boots made it much easier than before to keep your feet warm and dry. The plastic shell is an absolute barrier to snow and water, while the inner boot provides the insulation.

In some circumstances, bunny (or mouse) boots are an option. Developed originally for the military for arctic conditions, bunny boots rely on felt insulation sandwiched between airtight and watertight rubber inner and outer boots. The boot is not rigid and is best suited for non-technical routes. Because the rubber serves as a vapor barrier, keeping perspiration inside, it's necessary to dry your feet and change damp socks daily.

Gaiters are needed for keeping snow from entering the boot from the top. Standard gaiters cover the boot top and lower leg, while supergaiters add an additional layer over the entire boot. Overboots go one step further by including a layer, which quickly sheds snow, below the boot as well. Various brands of supergaiters and overboots offer insulation as well as a snow barrier.

Inside the boot, a vapor barrier sock will keep your foot warmer by preventing perspiration from evaporating. The energy required by evaporation robs warmth from your feet. The vapor barrier also keeps outer socks and boots drier. The sock is worn over a light pair of liner socks and beneath a heavier pair of insulating socks. The major disadvantage to vapor barrier socks is the necessity to change the liner socks and dry your feet each night. Apply foot powder and a strong anti-perspirant (not merely a deodorant) to help keep feet dry and comfortable—and watch out for blisters on the soft, moist skin.

The right socks are important in keeping your feet warm, but too many socks can do just the reverse. They can make the boot tight, restricting circulation and causing cold feet.

HEALTH

Surprisingly, dehydration is a winter hazard. Sweat may not pour from your brow the way it does in summer, but depending on your level of exertion and the dryness of the air, significant moisture loss occurs. Also, fluid intake normally drops because people don't crave cold drinks during the winter. Make a conscious effort to drink enough fluids to keep your urine output copious and clear. This need for fluids highlights the importance of a stove that can dependably melt plenty of snow for drinks.

Hypothermia and frostbite are more traditional winter health hazards. Both can be prevented by awareness of the hazards and by adequate clothing, food, and water. Avoid chills by staying as dry as possible and eating and drinking adequately. If you become chilled, do something about it. Put on more clothes or change damp clothes. If your feet are numb, wiggle your toes vigorously in the boot. If these actions don't work, it may be necessary to take a break to warm the numb body parts. When camp is established, inspect feet and fingers for frostbite and treat as necessary. (There is some general information on frostbite later in this chapter, but be sure to consult a first-aid text for details.)

As a member of a climbing party, you're responsible for taking good care of your own health and guarding against problems that could jeopardize the climb or endanger fellow climbers. At the same time, keep alert to any health problems of other team members.

WINTER CAMPING

Winter camping, more so than summer camping, demands well-developed rituals and habits. Efficiency and safety get a boost if everyone is familiar with their assignments. A tent goes up quickly and easily if two or three members of the party know exactly who does what: who holds the tent to keep it from blowing away, who threads poles through the sleeves, and who pushes the poles. Here's a look at the principal techniques and equipment that go into successful winter camping.

Snow shovels

The snow shovel (fig. 15-1) is a fundamental piece of equipment for the winter mountaineer, used to excavate climbers from avalanche debris, dig emergency shelters, prepare tent platforms, and—in some conditions—clear a climbing route. In choosing a shovel, a climber is torn between the heavy, bulky grain scoop, ideal for moving large amounts of snow quickly, and the compact folding or collapsing shovel, convenient to carry and therefore less likely to be left at home. A large party has the strength to carry both types. A small party will want to examine the route and expected uses before deciding which type or how many to take. If you expect to cut any sort of snow blocks for snow constructions, you will also need a snow saw.

Shelters

For overnight winter trips, you can stay in a tent or in a snow shelter. Tents are much easier to set up, but a good snow shelter is much sturdier. Both

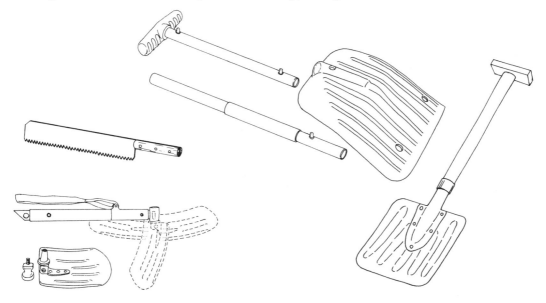

Fig. 15–1. Snow construction tools

have their virtues depending on the situation, and you should know how to set up either one.

Snow shelters

A well-made snow shelter is far more secure than a tent. In a storm, as the snow piles up, the snow shelter becomes even more secure while the tent must be continually cleared of snow. Sometimes a snow shelter is the only possibility, such as on a narrow, windy ridge with no space for a tent. A snow shelter requires no special equipment other than a shovel and, sometimes, a snow saw.

Even if you use tents for sleeping, a snow shelter is a useful addition for an extended stay in one spot. The snow shelter can be the communal hall where cooking and socializing take place without fear of spilling soup on a sleeping bag or tearing a hole in a tent wall. The extra shelter also serves as a warehouse for equipment and a place of refuge if a tent fails in extreme conditions.

On the negative side, snow shelters take time to build; 2 to 3 hours is common. If you'll only be there one night, it may not be worth the effort. Building a snow shelter is hard work and may leave the building crew wet from perspiration and from the snow. In some circumstances a snow shelter is warmer than a tent. But if it's midday and the sun is out, the inside of a tent can be 40 or 50 degrees warmer than the outside air, and makes a great place for drying sleeping bags and clothing.

There are pluses and minuses to a number of snow-shelter designs. Check back to Chapter 3 for a look at how to build some of them.

Snow caves require both adequate snow depth and the right topography. Look for a fairly steep slope to dig into; it's much easier than trying to dig a cave into a shallow slope. The snow must be deep enough so you won't hit ground before you can excavate a cave that's large enough.

With igloos, the depth of the snow is not as critical because they are constructed of snow blocks. Therefore it's usually easier to build an igloo with lots of space and headroom than a roomy snow cave. In addition to a shovel, igloo construction requires a snow saw, experience in the art of igloo building, and good block-cutting snow. If the snow isn't just right, and the snow blocks fall apart as you move them, forget about building an igloo.

You can also create hybrid snow shelters, combining igloo and snow-cave techniques. To make a typical hybrid shelter, dig into a snow slope through a relatively large opening; this makes it easy to excavate snow. When the cave is big enough, close the opening over with snow blocks. Then dig a smaller entrance for access to the shelter. Various types of trenches also provide shelter in the snow. (Chapter 3 also has details on snow trenches.)

Snow-shelter construction is a useful skill and it can be fun, but for short winter trips these shelters are not usually practical to build. It is on longer trips, where the investment in the snow shelter can be amortized over several nights or where conditions are too extreme for a tent, that snow shelters are most valuable.

Tents

Tents are the first choice in shelters for the typical weekend winter outing. A quality winter tent must be sturdy enough to withstand high winds and snow dumped during the night. Steep side walls aid in clearing snow off the tent, and an aerodynamic shape helps outwit the wind. Free-standing dome-type tents work well, and so do the tunnel-style (hoop) tents, which require a few stakes (fig. 15-2). Every winter tent, free-standing or not, needs multiple lashing points for tying into anchors to keep it from taking off like a box kite in a strong gust. The considerations that go into selecting and using a good winter tent apply likewise to tents used for expeditions.

Size: For extreme routes, where flat real estate is rare and weight is a supreme consideration, consider the compact and lightweight ''wedge'' tent, a free-standing design with two poles that go from corner to corner and cross in the middle. On most winter trips, however, you will want a tent that is roomy, though heavy. The extra room is used to store packs and personal gear as well as reduce feelings of claustrophobia during 15-hour nights in the tent.

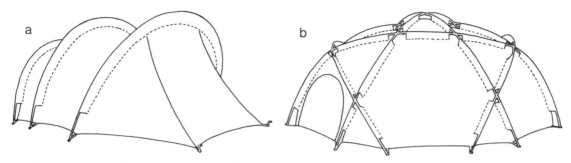

Fig. 15–2. Winter-quality tents: a, hoop style; b, dome.

Construction: Although single-walled tents of rainproof, breathable fabric are lighter, double-walled tents (with an integral or separate rain fly) are somewhat warmer and less subject to icing on the inside wall. Aluminum tent poles are usually stronger than fiberglass poles. High-tech poles of such materials as Kevlar or carbon fiber may some-day supplant aluminum.

Features: Certain conveniences simplify wintertime tent living. These include multiple entrances (in case one entrance bears the brunt of the weather), a vestibule for cooking or storage, gear pockets inside the tent for organizing small items, and inside loops for hanging clothes or a lantern.

You can't pitch a tent without giving some thought first to selecting and preparing a site. Some tips:

Use the terrain to your advantage. Select a spot that is as near to flat as possible to make site preparation easier. Watch out for hazards such as crevasses, avalanche paths, and cornices. Observe the local wind patterns: a rock-hard or sculpted snow surface indicates frequent wind, while a loose powdery area indicates a zone where wind-transported snow is deposited. Keep in mind that although the powdery area may be protected from the direct wind, the tent may have to be cleared of snow frequently.

Compact a large-enough area for the tent and for movement around the tent to check tie lines or clear snow. Flatten and smooth the tent platform thoroughly to keep you from sliding toward one wall or the other during the night and to get rid of any uncomfortable lumps. This is especially im-portant if you're staying for several nights, because the entire tent platform becomes rock hard with all features cast in ice after the first night. A ski does a great job of smoothing the tent platform.

Dig an entrance pit 1 foot or so deep once the tent is erected. The pit in front of the main tent door makes entering and leaving easier, as you can sit comfortably in the doorway and place your feet in the pit.

Build snow walls around the tent if the site is exposed to winds. The walls can be anywhere from about 3 to 6 feet high and will deflect some of the wind away from the tent (fig. 15-3). Keep the walls as far away from the tent as they are high (a 3-foot wall, for example, should be 3 feet away from the tent), because wind will deposit snow on the leeward side of the walls and fill this area quickly. Blocks cut by a snow saw make the easi-est, quickest walls, though you can also just shovel snow into a pile to serve as a wall.

A number of special items are useful in winter camping. Each tent should have a snow brush—a small broom with synthetic bristles to sweep snow from boots, packs, clothing, and the tent. Each tent also needs a sponge for cleaning up cooking or drinking-cup spills and removing condensation from the inside tent walls. A cheery addition to a tent, especially during the long nights near the winter solstice, is a candle lantern. You might even consider a gas lantern, which can repay its price in weight and bother by bringing tremendous bright-ening and warming to a tent.

For anchoring a tent, you can use wide-profile stakes, mini snow flukes, or regular snow anchors.

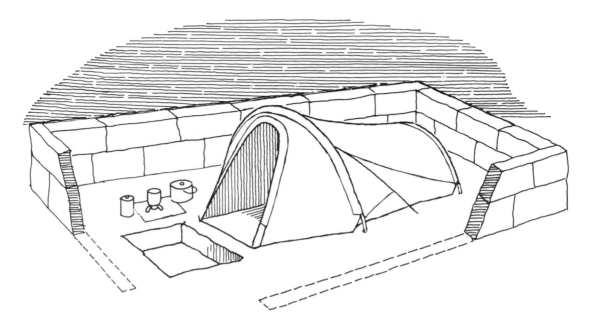

Fig. 15–3. Typical winter camp: kitchen area, snow walls, and well-placed tent.

Skis, ski poles, ice axes, and such also work well. Of course, whatever you use to hold down the tent won't be available for other uses. Tie the tent to a tree if there is one nearby.

To help make your winter tent-bound hours more pleasant, you need some house rules. They will depend on the weather, the size of the tent, and the experience of the occupants. For example, a small tent may mean that packs stay outside. If the tent is large enough and packs are brought inside, they should be thoroughly brushed of snow first. House rules may dictate that boots be taken off outside, brushed of snow, and placed in a waterproof boot bag inside the tent. Boots can bring in snow, and they also can cut or tear holes in the tent floor. Use stuff sacks or a large personal tent sack to help you organize and protect personal gear and keep it out of the way of your tentmates. It often helps to have one person enter the tent first to lay sleeping pads and organize gear before others enter.

During a storm, you'll face the necessary chore of keeping snow cleared away from the tent. In most storms, it isn't the snow falling from the sky that creates the problem, but rather the snow carried by the wind. Nature desires a smooth snow surface with minimal obstructions to impede the wind. When the wind encounters an obstruction, such as your tent or snow wall, wind-transported snow will be deposited in a way that minimizes its impact on the wind. Snow is deposited on the leeward side of tents and snow walls, and the tent begins to be buried. Even a partially buried tent poses the risk of asphyxiation, especially if you are cooking in the tent. Clear the snow regularly from around the tent. (Avoid cutting the tent with the shovel. Nylon cuts easily when it is tensioned by a snow load.)

In a severe or prolonged storm, your tent may begin to disappear into the hole created by neighboring snowdrifts. You may need to move the tent up on top of the new snow surface.

Stoves

As with winter tents, a stove suitable for winter must be tougher and more capable than a stove relegated to summer use. In addition to heating food, it is used to melt pots full of snow, providing your only reliable source of water. The stove must have a high heat output in order to melt snow quickly, stability so that it supports a full pot of snow, and relative ease of repairing when this becomes necessary. It also must operate well at low temperatures (which pretty much rules out self-pressurizing white gas stoves, which do not have a pump).

The most popular stove fuels are white gas, kerosene, or pressurized butane cartridges (see Chapter 3 for more details on stoves and fuels). White gas or its close equivalents, such as Coleman fuel or Chevron Blazo, are readily available in the United States, while kerosene is usually more common in other countries. Both fuels are inexpensive and efficient. Kerosene's lower volatility is both a virtue and a drawback. It necessitates priming your stove with something more volatile, such as alcohol or stove preheating paste. On the other hand, it lessens the chance of stove flare-up, a serious hazard if you're cooking in the tent.

A multifuel stove is useful for foreign travel, letting you burn such fuels as Stoddard solvent, stove oil, and alcohol when white gas or kerosene aren't available. Follow the manufacturer's instructions for using the selected fuel, as it may require changing fuel jets or burner heads.

Stoves that use pressurized gas cartridges are easy to use—just turn the valve and light—and there is less chance of a fuel flare-up. But these cartridges react to the lower temperatures of winter by putting out less heat, because the butane then does not vaporize as well. You can help out by prewarming the cartridge next to your body. Newer models burn a mixture of butane and propane, or isomers of butane, and do somewhat better at low temperatures. The problem is not as bad at greater altitudes, where lower atmospheric pressures mean higher relative pressure inside the cartridge to help vaporize the fuel. The disposable gas cartridges are expensive and heavy, and spent cartridges must be packed out. Another disadvantage of some cartridge stoves is poor stability because

of a high stance and relatively narrow base. A cook set that suspends the stove and pot combination from the tent ceiling can solve this problem.

The snow that you melt for drinking water should come from a "drinking snow" pit, well away from the designated toilet and cleaning areas. Be sure everyone understands where it is and what it is for. Collect the snow as small pot-size chunks rather than as loose snow in order to make stoking the melting pot simpler and neater. If you are cooking in the tent, the process also is easier and cleaner if you collect the snow in a sack and then just bring the sack into the tent.

Cooking in the tent

Cooking in the tent is risky; it's also a convenience and at times a necessity. The risks go from the relatively minor ones of spilling pots onto sleeping bags or increasing condensation inside the tent, to the deadly dangers of tent fires or carbon monoxide poisoning. Nevertheless, cooking inside may be required if it's so windy the stove will not operate outside, or if it's so cold the cook risks frostbite. A tent vestibule is a big advantage because it provides the protection of cooking inside, with fewer risks.

Inside or out, your stove must be set on a stable platform to insulate the tent floor or snow from the heat of the stove, and to keep it from tipping over. A fallen stove is more than a nuisance, as it may spill fuel over gear or even set a tent on fire. Also, some stoves work significantly better if the fuel is insulated from the snow. A piece of $1/4$-inch plywood is a good stove pad. A snow shovel or snow fluke also may be pressed into service as a platform.

Here are some additional tips on inside cooking:
• Light the stove outside (or near an opening so it can be tossed outside if it flares) and bring it inside only after it is running smoothly.
• Cook near the tent door or in the tent vestibule. This puts the stove near the best ventilation and lets you throw the stove outside quickly in an emergency.
• Provide plenty of ventilation. This is critical. Carbon monoxide is colorless and odorless, so you

can't detect it. It is better to err on the conservative side by cooling off the tent with too large a ventilation hole rather than risk carbon monoxide poisoning with too small an opening.

Sleeping bags

A comfortable sleeping system is critical for winter trips, when the climber may spend the greater part of each day in the sack. It's colder than summer, so you need more insulation. This can come from a heavier sleeping bag or an overbag with additional insulation. An overbag must be large enough that it does not restrict the loft of the insulation in the inner bag. A non-insulating overbag, such as a bivouac sack, provides some extra warmth and protects the main bag from spills, condensation, and snow. If you don't use any kind of overbag, it may be helpful to have a sleeping bag with a cover made of material such as Gore-Tex to help keep the bag dry and windproof.

The type of insulation you want in your sleeping bag can depend on how wet the climate is. In the mild damp cold of coastal areas, synthetic bags work well as they absorb little or no moisture. As the temperature drops, there is less moisture in the air and the high loft of down clearly excels.

A vapor-barrier liner inside the sleeping bag adds to the sleeping system's warmth, especially in cold, dry environments. As with vapor-barrier clothing, the liner adds warmth by halting evaporative heat loss from your body. Less evaporation means less water vapor condensing on the sleeping bag and, therefore, a drier bag. The liner reduces your perspiration during the night and the subsequent necessary drinking the next morning to replace the lost fluid. The liner may feel clammy next to your skin so wear a single layer of synthetic underwear, which retains very little moisture and dries quickly in the morning. As an alternative to the liner, you can wear a vapor-barrier suit (shirt and bottom). The suit provides advantages similar to the liner, but it can also be worn when you're not in the sleeping bag.

An insulated pad is a critical component of the sleeping system, as the snow is virtually an infinite heat sink held at a constant 32 degrees. Inflatable foam pads such as the Therm-a-Rest are an excellent choice. You can add a closed-cell foam pad beneath the inflatable pad for added comfort, warmth, and reliability. Two foam pads or an extra-thick foam pad are good but somewhat bulky. (Take a look at Chapter 3 for additional general information on sleeping systems.)

WINTER CLIMBING

Winter makes just about every route harder to climb than in the summer. The first winter outing is usually a humbling experience in comparison to summer expectations. The days are shorter, travel is slower, and routine tasks take more time. Allow for the short days: scale down your goals, get under way at first light, and carry a good head lamp.

You will need skis or snowshoes for support, except during the low snow of early season or the firm snow of late season. Whether you choose skis or snowshoes depends on your ability and the route. Are you a diehard skier who loves skis even if conditions are poor? Are you good enough to ski virtually any slope? Will you be moving along a broad ridge or logging road, which is good terrain for skis, or will you be traveling through forest and brush? Is the approach long but easy, where the speed of skis is a benefit? Will you encounter technical climbing, where skis would be more cumbersome to carry than compact snowshoes? Consult specialized texts on skiing or snowshoeing for details on equipment and techniques.

For additional information applicable to mountaineering in snow, see Chapters 4, 12, and 14.

Routefinding

Winter routefinding gets challenging when bad weather hides the destination or landmarks along the way. Study the map ahead of time and become familiar with the terrain you will cross. Note broad features such as ridges, ravines, streams, and changes in steepness of the slope so that when you encounter them, you'll have an idea where you are. An altimeter is a vital companion to a compass for routefinding. If you cross an obvious ravine, for example, an altimeter should be able to pinpoint your position in the ravine by giving you an elevation to check on the map.

When the visibility is good, route features often stand out more clearly than in the summer. Ledges and couloirs hold snow and show up sharply against dark surrounding rock features. Ridges or arêtes blown free of snow stand out against the white of a snow face.

Avalanche hazard often dictates changes in the usual summer route, which may lead through an active avalanche path. Heavy snowfall, warm temperatures, or wind can increase the hazard of slab and loose-snow avalanches. Ridges are safer from avalanche than gullies and broad open slopes; windward slopes are safer than leeward. Never underestimate the danger of avalanche.

Wands are a big help in finding the return route during winter's poor weather and limited visibility, and when wind-driven snow covers your tracks. (For more details on routefinding on snow, see Chapter 12.)

Climbing mixed terrain

If your winter goal is normally a summer rock climb, be prepared to climb in crampons. Although considerable rock may be showing, the surface could be slick with a thin veneer of snow or ice. Even more than in the summer, climb deliberately. Search for small holds or level spots on which the crampon points can rest. This mixed climbing rapidly dulls crampon points, but they should be able to withstand the abuse. Consider carrying a small file to sharpen points if difficult ice climbing is required after the mixed terrain.

An ice tool (axe or hammer) is useful even on a rock route. The tool can be placed in occasional ice or snow pockets and can even be hooked over the edge of rock holds. When it is not needed, holster the tool on your harness (be sure the tool is secured, perhaps by its own leash) or sling it between your back and the pack.

Protection for mixed terrain

Previous chapters have detailed the types of protection used on rock, snow, and ice. Mix them all together, however, for winter climbing and there are some additional considerations.

Given a choice between a rock anchor and a snow anchor, the rock anchor is usually the one to use. It's relatively easy to check the soundness of rock anchors; not so with most snow or ice anchors. Even a good anchor in snow or ice has less strength than one well-placed in rock.

You may have to do a good bit of digging and grooming to clear away snow and ice in order to place a piece of protection in the rock. Your hands can knock off powdery snow, but it will probably take an ice axe to clear hard snow or ice. If a crack is filled with ice, a piton may be the only possible method of protection. But keep in mind that a piton scar made in winter is just as damaging as one made in summer. Always use the least damaging yet secure anchor.

Ice screws and pickets used for protection in mixed terrain sometimes go in only partway because the snow or ice is shallow. In this situation, tie off to the protection at the surface of the snow or ice to minimize the danger that the protection will be levered out (fig. 15-4). Don't try to force an ice screw farther in than it can go, because this useless effort could shatter the ice.

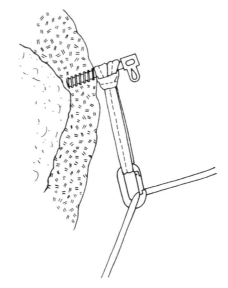

Fig. 15–4. Ice screw placement in thin ice over rock

Deep snow

The conventional wisdom is that loose snow will not stay long on a steep surface. But occasionally you encounter circumstances that seem to defy the rules, such as a short slope with snow well-anchored by boulders or by a wind-sculpted snow trough. Normal step-kicking won't work because the snow is too loose, nor is delicate footwork the answer. You must use your whole body to flail your way up the slope. An ice axe placed horizontally may be the only handhold, and you move upward on your knees rather than your feet. Rarely is the effort graceful.

At times, it takes a snow shovel to literally dig a path through the snow. Alternatively, teammates may pool their energies and toss the smallest member ahead in order to consolidate the path.

EXPEDITION CLIMBING

Expedition climbing does not represent a different type or standard of climbing as much as an expansion of the time scale for a climb. A weekend trip may involve several hours or a day for the approach to the peak, while an expedition can require two or three days of air travel followed by a day or two of land travel, followed by a ten-day hike into base camp. A rest break is not a 10- or 15-minute sit down, but may be an entire day spent lounging. The actual climbing is much the same as discussed in earlier chapters and in the winter climbing section of this chapter. The main differences between expedition climbing and other mountaineering come in the logistics of tackling a remote peak, the more severe weather likely to be encountered, and the challenge of climbing at high altitude.

The scope of this chapter is expeditions of three to four weeks, on relatively accessible 20,000- to 23,000-foot peaks, such as Alaska's Mount McKinley or Peru's Huascaran. Many of the techniques and considerations are similar to those of longer expeditions to higher peaks. However, there also are major differences in permits, hiring of porters, medical requirements, extremes of altitude and cold, use of oxygen, and so forth, that are beyond the scope of this chapter.

PLANNING AND PREPARATION

In deciding what peak to try and which route to climb, you will take a lot of factors into account:

Difficulty of the route: It's generally best to choose a route well within your climbing ability because the challenges of remoteness, changeable weather, and routefinding will add to the difficulties. Until you have gone on a few expeditions, think of the trip as an opportunity to apply well-practiced climbing skills in a new environment, rather than to push the limits of your ability.

Duration of the climb: Again, be realistic. Don't try to cram a twenty-five-day route into two weeks of annual leave.

Time of year: Study information on seasonal temperatures, winds, storms, rains, and amount of daylight. Your trip will be planned far in advance, so in choosing your dates you'll have to deal with probabilities and likelihoods, and hope that the realities will measure up when the time comes.

Costs: Major costs are equipment for the climb, transportation, and other expenses on the way to the peak, and hiring porters and pack animals to haul gear to base camp. In many cases, expenses within a country are minor compared with the cost of getting there. Estimate your costs based on research about the peak and/or area.

Location: Where to go? Alaska, Mexico, the Andes of South America, Europe, Nepal, Pakistan, India, the Soviet Union, and areas of Africa all boast difficult, remote peaks. The experience of traveling in a remote or foreign land is often one of the most enjoyable and rewarding aspects of an expedition.

After choosing your peak, research the mountain and its routes. Talk to climbers who have been there, look for write-ups in the journals of the American Alpine Club and of climbing organizations in Canada and Europe, and seek out guidebooks and stories in climbing magazines. Get all possible details on logistics, potential problems, where to buy fuel, what foods are available, objective hazards on the mountain, and so forth.

Have a backup route in mind in case the main objective is scratched because of avalanche hazard, bad weather, inability of some party members to continue, or any other reason. If you've chosen a highly technical route up your mountain, consider acclimating by climbing the standard route first, then taking on the tougher challenge.

Find out what permits and approvals are necessary. It helps to have typewritten itineraries, climbing resumes of party members, equipment lists, and medical information in hand ahead of time and while traveling to the peak. The appearance of good organization impresses bureaucrats the world around.

Choosing the team

Choosing a compatible team is the first step toward an enjoyable experience. Expedition climbing is full of stress, and climbers can be taxed to their physical and mental limits. Climbing literature abounds with "climb and tell" accounts of expeditions in which, it seems, team members despised their fellow climbers; you don't want your expedition to end up being another.

The skill of your team must, of course, be equal to the demands of the climb. Climbing with people of similar technical ability may improve compatibility. Team members need personalities that are compatible with each other, and must be able to live harmoniously with others in close quarters under stressful conditions. The climbers should agree on the philosophy of the trip in terms of climbing style, environmental impact, and degree of acceptable risk.

It's important to agree on leadership before the trip gets under way. If all climbers are of roughly equal experience, democratic decision-making usually works well. If one climber is clearly more experienced, that person can be given the leadership role. Even with a single leader, functional areas such as finance, food, medicine, and equipment should be delegated to others to lessen the leader's load and to keep everyone involved and informed. This also helps build expedition leaders for the future. (You might consider taking a guided climb if this is your first expedition or if you lack capable partners.)

The number of climbers in the expedition depends partly on what route you've chosen. A party of two or four climbers may be best on technically difficult routes because of the efficiency of two-person rope teams and the limited space at bivouac sites. However, climbing with a very small team means that if one person becomes ill or cannot continue, the entire team may have to abandon the climb.

When the route itself does not determine the optimum party size, logistics becomes the deciding factor. As the number of climbers increases, issues of transportation, food, lodging, and equipment become more complicated. The advantage is that parties of six or eight have strength and reserve capacity. If one climber doesn't continue, the rest of the party has a better chance to go on with the expedition. And larger parties usually are better able to carry out self-rescue than smaller teams. However, the logistics of an expedition with more than eight members can become more burdensome than many climbers are willing to accept.

Establishing a climbing style

Do you plan to climb "expedition style" or "alpine style" or somewhere in between? There's a big difference, and it's a question you need to resolve early, based on the route, the size and strength of your party, and the preference of the climbers.

Traditional expedition climbing style involves multiple carries between camps, during which food, fuel, and supplies are ferried to higher camps. Technically difficult sections of the route are often protected with fixed lines—ropes anchored in place to minimize danger during repeated trips up and down. It's a slow and measured campaign for the summit.

Alpine climbing style usually means moving camps up the mountain in a continuous push, so that the route is climbed only once. All equipment and supplies are carried with the team at all times.

It's a light, quick bid for the top.

Expedition-style ascents take longer because more time is spent hauling loads between camps. They are heavier because more food, fuel, and perhaps fixed line must be carried, and more costly because of the greater time, equipment, and food. Alpine-style trips tend to be riskier as there is less margin of safety in case of bad weather or injury.

The climbing itinerary

Once you've researched your mountain, you can set up an itinerary that makes a good estimate of the number of days to allow for the approach to the peak, for carrying loads up the mountain, for climbing, for sitting out storms and for resting. An average elevation gain of 1,000 feet per day is good for acclimatization, and this figure should be correlated where possible with good campsites. Rest days built into the schedule provide time for mental and physical recuperation, equipment sorting, and such. They can also serve as a time buffer for unplanned delays caused by storms, illness, or other problems. If a storm hits, try to reschedule a rest period for the same time, making the best of a bad day.

For moving camps expedition-style up the mountain, double carries are generally adequate on a three-week climb. The first carry hauls food, supplies and equipment to the site of the next camp. The second carry involves tearing down the current camp and resetting it at the next site. On bigger mountains, camps may need to be stocked pyramid style, with many carries between camps early in the trip and few if any carries between later camps.

When repeated carries are necessary, each load is usually cached at the next camp while the climbers go back down for more. Plan to set up a protected cache to avoid damage from the elements and from animals. Dig a hole, cover it with something an animal can't get through, such as a sled or snowshoes, and pile snow on top. Mark the cache with long wands. But beware. Ravens on popular peaks have learned to identify caches, so place the wands a little distance away and smooth the surface above the cache.

Food and equipment

On expeditions to the remote mountains of the world, you either take it with you or you do without it. Having the necessary equipment, in working order, is much more critical than on a weekend climb where home is a short drive away. Your expedition needs a complete equipment list, both group and personal, worked out in discussions with all team members. (See the sample equipment list at the end of this chapter.)

Supplies for the group

• Food

Food constitutes the heaviest single category of weight carried by an expedition. But who's complaining? Food provides the necessary fuel for your body to carry loads and climb the route, and it also can serve as one of the great pleasures of the trip.

Every climber has preferences in food, so conduct a team survey of strong food likes and dislikes before planning menus. Combat the danger of carrying unpopular foods by providing lots of variety. If some team members don't like one item, there should be several others they will find tasty, or at least palatable. A condiment and seasoning kit with the likes of Tabasco sauce, spices, soy sauce, margarine, and mustard will add interest to bland packaged foods and perhaps salvage the unpopular foods.

Although fats have the highest caloric density (9 calories per gram), carbohydrates (4.1 calories per gram) are easiest to digest and provide the quickest energy. Proteins have about the same caloric density as carbohydrates, but are not as easy to digest and are usually accompanied by substantially more fat. A reasonable expeditionary diet has about 50 percent of its calories from carbohydrates, 30 percent from fat, and 20 percent from protein.

Plan to provide about 35 ounces (roughly 2 1/4 pounds) of food per person per day. With no waste, 35 ounces would provide more than 5,000 calories. In reality—because of packaging, non-nutritive fiber, and the food's irreducible water—the food will provide only about 3,900 calories per day. Experience will tell whether this is just right, too much, or not enough. Too much food means extra-heavy loads between camps and possibly a slower trip. Too little means you will begin losing weight. On a trip of three or four weeks, weight loss shouldn't cause a problem. But on longer expeditions, too much weight loss may effect the team's strength and endurance.

Food is your major controllable weight factor. As you sit at home planning menus and calculating energy expenditures, you'll be tempted to throw into the menu an extra cracker at breakfast, an extra candy bar during the day, or an extra cocoa at dinner. Resist this temptation at all cost. Unless the extra food never gets past base camp, it will eventually find its way onto the climbers' backs or into their sleds, slowing their pace while fatiguing them faster. If you are planning a twenty-day trip, take food for twenty days, not twenty-one. On unplanned storm days, you will simply have to stretch your rations. Food can always be stretched on an expedition, and it's easier than suffering the consequences of overloaded packs.

You can plan foods for early in the trip that are different from those for later as you get up on the mountain. Candidates for lower elevations and warmer climes are foods that are time-consuming to prepare, such as pancakes; items that suffer from freezing, such as cheese and peanut butter; and canned foods. Foods carried to higher altitudes should be very light and require a minimum of preparation, such as freeze-dried items, instant noodles, instant rice, and potatoes. Try to eat local food on approach marches and at base camp so you don't tire too early of expedition food.

Packaging and organizing food is an important element of planning. Take the food you've bought for the expedition and get rid of as much of the commercial packaging as possible. Repackage the food to minimize this packaging, reducing the weight you have to carry in and the garbage to be carried out. Keep the preparation instructions from the packaging material. You should prepackage rations into person-days (put in one bag the food for one person for one day), or into group-days (put in one bag the food for the entire group for one day), or into tent-days (put in one bag the food for one

tent for one day). However you do it, measure the food into the correct portions and label it. Clear plastic sacks help organize the food while keeping the contents visible.

Adequate hydration is the first line of defense against altitude sickness. Bring lots of soups, hot drinks, and cold-drink mixes to help motivate you into drinking the necessary fluids. Contaminated water plagues nearly every part of the world. The expedition kitchen must be able to furnish adequate water for everyone through chemical decontamination, filtering, or boiling.

• Fuel

Fuel cannot be carried on airlines so it must be available at your destination. Multifuel stoves may be good insurance in foreign countries where white gas is not readily available. Even with a multifuel stove, check the fuel's compatibility with the stove before heading into the mountains. If you're using kerosene or a similar low-volatility fuel, be sure to buy alcohol or gas for priming the stove. The cleanliness of fuel in foreign countries is always questionable. Bring a filter and filter all fuel before using, and clean the stove often. Plan on using between $1/4$ pint and $1/2$ pint of fuel per person per day, depending on how much water must be boiled for purification or melted from snow.

Fuel containers are usually supplied in Alaska or Canada, but you must provide your own elsewhere. Aluminum containers as small as 1 liter are fine if you don't need to carry much fuel. For larger quantities, bring 1-gallon gas cans or sturdy approved plastic fuel containers. They should be new, as airlines object to containers with residual fuel vapors. Plastic bottles sold in foreign countries have a reputation for leaking.

• Community equipment

For communal cooking, take pots large enough for the group meal courses and for melting large amounts of snow. Filling water bottles is a common activity, so pots must be easy to pour from (a 2-quart coffee pot works well). Bring at least one cook pot per stove. Bring a metal gripper to use on pots that lack handles or bails, or use wool gloves as potholders. (Be careful using synthetic gloves, which will melt if they get too hot.)

To save a bit of weight, the party can carry an altimeter and a compass as pieces of group equipment rather than having each climber carry separate ones. Also among group equipment are wands, used for marking routes, camp perimeters, gear caches, and snow shelters. Carry long wands if there's a chance of significant snowfall. Tents are also community equipment. See the section on winter camping earlier in this chapter for guidelines on tents.

The party may carry radios to get weather information, call for emergency help, or communicate between climbers at different locations. The main choices are citizens' band, marine band, or FM. You'll have to do some investigating to determine both the technical feasibility and the legality of their use.

• Community climbing gear

The route determines the climbing gear you need. A route that involves only glacier travel may require just the basics: rope, crampons, and ice axe. Technical routes can take the whole gamut of equipment, from ice screws, snow flukes, and pickets to nuts and pitons.

Depending on the style and organization of the trip, climbing gear can be personal or community. On a technical route where climbers operate in self-sufficient pairs, climbing gear should be personal or left to each rope team to work out. In other cases, virtually all climbing gear—carabiners, runners, screws, and so forth—can be treated as group equipment. The choice is up to the team. Certain pieces of climbing gear, such as crampons and ice axes, are indispensable, and a large party may want to carry spares as insurance against equipment failure or loss.

The decision on what ropes to take also depends on the route and its difficulty. For technical pitches, you'll use use either a single rope (10.5 or 11 millimeters in diameter) or double or twin ropes (each 8 or 9 millimeters). On a glacier route, a single 9-millimeter rope may be adequate. Keep in mind, however, that an expedition puts extraordinary wear and tear on the rope because of its daily

use in bright sunlight. The team also needs to decide how much rope to bring for fixed line along the route. Fixed line is usually a polypropylene braided rope or a nylon kernmantle rope. Polypro is lightest and cheapest, but kernmantle is better for areas of high use.

• Repair kit

Equipment failure is common under the prolonged and rugged demands of an expedition, so count on needing to repair or substitute for failed gear. Put together a comprehensive repair kit, keeping in mind the relative importance of each piece of equipment to the progress of the group.

Among the repair-kit items should be:

• Tape. Gray duct tape seems to be the universal repair favorite, but other tapes, such as ripstop fabric tape or filament tape, are useful.
• Sewing kit for permanent repairs or those beyond the capability of tape.
• Extra stove parts and the tools to disassemble the stove.
• Tent-pole splices or extra tent poles. While the tent body or fly can be patched with tape, broken tent poles must be repaired or replaced.
• Extra crampon parts, such as screws, nuts, and connecting bars, and the necessary tools.
• Patch kit for inflatable foam pads that spring leaks.
• Also: crampon file, pliers, wire, accessory cord, pack buckle.

• First-aid kit

An expedition usually carries a comprehensive first-aid kit, which is assembled after everyone in the party has had input into the selections. Keep in mind the isolation of the peak, the specific medical conditions of team members, and their medical knowledge. Discuss your group's medical needs with a doctor who is familiar with mountaineering.

The first-aid kit may include such specialized or prescription items as a strong painkiller, antibiotics, a dental repair kit, and a suture kit. Be sure to carry a first-aid manual.

Personal gear

Expedition climbers need clothing and sleeping

bags that can stand up to prolonged use under severe conditions. The clothing and equipment suitable for winter climbing, outlined earlier in this chapter, works well for expeditions. The desired comfort rating for your sleeping system varies with the climate and season, but a good general rating for expeditions is about –30 degrees Fahrenheit (about –35 degrees Celsius).

Every person on an expedition team needs a big pack, with a capacity between 5,500 and 7,000 cubic inches, because there are times you will be called on to carry ''impossible'' loads. The pack also must be comfortable while you are wearing a climbing harness.

You may want mechanical ascenders, rather than prusik slings, both for crevasse rescue and for protection while climbing with a fixed line. The ascenders permit one-way movement by gripping or squeezing the line when your weight is on them but letting you move move them when they are unweighted. The ascenders, under such brand names as Jumar, Clog, and Gibbs, are necessary to handle the large, heavy expedition loads involved in any crevasse rescue. On fixed line, the prusik knots are unsafe because of the time required to unfasten and reattach them past each anchor you encounter on the way up or down.

Although two ascenders are the norm, one plus a prusik sling can work if you need to cut down on weight. Regardless of the choice, make sure the system can be operated while you're wearing bulky gloves or mittens.

Other items of personal gear to consider:

• Prescription glasses. Carry an extra set of prescription sunglasses.
• Journal. An expedition can make you introspective. A journal made of waterproof paper (look under surveyor supplies at a book store or stationery supply store) and some pencils can help pass the time.
• Books. You can catch up on reading while waiting for flights, or during rest days and storm days in the field. Coordinate your selection of books with other team members to avoid repetition and provide variety.

• Personal hygiene. On cold-weather trips where water is at a premium, chemical wash/wipes can provide a refreshing sponge bath.
• Pee bottle. During storms and cold nights, the pee bottle eliminates those unpleasant traipses to the latrine. Be sure the bottle has a secure top.

Physical and mental conditioning

Training for an expedition involves both physical and mental preparation. For the body, emphasize cardiovascular training and strength training equally. Cardiovascular conditioning is important for physical activity at high altitudes. Powerful leg muscles are needed to walk heavy loads up the mountain, and upper-body strength is needed to hoist and carry the large expeditionary packs.

Climbing itself is the best training. Climb often and in all weather conditions, carrying a heavy pack. If you can go on a typical two- to three-day climb packing gear for camping and climbing, gaining 3,000 to 5,000 feet per day, and feel you still have plenty of physical reserves, you're probably sufficiently fit for an expedition. An expedition climber needs the endurance to carry packs of 40 to 60 pounds (sometimes in addition to pulling a sled) for an elevation gain of 2,000 to 3,000 feet every day, day after day.

Your mind and spirit also need to get into shape for the rigors of an expedition. Learn about the special challenges of expedition travel and prepare yourself to accept them. Otherwise, you can be overwhelmed by the size and remoteness of the climbing area or lose your good spirits during a long storm or a bout with the flu.

Success on an expedition often goes to the person who has a greater desire or will to succeed, even though he or she may be physically weaker than another climber. It takes more than physical strength to deal with extreme cold, sickness, cramped quarters, poor food, conflict with teammates, the stress of technical climbing, and the lethargy brought on by high altitude.

You can work on both your physical and mental conditioning by seeking out experiences that come as close as possible to what you expect on the expedition. Prepare for the expedition by going on winter climbs and on longer trips. You may not be able to alter such objective conditions as cold or illness, but you can learn to exercise a great deal of mental control over your response and attitude toward them.

Before you leave home

Food and gear must be packed and frequently repacked to accommodate the various transportation modes used to get to the mountain. Become familiar with the requirements that face your expedition, such as airline regulations on bag sizes and weights, or muleteer requirements on load balancing. Keep lists of what went into each bag so any item can be retrieved readily. Before leaving home, plan travel arrangements for each leg of the journey and make reservations where possible. Try to work with a travel agent who has booked trips to the region before.

Be as healthy as possible when you leave town because, in all likelihood, you won't get better while traveling. For foreign travel, find out well in advance what inoculations are needed. Have a dental exam and leave no dental care pending. To stay healthy once you get to your destination, plan on purifying all water and be cautious about eating unpeeled fresh vegetables or fruit, dairy products, and uncooked food. And through all the complicated hurry and scurry of getting ready for a big expedition, try to remember that your goal is to get away from it all and climb a mountain.

EXPEDITIONARY CLIMBING TECHNIQUES

Expedition mountaineering calls for the rock, snow, ice, and winter climbing techniques that have been covered throughout this book. An expedition can add a couple of new techniques to your climbing repertoire: hauling sleds and using fixed lines.

Haul sleds

Expedition members often pull sleds or haul bags behind them on long glacier approaches as a way to move the loads of gear and supplies (fig. 15-5). A climber can transport a normal load in a backpack in addition to pulling a sled with another pack's worth of gear. Commercial haul sleds are available, with zippered covers to hold the load, a waist harness for you to wear, and rigid aluminum poles connecting the sled to the harness. These

Fig. 15–5. Sled and climber rigged for glacier travel

poles help control the sled when traversing or going downhill.

A cheaper but usable alternative is a plastic children's sled, with holes punched in the sides as rope attachment points. Load your gear into a duffel bag and tie it to the sled. Perlon (5 to 7 millimeters) is used to pull the sled, and most climbers prefer to attach the perlon to their pack, not their climbing harness. A final alternative is to drag a haul bag, constructed of durable, slick material to help it slide over the snow. A swivel connecter attaching the haul line to the haul bag will keep the rolling of the bag from putting twists in the line.

As the route steepens, the amount of weight you can pull in a sled decreases, and it can't be used at all on steep technical climbing terrain. Haul bags may then be what you need. (See Chapter 11 for techniques for using haul bags on technical routes.)

No special trick is involved in towing a sled behind you. It simply takes steadfast pulling. Where it can get complicated is during roped travel on glaciers, where any fall into a crevasse is made more treacherous by having the sled plunge down behind you. Even if you aren't injured by the plummeting sled, rescue is more difficult with the need to deal with you, your pack (perhaps weighing 60 pounds) and the sled (carrying another 50 pounds or so).

You can minimize the danger of getting hit by the sled during a crevasse fall with a simple preventive technique. Just take your climbing rope where it runs past the sled and tie it snugly with a clove hitch to a carabiner at the rear of the sled. In a crevasse fall, you will drop in, followed by the sled. But the sled will be stopped above you by the tie-in to the climbing rope. If you are using a hauling tether to the sled (instead of rigid aluminum poles), be sure the tether is long enough so you are well beyond the reach of the sled as it hangs from the climbing rope. This technique depends on having a team member behind you on the rope to arrest the fall of both you and the sled, so it won't work for the last climber on a rope. The last person either assumes the extra risk, or the team can decide to haul only two sleds for each three climbers.

Crevasse rescue

It takes some special procedures for crevasse rescue if you are hauling a sled (fig. 15-6), beyond those methods spelled out in Chapter 13. Imagine you have just fallen into a crevasse. The sled, attached to the climbing rope, dangles above you. Here is how you can help yourself get out.

First of all, get your weight onto the climbing rope. As you dangle in the crevasse, your weight may be on the sled haul line (or towing poles, if you are using a commercial sled). Transfer your weight to the climbing rope by standing in slings attached to your ascending system (mechanical ascenders, prusik slings, or a combination).

Then disconnect the attachment from you to the sled. If you are using a haul line attached to your pack, simply take off the pack and let it hang from the line.

Once free of the sled, you can try to rescue yourself or wait for your climbing mates to get you out. If you start up the climbing rope on your own, the sled probably will cause some complication. You may need to ascend around the climbing-rope knot that holds the sled. In this case, remove and reattach your ascenders above the knot, one at a time.

You may also need to untie from the climbing rope in order to move past the sled and reach the lip of the crevasse. To make it easier to disconnect from the climbing rope, many sled-pullers travel with the rope clipped to a locking carabiner on their harness, rather than tying directly to the harness itself. If you must unclip from the climbing rope, use extreme caution to ensure that the ascenders are secure.

Your fall into the crevasse can also mean extra effort for your teammates if they must pull you out. If you can't disconnect yourself from the sled or if there is no extra rescue rope available, they must haul both you and the sled at the same time. They will have to use a Z-pulley system to get the most mechanical advantage in pulling on the climbing rope. Far preferable is to use a spare rope to pull you out, and to then pull the sled out on the climbing rope it is already attached to.

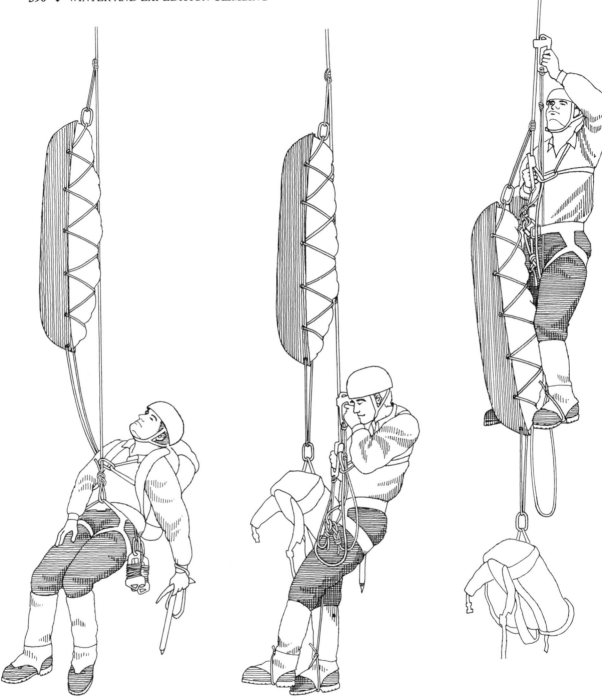

Fig. 15–6. Crevasse self-rescue with sled

Fixed lines

A fixed line is simply a rope that is anchored to the route and left in place. It allows safe, quick travel up and down a difficult stretch. Climbers protect themselves by tying into a mechanical ascender on the fixed line, eliminating the need for time-consuming belays. If you fall while climbing next to the fixed line, the ascender cam locks onto the line and holds the fall.

It's also possible in some cases to climb a fixed line directly by hanging from slings attached to two ascenders and moving them methodically upward. However, fixed lines are not generally used for direct aid in the situations discussed in this chapter.

The fixed line simplifies the movement of people and equipment, especially when numerous trips are required, and permits less-experienced climbers to follow a route. Fixed lines have been common on large expeditions to major peaks to provide protection on long stretches of exposed climbing or to protect porters while they make carries from camp to camp in the face of such obstacles as icefalls, glaciers, and steep rock or ice. The lines make it possible for climbers and porters to carry heavier loads than they could safely carry without them.

Fixed lines are sometimes used as a siege tactic on difficult rock and ice faces, with climbers retreating down the lines each night to a base camp, then reascending the next day to push the route a little farther. They also come into play on continuous multiday aid climbs of big walls, where the second climber follows on the line, removing protection and hauling up equipment. The climbers do not retreat down this line, but move it upward as they go. Thus it becomes a "moving" fixed line, only one rope length long.

Some climbers argue that fixing ropes is an outmoded technique, no longer required to climb any mountain or route. This is not the majority view, but the technique should not be abused. Fixed lines should not be used to supplement the climbing ability of an expedition team. If many of the climbers don't have the ability to climb a route without help from a fixed line, find an alternate route.

Fixed lines should not be added on popular routes or in regions where they are not normally used.

In the past, climbers often abandoned fixed lines when a climb was done. It was not uncommon to find several lines, one on top of the next, frozen into a route. This is no longer acceptable in a time of increasing environmental awareness, and each party needs to make a commitment to remove its fixed lines.

Equipment for fixed lines

To set up and use fixed lines, you need rope, anchors, and ascenders. Climbing ropes don't make good fixed lines because they are designed to stretch under a load, an undesirable characteristic in a fixed line. What you want is a more static rope, one with low elongation under load. Nylon is the most common material for fixed lines, though polypropylene and Dacron also are used. Kernmantle construction is best, though braided ropes can be used.

The diameter of fixed lines usually varies between 7 and 10 millimeters, with the size depending on the terrain and the amount of use the line is expected to get. Try to carry your fixed line in long lengths. The ropes are usually manufactured in lengths of somewhere between 300 and 1,000 feet, depending on rope diameter.

To anchor the fixed line to the mountain, employ any attachment points that are normally used in belaying and climbing on rock or ice: pitons, chocks, natural outcrops, ice screws, pickets, and snow flukes or other deadman anchors.

A mechanical ascender attached from your harness to the fixed line is the most efficient means of protecting you from a fall as you climb next to the line. Prusik knots can be dangerous because it is so time-consuming to untie and retie them as you move past an anchor, especially while wearing mittens. Prusiks are OK in an emergency or on very short sections of rope.

Anchors for fixed lines

Every fixed line needs an anchor at the bottom to hold the rope in place while climbers ascend, and a bombproof anchor at the top. Mark the location of the anchors with wands so you can find them after a snow storm.

Place a series of intermediate anchors between the bottom and top of the fixed line. The fixed line is tied off at each anchor so that every section of line is independent of the others. This permits more than one climber at a time on the line. In deciding where to place the intermediate anchors, take several considerations into account. Place an anchor at points where you would like to change direction of the line or prevent pendulum falls. An anchor at the top of difficult sections of the route is helpful. If possible, place the intermediate anchors at natural resting spots, making it easier to stand and move the ascenders past the anchor.

Always bury or cover snow and ice anchors and inspect them regularly for possible failure from creep or melting. Also keep a close eye on any rock anchors capable of creeping or loosening. Place anchors at locations that help keep the line from rubbing on rough or sharp surfaces, or pad the line at points of abrasion. Even small amounts of wear can multiply into dangerous weak spots on fixed lines, which usually use lightweight rope. Falls will also damage the line. After any fall on the line, inspect it for damage and check the anchors for any indications of possible failure.

How to set up fixed lines

There are many variations in how to set fixed line, each appropriate for certain conditions, climber preferences, types of line and so forth. The key is to think through a system prior to starting out and if possible test and refine it before you actually need it. Here are three possible methods:

1. The most common way is for two or three climbers to ascend the route—using a standard climbing rope to belay one another or to establish a running belay—and setting the fixed line as they climb. They can carry the whole spool of line with them and let it out as they ascend, tying it off at each intermediate anchor along the way. Or they can just pull the end of the line up with them as they ascend, clipping the line into each anchor with carabiners. Then after anchoring the top, they can go back down, tying off the line at each anchor as they

go. In either case, it can be a big job. Carrying the spool of line is difficult, but so is pulling up on the end of the line and trying to overcome the tremendous friction that develops as it travels through carabiners and over the route.

2. The entire fixed line also can be set on descent. The material for the fixed line must first be carried to the top of the route, of course. Tie the line into a bombproof anchor at the top. Then rappel or downclimb to tie the line off at intermediate anchors. These anchors can be the ones that were placed on the earlier ascent of the route, although new ones can be added just for the fixed line.

3. You can also use the fixed line as your climbing rope at the same time you are setting it in place. Use the line just as you would a normal climbing rope, clipping it into anchors as you climb, belayed from below. At the top, tie the fixed line into a bombproof anchor, and then it is ready to be tied off at each intermediate anchor. The problem with this method is that fixed line is usually thinner and has less stretch than climbing ropes. If you fall, there's a bigger chance the line could break. Even if it holds, the limited stretch in the line would make for a hard fall. An additional drawback is that the friction on the line as you pull it up through more and more carabiners will probably limit the maximum length of the run. This method is best saved for short sections of fixed line or for instances where a standard climbing rope is being used as a fixed line.

Attaching fixed line to anchors

For the final tie-off of the fixed line at each intermediate anchor, use a clove hitch or figure-8 knot in the line. Tie a sling directly to the anchor and clip a figure-8 loop or clove hitch into a carabiner attached to that sling (fig. 15-7a). Or better yet, minimize use of carabiners and have one less link in the system by retying the sling directly through the figure-8 loop (fig. 15-7b).

Ascending

Ascending with a fixed line simply involves

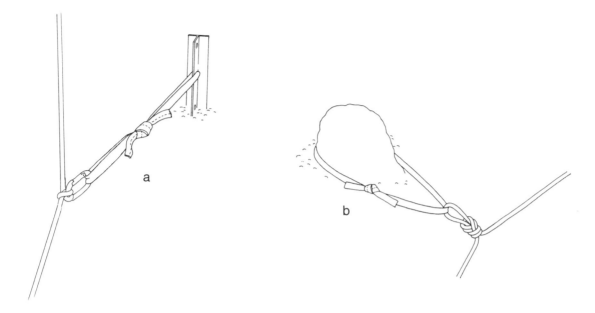

Fig. 15–7. Intermediate, fixed anchors: a, anchor with carabiners in system; b, anchor without carabiners.

climbing as usual, except that your harness is attached by a sling to the mechanical ascender on the line in case you fall (fig. 15-8).

Start by tying a sling from the ascender to your seat harness where you normally tie in with the climbing rope. (A less desirable way is to clip the sling into a locking carabiner attached to the harness.) Make the sling short so the ascender won't be out of reach if you fall. If you're climbing a near-vertical section or have a heavy pack, you may want to pass the sling through your chest harness as well to prevent tipping upside down in a fall.

Then attach the ascender to the fixed line, following the specific directions for your brand of ascender. The ascender should be oriented so that a fall will cause it to clamp the rope. It should slide easily up the line, but lock tight when pulled down. Test it before starting upward and also check the fittings on your seat harness.

You should attach a carabiner from the ascender sling or a separate sling to the fixed line to serve as a safety link as you move upward. If you fall and the ascender fails, the safety carabiner will slide down the rope but stop at the next anchor below and arrest your fall.

At each intermediate anchor, you have to remove the ascender from the fixed line and reattach it beyond the knot. This is the most dangerous moment in fixed-line travel, particularly if conditions are severe and you are exhausted. Be sure the safety carabiner stays on the line while the ascender is detached. Some ascenders can be configured so the safety carabiner can be moved and reattached above the anchor first, followed by the ascender. This order offers more security than moving the ascender first. Another safety option is to briefly clip yourself into the anchor as you relocate the ascender.

Whatever your procedure, it's urgent that you think it through in advance and practice it on a good day so you can perform it reliably under the worst possible conditions.

More than one climber can use a fixed line at the same time as long as there is at least one anchor between each climber. Also be sure that a fall by

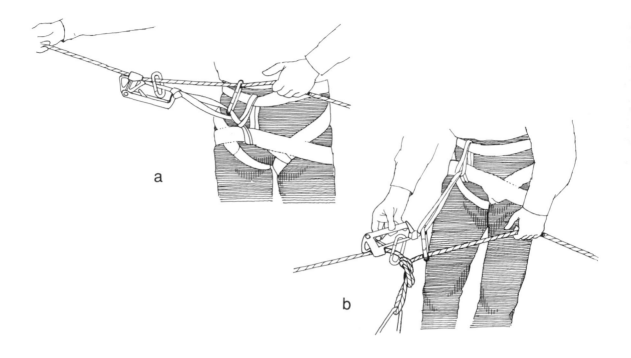

Fig. 15–8. Mechanical ascender attachment to fixed line: a, set up for normal movement; b, passing an anchor, move ascender separately from safety carabiner.

any climber would not cause rope movement, rockfall, or other activity that could endanger anyone else.

Descending

Climbing down with a fixed line is similar to climbing up. Again attach the ascender sling to your harness, then attach the ascender to the fixed line exactly the same as for ascending. Double-check that the ascender locks onto the rope when you pull down on it, and that it will be within reach if you end up hanging from it after a fall. Attach the safety carabiner.

Begin your descent. As you climb downward, you will be moving the ascender down the rope to stay with you. Use a light grip on the ascender release so that you can let go of it instantly to permit the ascender to grab the rope if you fall. It's

natural to try to hang onto something if you lose your balance, but the last thing you want to grab hold of at that moment is the ascender release.

Take extreme care as you climb past anchors, removing and reattaching the ascender. As in climbing up, never detach the ascender and the safety carabiner at the same time. Again, you can temporarily clip into the anchor while you relocate the ascender. On steep sections of fixed line, rappelling the fixed line may be a good alternative to downclimbing.

Removing fixed lines

Exhausted mountaineers at the end of a grueling climb often find it easier to abandon gear, garbage, and fixed line to the mercies of the mountain. This kind of behavior has become less and less acceptable, and expeditions now are learning to approach their climbs with a commitment to removing all signs of their passage.

Removing fixed lines will be easier if you keep it in mind as you plan where to put them up in the first place. In some cases you may be able to use a "moving" fixed line, removing it and moving it higher as you ascend the mountain, then descending via a safer route. If you are leaving the mountain and going down a fixed route for the last time, plan a downclimbing or rappelling procedure, or a combination of the two, that will permit the party to remove the fixed line.

What applies to fixed line also applies to all the other odds and ends of the expedition. Everything that goes in has got to come back out. Crevasses can't be used as garbage dumps because between wind and hungry ravens, the contents can end up strewn up and down the glacier. You can set fire to burnable garbage, but haul the ashes out. For human waste, set up a group latrine at each camp. In an exception to the use of crevasses, you can line the latrine with plastic garbage bags and then dispose of the waste in a deep crevasse.

EXPEDITION WEATHER

You need to become something of an amateur weather forecaster on an expedition because your safety and success are so closely bound to nature's moods. When you get to the climbing area, add to your knowledge of local weather patterns by talking to other climbers and to people who live there. Find out the direction of the prevailing winds. Ask about rain and storms. On the mountain, become a student of weather patterns. Your altimeter can serve as a barometer to signal weather changes.

Take clues from the clouds. Cirrus clouds (mare's tails) warn of a front bringing precipitation within the next 24 hours. Lenticular clouds (cloud caps) mean high winds. A rapidly descending cloud cap signals that bad weather is coming. And if you climb into a cloud cap, expect high winds and poor visibility. Be prepared for the fact that big mountains typically have storms and winds to match. Wait storms out if you can because of the risk inherent in descending under bad conditions. If it looks like you'll be stuck for some time, start

rationing food.

Fair weather poses problems too. If it's hot and solar radiation is intensified by protected glaciers, the result can be collapsing snow bridges, crevasse movement, and increased icefall. Then it's best to climb at night, when temperatures are lowest and snow and ice are most stable.

MEDICAL CONDITIONS RELATED TO HIGH ALTITUDE

Expedition climbing and a great deal of other mountaineering takes you to altitudes where your body no longer feels at home. Every climber is affected to one degree or other by the reduced oxygen of higher elevations. It often causes acute mountain sickness, and it can lead to the life-threatening conditions of high altitude pulmonary edema and high altitude cerebral edema. Frostbite is another danger, though it's not limited to high altitudes. It's important to learn how to prevent these conditions, and how to recognize and treat them when they occur. This chapter offers some general guidelines on these maladies, but consult your first-aid book, specialized texts, or physicians familiar with mountaineering for detailed information.

Altitude sickness (acute mountain sickness)

When you ascend rapidly to an altitude you're not accustomed to, your system works to adjust to the new conditions. Breathing becomes more rapid to extract enough oxygen from the thinner air, and the blood increases its proportion of oxygen-carrying red corpuscles. Climbing slowly and steadily upward, climbers routinely suffer uncomfortable symptoms from moving into this new environment. First comes a general malaise and loss of appetite, then headache, followed by increasing weakness and lessening of interest in the climb. If you continue on at that point, there's often increased apathy, nausea, dizziness, and sleepiness. A retreat to lower elevations usually brings about rapid improvement.

Symptoms of altitude sickness (mountain sickness) can occur at relatively low altitudes. Some people feel dizzy or tired or experience palpitations when riding in a car at 8,000 feet or so. Climbers generally have more time to acclimatize and, except for shortness of breath, usually feel only minor effects until after they reach 12,000 feet or more. In regions such as the Pacific Northwest, where climbers live at sea level yet ascend to over 14,000 feet for a weekend climb of Mount Rainier, altitude sickness of greater or lesser severity is the rule rather than the exception.

You can help moderate the more severe symptoms of altitude sickness by some relatively simple techniques. In ascending, use the rest step to give your leg muscles mini-rests all the way up the mountain and help you maintain measured, methodical breathing. Take occasional full rest stops with forced deep breathing. Drink lots of water and keep nourishment up by snacking often. Follow a program of careful acclimatization (outlined later in this chapter).

Medical experts and specialized texts can provide information on the current use of drugs in combatting altitude sickness. Two prescription drugs—Diamox and dexamethasone—are commonly used to aid in prevention and treatment of altitude sickness. They are not a substitute for proper acclimatization, or for immediate descent if you get sick.

High-altitude pulmonary edema and cerebral edema

High-altitude pulmonary edema is the leakage of blood into the lungs, which restricts the air sacs (alveoli) in exchanging oxygen and carbon dioxide in the blood. Pulmonary edema rarely occurs in healthy people below 9,000 feet. The average elevation at which it strikes in the United States is 12,000 feet, and the level of onset varies for mountain ranges in other parts of the world.

Early symptoms of pulmonary edema are similar to those of pneumonia, although it is not precipitated by an infection and there is no fever. Within 12 to 36 hours after reaching high altitude, the victim of pulmonary edema experiences extreme weakness, shortness of breath, nausea, vomiting, very rapid pulse (120 to 160), cyanosis (bluish color) of the fingernails, face and lips, noisy breathing which progresses to moist crackling breath sounds, and irritative coughing which produces a frothy white or pink sputum and later blood.

If untreated, the victim rapidly moves into the final phase characterized by unconsciousness and bubbles in the mouth or nose, and death will follow. The early symptoms may be mistaken for mountain sickness or fatigue, or may pass unnoticed during the night, with the morning finding the victim unconscious and in the final phase.

High-altitude cerebral edema is the accumulation of fluid in the brain. Symptoms begin with a severe, relentless headache resulting from pressure due to the swelling of brain tissue. They advance to difficulties with physical coordination, slurred speech, irrational behavior, collapse, and eventually death.

For both pulmonary and cerebral edema, you need to be alert to symptoms in yourself and others. The most effective first aid is rapid evacuation to lower altitude or constant administration of oxygen. Descending is the only way to recover, with a rapid descent of 3,000 feet usually bringing marked improvement. If the victim exhibits only minor symptoms, it may be OK to spend a few days at lower elevations and then go back up. But a climber who demonstrates advanced signs should not return to high altitude, as it takes weeks to recover from edemas.

Frostbite

Frostbite is a concern at high altitudes because of the cold environment and because reduced oxygen means your body is less efficient at generating internal warmth, making hands and feet more susceptible to freezing.

Frostbite is freezing of the tissues, and most commonly affects toes, fingers, and face. It occurs when an extremity loses heat faster than it can be replaced by the circulating blood, or it may result from direct exposure to extreme cold or high wind. Damp feet can freeze when moisture conducts heat away from the skin and destroys the insulating value of socks and boots. With continued cold or inactivity, circulation to the extremities is steadily reduced, accelerating the freezing process. If you're using good mountaineering clothing and equipment, frostbite is not likely to occur.

An area of superficial frostbite looks white or gray. Surface skin feels hard, but the underlying tissue will be soft. As the frostbite intensifies, the affected area becomes hard, cold, and insensitive.

You can warm superficially frostbitten areas by placing them against warm skin. Put your feet against a companion's abdomen or armpits. Warm your fingers in your own armpits. During rewarming, large blisters may appear on the surface, as well as in the underlying tissue. Two important cautions. You must not raise the temperature of the frostbitten area much above body temperature, such as by warming near a fire. And never rub the injured part, especially not with snow. The additional cooling and the abrasive action further damage devitalized tissues. Misguided efforts to give speedy relief invariably increase the injury.

You can thaw extensive or deep frostbite, in which the affected area is white, has no feeling, and appears deeply frozen. Immerse the damaged area in water that is at a temperature between 99 and 104 degrees Fahrenheit until it is thawed. But do not start the thawing unless you are sure you can thaw the part completely and without interruption. It's better to wait for medical help than risk incomplete thawing or refreezing. Sometimes it's better to make no attempt to thaw frozen feet until after you retreat from the mountains and can get transportation and medical aid. If you leave your feet frozen, it's still possible to walk on them and suffer little or no additional tissue damage. But once your feet are thawed, you won't be able to walk and you will probably experience severe pain.

ACCLIMATIZATION

The body needs time to acclimate to higher altitude. However, the time it takes to adapt varies from person to person.

Ascend at a moderate rate, averaging 1,000 feet a day in net elevation gain. If you are doing double carries, this may mean establishing camps at 2,000-foot intervals so that you carry one day and move camp the next, for a net gain of 2,000 feet every two days. If the suitable campsites are 3,000 feet apart, you can carry one day, move camp the next, and rest the third day, for a net gain of 3,000 feet every three days. Try not to overdo your efforts until you've become well acclimated, and schedule rest days after big pushes.

Hydration is critical in avoiding altitude sickness. Rather than relying on a figure for daily liquid consumption, such as 4 quarts per person, monitor your urine output and color. A good rule of thumb is that urine should be copious and clear, while dark urine indicates you're not drinking enough water.

Above 18,000 feet, most people begin to deteriorate physically regardless of acclimatization. Minimize the stays at high altitudes and periodically return to lower altitudes to recover. The old advice is good: Climb high, sleep low. The body acclimates much faster during exertion than during rest, and recovers more quickly at a lower altitude. Expedition-style climbing takes advantage of these concepts in carrying loads to a high camp, returning to lower altitude to recover, then ascending again.

AN EXPEDITION PHILOSOPHY

Members of an expedition need a common code to live by during the weeks they struggle together. A good one is summed up in three promises you and your teammates can make: To respect the land, to take care of yourselves, and to come home again.

Every day, your expedition will have the chance to put the health and beauty of the land ahead of your immediate comfort. The easy way out might be to burn wood fires or set up camp in a virgin meadow or abandon heavy gear. But if you've promised to respect the land, you'll be able to do the right thing.

If you and your partners have promised to take care of yourselves, you've made a commitment to group self-reliance. You may have no choice in the matter, anyway, as you will likely be a long way from rescuers, helicopters, hospitals, or even other climbers. You can prepare by thinking through the emergencies the expedition could face and laying plans for saving the day. You'll be happy the plans are ready if you have to use them, and grateful if you don't.

The third promise might be the hardest to keep because it can conflict with that burning desire for the summit. It's really a promise to climb safely and to sacrifice dreams of the summit before laying your life on the line. But expedition climbing is, after all, about pushing limits and testing yourself in a very tough arena. Each person and each team must decide what level of risk they wish to accept. Out of that flows daily decisions on how fast to ascend, what gear to carry, when to change routes, when to back off. Most climbers would rather return home safely than push for the summit under unsafe conditions. But how do you define "unsafe"? You'll keep the third promise by being sure you find the definition that is just right for your expedition.

A SAMPLE EXPEDITION EQUIPMENT LIST
GROUP GEAR

Shelter
- ☐ Expedition-quality tent
- ☐ Snow stakes and/or tent flukes
- ☐ Sponge and whisk broom
- ☐ Snow shelter construction tools: large snow shovel (for moving lots of snow); small snow shovel (for delicate trimming); snow saw (for cutting blocks)

Group climbing gear
- ☐ Ropes
- ☐ Hardware: snow and ice gear (pickets, flukes, ice screws); rock gear (pitons, spring-loaded camming devices, chocks); carabiners; runners; fixed line; extra climbing equipment (spare ice axe or tool, spare crampons)

Kitchen
- ☐ Stove gear: stove; wind screen and stove pad; fuel containers and fuel filter; matches and/or butane lighters
- ☐ Cook gear: pots; pot gripper; sponge/scrubber; dip cup and cooking spoon; snow sack

Repair kit
- ☐ Tent repair kit (pole splices, spare pole)
- ☐ Stove repair kit
- ☐ Crampon repair kit (extra screw, connecting bars, straps)
- ☐ Tape (duct, filament, ripstop fabric repair tape)
- ☐ Tools (standard, Phillips, and Allen screwdrivers, small pliers, small wire cutter/shear)
- ☐ Sewing kit: assorted needles and thread; assorted buttons, snaps, buckles, and "D" rings; Velcro (hook and rug); fabric (cordura, ripstop); flat webbing
- ☐ Miscellaneous: extra ski pole basket; wire and cord

First-aid kit

- [ ] Most expeditions will have a comprehensive group first-aid kit. In addition to the normal first-aid items, the kit should include the following drugs, plus others recommended by a physician.
- [ ] Prescription drugs. This will vary with the destination but should include antibiotics, strong analgesics, anti-diarrhetic, laxatives, and altitude medication (Diamox, dexamethasone).
- [ ] Non-prescription drugs. This will vary with the destination but should include a cough suppressant, decongestant, and mild analgesic (aspirin, ibuprofen).

Miscellaneous group gear

- [ ] Altimeter and compass
- [ ] Radio transceiver
- [ ] Latrine equipment (plastic sacks, rubber gloves)

PERSONAL GEAR

Clothing

- [ ] Synthetic fabric underwear
- [ ] Insulating layers
- [ ] Down clothing
- [ ] Wind protection garments (top and bottom)
- [ ] Extremities: hands (liner gloves, insulating gloves, and mittens); feet (liner socks, insulating socks, vapor-barrier socks); head (balaclavas, sun hats, face masks)
- [ ] Miscellaneous: bandannas; sun shirt; plastic double boots; supergaiters and/or overboots

Sleeping

- [ ] Sleeping bag
- [ ] Bivouac sack
- [ ] Vapor-barrier liner
- [ ] Inflatable foam pad
- [ ] Closed-cell foam pad

Climbing

- [ ] Ice axe
- [ ] Second ice tool
- [ ] Ski pole
- [ ] Seat harness with ice tool holsters
- [ ] Chest harness
- [ ] Crampons
- [ ] Personal carabiners
- [ ] Personal runners
- [ ] Ascenders and/or prusiks
- [ ] Helmet
- [ ] Large-volume pack
- [ ] Snowshoes or skis
- [ ] Sled with associated hardware (haul lines, carabiners, prusiks)

Miscellaneous gear

- [ ] Avalanche beacon
- [ ] Sunglasses and goggles
- [ ] Spare prescription glasses
- [ ] Personal hygiene: toilet paper; pee bottle; toothbrush; comb; chemical wash/wipes; sunscreen; lip balm; foot powder; ear plugs
- [ ] Personal recreation: camera and film; books; journal (waterproof paper); personal stereo

· 16 ·

SAFETY AND LEADERSHIP

Mountaineering is a sport of controlled risk. Climbers deal with the hazards of nature and their own shortcomings by cultivating knowledge, skill, and good judgment. A list of dangers in the wilderness reads like a catalog of disaster unless you've studied the hazards and know how to avoid them in order to establish control over your own safety. Climbers also need to develop leadership ability to help promote their group's safety, comfort, and success.

ACCIDENTS

One way to prevent accidents is to study incidents that have happened and try to learn from them. The American Alpine Club does just that in its annual publication "Accidents in North American Mountaineering." The publication includes only actual climbing accidents, as distinguished from other mishaps that occur in mountainous regions. It describes only those accidents that are voluntarily reported, so it doesn't include numerous unpublicized incidents. The accidents represent only a fraction of those in mountaineering areas throughout the world.

More than 1,100 climbers have been killed in North American mountaineering accidents since 1947, when the American Alpine Club began its annual reports. Despite advances in equipment, skills, and techniques, a number of climbers are killed or injured each year. Every accident is a little different from every other, but there are many common causes and most involve human error. For example, modern gear rarely breaks by itself. Equipment failure is usually related to improper use or to poor placement of protection. Climbers also cause accidents when they try to exceed their climbing abilities by relying on incompletely learned techniques.

There are some limitations to the American Alpine Club statistics because the types of causes change as climbing practices evolve, and the classification of accidents is a difficult judgment call, especially in deciding the relationship of immediate and contributing causes. But in spite of these limitations, the annual reports roughly indicate the elements of danger in climbing by showing recurring patterns.

The most common immediate causes of accidents reported were (1) fall or slip on rock, (2) slip on snow and ice, and (3) falling rock or other object. The most common contributing causes were (1) climbing unroped, (2) attempting a climb that exceeded abilities (inexperience), and (3) being inadequately equipped for the conditions or climbing situation.

An accident victim may feel that a mishap occurred "like a bolt out of the blue." But it's clear, in retrospect, that many accidents moved step by step toward an almost predictable incident. The climber who takes off on an ascent without an ice axe because it was forgotten in the rush of leaving home may do fine all day in soft snow. If this climber slips during the descent on the firmer snow of evening and is injured, it's an accident—but it's no ''bolt out of the blue.'' An alert leader tries to spot potential accidents, and takes such precautions as turning back a minimally equipped party in the face of worsening weather.

CLIMBING HAZARDS

Mountaineers face hazards of two sorts: the objective dangers of the mountain environment, and the subjective factors that are dependent on the climber. The objective, physical hazards of the mountains—the storms, the cold, the high altitude—are easy to recognize. No less important, but far harder to evaluate, are the subjective factors involving the climber's knowledge, skill, and judgment.

OBJECTIVE HAZARDS: THE MOUNTAIN ENVIRONMENT

Objective hazards are the natural processes that exist whether humans are involved or not. Darkness, storms, lightning, cold, precipitation, high altitude, avalanches, and rockfall are powerful, impersonal environmental conditions that can easily overwhelm humans. These objective hazards of the mountains are eternally persistent and changeable. We cannot control these forces, but we can learn to recognize them and act to minimize their dangers.

You will find detailed information throughout this entire book on dealing with objective hazards, especially in the chapters on wilderness travel and on the various types of climbing—rock, snow, ice, winter, and aid. They spell out ways to confront objective hazards ranging from fearsome exposure and rotten rock to avalanches and steep snow slopes with poor runout. They give advice on avoiding rockfall, icefall, cornices, crevasses, and other environmental dangers.

Many of the hazards of the terrain are relatively easy to spot, such as rotten rock or a steep cliff. The hazards of weather can be somewhat more difficult to identify because they change so quickly. When they do, it often adds significant risk to the climb. Rain or snow turns warm, dry rock into wet or icy surfaces difficult to climb. Wind blows ropes around and also makes communication more difficult. Fog or whiteout obscures the route, forcing you to rely on compass and altimeter for navigation and increasing the danger of falling into a crevasse or off of a cornice.

Cold weather, especially if it is abetted by wind and rain, can bring deadly hypothermia. Hot weather, on the other hand, poses the dangers of dehydration and hyperthermia. (Specialized courses and publications on mountaineering first aid provide information for diagnosis and treatment of these conditions.) Lightning, although not one of the principal hazards of mountaineering, has caused a number of serious accidents. The peaks and ridges that climbers seek generate the vertical updrafts and rain-cloud conditions that generate lightning.

Reducing the risk

To reduce risk, you need to recognize objective hazards and learn how to avoid them. If you recognize the possibility of rockfall, for instance, you will wear a hard hat and take extra care to prevent knocking rock loose with the rope or with your body. If you recognize an avalanche-prone slope, you will follow the correct procedures to avoid it and will know what to do in the event you or someone in your party is caught in a slide. If you see a white-out or other extremes of weather developing, you will have the training and equipment to deal with it.

It's simple to recognize the objective hazard of high exposure—that is, being in a steep and exposed place. There are exposed places where you can sit or stand without serious danger, but loose footing or a moment of inattention can bring tragedy. The safest response to exposure is to rope up so you are on belay or tied into the mountain. If you are the belayer, estimate the direction and magnitude of any force you may have to absorb if your partner falls and set up an anchored belay station where you can handle such a fall.

It's not so easy to recognize the hazard of a crevasse that is hidden beneath a layer of snow. But if you have studied glacier travel and learned the external signs of hidden crevasses, you will know when to rope up and how to choose routes that minimize the danger of falling into one. You and your companions also will have the training and equipment to carry out a safe, efficient crevasse rescue if that becomes necessary.

Help fortify yourself against objective hazards by always carrying the proper clothing, food, and equipment, because any trip can bring unexpected danger or an emergency bivouac. Protective gear, whether it's for technical climbing or bivouac survival, doesn't do any good if it is left at home, and it cannot often be replaced merely by nerve or skill.

You can use this book as a basic guide to proven gear and techniques, by studying the chapters on the various types of climbing and wilderness travel in addition to the specialized chapters on clothing, equipment, camping, navigation, knots, belaying, and rappelling. Then work to develop the experience and judgment to make the right decisions at the right time in order to avoid what are generally called accidents.

SUBJECTIVE FACTORS: THE CLIMBER

Subjective human factors share the blame for many accidents along with the objective physical hazards of the mountain. The climber without a bivy sack or extra clothes wouldn't have become hypothermic if it were not for that unexpected snowstorm. Conversely, the snowstorm wouldn't have caused any grief if it had not crossed paths with the climber.

The natural forces constantly at work on a mountain are usually harmless unless a human being is in their way at a critical instant. Then a small mistake—the subjective human factor—can cost dearly. A slope may be ripening to an avalanche tomorrow, but a climber ignorant of snow structure can trigger it today. A rock weakened by natural processes may be preparing to fall next week, but the weight of a climber can pull it loose today. This subjective factor, which brings a particular climber to a given danger point at just the perilous moment, is nearly always at the root of a climbing accident.

Although we can't alter the objective hazards, we have considerable control over the subjective factors that can reduce their risk. These subjective elements affect every phase of a climb, including choice of route, skill of the climbers, equipment quality, physical conditioning, leadership, and climbing techniques. In the final analysis, everything goes back to a climber's knowledge, skill, and judgment. Any shortcomings will eventually show up in the reality of a climb.

Knowledge

A beginner ignorant of mountaineering gains knowledge from books, courses, mountain climbers—and from climbing. At the start, beginners won't even know they don't know: a novice might look at an avalanche-prone slope warming in the sun and not even be aware the party needs to ask itself whether there is a risk. But as they study and as they climb, beginners can add to their knowledge by keeping alert and asking questions.

A climber won't learn much by simply tagging along without paying attention to the climb, relying on others to make all the decisions and ending the day with not much more mountaineering knowledge than at the start. A climber with inadequate knowledge can mean danger to a climbing party, which may need to count on every member in an emergency—a poor time to have to unmask a climber's failings.

Skill

A great many climbers are skilled, but some are more skilled than others. The point is that it's important to match a climber's skill level with the particular climb. A good match and you have a safe, satisfying climb. A poor match and you could have disaster. An excellent climber trying to raise a personal level of skill faces increased risk; so does a novice moving up to an intermediate-level climb. A climber who does well on warm, dry rock may be in trouble if the rock is wet.

It takes practice and more practice to raise your level of skill. Practice under forgiving conditions. Try making those harder moves first at a practice area with a top rope, rather than on a long run-out at the end of a strenuous pitch. Keep working at it. A great part of climbing safety lies in competence that embraces a commitment to better methods, an eagerness to study and to learn, and a determination to practice and perfect the skills of mountaineering.

Judgment

Good judgment can be a climber's most valuable ally. Good judgment is the quality of using knowledge gained from study and experience to make sound decisions. Your mountaineering judgment should get better and better as you read and as you climb. Watch experienced climbers at work and try to determine what decision they will reach in a particular situation, and why. Learn to think, question, and reach informed decisions.

Experienced climbers won't always agree on what constitutes good judgment in a particular case. Some climbers demand a conservative high level of safety and would consider a decision that results in moderate risk to be evidence of poor judgment. Others would find the decision correct based on all the conditions of the climb and the abilities of the climbers. Each person has an individual definition of an acceptable level of risk, so climbers need to discuss this question with their teammates before a climb. The start of good judgment is to decide on an acceptable level of risk for yourself and to match your known skills with the difficulties of the climb.

A common form of poor judgment is underestimating the skills needed for an objective, whether it's a single move or a major mountain ascent. It's poor judgment to climb beyond your present ability and knowledge during a demanding climb. Try new moves and techniques in a practice situation. But if they come during a climb, be sure you have extra protection—good enough to prevent injury in case you fall and to permit you to get back on route afterward.

It's also poor judgment to let desire for the objective overwhelm an accurate assessment of the risk. Desire is a very useful element in climbing; it helps you forget weariness and calls forth your best efforts. But if it's not restrained, it can end in disaster. It can delude you into thinking that a far-away summit is close, that a questionable placement will hold, that a weakened team is strong enough. This is wishful thinking. Be rigorous in making a rational evaluation of weather, party strength, and other factors in deciding whether or not to turn back.

Good judgment in mountaineering also means acknowledging when you or your team are having a bad day. All experienced mountaineers remember days when their climbing lacked the usual feel; when easy pitches felt hard. Take any bodily limitations into account, such as fatigue, cramps, blisters, altitude sickness, or poor conditioning. If you're honest with yourself, you'll recognize that occasional bad day and scale back your plans accordingly.

LEADERSHIP

The safety, success, and fun of a climb depend in large part on leadership and organization. These formal concepts may sound a bit stuffy for the out-of-doors, but they exist in any successful climbing party. A small group of longtime climbing companions probably incorporates all the elements of leadership and organization with no conscious thought or effort because they have become habit over the years. It's a different matter with a party that includes beginners and whose members have never climbed together.

Leadership starts with each individual. Individual leadership means being aware of the group and its progress, whether or not you are the formal climb leader. Assume responsibility for your own knowledge and skill, and make personal judgments based on how they can support the group's objective. Be willing to speak up when you feel the risks of the climb may exceed the abilities of the party. Don't be deterred by fears that others know more than you and may consider you weak. By asserting personal leadership, you can contribute to group decision-making within the framework of the established organization.

The complexities of leadership grow as party size and trip length increase. On a weekend climb by two close friends, it's possible for one of them to take on all the organization and leadership chores: planning the menu, selecting the route, supplying the gear, and so forth. In a group of several friends, leadership may be by consensus. As the trip becomes more complex, one person may be designated the formal leader, charged with coordinating the group's activities.

The leader of a climb cannot do everything, nor is that desirable. A leader delegates duties and responsibilities in order to maintain an overview of the trip and ensure that all tasks are carried out. This also helps build morale as party members become more involved in the climb by taking on specific jobs such as planning meals, arranging transportation, or coordinating equipment. In a group that is large or in which the members are not well acquainted, the leader should appoint an assistant who can assume the role of leader if that becomes necessary.

A leader is also a teacher. Beginning mountaineers need help with climbing techniques, and experienced mountaineers may appreciate help in learning leadership. The best leaders exhibit the patience, empathy, and generosity that it takes to give members of their party experience in all phases of leadership.

Leaders prepare carefully to meet any major disaster that could befall their party. But the most common, and the most vexing, problems of leadership are the less dramatic, exasperating little mishaps that arise at the most inopportune moments—a lagging, footsore climber who is breaking in new boots, or another too ill or fatigued to continue the climb. There is no set answer for these trying situations. The leader is called on to use good judgment in evaluating the predicament, and then make a decision firmly and

unequivocally. An effective leader recognizes the potential for serious consequences in such seemingly trivial problems.

Mountaineering trips bring a rich spectrum of choices and make continual demands on a climber's will. Without leadership, even a strong party may wander aimlessly or sit paralyzed with indecision. But with good leadership, even a relatively weak party may achieve its goals.

THE STRENGTH OF THE CLIMBING PARTY

Whether a party is up to the challenges of a particular climb depends on its overall strength, which in turn involves the proficiency of the climbers, the size and speed of the group, and other important factors. Good leadership is central to maintaining a party's morale and making the most of its attributes.

Mountaineering proficiency

The strongest party consists of several climbers with a high degree of mountaineering proficiency—experienced, well-equipped, in good physical condition, with every skill for the climb at hand. What constitutes a weak party is not so easy to define. In some cases, a party is strong enough if it has only two strong climbers in addition to many weak members. In other situations, a group of ten strong climbers and one ineffective climber is too weak a party. A group with no experienced members is a weak party in any case.

The leader should be familiar with the climbers' abilities in order to know how to assign them. The leader may need a patient, reliable climber to encourage slow members at the rear of the group, or a pair of sharp routefinders to scout out the way ahead. If the leader is traveling near one end of a large party, an assistant should be assigned to help near the other end.

The leader also uses knowledge of the climbers' skills in setting up rope teams. In small parties, rope teams are usually formed by tacit agreement among members of the group. But in larger parties or in groups where the people are relative strangers, the leader may set up teams based on the climbers' experience, speed, and personality. Each team of experienced climbers should have enough strength to rotate the lead, sharing the work and giving less proficient climbers a chance to expand their experience.

Size of the climbing party

The minimum size for a mountaineering party is considered to be the number of people who can handle an accident situation adequately. Traditionally, a minimum party of three has been standard. Thus, if one climber is hurt, the second can stay with the victim while the third goes for help.

Variations from the basic unit of three depend on the situation. On difficult terrain or in adverse weather, when it would be dangerous for one person to go alone for help, four may be the safe minimum. On the other hand, the complexity of the route may make more then a single rope team of two a liability.

A glacier climb calls for four to six people, divided into two rope teams, in order to carry out an efficient crevasse rescue. A climb in a remote area where there may be no help within 100 miles must be planned for complete self-sufficiency and, therefore, may become an expedition of relatively large numbers. A small party in a remote area must consciously accept an increased level of risk.

It's a mistake, however, to believe that a larger party is always a safer party. A larger party can start bigger avalanches and kick down more loose rock. It will generally be slower and more unwieldy, both in camping and climbing. A party of ten to twelve is considered the largest that can impose itself on the wilderness without serious damage to the ecosystem—and even this is too large a group for some areas.

Backup support

A party gains in strength if it has a support team nearby or if there are other climbers in the area. To be useful, a support team must be willing and able to come to your aid, and ready to initiate rescue automatically at a prearranged time. Then, if your party doesn't report in by a certain time, a rescue effort will get under way.

At the very least, be sure to leave a written description of your plans with a responsible person who will dispatch help if you don't return on time. Leave enough information so rescuers have a fair idea where to look, but there's no need to make it so detailed that you limit your own choices when you get to the area. If you do deviate from the schedule you left behind, keep in mind that you may be complicating any rescue effort. Give an estimated time of return, but build in enough leeway so that a few hours' delay from a routefinding error or other minor problem won't result in having the rescuers called out. Don't forget to check in when you return.

Keeping the party together

A critical responsibility of leadership is keeping the party together in order to concentrate strength and maintain communication. It's easy to divide up in the course of the trip, drifting into weak splinter groups. Some parties are large enough to divide into self-sufficient subgroups, but each subgroup must have adequate strength and leadership to meet its goals.

In small parties of equally proficient climbers, it's fairly simple to keep people together; if one lags, the others usually recognize the problem and slow their pace. In larger parties, the leader and assistants must work together to keep their group from splitting into independent fragments. This situation arises most often within organized club outings and climbing courses. Leaders of these groups may need to exert considerable control to keep the lead rope team from charging ahead, losing contact with climbers on the last rope.

It's even harder to keep a party together on the descent than it is on the way up. The leader, normally the last person off the mountain, must lay out crystal-clear instructions for where and when the party will meet in case of a separation. Glissading often results in breaking up parties. The fast, experienced glissaders are off the bottom of the run and on their way long before the last members of the group can overtake them. The leader should require a rendezvous of the entire party reasonably near the end of any major glissade. If the leader can hold the group to a pace everyone can maintain, there's little danger the party will be weakened by fragmentation or by having to search for a missing climber.

Time management

Speed is often equated with safety, and this can be true in crossing an area of rockfall hazard or trying to reach camp before dark. Speed also has its dangers. A quick, hard push can get climbers to a place where retreat is difficult in the face of deteriorating conditions, whereas a more measured, cautious approach would have left them with an easier withdrawal. Speed for its own sake can be a hazard if it comes at the expense of proper technique or safety precautions. The important thing is not how fast you go, but how wisely and well you use your time.

A climbing party's use of time should be planned out in advance, at least roughly. You can figure out the best time to get under way in the morning by mentally working through the various sections of the climb and estimating how long each will take. It's a good idea to set a time for turning back even if the summit hasn't been reached. The turn-around time will help prevent the party from pushing onward after it's too late to reach the summit and still get back to the camp or trailhead in daylight.

BECOMING A LEADER

Becoming a leader is a do-it-yourself project, requiring desire and initiative. The best way to become a good leader is to lead and to watch others lead, to organize informal private trips with friends on short, familiar climbs, and to gradually work up to more ambitious projects. Climb with experienced leaders and observe how they plan and how they work with their teams. Ask for assistant-leader positions on these climbs and become involved in the planning and decision-making.

Self-appraisal is a big part of becoming a good leader. Effective leaders take the time to assess their own performance, asking themselves: Did I do as well as I could? What went right? Why? What went wrong? Why? How could things have been improved?

Leadership brings pleasures as well as burdens. As awesome as the duty may appear, the exercise of competent leadership can become surprisingly easy if you prepare for it, fully accept the responsibility, and use common sense and good judgment to deal with rapidly changing situations.

• 17 •

ALPINE RESCUE

Mountaineer training emphasizes techniques for staying safe and healthy. But when injury or illness strikes, it's likely to be a long way from professional medical aid or rescue. Climbers are usually rescued by other climbers, often at great risk and sacrifice. So high a degree of mutual responsibility requires that every mountaineer be able to help in a rescue. This chapter focuses on efforts that can be mounted by a small climbing party without specialized equipment.

SEARCH

Searching for a missing person is one of the most common rescue activities. Start a search only if you can answer "yes" to this question: "Does the missing person need help?" If the person is healthy, well-equipped, traveling where injury is unlikely, and experienced in climbing and route-finding, there's a good chance he or she will find the way back to the party within a few hours. You may decide to defer a search until the next morning to give the missing person time to return.

Start the search immediately if the missing person might have wandered onto steep rock or a crevassed glacier, or is fatigued, inexperienced, or poorly equipped. Also get the search started right away if a physical problem, such as diabetes, is a factor, or if the missing person is a child. Search immediately if an entire rope team is missing after a severe storm, or in avalanche conditions, or on difficult terrain.

The thoroughness of a search will depend partly on how many searchers are available. A small party may be able to mount no more than a narrow search along a limited track. With a half dozen people, there probably can be a perimeter search. A large group can thoroughly comb a considerable area.

Regardless of the method, each person must know the full plan before the search begins. If the party decides to split up, each group must know where the others are. Arrange signals ahead of time: sounds such as yodels, yells or whistles, or visible signs with mirrors or lights. Establish a time and place for everyone to meet, whether or not they have found anything.

For safety, searchers should travel in pairs or remain within earshot of one another. Of course, this means that a search party of only two or three people can cover no more than a narrow strip of ground at a time. The best chance in this situation is to outguess the missing person. Put yourself in that person's place and visualize errors that might logically have been made. Check likely places such as the exits of off-route gullies and ridges.

If that doesn't work, retrace your party's original trail, searching all the way for tracks that indicate where the missing person wandered off. When such a point is found, proceed along the most likely path, watching for more footprints in snow, mud, sand, or on foot logs. In the absence of frequent footprints, searchers must fan out at broad intervals, calling to each other regularly and pausing frequently to listen for calls from the missing person. If no clues turn up after several hours of searching, it's probably time to go for outside help.

WHEN AN ACCIDENT HAPPENS

Leadership and discipline are key elements of success in alpine rescue. If your party has no recognized leader, select one to take charge in an emergency. The leader should consider suggestions from other members of the party, but the leader's decisions must be accepted without argument.

Go to the aid of an injured climber quickly—but move carefully to avoid any further accidents. On difficult terrain, dispatch only one or two rescuers, who are on belay and packing all the needed aid and rescue gear. As you climb or rappel down to an injured climber, keep to one side to avoid the danger of knocking rocks onto the victim. Stay calm; frenzied activity only complicates the rescue.

Urgent first aid should be rendered as soon as possible: bleeding stopped, breathing restarted, shock relieved, fractures immobilized. If it becomes necessary to move the victim to another spot because the accident site is too hazardous, use methods that will not compound the injuries.

It's important to keep close watch over the injured climber. A victim who is left unguarded, even for a few moments, must be tied to the mountain to prevent the danger of falling or wandering off, perhaps due to confusion or irrationality. Design the tie-in so that the climber cannot unfasten it.

In dealing with an emergency, swift action may be less effective than correct action. A hasty splitting up of the climbing party or any other spontaneous but shortsighted effort has less chance of ultimate success than one more deliberately considered. Therefore, after the initial demands of safety and first aid are satisfied, the leader and party sit down to plan. Everything must be thought through to the very end, everything prearranged, including what each person is to do under all circumstances throughout the rescue operation.

Every aspect of the situation needs cool analysis. How serious are the injuries? What measures are necessary to sustain the victim during evacuation? What is the terrain like and how far is it to the road? What are the strengths and resources of the party? Only after careful analysis of such questions should your party select a course of action.

EVACUATION BY THE CLIMBING PARTY

A climbing party can sometimes evacuate an ill or injured party member with no outside help. If the injured person can walk and the injuries are relatively minor, a lightened pack and moral support may be all that is needed. The party also may be able to evacuate a climber who has minor but disabling injuries such as a sprained ankle or injured knee.

An injured person generally benefits from a period of rest following an accident. Because the further trauma of immediate evacuation is seldom justified, postpone the move until the victim's condition has stabilized. The injured person can probably offer the best indications of when to begin the evacuation. Consult the victim and monitor the injuries closely, before and during the evacuation, and always keep the person's comfort in mind.

Some medical conditions require immediate evacuation: pulmonary edema, cerebral edema, unconsciousness for unknown cause, diabetic coma, and progressively deteriorating conditions such as appendicitis. Immediate evacuation also is necessary if circumstances of weather or terrain are life-threatening. Certain other conditions require that evacuation be delayed until trained medical help arrives (unless it will be more than 24 hours): head injuries, neck and spinal fractures, heart attack, apoplexy (stroke), and internal injuries. Evacuation is required but not urgent for all other serious injuries and illnesses.

OUTSIDE HELP

There are times a party can't cope with its own emergency. Outside help probably will be needed if a climber's injuries are severe, if the evacuation requires long stretches of lifting or lowering, or when circumstances—party size, condition of party, terrain, and distance to the trailhead—combine to make transport difficult. Thirty or more rescuers may be needed to carry a disabled victim for more than 2 or 3 miles on even the best of trails.

After your party decides that outside aid is needed, send for help as soon as the victim is stabilized and the persons going for aid are no longer needed at the accident site. In many areas, help by helicopter is usually no more than 3 hours away once word gets to the proper authorities, though this will depend on weather, terrain, and local politics. Ground rescuers often can be at the scene in 8 to 16 hours. If the climbing party is in a sheltered area accessible by helicopter and the weather is good, don't move the victim unless the injuries require doing so.

If your party needs help, don't hesitate in asking it from climbers on nearby peaks, from people living or working in the region, or from local authorities. A climbing party should know in advance where to turn for help if its own efforts fail and how to cooperate with rescuers and authorities.

It is sometimes not possible to send anyone from your group for help. Your only alternative then is to try to signal rescuers with noise or visual signals. Such a situation dramatizes the need to leave information about your intended route and estimated time of return with a responsible person, who will notify authorities if you don't show up.

GOING FOR HELP

If possible, send two climbers out together for help—partly for safety and partly because two people can do a better job of obtaining aid. Be sure they have a clear understanding of the party's situation and requirements so they will know exactly what aid to seek. They should take with them a list of the names and phone numbers of everyone in the party, a completed accident report form, and a map that pinpoints the accident site. Fill out an accident report form (fig. 17-1) for each injured person, with one copy going out with the messengers and the other being kept by the party leader.

Messengers need to carry enough gear to handle their own emergencies but not so much that they cannot move swiftly. However, the certainty, not the swiftness, of getting the message out is the most important consideration. The messengers must travel in a safe manner. The victim and other members of the party are relying solely on them, assuming authorities will get the word and that help will soon be on its way. The messengers should mark the route to help in finding the way back.

The messengers have several vital responsibilities once they get out of the wilderness. First of all, they contact the appropriate local authorities, such as the county sheriff or park personnel. They ask them to help in a rescue, or to relay the need for help to the local Mountain Rescue organization. If evacuation will take place over technical terrain, the authorities must know this so they will dispatch rescuers with the proper training.

The messengers' job is not ended at this point. They must make certain that messages are sent at once, accurately, and that they reach their destination. Often the organization of a rescue depends upon a chain of communication, messages relayed from person to person via telephone and radio, until finally a rescue leader is reached. Along the way, vital information may be ignored by non-mountaineers who do not understand the words they are asked to convey. The messengers should talk directly with a trusted fellow climber so that the line of communication is not broken. If the messengers can't speak personally to the rescue leader, they must be insistent with intermediaries—perhaps to the point of being obnoxious—to assure that a garbled message does not result in a tragic rescue failure.

The messengers then wait by the telephone at a meeting point, where they will get together with the rescue party. The messengers turn the accident report, map, and list of names over to the rescue leader and assist in devising a rescue plan. Unless

Fig. 17–1. Accident report form

FIRST AID REPORT FORM

© The Mountaineers

START HERE — **FINDINGS** — **FIRST AID GIVEN**

AIRWAY, BREATHING, CIRCULATION

INITIAL RAPID CHECK
(Chest Wounds, Severe Bleeding)

ASK WHAT HAPPENED:

ASK WHERE IT HURTS:

TAKE PULSE & RESPIRATIONS | PULSE | RESPIRATIONS

HEAD-TO-TOE EXAMINATION

HEAD: Scalp — Wounds
Ears, Nose — Fluid
Eyes — Pupils
Jaw — Stability
Mouth — Wounds

NECK: Wounds, Deformity

CHEST: Movement, Symmetry

ABDOMEN: Wounds, Rigidity

PELVIS: Stability

EXTREMITIES: Wounds, Deformity
Sensation & Movement
Pulses Below Injury

BACK: Wounds, Deformity

SKIN: Color
Temperature
Moistness

STATE OF CONSCIOUSNESS

PAIN (Location)

LOOK FOR MEDICAL ID TAG

ALLERGIES

VICTIM'S NAME | AGE

COMPLETED BY | DATE | TIME

RESCUE REQUEST

Fill Out One Form Per Victim

TIME OF INCIDENT
AM   PM | DATE

NATURE OF INCIDENT
FALL ON: ☐ ROCK ☐ SNOW ☐ FALLING ROCK
☐ CREVASSE ☐ AVALANCHE
☐ ILLNESS EXCESSIVE ☐ HEAT ☐ COLD

BRIEF DESCRIPTION OF INCIDENT

DETACH HERE – SEND OUT WITH REQUEST FOR AID

INJURIES
(List Most Severe First) | FIRST AID GIVEN

SKIN TEMP/COLOR:

STATE OF CONSCIOUSNESS:

PAIN (Location):

RECORD: | INITIAL | WHEN LEAVE SCENE
Time
Pulse
Respiration
VICTIM'S NAME | | AGE

ADDRESS

NOTIFY (Name)

RELATIONSHIP | PHONE

TEAR HERE – KEEP THIS SECTION WITH VICTIM

VITAL SIGN RECORD

Record TIME	BREATHS		PULSE		PULSES BELOW INJURY	PUPILS	SKIN	STATE OF CONSCIOUS- NESS	OTHER
	Rate	Character	Rate	Character					
		Deep, Shallow, Noisy, Labored		Strong, Weak, Regular, Irregular	Strong Weak Absent	Equal Size, React To Light, Round	Color Tempera- ture Moistness	Alert, Confused, Unresponsive	Pain, Anxiety, Thirst, Etc.

TEAR HERE –KEEP THIS SECTION WITH THE VICTIM

DETACH HERE –SEND OUT WITH REQUEST FOR AID

SIDE 2 RESCUE REQUEST

EXACT LOCATION (Include Marked Map If Possible)

QUADRANGLE: SECTION:

AREA DESCRIPTION:

TERRAIN: □ GLACIER □ SNOW □ ROCK
□ BRUSH □ TIMBER □ TRAIL
□ FLAT □ MODERATE □ STEEP

ON SITE PLANS:
□ Will Stay Put
□ Will Evacuate To
Can Stay Overnight Safely □ Yes □ No
On Site Equipment: □ Tent □ Stove □ Food
□ Ground Insulation □ Flare □ CB Radio

LOCAL WEATHER

EVACUATION: □ Carry-Out □ Helicopter
□ Lowering □ Raising

EQUIPMENT: □ Rigid Litter
□ Food □ Water □ Other

PARTY MEMBERS REMAINING:
_____ Beginners _____ Intermediate _____ Experienced

NAME   NOTIFY (Name)   PHONE

NOTIFY:
IN NATIONAL PARK: Ranger
OUTSIDE NATIONAL PARK: Sheriff/County Police.
RCMP (Canada)

they are injured or extremely fatigued, they lead the rescuers back to the climbing party.

The messengers also have the job of seeing that information gets to relatives of people in the climbing party. Because of the urgency of seeking aid and the need to keep phone lines available, this job may have to await arrival of the rescue leader, who probably has had considerable experience in working with concerned relatives and with the news media.

TRANSPORT ON TECHNICAL TERRAIN

On steep terrain that demands technical climbing, even a minor illness or injury can make a person unable to travel without help. A large, well-equipped rescue party has a lot of options for safe and efficient evacuation of the victim. A small climbing party, however, will find it difficult to take any route that involves much raising or traversing. The small party usually will take an evacuation route straight down the fall line, which uses the least energy and equipment. Rescue on class 4 and 5 terrain usually requires more equipment than on the easier class 2 or 3 ground, where people rather than gear can provide most of the help.

Raising or lowering an injured person on technical terrain is a serious undertaking, with any number of things that can go wrong. A small climbing party should be prepared with prior training in rescue techniques and their complications, in order to avoid errors that make matters worse. A rescue is inherently more dangerous than a normal climb over the same ground because attention is focused on the victim instead of on the climbing. Often, the climbers must descend by a route unknown to them.

The prime object—moving the victim without further injury—is naturally uppermost in everyone's mind, yet the safety of each individual must never be forgotten. Solidly anchored belays may be required both for the victim and for the rescuers, even if they wouldn't be set up under ordinary climbing conditions. If ropes are in short supply, rescuers can be safeguarded by a fixed line to which they attach themselves with prusik slings.

A small party uses its available climbing hardware for rescue work and must think through the limitations of this equipment. Be sure the equipment can safely do what you plan to ask of it. The party's standard 11-millimeter climbing rope is usually adequate for rescue raising and lowering of single-person loads, although keep in mind that it will stretch. If the rope was involved in the accident, check it carefully for damage before using it in the rescue. Climbers in small parties often carry emergency items to help in a rescue. Depending on the climb, such items might include extra slings and carabiners, a pulley, folding saw, snow shovel, whistle, plastic tarp, and emergency smoke.

THE RESCUE BELAY

The belay is an important component of the system of raising and lowering persons who are ill or injured. Whenever possible, the person being moved should be on a belay that is independent of the mechanism that is being used for raising or lowering (fig. 17-2). With this independent belay, the victim is safeguarded in case of any disaster to the raising/lowering system, such as failure of the main anchor, rockfall damage to the rope, loss of the lowering brake or of the raising pulley, or injury to anyone operating the system. The belay anchor, independent of the main system anchor, should be constructed of multiple self-equalizing placements.

For belaying one person who is being raised or lowered, the belayer can use any standard belay device, maintaining it in a position that ensures maximum friction. Do not use a hip belay. For belaying two people at once, only the Münter hitch provides a safe enough degree of friction. (For a review of the Münter hitch, see Chapter 6.) The belayer should have the ability to continue lowering the victim if the original descent system fails. The belayer also should be able to safely carry out a knot bypass of the belay device (described later

Fig. 17–2. Typical lower with belay

in this chapter) if two or more ropes must be tied together for lowering.

LOWERING THE VICTIM

Before deciding to lower a victim, be sure that's exactly what you want to do. Once started, it's very hard to reverse. It can be especially tricky with a small party, in which there are not enough people to provide an independent belay or help out if complications arise. If you go ahead with lowering, watch that the rope doesn't dislodge dirt or rocks.

There are several possibilities for getting the affected person down the mountain, depending on the extent of illness or injuries:

Downclimbing: A person with slight injuries can climb down under tension from a tight belay, assisted by a companion who helps with placement of hands and feet. On snow or ice, large platform steps can be prepared.

Rappelling: If the victim has no head injury or symptoms of shock and is not seriously hurt, a rappel is possible. You can belay the rappel from above with a separate rope. Alternatively, you can offer a belay from below by holding onto the rope strands from the victim's rappel device. (However, don't pull down on the strands unless the injured person loses control of the rappel. Otherwise, you could interfere with the rappel, especially if the person is using a hip wrap for additional friction.)

Lowering in the seat harness: You may be able to lower the injured climber by the seat harness if neither downclimbing nor rappelling is possible. The victim must have no serious leg or upper-body injuries. Use a rope with a lowering device (described in the next section) to lower the victim, who uses hands and feet against the terrain to help guide the way down. The person will stay upright more easily by wearing a chest harness with the rescue rope going up through a carabiner at the harness. The injured person should be on an independent belay.

Back carry: This is a good technique if the victim has a minor but disabling lower body injury or is uneasy about rappelling or being lowered. Keep in mind that the rescuer must be strong enough to take the weight of the other person and still be able to maneuver. This will be especially difficult on low-angle rock. Connected like this to the victim, the rescuer will find it almost impossible to give first aid if medical problems arise. Do not use the back carry in cases that involve back or neck injuries, suspected internal injuries, serious head injuries, or other conditions requiring constant monitoring. For these, a rigid stretcher must be used.

Two common methods of back carry are the coil carry and the nylon-webbing carry. If possible, have the rescuer and victim on an independent belay, regardless of the method.

In the coil carry, the rescuer slips half the loops of a coiled rope over one shoulder and half over the other, with the coils looping down the back to form a seat for the injured climber (fig. 17-3). Tie a short piece of webbing around both loops over the rescuer's sternum to keep the coils from slipping off the shoulders. Run a prusik loop from the lowering rope to the injured person's chest harness to take some weight off the rescuer's shoulders and help keep the victim upright.

Another method of back carry employs nylon webbing to support and distribute the victim's weight (fig. 17-4). The webbing should be extremely well padded, especially under the victim's thighs, to prevent concentrated pressure that will cause a loss of circulation.

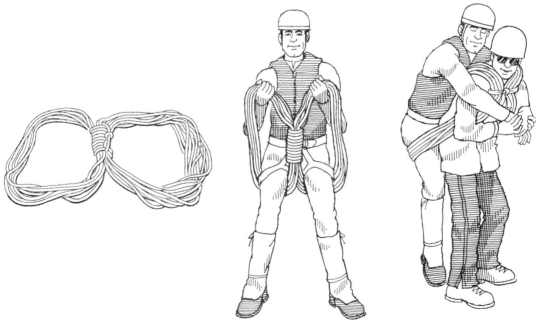

Fig. 17–3. Rope coil carry

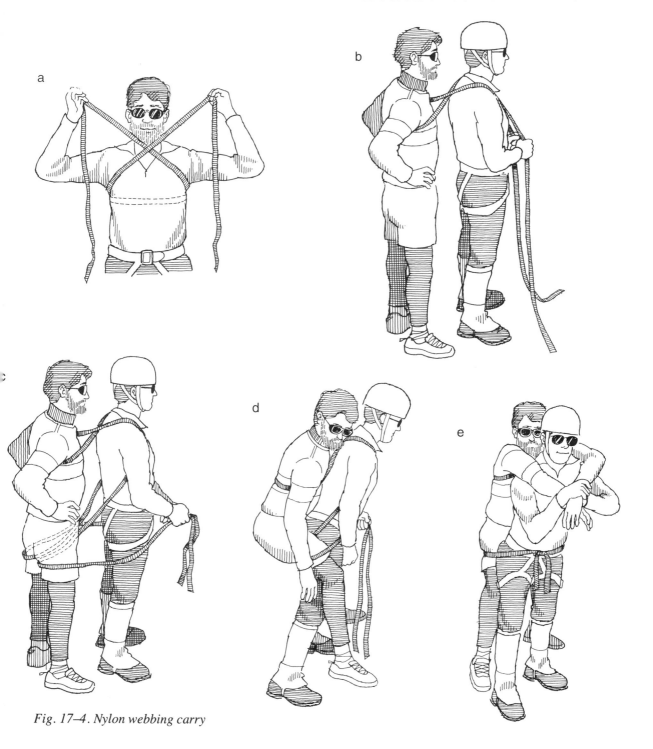

Fig. 17–4. Nylon webbing carry

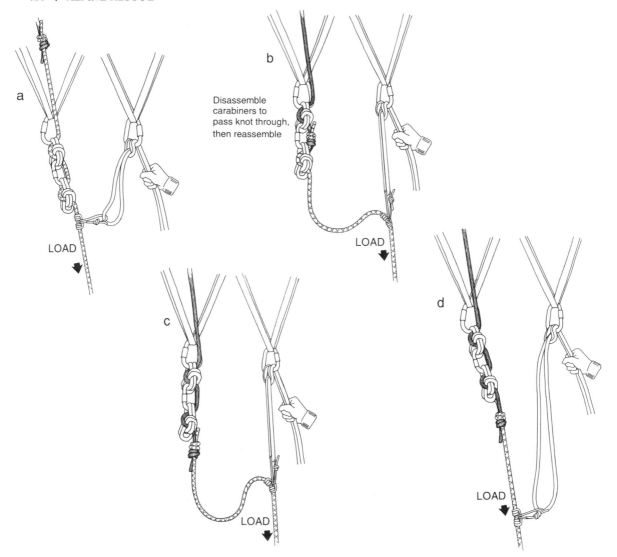

Fig. 17–5. *Passing the knot in a two-rope lower through a doubled carabiner brake system*

The lowering device

The best lowering device for use by a small party without specialized rescue gear is the standard carabiner brake system, as used in rappelling—but doubled (fig. 17-5). Simply construct two carabiner brakes, and join them with a locking carabiner. (Chapter 8 gives details on putting together a carabiner brake.) Each brake should include two braking carabiners (the crosswise carabiners).

The rescue rope runs through both brakes, providing increased friction for holding weight during lowering. The use of a standard belay device for technical lowering is not recommended because these devices were designed for single-person loads and may not provide sufficient friction for all the conditions of lowering. A doubled carabiner brake, on the other hand, provides enough friction for lowering two people at once.

Please note that the doubled brake system calls for a locking carabiner—not a pair of opposed regular carabiners—to join the two carabiner brakes. The single locking carabiner eliminates the possibility the rope could be pinched between a pair of carabiners. For the brakes themselves, standard symmetric oval carabiners work best.

Passing the knot

On a long pitch, you may want to tie two or more ropes together to permit a long uninterrupted descent for the injured person. As the knot approaches the lowering device (the doubled carabiner brake), it's necessary to stop lowering and perform a careful procedure to pass the knot safely through the device (fig. 17-5). Otherwise, the knot would jam.

It usually takes two people to carry out this procedure. Stop the descent when the knot gets to within 2 or 3 feet of the braking device. One person holds the lowering rope while the other attaches a prusik sling to the rope just below the brake, and then wraps this sling several times around one side of a carabiner that is anchored above the brake. (You can also connect to this carabiner with a Münter hitch if you wish.) The second person holds tight to the loose end of the sling while the first person gently eases the load onto the prusik by slacking off the lowering rope. The first person then passes the knot through the braking system one brake at a time: the upper brake is disassembled, the knot brought through, and the brake reassembled; then the same procedure follows with the bottom brake.

Once the knot has been passed through the entire system and the brakes are reset, the second person loosens the hold on the sling that is wrapped around the carabiner (or connected with a Münter hitch). This allows the load to slowly transfer back to the lowering rope, so the descent can continue. (The prusik sling must be long enough to allow for the slack introduced into the system when passing the knot.)

RAISING THE VICTIM

Lowering a person puts the force of gravity on the side of the rescuers, and therefore it's the preferred way to go, but sometimes there's no alternative to raising a victim up a steep face. Rescuers then have a choice of two general methods: the prusik system, which depends upon the victim's own efforts, and the pulley system, in which rescuers do the lifting.

These systems work on steep rock, snow, or ice, but they are usually associated with crevasse rescue. (Several versions of these systems are described in full in Chapter 13.) The same safety precautions that apply to lowering injured climbers apply to raising them. Whenever possible, safeguard the injured person with the use of backup anchors, safety prusiks, independent belays, and with padding or other measures to prevent ropes from being cut on sharp edges.

In the prusik system, the climber carries out a self-rescue by ascending in slings that are tied to the rope with prusik knots or other friction knots or that are attached with mechanical ascenders. This is an exhausting technique and has limited use in evacuating a seriously ill or injured person.

For a pulley system, rescuers usually use the Z-pulley, the most mechanically efficient of the basic pulley methods. There are some precautions to observe in using the Z-pulley: establish a main anchor that is bombproof. Keep extra prusik slings handy for replacements if a prusik in the system jams—and have a knife ready to cut away the jammed sling. (Caution: ropes and slings under tension cut very easily, so always cut away from other ropes.) Keep in continuous communication with the person you are raising.

Also be careful that the haulers don't pull too zealously on the rope. The Z-pulley is a powerful multiplier of forces, and it's possible to yank out an anchor, break a rope, or further injure the climber by pulling too hard against excessive friction or an unexpected obstruction.

Many rescuers prefer prusik knots to mechanical ascenders in a Z-pulley, because of the possibility the ascender could fail or could damage the rope. Give the prusik at least three wraps around the rescue rope. Each time you reset the Z-pulley, check that the prusik is holding securely.

TRAVERSING

If the descent deviates much from a route that is straight down the fall line, moving an injured person becomes very difficult. Try to avoid highly technical, exposed traverses, using them only as a last resort.

A pendulum technique is useful on terrain where rescuers can traverse overhead. For this method, suspend the injured person from an anchored rope. With a second rope, also anchored above, pull the victim sideways. Gradually release tension on the first rope as the victim pendulums to a position beneath the anchor of the second rope. Repeat the procedure if you need to traverse farther. As you pull on the pendulum rope, remember that ropes stretched horizontally have a tendency to snag and to knock rocks loose, and that they develop high stress under load. Victim and rescuers alike should be wearing helmets.

HAZARDS

Rescuers face the same hazards as climbers in general—hazards from objective environmental conditions such as storms, rockfall, cold, and high altitude, or from subjective human factors such as inadequate training and poor judgment. Dealing with any of these hazards greatly complicates a high-angle rescue.

Rescuers and climbers can minimize the impact of a storm or other objective hazard with proper equipment and contingency training. Ask the big ''What if'' questions before you leave on a trip, to be sure you have thought through the possible consequences of cold weather or high altitude or other hazards and are ready for them.

Take every possible precaution to guard against hazards as you raise or lower a person. If there is any doubt, confusion, or major disagreement on what is to be done, stop and reconsider the entire situation. Be especially wary of rockfall during raising and lowering operations. Wear helmets.

Subjective hazards exist when a person's skill, conditioning, or other qualities fall short of what is needed for safety on a particular climb. You can exercise a good deal of control over subjective hazards through planning and training before a climb, and by keeping alert during a climb to such hazards in yourself or others in the party. Dealing with the subjective hazards at the start of a rescue can minimize problems from objective hazards.

TRANSPORT ON NON-TECHNICAL TERRAIN

In many rescues the hardest job begins when the steep terrain is past and the ropes are put away. No longer aided by gravity, the party must carry its burden, very fatiguing work on rough ground. Under some conditions, however, a few simple techniques extend the capacity of the small party so that it need not call for help.

SHORT-DISTANCE CARRIES

Four-hand seat: This technique, useful for very short distances, requires two carriers who are the same height. The carriers grasp their own right wrist with their left hand, palms down. With the right hand, they grasp their partner's left wrist, forming a seat for the incapacitated person (fig. 17-6).

Ice-axe carry: This method permits longer carries than the four-hand seat. Carriers wearing rucksacks stand side by side, with the bundled shafts of two long-shaft ice axes supported between them in their pack straps. The person being carried sits on the padded shafts, arms over the carriers' shoulders (fig. 17-7).

Back carries: A strong climber can carry a person on his back for a considerable distance if the weight is distributed properly. The two back carries described earlier in this chapter—using webbing or a coiled rope—work well. The rucksack carry is another useful type of back carry. In this method, a large backpack is slit on the sides near the bottom so the carried person can step into it like a pair of shorts.

Fig. 17–6. Four-hand seat carry

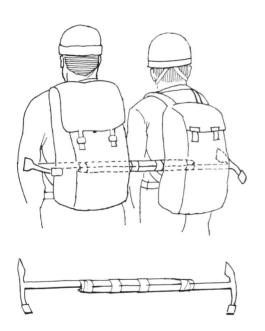

Fig. 17–7. Ice-axe carry

LONG-DISTANCE CARRIES

A stretcher improvised from rope can make it possible to carry a person long distances over non-technical ground. But before doing this, carefully consider the fact that evacuation on an improvised stretcher is usually very rough on the victim. If there is a chance that further injury will result, wait until trained rescuers with proper equipment get there.

Here is how to make a stretcher from a climbing rope, as shown in figure 17-8: Place the rope (150 feet is best) on the ground. From its exact center, make sixteen 180-degree bends, eight extending on each side of the center. The distance between bends should be about as wide as the person who will be carried, with the full sixteen bends approximately as long as that person.

Bring one rope end around each side of the stretcher, next to the bends. Tie a clove hitch in the rope section adjacent to each bend; insert the bend through the loops of the clove hitch. Continue tying clove hitches and inserting bends until all the bends are bound within clove hitches. Leave a small loop between the apex of each bend and the knot; insert the remaining rope through these loops until the entire remainder is strung around the stretcher. Snug up the knots, tie off the rope ends, and pad the area that will support the person from neck to hips.

Have one of the rescuers try out any improvised stretcher to decide if it needs more padding or support, keeping the victim's comfort in mind.

EVACUATION ON SNOW

On snow, it's particularly urgent to protect an injured person from heat loss while you give first aid and plan the evacuation. Wrap the person in

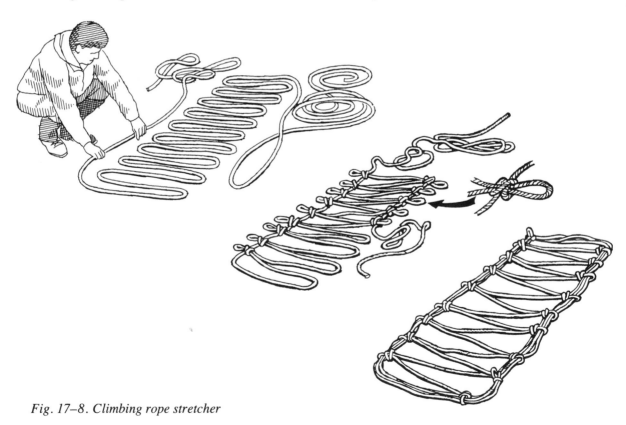

Fig. 17–8. Climbing rope stretcher

extra clothing. Use pads, packs, or ropes as insulation from the snow. If the victim cannot be moved quickly, build a trench or low wall as a temporary wind shield. Of course, if you must stay overnight, the party will put up a tent or dig a snow cave.

If possible, move the victim to a sheltered location, preferably below timberline. Do this as soon as you have given first aid and prepared the person for travel.

An ill or injured climber may be able to get down a snow slope by using some form of assisted sitting glissade. Sometimes the climber can be lowered in a sitting glissade position. Or a rescuer can sit in front of the victim, smoothing the track, the two tied together and on belay. A victim in relatively good condition can be roped in with two or three companions who then glissade slowly as a team, constantly under control.

Rescuers can set up anchors for belays and for braking devices by using pickets, bollards, or deadman anchors such as snow flukes or buried ice axes. (Chapter 12 gives the details on setting up these anchors.) The boot-axe belay usually is not strong enough for use in rescues. Moats often provide superb anchor positions for lowering.

Snow evacuations often involve climbers rescued from an avalanche or a crevasse. (Techniques of avalanche rescue are covered in Chapter 12, and crevasse rescue is explained in Chapter 13.)

ORGANIZED RESCUE OPERATIONS

Mountain rescues are often mounted by professional rescue agencies or by highly trained volunteers. This chapter has emphasized rescue efforts that can be undertaken by climbing parties themselves. Organized rescue groups bring the benefits of wide experience and training, plus specialized equipment and techniques, including air rescue.

RESCUE ORGANIZATIONS

In the Alps, with its large corps of professional guides, organized rescue is all part of the business. In North America, mountain rescues are commonly carried out by volunteer organizations. The volunteers use their rescue training and knowledge of the local mountains to analyze a situation, decide a course of action and carry it through. They round up the needed equipment and rescuers from among local climbers who are on call for emergencies. In the state of Washington, for example, Mountain Rescue units are headquartered in the major cities. Rescue evacuations usually require a leader and from eighteen to twenty-four stretcher bearers, unless a helicopter does the job.

In most areas, official responsibility for rescue rests with an agency such as the county sheriff's department or the National Park Service, and volunteer rescue units work closely with these authorities.

SPECIALIZED EQUIPMENT

Rescue organizations use equipment specially designed to make their task easier. Although these items are not standard climbing gear, every climber should know what they are and what can be done with them.

Most important is a rigid stretcher of fiberglass or metal. A well-known design is the Stokes litter, which has a framework of metal tubing and a wire-mesh basket that closely fits the outlines of a person's body. The Stokes, although heavy, works well on technical evacuations and general carryouts. Fiberglass stretchers with a metal framework are lighter and can be broken down into sections for ease of carrying, especially valuable attributes for technical rescues. They are widely used on snow because they slide easily. Many stretchers permit attachment of a wheel for trail or snow carryouts.

For raising and lowering, rescuers sometimes employ hand-operated or engine-powered portable winches with wire cables or non-stretch ropes that are several hundred feet long. The ropes are lighter than wire cable and require no specialized equipment to use other than standard climbing gear.

Two-way radio communication greatly facilitates mountain rescue, if the gear is lightweight and efficient. However, it can be difficult to get reliable transmission and reception through heavy timber, intervening ridges, long distances, and bad weather.

HELICOPTER RESCUE

Climbers can communicate with air rescuers by constructing international ground symbols, which are familiar to most pilots (fig. 17-9). The symbols, signaling such information as the need for a doctor, should be 8 to 12 feet high with lines 1 foot wide. It's a good idea to keep a copy of the symbols in your first-aid kit.

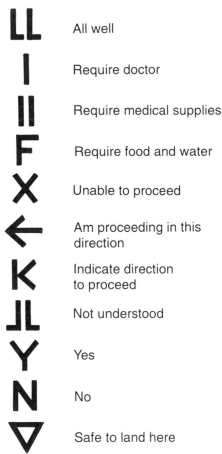

LL	All well
I	Require doctor
II	Require medical supplies
F	Require food and water
X	Unable to proceed
←	Am proceeding in this direction
K	Indicate direction to proceed
⅃L	Not understood
Y	Yes
N	No
▽	Safe to land here

Fig. 17–9. Ground-to-air signals

The helicopter revolutionized mountain rescue. It can pluck climbers from cliffs and glaciers and get them to hospitals in hours rather than the days sometimes required by ground transport, often meaning the difference between life and death. A helicopter takes on a load by landing, or by hovering and lowering a sling or a stretcher on a cable attached to a power winch. Climbers need to know some of the requirements and limitations of helicopter operation.

The most important factors governing a helicopter's ability to evacuate are visibility, wind velocity and turbulence, and air density. In mountain flight, continual visual contact with the ground is essential, so a helicopter can't operate in poor weather. It can maneuver safely in winds up to about 35 miles per hour, with a wind of about 10 miles per hour being better than still air. A dangerous turbulence usually accompanies high wind. The altitude to which a helicopter can fly depends on air density, which decreases as either altitude or temperature increases. Thinner air reduces the lifting force of the rotor blades.

The people on the ground should try to prepare a helicopter landing zone that has a 360-degree choice of landing and takeoff direction, so the pilot can land or take off into the prevailing wind. Clear an area at least 100 feet in diameter around the touchdown pad, removing obstacles such as brush and loose objects. Make the area as level as possible, with a slope of not more than 8 percent. Try to establish a landing zone where the helicopter can drop downward as it takes off rather than having to fly upward.

Mark the landing area with colored tape or brightly colored objects, and use streamers, plastic ribbon, or smoke to indicate wind direction. Put the wind indicators at the edge or downwind of the landing area so they don't obstruct the pilot's vision. It is urgent that all loose items near the landing zone be well secured, especially those used to mark the boundaries. If the helicopter lowers equipment, allow it to touch ground first to dissipate static electricity.

A couple of arm signals can be important. If there is a last-minute danger to the helicopter, signal "do not land" by holding your arms straight out horizontally from your sides and moving them to over your head several times. If your party has been unable to mark wind direction or landing site, members of the group should stand with arms extended toward the landing area and the wind at their backs. This signals to the pilot: "Land where we are pointing; our backs are into the wind."

Several safety precautions will minimize hazards from a helicopter. Stay away from cliff edges or anywhere else where you might be injured if you are knocked over by the helicopter rotor's powerful down-wash winds. Watch out for flying debris, use eye protection, and have all gear safely secured. Approach the helicopter only after signalled to do so by the pilot or a crew member, and then duck down and approach or leave from near the front so the pilot can always see you. Don't approach or leave the helicopter from any side where the ground is higher than where the helicopter is standing, and beware of the rear rotor, which is nearly invisible when spinning. If you're not needed near the helicopter, stay at least 75 feet away from the landing area.

Keep the victim's safety in mind as you prepare for the helicopter evacuation. Secure the person and any gear so there are no loose straps, ropes, or clothing; shield the person's face and eyes from flying debris and assure proper respiration. It takes time to secure an ill or injured climber to a stretcher. Remember that the person's safety is at stake and don't be rushed into this critical job just because the helicopter is waiting. Rescuers who put their training to use in a caring and efficient manner can often bring a happy ending to what may have been a long and difficult rescue effort.

• Appendix 1 •
THE CYCLE OF SNOW

Snow crystals form in the atmosphere when water vapor is precipitated at temperatures below freezing. They form around centers of foreign matter, such as microscopic dust particles, and grow as more ice formed from atmospheric water vapor is deposited on them. Tiny water droplets may also contribute to snow crystal growth. The crystals generally are hexagonal, but variations in size and shape are almost limitless and include plates, columns, and needles. The particular shape depends on the air temperature and the amount of water vapor available.

When a snow crystal falls through air masses with different temperature and water-vapor conditions, more complex or combined types may develop. Crystals in air that has a temperature near freezing stick together to become snowflakes, aggregates of individual crystals. When snow crystals fall through air that contains water droplets, the droplets freeze to the crystals, forming the rounded snow particles called graupel (soft hail).

The density of new-fallen snow depends on weather conditions. The lowest-density snow (lightest, driest) falls under moderately cold and very calm conditions. At extremely low temperatures, the new snow is fine and granular, with somewhat higher densities. The general rule is that the higher the temperature, the more dense (heavier, wetter) the snow, though density varies widely in the range of 20 to 32 degrees Fahrenheit (–7 to 0 degrees Celsius). The very highest densities are associated with graupel or needle crystals falling at temperatures near freezing. The percentage of water in new-fallen snow ranges from 1 to 30 percent, sometimes even higher, with the average for mountain snowfall being 7 to 10 percent. Wind affects snow density, for high winds break up falling crystals into fragments that pack together to form dense, fine-grained snow. The stronger the wind, the denser the snow.

Two types of snow form right at ground level.

Rime is the dull white, dense deposit formed from the freezing of droplets of water on trees, rocks, and other objects exposed to the wind. Rime deposits build up toward the wind. Rime may form large feathery flakes or a solid incrustation, but

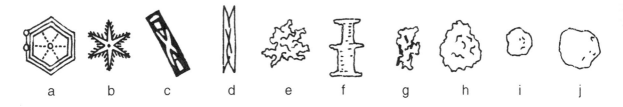

Fig. App. 1–1. Snow crystal forms: a, plates; b, stellar crystals; c, columns; d, needles; e, spatial dendrites (combinations of feathery crystals); f, capped columns; g, irregular particles (compounds of microscopic crystals); h, graupel (soft hail); i, sleet (icy shell, inside wet); j, hail (solid ice).

424

lacks regular crystalline patterns.

Hoarfrost, on the other hand, displays distinct crystalline shapes: blades, cups, and scrolls. Hoarfrost forms on solid objects by the process of sublimation—the direct conversion of atmospheric water vapor to a solid. Deposited on top of snow, it is known as surface hoar and is generally produced during a cold, clear night. The crystals appear fragile and feathery, and sparkle brilliantly in sunlight. A heavy deposit of surface hoar makes for fast, excellent skiing.

AGING OF THE SNOWCOVER

Snow that remains on the ground changes with time. The crystals undergo a process of change—metamorphism—that results in smaller, simpler forms and a snowpack that shrinks and settles. Because the snowpack generally becomes more stable over time, mountaineers find it useful to know the recent history of weather and snow conditions in an area.

Metamorphism begins the moment that snow falls and lasts until it melts. The equilibrium growth process gradually converts the varied original forms of the crystals into homogeneous rounded grains of ice (old snow). Both temperature and pressure affect the rate of change. When temperature within the snow is near the freezing point (32 degrees Fahrenheit; 0 degrees Celsius), change is rapid. The colder it gets, the slower the change, and it virtually stops below –40 degrees Fahrenheit (–40 degrees Celsius). Pressure from the weight of new snowfall over an older layer speeds changes within the layer. Snow that has reached old age—surviving at least one year and with all original crystals now converted into grains of ice—is called firn (or névé). Any further changes to firn snow lead to formation of glacier ice.

Another type of metamorphism takes place when water vapor is transferred from one part of the snowpack to another by vertical diffusion and is deposited in the form of ice crystals with different characteristics than those of the original snow. This kinetic growth process produces faceted crystals. When the process is carried to completion, the crystals often have a scroll or cup shape, appear to be layered, and may grow to considerable size. They form a fragile structure that loses all strength when crushed, and becomes very soft when wet. This weak and unstable snow form is known as depth hoar, popularly referred to as sugar snow. The necessary conditions for its formation are a large difference in temperature at different depths in the snow and sufficient air space so that water vapor can diffuse freely. The conditions are most common early in winter when the snowpack is shallow and unconsolidated.

As the snowpack on a slope moves very slowly downhill under the influence of gravity, the upper layers travel faster than those next to the ground. This internal deformation, called creep, proceeds most rapidly at the freezing point and diminishes with decreasing snow temperature. The entire snowpack also glides on the ground when

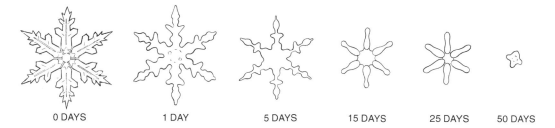

0 DAYS 1 DAY 5 DAYS 15 DAYS 25 DAYS 50 DAYS

Fig. App. 1–2. Destructive metamorphism of a snow crystal

the interface between snow and earth is at the melting point. If the ground is smooth (covered with grass, for instance), gliding is the dominant form of snow motion. The slow combined motions of creep and glide are so unhurried that they can't be noticed by the casual observer, but they cause the snowcover to exert enormous forces on obstacles in its path. The stresses produced by uneven snow creep are an important factor in avalanche formation.

Variations in the strength of snow are among the widest found in nature, with strength continually changing due to metamorphism, temperature differences, and wind. The hardness of wind-packed old snow may be fifty thousand times that of fluffy new snow. An increase in hardness is always associated with wind-drifted snow, or snow mechanically disturbed in any fashion, which undergoes a process known as age-hardening for several hours after it is disturbed.

SURFACE FORMS OF SNOWCOVER

Snow and ice undergo endless surface changes as they are worked on by wind, temperature, sun, freeze-and-thaw cycles, and rain. Following is a rundown on most of the surface permutations mountaineers typically encounter.

Powder snow: This is a popular term for light, fluffy new-fallen snow. However, powder snow is more specifically defined as new snow that has lost some of its cohesion due to the recrystallizing effects of steep temperature differences in the surface layers. These changes occur only during periods of persistent low temperatures. The changed snow is loose and powdery, commonly affords good skiing, and may form dry loose-snow avalanches.

Corn snow: After the advent of melting in early spring, a period of fair weather may be followed by formation of coarse, rounded crystals on the snow surface, often called corn snow. The crystals are formed from the daily melting and refreezing of the snow. Only when the same surface layer continues to melt and refreeze does true corn snow develop. When corn snow thaws each morning after the nighttime freeze, it's great for skiing and step-kicking.

Rotten snow: Rotten snow is a spring condition characterized by soft, wet layers that offer little support to the firmer layers above. In its worst forms, it will not support even the weight of a skier. Snow that promises good spring skiing in the morning, while there's some strength in the crust, may deteriorate to rotten snow later in the day. Rotten snow forms when lower layers of depth hoar become wet and lose what little strength they

have. It's a condition that often leads to wet loose-snow or slab avalanches running clear to the ground. Continental climates, such as those of the American Rockies, often produce rotten snow, which is much less likely to occur in the more stable maritime snowcovers of the Pacific coastal ranges of the United States and Canada.

Meltwater crust: This is a snow crust formed when water melted at the surface is refrozen and bonds snow crystals into a cohesive layer. A common variety is sun crust, so called because the source of heat for melting is solar radiation. Heat to permit meltwater crusts also comes from warm air or condensation at the snow surface. In winter and early spring the thickness of a sun crust is usually determined by the thickness of the surface layer where meltwater is formed in otherwise dry snow. In later spring and summer when free water is found throughout the snowcover, the thickness depends on how cold it gets at night.

Wind crust: In contrast to meltwater crust is the crust caused by action of the wind. After the surface snow layers are disturbed by the wind, age-hardening takes place. Fragments of snow crystals broken by the wind are compacted together when they come to rest, adding to the process. The hardening is compounded when the wind provides heat, particularly through water vapor condensation. Even when there is not enough heat to cause melting, the warming of the disturbed surface layer, followed by cooling when the wind dies, provides additional metamorphic hardening.

Firnspiegel: The thin layer of clear ice some-

Fig. App. 1–3. Surface features on snow: left, suncups; center, sastrugi; right, nieve penitentes.

times seen on snow surfaces in spring or summer is called firnspiegel. In the right conditions of sunlight and slope angle, its reflection produces the brilliant sheen of "glacier fire." Firnspiegel forms when solar radiation penetrates the snow and causes melting just below the surface at the same time that freezing conditions prevail at the surface. Once formed, it acts like a greenhouse, bringing melting of the snow beneath while the transparent ice layer remains frozen at the surface.

Verglas: This is a layer of thin, clear ice formed from water freezing on rock. It is most commonly encountered at higher elevations in the spring or summer when a freeze follows a thaw. The water comes from rainfall or melting snow. Verglas may also be formed directly by supercooled raindrops freezing as they fall onto exposed objects ("freezing rain," also sometimes inaccurately called "silver thaw").

Drainage patterns: After melting has begun in spring, drainage patterns formed by the runoff of water appear on snowfields. However, the actual flow takes place within the snowpack, not on the surface. As snow melts at the surface, the water formed percolates downward until it encounters impervious layers, which deflect its course, or highly permeable layers, which it can easily follow. Much of the water also reaches the earth beneath. The water that flows along within the snow often causes a branching pattern of channels on the surface. This happens because the flowing water accelerates the snow settlement around its channels, which are soon outlined by depressions at the surface. The dirt that collects in these depressions absorbs solar radiation and accentuates them further by differential melting.

Suncups: Suncups are depressions in the surface of summer snowfields, and they can vary in depth from 1 inch to 2 feet or more. They always occur as an irregular pattern covering an entire snowfield and form whenever weather conditions combine to accentuate surface irregularities. There must be motion of air to cause greater heat and mass transfer at high points of the snow than at the hollows. The air must be dry enough to favor evaporation, and there must be an additional source of external heat, usually the sun.

Under these circumstances, more heat reaches the points than the hollows but a larger proportion causes evaporation rather than melting. Because evaporation of snow demands more than seven times as much heat as melting, less snow is lost from the high points in the form of vapor than is lost from the hollows in the form of meltwater. The hollows melt faster than the points evaporate, and suncups form. They are enhanced by differential melting when dirt in the hollows absorbs solar radiation. The suncups also melt faster on the south (sunny) side in the Northern Hemisphere, so the whole suncup pattern gradually migrates northward across its snowfield.

Warm, moist winds tend to destroy suncups by causing faster melt at the high points and edges. A prolonged summer storm accompanied by fog, wind, and rain will often erase a suncup pattern completely, but they start to form again as soon as dry, fair weather returns.

Nieve penitentes: When suncups grow up, they become nieve penitentes (Spanish for "penitent snow"). They are the pillars produced when suncups intersect to leave columns of snow standing between the hollows. They are peculiar to snowfields at high altitudes, where radiation and atmospheric conditions conducive to suncups are intense. Nieve penitentes reach their most striking development among the higher peaks of the Andes and the Himalaya, where they may get several feet high and make mountain travel very difficult. The columns often slant toward the midday sun.

Wind and erosional features: The surface of dry snow develops a variety of erosional forms from the scouring of wind, such as the small ripples and irregularities on winter snowcover. On high ridges and treeless arctic territory, under the full sweep of the wind, these features attain considerable size. Most characteristic are the wavelike forms, with sharp prows directed toward the prevailing wind, known as sastrugi. A field of sastrugi—hard, unyielding, and as much as several feet high—can make for tough going. High winds over featureless snow plains also produce dunes similar to those found in desert sand, with the crescent-shaped dune, or barchan, being most common.

Cornices: Cornices are deposits of wind-drifted snow on the lee edge of ridges or other features. They offer a particular hazard as they overhang, forming an unstable mass that may break off

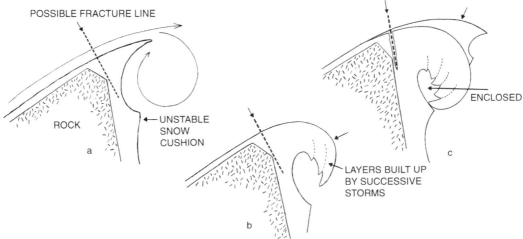

Fig. App. 1–4. Formation of cornices

from human disturbance or natural causes. Falling cornices are dangerous in themselves and also can set off avalanches.

During storms the precipitated snow furnishes material for cornice formation. Cornices also are formed or enlarged by material blown in from snowfields that lie to windward. As a general rule, cornices formed during snow storms are softer than those produced by wind drift alone.

THE FORMATION OF GLACIERS

Glaciers form for a rather simple reason. Snow that does not melt or evaporate during the year is carried over to the next winter. If snow continues to accumulate year after year, eventually consolidating and beginning a slow downhill movement, a glacier is formed.

Within the old snow (the firn, or névé), the metamorphic conversion of snow crystals into grains of ice has been completed. Now the grains of ice are changed into glacier ice in a process called firnification. Firn turns into glacier ice when the air spaces between the grains become sealed off from each other so that the mass becomes airtight.

Part of the glacier ice is formed by refreezing of percolating meltwater each spring when the lower snow layers are still at temperatures below freezing. This refrozen meltwater forms ice layers within the firn. Therefore, by the time compaction and metamorphism have prepared an entire area of firn for conversion to glacier ice, it may already contain irregular bodies of ice.

Once glacier ice has formed, metamorphism does not cease. Through crystallographic changes, some of the ice grains packed in the glacier continue to grow at the expense of their neighbors, and the average size of the ice crystals increases with age. Large glaciers, in which the ice takes centuries to reach the terminus, may produce crystals more than 1 foot in diameter, gigantic specimens grown from minute snow particles.

In our imagination, we can follow the birth of a simple valley-type alpine glacier. Picture a mountain in the Northern Hemisphere that has no glaciers. Now suppose climatic changes that cause snow to persist from year to year in a sheltered spot on a northern exposure.

From the first, snow starts to flow toward the valley in the very slow motion called creep. New layers are added each year, the patch of firn snow grows deeper and bigger, and the amount of snow in motion increases. The creeping snow dislodges soil and rock, while the melting, refreezing, and flow of water around and under the snow patch add to impact on the surroundings. This small-scale process of erosion eventually leads to formation of a hollow where the winter snows are deposited in deeper drifts. The snow gets to be 100 feet deep or so. The lower layers have nearly turned to glacier ice, while the increasing pressure of the many upper layers of firn causes the flow to accelerate. A glacier is born.

With continued nourishment from heavy winter snows, the glacier flows toward the valley as a stream of ice. At some point in its descent, the glacier reaches an elevation low enough and warm enough that no more new snow accumulates. The glacier ice begins to melt. Eventually the glacier reaches the point, even lower and warmer, at which all ice carried down from above melts each year. This is the lower limit of the glacier.

Glaciers vary from stagnant masses with little motion to vigorously flowing rivers of ice that transport large masses each year from higher to lower elevations. Glaciers in relatively temperate climates flow both by internal deformation and by sliding on their beds. Differences in speed within the glacier are somewhat like that in a river, fastest at the center and surface and slower at the sides and bottom where bedrock creates a drag. Small polar glaciers present a striking difference in appearance from their temperate cousins, for they are frozen to their beds and can flow only by internal deformation. The polar glaciers look much like flowing molasses, while temperate glaciers are rivers of broken ice.

• Appendix 2 •
RATING SYSTEMS

The development of rating systems began in the late-nineteenth and early-twentieth centuries in Britain and Germany. In the 1920s, Willo Welzenbach defined a rating system, using Roman numerals and the British adjectival system to compare and describe the routes in the Alps, which today forms the basis of the UIAA rating system. Today there are more than seven major rock, four alpine, four ice, and two aid-climbing rating systems used worldwide. This appendix will briefly describe some of these.

A rating system is a tool that helps a climber choose a climb that is within his or her abilities or presents a desirable level of challenge. The rating of a climb also reflects the type of equipment needed for the climb.

Rating climbs is a subjective task, which makes consistency between climbing areas elusive. The rating of climbs assumes good weather and the best equipment available. Variables that affect the rating of climbs include: how the local climbers who put up the routes interpret the rating system, how they want the area to be recognized, the type of rock or ice, and the type of climbing (e.g. face, crack, or friction rock climbing; front pointing or French technique ice climbing). The physical size and strength of the climber also affects how he or she thinks a climb should be rated. Ideally, a route is rated by consensus. A guidebook author typically has not climbed every route described and therefore has to rely on the opinions of others. In some cases, a route may have been done only once. When climbing in an area for the first time it is best to start at a lower level than normal in order to become familiar with the rock or ice, the type of climbing, and how the rating system reflects the qualities of the climbing.

NORTH AMERICAN RATING SYSTEMS

Rock climbing

Free climbing

In 1937, a modified Welzenbach rating system was introduced in America as the Sierra Club System. In the 1950s this system was modified to more accurately describe the technical climbing that was being done at Tahquitz Rock in California by adding a decimal figure to class 5 climbing. This has become known as the Yosemite Decimal System (YDS). This system categorizes terrain according to the techniques and equipment required to travel that terrain.

Class 1: A hiking scramble to a rocky gradient; generally hands are not needed.
Class 2: Involves some scrambling and likely use of hands; all but the most inexperienced and clumsy will not want a rope.
Class 3: Moderate exposure may be present; simple climbing or scrambling with frequent use of hands. A rope should be available.
Class 4: Intermediate climbing is involved and most climbers want a rope because of *exposure*. A fall could be serious or fatal. Another definition is that it begins when all beginners and most average climbers will want and should have a *belay*. Usu-

ally natural protection is easily found.
Class 5: Climbing involves use of a rope and natural or artificial protection by the leader to protect against a serious fall.

The extension of fifth-class climbing originally was meant to be a closed-ended scale of 5.0–5.9. The rising standards in the 1970s, however, led to a need for an open-ended scale. Strict decimal protocol was abandoned and 5.10 (pronounced ''five ten'') was adopted as the next highest class. Classes 5.10–5.14 (as of 1991) have been subdivided into four parts, a–d. (See Table 1.) A (+) or (–) is sometimes used as a rougher means to refine a classification. For example, 5.12(+) equates to 5.12c or 5.12d. It also can be used to indicate a sustained pitch (+) or a pitch of one or two moves of a given rating (–) (e.g. 5.8(–)).

The extension of fifth-class climbing cannot be defined accurately, either quantitatively or qualitatively. The following general guidelines to the extension of fifth-class climbing will aid the climber who is unfamiliar with the YDS descriptions.

5.0–5.4: A physically fit climber can usually climb at this level with little or no rock climbing skills, using only natural ability.
5.4–5.7: Requires use of rock-climbing techniques such as hand jamming and/or strength.
5.7–5.9: Rock-climbing shoes, good skills, *and* some strength are usually necessary at this level.
5.10 and above: Beyond rock shoes, excellent skills, and strength, this level requires training for climbing techniques and commitment of time to maintain that level.

The YDS rates only the hardest move on a pitch. The YDS gives no indication of overall difficulty, protection opportunity, exposure, runout, or strenuousness. Some guidebooks, however, will rate a pitch harder than the hardest move if it is very sustained at a lower level. A guidebook's introduction should explain any variation of the YDS used. Some guidebooks give routes two ratings, one for the hardest move and one for the overall difficulty of the pitch.

Because the standard use of the YDS defines only the hardest move, a *seriousness rating* was introduced by James Erickson in 1980 to indicate relative danger of a climb:
PG-13: Protection is considered adequate, and if properly placed, a fall would not likely be long or of consequence.
R: Protection is commonly considered inadequate. The possibility exists of a long fall onto good protection or a shorter fall onto poor protection, which may pull. A falling leader will probably suffer injuries.
X: Protection is commonly considered extremely poor. There exists the possibility of long falls, pulling several pieces of protection and causing serious injury or death.

Quality ratings are common in many guidebooks. The number of stars indicates the aesthetics of a particular climb. No standard has been set, so each area and guidebook have their own definitions. These star ratings are useful in guiding a climber who is new to the area to the quality routes.

The National Climbing Classification System (NCCS) for rating free climbing proposed in 1963, and using F1–F10, is largely out of use. Many old guidebooks used this system (see Table 1).

Aid climbing

Rating aid moves or climbs is different than rating free climbing in that it is not an open-ended system, nor do the ratings change with improved technology. The aid-climbing rating system indicates quality of protection and the difficulty of placing that protection. The scale is A0 or C0–A5 or C5, with A referring to the use of pitons and/or chocks, and C referring to clean aid climbing (chocks only), although the use of C has not been universally accepted. This system is used throughout the world except in Australia, which uses M0 (mechanical) to M8, with similar definitions as A0–A5.

A0 or C0: Aid points are fixed.
A1 or C1: Aid placements are solid and easily placed.
A2 or C2: Placements are awkward to place and

Fig. App. 2–1. Comparison of rock classification systems

UIAA	French	YDS	Australian	E. German	Brazilian	NCCS	British
I	1	5.2		I		F4	3a — VD
II	2	5.3	11	II		F5	3b
III	3	5.4	12	III	II		3c — HVD
IV	4	5.5		IV	IIsup	F6	4a — MS/S/HS
V-		5.6	13	V	III		4b
V	5	5.7	14	VI	IIIsup	F7	4c — VS
V+			15				
VI-		5.8	16	VIIa	IV	F8	HVS
			17	VIIb			
VI	6a	5.9	18		IVsup	F9	5a
VI+	6a+	5.10a	19	VIIc	V	F10	E1
VII-	6b	5.10b	20	VIIIa	Vsup		5b
		5.10c	21	VIIIb	VI	F11	
VII	6b+	5.10d	22	VIIIc	VIsup		5c — E2
V11+	6c	5.11a	23	IXa	VII	F12	E3
	6c+	5.11b					
VIII-	7a	5.11c	24	IXb	VIIsup	F13	6a — E4
VIII	7a+	5.11d	25	IXc	VIII		
VIII+	7b	5.12a		Xa	VIIIsup	F14	6b — E5
	7b+	5.12b	26				
IX-	7c	5.12c		Xb		F15	6c — E6
		5.12d	27				
IX	7c+	5.13a	28	Xc		F16	7a — E7
IX+	8a	5.13b	29				
X-	8a+	5.13c	30				
			31				
X	8b	5.13d	32				
	8b+						
X+	8c	5.14a	33				

holds less.

A3 or C3: Aid placements will hold a short fall.

A4 or C4: Aid placements hold only body weight.

A5 or C5: Entails enough A4 placements to risk a very substantial fall.

Bouldering

Bouldering has its own rating system. It is a floating scale that moves upward as the standards rise. B1 is always the hardest YDS classification in existence, and B3 is always a climb that has never been repeated. In 1991, the bouldering ratings could be compared to the YDS as follows:

B1: 5.14
B2: above 5.14
B3: the climb is unrepeated

Alpine climbing

The National Climbing Classification System (NCCS) describes the overall difficulty of a multi-pitch alpine climb in terms of time and technical rock difficulty. It takes the following factors into account: length of climb, number of hard pitches, average pitch difficulty, difficulty of hardest pitch, commitment, routefinding problems, ascent time, rockfall, icefall, and weather problems. The approach and remoteness of an area also influence the grade of a climb, which will be regional and, thus, guidebook-dependent. It should be emphasized that with increasing grade an increasing level of psychological preparation and commitment is necessary. This system assumes a competent party for the level of climbing expected.

Grade I: Normally requires only several hours to do the technical portion; can be of any technical difficulty.

Grade II: Normally requires a half day for the technical portion; can be of any technical difficulty.

Grade III: Normally requires a full day for the technical portion; can be of any technical difficulty.

Grade IV: Expected to take one long hard day of technical climbing (longer on the first ascent); the hardest pitch is usually no less than 5.7.

Grade V: Expected to take an average one-and-a-half days; the hardest pitch is rarely less than 5.8.

Grade VI: Usually takes two or more days; generally includes considerably difficult free climbing and/or aid climbing.

The times given do not especially apply to glacier/snow/ice climbs. The type of climb affects which factors are emphasized. It is important to study a route description to understand which factors make it the grade that it is.

Ice climbing

The variable conditions of snow and ice climbing make rating climbs difficult. The only two factors that do not vary greatly from year to year are length and steepness of the ice. Snow depth, thickness of ice, and temperature affect the condition of the route; these factors plus the nature of the ice and whether or not it offers good protection affect its difficulty.

Three rating systems have been introduced in North America: the New England Ice Rating System, first described in the early 1970s by Rick Wilcox, another in 1979 by Jeff Lowe, and the third in 1988 by Albi Sole. All use a modified version of the Scottish system (composed of Grades 1–6), which consists of two elements referred to as the *seriousness grade* (or *overall grade* [Lowe] or *commitment rating* [NEI]) and the *technical grade*.

Depending on the terrain being rated, water or alpine ice may be denoted as WI or AI, respectively. *Water ice* may be a seasonal frozen waterfall or nonporous ice found in the alpine environment. *Alpine ice* is permanent ice of a porous nature generally in the form of consolidated snow such as that usually found in glaciers.

The *technical grade*, as defined by Sole, rates the single most difficult pitch, taking into account the sustained nature of the climbing, ice thickness, and natural ice features, such as chandeliers, mushrooms, or overhanging bulges.

Grade 1: Walking up ice with only the use of crampons.

Grade 2: A pitch of 60–70 degree ice, reasonably

consistent, with few short, steep steps. Good protection and belays.

Grade 3: Sustained 70–80 degree ice, usually thick and solid. May contain short, steep section, but will have good resting places and offer good protection and belays.

Grade 4: Sustained 75–85 degree ice, separated by good belays or a less steep pitch with significant vertical sections. Generally good-quality ice, offering satisfactory protection.

Grade 5: A noticeably more strenuous pitch of good but steep (85–90 degree) ice. May be considered the equivalent of 5.9 rock in terms of relative technical ability required.

Grade 6: A very steep, strenuous pitch with few resting places and often a hanging belay. The ice may not be of top quality and protection may be dubious.

Grade 7: A pitch of near vertical ice, which may be thin, of poor quality, and doubtful adhesion to the rock. Protection difficult or nonexistent.

The *Seriousness grade*, as defined by Sole, takes into account the length, continuity, remoteness, hazards, and difficulty of descent; it is not, however, totally unaffected by technical difficulty.

Grade I: A short climb close to the road with bombproof belays and an easy descent.

Grade II: A 1- or 2-pitch climb within easy reach of a vehicle, little objective danger, and easy descent by rappel or downclimbing.

Grade III: A multipitch route at low elevation, which may take several hours, or a route with a long approach on foot or ski, demanding good winter travel skills, or a route subject to occasional winter hazards. Descent usually by rappelling.

Grade IV: A multipitch route at higher elevations or in a remote region requiring mountaineering and winter travel skills. May be subject to objective hazards such as avalanches or rockfall. Descent may present difficulties and usually involves rappelling from bolts.

Grade V: A long climb on a high mountain face requiring a high level of competence and commitment. Subject to hazards of bad weather and avalanches. May have long approach or difficult descent.

Grade VI: A long multipitch route on a high alpine face, which only the best climbers will complete in a day. May include the logistical problems of winter alpine climbing.

Grade VII: The biggest and hardest Himalayan alpine-style climbs (Lowe definition).

The *New England Ice Rating System* is used extensively in New England and was developed for the water-ice climbing found there. This system applies to a normal winter ascent of the route in moderate weather conditions.

NEI 1: Low-angle water ice of 40–50 degrees, or long, moderate snow climbs requiring a basic level of technical expertise for safety.

NEI 2: Low-angle water-ice routes with short bulges up to 60 degrees.

NEI 3: Steeper water ice of 50–60 degrees with 70–90 degree bulges.

NEI 4: Short, vertical columns, interspersed with rests, on 50–60 degree ice; fairly sustained climbing.

NEI 5: Generally multipitch ice climbs with sustained difficulties and/or strenuous vertical columns, with little rest possible.

NEI 5 + : Multipitch routes with a heightened degree of seriousness, long vertical sections, and extremely sustained difficulties—the hardest ice climbs in New England to date.

The *commitment rating* shows the time and logistical requirements of the climb.

I: Up to several hours.

II: About half a day.

III: A full day, up to 7 or 8 hours.

IV: A substantial undertaking; a very long day, possibly including a bivouac.

V: A big-wall climb of one and a half to two days. Could be done in a single day by a very fit team.

VI: Multiday big-wall climbs requiring more than two days.

VII: Big-wall ascents in remote alpine situations.

Ice climbing is relatively new in America so standards vary from area to area and guidebook to guidebook. Some guidebooks define their own rating system: *Bob's Route* IV, 5 (indicating seriousness and technical grade), *Bob's Route* (5) (indicating technical grade), and *Bob's Route* IV, WI5 (indicating overall grade, technical grade, and water ice). Most guidebooks do give the length of the technical ice climbing.

OTHER MAJOR RATING SYSTEMS

Many of the rating systems used throughout the world are very similar to one another, especially in Europe. Table 2 indicates which rating systems are used in which country.

Rock climbing

Australian

The Australian system uses open-ended numerics 1–33. See Table 1.

Brazilian

The rating of climbs in Brazil is composed of two parts. The first number gives the general level of difficulty of the route ranging from first to eighth grade (or degree), which is written as grade $5°$. There is no comparison to the YDS for this part of the system. The second part gives the difficulty of the hardest free move (or sequence of moves

Fig. App. 2–2. Rating systems used throughout the world

COUNTRY	RATING SYSTEM
Australia	Australian
Brazil	Brazilian
Britain	British, IFAS
Canada	YDS, NCCS
East Germany	E. German, IFAS
France	French, IFAS
West Germany	W. German = "UIAA," IFAS
Italy	French, IFAS
Japan	UIAA, "NCCS"
Spain	"French," IFAS
United States	YDS, NCCS

Quotation marks denote that only slight modifications have been made to the system indicated.

without a natural rest) in roman numerals with sup (superior) added for greater accuracy. See Table 1 for comparison to the YDS. Ratings of climbs are written as 5° VI.

British

The British classification system is comprised of two elements, the adjectival grade and the technical grade, and is expressed as, for instance, HVS 5a.

The *adjectival grade* describes the overall difficulty of a route, including factors such as exposure, how sustained the route is, seriousness, strenuousness, protection opportunities, and runout. Acronyms are used up to Extremely Severe. The need for an open-ended, less cumbersome system led to an alphanumeric adaptation, hence E1, E2, E3, etc.

Easy	E
Moderate	M
Difficult	Diff
Very Difficult	V. Diff
Hard Very Difficult	HVD
Mild Severe	MS
Severe	S
Hard Severe	HS
Very Severe	VS
Hard Very Severe	HVS
Extremely Severe	ES
subdivided as:	E1, E2, E3, etc.

The *technical grade* is defined as the hardest move on a particular route. This numeric component of the British system is also open-ended and is subdivided into a, b, and c (see Table 1).

The two grades are linked to each other. For example, the standard adjectival grade for a well-protected 6a, which is not particularly sustained, is E3. If the route is a bit run out then it would be E4; if it is really run out then it would be E5.

French

The French open-ended rating system currently extends from 1–8c. Starting at level 6, the ratings are subdivided a, a(+), b, b(+), c, and c(+). See Table 1.

Soviet Union

Currently, there is no rock-climbing classification system used in the Soviet Union. First ascents are often done by climbers from other countries who rate the climb according the rating system used in his or her own country.

UIAA

The UIAA rating system currently extends from I–X(+) with levels V–X subdivided into (–), (nought), and (+). It does not express length, time, seriousness, and dangers of the climb. See Table 1.

West German

The same as UIAA except uses arabic numbers (see Table 1).

Alpine climbing/ice climbing

Europe

The International French Adjectival System (IFAS) is an overall rating of alpine and ice climbs used primarily in the Alps. It expresses the seriousness of the route, including factors such as length, objective danger, how sustained it is, commitment, altitude, runouts, descent, and technical difficulty in terms of *terrain*. It has six categories that are symbolized by the first one or two letters of the French adjective used. It is further subdivided with the use of (+) or (–) or sup (superior) or inf (inferior).

F: *Facile* = easy. Steep walking routes, rock scrambling, and easy snow slopes. Crevasses possible on glaciers. Rope not always necessary.
PD: *Peu difficile* = moderate. Rock climbing with some technical difficulty, snow and ice slopes, difficult glaciers, and narrow ridges.
AD: *Assez difficile* = fairly hard. Fairly difficult and serious climbs, steep rock climbing, long snow/ice slopes above 50 degrees.
D: *Difficile* = hard. Sustained hard rock and snow/ice climbing.
TD: *Trés difficile* = very hard. Very difficult technical climbing on all kinds of terrain.
ED: *Extrêmement difficile* = extremely difficult. Extremely serious climbs with long sustained difficulties of the highest order.
ABO: *Abominable*

Soviet Union

The Soviet Union has an alpine rating system somewhat comparable to the NCCS system used in the United States. The scale is 1–6, with a and b subdivisions.

◆ Appendix 3 ◆
LIGHTNING

Though not one of the principal perils of mountaineering, lightning has caused a number of serious—and mostly avoidable—accidents. The very nature of their sport places climbers on or near the most frequent targets: peaks and ridges produce the vertical updrafts and raincloud conditions that generate lightning; the prominences serve to trigger the strokes. Climbers therefore should understand the basic mechanisms involved and fix in their minds the fundamentals of evasive action.

For all practical purposes the hazards are three: (1) a direct strike, (2) ground currents, and (3) induced currents in the immediate vicinity of a strike.

Electrical potential builds up in a cloud in somewhat the same manner one's body picks up an electrical charge on a dry day. Air is normally a very poor conductor (good insulator) of electricity; trees, rock, or earth are better conductors, more so when wet; the human body is still better; and most metals are best of all. Lightning seeks the path of least total resistance between the cloud and earth—the shortest possible line through the air. Ordinarily the closest ground point is directly below the cloud, but a summit off to one side can be closer and become the bull's-eye.

Air ceases to be a good insulator when subjected to a sufficiently high electrical pressure; it *ionizes* and thereupon loses its insulating quality and becomes a conductor. The ionizing breakdown around a conducting projection often gives off a crackling noise (notorious in the Alps as the "buzzing of bees") caused by small sparks. The distinctive odor of ozone is usually noted. A bluish glow or *corona* (St. Elmo's fire) may be seen. If a person's head is the projection, the hair (if any) crackles and stands on end. Corona discharges have often been observed when the nearest cloud seemed too far away to be at all relevant. The sound or sight of corona does not necessarily indicate danger, but lacking more precise indication should be regarded as a warning, especially when thunderclouds are nearby. Additonally, any atmospheric activity symptomatic of commotion should stir suspicion. A sudden rush of cold air perhaps announces a strong cold front with possible lightning. A cloudburst of enormous raindrops or monster snowflakes or huge hailstones almost certainly means a cumulonimbus is overhead.

Lightning is, of course, electricity, which is a stream of electrons. When the more than 100 billion billion electrons in an average bolt strike a peak or a tree they do not just lie there in a puddle, but immediately spread out in all directions. In the process considerable damage can result. Two factors determine the extent of human injury: the quantity of current, and the part of the body affected.

The worst threat is the passage of electricity *through* the body in a way which impairs some vital function such as heart, brain, or breathing action. A current from one hand to the other through the heart and lungs, or from head to foot through virtually all organs, is most dangerous, even if relatively small; one can survive a larger current from one foot to the other through the legs.

Climbers face other potential hazards: large currents can cause deep burns at points of entry and exit; a mild shock may momentarily startle them or set off muscular spasms, or they may move about in semiconsciousness, and in either case may fall off a cliff.

First thought should be given to avoiding areas which might be hit. The governing rule is to seek a location with nearby projections or masses that are somewhat closer than one's own head to any clouds which may drift by. In a forest the safest shelter is amid the shorter trees. The middle of a ridge is preferable to the ends; avoid shoulders.

An electrical discharge at a strike point instantly radiates outward and downward, with the intensity of the flow, and consequently the danger to climbers, decreasing rapidly as the distance from the strike increases. On firm rock, especially when wet, the major path in most cases is along the surface. Lichen patches, cracks, or soil may hold moisture and thus provide easy paths. High-voltage currents tend to jump across short gaps, as in a spark plug, rather than take a longer path around.

Current flows because of a voltage difference between two points along its path. A person bridging two such points with some part of his or her body presents a second and probably better path for the current, some portion of which is therefore diverted through his or her body. The wider the span, the greater the voltage difference and the greater the flow through the body.

With this background, several precepts can be listed:

1. Avoid moist areas, including crevices and gullies.
2. Span as small a distance (occupy as little area) as possible. Keep the feet close together; keep the hands off the ground.
3. Sit, crouch, or stand on insulating objects if possible—a coiled rope or a sleeping bag, preferably dry.
4. Stay out of small depressions; choose instead a narrow slight rise. A small detached rock on a scree slope is excellent.
5. Stay away from overhangs and out of small caves. Large caves are very good if one keeps clear of the walls and entrance. However, a cave might well be the lower terminus of a drainage crevice, and in such case should be avoided.
6. When on a ledge, crouch at the outer edge, at least 4 feet from the rock wall if possible. If there is danger of falling off in event of a shock, tie in *crosswise* to the prospective flow of current. Make the tie short and avoid placing the rope under the armpits.
7. Rappelling when lightning is imminent should be avoided, but may be a valid calculated risk if it is the quickest way to escape a danger zone. Dry synthetic rope presents the minimum hazard.
8. Contrary to popular belief, metal objects do not attract lightning as such. However, in the immediate vicinity of a strike, metals in contact with one's person may augment the hazard from *induced currents*. Induced currents usually are quite small, but when added to ground currents may mean the difference between life and death. Thus it is best to set aside all metals, but to keep them close by (don't worry about an article buried in the pack). A metal pack frame might well be positioned to provide a more attractive path for ground currents beside and past one's body. At distances greater than 100 feet from a possible strike there is no need to divest oneself of metal objects.

◆ Appendix 4 ◆
SUPPLEMENTARY READING

Chapter 3: Camping and food

American Heart Association. *Nutrition, Health and Athletic Performance*. Seattle: AHM, 1986.

Axcell, Claudia, Diana Cooke, and Vikki Kinmont. *Simple Foods For The Pack*. San Francisco: Sierra Club Books, 1986.

Berglund, Berndt and Clare Bolsby. *Wilderness Cooking*. New York: Charles Scribner's Sons, 1973.

Bergstrom, J., E. Hultman, L. Hermansen, and B. Saltin. ''Diet, Muscle Glycogen and Physical Performance.'' Acta Physiol. Scand. 71:140, 1967.

Dairy Council. *Nutrition and Athletic Performance*. 46(2), March/April, 1975.

Fleming, June. *The Well-Fed Backpacker*. Portland, Oregon: Victoria House, 1978.

Food and Nutrition Board. *Recommended Dietary Allowances*, 19th ed. Washington, D.C.: 1980.

Gunn, Carolyn. *The Expedition Cookbook*. Denver: Chockstone Press, 1988.

McHugh, Gretchen. *The Hungry Hiker's Book of Good Cooking*. New York: Alfred A. Knopf, 1982.

Peterson, M. S. and C. M. Martinsen. *The Athlete's Cookbook*. Seattle: Smuggler's Cove Press, 1980.

Peterson, M. S. and K. Peterson. *Eat to Compete*. Chicago: Year Book Medical Publishers, Inc., 1988.

Prater, Yvonne and Ruth Dyar Mendenhall. *Gorp, Glop & Glue Stew: Favorite Foods from 165 Outdoor Experts*. Seattle: The Mountaineers, 1981.

SCAN. *Sports Nutrition*. Chicago: American Dietary Association, 1986.

Wallace, Aubrey. *Natural Foods for the Trail*. Yosemite, California: Vogelsang Press, 1977.

Chapter 4: Routefinding and navigation

Carrington, David and Richard Stephenson. *Map Collections in the United States and Canada—A Directory*, 4th ed. New York: Special Libraries Association, 1985.

Cobb, David. *Guide to U.S. Map Resources*. Chicago: American Library Association, 1986.

Dodd, K. *Guide to Obtaining USGS Information*, U.S. Geological Survey Circular 900. Washington, DC: U.S. Geological Survey, 1986.

Fleming, June. *Staying Found*. New York: Vintage Books, 1982.

Kals, W. *Land Navigation Handbook*. San Francisco: Sierra Club Books, 1983.

Makower, Joel, ed. *The Map Catalog*. New York: Vintage Books, 1986.

Miller, Victor C. and Mary E. Westerback. *Interpretation of Topographic Maps*. Columbus, OH: Merrill Publishing Company, 1989.

Moore Moffat, Riley. *Map Index to Topographic Quadrangles of the United States 1882–1940*.

Nicholson, N and L. Sebert. *The Maps of Canada*. Hamden, CT: Archon Press, 1981.

Parry, R. and C. Perkins. *World Mapping Today*. London: Butterworths, 1987.

Thompson, M. *Maps for America*, 3d ed. Washington, DC: U.S. Geological Survey, 1987.

Chapter 7: Belaying

Leeper, Ed. ''Belaying: The European Connection.'' *Summit*, 25, no. 4 (August–September 1979): pp. 11–29.

——. ''Belaying: Forces and Stopping Distances.''
Summit, 25, no. 6 (December–January 1980):
pp. 6–13.

——. ''Belaying: The Occupational Hazards.''
Summit, 26, no. 3: pp. 20–27.

Loughman, Michael. ''Ropes, Anchors and Belayers.''
In *Learning to Climb*, pp. 64–104. San
Francisco: Sierra Club Books, 1981.

Steele, George. ''Equipment Notes: Some Thoughts on
Belaying.'' *Mountain*, 32 (February 1974): pp.
35–37.

Chapter 8: Rappelling

Martin, Tom. *Rappelling*, 2d ed. Sterling, Kentucky:
Search, 1988.

Chapters 9 and 10: Rock climbing and Leading and placing protection

Long, John. *How to Rock Climb*. Evergreen, Colorado:
Chockstone Press, 1989.

Loughman, Michael. *Learning to Rock Climb*. San
Francisco: Sierra Club Books, 1981.

March, Bill. *Modern Rope Techniques in
Mountaineering*. Manchester/Milnthorpe,
England: Cicerone Press, 1985.

Ontario Rock Climbing Association. *Rock Climbing
Safety Manual*. Toronto: Ontario Rock Climbing
Association, 1985.

Robbins, Royal. *Basic Rockcraft*. Glendale, California:
La Siesta Press, 1971.

Chapters 12, 13, 14, and 15: Snow travel and climbing, Glacier travel and crevasse rescue, Ice climbing, and Winter and expedition climbing

Barry, John. *Alpine Climbing*. Seattle: Cloudcap Press,
1988.

——. *Snow and Ice Climbing*. Seattle: Cloudcap Press,
1987.

Chouinard, Yvon. *Climbing Ice*. San Francisco: Sierra
Club Books, 1978.

Cliff, Peter. *Ski Mountaineering*. Seattle: Pacific Search
Press, 1987.

Collister, Rob. *Lightweight Expeditions*. Seattle:
Cloudcap Press, 1989.

Daffern, Tony. *Avalanche Safety for Skiers and
Climbers*. Seattle: Rocky Mountain Books, 1983.

Everett, Boyd. *Organization of an Alaskan Expedition*.
Pasadena, California: Gorak Press, 1984.

Fawcett, Ron, Jeff Lowe, Paul Nunn, and Alan Rouse.
The Climber's Handbook. San Francisco: Sierra
Club Books, 1987.

Houston, Charles. *Going Higher: The Story of Man and
Altitude*. Burlington, Vermont: self-published,
1983.

LaChapelle, Edward. *ABC of Avalanche Safety*, 2d ed.
Seattle: The Mountaineers, 1985.

Lowe, Jeff. *The Ice Experience*. Chicago:
Contemporary Books, 1979.

March, Bill. *Modern Snow and Ice Techniques*.
Manchester, England: Cicerone Press, 1973.

Prater, Gene. *Snowshoeing*, 3d ed. Seattle: The
Mountaineers, 1988.

Selters, Andy. *Glacier Travel and Crevasse Rescue*.
Seattle: The Mountaineers, 1990.

Chapter 17: Alpine Rescue

May, W. G. *Mountain Search and Rescue Techniques*.
Boulder, Colorado: Rocky Mountain Rescue
Group, 1973.

Padgett, Allen and Bruce Smith. *On Rope*. Huntsville,
Alabama: National Speleological Society, 1987.

Setnica, Tim. *Wilderness Search and Rescue*. Boston:
Appalachian Mountain Club, 1980.

Appendix 2: Rating systems

Fawcett, R., J. Lowe, P. Nunn, and A. Rouse.
Climbing. London: Bell and Hyman Limited,
1986.

Lowe, Jeff. ''Rate Your Turn, A System for Grading
Ice Climbs.'' *Climbing*, no. 51
(November–December 1978): pp. 14–17.

Roberts, Eric. *Welzenbach's Climbs*. Seattle: The
Mountaineers, 1980, pp. 38–41.

Smith, Craig. ''Twigging the Grades.'' *Climbing*, 109
(August 1988): pp. 38–41.

Wiessner, Fritz. ''UIAA Grading.'' *AAJ*, 16, no. 2
(1969).

Index

Boldface numbers indicate pages where illustrations occur.